IDEAS OF ORDER:

A Formal Approach to Architecture

IDEAS OF ORDER:

A Formal Approach to Architecture

Jacqueline Gargus

KENDALL/HUNT PUBLISHING COMPANY
4050 Westmark Drive Dubuque, Iowa 52002

ISBN 0–8403–8397–5

Printed in the United States of America
10 9 8 7 6 5 4 3 2 1

For Emma

Table of Contents

Acknowledgments			*ix*
Introduction			*1*
PART I.	*ELEMENTS OF ARCHITECTURAL THEORY*		7
	Chapter 1	Basic Terms: Point, Line, Plane, Volume	8
	Chapter 2	Space and Mass: Figure / Ground Relationships	20
	Chapter 3	Basic Organizations: The *Parti*	38
	Chapter 4	Typology versus Morphology	56
	Chapter 5	Precedents and Transformation	66
PART II.	*THE ARCHITECTURE OF ANTIQUITY*		85
	Chapter 6	Ancient Egypt: Axes, Symmetry, Hierarchy	86
	Chapter 7	Ancient Greece: Ideal Form and Mythic Landscape	100
	Chapter 8	Ancient Rome: Urbanism and Figural Space	118
PART III.	*THE ARCHITECTURE OF CHRISTIANITY*		143
	Chapter 9	The Middle Ages: Spiritualized Mass & Space	144
	Chapter 10	The Renaissance: Proportion & Ideality	166
	Chapter 11	The Baroque Period: Theater & Rhetoric	196
PART IV.	*THE ARCHITECTURE OF MODERNITY*		221
	Chapter 12	Enlightenment Town Planning in America	222
	Chapter 13	The 18th &19th Centuries: The Crisis of Style	244
	Chapter 14	The Twentieth Century: High Modernism	260
	Chapter 15	Architecture in the Post-Industrial Age	292
Appendix:	Ways of Seeing and Ways of Representing		324
Glossary			347
Select Bibliography			363
Sources of Illustrations			371
Index			379

Acknowledgments

I would like to thank all my colleagues and friends who have helped in the making of this book. In particular I would like to acknowledge my assistant, Jenifer Simons Syed. Without her help this book would not have been realized. Her tireless work, good cheer and careful suggestions about style and content have been most valued. I would also like to thank Karen Bokor who helped me get started on this project and only left to gestate twins. Kari Jormakka has been a constant source of support in all aspects of book preparation. His extraordinary erudition has been an invaluable resource and conversations with him have helped me formulate many of my arguments. He has kindly read the manuscript and made many witty yet scholarly contributions to expand its scope and focus. He moreover provided valuable counsel on graphics and cover design. I wish to thank Jon Bevington Stephens for his careful and exacting work in preparing many of the drawings. All errors and omissions are my own; all that is of interest I owe to my collaborators.

Robert Livesey deserves special mention. My instructor at graduate school, my former chairman at the Ohio State University, and my friend, it was he who persuaded me to teach architecture, and who first asked me to give the lecture course upon which this book is based. He has generously permitted me to make use of his extensive slide collection in my lectures, and to include many of his photographs in this text. He is responsible for all the good photographs in this book. Douglas Graf has been an unwitting mentor. Discussions and travels with him have opened my eyes to architecture in new ways, and helped me to see architectural order in the vernacular landscape as well as in the great cities of the world. Many of the ideas in this book imperfectly reflect insights gleaned from him. I am indebted to José Oubrerie, Chairman of the Department of Architecture, and Jerrold Voss, Director of the School of Architecture at the Ohio State University for their support and encouragement in this endeavor.

I give special thanks to my parents, who instilled in me a love of knowledge and a passion for travel, traits which have stood me in good stead in the study of architecture. Lastly, I thank my daughter Emma, who has patiently endured my neglect during her first few months of life while I finished work on this project.

Introduction: Ideas of Order

"...Ramon Fernandez, tell me, if you know,
Why, when the singing ended and we turned
Toward the town, tell why the glassy lights,
The lights in the fishing boats at anchor there,
As night descended, tilting in the air,
Mastered the night and portioned out the sea,
Fixing emblazoned zones and fiery poles,
Arranging, deepening, enchanting night..."
-WALLACE STEVENS

The title of this book, *Ideas of Order*, comes from a poem by Wallace Stevens, "The Idea of Order at Key West". Stevens' poem elegantly and compactly addresses issues which in this text are drawn out over three hundred pages. The poem recounts the tale of a woman singing by the shore. The words of her song and the natural rhythms of the sea mimic one another, yet the gulf between language and the grinding water keep them from ever forming a dialogue. Instead, the contrast between the song and the sounds of the wind and sea provides a frame which reveals both with new clarity. When the singing ends, the sea still cannot be grasped as an autonomous, independent entity. Instead, a new frame emerges; the lights of the fishing boats mark out a visual structure which fixes a new order for the sea.

The primary aim of *Ideas of Order* is to provide conceptual and historical frames of reference which can be used to 'portion out' the order of architecture, a task that is by no means easy. Most of our training prepares us to decipher linguistic and numeric information. We have little training in making sense out of visual and graphic material. Ground rules in visual literacy are presented in this book in an attempt to demystify the study of architecture, a discipline which is so fraught with jargon and specialized argot that without a primer, the novice may become hopelessly muddled, or worse, indifferent to the built environment. The intent is not to develop an historical or art historical argument, but rather to provide insight into the way architects make decisions so that the reader may better appreciate the richness of the material world.

We do not presume to divine the intentions of architects nor to understand the precise reasoning followed in their design processes. Instead, we shall examine objective data: the physical forms of buildings and the interrelationships among the whole, the constituent parts and the broader context. Formal analysis of buildings and drawings shall act as a springboard for our discussion, although excurses may range into more abstruse theoretical territory. Many complementary and contradictory readings may be proffered. That is why the book is called *Ideas of Order*, rather than *The Idea of Order.* In Stevens' poem, an interpretation of the sea which emphasizes its auditory structure is supported by the song; another interpretation which emphasizes its spatial characteristics is supported by the cadence of lights and fishing boat masts. So too in architecture, multiple orders can be found and ambiguous, overlapping strata do not diminish the interpretations, but rather create reverberations among them which strengthen the whole. Apparent disorder may yield a higher kind of order.

As Stevens suggested, order is discernible only through contrast and framing; and frames, by their nature, include some things and exclude others. A theoretical scaffold acts as a frame to sharpen critical focus so that the structure of a verbal or graphic idea is more easily discerned.

Meaning is conferred in many ways. In language, the order of words, the choice of vocabulary, the particularities of syntax and tone signify more than the literal denotation of a phrase. In architecture the most straightforward function, that of making shelter, carries only a small part of the building's meaning. Architecture is not just about shelter and accommodation; it also conserves rituals and mediates between the condition of humankind and the forces beyond our control.

The first five chapters of the book set forth methods of examining buildings and provide tools for formal analysis. Categories, vocabulary and criteria are presented which identify some organizing principles of architectural works. With an understanding of how architectural ideas are structured, it is hoped that the reader will gain insight into why one choice was made and not another, and how different arrangements of form can shape their attendant meanings.

The last ten chapters loosely follow an historical time line, although the approach in this book is not historical. Rather, an historical sequence is used as a convenient armature for the discussion of broader architectural ideas. Our methodology diverges from that of most architectural histories in another way. Architectural historians explore temporal chains of relationship. Here, we shall concentrate on the spatial, not the temporal context. Buildings will not be looked at as autonomous specimens, responsible only to their own logic and limited by their own boundaries, but as elements in dialogue with a context. A building's design does not end with its walls and roof but extends to engage the entire site. Similarly, the true site of a building does not end at the property lines but includes a larger context of elements in the environment. Within this extended context, the building partakes in a sequence of events. Repetition, rhythm, juxtaposition, patterns of light and darkness, solid and void, large and small, articulate an architectural procession and construct a frame of reference in which a building is seen and understood.

The scope of this book concentrates on buildings but is not limited to buildings alone. Landscapes and cities are looked at as extensions of architectural ordering systems, for architecture comments upon and makes intelligible the landscape and the context. Another poem by Wallace Stevens, "Anecdote of the Jar", deals with the theme of context and the power of architectural interventions to define place by calling out difference and thereby instituting hierarchy:

"I placed a jar in Tennessee,
And round it was, upon a hill.
It made the slovenly wilderness
Surround the hill..."

Sequence, time and memory set architecture apart from other visual arts, such as painting or sculpture. The painters' canvas defines a frame which clearly circumscribes their work from its surrounding environment. The entirety of a painting can be apprehended in an instant. Moreover, the two-dimensionality of painting calls it out as alien and artificial in the three-dimensional world we inhabit. Sculptors work in three-dimensions, but their creations are usually independent objects which can be bought, sold and moved to any site. As objects in environments, paintings and sculptures engage in a dialogue with their surroundings, but unlike the architect, the sculptor and the painter are usually not able to control these relationships.

As in poetry and music, no single part of an architectural work can be considered except in relation to that which immediately precedes it. To quote an old adage, 'architecture is frozen music'. As such, architecture is a pure art; architecture is about architecture; its task is to formulate an internal order which gives it significance, although its meaning may be inaccessible to the general public. At the same time architecture has a public nature. Every architectural act is a civic gesture loaded with political and social implications. Buildings do not only provide shelter for the simple functions of everyday life, but they also act as repositories for the collective history and memory of a culture. An Egyptian pyramid evokes the grandeur of the pharaonic age and the capabilities and values of the society more powerfully than a hieroglyphic inscription or any other written text. Histories are constructed by authors whose viewpoints may color the material, but stones never lie. In examining architectural artifacts we can make fresh assessments of a culture, free from the interposed lens of the historian's vision. Architecture is a palimpsest, each built layer inscribing its form and meaning on subsequent interventions, the assembled whole mapping out the trajectory of a civilization.

Part 1.

Elements of Architectural Theory

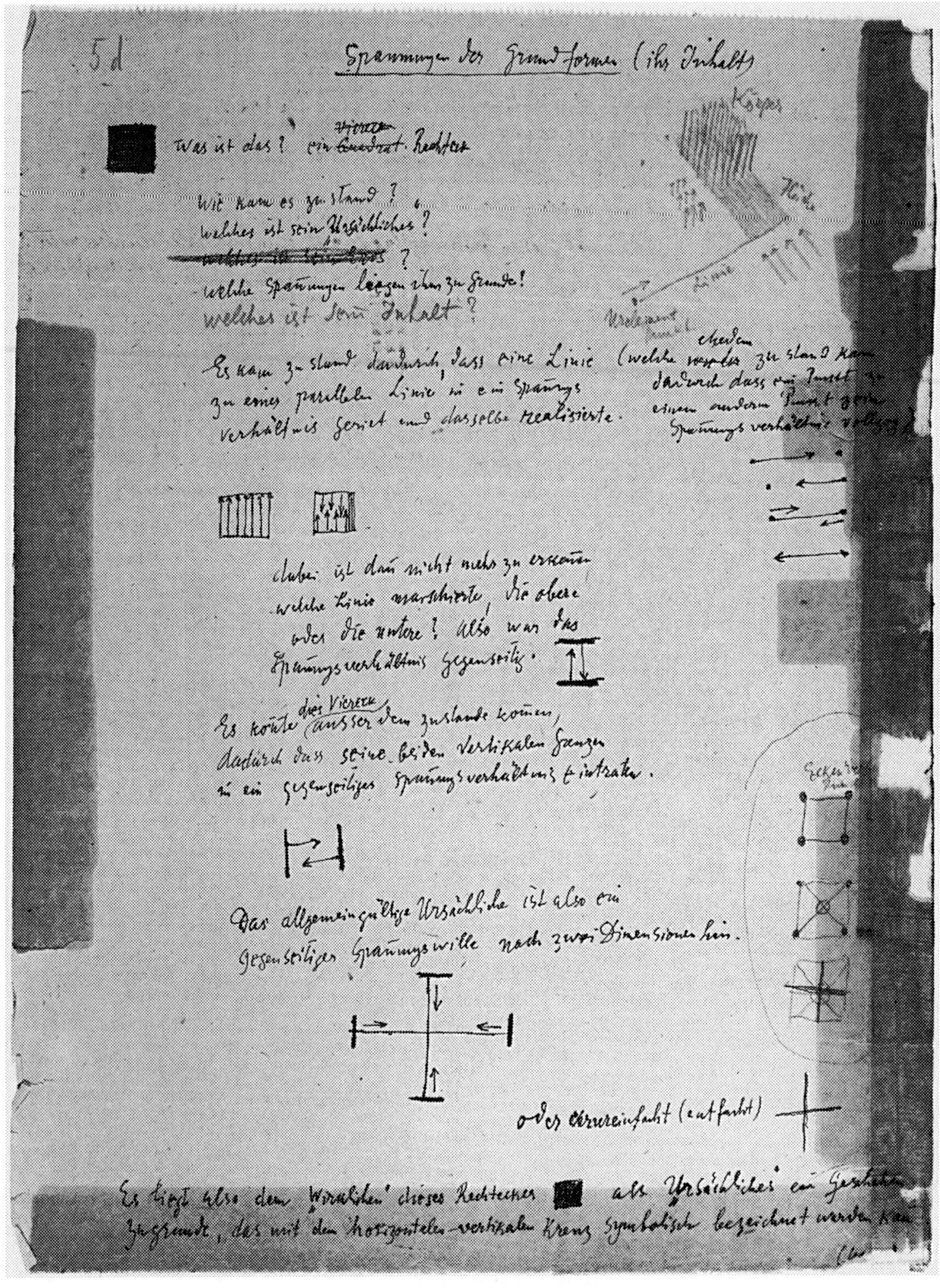

1.0
Paul Klee, "Point, Line, Plane, Volume," (upper right.) Paul Klee-Stiftung. Kunstmuseum, Bern, Switzerland.

Chapter One

Basic Terms: Point, Line, Plane, Volume

Geometry is the means, created by ourselves,
whereby we perceive the external world
and express the world within us.
-Le Corbusier

Four centuries separate **Sebastiano Serlio's** (1475-1554) *Five Books on Architecture,* 1545 from **Le Corbusier's** (1887-1965) *The City of Tomorrow,* 1924. Yet both books begin in exactly the same way, with illustrations of the basic geometric elements. The two architects worked in remote time periods, designed buildings of widely diverse character, made use of different structural and constructional technologies, and related to very different political, social, and cultural pressures. Yet for both, simple geometry and the basic **Pythagorean progression** of point, to line, to plane, to volume constituted the fundamental ingredients of all architectural form.

Why were these terms useful to Serlio and Le Corbusier? Geometry did not provide specific solutions to questions of style, building program, or construction, since the two architects were as far apart as possible on these issues. Instead, both architects used geometry to establish an architectural order. A geometrically determined definition of form and arrangement of parts made it possible for both

A Poynt.
A Line.
Parable.
Superficies.
Perpendicular.

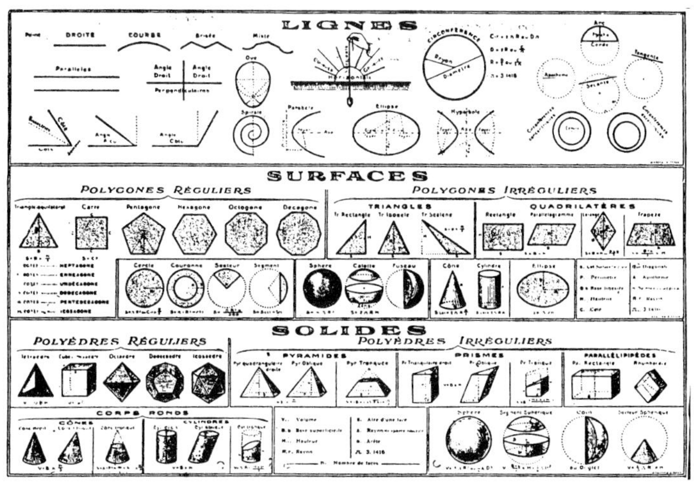

1.1 *Left: Sebastiano Serlio, Five Books on Architecture, Book I, Plate 1, 1545.*

1.2 *Right: Le Corbusier, The City of Tomorrow, Frontispiece, 1924.*

architects to express architectural ideas clearly, and further, to allow for the development of sub-themes and variations which could be understood against the strong underlying formal order, or **datum**.

In discussing the role of geometry in architecture we shall begin, like Serlio and Le Corbusier, with a point. Equal in their relationship to all surrounding directions, points establish centers for groupings of form. While geometers define a point as dimensionless, in our discussion of architectural form we understand a point as any simple, singular thing: a pin point, a dot on a page, a sugar cube, a cylindrical oil drum, etc.

The line, mathematically defined, is a one-dimensional entity which can be infinitely extended in two directions. Rather than consider a line to be of a wholly different nature than the point, one can imagine a transformational relationship which links the two. In other words, a line can be understood as a point which has been dragged or 'translated' in space.

The next term in the Pythagorean progression is the plane, a two dimensional, unbounded surface which extends infinitely in all directions. How does a plane relate to the previous term, the line? Just as the idea of transformation helps us to understand the relationship between the point and the line, the same strategy can be used to clarify the relationship between the line and the plane. A plane can be understood as a line that has been dragged in space.

In discussing architecture, lines and planes do not have infinite extension: nothing in the physical world has that property. Still, the implication of extension gives power to the form, and establishes a potent demarcation between front and back, above and below, inside and outside, etc. Such distinctions permit further levels of spatial stratification to take place. Linear and planar structures can act in many different ways. As solid components of the built environment, walls separate one precinct from another; slabs establish boundaries between vertically stacked spaces; filters effect a transformation of spatial experiences from one side to the other; the neutral plane, or datum, acts as a background against which a free play of form can be deciphered.

As voids, linear elements often have even greater power to organize form. Axes can forge clear relationships across long distances without the requirement of adjacency; views or vistas make possible an understanding of connection between even more loosely grouped elements; paths orchestrate a sequence of experiences along the procession and enlist memory in the task of reconstructing and assembling the experience as an entirety.

The last term in the Pythagorean progression is the volume. Again, we can use our notion of transformation to understand the relationship between the three-dimensional volume and the preceding two-dimensional term. If a plane is dragged through space the resulting form is a cube or some other rectangular prism. Hence point, line, plane, and volume, the primary terms needed to establish an architectural order, are all related by a one simple act of transformation, as **Paul Klee's** (1879-1940) drawing, ***"Point, Line, Plane, Volume"*** illustrates.

Further affinities and distinctions can be found among these four basic elements. A line has only one more dimension than a point, yet

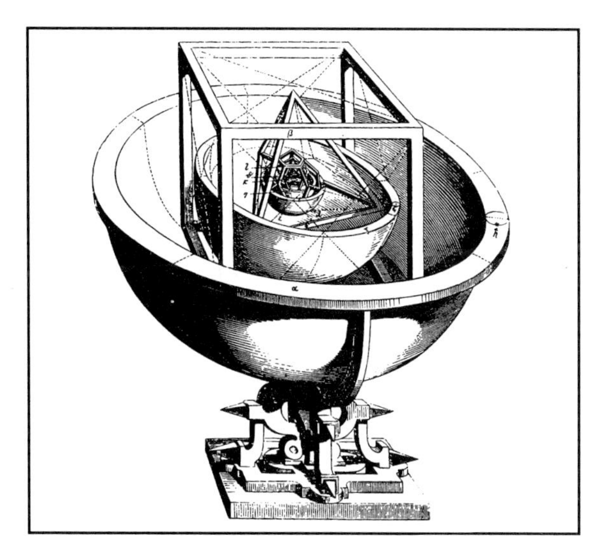

1.3 Left: Johannes Kepler, Harmony of the spheres, Mysterium Cosmographicum, 1621.

1.4 Right: J. de Barbari, 'Luca Paccioli,' (author of Divina Geometria), detail, c.1500, Capodimonte Museum, Naples.

they function very differently in the making of space. The primary task of points is the definition of center, while the primary task of lines is the definition of edge or perimeter. Points are finite and bounded; lines are by definition extensible. Volumes and points, on the other hand, play similar roles in spatial organizations. Even though volumes are three dimensional and points are conceptually dimensionless they can be thought of as equivalent, but for the matter of scale. The farther we are away from something, the more it tends to have qualities of a simple, dimensionless point. When seen from the earth, stars appear to be minuscule points, although we know they are of vast size. When examined under a microscope, grains of sand appear to be volumetric, although under ordinary circumstances they appear as mere specks. Both points and volumes are bounded, finite and neutral towards the various directions which surround them. Hence, both can act as centers to organizations. On the contrary, lines and planes are defined both by extension and by their ability to set up distinctions between one side and the other. They do not act as centers but as edges to organizations of form.

Let us examine two structures which are bounded and crisply defined in form, an **Egyptian pyramid** from more than four thousand years ago, and a **cylindrical corn crib** from a Midwestern farm in the 1990's. Both are understandable as almost pure **Platonic solids,** or elemental three dimensional forms. The term 'Platonic solids' derives from the writing of Plato, the Greek philosopher who speculated that the four elements in nature, earth, air, fire and water, corresponded to geometrical solids whose faces are regular polyhedrons. For Plato, these were the tetrahedron, the cube, the icosahedron and the dodecahedron. The sphere was reserved as the shape of the heavens above. Believing in the cosmological significance of Platonic solids, **Johannes Kepler** constructed a model of the universe by nesting the Platonic

1.5 Cylindrical corn crib, Midwestern farm, 1990's.

forms around a center. **Luca Paccioli** wrote a treatise on the innate proportional relationships among simple solids in *Da Divina Proportione*. Both sought to reveal the underlying order in the **"Harmony of the spheres"** which governed relationships of everything from astral bodies to musical harmony.

In every day discourse, 'Platonic forms' have come to mean volumes like spheres, cylinders, cones, pyramids, cubes, tetrahedrons, and the like which are generated when idealized two-dimensional forms (circles, squares, isosceles triangles, etc.) have been extended, rotated or reflected around their centers or axes. Both the cylinder and the pyramid, by their own mathematical definitions, make reference to their centers. Both are organized by a vertical **axis,** or conceptual center line, running from the ground through the top of the roof. Indeed, one symbolic purpose of the pyramid was to gather up the earth into a single point to meet the sun. Hence, at changing scales, the function of these

1.6 The Pyramids of Cheops (c. 2570 B.C.), Chefren (c. 2530 B.C.), and Mycerinus (c. 2500 B.C.) at Giza, Egypt.

structures as points or volumes is interchangeable.

A more complex organization takes place in the next figure, the **Pantheon,** a circular Roman temple. Like the corn crib in the previous example, the Pantheon is essentially a domed cylindrical volume, but here the form is hybrid. A cylindrical drum is united with a temple front, joined together by a thick masonry block. Unlike the previous example in which all surrounding directions were addressed with equanimity, the addition of the temple portico introduces an axis into the centralized organization. The axis stems from the elongation of the structure in one direction, and the path of movement into the buildings. Even so, the axiality of the path is resolved in the vast centralized interior space. In the interior another axis is revealed: the **axis mundi**, or the vertical axis which links the earth to the sky, framed by the circular window or **oculus** at the top of the dome.

1.7 The Pantheon, Rome, Italy, 1st century A.D.

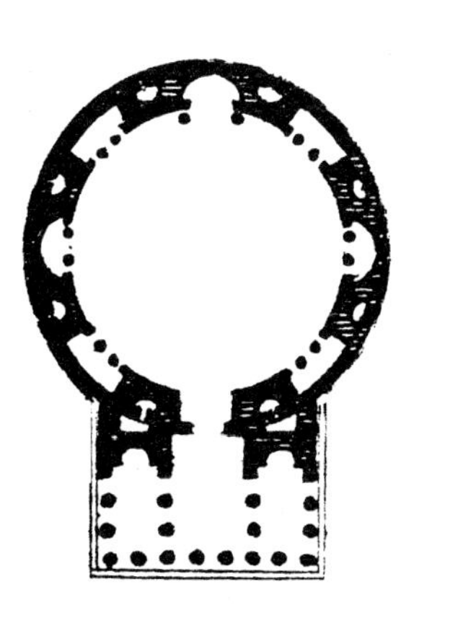

1.8 The Pantheon, elevation and plan.

1.9
Stoa of Attalos II, c. 150 B.C. the Agora, Athens, Greece.

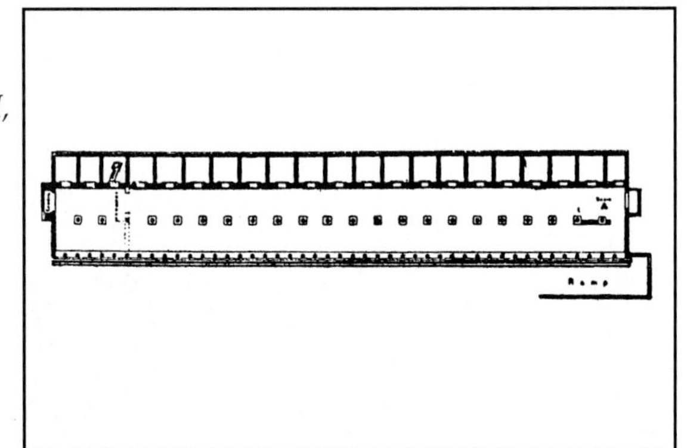

1.10
Stoa of Attalos II, plan.

Centralized buildings may grow complex but still make reference to the central point around which they are organized. Linear buildings may also have more elaborate internal configurations. The simplest form of a linear structure is a wall; a bar of matter which is consistent throughout its length, like a bar of chocolate. However, the width of the bar itself may yield a more intricate organization. The space between the two exterior surfaces of a wall, called **poché,** can be carved to shape spatial figures, like the holes formed in a thick mass of Swiss cheese. A linear or 'bar' building can be permeable, like a comb, in which the surface is not continuous but marked by a regular rhythm of vertical members. A bar-building can be cellular, like a Tootsie Roll, in which the line is comprised of like units which are serially repeated. A bar-building can be layered, like a Snickers bar, with one surface treatment on the outside, then another, and another to comprise the whole. A Greek **stoa** is an example such a

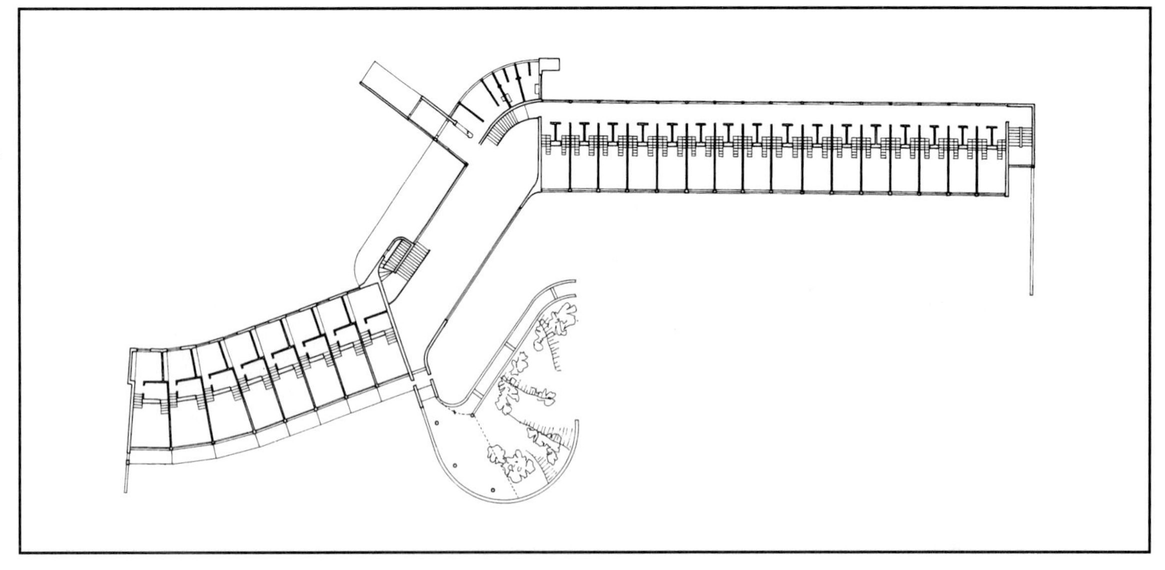

1.11
Hans Scharoun, Hostel, Wroclaw, Poland, 1927.

structure. The side facing the market square or **agora** is columnar in structure. The outer wall, on the contrary, is solid and frequently houses a cellular band of shops. The **Greenhouse at Chatsworth** by **Joseph Paxton** (1801-65), is another example. Attached to a heavy stone wall which girdles the estate is a delicate glass and metal structure. The transparency of the greenhouse enclosure allows both surfaces to be read simultaneously and strongly differentiates the inside from outside.

While centralized buildings insist on the equality of all space surrounding them, linear buildings clarify difference from one side of the line to the other. When a line bends or deflects it no longer simply describes a boundary but it begins to define a space. **Alvar Aalto's** (1898-1976) **Baker House Dormitory** in Cambridge, Massachusetts, gently curves in response to the natural form of the Charles River, forming a garden on the river side of the complex. Differences between inside and outside are further

1.12 Joseph Paxton, Chatsworth, England, the Greenhouse, 1836-40.

1.13 Alvar Aalto, Baker House Dormitory, Cambridge, Massachusetts, 1947-48.

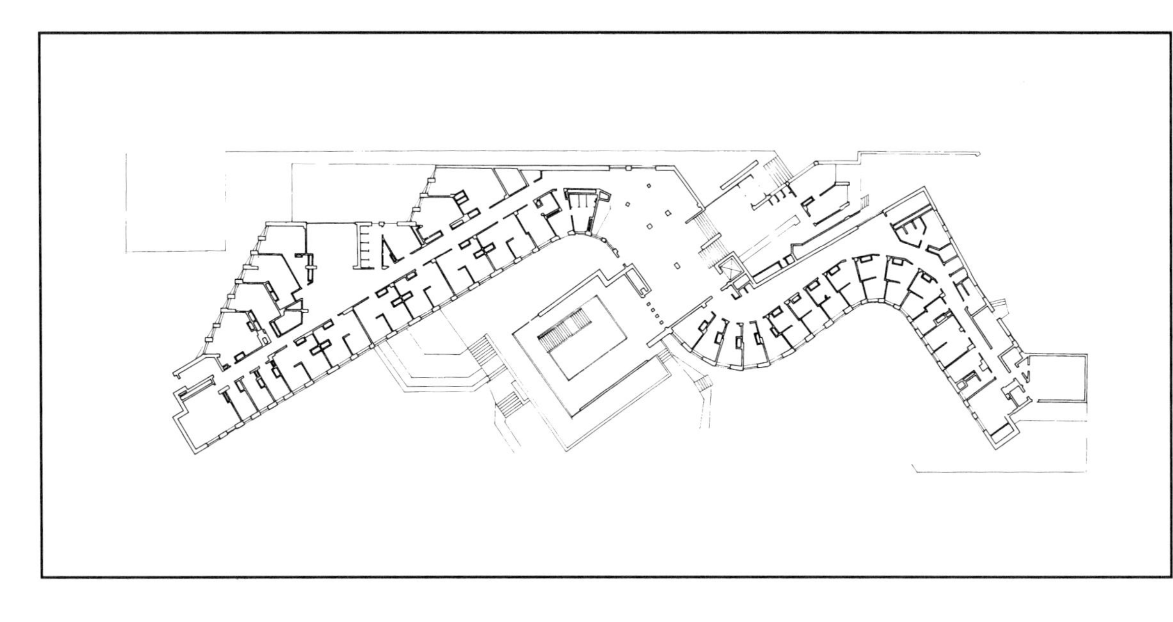

1.14 Baker House, plan.

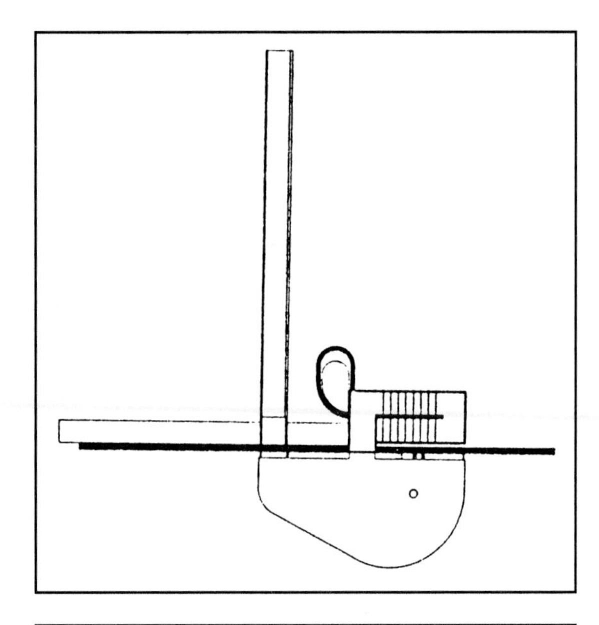

1.15
John Hejduk, Wall House I, plan, 1968-74.

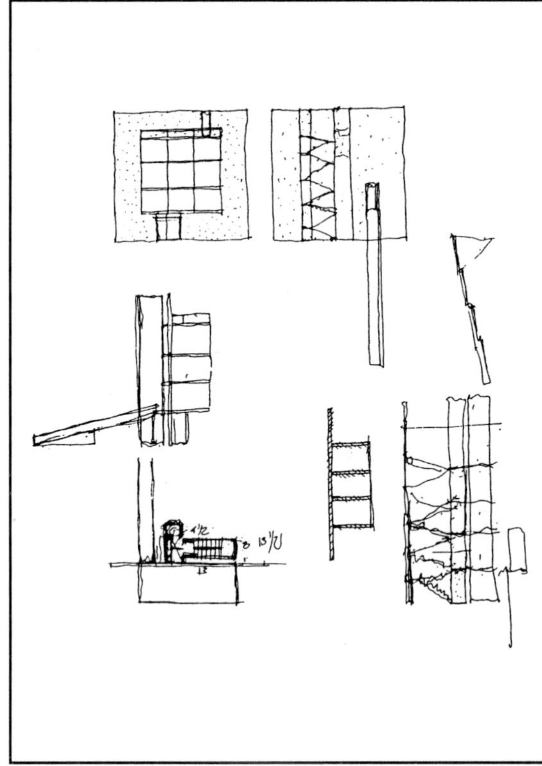

1.16
John Hejduk, Wall House I, preliminary sketches.

refined by the use of hard, angular forms on the street side in contrast to the gentle undulations of the river side. Moreover, the river side collects private dormitory rooms while the city side is mostly comprised of **circulation**, (corridors, stairs, and elevators,) and collective spaces such as living rooms and bathrooms. At entry, a shaft of space cuts a void through the building, pushing matter out from the bar to form a dining pavilion. Hence, all components of the dormitory derive from transformations of a simple bar.

In **Hans Scharoun's** (1893-1972) **Hostel** in Wroclaw, Poland, the bar of dormitory rooms frames exterior space not so much by bending as by 'twisting.' The open, balconied edge of the long wing threads through the irregularly shaped central hall and reemerges on the opposite side of the short wing, almost as if the particularity of the central space arose through the pressure of the deformation. As in the Baker House, not only form but also **program,** or the functional requirements of a building, are satisfied through this move. Rooms for couples are arranged in the wider bays of the short wing and rooms for bachelors are arranged in the narrower bays of the long wing. The specially shaped central piece houses common living and dining activities.

In the previous two examples we observed how a relationship between linear elements and centric objects can arise from a transformative process. In the Baker House, the trajectory of the entry path pushed the rooms at the lower floor outside the bar to form a pavilion piece in the garden. In the Hostel, a twisting of the bar yielded a special condition, much as in the twisting of a Mobius strip. In **Wall House I,**

John Hejduk (b. 1929) reduces the wall to the simple condition of datum. Against the neutral surface of the wall a more particular collection of objects is arranged, not through transformation but through **collage.** The wall emphasizes the difference from one side to the other. Public activities are arranged on one side, private spaces on the other; one side confronts an urban condition, the other side a landscape; one side makes use of a **tectonic,** or constructional system, of heavy, compressive materials, while the other side uses a tectonic system of light, tensile materials, suspended from the wall; one side is comprised of opaque, neutrally colored materials, while the other side is comprised of reflective, transparent surfaces. Hejduk describes his project in the following way: *"on one side of the wall (the past), the circulatory elements— ramp, stair, elevator— were placed. They were volumetric, opaque, monochromatic, in perspective with the structure grounded. The color was white, grey, black; the materials reinforced concrete, steel and cement. Once the single inhabitant passed through the wall he was in a space overlooking a landscape (trees? water? earth? sky?) which was basically private, contemplative and reflective. There were three suspended floors cantilevered from the collective elements. The materials on this side of the wall were glass and reflective metal; a fluidity was sought after. Whereas the collective side was hard, tough, concrete, the private side was inwardly reflective, a light shattering into fragments, mirror images moving along polished surfaces of metal."* (*Mask of Medusa*, by John Hejduk.)

The plan of the Hellenistic town **Pergamon** illustrates an entire context that can be deciphered as a transformation of very simple objects and linear forms to yield a much more

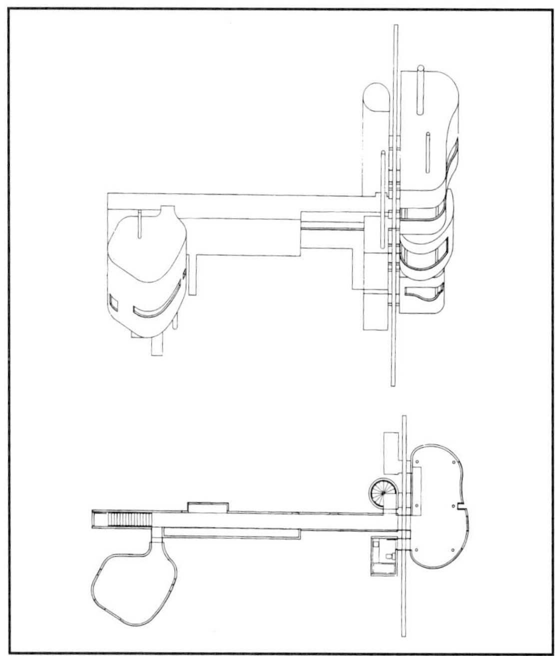

1.17 John Hejduk, Wall House II, axonometric and plan, 1968–74.

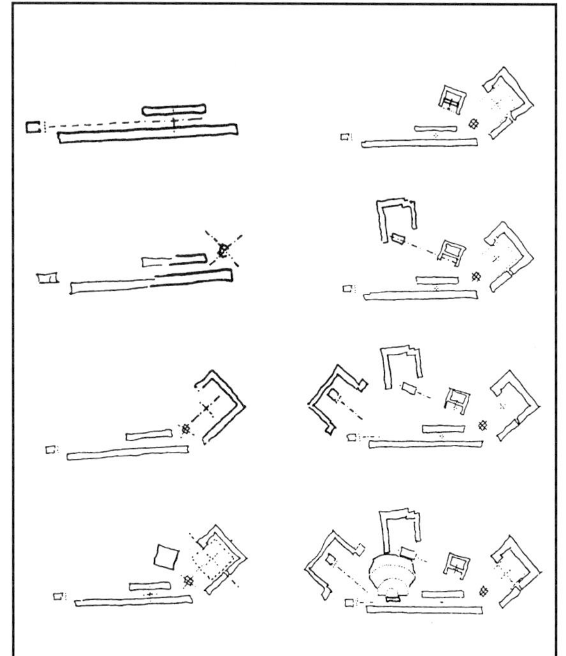

1.18 Douglas Graf, Diagrams of the Upper City, Pergamon.

1.19 Pergamon, Hellenistic.

complex order. In the broadest terms, the urban form of Upper Pergamon can be described as radial, taking advantage of the slope of the hill to carve out the fan-shaped space of the theater, around which secondary spaces splay out like plumes in a fan. A more precise description of interconnections among various spaces in the plan can be construed by imagining acts of formal transformation, just as we earlier read relationships between points, lines, planes and volumes by positing spatial translation from one dimension to the next.

Our reading of the plan begins with the Caracalla Temple at the lower left. The Temple, much like a sugar cube, is a discrete, bounded object, although its permeability along the axis of entry implies extension and organizes a shaft of space in front of it. Just beneath the Temple, a bar-like building, or stoa, extends rightward, as if the temple had been dragged to yield a new linear form. The next element, moving counter-clockwise, is the Market. Here the stoa bends, enveloping in its perimeter the plane of the market area. A few isolated buildings flank the lower edge of the Market, as if the bar had been fragmented to yield discrete objects once again. The plane defined by the Market stoa slips to the left to act as a platform for the Pergamon Altar. Meanwhile, the stoa, which defined perimeter in the Market Complex, shrinks inwards to define the Altar itself. The voided center of the Altar is as bounded and figural as the first term in our progression, the Temple. However, now the figure is defined by an enclosed void rather than a space-displacing solid. While the Temple had a voided perimeter defined by the space of the colonnade and a solid center, the cella, the Pergamon Altar has a solid perimeter and voided center. Hence, form presents itself in its two purest manifestations, as pure solid and pure void. In the Library Complex the bent bar of the Altar splits apart,

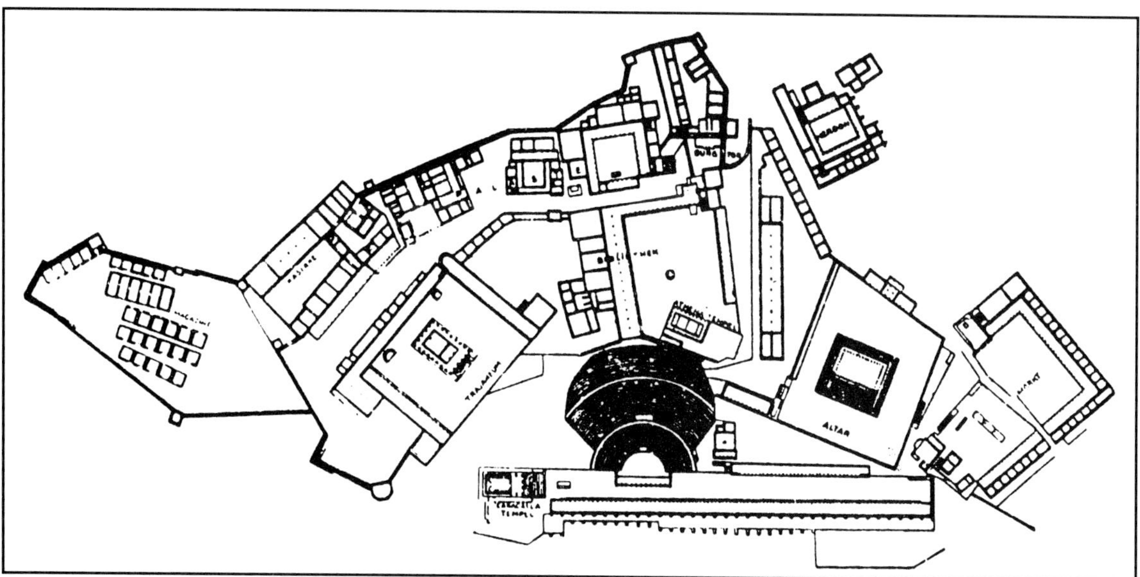

1.20
Pergamon, plan.

shattered by the path from the Citadel Gate. In the process, the center is freed from the engirdling wrapper. A monument marks the original location of the center while the true center, the Athena Temple, shifts downwards to align with the central void of the Pergamon Altar to which it formally relates as a figure/ground reversal. The last major space, the Trajaneum, reconstitutes the wrapper and ideal centering of the Pergamon Altar at an expanded scale. However, here a solid object, the temple, marks center. To complete the circuit, one merely needs to slip the temple of the Trajaneum downwards to yield the Caracalla Temple, our starting point.

Reading the plan of Pergamon as a series of transformations performed on fairly straightforward elements makes it possible to decipher order in a plan that at first glance might seem chaotic and without structure. Understanding the various spaces as the product of translations of objects in space, the foldings of edge-defining bars, scale changes, and reversals of figure and ground makes it possible to see how affinities of form and meaning might be constructed. It is worth mentioning that Pergamon did not historically emerge according to an overarching urban strategy of constructing variations on center/perimeter relationships. Pergamon grew up over time, responding not only to the inherent pressures that buildings have upon one another; but also to complicated landform, or **topography**; to precise religious, political and social orderings or **hierarchy;** and to the necessity to make connections to other parts of the town. Still the formal structure yields a 'reading' of the relationship among elements on the site.

2.0
G.B. Nolli, Map of Rome, 1748, engraved by G.B. Piranesi, detail.

Chapter Two

Space and Mass: Figure/ Ground Relationships

The basic ingredient of architectural design consists in two elements, mass and space. The essence of design is the interrelation between these two. In our culture the preponderant preoccupation is with mass, and to such an extent that many designers are "space blind."
-Edmund Bacon

Mass and space are essential components of architecture: one cannot be understood independently of the other. They define one another. Only through the differentiation of mass from space can one perceive objects, discern outlines, and grasp the limits of a void through reference to its boundaries. Space can be figural, capable of organizing forms around it. Space can be extensible, capable of sweeping out a swath to connect distant elements with each other or with the plane of the earth, the sky, or the horizon. While things, even very large things, are in some way limited in their extent, space is by definition boundless.

Indeed, a nineteenth-century theoretician, Alois Riegl, posited that the production of art in different historical epochs was governed by the different sensory organs which were primary in perception. According to Riegl, in the early history of aesthetic production the sense of touch was dominant. **Haptic** artifacts, produced in response to this predilection, were frequently heavy, solid volumes with clearly defined boundaries. The Egyptian pyramids are examples of haptic structures. Such objects can be well represented by small solid models or axonometric drawings since they are closed, isolated, discrete forms. Some time around the Renaissance, a shift occurred which favored the sense of sight as the primary receptor of perception. The emphasis of **optic** architecture moved away from the description of things to the description of spatial relationships between things. Perspective drawing is a good vehicle for investigating such designs: not only the space enframed by the architecture is represented, but the location of the **vantage point** further implies the space between the viewer and the depicted scene.

Optical puzzles which allow an interchangeability of figure and background are familiar from children's books. Proper interpretation of the images depends on whether one reads the dark part as the primary figure and the white part as background, or the reverse. Stare at the white vase in Figure 2.1 and the black area ap-

2.1
A vase or two faces.

2.2
A black square or a white ell.

2.3
M.C. Escher, "Sky and Water I," 1938, M.C. Escher Foundation, Baarn, Holland.

pears only as a plain background. Stare at the black facial profiles at the edges and the white looses its figurality, likewise appearing as a simple background. In the second drawing the image is even simpler, consisting of pure rectilinear fields of black and white. What is it? A white ell? A black square? The interlocking of figure and field gives the image its capacity to sustain multiple, reversible readings. In ***Sky and Water 1,*** **M.C. Escher** (1898-1972) makes the shifting play between figure and ground thematic in his drawing. Almost indiscernibly fish becomes fowl and foreground exchanges places with background.

We can extend the discussion of these drawings to include architecture. In three-dimensional objects, as in two-dimensional drawings, form makes itself manifest through contrast to a background or a surrounding space. Buildings do not exist as pure entities in abstract, characterless space. Rather, they are situated in elaborate relationships to complex environments. In some instances, buildings function primarily as edges to define a greater collective space. This is the case in **Eliel Saarinen's** (1873-1950) **Cranbrook School** of 1925. While all the buildings at the Cranbrook School are carefully crafted and architecturally distinctive from one another, it is not the individual buildings but the collection of quadrangles, courtyards, pathways and lawns that provides the most memorable image of the campus. The shaping of exterior space is the primary task of the architecture.

In other instances, buildings are perceived as objects in their surroundings, acting as centers, monuments, or landmarks. Here space is much more neutral. The **plasticity**, or three-

2.4
Eliel Saarinen, Cranbrook School, Bloomfield Hills, Michigan, c. 1925.

2.5, 2.6
Left and Right: Eliel Saarinen, Cranbrook School.

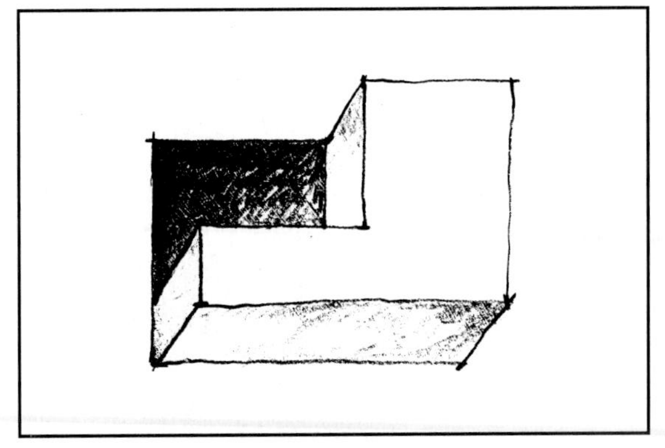

2.7 A white ell-shaped building on a black surface.

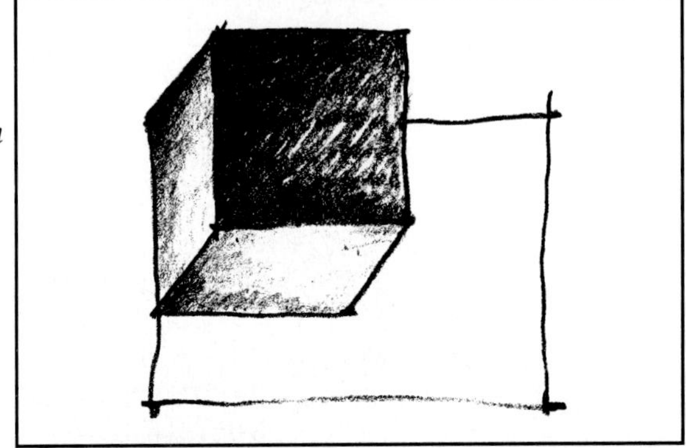

2.8 A black box-shaped building on a white surface.

2.9 Aerial photograph, the Ohio State University Oval, 1948, The Ohio State University Archives.

dimensionality, of the structure displaces space rather than defines its boundaries. Even in these cases, the building is engaged in a taut relationship with its surroundings. Tensions are created between object-buildings and edges, among several object-buildings on the site, among natural features in the landscape and even by the varied sweep of the topography. Nothing in the built environment operates in true isolation from context. An important task for architects is to understand what relationships are present on the site and how the placement of their buildings can enhance these relationships and make apparent even more affinities of space, form and order.

While some buildings clearly function to define space and others function as free-standing objects, even more frequently buildings have a hybrid character. Such buildings act partly as edges and partly as objects. This is true of elements at the Cranbrook School like the central tower, whose extreme verticality sets it off from the edge-building it adjoins. The tower also acts as a center to the space in front of it. A clearly delineated, rectangular extension of space is aligned with the tower, distinguishing the ideal order established by the tower from the more rambling, picturesque assemblage of space that characterizes the campus as a whole.

Returning to Figure 2.2, it is now possible to interpret the drawing as a very simple architectural plan indicating the interplay of open and occupied space. This kind of drawing is called a **figure/ground** diagram. If one identifies the black area as mass and the white area as open space the drawing reveals an ell-shaped building and the land it sits upon. By reversing the assignment of mass and void in the drawing, the diagram yields a free-standing rectangular building at the corner of its site. Yet another reading of the drawing is available if we are more abstract in our interpretation. The diagram can represent a large exterior space like the **Oval at the Ohio State Campus.** Even though the space is of a vast urban scale and the edges are not defined by a continuous, unbroken wall of buildings, the Oval is more imagible and memorable than any of the buildings that bound it.

A drawing by **Paul Klee, *"Innerspatial-Outerspatial,"*** illustrates the ability of a single two-dimensional form, the rectangle, to describe opposite spatial conditions. The topmost rectangle shows how a crisply defined center can organize a loosely structured perimeter, rather like a fried egg, ("outer-spatial," in Klee's terms). The middle drawing, on the contrary, shows how a clearly drawn perimeter can hold within it a loose arrangement of form, rather like a sliced tomato, ("inner-spatial" in Klee's terms). The lowest rectangle is ambiguous. The two-dimensional drawing does not give us sufficient information to determine whether we are seeing a dark void cut out from a light background or the reverse, a black rectangle placed on a white background.

It is easy to read Klee's drawing architecturally. Two paradigmatic building types can be defined respectively by Klee's top two drawings; the **palazzo** and the **villa**. The third illustrates the interrelationship of the two building types through a figure/ground reversal.

Unlike American cities and suburbs which are frequently comprised of free-standing buildings surrounded by lawns or parking lots, the built fabric of old European city centers is very

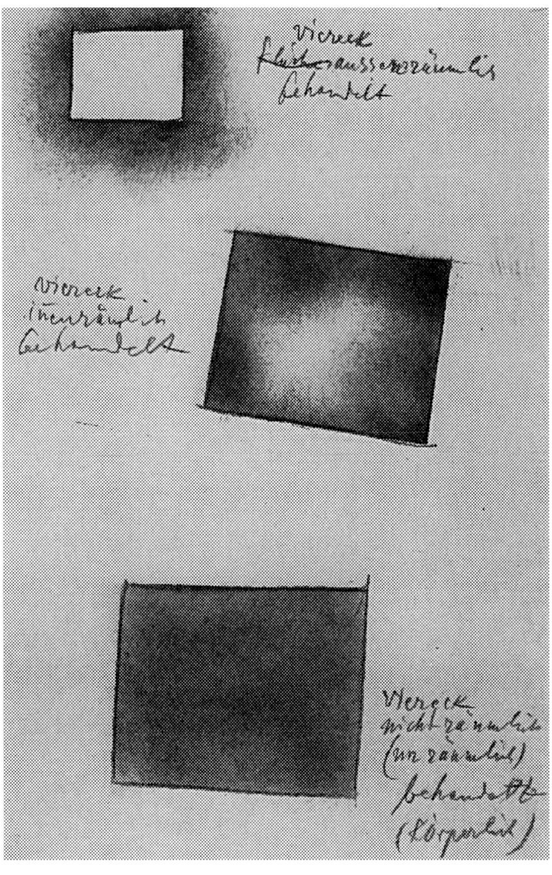

2.10 Paul Klee, "Inner Spatial-Outer-spatial." Paul Klee-Stiftung, Kunstmuseum, Bern, Switzerland.

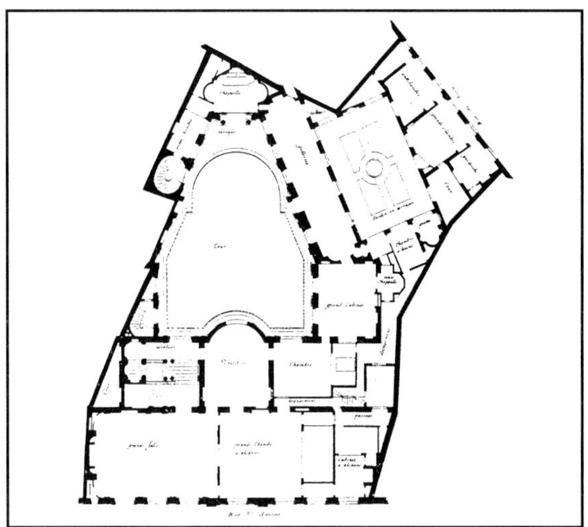

2.11 Antoine Le Pautre, Hotel Beauvais, Paris, France, c. 1654.

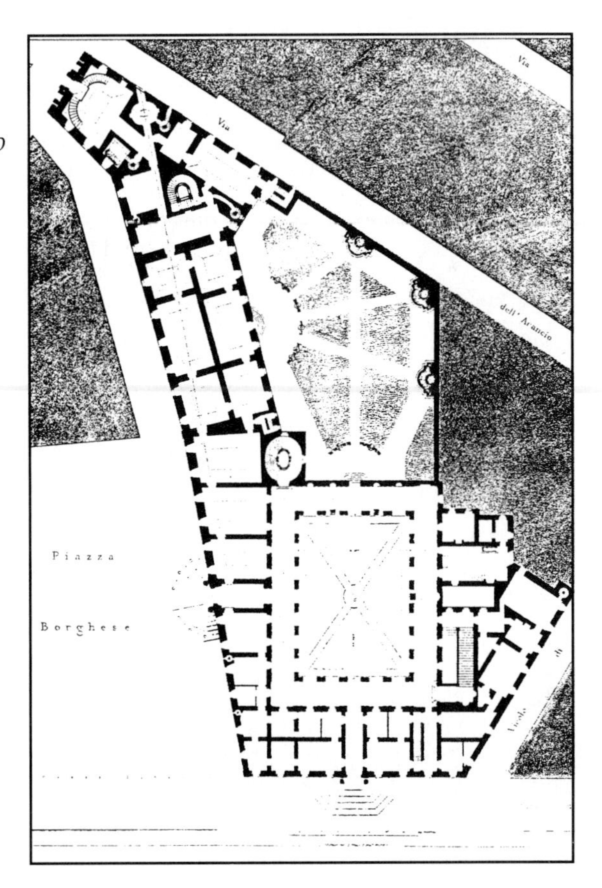

2.12 M. Longhi & C. Rainaldi, Palazzo Borghese, Rome, Italy, c. 1671.

dense. Streets are often quite narrow, buildings share common 'party walls,' facades of buildings join together to define a continuous edge along the street, making them seem like canyons. It is difficult to situate clearly defined object-buildings into such a fabric. Instead, the urban fabric is punctuated by shaped voids. The clear geometric form of courtyards and squares is preserved while the internal organization of buildings may be irregular in response to contingencies of site or program.

The **Palazzo Farnese** by **Antonio da Sangallo the Younger** (1485-1546) and **Michelangelo Buonarotti** (1475-1564), clearly illustrates the formal organization of the palazzo type. Like all palazzos, it is organized around a very clearly defined central courtyard. However, unlike most palazzos, the site of the Palazzo Farnese occupies an entire city block. The perimeter wrapper of the palace reflects the form of the center, resulting in a kind of extruded 'square doughnut.' More typical are palazzos in which the perimeter is rendered ir-

2.13 Left: Michelangelo Buonarotti and Antonio da Sangallo the Younger, Palazzo Farnese, Rome, Italy, c.1517, perspective.

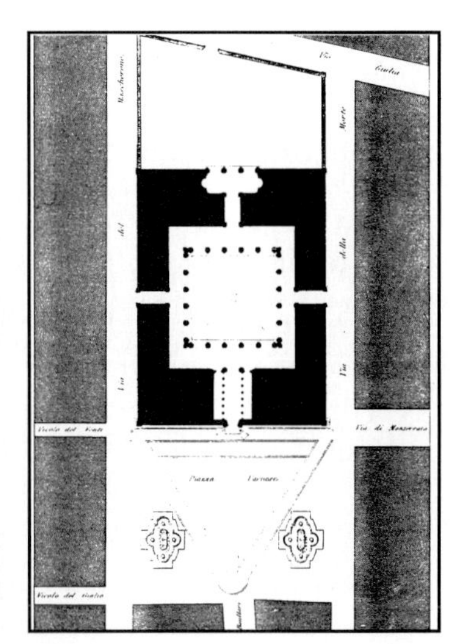

2.14 Right: Palazzo Farnese, plan.

regular to effect a gradual transition from the perfect geometry of the center to the more irregular adjacent conditions. The **Palazzo Borghese** and the **Hotel de Beauvais** are extreme examples of urban buildings which are organized around idealized centers. In contrast to the regularity of the center, the perimeter is stretched, bent and pulled to adjust to local site conditions.

Baldassare Peruzzi's (1481-1536) **Palazzo Massimo,** is a double palace for the brothers Pietro and Angelo Massimo, with Pietro's palace at the right and Angelo's at the left in the complex. Idealized central courtyards organize a highly irregular wrapper. The facade of the Palazzo Pietro Massimo bends gently along the curving street. Its main entrance is carved into the block of the building, allowing the street wall to remain undisturbed by the intrusion of a porch. This recessed entrance vestibule, or *portico in antis,* does not align with the center of the courtyard, but shifts beyond the boundaries of the palace to align with the axis of a minor street. A new center to the building is established. As the path slips into the side of the courtyard, yet another re-centering takes place. At the far end of the courtyard a slight rotation of the building's axis occurs in response to the site conditions at the back of the building. Palazzo Angelo Massimo likewise undergoes subtle readjustments as the building wrapper mitigates between the ad hoc order of the surroundings and the clear geometry of the courtyard. Two ordering systems are operating at the same time. An urban order of street alignments, axes, open spaces, property lines, and adjacencies exerts pressure on the exterior envelope of the building, causing many local

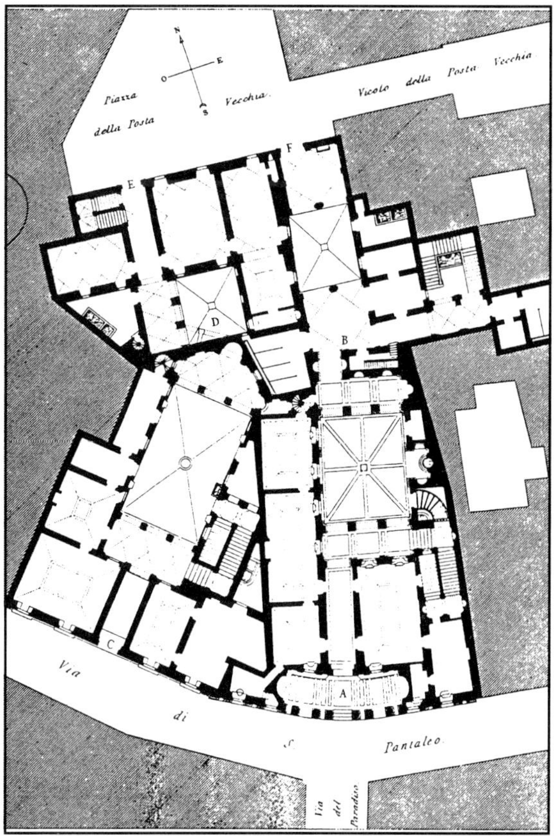

2.15
Baldassare Peruzzi, Palazzo Massimo, Rome, Italy, c. 1532.

2.16
Palazzo Massimo, elevation.

2.17 *Le Corbusier, Villa Savoye, Poissy, France, 1928-31.*

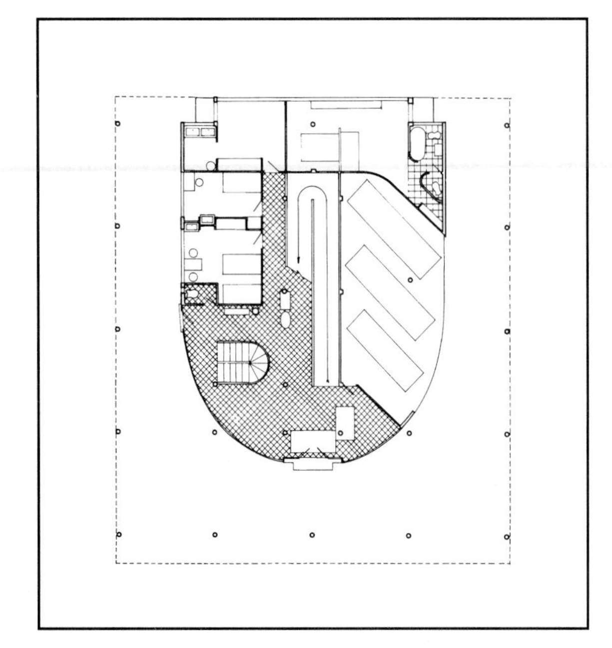
2.18 *Villa Savoye, ground floor plan.*

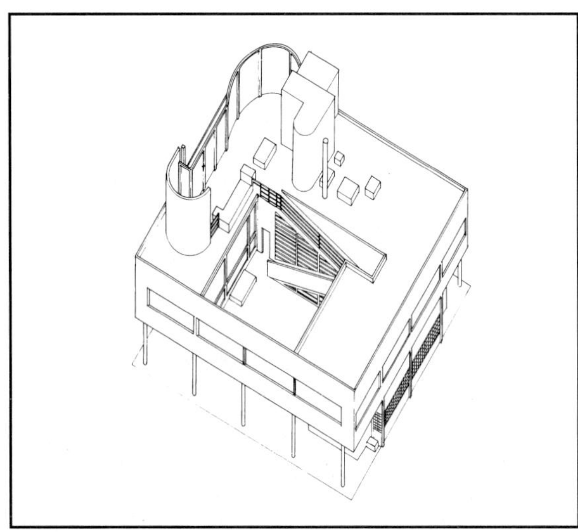
2.19 *Villa Savoye, axonometric.*

adjustments to be made. Yet the ideal order of the void, the palazzo courtyard, governs the spatial organization of the interior of the building. The two systems are melded together through the use of hinge-like spaces carved into the poché, **local symmetries**, and a series of deformations and re-centerings.

The carving out of figural spaces is a strategy for bringing order into dense, congested urban fabrics. When operating in the countryside, the task of the architect is quite different. Here open space is abundant and order is established through an opposite gesture: the insertion of figural, free-standing buildings into the open spatial continuum. **Le Corbusier's Villa Savoye** at Poissy is an example of such a building. As a form, the Villa Savoye is almost a perfect white rectangular prism, a platonic solid, whose sharply defined geometry sets it off as an alien entity on the open meadow. The pristine purity of the villa is carried so far that the box does not even touch the ground. Rather, the main volume of the building is suspended off the ground on a field of columns called **piloti**.

While the perimeter of the villa is strongly determined by the geometry of the box, the interior is not. As in Klee's second diagram, the clarity of the perimeter acts as a datum which makes possible a freer arrangement of walls and objects within its boundaries. Indeed, the architectural critic **Douglas Graf** has constructed a series of fanciful **transformational diagrams** which suggest that the plan of the Villa Savoye was generated through the operation of turning the Palazzo Farnese inside out. The Palazzo, a void ringed by a colonnade and a 'solid' cellular band of rooms reverses to yield a 'solid' center ringed by a colonnade held within a voided boundary.

The **Villa Rotonda** by **Andrea Palladio** (1508-80), c. 1566, is a more classic representation of the villa than Le Corbusier's contemporary rendering of the same theme. A free-standing object with identical porches on all four sides, it is an autonomous object on an open landscape. Inscribed within a perfect square, the disposition of interior space is governed by a nine-square grid whose central cell is expanded to receive the dome, further reinforcing its centrality around a point.

The simple nine-square order of the villa permits a wide range of variation so that the ideal paradigm may transform into a more hybrid condition. Like The Villa Rotonda, **Palladio's Villa Emo** of 1564 is a pure rectangular volume whose interior is organized by a nine-square grid. However, in the Villa Emo instead of a spatial expansion at the center, there is a contraction as the service stairs pinch inwards. The nine-square grid no longer operates with equanimity in all four directions. The pinched center sponsors an extension of the central bar into lateral wings. A clear division between front and back is established, engaging object and edge.

At **Filippo Juvarra's** (1678-1736) **Villa Stupinigi** of 1729-33, the status of the villa as an autonomous, free-standing object is even further called into question. The central structure can still be understood as a nine-square grid, but the corner cells have been pulled diagonally, engendering a radial disposition around an enlarged center. Indeed, the extended diagonal arms spawn new clusters of radial arms so relentlessly that a great figural space enclosed

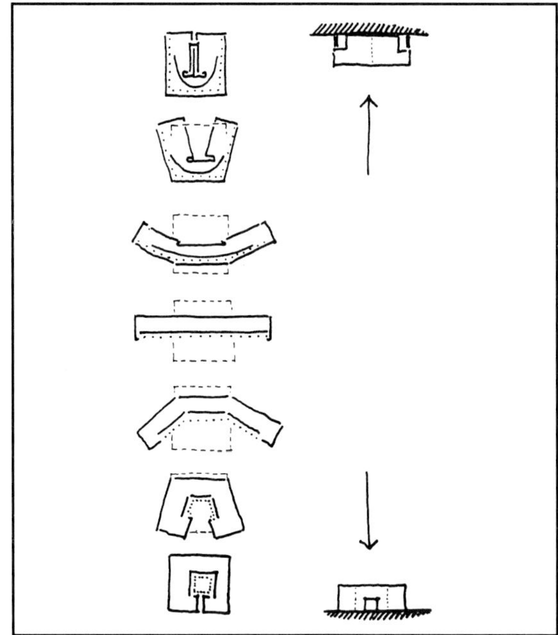

2.20 Douglas Graf, Transformation of Palazzo Farnese into the Villa Savoye.

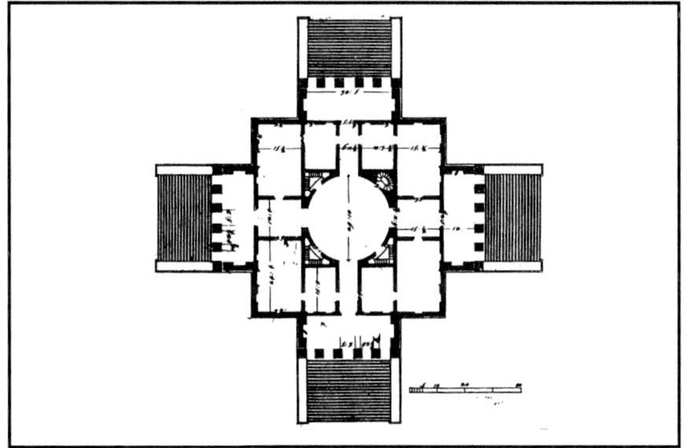

2.21 Andrea Palladio, Villa Rotonda (Villa Capra), Vicenza, Italy, c. 1566.

2.22 Villa Rotonda, view.

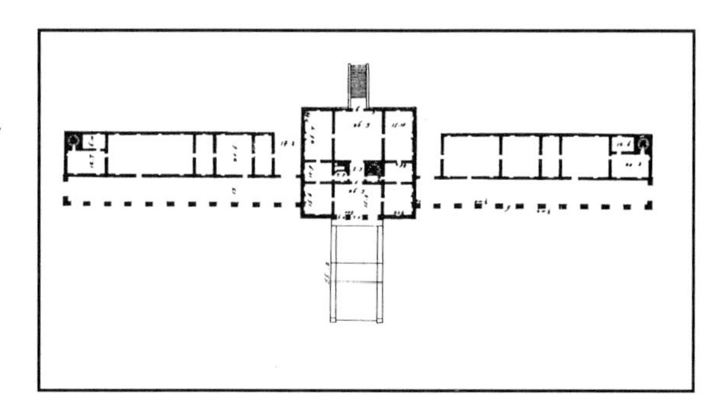

2.23
Andrea Palladio, Villa Emo, Fanzolo, Italy, 1564 .

2.24
Villa Emo, view.

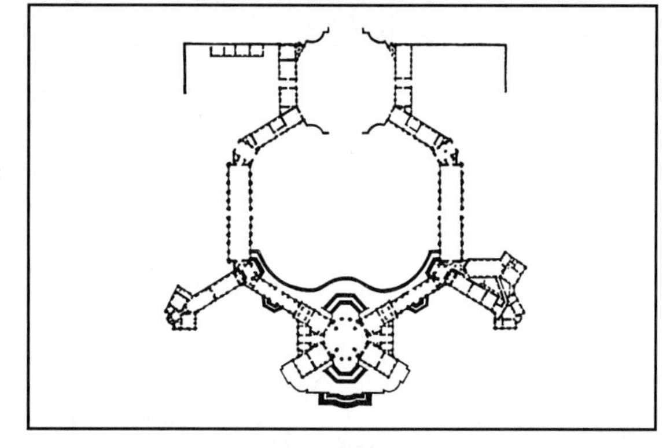

2.25
Fillippo Juvarra, Villa Stupinigi, near Turin, Italy, c.1729-33, plan.

2.26
Villa Stupingi, view.

by the arms dominates the central pavilion, which becomes simply a special event in the wrapper.

A figure ground shift occurs from the clarity of the object at the Villa Rotonda, to the ambiguity between object and edge at the Villa Emo, and finally, to the clarity of the spatial figure and ambiguity of the object at the Villa Stupinigi.

An analysis of figure/ground relationships is useful in the study of buildings but it is even more valuable in understanding urban space. In cities, the space between things often is more legible and distinctly characterized than the buildings that bound the spaces. A visitor to London, Paris or Rome remembers the great public squares long after the surrounding buildings have been forgotten. Moreover, an analysis of figure/ground relationships leads one to understand the progression of open and closed spaces that characterizes movement through the city. It also shows how some structures are able to stand out as special or monumental within their context.

An examination of maps of Rome illustrates this point. A sixteenth century drawing of the city emphasizes objects and buildings. Major churches and monuments from antiquity are portrayed, almost as if to catalog the sights of the city rather than to provide a map for navigation. **The Nolli Plan of Rome** from 1748 instead emphasizes the interplay of solid and void space and helps to identify a sequence of public spaces throughout the city.

If we go back to Riegl's distinction between the 'haptic', or an object-oriented vision of the world, and the 'optic,' or a space-oriented vision of the world, we begin to understand the that

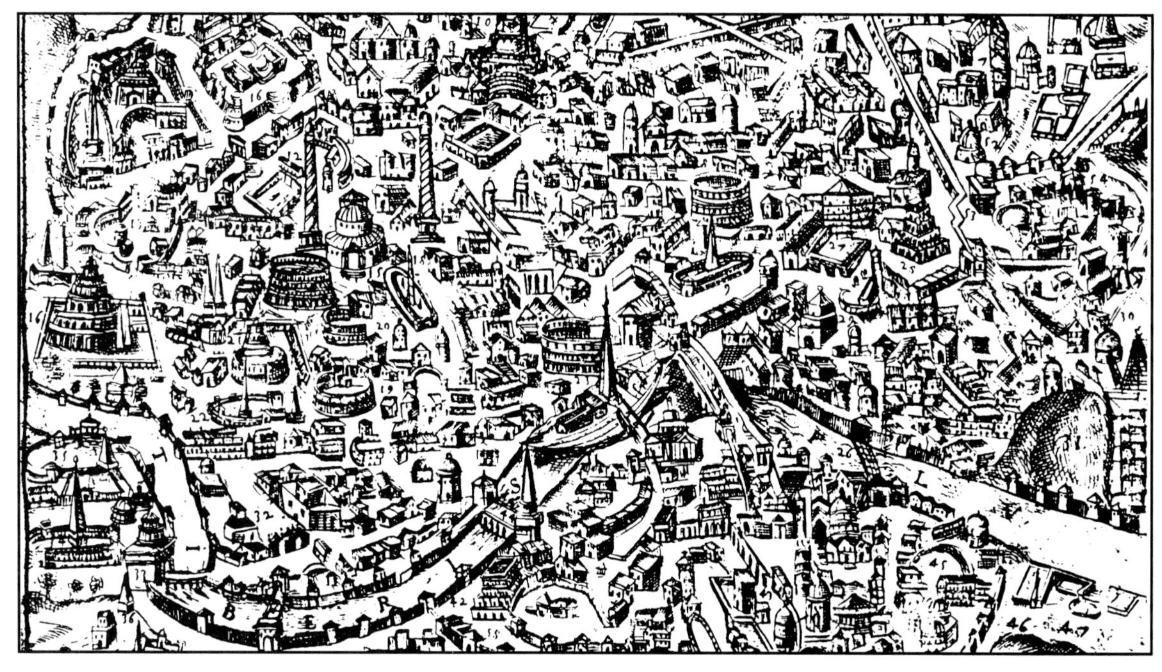

2.27
Pietro Bertelli, 1599, "Plan of Ancient Rome," detail.

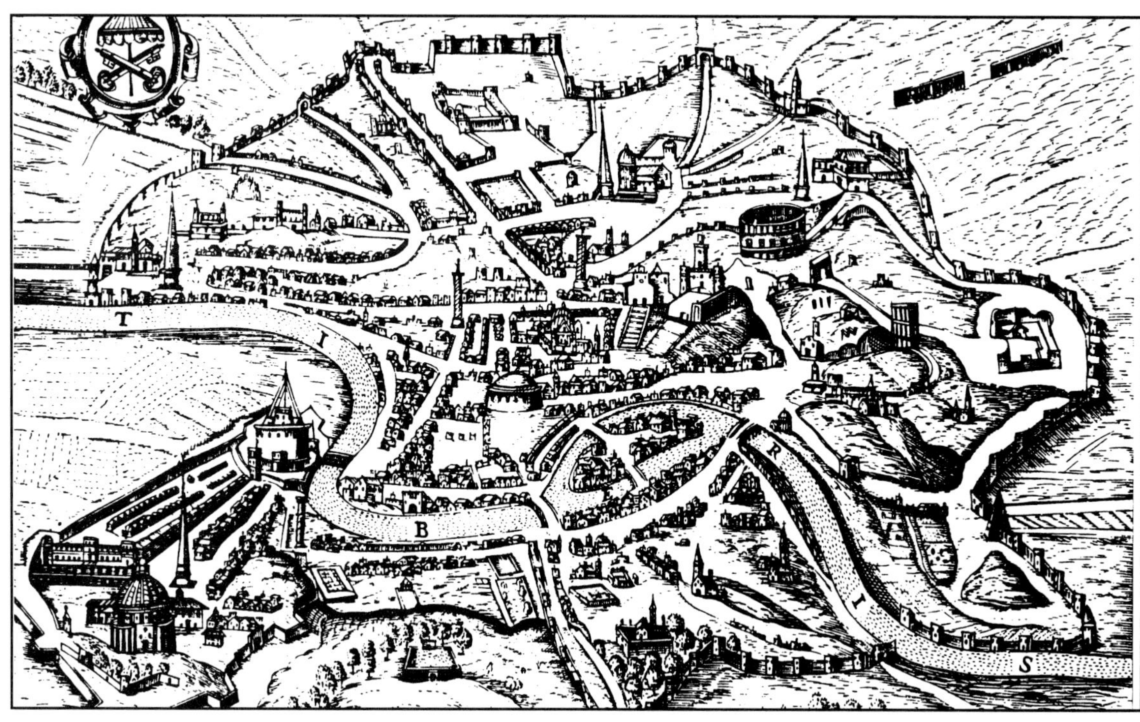

2.28
Pietro Bertelli, 1599, "16th Century Rome."

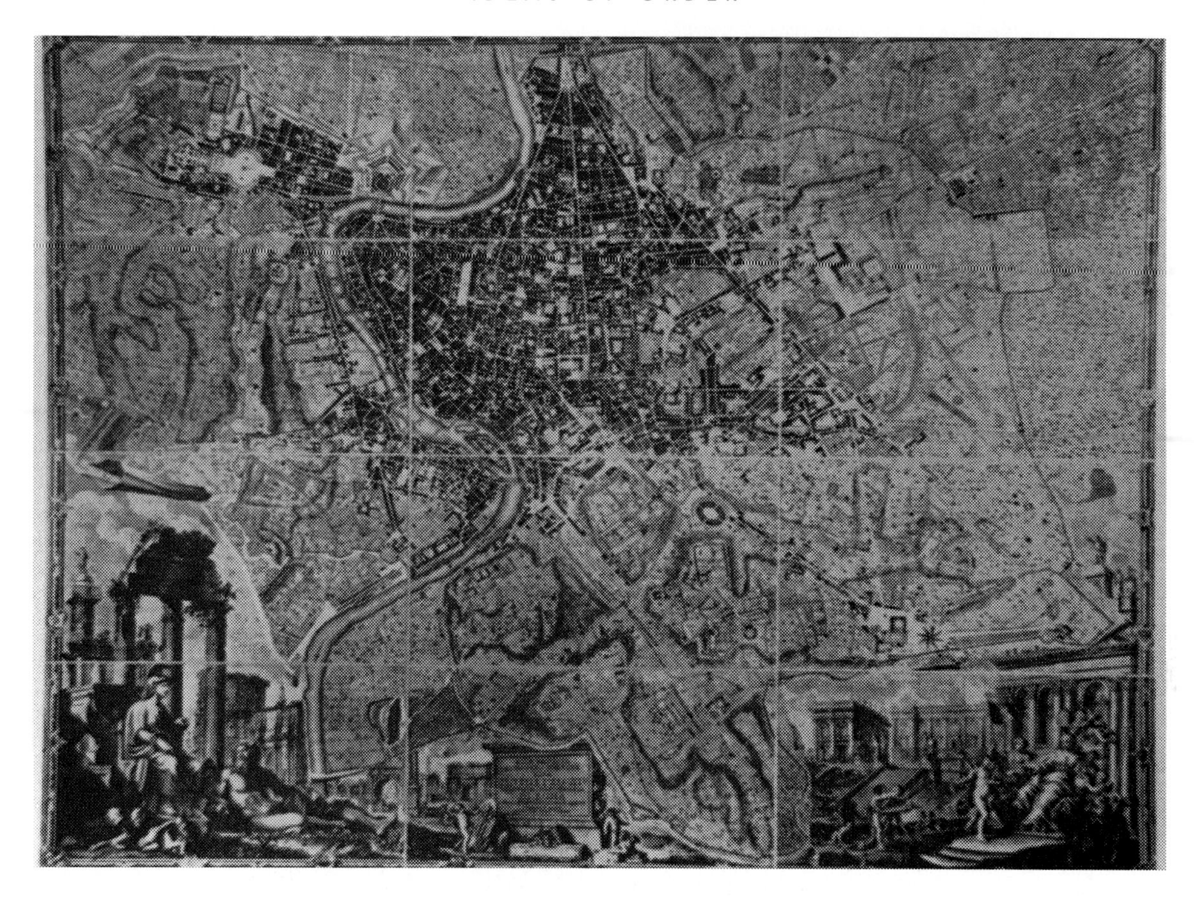

2.29 Nolli Plan, showing Piazza Navona and the Pantheon.

the emphasis on space in the Nolli Plan implies a perspectival vision of the city which is no longer understood as a collection of objects, but rather as a great stage set against which the denizens of the city enact the drama of their daily lives.

The black areas in the Nolli Map depict the 'urban fabric;' the parts of the city occupied by buildings. It is possible to think of it as the 'solid' out of which the 'void' of the piazzas, streets and courtyards have been carved, rather like carving the face of a jack-o-lantern out of the orange pulpy fabric of a pumpkin. Unlike other representations of the city, the Nolli Map assigns equal or greater value to the spaces between things than to the built elements in the city. The Nolli Map also represents the continuity between interior public spaces, the great public rooms of churches, theaters and government buildings, and exterior public spaces. A clear distinction is made between the public and private realms of the city. In this way, an imaginary reconstruction of the sequence of experiences available in the city can be made. The two dimensional drawing provides precise information about the contrast between the con-

2.30 *Giambattista Nolli, Plan of Rome, 1748.*

2.31
Giorgio Vasari, The Uffizi, Florence, plan, c.1550.

2.32
The Uffizi, view towards the Palazzo Vecchio.

stricted space in a narrow alley-way, the expansion of space in a large, sun-filled square, the cool, soaring space of a church, and so forth.

Against the background of the built fabric of the city some special figures emerge. A shaped space, like the elongated horse-shoe void of the **Piazza Navona**, provides contrast and relief from the narrow alleys which surround it. A shaped object, like the circular Pantheon, also stands out from its surroundings by virtue of its idiosyncratic shape and plastic volume. The insertion of such special figures into the city fabric sets up hierarchy and identifies places of great importance. Such 'jewels' are supported by and shown to advantage by the neutrality of the surrounding urban fabric.

The **Uffizi** in Florence by **Giorgio Vasari** (1511-74) is another example of a building defined more clearly by the space it surrounds than the actual mass of inhabited rooms. Indeed, the Uffizi almost disappears to create defining edges for a street which links the Palazzo Vecchio with the Arno River. The inward facing arcaded facades of the building suppress all information about the rooms behind them, presenting instead a uniform mask to the city. An uneven, irregular collection of differently shaped rooms emerges on the outer edge of the building, invisible because this rough edge is completely embedded in the surrounding urban fabric.

Colin Rowe has shown that the majestic voided rectangle of the Uffizi is of almost identical proportion to the footprint of the solid rectangular volume of **Le Corbusier**'s **Unité d'Habitation**, a free-standing, slab apartment block in Marseilles, France. But while the Unité is sited in a field of open space the Uffizi is inserted into the midst of the city. Hence, while the Unité can be unequivocal in the expression of its form, the Uffizi must use a siting strategy which accepts and transforms the surrounding built context. Rowe observes that the different arrangements of mass and space in the Uffizi and the Unité have social and political as well as architectural implications: *"For if the Uffizi is Marseilles turned outside in, or if it is a jelly mould for the Unité, it is also void become figurative, active and positively charged; and while the effect of Marseilles is to endorse a private and atomized society, the Uffizi is much more completely a "collective" structure. And to further bias the comparison: while Le Corbusier presents a private and insulated building which, unambiguously, caters to a limited clientele, Vasari's model is sufficiently two-faced to be able to accommodate a good deal more. Urbanistically it is far more active."* (Colin Rowe, *Collage City*.)

The Uffizi was built at a time in which it was possible to reach a consensus on the values and aspirations of a society. The insertion of the Uffizi into the fabric of Florence responds to these collective needs and reveals relationships between the city's center of power, the Palazzo Vecchio, and the source of wealth and commerce: the river. At the same time, the building suppresses its own private identity to shape a common space for the enjoyment of the whole citizenry. In contemporary times, no such consensus exists.

The atomization of the urban fabric into discrete, self-involved object-buildings, like the Unité, responds to a like disillusion of common social aims typical of the modern sensibility. With the many benefits of democracy comes a reduction in the hierarchy needed to give

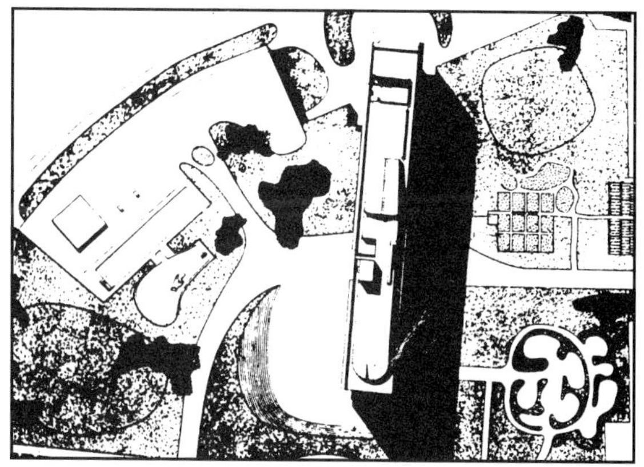

2.33 Le Corbusier, Unité d'Habitation, Marseilles, France, c.1948, site plan.

2.34 Unité d'Habitation, elevation.

2.35 Unité d'Habitation, roof terrace.

2.36 Left: Place des Vosges (Place Royale), Paris.

2.37 Right: Place Dauphine, Paris.

memorable structure to a city. With the privatization of land comes a diminution of the power of the collective and a decreasing likelihood that great public spaces will be created. The wealth and authority of French kings made it possible to reconfigure parts of the city of Paris into magnificent public squares like **the Place des Vosges** and the **Place Dauphine**. Today, individual land ownership, market pressures, and the disruption of traditional scale in order to accommodate the scale and speed of the automobile has generated a very different urban structure. Motor ways and parking lots transform cities into great asphalt expanses. Modern transportation systems call for buildings which can be seen and understood instantaneously as cars whiz by. Refined detail and nuanced relationships to context are replaced by ostentatious object-buildings, the idiosyncrasy of whose designs insures their memorability from the highway.

The composition of solids and voids in the contemporary city is a figure/ground reversal of that of the traditional city. Dense, continuous fabric gives way to superstrings of oddly shaped buildings arrayed along highways, surrounded by parking, and utterly disinterested in the architecture of their neighbors. A late twentieth-century American interpretation of the Nolli map would not suggest a system of squares and avenues carved into the mass of the city, but rather a scattering of convenience stores surrounded by asphalt lots.

2.38
The Marlboro Man, Hollywood Boulevard, West Hollywood, California.

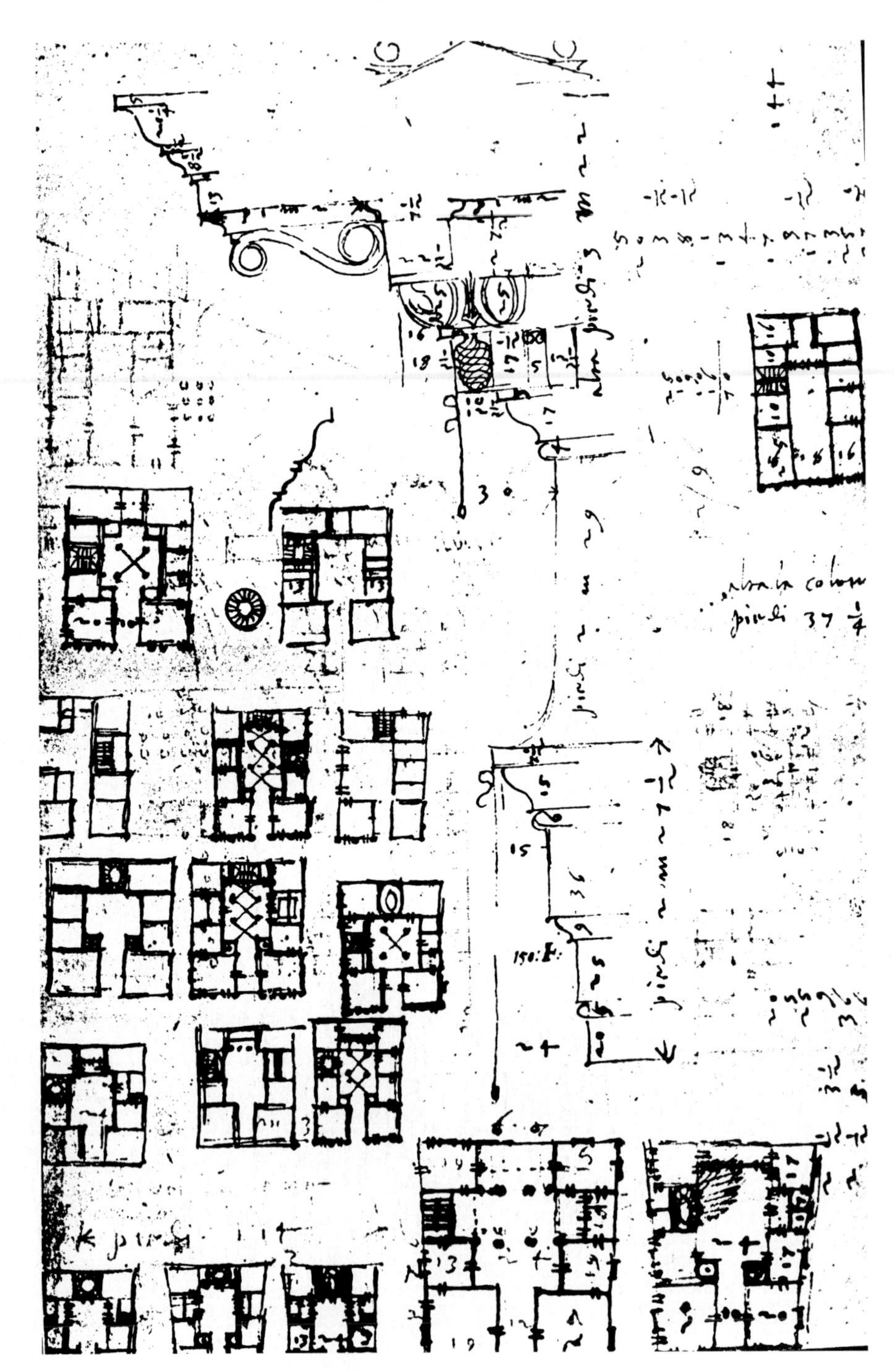

3.0 Andrea Palladio, Alternative Plans for a Palace, c. 1560, courtesy of the R.I.B.A.

Chapter Three

Basic Organizations: The Parti

Before all else, an aesthetic, a work of art, are systems. An attitude is not a system. Genius is a separate and fated thing. Genius gains utterance with the aid of systems. There is no work of art without system.
-Amedée Ozenfant and Le Corbusier

Thus far, we have looked at strategies for formal organization which deal with simple configurations; conditions in which buildings act as objects or centers against a neutral background of continuous space; or conditions in which buildings form edges to define positive, spatial figures. However, it is rare to find either condition operating in its purest form. In the world around us nothing is wholly isolated from its environment. Most organizations of form are hybrid, comprised of multiple and mixed elements. The concept of the **parti** is used to simplify our understanding of formal organizations. Deriving from the French word *partir* (to depart), a parti is a point of departure for an architectural idea. In the *Ecole des Beaux Arts*, the French school of the arts, the term referred to organizational ideas used in quick sketches, or *esquisses*, which the students prepared in a few hours, and then elaborated for the next few months.

A parti is a clear, strong, abstract diagram which is used as the organizational armature for a more complicated arrangement of form. Partis can be drawn from elemental geometry: for example, organizations can be cubic, linear, or circular. Partis can make use of a datum or a neutral ground against which variations can be understood. In musical notation, the relative position of notes with respect to the five lines of the musical staff make it possible to read the different notes with precision. In architecture, diverse structures can serve as data, such as planes, lines, grids, and walls. Partis can be metaphorical, borrowing structures that are essentially zoomorphic, vegemorphic, mechanistic, or whatever. A very crude example of a parti is the lay-out of a typical shopping mall. Malls usually adhere to a 'dumb-bell' parti in which anchor department stores occupy each end of a linear system and rows of smaller shops stretch between them. Without the use of formal concepts like 'dumb-bell' or 'bar' the task of arranging a hundred stores can be overwhelming. With such a model in mind, the architect has solved basic issues of organization and can concentrate on refinements.

3.1
Persian rug.

Transformations of simple formal organizations often serve as the major idea of a design scheme. Actions like 'rotation,' 'reflection,' 'shifting,' 'shearing,' 'translation,' 'displacement,' 'repetition,' 'variation,' 'reversal,' 'scaling,' 'inversion,' 'recursion,' etc., are often applied to an initial organization to create more complex arrangements of parts which nonetheless are logically connected to one another. Later on in this text we shall see that sometimes the structure of an architectural idea is not drawn from form and geometry but from reference to story lines, or 'narratives,' methods of literary criticism, or the very *process* of manipulating form itself. However, we shall stick to basics for the moment.

Just as a datum serves as a ground against which subsequent arrangements of elements can be understood, it is useful first to establish a simple, legible order before a transformation can be meaningful. Hence, designs make use of **paradigms** or ideal models. The most basic, elemental paradigm derives from the ancient structure of the 'Paradise garden,' often represented in the design of traditional **Persian rugs**. Essentially a four-square grid, the carpet pattern is divided by stripes representing the four rivers flowing from Paradise. The rivers extend outwards in each of the cardinal directions until they encounter the surrounding garden wall. The intersection of the four rivers marks the center, which fixes the location of a fountain pool, the source of all fruitfulness. The four-square organization of the overall composition recurs at reduced scale in each of the four quadrants, setting up a more complex nesting of dominate and secondary formal orders. This perfect balance between center and perimeter and the suggestion of an organizational hierarchy which extends from the whole to the detail was considered for millennia to be a model of earthly harmony: Paradise.

The **Vitruvian Man** is another classic paradigm of formal order. While the present example by **Leonardo da Vinci** (1452-1519) comes from the Renaissance, its origins date back to the writings of **Vitruvius**, a Roman architect whose *Ten Books on Architecture* is the only extant architectural treatise from antiquity. As in the paradise garden, geometrical figures are subdivided into four parts, but this time the imposition of cross axes on the centralized scheme reflects the order inherent in the human body. In Leonardo's drawing, the human figure is simultaneously inscribed into the ideal forms of the square and circle. Indeed, the human form can almost be seen to generate these perfect forms through its own perfection. Leonardo's Vitruvian Man is positioned two ways in this drawing. A y-axis is described by the legs, torso and head while an x-axis is described by the outstretched arms. This position generates the square and reflects the order of the square at the same time. Superimposed on this drawing is another human figure with his feet outstretched and his arms raised upwards at an angle. This position generates the circle and reflects the shared radial disposition of the circle and the human body.

Leonardo's genius in his design of the Vitruvian Man comes from the slipping of the circle with respect to the square, creating two centers. The circle, the form connected by Platonic and Pythagorean tradition to the heavens, is arranged around a sacred center, the navel. The square, the form likewise connected to the earth, is arranged around a profane center, the phallus. Moreover, the arithmetically modulated scale at the bottom of the drawing gives measure to the square but further breaks down its dimensions to reflect correspondence with those of the body. The human figure itself is articulated into a series of rectangles related by harmonic proportion, considered in the Renaissance to be the proportional system which governed the distribution of the heavenly bodies. Hence, Leonardo's scheme not only links the proportions and lineaments of the human figure to divine geometry, but also connects the

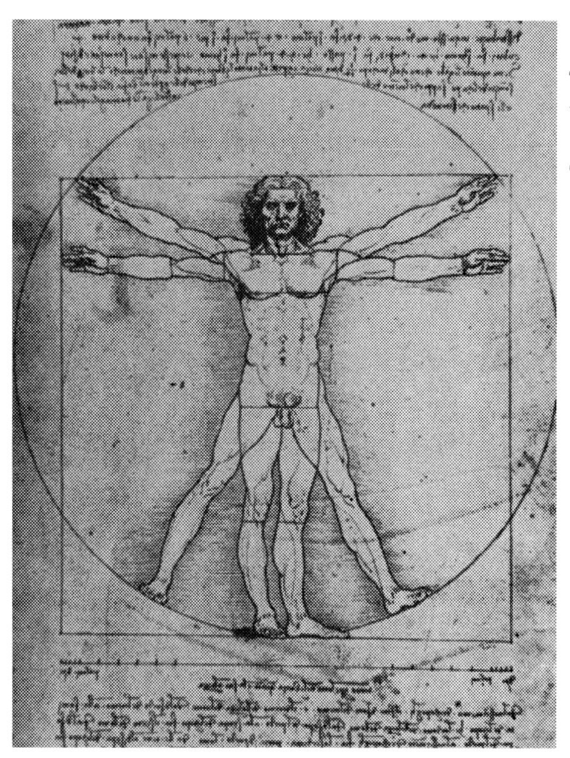

3.2 Leonardo da Vinci, Vitruvian Man, c.1500

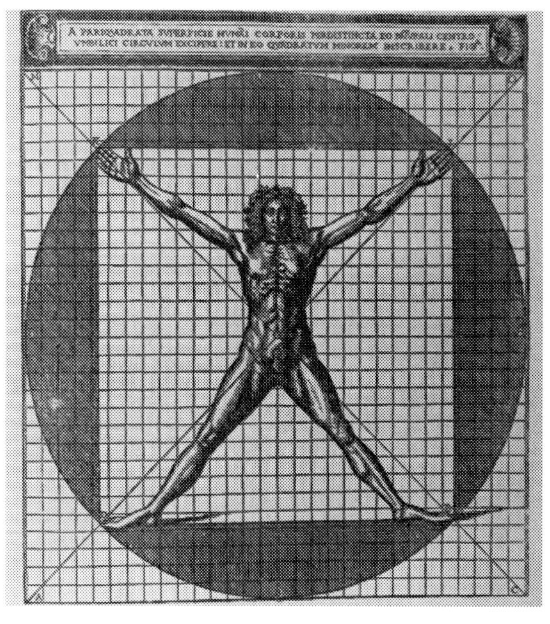

3.3 Cesare Cesariano, Vitruvian Man, 1523.

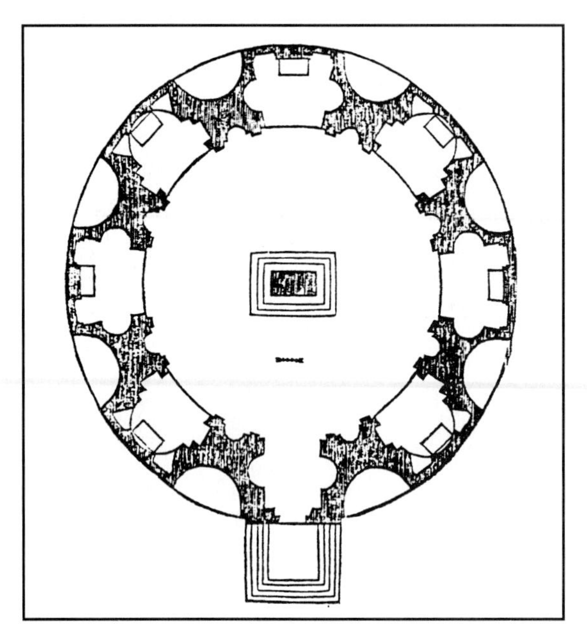

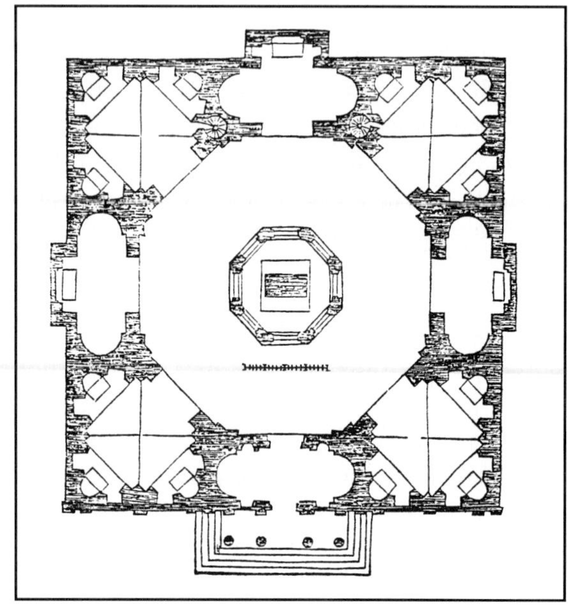

3.4 Left:
S. Serlio, Round Temple plan, c. 1537.

3.5 Right:
S. Serlio, Square Temple plan, c. 1537.

cosmological, ideal harmony of divine order to natural, earthly form.

By comparison, **Cesare Cesariano's** (1483-1543) **Vitruvian Man** nests the circle, square and human figure around a single center, yielding a diminished range of meanings and an 'ideal man' with something less than ideally proportioned hands and feet, stubby legs, and a tiny head. To derive subsequent measure related to the overall scheme, Cesariano applied a neutral grid to the entire background. While the grid sheds light on the dimensional properties of the geometrical figures, it does not succeed in reconciling these dimensions with those of the human figure.

While seldom used with the incisive precision of Leonardo, the basic paradigms of the four-square grid and a centralized, radial organization occur over and over again in architecture. **Sebastiano Serlio** includes many examples of each in his treatise. The **round temple complex** is radial, a scheme which by definition places greatest emphasis on the central point. The primacy of center is further reiterated by the concentric arrangement of rings outward from the center. The **square palace plan**, on the other hand, is organized by cross axes, much like the Paradise garden. Unlike a radial scheme which privileges only the center, the crossing of the X and Y axes locates one special point, but implies the possibility of an extensible coordinate system in which all points can be identified with equal precision.

Using the concept of parti, relationships can be constructed between buildings of different epoches and for different purposes. Hence, it is possible to learn lessons from historical examples which are divorced from issues of historical style and can be used by designers today.

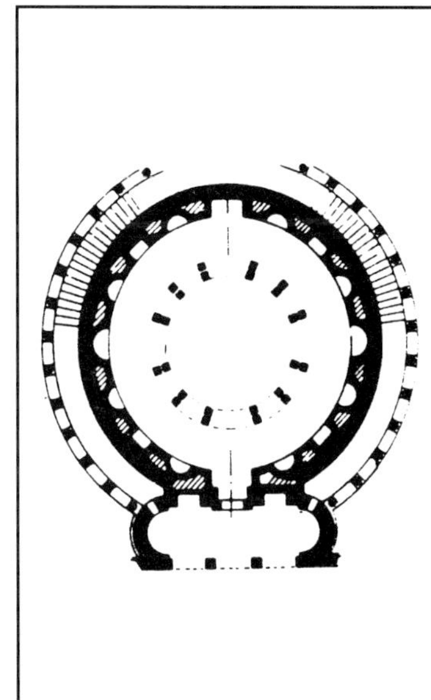

3.6 Left: Anonymous, Santa Costanza, Rome, Italy, c. 345, section.

3.7 Right: Santa Costanza, plan.

3.8 G.B. Piranesi drawing, c. 1745, Santa Costanza, interior.

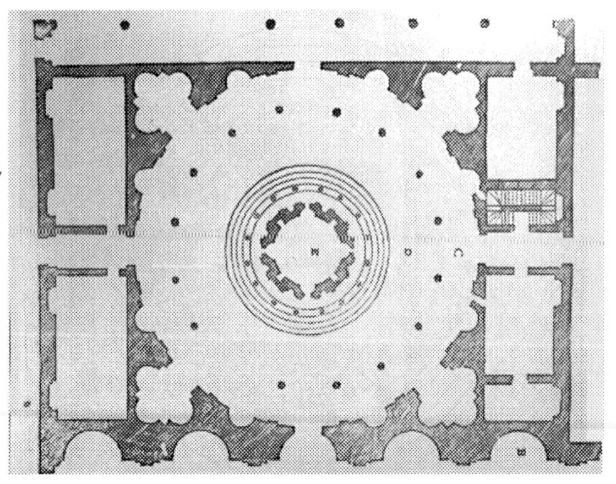

3.9
Donato Bramante, Tempietto, San Pietro in Montorio, Italy, 1502.

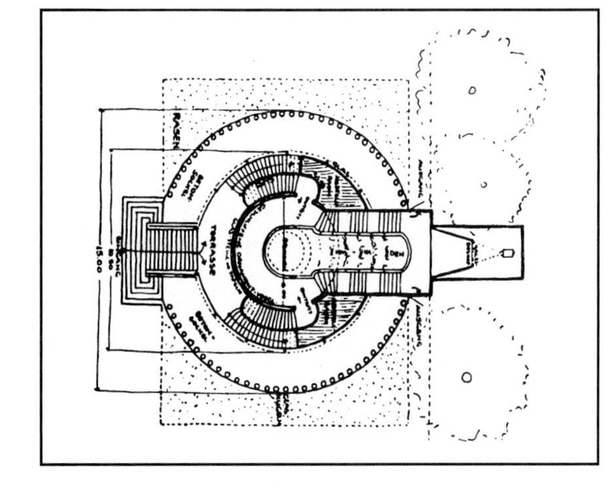

3.10
Bruno Taut, Pavilion for the Glass Industry, Cologne, Germany, 1914.

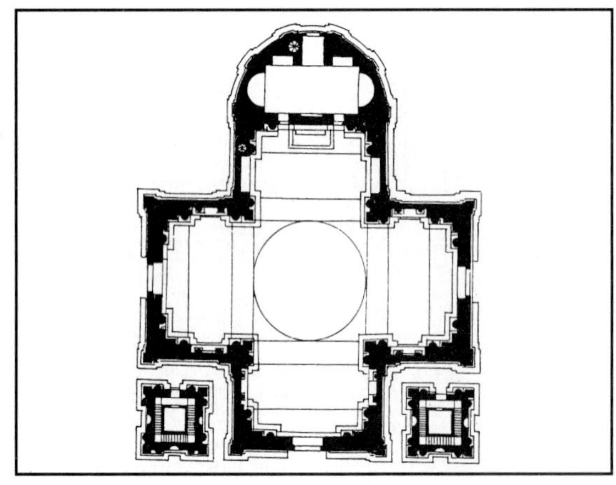

3.11
Antonio da Sangallo the Elder, San Biagio, Montepulciano, Italy, c. 1518.

For example, the formal structure of a sliced onion, in which a centralized scheme is elaborated through the use of concentric bands of material, acts as the organization for the following buildings: the early Christian Mausoleum of **Santa Costanza**, A.D. 345; the Renaissance **Tempietto of San Pietro in Montorio,** by **Donato Bramante** (1444-1514), c. 1502; and the twentieth-century exposition **Pavilion for the Glass Industry** by **Bruno Taut** (1880-1938), Cologne, 1914. Given the common structure, the schemes develop in many different ways.

Santa Costanza is insular and inward-looking. Tucked behind a blank, mask-like wall, it is comprised of an **ambulatory** ring formed of single columns, the encircling thick, masonry wall, and a ring of paired columns which support the taller central domed drum. There is a progression in scale towards the center, paradoxically allowing the innermost shell to be the most brilliantly illuminated. In Bramante's scheme, the basic elements of Santa Costanza are present, but in such a compressed space that the space between the rings of the building cannot be occupied. Rather, the concentricity of the building expands outwards to organize the surrounding courtyard, setting the Tempietto off as a jewel in an ideal display case. While the previous two examples use the rings as layers which are moved through in sequence, Taut's scheme makes use of concentric rings to organize the path through the building. The axis introduced by the entry stairs is wrapped around the center so that one ascends through the glass-block shells of space on glass block and metal stairs to a special room beneath the glass dome. The axis reappears at the opposite side of the pavilion as a cascade of water, flanked by two sets of stairs which appear to have been 'unwound' from the center.

Both the Paradise Garden and the Vitruvian Man rely on 4-square grids, organizations in which center is defined by two crossing lines. The 9-square grid differs from this in that the center is void, and hence occupiable. **Antonio da Sangallo the Elder's** (1455-1534) **Church of San Biagio** can be seen as an incident in the manipulation of the 9-square grid. The grid clearly structures the overall lay-out of the building. The central square is most vertical and given further prominence by its crowning dome. Implied by the spatial envelope, the corner squares are left void to yield a cruciform plan. **Andrea Palladio's** plan for the **Villa Thiene** also uses the nine-square grid as a formal armature. The schematic plan diagram yields a nine-square tartan grid, composed of wide and narrow bands of space. While the basic nine-square organization establishes a firm overall order, the narrow, intermediary bands of space can house the stairs or be absorbed into adjoining spaces. Hence, variation can occur in the development of the plan without compromising the clarity of the parti. As in San Biagio, the central space is given primacy. However, unlike San Biagio, the perimeter of the rectangle is left intact. In a famous essay, the architectural historian **Rudolph Wittkower** prepared a **diagram** which connects all of Palladio's villas back to simple variations on the nine-square plaid grid, showing how a simple parti can be elaborated to achieve many different results. (Rudolph Wittkower, *Architectural Principles in the Age of Humanism*, Rudolph Wittkower, 1949).

A contemporary building which uses the parti of the nine-square grid is **Louis Kahn's**

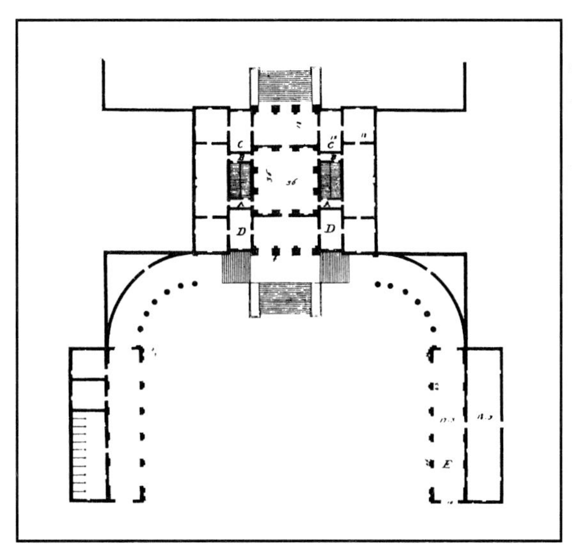

3.12 Palladio, Villa Thiene, Cirogna, Italy, c.1550.

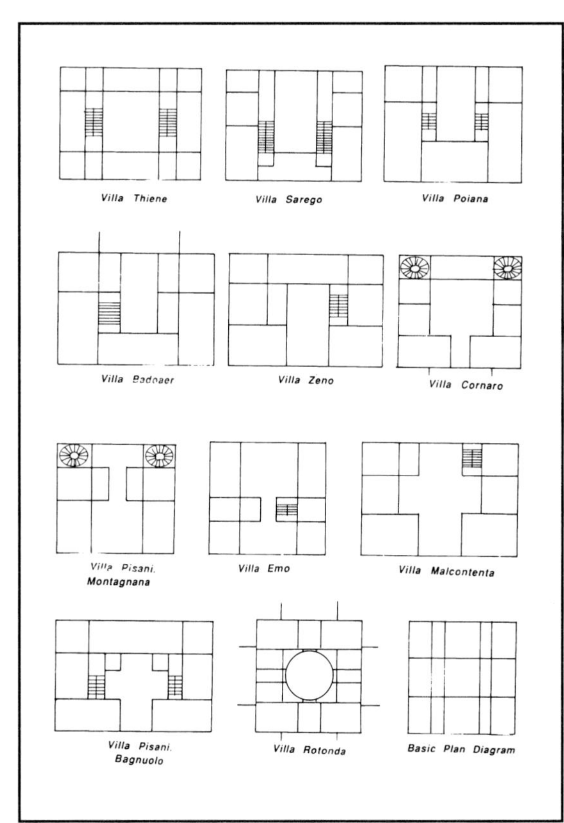

3.13 Rudolph Wittkower, diagram of the basic grid structure of Palladian villas.

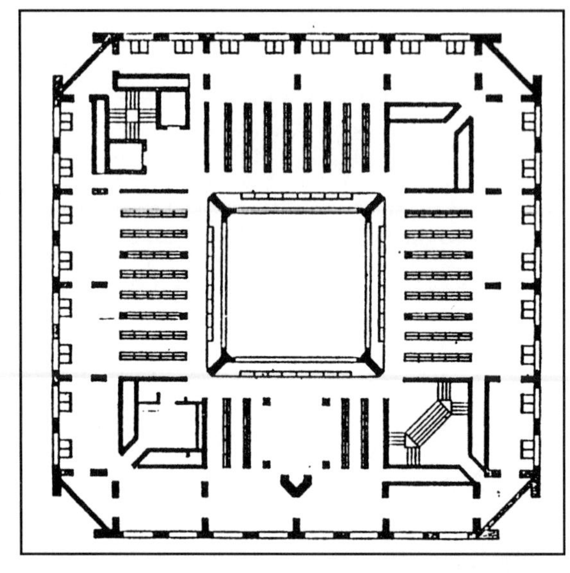
3.14 Louis Kahn, Exeter Library, Exeter, New Hampshire, 1972, plan.

3.15 Exeter Library, ceiling.

3.16 Exeter Library, interior view.

(1902-74) **Exeter Library** in Exeter, New Hampshire. Here the basic nine-square organization is expanded to include other ordering devices. Cubic in general form, the building is like a palazzo, with a voided interior cubic volume wrapped by the perimeter spaces. The wrapper itself is layered, providing double-height bands of space at the **fenestrated** edge for reading carrels, a denser zone away from the light for the shelving of books, a swath of space for circulation around the center, and a very narrow shaft of space between the outer edge of the corridor and the concrete structural element that defines the center. The exterior walls of the library do not meet at the corners, but are pulled apart, voiding the corners and introducing diagonal axes into the building. These diagonal axes are reinforced by the disposition of interior stairs, services, and angled structural piers. The arrangement of structural members and sky-lights of the ceiling plan clearly map out the simultaneous presence of the nine-square grid and the diagonal cross-axes.

Richard Meier also uses a nine-square grid to organize his **High Museum** in Atlanta, Georgia. Like Kahn at Exeter, Meier elaborates the internal structure of the nine-square grid, but he also manipulates the grid itself through a series of transformations. Starting with the simplest idea of the nine-square grid, Meier's first elaboration is to expand the width of the central areas of the grid to three column bays while the outer bands are comprised of two column bays. Within the central band, the outer bays are used for circulation and the inner for services such as bathrooms. Next, the corners of the grid are given their own definition through a system of enclosing walls making them read as special pavilions. Entry is established by pulling one corner pavilion out of the matrix. The displacement is mapped by the double, shifted wall of the auditorium and the irregular, organically-shaped space of the entry lobby which appears almost as if the taut fabric held between two pavilions in the undisturbed condition had been snapped like elastic and assumed a new, relaxed form.

The violent displacement of this corner reverberates throughout the organization of the building. Along the trajectory of the displacement, a path is extended to the street. This diagonal axis sponsors the radial organization of the atrium. The circulation bays at the remote corners are voided as corridors, making possible the reading of a four-square grid; while the remaining circulation bays are rendered solid and used for vertical circulation. The crossing of circulation paths marks the center of both the four-square and the radial organization, while the center of the nine-square organization has become distended and pie-shaped.

The spatial neutrality of the nine-square grid has been shattered, resulting in a highly site-specific arrangement of form. The hard, ell-shaped edge of the wrapper addresses the back of the site and serves as a background for the figural volumes towards the main street. Hence, a building organization which seems at first glance to be impossibly complex is understandable and clear through reference to a simple spatial paradigm and its transformation.

The **Ozenfant Studio** in Paris by **Le Corbusier**, 1922, is another building whose complexities are governed by simple geometric figures placed into dynamic relationships with

3.17 Richard Meier, High Museum of Art, Atlanta, Georgia, c. 1982.

3.18 High Museum, diagrams.

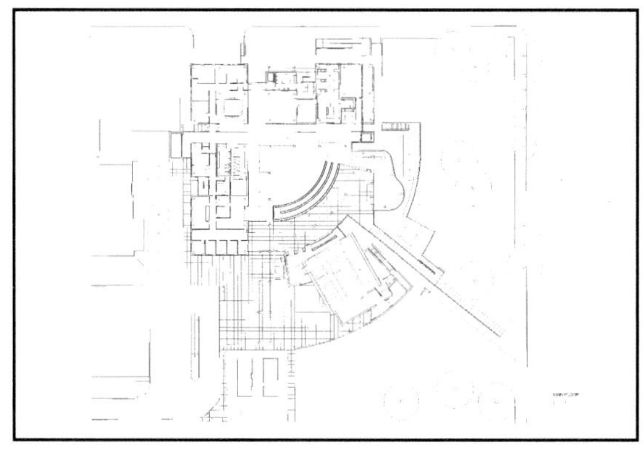

3.19 High Museum, atrium.

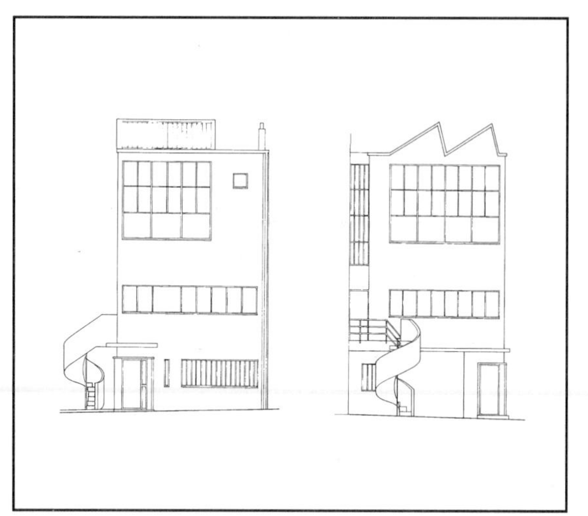

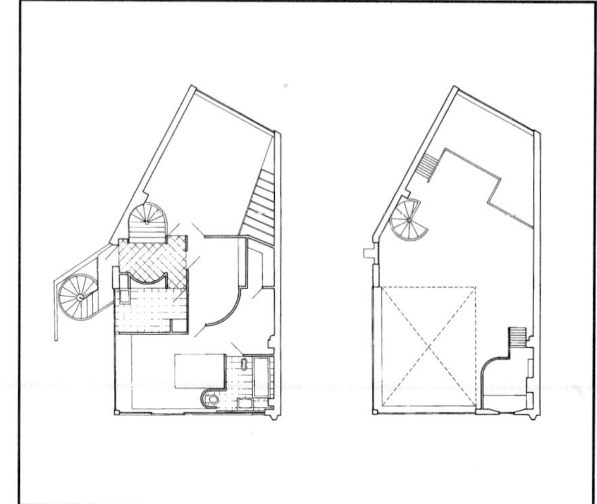

3.20 Left:
Le Corbusier,
Ozenfant Studio,
Paris, France,
1922, elevations.

3.21 Right:
Ozenfant Studio,
plans.

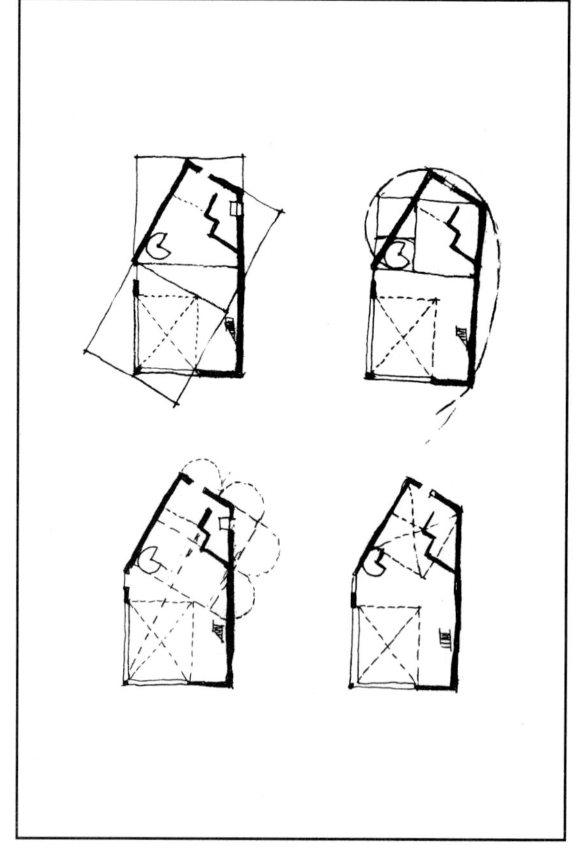

3.22 Left:
Ozenfant Studio,
exterior view.

3.23 Right:
Ozenfant Studio,
diagrams.

each other and the site. At first glance, the footprint of the plan appears to be an irregular polygon. Upon closer analysis we see that the plan is comprised of a primary square and canted trapezoid. Further analysis reveals that a relationship exists between these two forms: the trapezoid can be seen as the remnants of another square, folding out from the first, generative square along a hinge-point marked by the spiral stairs and truncated where the property lines are met. Further elaborations of the diagram connect back to the ideas of rotation, hinging, and spiraling. Proportional relationships between the long and short sides of the rectangle describe a **golden rectangle**, wherein B/A = A/(A+B). An infolding of the golden rectangle progression towards the spiral stair locates other main elements of the plan, such as the balcony and ladder.

The corner of the primary square is voided, wrapped by windows not only on the corner walls but on the ceiling as well. Function, light, views and ventilation are optimized. Formally, the erosion of the corner responds to the angle of the oblique wall. Ordering devices which implicitly govern the plan, such as the golden rectangle progression, are used to generate the section and elevations of the building. Drawings of elevations explicitly note proportional strategies through the use of **regulating lines**, a network of parallel and perpendicular lines, lightly drawn over the elevation to reveal the presence of similar rectangles.

Metaphor can serve as the basis of a parti. The Renaissance architect **Pietro Cataneo** explicitly links the form of a **longitudinal church plan** to that of the human figure. **Eero Saarinen's** (1910-61) inspiration for the **TWA Terminal** at

3.24 Pietro Cataneo, Anthropomorphic Church Plan, 1567.

3.25 TWA Terminal, exterior view.

3.26 Eero Saarinen, TWA Terminal, New York, 1958-62, interior view.

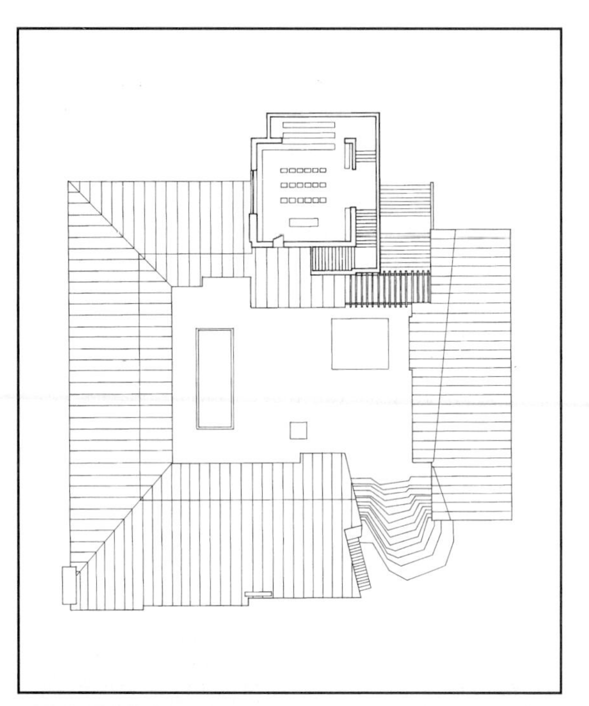

3.27 Left: Alvar Aalto, Säynätsalo Town Center, Säynätsalo, Finland, plan.

3.28 Right top: Säynätsalo Town Center, model.

3.29 Right bottom: Säynätsalo Town Center, view.

3.30 Left: Antoni Gaudi, Crypt of the Chapel of the Colonia Güell, Santa Coloma de Cervelló, Spain, c. 1908, view.

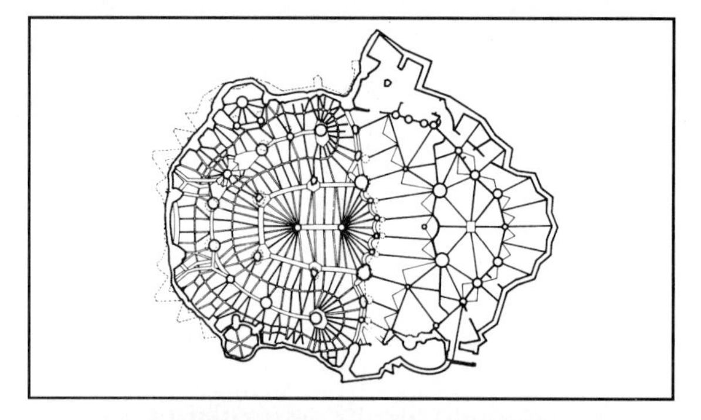

3.31 Right top: Crypt of the Chapel of the Colonia Güell, plan.

3.32 Right bottom: Crypt of the Chapel of the Colonia Güell.

Kennedy Airport was the idea of flight. The arched concrete shell of the building mimics the wings of a bird. Alvar Aalto's **Säynätsalo Town Center** in Säynätsalo, Finland follows a 'head/tail' organization. Just as the head and tail of a snake are differently shaped and perform different functions than the body, which is more or less equal across its length, so too does Aalto's scheme begin and end with special, figural elements. The head-piece is the council chamber, the most important space in the complex. The bent bar of offices is repetitive, neutral and edge-like along its length until it terminates in a special condition. The library separates itself from the main building like the rattle at the end of a snake's tail.

In his design for **Santa Coloma de Cervello**, **Antoni Gaudi** (1852-1926) goes beyond Cataneo's two-dimensional equation between the human form and architectural space. For Gaudi, the three-dimensional development of space is mimetic of the decaying carcass of a large animal. Structural ribs in the ceiling vault are analogous to ribs. Roughly hewn, primitive shafts look more like bleached bones than col-

3.33 Pablo Picasso, Green Still Life, 1914, Museum of Modern Art, New York.

3.34 Le Corbusier, Cité de Réfuge (Salvation Army), Paris, France, 1931-33.

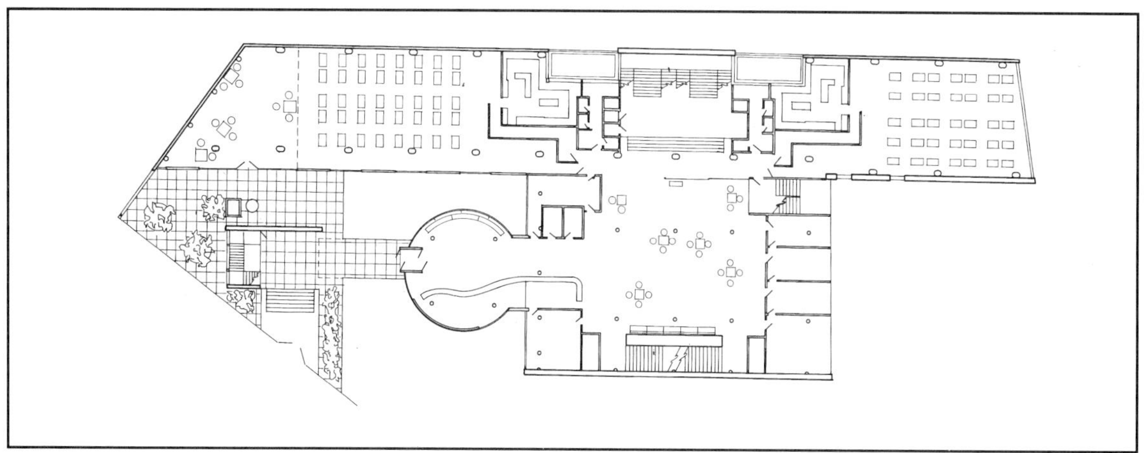

3.35 Cité de Réfuge, plan.

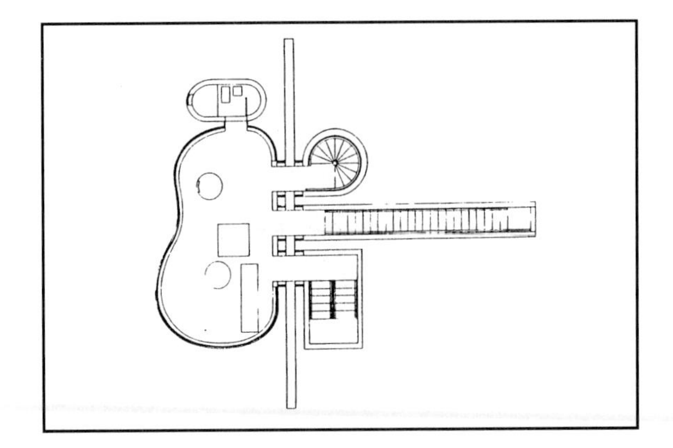

3.36 Left: John Hejduk, Wall House III, project, 1968-74, plan.

3.37 Right: Wall House III, elevation.

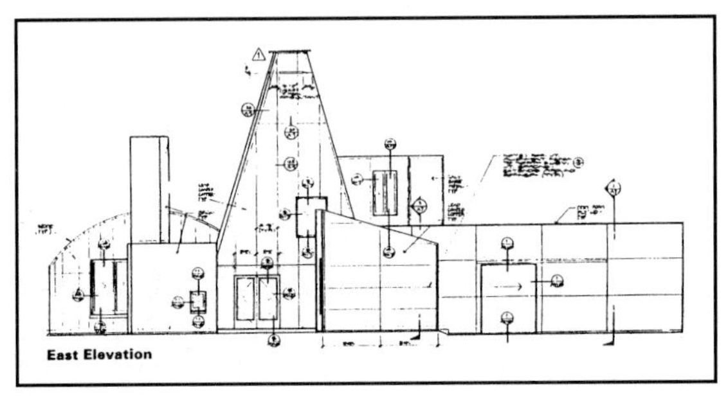

3.38 Frank Gehry, Winton Guest House, Wayzata, Minnesota, 1983, elevation.

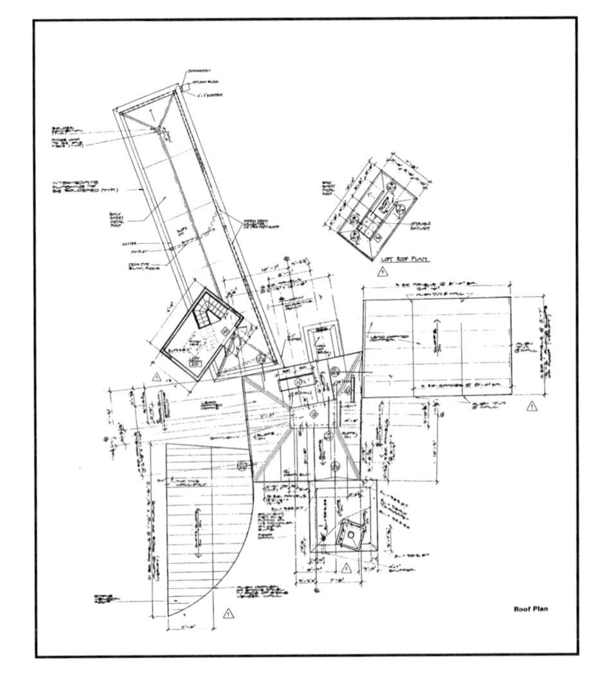

3.39 Winton Guest House, plan.

umns of any known order, evoking a sense of horror and piety in the observer.

When the program of a building is complex, parti strategies which accommodate diverse elements and diverse scales are often adopted. **Le Corbusier's Salvation Army Building**, or Cité de Réfuge, in Paris, 1931-33, organizes repetitive elements, dormitory rooms and workshops, in a tall slab which acts as a datum for smaller, more figural pieces. The neutrality of the slab acts almost like the continuous surface of a table top to organize diverse elements in a still-life composition similar to that achieved by **Pablo Picasso** (1881-1973) in his ***Green Still Life*** of 1914. The cubic and cylindrical volumes at the Salvation Army Building set up the entry sequence into the building.

In Le Corbusier's 'bar/object' organization for the Salvation Army Building, the bar is one-sided, embedded into the fabric of Paris. **John Hejduk** uses the wall as a datum to organize figural objects in his **Wall House III,** but in this case, the wall is two sided. Instead of using a neutral vertical element like a wall or a slab as a datum for the organization of disparate pieces, **Frank Gehry** collages and collides discrete vol-

3.40 Left: House, Los Angeles.

3.41 Right: House, Los Angeles.

umes together on a common ground plane in the assemblage of elements which comprise the **Winton Guest House** in Wayzata, Minnesota.

It would be impossible to catalogue all possible parti configurations, they are numberless. Nor are partis selected solely because of their ability to accommodate programmatic demands. All houses are used for dwelling, yet the forms they take are myriad. Sometimes they are linked to the specific customs of a place, like the **vernacular housing on Mykynos**, and sometimes linked to more subtle representations of the aspirations and pretensions of the clients.

The **Paris Opera House** by **Charles Garnier** (1825-98), 1860-75, and the **Berlin Philharmonic Hall** by **Hans Scharoun**, 1956-63, are both theaters for the performing arts. However, both buildings respond to very different political and cultural pressures which influence the arrangement of forms. In nineteenth-century France, Charles Garnier chose a strongly axial, layered organization which emphasized the hierarchy of a highly stratified society. In post-World-War II Germany, the recent experience of the Third Reich made authoritarianism suspect.

3.42 House, Mykonos, Greece.

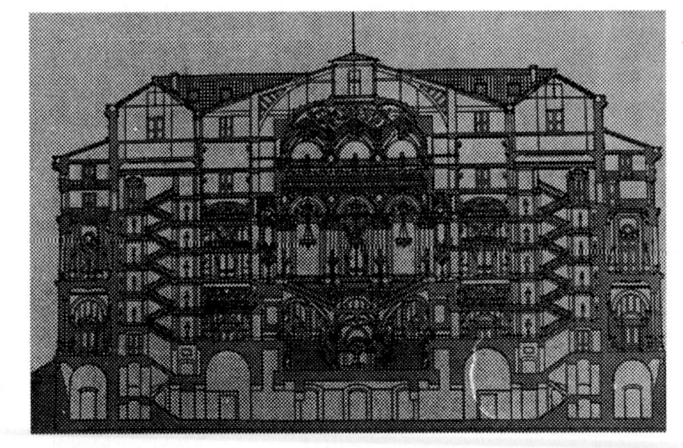

3.43 Left: Charles Garnier, Paris Opera House, Paris, France, 1860-75, section.

3.44 Right: Paris Opera House, the grand stair.

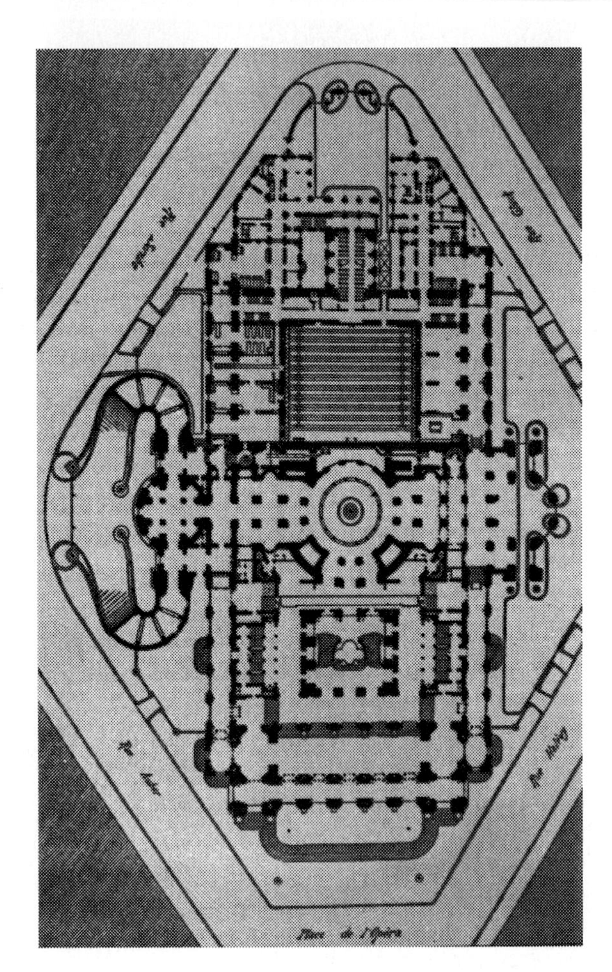

3.45 Paris Opera House, plan.

Scharoun sought a deliberately non-hierarchical arrangement of form. In Berlin, the grand stair of the Paris Opera House is shattered, atomized, rendered non-hierarchical and democratic through its multiplicity and equality throughout the theater. Even the strong division between front and back, the stage and the audience, which is so important in Garnier's scheme, disappears in Scharoun's. In the Philharmonic, the stage acts as an instable center enveloped by tiers of seating, like shards of a broken vessel. The fragmented disorder of the interior extends outward and is mapped on the exterior of the building. Here, unlike Paris, no singular, monumental entry is provided. Like the stairs, entry is diffused and reiterated throughout the plan.

The location of the buildings in the fabric of the city further enforce these meanings. Situated at the terminus of the grand l'Avenue de Opéra, the monumentality of Garnier's building commands views across the entire city. Scharoun's building, situated near the old Berlin Wall, deliberately disrupts traditional street patterns of the city and is positioned to interrupt the flow of the old Potsdammer Straße,

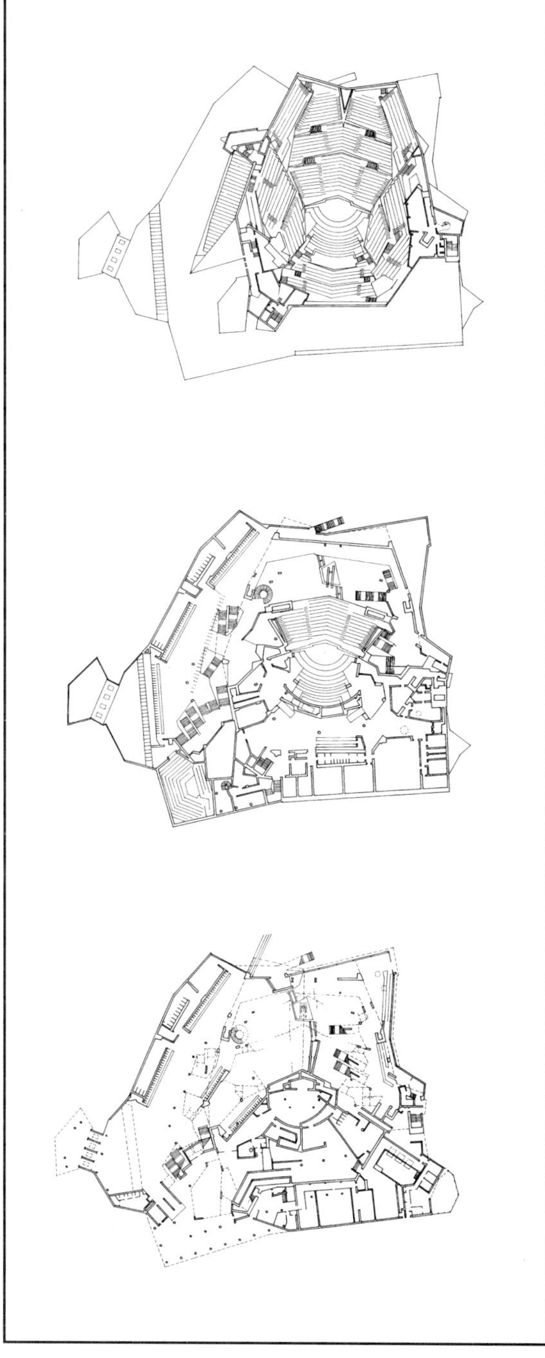

3.46 Left: Hans Scharoun, Philharmonic Hall, Berlin, Germany, 1956-63, stairs.

3.47 Right: Philharmonic Hall, plans.

once a grand boulevard which extended across the length of Germany signifying and helping to consolidate the authority of the capital.

In discussing partis we have observed that simple organizational structures can be elaborated to yield very different buildings and to communicate very different messages about their client, culture and world view. As building programs or site relationships grow more and more complex, the utility of the parti increases. Without a governing, overarching order, the designer confronts an impossible task; every design decision, even fairly trivial ones, must be made from an infinite range of possibilities. The parti provides a structure which limits the range of choice and assures cohesion of the whole. The parti is a graphic device which holds within it the germ of an architectural idea. Rather than enforcing rigidity on an architectural solution, the parti is sufficiently flexible to accommodate great variety. In this way, complex buildings can have coherence and clarity, abiding by an order which extends from the general concept to the detail.

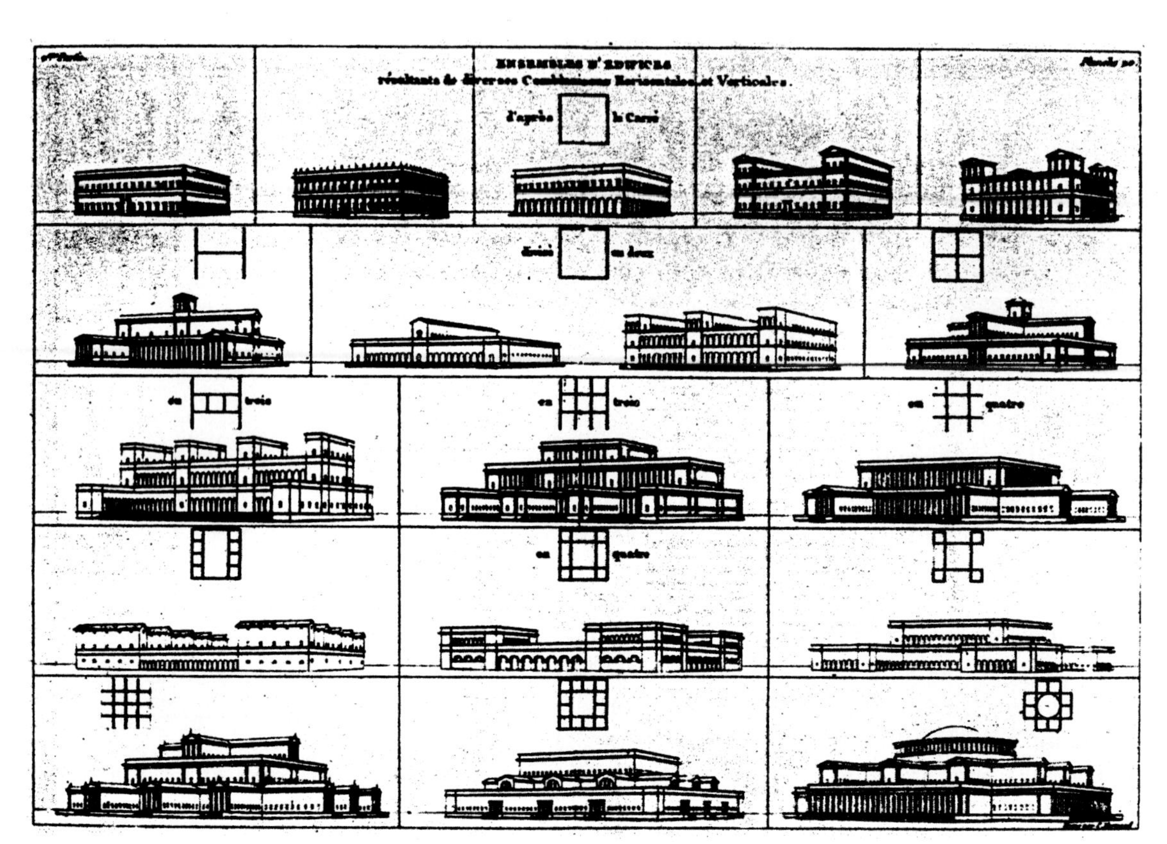

4.0
J.N.L. Durand,
Precis des leçons.

Chapter Four

Typology versus Morphology

The Art of Building is born out of a pre-existing germ; nothing whatsoever comes out of nothing- the type is a sort of kernal around and in accordance to which variations the object is susceptible are ordered.

-Quattremère de quincy

Our discussion of partis has concentrated on the formal analysis of buildings, deliberately avoiding historical or stylistic analysis. The study of forms and their manipulation is sometimes called **morphology.** While morphology suggests an examination of formal relationships in their purest, most abstract sense, it is difficult to disassociate forms from traditions of use. For example, a small building surrounded by a parking lot and flanked by golden arches is difficult to understand as pure form and color. It is immediately understood as an example of a class or **type** of building, a McDonald's Restaurant. It is then possible to make subtle judgements about the development and refinement of the example at hand. We may speak of a 'nice McDonald's' or an 'awful McDonald's' without holding either to the standards of excellence one would use to judge a palace or a cathedral.

Building types have been defined in purely formal terms. Raphael Moneo states that *"type... can most simply be defined as a concept which describes a group of objects characterized by the same formal structure. It is neither a spatial diagram nor the average of a serial list. It is fundamentally based on the possibility of grouping objects by certain inherent structural similarities."* (Raphael Moneo, "On Typology," *Oppositions 13,* Summer, 1978). Yet unlike morphological manipulations of form and structure, building types arose in response to specific vernacular, programmatic or ritualistic uses. They therefore carry with them a memory of those original meanings. Architects can make use of **typology** to tap our collective cultural understanding of traditional built form and to connect the meaning of their buildings to that tradition.

Antoine-Chrysostome Quattremère de Quincy, (1755-1849), formalized the theory of typology in his *Dictionaire d'architecture encyclopédie méthodique*, Paris, 1788-1825, vol. III, part 2. Here he proposed that there was a collective patrimony of architectural forms which

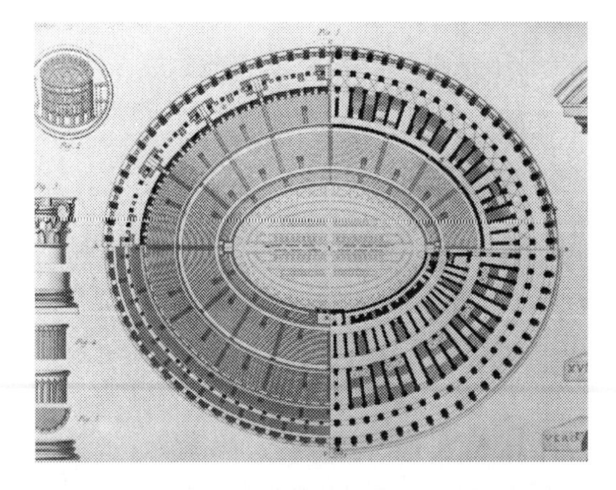

4.1 The Colosseum, Rome, Italy, A.D. 75-80.

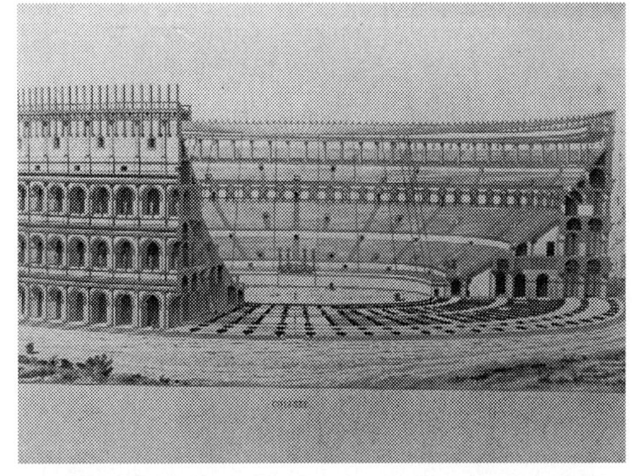

4.2 The Colosseum, section.

4.3 Thomas Jefferson, University of Virginia, Charlottesville, Virginia, 1817-26.

derived from the Greeks and which was promulgated and diffused by the Romans. These normative building 'types' were distinguished from specific 'models.' A building 'type' provides a formal armature for the selection and configuration of constituent elements in a building, but it also provides latitude for variation. A 'model', on the other hand, serves as a direct source to be imitated, down to the detail. While Quatremère himself subscribed to a rigid classicism, his theory of typology did not exclude invention on the part of the architect. Rather it used the concept of building type to define a framework in which architectural invention could take place, just as the structure of a sonnet limits the form of the poem but not its content.

The utility of 'type' as an architectural construct hinges on how broadly or how narrowly 'type' is defined. If it is too broad, all buildings can be grouped under the aegis of a single type. This all-embracing type might be something like 'built structures.' If it is too narrow, then every building exemplifies and defines a type particular to itself. An example of a too-narrow type might be something like 'yellow clapboard three-bedroom houses with garage doors embellished with eagles.' Quattremère solved the problem by concentrating on only building types which arose historically within the Graeco-Roman tradition. Yet every culture has placed new demands on the built environment and new building types have emerged. We have already discussed examples of many such building types, such as the palazzo, the villa, and the longitudinal church. Even newer building types have been sponsored by our mechanized society, such as the train station, the airport, the gas station, the factory, etc. The definition of each building type must be sufficiently broad as to allow great variety to be absorbed within the type, but not so broad as to encompass buildings with significant differences among them.

Specific buildings and historical types can be used as **precedents** for contemporary building. Architects can use and manipulate reference to previous works and the normative types they exemplify to create even further nuances of meaning in their buildings. Variations made with reference to an established building type are meaningful because the original significance of the type is already known, imbedded in our culture.

Sometimes when building types are adopted, the function of the original type is conserved. Modern sports stadia are not essentially different in form and function from their Roman predecessors, although their constructional and mechanical systems differ greatly. A type may also be adopted for associative or merely decorative purposes, and reference to the original function is all but lost. Few cults worship Olympian gods in the modern world, yet examples of Graeco-Roman temple porches can be found in almost every town. The building type of temple, or at least the temple portico, has been used by banks, post offices, churches, schools, etc., and assigned a new function, while its ancient significance of stability, power, authority, and dignity have been appropriated by the institutions which aspire to the stature and timelessness of the original. Sometimes the inappropriate use of a type can be amusing, as in the case of the temple-like **Grain elevator**, **Gas station** and **Outhouse**.

4.4
K. F. Schinkel, Neuewache, Berlin, Germany, 1817.

4.5
Leo von Klenze, Glyptotek, Munich, Germany, 1816-31.

4.6
Leo von Klenze, Propylaea, Munich, Germany, 1846-60.

4.7 Left: Doric Outhouse, Ellicott City, Maryland.

4.8 Right: Doric Grain elevators, Texas.

4.9 Right bottom: Doric Gas Station, Dayton, Ohio.

4.10 Left: Andrew Gargus, age 8, 'House'.

Both morphology and **typology** provide the architect with *a priori* forms which can be adapted in the design of a given building. However, while morphology deals with abstract, ideal geometries, typology deals with form laden with cultural, functional and historical associations. A comparison between two twentieth-century houses may prove instructive. **Frank Lloyd Wright's** (1869-1959) **Robie House** and **Le Corbusier's Villa Savoye** both pushed the conventional form of 'house' to the limit in the early part of the twentieth century. Using the new constructional technology of re-

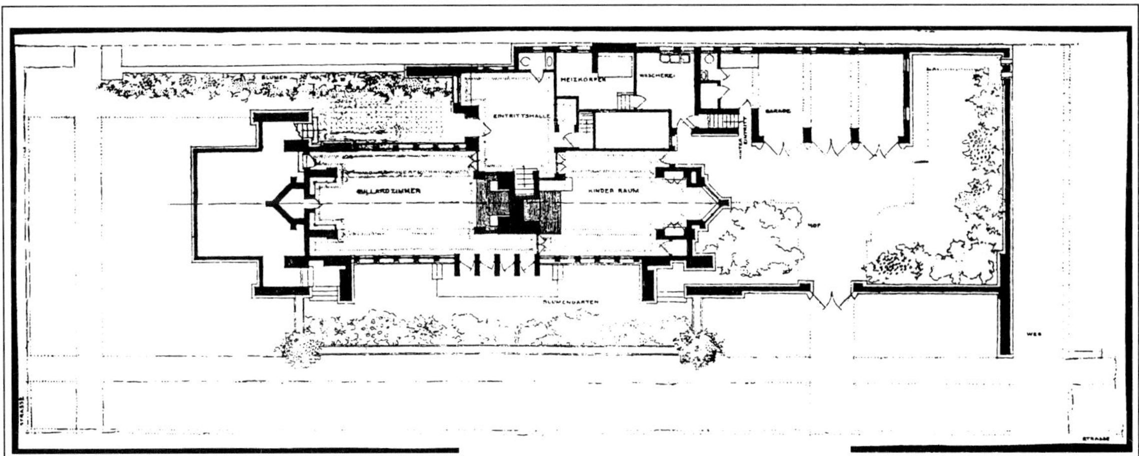

4.11 Frank Lloyd Wright, Robie House, Chicago, Illinois, 1909, plan.

4.12 Robie House, perspective drawing.

inforced concrete, both architects sought to reinvent the house. They eschewed traditional spatial and ornamental schemes in an effort to find a form more appropriate to the specific time (Le Corbusier) or place (Wright) in which they were building. Both architects challenged conventional notions of interior space. Departing from a conception of the house as a series of discrete rooms, both developed open interiors comprised of interlocking, interdependent spaces and extended their investigation of spatial openness to include a blurring of the limits between interior and exterior space. However, they proceeded along very different paths and therefore achieved very different architectural expression for their ideas. Le Corbusier approached the task of reinventing the house from a morphological standpoint while Wright made use of house typology to recompose the constituent elements of the traditional house.

The Villa Savoye is a pristine white box, its envelope fully explicable through geometric description. The white stucco surface of the building succeeds in neutralizing color and material and removing any hint of ornament. The development of proportions is self-contained in

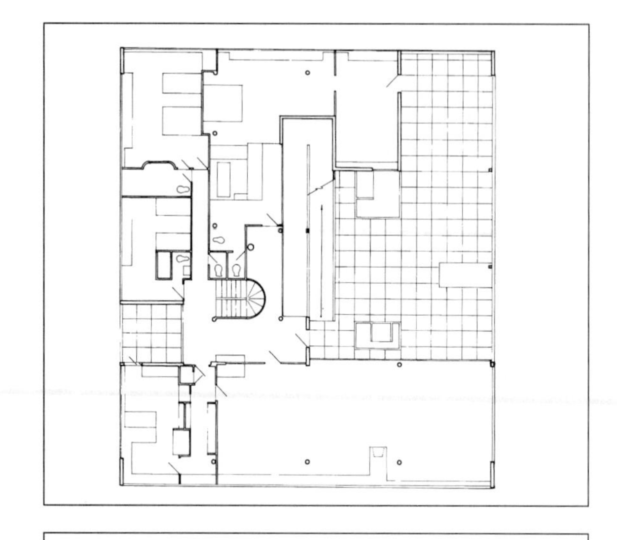

4.13
Le Corbusier, Villa Savoye, Poissy, France, 1928-31, piano nobile plan.

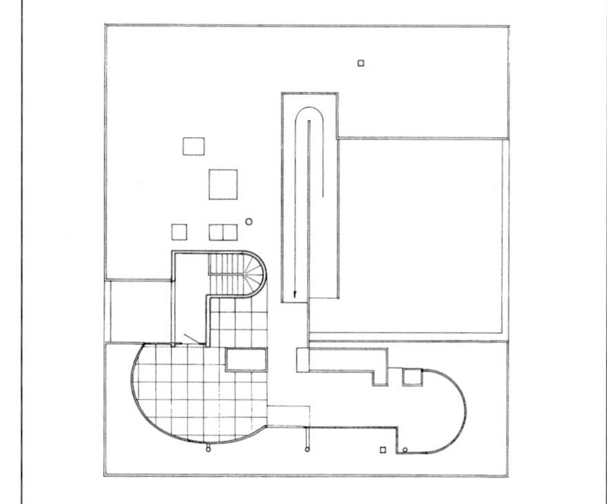

4.14
Villa Savoye, roof terrace.

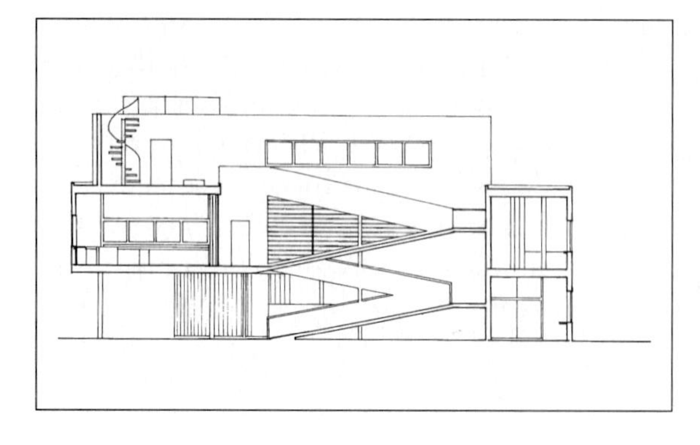

4.15
Villa Savoye, section.

the Villa Savoye. Legible scale references to the human body is eradicated: no material joints, windows or doors are visible to provide clues to the relationship between the building and the human body. Ribbon windows, which wrap the building, render the building box even more abstract. Rather than adding elements like porches or terraces, the elemental box of the Villa Savoye is elaborated through subtraction. Terraces are scooped out of the mass of the box and figural elements are allowed to emerge only within its taut frame. It is a morphological exercise in the manipulation of pure form.

Wright, on the other hand, seems to celebrate the very elements that Le Corbusier seeks to neutralize. His exaggerated emphasis on roof, window, chimney and natural materials seems to have been extracted from the standard image of houses drawn by children. Wright first identifies the elements which define the type. He then pulls them out of context and reassembles them as a collection of horizontal and vertical planes, this time in a new dynamic relationship with each other and the ground plane. Yet the meaning of the house remains strongly rooted to these defining elements drawn from tradition. The chimney pins together the two shifted bars of the plan and acts as an axis mundi, establishing the connection between ground and sky, uniting the physical center of the house with its center of meaning, the hearth. The roofs sweep out beyond the built enclosure to embrace the landscape, making specific the connection of building to site. The horizontal extension of the Midwestern prairie was more an inspiration for Wright's broad terraces and roof overhangs than an abstract interest in shifting planes. Le Corbusier,

4.16
Villa Savoye, exterior view.

4.17
Villa Savoye, roof terrace.

4.18 Lewis Cubitt, King's Cross Station, London, England, 1850-2, street facade.

4.19 Kings Cross Station, train shed.

4.20 Sir George Gilbert Scott, St. Pancras Station, London, 1865-74.

on the other hand, seeks to make a new kind of dwelling which is 'typical,' repeatable, and mass-producible: a *"machine for living."*

The emergence of new building types has long posed a challenge to architects grounded in a traditional practice of architecture. Some recent eighteenth century building types, like the museum, adopted the classical language of the Greeks and Romans in response the character of the antiquities held within. Other new building types, like the train station, proved more challenging as architects tried to reconcile the classical idea of a gateway to the town with the mechanical scale and velocity of the locomotive. **St. Pancras Station**, London, by Sir George Gilbert Scott (1811-78) subscribes to the belief that an elegant, urbane facade must intermediate between the clamor of the train sheds and the city. **Kings Cross Station**, by Lewis Cubitt (b.1799) on the other hand, directly expresses the engineered features of the train shed on its front facade, juxtaposing an architecture based on the colossal scale of the locomotive to the more demure, human scale of the surrounding buildings. Both strategies for the design of new building types posed problems: the appropriation of historical building types for new functions communicated confused messages about the meaning of the building; the reliance on engineering and radically new forms ran the risk of providing no intelligible meanings at all.

In his **AEG Turbine Works**, 1909, **Peter Behrens** (1868-1940) forged a solution to the new building type of factory by layering references to traditional and historical building types over a functionally derived solution to the problem. The engineering task Behrens confronted was enormous. The AEG factory was the largest steel-frame building in Berlin at the time. Moreover, the construction of steel turbines required a clear span of 50 feet and the accommodation of two gantries, each capable of lifting 50 tons and travelling at a speed of over six feet per second while fully loaded. The gambrel roof form derives its shape from the structural system of hinged trusses which were able to slightly deform in response to climate changes and the different loads placed on the structure during different phases of assembly. At the same time, the form is evocative of barns, providing a familiar and amiable association for factory workers, many of whom were displaced from agricultural communities. Additionally, the **massing** and **columniation** of the structure recalls that of a Greek temple, further associating the drudgery of factory work with heroic ritual and the grandeur of classical civilization. The ornament of the building does not derive from ancient or vernacular sources, but is rather a direct expression of construction. Hence, Behrens solves a difficult, modern constructional task with the rigor of engineering, while enhancing the meaning of form through typological associations to the agrarian life of pre-industrial Germany and to the heroic stature of the factory.

4.21
Peter Behrens, AEG Turbine Works, Berlin, Germany, 1909, exterior.

4.22
AEG Turbine Works, steel column, hinged connection.

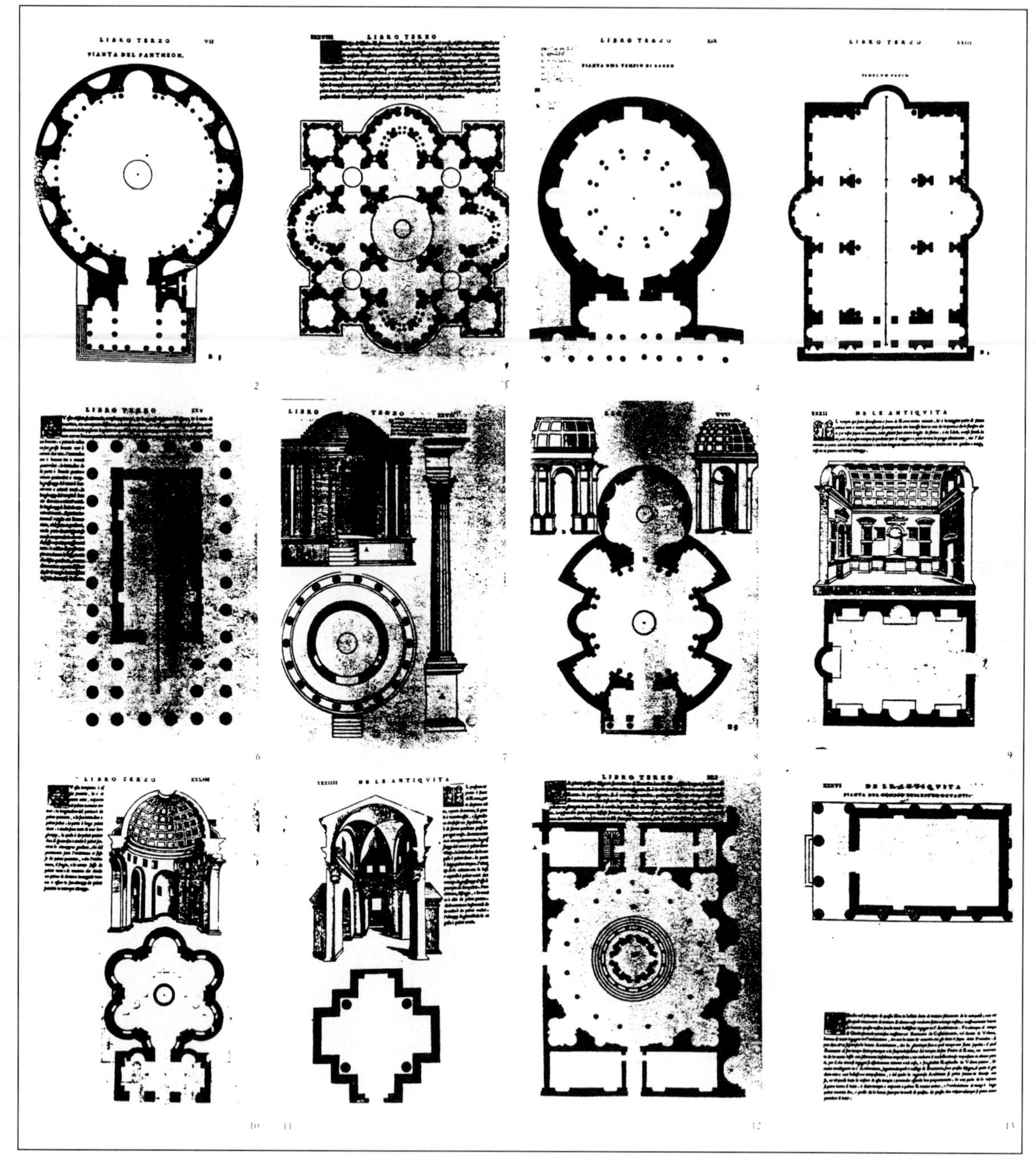

5.0
Sebastiano Serlio, Temples, c. 1545.

Chapter Five

Precedents and Transformation

Nothing old is ever reborn. But it never completely disappears either. And anything that has ever been always emerges in a new form.

-ALVAR AALTO

A myriad of structures, landforms and urban organizations have been constructed throughout history. Some are specific to their own culture, such as **Stonehenge,** or the **Treasury of Atreus**; some are universal and invariable, such as the circular plan, which embraces the previous examples within its definition. Related to the question of how such a plenitude of forms could be designed is the equally puzzling question of how so many different forms can mean anything. The greater the range of inventive possibilities, the more diverse the formal, spatial, and constructional solution, the more idiosyncratic and unique the project, the less likely it is that anyone other than the author will have access to its meaning. Architecture, like language, is a medium through which culture articulates and conveys its messages. To be successful in communicating, the architect must find a way to embed decipherable meanings in the architectural project, which is not an easy task.

5.1
Stone Henge, 2600-1800 B.C., view.

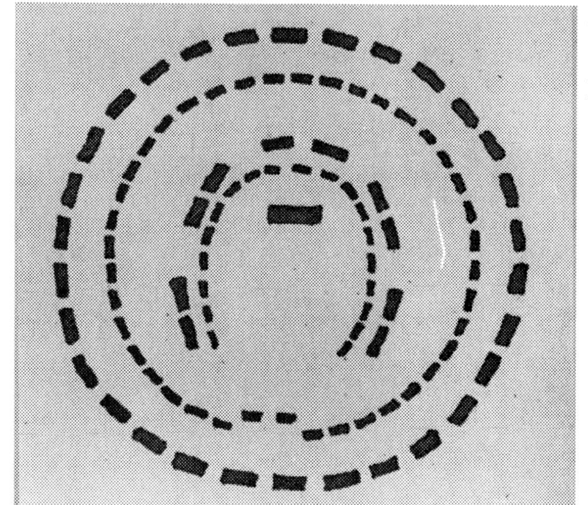

5.2
Stone Henge, plan.

5.3
Treasury of Atreus, c. 1350 B.C. interior view.

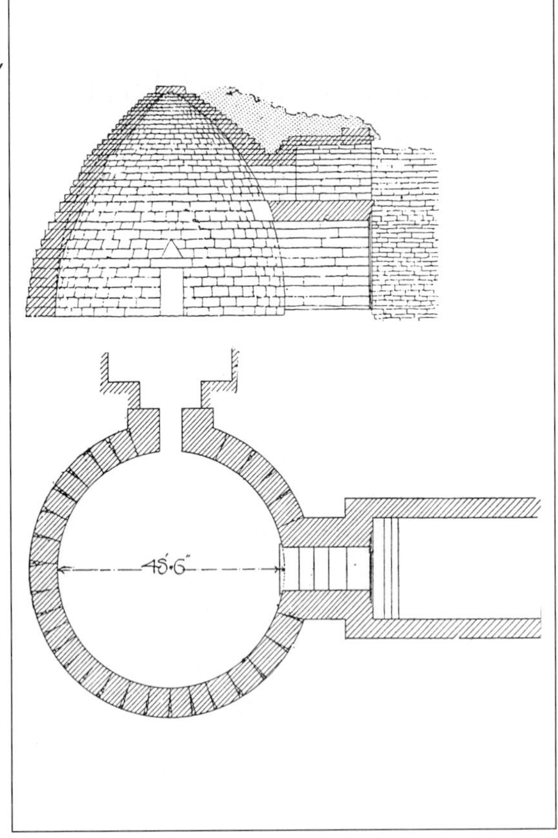

5.4
Treasury of Atreus, plan and section.

One temptation is to ascribe to the cult of novelty and self-expression, resulting in willfully flamboyant arrangements of form which defy connection with the surrounding world. For all its exuberance, such arbitrary Expressionism risks muteness *vis a vis* the culture with which it purports to communicate. Expressionist fabrications, such as **Bruno Taut's** design from ***Auflösung der Städte*** is more intelligible as a botanical study than an architectural proposal. Another temptation is to abnegate the task of design altogether and timidly clone forms from an earlier age. Such architecture fails to engage the concerns and aspirations of the present age and the built world may become likewise mute and impoverished.

Neither the fetishism of novelty nor slavish historicism provides a solution for the designer. Invention grounded in tradition, on the other hand, provides a method whereby the architect may exercise originality within a field already saturated with meanings and associations. Traditional sources need not be taken as invariables. The richness of the architectural project may stem from transformation. Transformations of elements drawn from tradition may be so extensive that the resultant product no longer resembles the starting point, and the original may be unrecoverable in the end. Yet because of the specificity of its origins, the meaning of a building so generated remains embedded in the culture. The transformation of building types and spatial paradigms makes it possible to vary the form of a building greatly while conserving those aspects of the type which carried important, decipherable cultural messages. For Plato, formless, protean matter makes itself manifest in the physical world only through the intercession of the *chora* or 'receptacle.' So too can architectural ideas make themselves manifest through reference to typological or morphological paradigms.

Type, precedent and their transformation address not only questions of form but also questions of meaning, as illustrated by a brief examination of religious buildings from antiquity to the present. We shall begin with the classical Greek temple, although it is possible to find historical precedents for the Greek temple type as well. The Roman architectural theoretician Vitruvius connected the origins of classical architecture back to the **primitive hut,** the mythical first work of architecture. According to the legend, this simple shelter was built by twining together tree trunks and branches. Its organic forms and members were frozen and eternized in the stones of Doric architecture, the language of which is still mimetic of its timber ancestors. The building type 'Greek temple,' best exemplified by the **Parthenon** in Athens, consists primarily of an inner chamber built on a platform, surrounded by columns and surmounted by a **pediment**, or gable roof. An altar to the cult god was housed in the **cella,** an inner room entered only by the priests. The same assortment of parts: inner sanctum, platform, colonnade, and roof, comprises the circular temple, or ***tholos***, such as the **Tholos at Delphi**.

Roman civilization borrowed many architectural forms from the Greeks, but organized these forms according to different spatial principals. In Rome, sacred complexes were frequently engaged in denser urban settings. Roman temples faced specific courtyards and were organized frontally rather than as figures-in-the-round. The Greek temple type was

5.5
Bruno Taut, Die Große Blum, from Auflösung der Städte, c. 1920.

5.6
Marc-Antoine Laugier, Essay sur l'architecture, Frontispiece to the Second Edition, 1755.

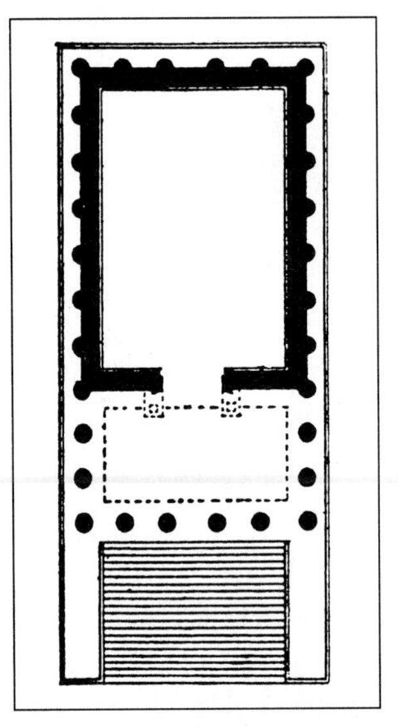

5.7 Left: Maison Carrée, Nîmes, France, A.D. 117-138, plan.

5.8 Right: Maison Carrée, perspective.

5.9 Maison Carrée, view.

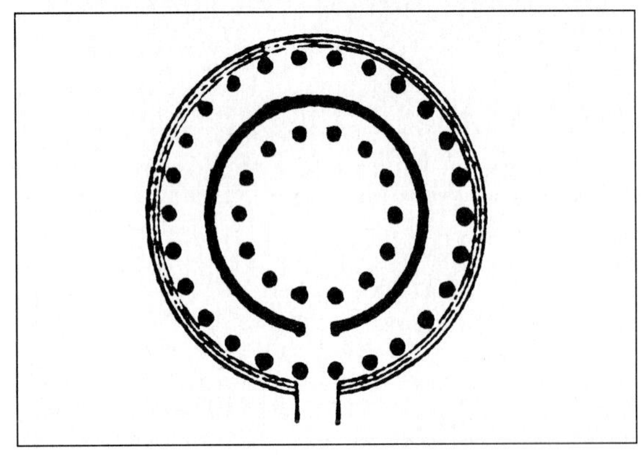

5.10 Tholos at Delphi, Greece.

adequate for the Romans because the function remained the same. The Roman temple **Maison Carrée,** borrows the temple type with only minor transformations: the dominance of the front facade is so strongly emphasized that the surrounding colonnade is absorbed into the wall on the back and sides of the building. In the case of the **Temple of Venus and Rome,** a temple dedicated to two gods, a transformation takes place in the organization of interior space. The inner chamber splits down the middle, and the inner sanctum for the cult altar is presented twice, reflected on each side of the dividing line. The binary organization of the temple is well suited to its site, for it does not only address one space, as did the Maison Carrée, but two. One portico aligns with the Colosseum and the other terminates the main axis of the Roman Forum. A conceptual extension of the Forum axis is threaded through the temple, and a linkage of the Colosseum to the Forum is established.

5.11 Left: Temple of Venus and Rome, Rome, Italy, A.D. 123-135, elevation and section.

5.12 Right: Temple of Venus and Rome, plan.

The **Pantheon** is a circular Roman temple to all the gods. Because the Pantheon needed to house a number of altars rather than one or two, a more radical transformation of the temple type was required. The modest interior space of a Greek cella had to be replaced by something much more capacious. Roman society connected specific forms with specific meanings. How could a new kind of building still be understandable as a temple? In the case of the Pantheon, the meaning of temple is conserved through the inclusion of a temple portico, grafted onto a cylindrical volume almost as a sign. The new elements in the temple expand the repertoire of meaning. Because the temple honored all gods, it served as a **microcosm,** or miniature model reflective of the organization and structure of something much larger. The circle and sphere represented the cosmos in Pythagorean and Platonic tradition. In the Pantheon, those ancient meanings are tapped: a

5.13 Parthenon, Athens, Greece, Ictinos and Callicrates, c.438 B.C.

5.14 Acropolis, view, showing Propylaea, Athena Nike Temple and Parthenon.

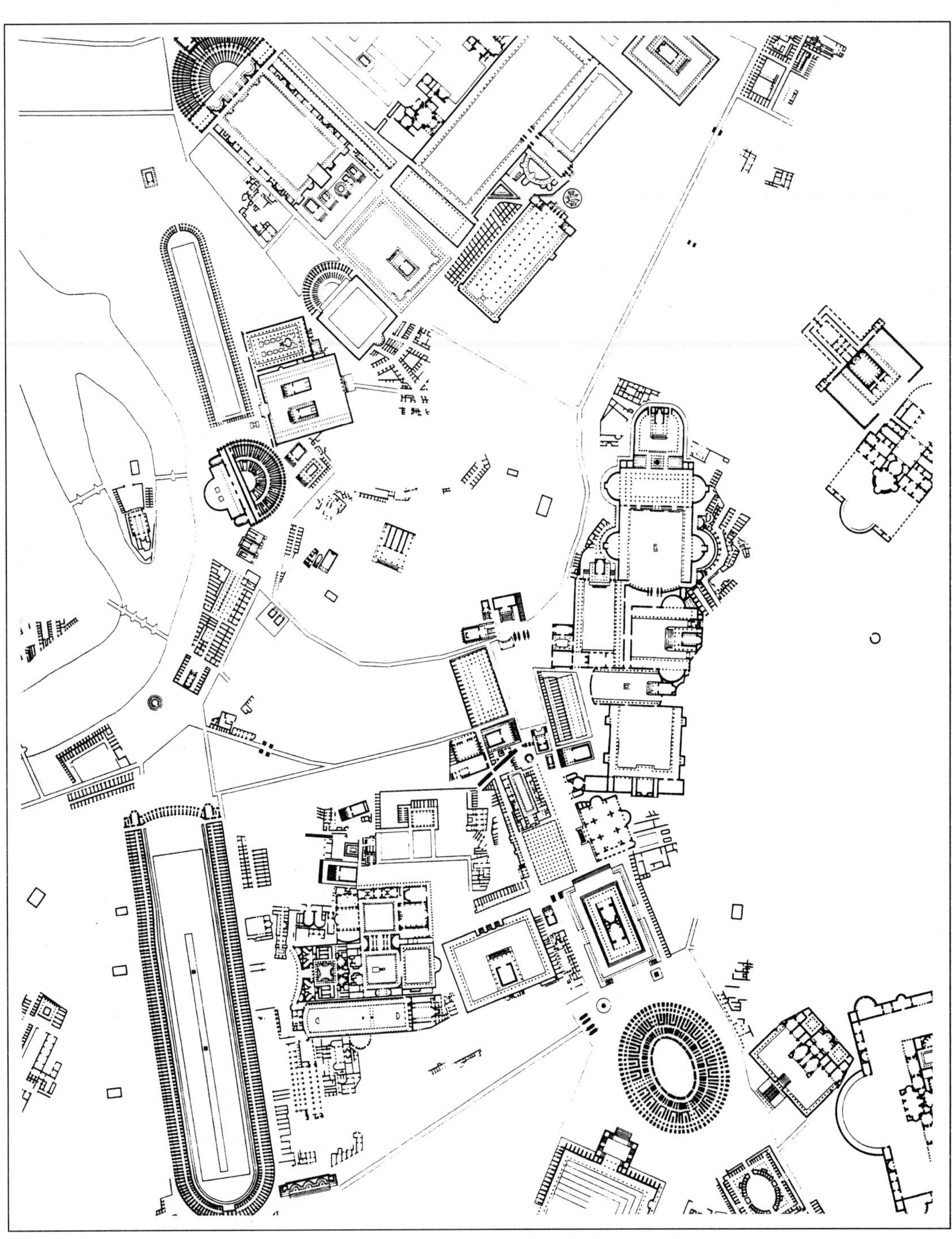

5.15
Plan of the Roman Forum showing the Temple of Venus and Rome and its relationship to the colosseum.

5.16 Left: The Pantheon, Rome, Italy, A.D. 118-28, exterior.

5.17 Right: The Pantheon, oculus.

sphere could fit perfectly within its volume. The oculus, or round opening at the top of the dome, provides yet another meaning. The voided axis mundi runs through the oculus and connects the heavens to the earth, and serves as an eye that allows a gaze from earth to contemplate the sky, and the reverse.

In its early history, Christianity was a secret religion, practiced at the peril of gladiatorial confrontation. Worship took place in houses, meeting halls, or even in underground catacombs. When Christianity was finally adopted as the state religion of the Roman Empire and churches were built specifically for Christian worship, the precedent of pagan temple architecture was hardly deemed appropriate. Early Christians favored the **basilica**, a Roman longitudinal building type used originally for public assembly. In Early Christian basilicas, such as **St. Paul's outside the Walls** in Rome, the A-B-A disposition of tall central **nave** flanked by lower **aisles** accommodated elaborate liturgical processions. Sectional change from aisle to nave made it possible for **clerestory** windows above the nave to introduce light directly to the center of the building. Early Christian basilicas were introverted structures whose facades were

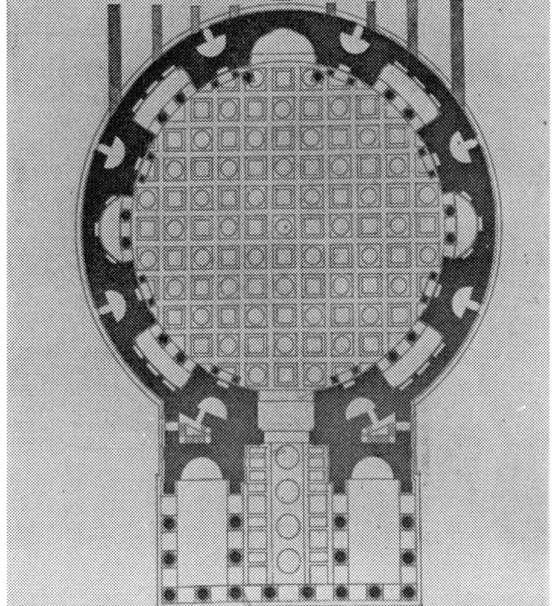

5.18 The Pantheon, plan.

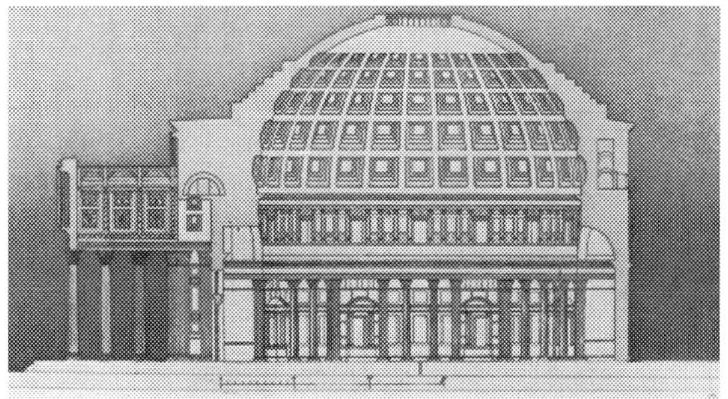

5.19 The Pantheon, section.

5.20
Saint Paul's outside the Walls, Rome, Italy, A.D. 380, section.

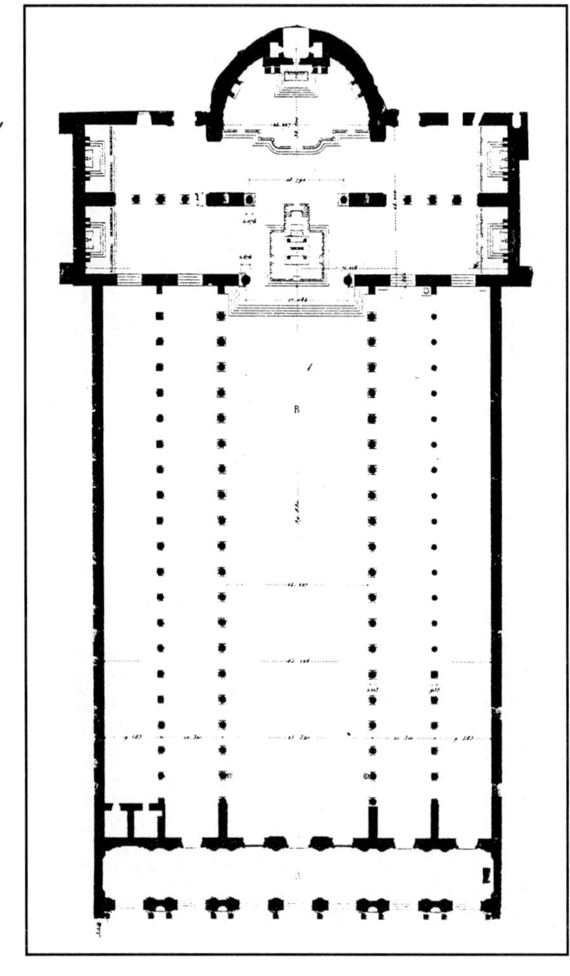

5.21
Saint Paul's outside the Walls, plan.

screened from the surrounding neighborhoods by modest courtyard walls. The symbolism of the church is more subtly developped: the profane building type of basilica is sanctified through the expression of a cross within the plan, imprinting it with the symbol of Christ.

In A.D. 330 the Emperor Constantine moved the capital of the Roman Empire from Rome to Constantinople, now Istanbul. The site for the new town mediated between the locations of Rome and Jerusalem, signifying a union of the two traditions under a new Holy Roman order. The construction of this 'Second Rome' did not reach full flower until the reign of Justinian and the building of the great church, **Hagia Sophia**. The Hagia Sophia can be understood as a representation of the Pantheon, although Justinian himself likened it favorably to the Temple of Solomon. Just as the Early Christians transformed and appropriated the profane historical type of basilica through the expression of a cross within the basilican plan, the architects of the Hagia Sophia sought to incorporate the symbolic and spatial values of the Pantheon, symbol of Rome's grandeur, while transforming the pagan references into something more purely Christian.

The space of the Hagia Sophia results from manipulations on a centralized domed cylinder, similar to that of the Pantheon, which is then split apart to reveal another perfect dome at the center. A longitudinal space emerges. At its center a perfect circle is found, bracketed between the two half domes. The church is at once centralized and longitudinal. As a centralized structure, ancient traditions of the circle and the microcosm of the heavens are conserved; as a longitudinal structure, processions

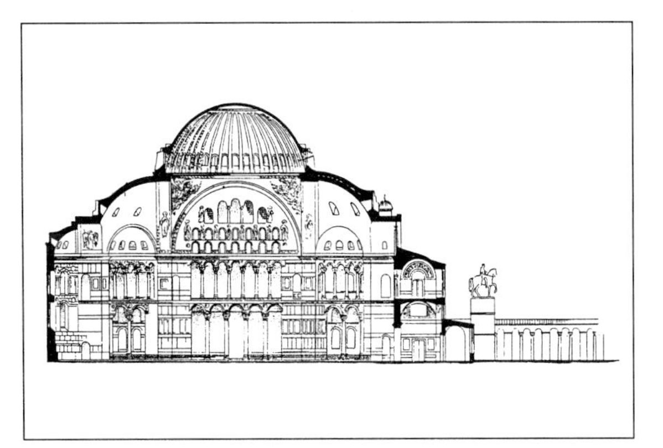

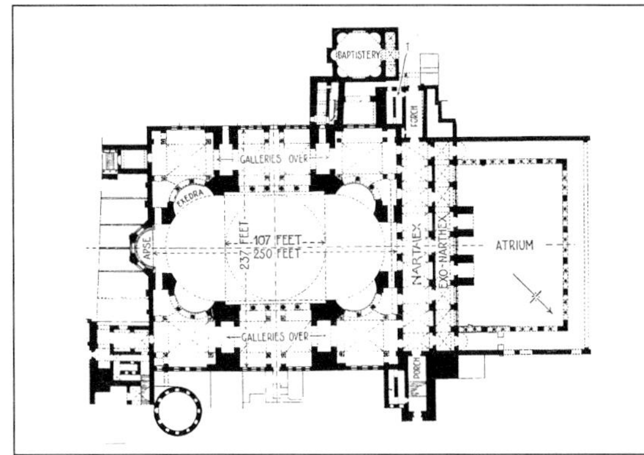

5.22 Left: Hagia Sophia, Isidorus of Miletus and Athemius of Thralles, Istanbul, Turkey, A.D. 532, section.

5.23 Right: Hagia Sophia, plan.

and pageantry involved in Christian liturgy are accommodated and the memory of Early Christian basilican space evoked. Furthermore, because the Pantheon is free-standing, its closed perimeter makes possible only one spatial reading. On the contrary, the main sanctuary of the Hagia Sophia is embedded in a rectilinear wrapper and can be seen as a development of a nine-square grid. The presence of the grid makes possible multiple readings of the space. The flanking subordinate chambers on either side of the main space behave much like the aisles in a true basilica. At the same time, the walls in the opposite direction of the vault extension are perforated, so that space can flow outwards and complete a cruciform reading.

The Hagia Sophia also develops another theme, that of light. While the center of the dome of the Pantheon is open to the sky, the perimeter remains tightly rooted on the supporting masonry walls. At the Hagia Sophia, the center of the dome is solid but a ring of windows perforates the base, resulting in an apparent dematerialization of the supporting wall. The ability of the vast dome (30 meters wide) to hover effortlessly over the space seemed mi-

5.24 Hagia Sophia, view.

5.25 Hagia Sophia, view.

5.26 G.B. Piranesi, Engraving of the oculus of the Pantheon.

5.27 Pantheon, oculus from the roof.

5.28 Pantheon, exterior detail.

raculous, as if it were a demonstration of divine glory. Moreover, the construction of the dome relied on the insertion of a circular dome on a square base by means of triangular structural braces called **pendentives**. The simultaneous presence of the circle, square and triangle seems to manifest the nesting of divine and mathematical order. In the Pantheon, the spherical space alone sufficed to represent the cosmos. In the Hagia Sophia, the extended domical structure is made possible only through the intercession of triangular pendentives, as if to suggest that the earthly and divine realms can only come together through the power of the Christian Trinity.

Although there were some exceptions, the **Romanesque** and **Gothic** periods were characterized by increasingly flamboyant developments of the basilican plan and section, each generation trying to outdo their predecessors in the development of vertical space, the dematerialization of wall, and the manipulation of light. Centralized plans were reserved for the architecture of baptistries and chapter houses, although divine geometry was used to generate networks of lines or a schemata to determine the location of elements within the cathedral. For cathedral architecture, the most profound expression of center was the crossing of the nave and transept, sometimes surmounted by a tower.

In the **Renaissance**, a 're-birth' of the classical tradition took place and there was again direct borrowing from ancient sources. However, the Roman basilica as a precedent for sacred architecture was eclipsed by a renewed interest in centralized temples. Through an elaborate literary tradition, the stories of the

Old Testament and finally all of antiquity were embraced as allegories of Christian themes. Hence reference to pagan gods and pagan temples was not blasphemous, but pious. **Sandro Botticelli's Birth of Venus** was conceived of as a serious religious painting, an allegory on the life of the Virgin, although it appears to be a sensual representation of the Roman goddess of love. So too could the form of temples originally dedicated to pagan Gods be reappropriated as houses of Christian worship. Indeed, the Renaissance theoretician **Leonbattista Alberti** (1404-72) pronounced the superiority of centralized temples in his treatise.

The Renaissance brought not only a re-birth of interest in the architecture of antiquity, but a renewed interest in classical ideas as well. Among the ideas resurrected from antiquity were Neo-Platonism and Humanism. The latter was a school of philosophy which emphasized the centrality of the human being in the divine scheme of things, as illustrated in Leonardo's drawing of the Vitruvian Man. The former held that the contemplation of any beautiful creature, construction, or idea could provide insight into the beauty of the divine order. Hence, the quest for beauty was neither sensual nor aesthetic, but spiritual. Beautiful form, beautiful color, beautiful proportions all served as a microcosm of an eternal, limitless, heavenly beauty too vast to be apprehended by humankind. The contemplation of all beautiful things was believed to point to the same truth. The beauty of God was a perfect mirroring of earthly and divine beauty, so that the length of strings required to strike a harmonious chord found its correspondence in the length of measurements in a well-proportioned composition, and indeed, the relative

5.29 Sandro Botticelli, "Birth of Venus", 1480.

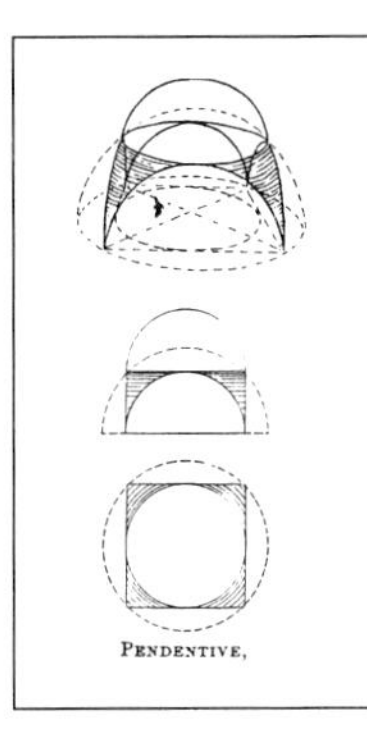

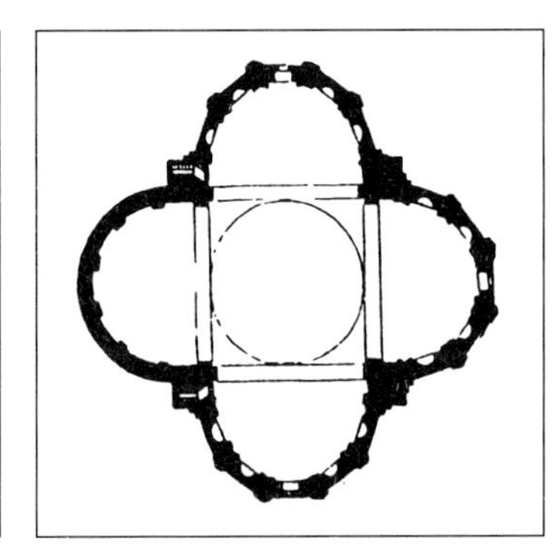

5.30 Left: Pendentive diagram.

5.31 Right: Anonymous, S. Maria della Consolazione, Todi, Italy, c. 1508, plan.

5.32 Santa Maria della Consolazione, view.

5.33 Antonio da Sangallo the Elder, San Biagio, Montepulciano, Italy, c. 1518.

5.34 Donato Bramante, Tempietto of S. Pietro in Montorio, Rome, Italy, 1502.

lengths of planetary orbits, called the *"harmony of the spheres."* Renaissance architecture aspired to perfection of form and proportion so that its contemplation might provide an intelligible model of the universe. In so doing, it went directly back to antique precedent, namely, the Pantheon.

Perhaps the most famous and most beautiful Renaissance centralized church was **Donato Bramante's Tempietto of San Pietro in Montorio**, in Rome. A variation on the *tholos* temple type, the Tempietto was greatly admired by contemporaries in the Renaissance. In 1537 Sebastiano Serlio included it in his treatise among the most perfect examples from antiquity, blurring the line between precedent and copy. Unfortunately, in spite of the theoretically grounded impetus to build centralized churches, very few were ever constructed. The Tempietto is able to attain its perfect form for several unusual reasons. One, it functions more to mark a spot, that of Saint Peter's crucifixion, than to house any particular ceremony. Two, it was designed to be installed in an ideal, circular courtyard where the thick walls of the courtyard mitigated between the exterior world and the perfect, inviable, round church. Other centralized churches, such as **Santa Maria della Consolazione** in Todi and **San Biagio** in Montepulciano were able to attain their ideal form because they were located in sites remote from the town centers. In cities, where pressures from the existing urban fabric were exerted against the ideal symmetries of the churches, more compromised building types were the rule. One example is **Bramante's** urban church **Santa Maria presso San Satiro** in Milan. In an irregular T-shaped space, the extension of the fourth arm of a centralized Greek Cross plan is implied in a shallow niche behind the altar through perspectival tricks.

The re-emergence of the classical temple type not only posed theological difficulties, but functional ones as well. In antiquity, the inner sanctum was meant to house only the cult altar and a few priests. In the Renaissance, a sizable congregation needed to be accommodated as well. Even when the churches weren't impossibly small, as in the case of the Tempietto, the question of what would occupy the center remained unresolved. Placing the altar in the center made a potent link between the microcosmic structure of the temple and the point at which worship was celebrated, but made it impossible for the congregation and priests to position themselves in a way appropriate to the ceremony. Placing the altar in one lobe of a centralized **Greek Cross** plan made it possible spatially to establish an appropriate hierarchical relationship between the congregation and the priests, but the meaning of the center was diluted. Lastly, the clear, legible exposition of geometry and proportion, meant to appeal to reason and intellect, implied that the priesthood was no longer necessary as an intermediary between God and man.

Such heretical thinking was espoused by Martin Luther and other founders of Protestant sects. After the power of the Catholic church in Rome reached its nadir with the Sack of Rome in 1527, the Council of Trent convened in 1564 to determine ways to rebuild the institution. Primary among these involved the design of churches. It was mandated that the longitudinal form, or **Latin Cross** plan, of early Christian churches be adapted in eschewal of pagan, hu-

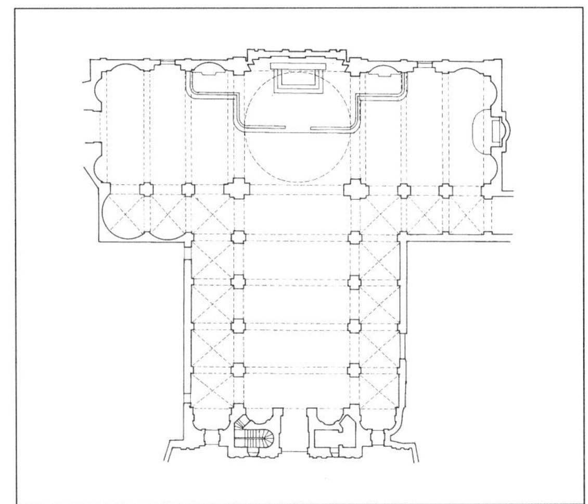

5.35
Donato Bramante, Santa Maria presso San Satiro, Milan, Italy, 1480-81, plan.

5.36
Santa Maria presso San Satiro, view.

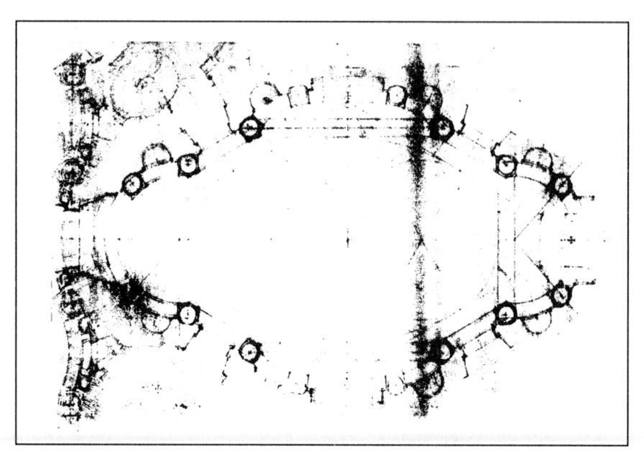

5.37 Francesco Borromini, San Carlo alle Quattro Fontane, Rome, Italy, 1637-41, plan, Albertina, Vienna.

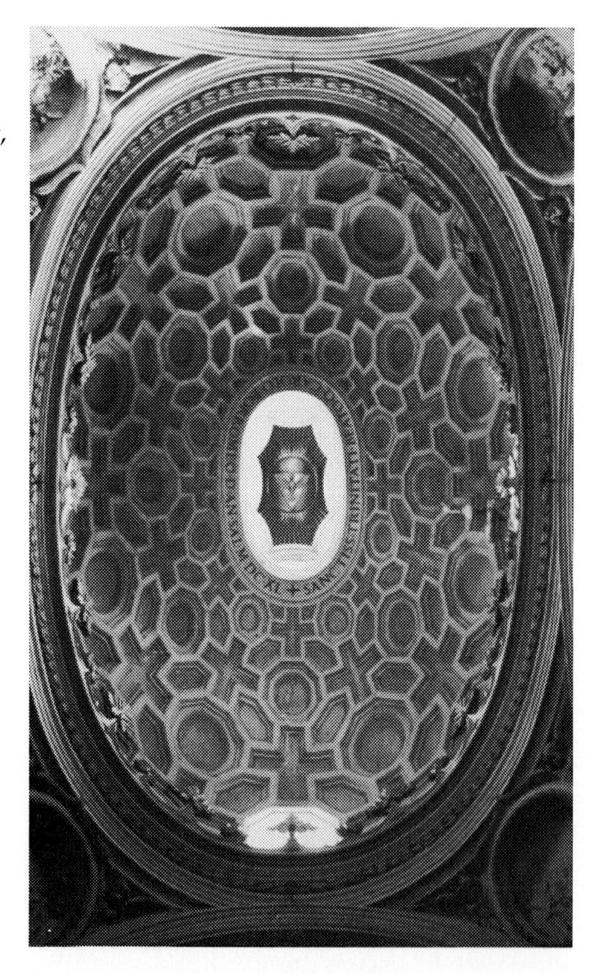

5.38 San Carlo alle Quattro Fontane, dome.

manistically derived centralized forms. Such churches would allow the true liturgy of the church to be practiced, and lead worshippers towards a mystical, faith-inspired appreciation of God. Through the rhetorical, persuasive power of architecture, it was believed that the power of the catholic church could be preserved and extended.

In the **Baroque** era, the message of Renaissance Humanism and the architecture it sponsored was still too current to be dismissed by architects, even though the client churches were calling for a traditional, longitudinal arrangement of plan. In a tiny church in Rome, **Francesco Borromini** (1599-1667) forged a compromise between centralized and longitudinal church typologies. **San Carlo alle Quattro Fontane**, 1637-41, is at once centralized and longitudinal. The form of the church evolves around the simultaneous presence of the oval, cross, and octagon, as fully discussed in Leo Steinberg's *Borromini's San Carlo alle Quattro Fontane: A Study in Multiple Form and Architectural Symbolism.* As in Bramante's Santa Maria presso San Satiro, illusionistic devices are at play. **Coffers** of the niche vault above the altar diminish to create a ***trompe l'oeil*** effect of perspectival recession in depth, enhancing the apparent longitudinality of the church.

The delicate synthesis of contradictory spatial paradigms and multiple geometries implicit in San Carlo is made explicit in **Guarino Guarini's** (1624-83) **Santa Maria della Divina Providenza**, Lisbon, c. 1656-59. The undulating perimeter of the church is caused by a progression of domed spaces within the nave of the church. The fusion and distension of domes in tense relation to one another looks almost like cell division, wherein a centric organism replicates itself within a single membrane. The plan of the church is at once a centralized Greek cross, a longitudinal basilica, and a highly developed moment in a grid of ovalized chambers. The sinuous line that emerges from the intersecting domes extends to the ornamental scheme of the church. The undulations of the vault give character to the columns, pilasters, and entablature as well.

Balthazar Neumann's (1687-1753) **Vierzehnheiligen** takes Guarini's exercise in synthesized polymorphism even further. In Vierzehnheiligen, as in Santa Maria della Divina Providenza, the vault is comprised of a series of autonomous domes. In Guarini's church, the heavy structural piers which support the vault are configured to define both the space of the nave and the aisle chapels. In Neumann's church, the vault is supported by slender, freestanding columns. These columns are indifferent to the spatial definition of the aisles and are disposed according to the structure of the dome. The serially domed spaces seem to detach from the encircling walls, leaving a vestigial plenum of space which evokes the aisles in a basilican plan. The reliance on columns rather than the thick poché of walls to accomplish spatial differentiation is particularly modern. Like the other examples we studied, the church of Vierzehnheiligen is simultaneously longitudinal and centralized. The center in the Latin Cross plan has slipped from the crossing of nave and transept to the true central body of the church. Instead of expressing the section at the crossing with a tower, as in Gothic examples, or a dome, as in Renaissance and Baroque examples, it is suppressed and residual to the forms which

5.39 San Carlo alle Quattro Fontane, niche above altar.

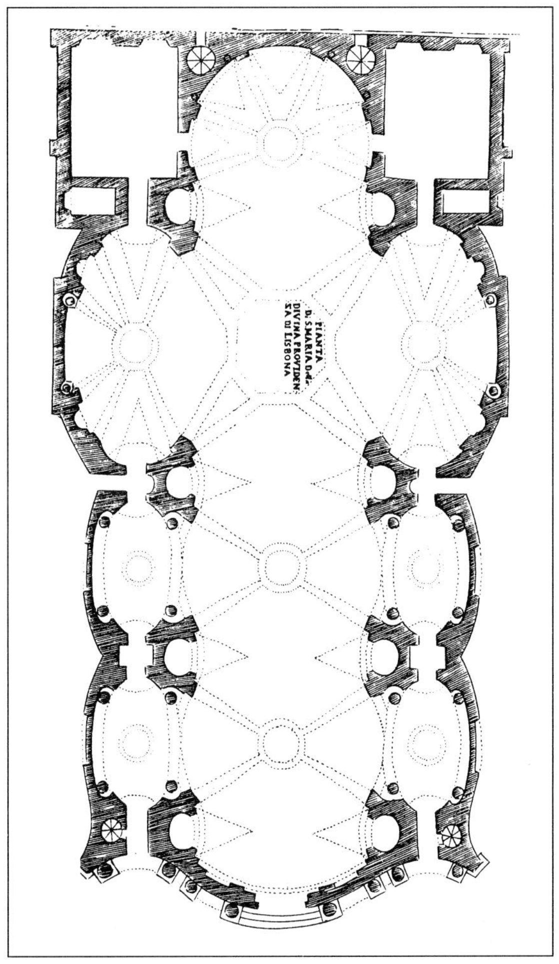

5.40 Guarino Guarini, Santa Maria della Divina Providenza, Lisbon, Portugal, c.1656-59.

5.41
Balthazar Neumann, Vierzehnheiligen, Lichtenfels, Germany, 1743-72, section.

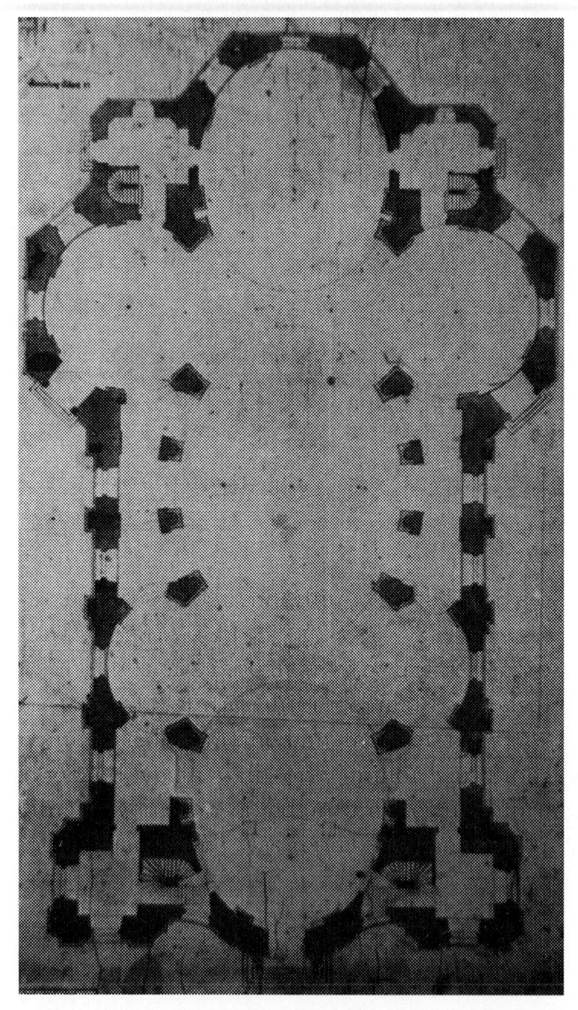

5.42
Vierzehnheiligen, plan.

flank it. The dilemma of how to occupy center in a centralized plan is resolved by the multiplication and displacement of center, fusing together the two readings of the church so tightly that they cannot be separated.

The last building we shall examine is **Le Corbusier's Notre-Dame-du-Hau**t, Ronchamp, France, 1950-55. At Ronchamp, the form of the church appears wholly new, never the same from any vantage point. Indeed, it seems to transform before your eyes as you walk around it. With stark, white, heavy walls and an oppressive roof, Notre-Dame-du-Haut manifests its spirituality not through dematerialization but through a superabundance of material. Light pierces through a thick wall, which then curls in upon itself to form towers, vestries, and chapels. A sliver of light at the joining of roof and wall reveals that the roof is not pushing down on the structure beneath it, but actually hovers very lightly above.

Finally, at Ronchamp it seems that the architect is free from reference to type and precedent which governed so many decisions in the previous examples. However, Notre-Dame-du-Haut too is engaged in a debate with tradition and gains much of its power by manipulating familiar themes. Like the earlier examples, the church is simultaneously longitudinal and centralized. Instead of developing these contrary themes along a single axis, Le Corbusier affects the transformation along a constantly changing perimeter. The reflection of half the church yields a centralized plan; the reflection of the other half results in a longitudinal plan. Additional references to traditional ecclesiastic architecture emerge as the perimeter effortlessly transforms from the abstraction of a razor sharp

5.43 *Left:* *Le Corbusier, Notre-Dame-du-Haut, Ronchamp, France, 1950-55, view.*

5.44 *Right: Notre-Dame-du-Haut.*

line to paired towers, reminiscent of the **westworks** in a cathedral. The asymmetrical inversion of the plan is signaled by the misplacement of the apsidal wall of the church: instead of serving as a back drop to the altar, it faces the altar. The altar itself backs against a convex wall which forms the screen for an outdoor chapel. It is almost as if the church had been turned inside out, the twist yielding strange distortions which nonetheless harken back to the original type.

There is nothing new under the sun. Architecture does not arise from the creation of the novel forms, but from significant transformation within a tradition. The transformation can be modest, as in the development from the Greek to the Roman temple, or enormous, as in Le Corbusier's design at Ronchamp. In both cases density of significance is created through overlaying the meaning of the original type with the specific, personalized meanings of the architect's transformative act.

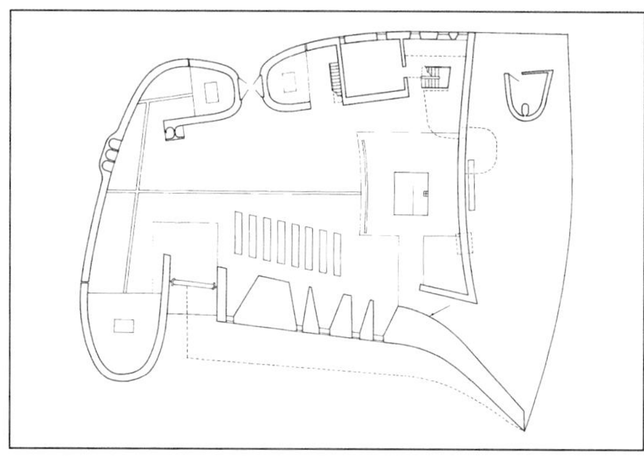

5.45 *Notre-Dame-du-Haut, plan.*

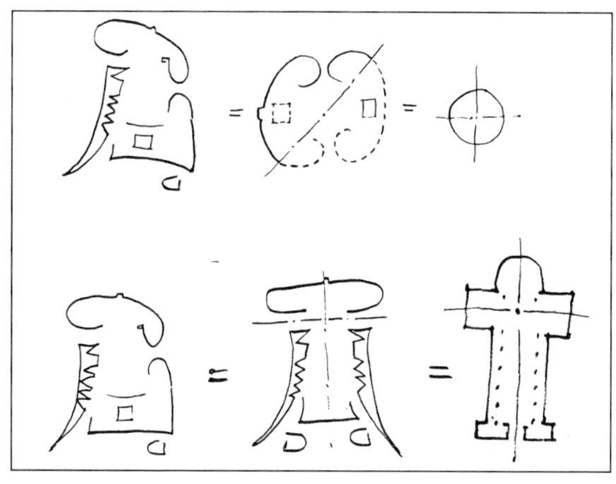

5.46 *Notre-Dame-du-Haut as a longitudinal church, and as a centralized church.*

Part II.

The Architecture of Antiquity

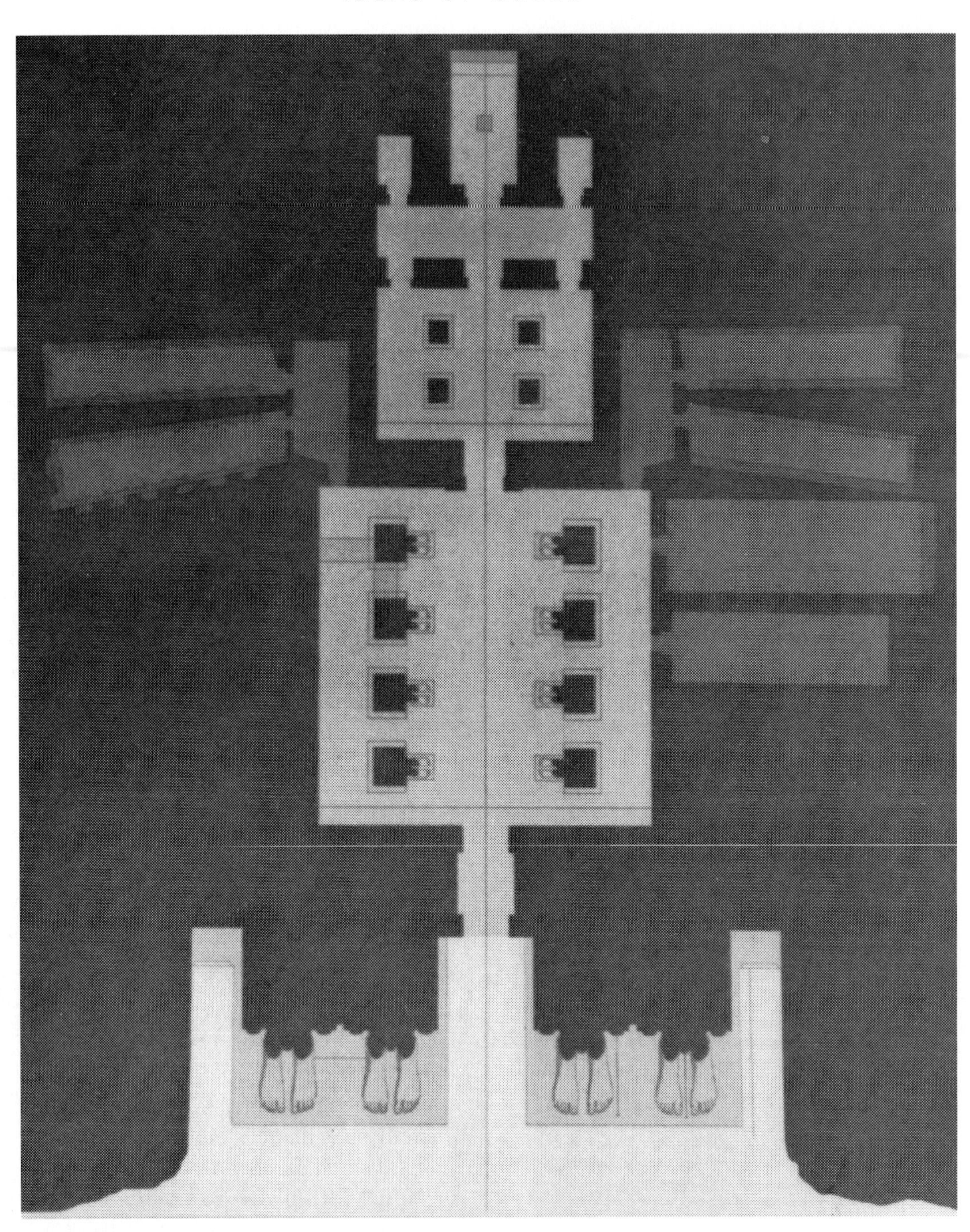

6.0
Temple of Ramesses II, Abu Simbel, Egypt, 19th Dynasty, c.1250 B.C., plan.

Chapter Six

Ancient Egypt: Axes, Symmetry, Hierarchy

It is one of the greatest things in Egyptian art that all the statues, paintings and architectural forms seem to fall into place as if they obeyed one law. We call such a law, which the creations of all peoples seem to obey, a 'style'.

-Ernst Gombrich

The examples we have looked at thus far have been gathered from many different parts of the world and many different time periods. There was little emphasis on the contextual or cultural pressures that helped shape the artifacts. Buildings were pulled from their natural frame of reference and placed into another, much like a scientist putting tissue samples under a microscope. In the coming chapters, we shall focus on the ancient civilizations of Egypt, Greece and Rome and try to look more closely at the relationship between landscape, buildings, urban settlements and the culture that sponsored them. Our attempt is not to provide thorough historical, archeological, or art historical accounts of these ancient civilizations. Rather, we shall focus on how aspects of their culture have been embodied by architecture and how principles of order from those cultures can be extended to illustrate universal architectural principles.

Let us begin with Ancient Egypt, considered by many to be the birthplace of western civilization. The landscape of Egypt is characterized by a vast expanse of desert, slashed by the thin green band of the Nile in whose fertile valleys the great civilization arose. As a spatial organizer, the powerful north-south ribbon of the Nile is equalled only by the east-west path of the sun. The Egyptian hieroglyphic for 'world' comprises these two markings. It is therefore not surprising that rigid axial organization is so important in Egyptian art and architecture. Annual flooding of the Nile encouraged the development of accurate techniques in applied mathematics and land-surveying. Little remained after the flooding to distinguish one property from another, save the mathematical description of boundaries provided by the orthogonal grid of the surveyors. Hence, the elements which give order to the landscape, the dominate axis of the Nile, the solar path, and the gridded agricultural fields, are the very elements which governed artistic production.

A good part of Egyptian art and architecture was dedicated to the glorification of the ruler, either through the construction of palaces or the inscription of historical narratives in hieroglyphic script. Yet an even greater amount of attention was given to the creation of works which had mystical, religious value. The Egyptians believed in the immortality of the *Ka*, the 'soul' or 'vital force' of a human being, but it needed a ready supply of provisions to assure the continuity of life after death. Art and architecture magically re-created all physical implements required to carry on every day life. Tombs provided eternal dwellings for the *Ka*, statuary and mummification provided surrogate bodies which could be inhabited by the *Ka* of the deceased. Indeed, the Egyptian word for sculptor meant 'he-who-keeps-alive'. Art and architecture served a ritual function and were intended to last for eternity.

We shall begin by looking at a few statues, the **Statue of Senmut** and the **Statue of Ranofer**. In both statues, life-like, naturalistic portraiture is suppressed. Emphasis is placed on the elemental, stereometric properties of stone, geometric regularity, and the timeless, static constancy of the image. The carved figures are not totally liberated from the blocks of stone. Only the front of the Ranofer figure has been hewn from the rectilinear granite block: the back is fully engaged. Senmut's entire body is encompassed within a cubic block which remains unaltered, save for the surface inscription of hieroglyphics and the trapezoidal head which surmounts it. A selective process of abstraction takes place as the sculptor strives to include a clear depiction of all essential body parts which will be necessary for the resurrection of the *Ka*. The forms are subtractive, like figures carved into a bar of soap. Both statues are organized by a rigid axiality; the symmetry is broken only by the forward thrust of Ranofer's foot.

An emphasis on axiality, symmetry, geometric description, magical embodiment, and bold stereometric massing also characterizes the most famous work of Egyptian architecture, the **Great Pyramids** at Giza, a complex of Fourth Dynasty royal tombs. The Pyramids, whose shared orthogonal orientation aligns with the Nile, appear to be free-standing objects organized around their centers, and evocative of an artificial mountain range. In fact, they culminate a progression of funerary temples which began at the banks of the Nile. The corpse arrived on a barge at the 'Valley Temple', where it underwent ritual purification and mummification. A long axial causeway links the Valley Temple to a 'Mortuary Temple' at the base of the pyramid. Here mourners could worship and make offerings to the dead. Finally, the pyramid served as a tomb for the Pharaoh. The remains of the ruler were buried deep within the massive stone tomb, and the great horizontal axis which extends from the river to the pyramid is bent upwards, the apex of the pyramid addressing the sun. The enormous scale of the pyramid complex testifies to the extent of Pharaonic power, a power capable of enlisting thousands of workers to haul stone from distant quarries and lay it in place with extraordinary precision.

The Cheops pyramid is the oldest and largest (755 feet square and 475 feet in height) of the

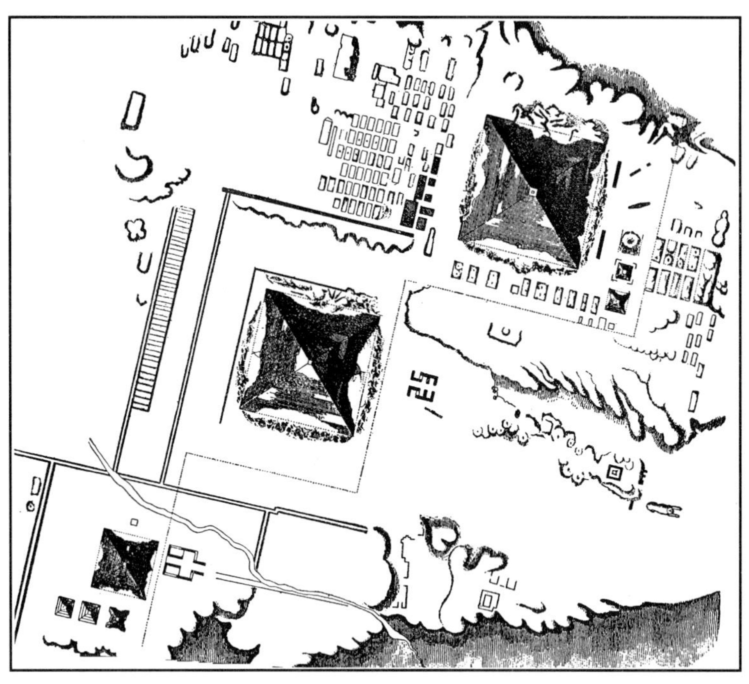

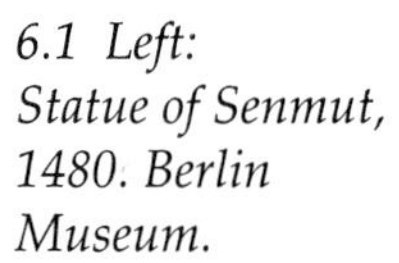

6.1 *Left: Statue of Senmut, 1480. Berlin Museum.*

6.2 *Right top: The Pyramids of Cheops, Chephren and Mycerinus and the Great Sphinx, Giza, Egypt, plan.*

6.3 *Left bottom: Statue of Ranofer, Fifth Dynasty, Cairo Museum.*

6.4 *Right bottom: The Great Sphinx, c. 2530 B.C. and the Pyramid of Chephren, c. 2530 B.C.*

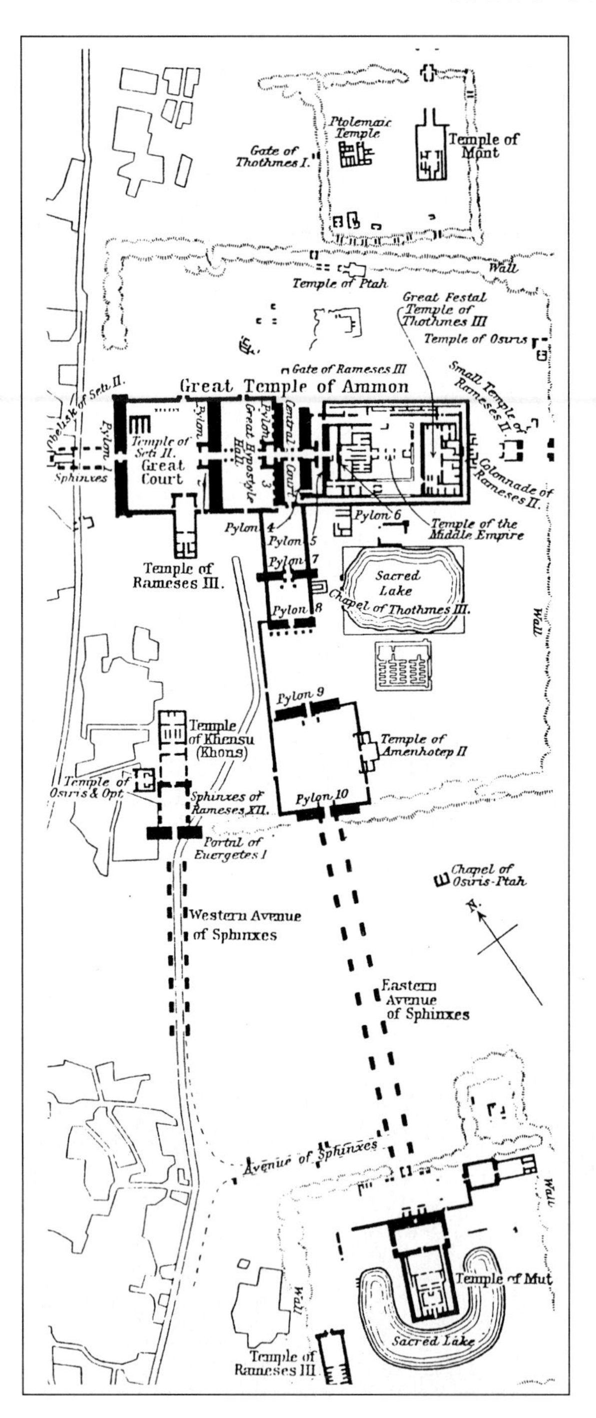

6.5
Plan of the Ruins of Karnak (Thebes), Egypt.

three. The Chephren pyramid is slightly smaller. The Mycerinus pyramid is the most recent and the smallest of all. Moreover, unlike the larger pyramids, here the alignment of the Valley Temple, causeway, and Mortuary Temple is axially disposed, allowing the progression through the landscape to proceed symmetrically.

The ritual voyage of the corpse from life to death to afterlife is reflected by the importance of the path in unfolding spatial experiences in Egyptian funerary temples. In later mortuary complexes, the pyramid disappears completely but the dominance of the axial path and the progression along it becomes even greater.

At the **Temple of Khons** in Karnak, the progression unfolds along a strong central axis. An avenue of sphinxes terminates at a massive temple gateway, or **pylon**, the first in a series of heavy walls that mark thresholds between spatial precincts in the temple. The pylon is at once a walled boundary, pierced by a door at the bottom, and an open passageway with two halves cleaving apart at the top to frame the axis. Division and unity are stated simultaneously in response to the double line of the sphinxes and the single line of the path. Beyond the first pylon there is a large colonnaded court; then a **hypostyle hall**, densely filled with colossal columns; and finally, ever-diminishing in size, a sanctuary. The spatial compression in plan has its counterpart in section. Floors rise and ceilings drop down so that the entire space telescopes down to a single, sacred space.

In several ways the axis helps to establish hierarchy, a system of ranking the relative significance of elements from most to least important. One, importance is conferred to

6.6 Left: Temple of Khons, Ramesses III, Karnak, Egypt, Twentieth Dynasty, c.1150 B.C., view.

6.7 Right: Temple of Khons, axonometric.

those things nearest the center-line of the scheme; two, the farther along the linear progression one goes, the more important the space; three, the terminus of the axis is reserved for the most special element of all, the sanctuary.

The Khons Temple is an axially organized progression of telescoping spaces. However, the closed perimeter wall mediates among the differences and creates of the temple a unitary volume. Because it is representative of a building 'type' its basic organization can be conserved while allowing for great diversity. **The Mortuary Temple of Amenhotep III** at Luxor is likewise organized by means of a strong central axis which threads through a series of diminishing courtyards. In contrast to the Khons Temple, here the unequal dimensions and orientations of the various courtyards are not absorbed by a neutral perimeter wall. Rather, the constituent forms are autonomous and explicitly defined, creating a series of linked volumes rather like a train consisting of boxcars. **The Mortuary Temple of Ramesses III** at Medinet Habu is an even more elaborate

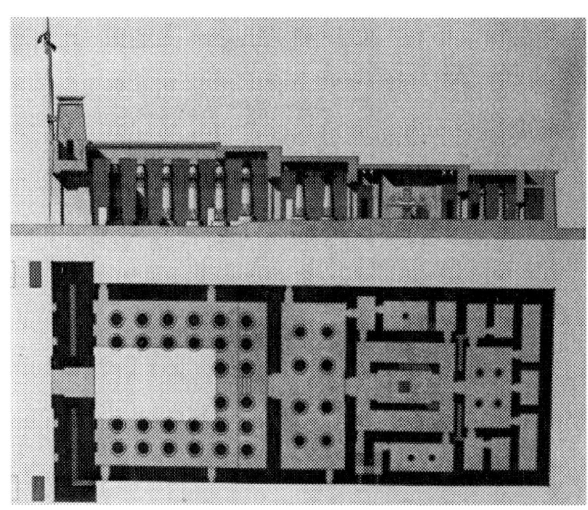

6.8 Temple of Khons, plan and section.

6.9 Temple of Khons, interior view.

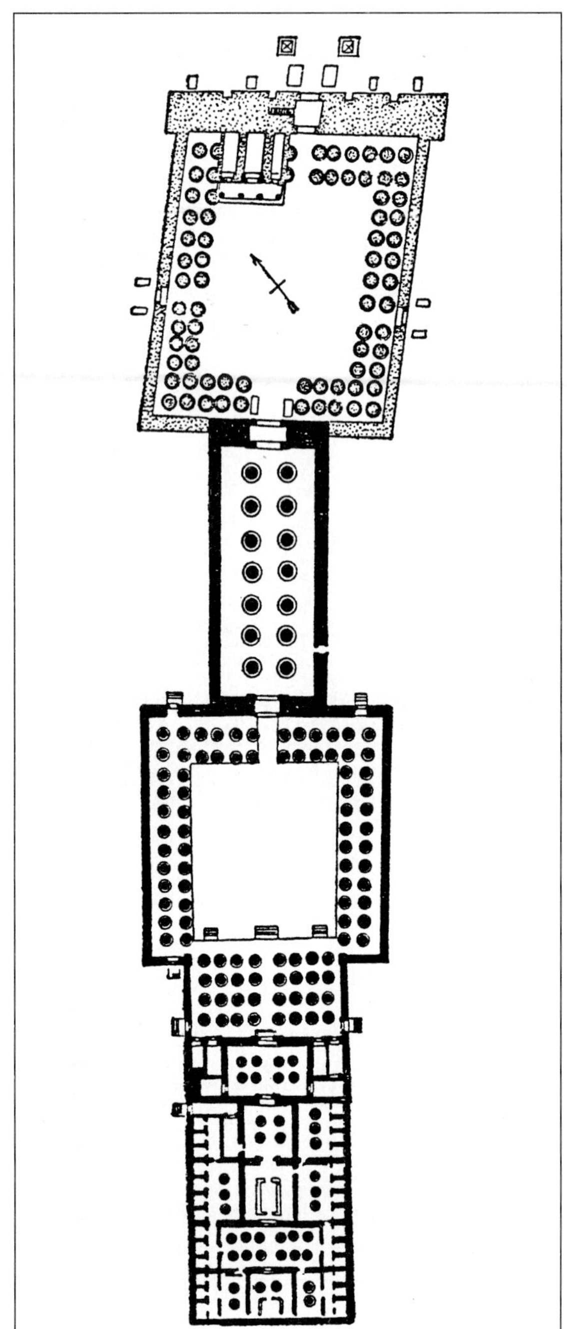

6.10 Left: Temple of Amenhotep III, Luxor, Egypt, 18th Dynasty, c.1370 B.C., plan.

6.11 Right: Temple of Amenhotep III, Luxor, view.

version of the same temple type. Here the temple is but the center of a larger complex for a holy city. The basic principles governing the smaller temples are again at play. A series of pylons marks a progression along a central axis, but this is not the only ordering device in operation. Massive walls are concentrically disposed, the outermost measuring 33 feet in thickness and 60 feet in height. The sanctuary's position at the terminus of the axis and at the center of the nested spatial envelopes enforces its hierarchical stature in the scheme.

The Great Pyramids and the three funerary temples we have thus far examined are all built near the Nile on the expansive plane of the desert. Free-standing compounds, their connection to the landscape is expressed symbolically. The meaning of the Pyramids relies on a geological metaphor which associates them with petrified rays of sun or ritualized mountains, landscapes more hospitable to the gods than the flat terrain of earth. To properly claim their landscape, the Middle-Kingdom funerary temples make use of path, procession, and a sympathetic alignment with the Nile. The architecture is constructed through an additive

6.12 Left: Mortuary Temple of Ramesses III, Medinet Habu, Egypt, 1198-1166 B.C., view.

6.13 Right: Mortuary Temple of Ramesses III, Medinet Habu, view.

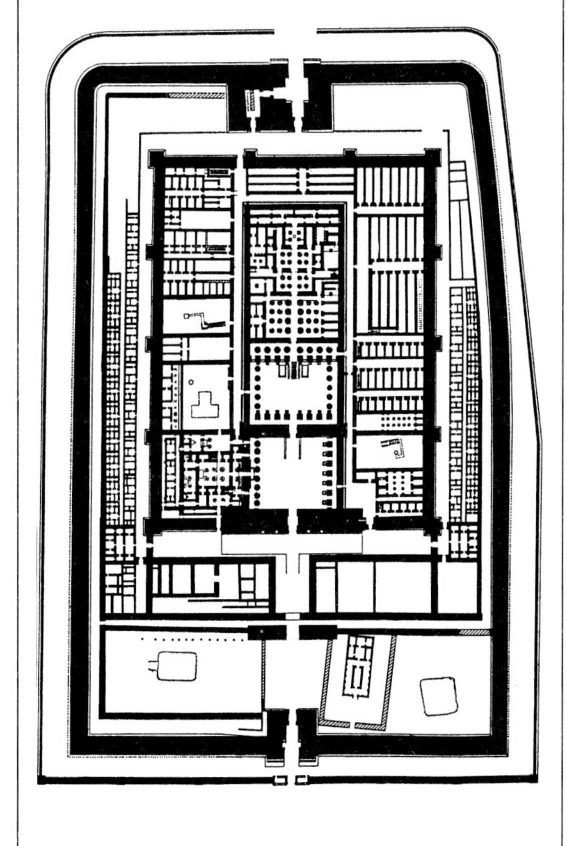

6.14 Mortuary Temple of Ramesses III, Medinet Habu, plan.

system of posts and beams, which we shall discuss later on. Another possibility exists in the repertoire of Egyptian architecture: structures which are carved from the great mass of earth, much like the statues, rather than through the assemblage of elements upon the surface.

The **Rock Temple of Ramesses II** in Abu Simbel is an example of an architecture which reveals itself through carving rather than through the aggregation of parts. The cliff, sacred in its own right, was converted into a temple by Ramesses II. Four great Colossi guard the gate. Oriented towards the sunrise, the face of the cliff is transformed into one gigantic pylon, and the significance of the mountain reverses the metaphorical connection to the landscape of the Great Pyramids. While the latter were geometrized, man-made evocations of great natural landforms, the former is a natural mountain evocative of the Pyramids in Giza. Within the mountain the disposition of carved rooms corresponds to that of Theban mortuary temples. As in Luxor, Karnak and Medinet Habu, the dimensions of rooms gradually diminish in both plan and section from an ample forward chamber, to a hypostyle hall,

6.15 Left: Temple of Ramesses II, Abu Simbel, Egypt, 19th Dynasty, c.1250 B.C., view.

6.16 Right: Temple of Ramesses II, Abu Simbel, section and detail.

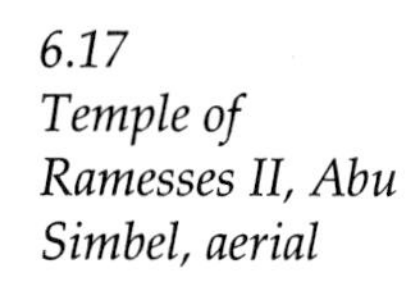

6.17 Temple of Ramesses II, Abu Simbel, aerial

and finally to the most compressed space, the holy-of-holies. The question of perimeter wall is not at issue: the mass of the mountain constitutes the wall which bounds the temple.

The last temple complex we shall discuss is the **Mortuary Temple of Queen Hatshepsut** in Deir-el-Bahari. As in the other funerary temples we have examined, an axial processional path organizes the scheme, but here the relationship of building to landscape is more finely resolved. The temple redefines the edge of the cliff and allows the desert and the broad face of the cliff to be married together. As the processional path gradually rises across diminishing ramped terraces, the architecture transforms from post-and-beam colonnades to carving in the megalithic mass of stone. The first terrace directly rests on the surrounding desert floor, and is presented as a pristine, geometrized moment in a vast planar continuum. The scale of terraces funnels down, while the narrow ramped path continues the movement up into the rising cliff. At Abu Simbel, the face of the cliff is transformed into an architectural element, a pylon. At Deir-el-Bahari, there is a blurring between

6.18 Left: *Mortuary Temple of Queen Hatshepsut, architect, Senmut, Deir-el-Bahari, Egypt, 18th Dynasty, 1480 B.C., view.*

6.19 Right: *Mortuary Temple of Queen Hatshepsut, view.*

landscape and architecture. The enormous scale of the mountain is engaged and appropriated by the architectural intervention. Modest porticos of stark, simplified columns abandon the traditional language of temple architecture and become rather a reiteration of the vertical striations of the cliff wall. From a distance, it is hard to tell where the architecture stops and the land begins. The use of local stone in the temple construction helps sustain this reading, for the color and material of the hillside and temple are one.

Two constructional techniques characterize Egyptian architecture. Forms are generated through subtraction, as at Abu Simbel, or forms are generated through addition, as in the trabeated structures of the Theban temples. At Deir-el-Bahari, both carving and trabeation are used. Royal temple and tomb projects were constructed of stone, a material as unchanging and eternal as the afterlife of the souls to be housed. However, stone is not the best material for trabeated architecture. Strong in compression (bricks, paving or columns), it is very brittle in tension (beams or slabs). This simple

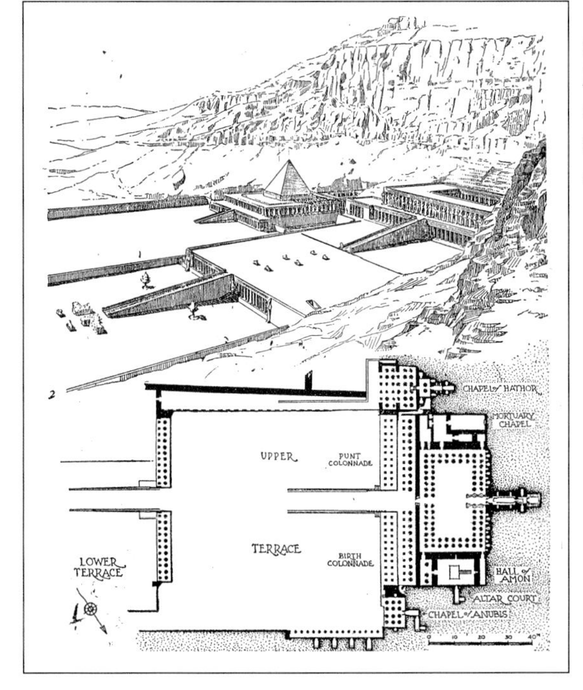

6.20 Mortuary Temple of Queen Hatshepsut, plan and axonometric.

6.21
Khons Temple, Karnak, construction techniques.

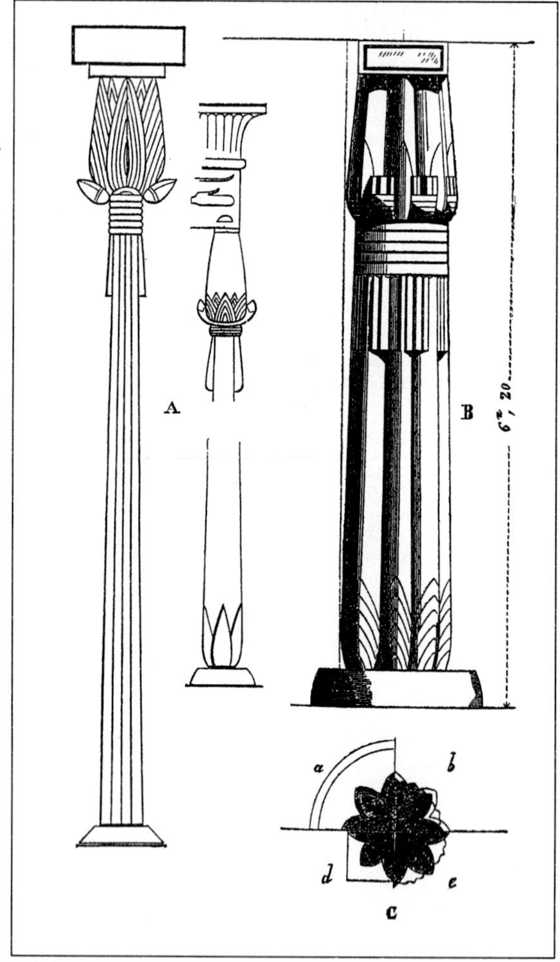

6.22
Origin of an Egyptian Column.

principle is easy to demonstrate by standing on a piece of glass which rests squarely on the ground. When compression is the only force exerted on the material, it is able to withstand great pressure before crushing. If the same piece of glass were supported at either end and a load applied, it would be likely to break. Tension exerted in small loads can cause deflection and fracture in a material that can sustain great compressive loads. The limitations of available construction methods are evident in the spatial development of Egyptian architecture. Because stone can only span small distances, there are dense fields of enormous columns in Egyptian temple architecture and little development of interior space. The form of the columns is mimetic of bundled papyrus, lotus or reeds. In temple architecture, these ephemeral materials are eternized in stone. The stylistic allusion to plant forms causes the columns to be differentiated at the top, where the flowers and leaves are most abundant. The broadening of the **capital** of the column also provides for greater structural efficiency. **Shear**, the tendency of one stressed material to pass through another, can cause a thin column shaft to pierce through the horizontal member it supports when the loads are great. The tri-partite division of the column into base, shaft, and capital is **anthropomorphic**; suggestive of the division of the human body into feet, body and head. The ornamental program of Egyptian temples may seem elaborate, but there is a strong correlation between constructional necessity and decoration, lending a reserved elegance and clarity to the whole.

Some aspects of Egyptian architecture are specific to the rituals they celebrate, the landscape they inhabit, the constructional properties of their material and the culture for which they were constructed. Still, there are universal lessons that can be extracted from the architecture of ancient Egypt, and these lessons are still applicable today.

An understanding of the role of procession and path, so critical in Egyptian architecture, is essential in the appreciation of any architectural experience. Architecture does not rely on a single static image. Works of architecture unfold in time, serially, as one moves through a space and observes changing views, changing definitions of enclosure, changing materials, light, and even smells, textures and sounds. The Great Pyramids, the most haptic, centered, object-like constructions conceivable, are in fact but the final term of a progression across a landscape. The power of the massive Pyramids is indisputable, but the experience gains in richness by means of the juxtaposition of different spatial and physical experiences as one approaches them from the river bank.

Pylons help mark and celebrate thresholds and transition spaces in Egyptian architecture. The cadenced rhythm of gateways along the processional path underscores the hierarchy of the scheme as it develops along the axis and defines precincts of different significance. Sometimes the path links a progression of spaces, as in the telescoping spaces of Theban temples. Sometimes the path permits a stark juxtaposition between spaces of very different natures, as in the Gizan procession. The orchestration of experience creates a total effect greater than the sum of the individual parts.

Taut parameters are described by the temple type and axial symmetry is, by nature, inflexible. Still, in Egyptian temple architecture and in any axial scheme, there is room for subtle refinement and minor deviations from the norm. The Khons Temple allows symmetry to govern every element in the scheme, but at Medinet Habu, local differences are accommodated on either side of the center-line without compromising the symmetry of the whole. At Luxor, the axis of the Amenhotep II temple is able to sustain a shift and transformation. The great rhoboidal court added on by Ramesses II to the north is curiously misaligned. The changed orientation is not a constructional error, but an attempt on the part of Ramesses II to make a stronger link between the Amenhotep II temple in Luxor and the nearby temple complex in Karnak, from whence the new axis is adopted.

The scale and physical properties of a landscape enhance the presence and meaning of a work of architecture. In Egyptian architecture the engagement of building and landscape is never casual. Use of local stone affords the building and the landscape a common materiality: they are of one substance, one color, one texture and one scale. The placement of buildings underscores sacred ritualized meanings of the landscape. The path of the sun or the flow of the Nile orient most structures and supply the coordinates for the grid of fields in the Nile valley. The Pyramids themselves take on the scale and ritual function of landscape in their evocation of sacred mountains. Works of lesser physical presence, like the humanly-scaled Temple of Hatshepsut, gain in stature from its delicate placement on the edge of a cliff, making one continuum of building and landscape. Not until the twentieth century did Western architecture again achieve such a masterful synthesis

6.23 *Left:* *Column detail.*

6.24 *Right:* *Papyrus column*

of landscape and architecture with the works of Frank Lloyd Wright.

The style of Egyptian architecture: axial, progressional, static, hierarchical, colossal, symmetrical, remained in tact for over two thousand years with only minor variations. Rituals were conserved in architectural form and the landscape was represented in each architectural act. Never again in western culture was a way of building to enjoy such a long life. Indeed, as we grow closer and closer to the present in our examination of architectural form, we shall see that the generation, consumption, and disposal of architectural styles proceeds with greater and greater speed.

6.25
Avenue of the Sphinxes, Temple of Ramesses II, Luxor, XIX Dynasty.

6.26
Avenue of Sphinxes, Temple of Ammon, Karnak, XIX Dynasty.

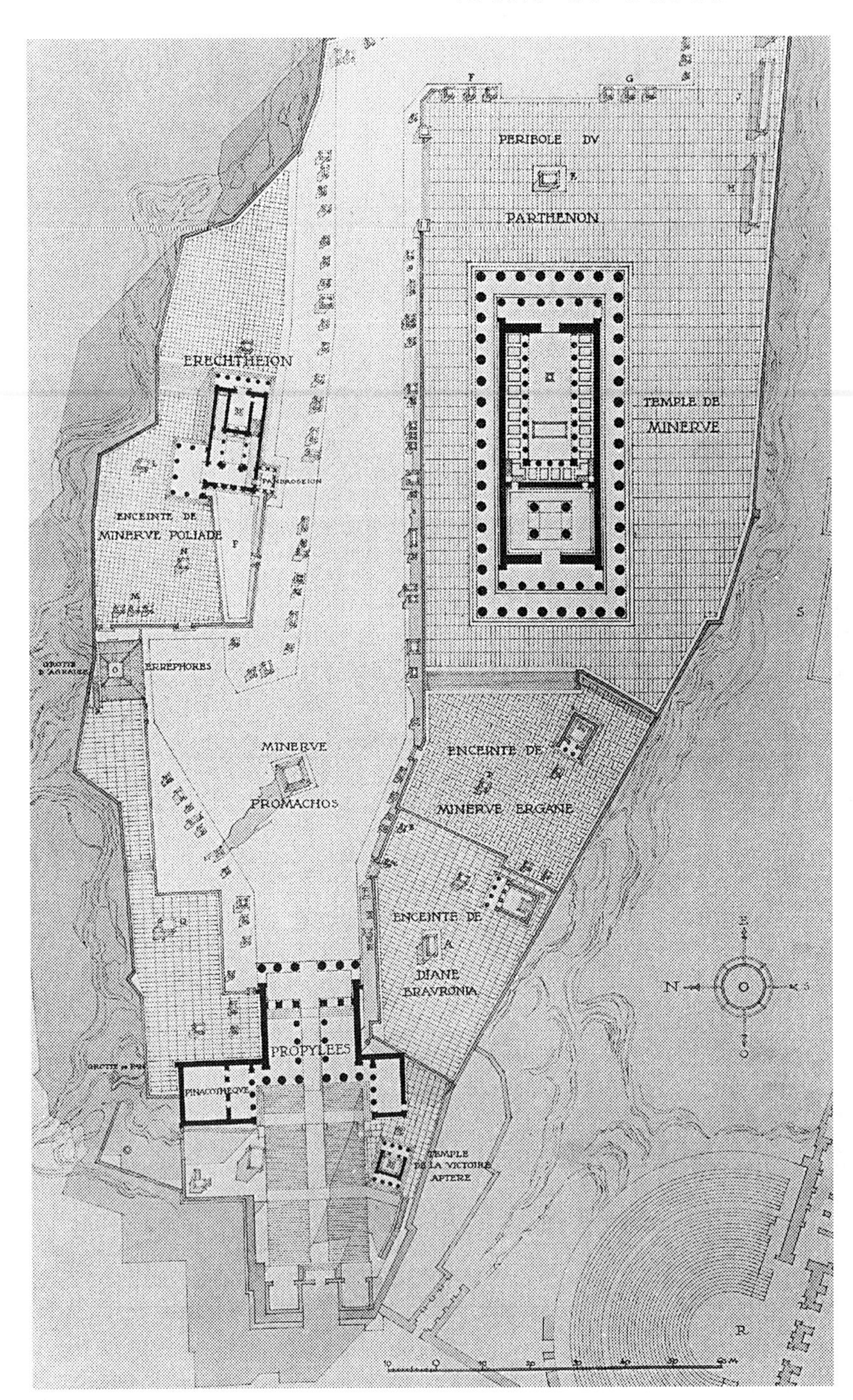

7.0
Acropolis, plan.

Chapter Seven

Ancient Greece: Ideal Form and Mythic Landscape

Art is produced when from many notions of experience a single universal judgement is formed with regard to like objects.

-Aristotle

A profound relationship exists between ritual, landscape and building in ancient Greece, as in ancient Egypt. The underlying myths and beliefs which sponsored artistic production in each society differed greatly, and the result of these varied world views produced different attitudes towards form, settlement, and order. The landscape in Egypt is an expansive, unchanging desert; Greece has a complex topography with mountains, valleys, harbors, and promontories. Egypt was governed by a powerful kingship; Greece was the birthplace of Democracy. The Egyptians believed in a continuum from life to the afterlife and the apotheosis of the Pharaoh; the Greeks believed in clear division between the realm of the living, the dead, and the immortals, although heroes, like Prometheus transgressed the boundaries and paid their penalty. The Egyptians believed in a divine, immutable order, dictated from above and symbolized by the permanence of the sun disk; Greek mythology is characterized by the supersedance of the rival cults. The mystical, dark, frenzied ritual of older earth deities, like the cults of Dionysius and Demeter, was overtaken by Olympian cults which championed rational thought, light, and measure, such as the cult of Apollo. Static timelessness characterized the Egyptian ideal; the tension of the heroic struggle, or *Agon,* characterized that of Greece.

Art and architecture conserve and make manifest cultural beliefs. In Egypt, architecture re-created the ceremonial journey of the dead and made provisions for the afterlife. The result was a highly structured, hieratic, hierarchical, and ritualized development of space. With the unerring regularity of the rising sun and the flooding Nile, a clearly defined path marked out a procession which never varied. Thresholds were marked by giant pylons, and paths were flanked by towering obelisks and avenues of colossal statues. Human scale was dwarfed and one entered the changeless land of immortal giants. The three-dimensional properties of the temples mattered much less than their geometrical description and the unfolding sequence of spatial events along the axis. In ancient Greece, the variety of landforms and the fecundity of nature inspired a belief that each particular place was inhabited by its own *genius* or special spirit. The purpose in constructing a temple was not to consecrate a site or make a shrine, but rather to reveal the inherent holiness of the site. While Egyptian temples describe a progression, Greek temples mark a point. Hence, they are conceptualized as objects-in-the-round. Archetypal, severe and repetitive in their formal description, the tense relationship among structures on a holy site with the surrounding landscape re-enacts the heroic *agon.*

The Greek way of conceptualizing form and space can best be understood by looking at a Greek statue, such as that of **Poseidon** from c.460 B.C. and comparing it with the Egyptian statuary we earlier examined. The Egyptian statue of Ranofer is axial in organization and characterized by a frozen, timeless stasis. The form is closed and compact, fully contained within the rectilinear boundaries of the stone block. The Poseidon statue is just the opposite. The figure is caught at a critical moment of action, as he is about to hurl his spear. In the statue dynamism and action are arrested. The portrait of the god is idealized and his features and lineaments strive to describe the archetypal, rather than any particular individual. Nonetheless, the figure is naturalistically portrayed and eminently human. Taut, muscular limbs flex under the stress of action. Human scale, human proportions and the beauty of the human figure are celebrated in the work. While the Egyptian statue is frontal, the Poseidon statue is a fully **plastic** object, meant to be appreciated three-dimensionally. The dynamism and plasticity of the figure are emphasized by the outward extension of the arms and the open stride of the legs. The torsion in the body causes the muscles to stretch and the three-dimensionality of the figure to be shown off to full advantage.

The very terms which characterize Greek sculpture can be applied to architecture: plasticity, tension, muscularity, archetype, human scale, proportion, dynamism. At first glance those claims may seem preposterous. The internal organization of Greek temples is axial and perhaps even more highly codified than that of Egyptian funerary temples. The classical language is moreover canonical and prescriptive. Models or proportional relationships govern everything from the over-all description of building type to the **intercolumniation**, or the spacing between columns. In appreciation of this extravagant, all-embracing order, eighteenth-century Graecophiles claimed that they could accurately reconstruct an entire temple from a fragment of a fluted column.

Drama and poetry were the most highly esteemed art forms in ancient Greece. It is possible to gain further appreciation of architectural organizations by comparing their structure to those of Greek plays. In ancient Greece, theater had ritual significance and the location of amphitheaters in landscapes had the same sacred revelatory properties as the siting of temples. Actors, chorus, and audiences all took part in the spectacle of dance and rhythmic chanting. In the early days of Greek theater, dramas were enacted on a round stage, eschewing notions of the frontal proscenium which dominated theater at a later period. Dramatic personae represented idealized archetypes rather than individuals. The conflicts they meet were likewise archetypal.

Greek buildings, like actors on the stage of an amphitheater, must be understood as figures-in-the-round. Moreover, like the antagonists and protagonists of classical drama, Greek building types strive for archetypal clarity in their definition and articulation. Their forms are simple, abstract, repetitive and rule-bound. We described many of these types in our analysis of Pergamon: the temple, treasury, stoa, theater, **megaron**.

The temple is best able to rival the stature of the hero in Greek drama. The basic description of a temple remained constant for hundreds of years and survived for hundreds more in Roman architecture with only slight transformations. As Vincent Scully observed: *"...No study of Greek temples can be purely morphological, of form without theme, nor purely iconological, of theme regardless of form, since in Greek art the two are one. The form is the meaning..."* (Vincent Scully, *The Earth, The Temple and The Gods*) Loosely speaking, a Greek temple consisted of the following: an elevated platform or **stylobate**, an inner chamber or **cella**, surrounded by flanking columned porticos or **pteron** which support a triangular roof, or **pediment**. The language in which these elements were articulated was clearly prescribed by the classical orders, which we shall discuss shortly.

Because the holy-of-holies was intended to be entered only by the cult priests, the development of long clear spans and interior space was not a major concern in Greek architecture. Temple walls and porticoes were made of stone,

*7.1
Poseidon, c. 460 B.C., National Museum, Athens.*

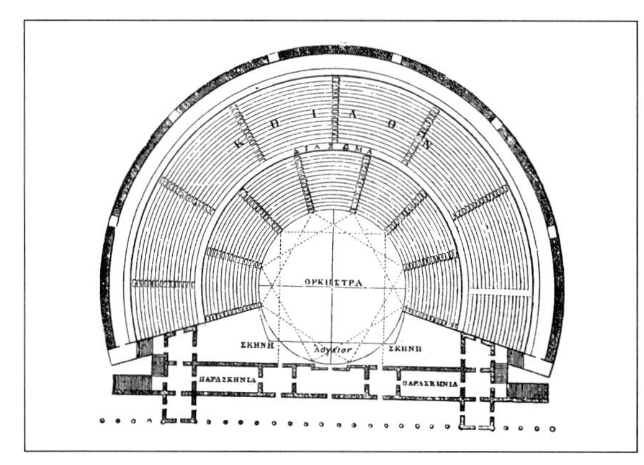

*7.2
Theater at Epidaurus, Greece, c. 300 B.C., plan.*

*7.3
Theater at Syracuse, Sicily, view.*

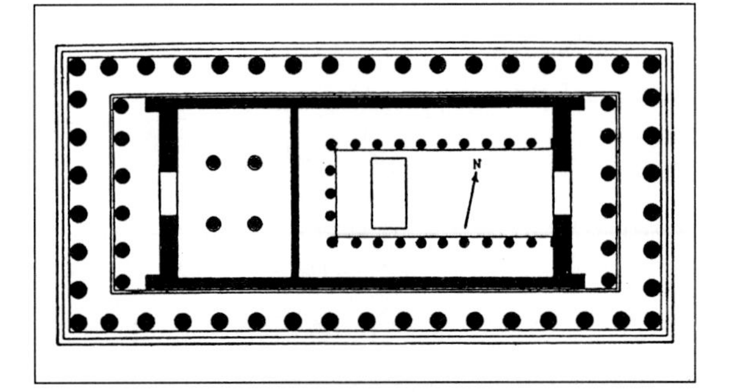

7.4
Parthenon, plan.

7.5
Parthenon, elevation.

7.6
Parthenon, section.

7.7
Parthenon on the Acropolis.

but the roof of the cella was structured with wood trusses. The overall size of a temple was related to the size of the cella. Hence, the length of available timber for roof trusses limited the size of structures. When majestic Lebanon cedars were available, buildings could grow very large indeed, as may have been the case with the Temple of Olympian Zeus, Agrigentum, 480 B.C., in which the cella spans over 68 feet; or the Council Chamber in Miletus, whose span is even greater. Still, even in the case of the latter building where interior space does have a public function, little attention is lavished on its design.

The language used by the Greeks to provide measure and constancy to their buildings was based on the three **Greek Orders: Doric, Ionic, and Corinthian**. Frequently used to describe only the column, or indeed, only the column capital, the Orders govern far more. Greek architecture was **trabeated**, that is based on a post and beam system of construction. Each Order consisted of both vertical and horizontal elements; the column, composed of **base, shaft** and **capital,** and the **entablature,** composed of **architrave, frieze** and **cornice**. Etymologically the word 'order' derives from 'ornament'. What may at first seem like an inessential ornamental program in fact defines the temples and gives them substance. The Orders dictate a proportionally related series of elements from the whole down to the detail. Given the archetypal fixity of the temple type, nuances of proportion and elaboration of detail held tremendous meaning. The great Greek sculptor Polyclitus propounded the need for finely resolved proportionate relationships in his *Kanon,* a lost rule book on proportion whose only extant fragment states *"perfection lies in many numbers."* Writing specifically about the human figure, he is thought to have meant that physical beauty is achieved through commensurate proportions among all parts of the body with respect to each other and with respect to the whole.

Anthropomorphic qualities are ascribed to the classical orders by Vitruvius, 1st century A.D., in his *First Book of Architecture.* Although Vitruvius was a Roman, he based his text on many, now lost, Greek sources. Doric, the stoutest, most severe and most muscular of the orders rests squarely on the ground without a base and is associated with masculine deities. The simple, disk-like capital flares out to meet the entablature. The flexing of an athlete's muscles has correspondence in the exaggerated flexure of architectural members. Most pronounced is the bulge one third up the shaft of the column, called the **entasis**. The Doric entablature is adorned by band of **triglyphs**, a pattern of three vertical bars, perhaps mimetic of the ends of beams used to construct wooden temples. Ideally, the triglyphs fall above columns and at the mid-point between columns. A classic problem in Doric architecture is the difficulty of achieving these relationships at the corner of the building. In his 1929 book. D.S. Robinson rhapsodized: *"It is not surprising that the triglyph problem killed the Doric tradition. Who shall blame the third and fourth century architects, who (as Vitruvius tells us) declared that for this reason, and this only, Doric, despite its acknowledged beauty and dignity, was not a fit style for temple architecture? Men will not wear inherited chains forever."*

The Ionic Order rests on a base. Its shaft is more slender than that of the Doric Order and

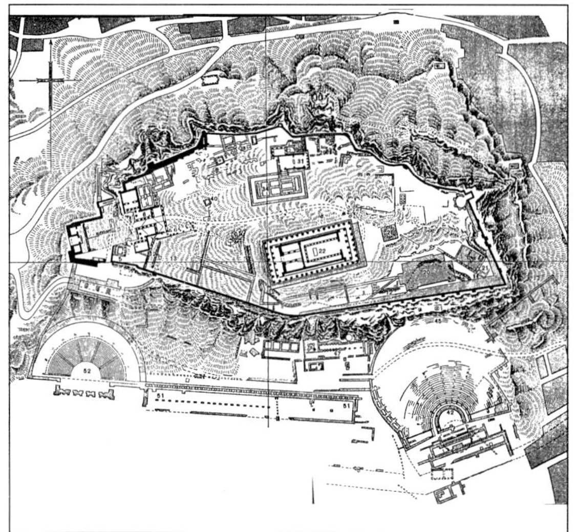

7.8
The Acropolis, plan.

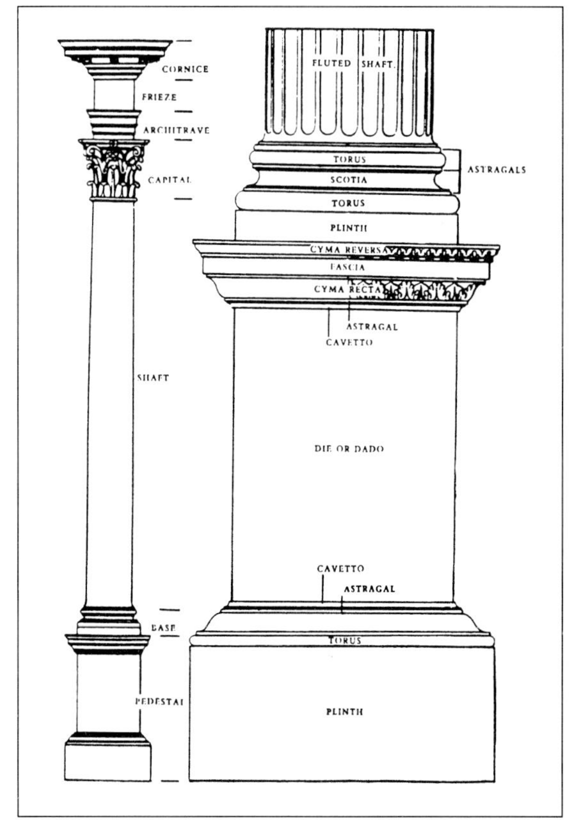

7.9
The Corinthian Order, after James Gibbs, 1722.

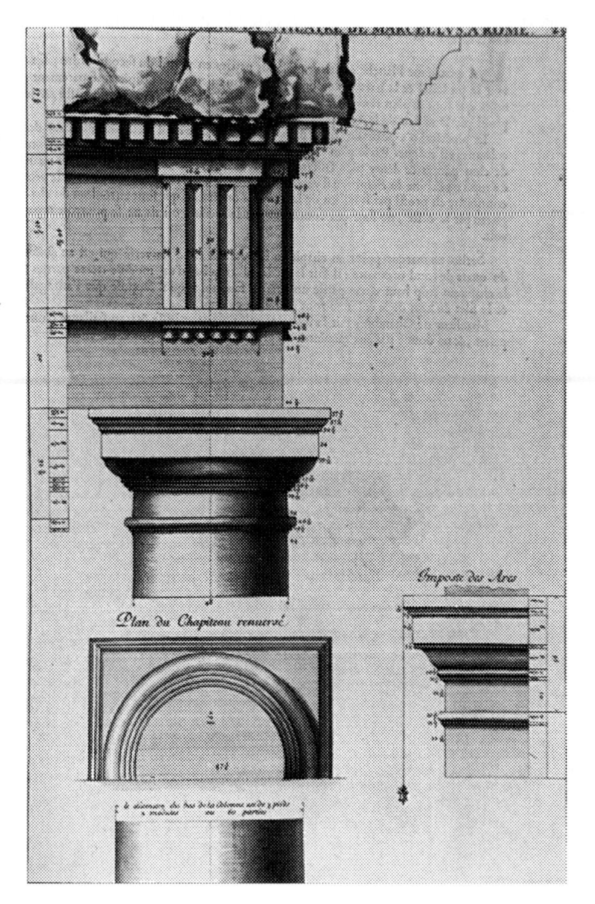

7.10 Left: The Doric Order, according to A. Desgodetz, 1695.

7.11 Right: The Ionic Order, according to A. Desgodetz, 1695.

the capital is more elaborate. The inward curl of the **volutes** on the capital is at once reminiscent of a ram's horns and the curving locks of a matronly deity, with whom the order is conventionally associated. Remarking on the delicacy of Ionic proportions, Le Corbusier said: *"there was a breath of tenderness when Ionic was born."* The ornamental program for the Ionic entablature is not as formulaic as it is the Doric, but there is nonetheless a problem when columns meet the corner of buildings. The twin volutes describe a plane and enforce a dominant, frontal orientation which makes an awkward transition as the colonnade wraps the cella.

The Corinthian Order is the most slender and graceful of all. The tall, fluted shaft rests on a base and is surmounted by a capital adorned by acanthus leaves and other flora. The abundant foliage of the Corinthian capital evokes a woven headdress or garland atop the head of a maidenly goddess, with whom the Order is conventionally associated. The anthropomorphism of the Orders goes beyond the association of specific Orders and mythical per-

7.12 Left: The Corinthian Order, according to A. Desgodetz, 1695.

7.13 Right; Doric corner detail, from the Parthenon, Ictinos and Callicrates, Athens, c. 438 B.C.

sonages. Human attributes are projected directly on to the column. **John Shute** emphasized this connection in his illustration of **The Orders** for his 1563 treatise.

Elaborate attention to proportion and the codification of temple type, parts and assembly suggests a very rigid, rule-bound method of construction for the ancient Greeks. This was hardly the case. Greek architecture was imbued with strange deviations from the norm, some of which Vitruvius attributed to *"optical corrections,"* so that perspectival foreshortening would not distort the true beauty of well-proportioned rectangular structures. In addition to entasis in the columns, refinements include curving stylobates (platforms), columns which taper and tilt inwards, and corner columns which are thickened. J.J. Coulton has offered the following explanation: *"The stylobate of the Parthenon is set out with extreme accuracy, parallel sides differing from each other by less than one part in 5000, but the columns are placed on it with much less precision, some intercolumniations varying from the mean by as much as one part in 250. Such un-*

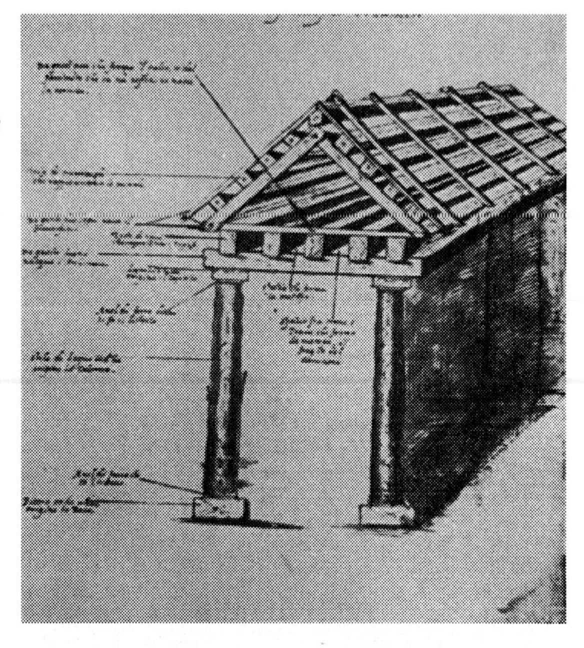

7.14
Doric Primitive Hut, according to Gherardo Spini, c. 1568.

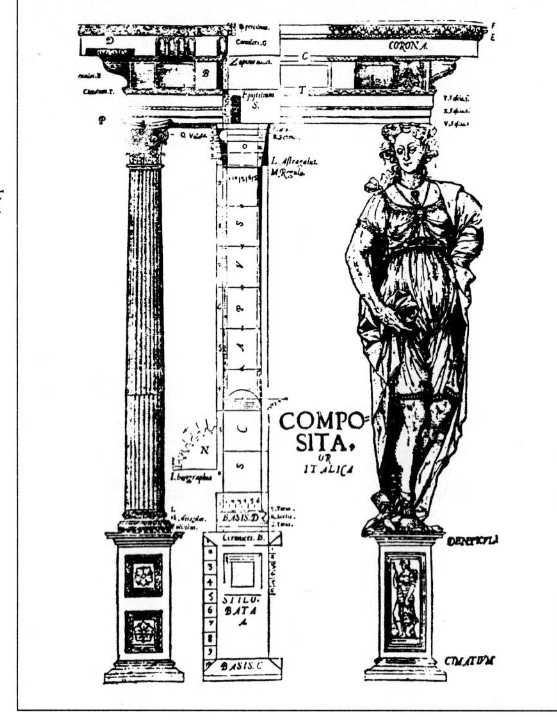

7.15
The Composite Order, according to John Shute, from First and Chief Groundes of Architecture, London, 1563 .

avoidable variations in column spacing must, at the very least, have been intentionally tolerated, and since they correct no optical illusion, they must have been intended to relax slightly the stiffness of complete regularity; if so, then other variations from regularity may well have had the same intention." (J.J. Coulton, *Ancient Greek Architects at Work*).

The **Temple of Ceres** in Paestum is an early example of a Doric Greek temple in which all the features of the fully developed type are present, albeit in an extreme form. Columns are fat with narrow necks and exaggerated entasis. Capitals mushroom out to engage the architrave. The oppressive heaviness of the membrature is the very opposite of the lightness and grace achieved by the Doric order when it reaches its height in the Parthenon

It is impossible to discuss any Greek building without also discussing its site and the relationship of buildings upon the site. At first glance, the disposition of buildings in the sacred precinct or ***temenos*** seems irregular and haphazard. The clear geometric alignments we have come to expect from our earlier study of Egyptian architecture is replaced by a scattering of buildings upon the land. In his book on Greek sacred architecture, Vincent Scully has observed that the placement of buildings is not at all random nor neglectful of context. Rather, context is understood to include local adjacencies to buildings and landscape features but in much broader terms. Curious alignments are often made in deference to distant peaks and valleys, whose special powers connect directly to those of the temple and whose meaning is revealed by the location of the temple. Scully states: *"all Greek sacred architecture explores and praises the character of a god or group of gods in a*

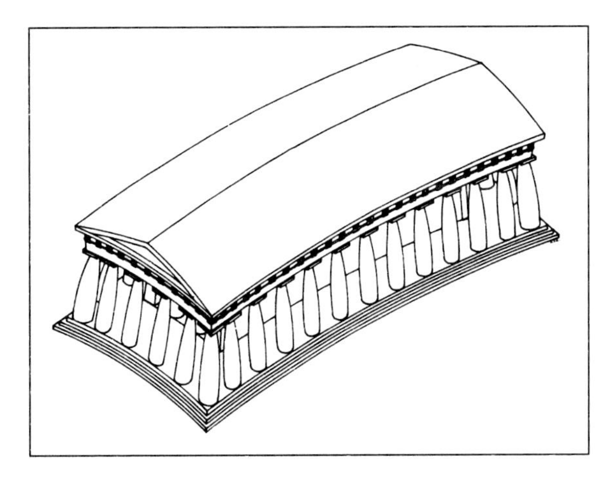

7.16 Left: Doric temple showing exaggerated refinements according to J. J. Coulton.

7.17 Right: Temple of Ceres, Paestum, mid Fifth Century B.C.

specific place. That place is itself holy and, before the temple was built upon it, embodied the whole of the deity as a recognized natural force... Therefore, the formal elements of any Greek sanctuary are, first, the specially sacred landscape in which it is set and, second, the buildings that are placed within it..." (Vincent Scully, *The Earth, the Temple, and the Gods*).

K.A. Doxiadis proposed another system of sacred site planning in *Architectural Space in Ancient Greece.* Surveys and studies of many sacred precincts led Doxiadis to the conclusion that Greek site planning only seems random if we attempt to understand it in terms of a neutral, gridded network of lines which evenly assign orientation and related measure to all elements on the site. If one examines the sites the way the ancient Greeks would have, that is, based on the theory of a circular universe and a 180 degree arc of vision, it is possible to read a different order into the sites. Doxiadis showed that from the gateway to a sacred precinct a point could be determined five feet off the ground, at eye level. From this point, lines radiated at regular intervals and located all major

7.18 Temple of Ceres, Paestum, column detail.

7.19 Left: Temple of Concord, (Temple F), Agrigentum (Akragas) second half of the fifth century B.C., view.

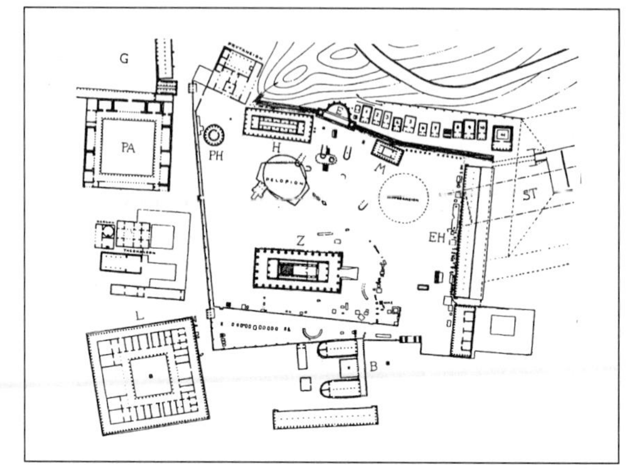

7.20 Right: Olympia, fifth century, site plan.

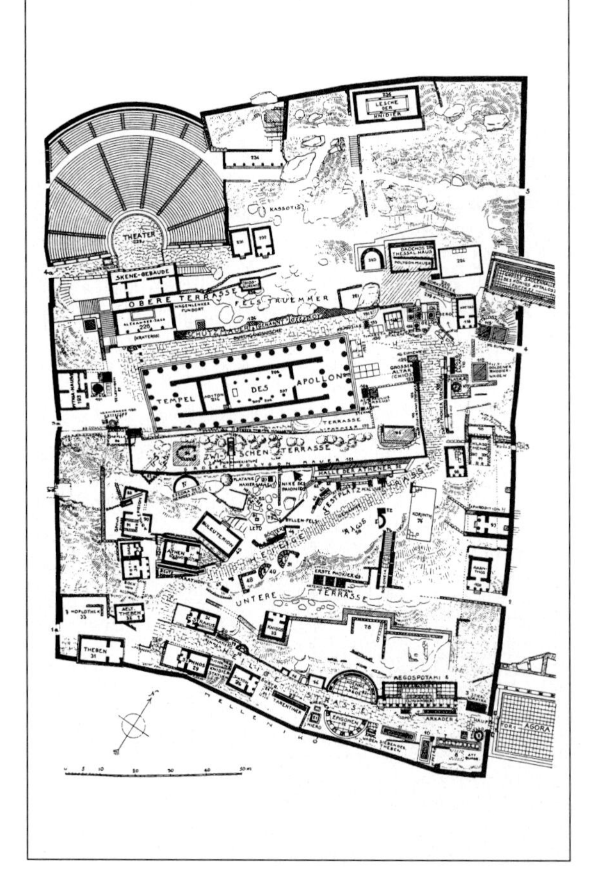

7.21 Sanctuary of Apollo, Delphi, Greece, c. 150 B.C., site plan.

elements and edges on the site. Furthermore, the infinite extension of radial lines-of-sight from their origin connects the buildings in the precinct to the distant landscape beyond. Within the precinct, individual buildings exert enormous tension on one another as their orientations skew and the space between them compresses. The peculiar characteristics of each site are rooted in the topography and also in the nature of the local cults. At **Olympia**, home to the gods, each city state kept a treasury to assure their protection by the residing gods. At **Delphi**, the embracing valley of the site sponsored its association with the *omphalos*, or naval of the world.

The most famous of all Greek sacred sites is the **Acropolis**. High on a plateau overlooking Athens, a sacred terrain was claimed by the cult of Athena. The largest and most majestic temple on the Acropolis is the **Parthenon**, a Doric temple dedicated to the cult of Athena, patron goddess of Athens. Other cults also laid claim to the site, and their connection to the land is revealed in an assortment of shrines. While the experience of Greek space is not organized by an axial path, as in Egypt, it is nonetheless processional. A serpentine path, the Panathenaic Way, winds up the sacred hill and terminates the ceremonial path that extends across Greece. There is a continual reorganization of elements and landscape throughout the progression, as views are framed, concealed and revealed according to the diverse vantage points along the trail. When seen from the base of the Acropolis, the buildings seem to grow out of the hill and assume the scale and power of the landscape. Structures are revealed obliquely as one approaches the site, enhancing their sculptural, plastic value.

A great pedimented gateway, the **Propylaea**, marks the entrance to the sacred precinct. The undulations of the path are embraced in the colonnaded arms of an open fore-court, and further compressed into a single line through the symmetrically organized gate. There is an expectation that such symmetry would sponsor an over-all site symmetry, but this is not the case. The center line of the Propylaea located a colossal cult statue of Athena, 23 feet high, by the great sculptor Phidias. One's view is then deflected to the left where the full plasticity of the Parthenon is revealed at three-quarter view. Canted inwards in front of the Propylaea is the **Temple to Athena Nike**, a tiny but elegant Ionic temple. When viewed from the top of the hill the diminutive size of the temple seems in stark counterpoint to the grandeur of the Parthenon. When seen from below, the tiny temple conjoins with its base and engages the expanse of the cliff.

If the Parthenon is the most masterful building on the Acropolis, the **Erechteion** is certainly the most curious. We think of Greek temples as

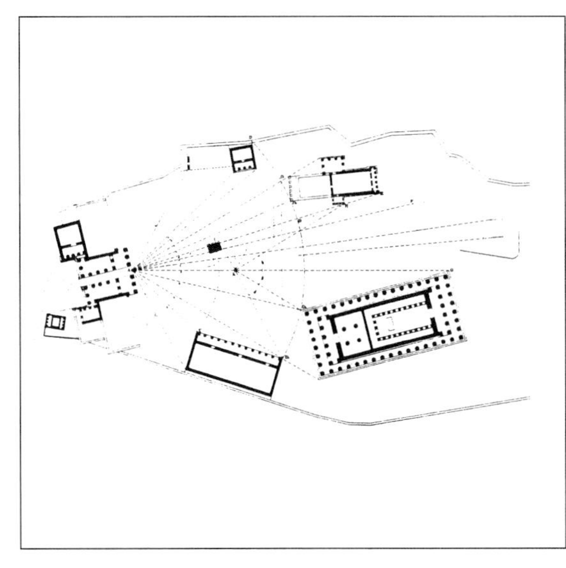

7.22 The Athenian Acropolis, according to K.A. Doxiadis' principal of Greek site planning.

7.23 Acropolis, Athens, Greece, 530 B.C., view of the Erechteion from the Propyleaea.

7.24 Left: Acropolis, elevation.

7.25 Right: Acropolis, view.

7.26 Parthenon, view.

7.27 Left: Temple of Athena Nike, Callicrates, Athens, 438 B.C., elevation.

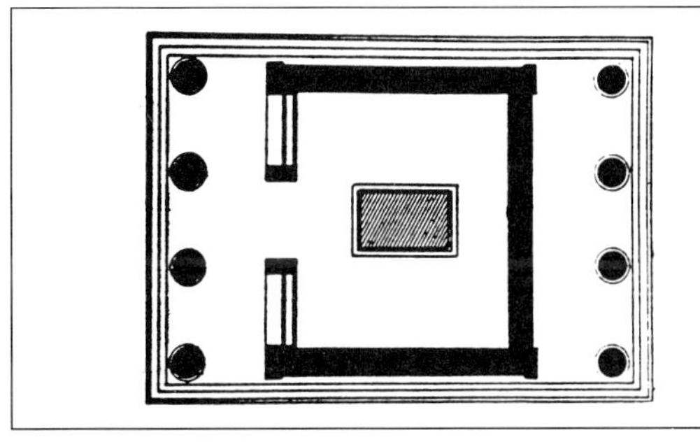

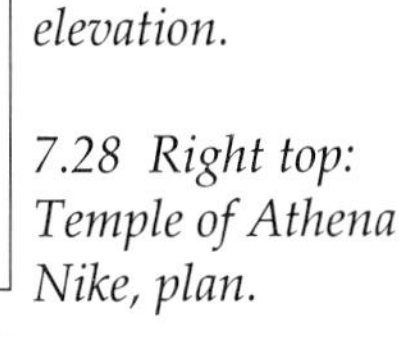

7.28 Right top: Temple of Athena Nike, plan.

7.29 Right bottom: Temple of Athena Nike, view.

pristine, rectangular volumes, elaborated in strict accordance with the rules governing the type and the Orders. Variations come from small, delicate refinements, like the profile of the moldings, the carving of the capitals, or the rhythm of intercolumniation. On the contrary, the Erechteion has a hybrid nature. Built on a sloping site, it commemorates three distinct shrines and accommodates a precinct for a long-vanished sacred olive tree. One small porch is supported by female figures called **Caryatids**. Many of the idiosyncrasies of the temple relate to the unusual function, but it is also possible to read the strange arrangement of parts as a decorous response to different site constraints. As the topography falls off towards the edge of the cliff, the scale of the Poseidon porch expands to rival the scale of the Parthenon and to engage distant views from below. Meanwhile, on the uphill side, the scale of the Caryatid porch shrinks, emphasizing the subordinate role of the temple with respect to the Parthenon. Both porches are orthogonally clipped onto the sides of a more conventional Temple to Athena Polias. This temple is aligned to view the distant mountains which orient the Parthenon. Indeed, the Athena Polias temple and the Parthenon frame the mountain thereby bringing it into the space of the Acropolis.

We earlier mentioned the **Panathenaic Way**, the great processional route through Greece. Just before its termination atop the Acropolis, it passes through the **Athenian agora**, or marketplace, at the base of the hill. **Edmund Bacon** has

7.30 Left: Erechteion, Mnesicles, Athens, Greece, 420-393 B.C., view.

7.31 Right: Erechteion, view.

7.32 Left: Erechteion, plan.

7.33 Right: Erechteion, detail of carydid porch.

shown how the character of the agora transformed from 500 B.C. to the second century A.D. At the earliest period, the agora was comprised of free-standing buildings, loosely arranged with respect to one another, and very loosely defining the space between them. By 420 B.C. the addition of stoas and additional structures gave stronger definition to the central space. Equal in force to the solid edges and objects in the complex are powerful shafts of space. The swath of space cut by the Panathenaic road divides the site into triangular halves. The **Hephasteion Temple**, pulled outside of the precinct, generates through its axiality a shaft of space which projects into the agora and influences subsequent additions to the agora. By the Hellenistic period, the edges are completely defined and a figure/ground reversal had taken effect. The character of the space shifted from one comprised of figural solids to a great bounded figural void. By the second century A.D., when Greece was fully under Roman dominion, the density of buildings in the agora made unequivocal the dominance of the shaped space over the plasticity of the buildings. In our discussion of ancient Rome, we shall see that this changed attitude towards space is precisely what makes Roman building complexes so different from their Greek predecessors.

The architecture of ancient Greece should not be looked at as a quaint historical artifact from more than two millennia past. Important lessons about landscape and building can be learned from the ancient Greeks that apply to contemporary design. Although today we would not assign religious meaning to the specific character of topography and landform, it is

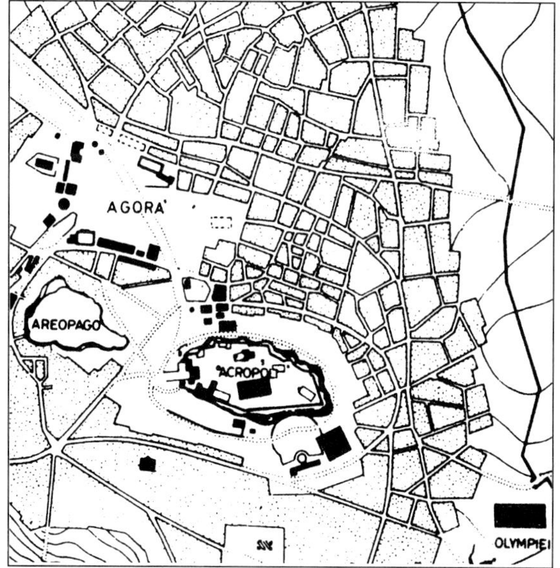

7.34 The Agora and the Acropolis.

7.35 Hephasteion Temple in the Agora.

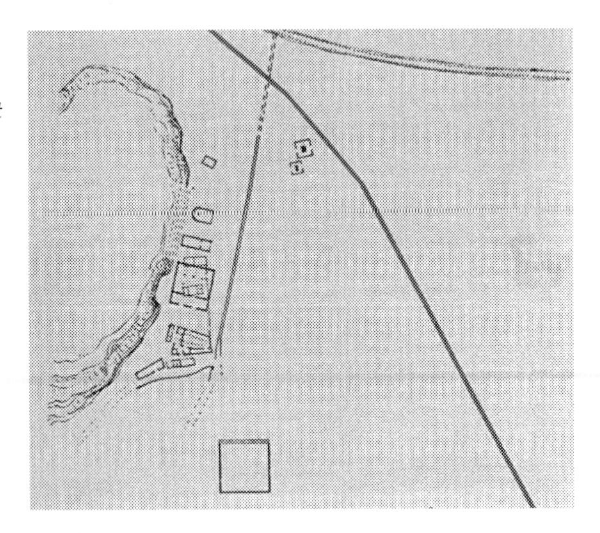

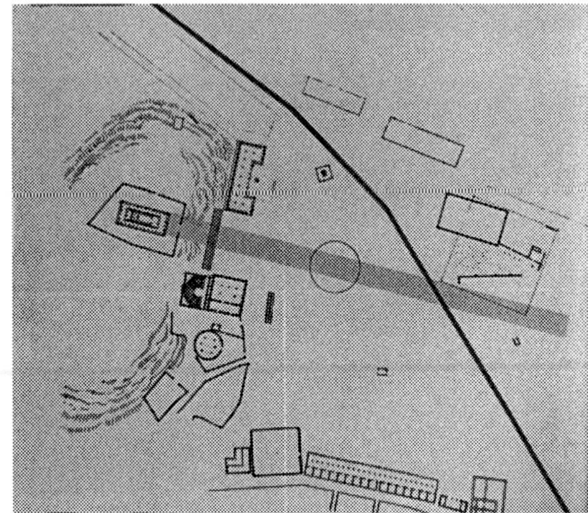

7.36- 7.39 The development of the Athenian Agora.

7.36 Left: 500 B.C.

7.37 Right: 420 B.C.

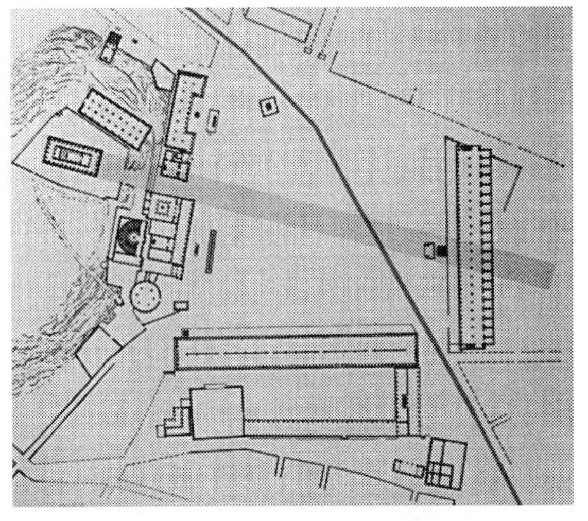

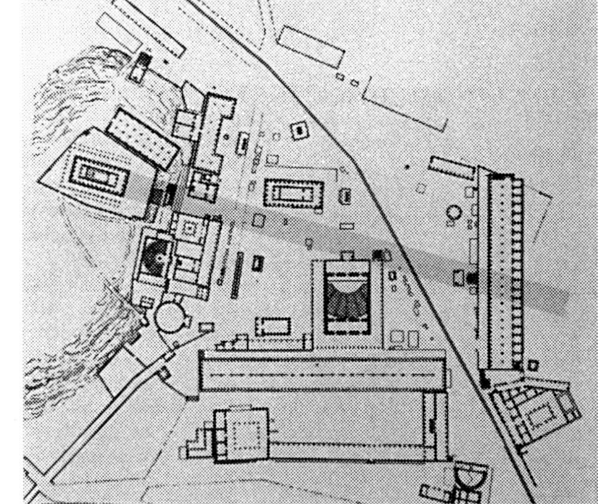

7.38 Left: Hellenistic Period.

7.39 Right: Second Century A.D.

nonetheless true that each site has its own qualities which are enhanced by some architectural interventions and obliterated by others. The Greeks realized that site was not limited to local conditions, be they defined by the *temenos* of a sacred site, or by the property lines on a plot plan. Context involves the relationship among features particular to the site and features which order the region. In the Erechteion, we observed that a compromise or hybrid solution, which may seem puzzling in terms of a very narrow analysis of site and program, yields a greater synthesis in terms of the whole.

The classical language of architecture, born in Greece, set forth a method which related the proportions and scale of all aspects of a building, extending from its overall composition to tiny, fine-grained ornamental details. Such an all-inclusive mastery of scale is seldom present in architecture today, except in that of the greatest masters. The Greek method of determining proportion was not additive, whereby the combination of equal modules yielded structures which were one, two, or three times the size of their predecessors. Rather geometric systems were used which relied on the nested generation of related parts within the whole. The golden rectangle is the best known example of such a self-regenerating geometry. Le Corbusier looked to the Greeks and their 'dynamic symmetries' for inspiration when he developed his own system of proportions, the **Modulor**. Such a system allows a marriage of standardized measure and compositional freedom.

In Greek architecture free-standing buildings are grouped with sympathy to each other and the landscape. Given the fact American cities seldom have sufficient urban density to create figural spaces like those in Europe, it is instructive to see how tension and order can be established through voids as well as through mass.

7.40
Le Corbusier in Athens, sketch, from Journey to the East.

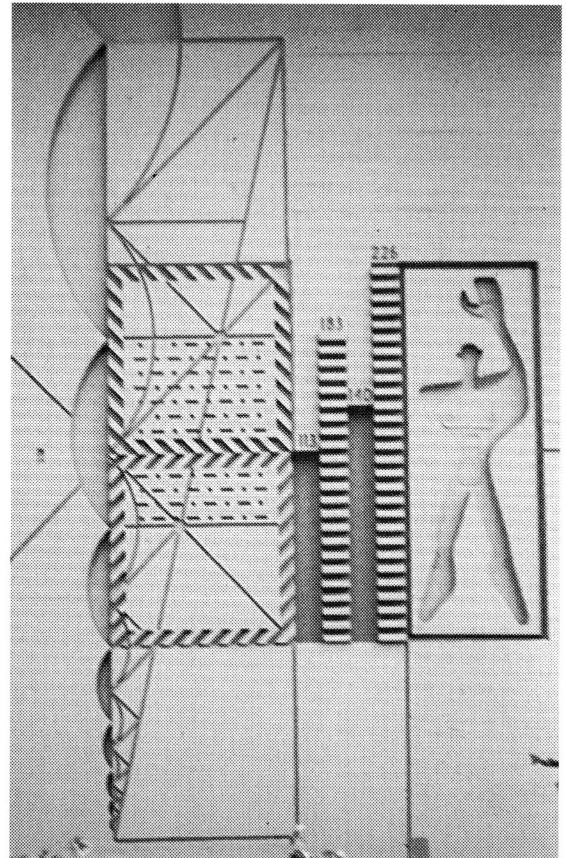

7.41
Le Corbusier, 'The Modulor', imprinted on the wall of the Unité, West Berlin.

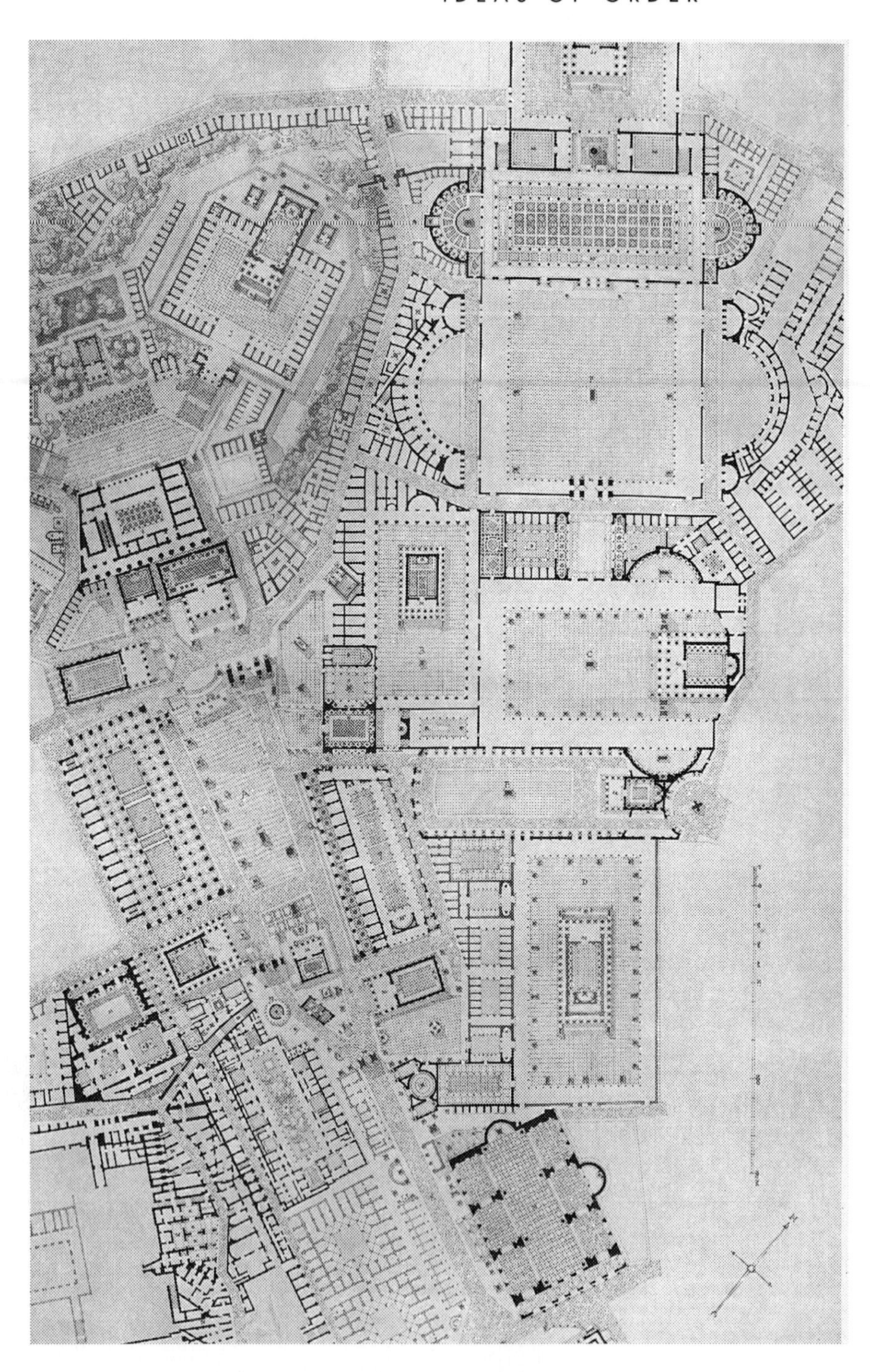

8.0
The Roman and Imperial Fora, reconstruction.

Chapter Eight

Ancient Rome: Urbanism and Figural Space

Greece had a genius, Greece had eloquence,
for her ambition and her end was fame.
Our Roman youth is diligently taught
the deep mysterious art of growing rich,
and the first words that children learn to speak
are of the value and the names of coin:
can a penurious wretch, that with his milk
hath suck'd the basest dregs of usury,
pretend to generous and heroic thoughts?
And can rust and avarice write lasting lines?

--Horace

Roman architecture, like Roman philosophy, drama, and poetry, owes a great debt to the Greek culture they vanquished. Even the Olympian gods and the myths that surround them were adopted by the Romans and incorporated into local cults. Building types established in Greece were taken over by the Romans and amplified with the addition of many new types, such as basilicas, baths, atrium houses, theaters, circuses, and arenas, to name a few. Likewise, the Greek Orders and the classical language were adapted and expanded by the Romans. Indeed, if the Greeks had a genius for the lyric and the dramatic, for the exquisite refinement of physical and intellectual constructs, then the Romans had a genius for discursive argument, rhetoric, engineering and administration. In other words, while the Greeks excelled at the theoretical and the original idea, the Romans excelled at the practical and the promulgation of ideas borrowed from elsewhere.

To the three Greek Orders, two more were added: a simpler and more modestly propor-

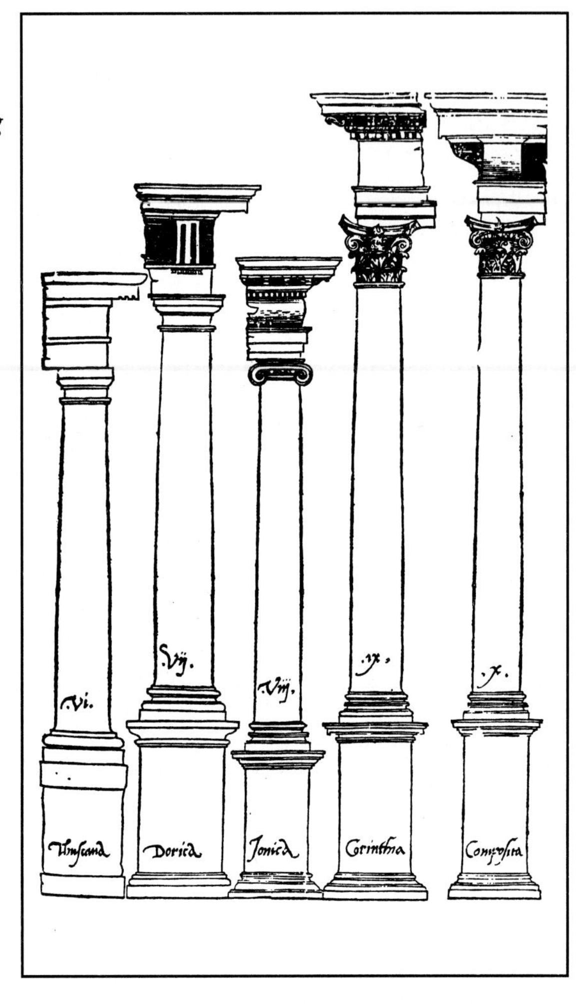

8.1
The Five Roman Orders, according to Sebastiano Serlio.

tioned **Tuscan Order**, and a grander, slenderer and more ornate **Composite Order**, which joined together elements of the Ionic and Corinthian. Columns were structural and free-standing in Greece; in Rome, they were frequently non-structural, engaged in walls as ornament. Large expanses of wall were broken up into agreeably proportioned units through the surface application of reticulated columnar grids. The greater urban density of Rome and a taste for colossal scale made it necessary to develop a language for multi-story buildings. The Romans did this through the superposition of the Orders. The **Colosseum** is the best known example of a structure in which the different Orders are progressively stacked, stoutest at the bottom and slenderest at the top.

A comparison of Egyptian and Greek statues revealed most of the significant attitudes towards space and form which permeated artistic production in those cultures. Roman statuary, on the contrary, is largely borrowed from the Greeks. Many of the most important works of Greek sculpture are now known only from accurate Roman copies, such as the **Doryphoros of Polyclitus**. While accurate in their representation of the figure, Roman copies tend to be frozen and rigid when compared with the Greek originals. More indicative of a peculiarly Roman sensibility are the strange colossal heads, feet, and hands which date from the Constantinian period. Delicacy of scale and the celebration of human proportions, so essential to the Greek works, are replaced by sculpture whose very size makes it approach engineering. The purpose is rhetorical; the statues manifest a physical testament of the grandeur and power of the Empire, rather than an exercise in **mi-**

8.2
Colosseum, Rome, Italy, A.D. 75-80.

8.3 Left: Constantinian Head, Fourth century A.D., Capitoline Museum, Rome.

8.4 Right: Doryphoros of Polyclitus, Roman copy in marble of a bronze original, c. 450-440 B.C., National Museum, Naples.

metic or **heuristic** art, as in ancient Greece. In the nineteenth century, it was commonplace to view Roman art and architecture as a degeneration from the height of classicism attained in ancient Greece. Contamination of a cultural patrimony works both ways, however. The Roman poet, Juvenal, expressed his distaste for the Hellenization of Rome in the following lines: *"...I hate, in Rome, a Grecian town to find: To see the scum of Greece transplanted here, Receiv'd like gods..."*

The Romans excelled at government and the sponsorship of vast public works projects. The administration of the largest empire ever assembled on earth required systematization and ingenuity. Roman roads, aqueducts, sewers and bridges, many of which are still operable today, were mechanisms by which Roman culture could be exported and Roman political hegemony maintained. Good roads made possible efficient troop movement, and aqueducts assured fresh supplies of water.

Greek reliance on free-standing buildings in dynamic tension with each other and the landscape had correspondence in the staging of Greek plays. In Rome, a transformation occurred in the design of theaters. The **proscenium,** or framed stage, was introduced, instituting a clear division between audience and actors, and an axial relationship between

8.5
G.B. Piranesi, Engraving of a cross section of Castel S. Angelo, Rome, c.1755.

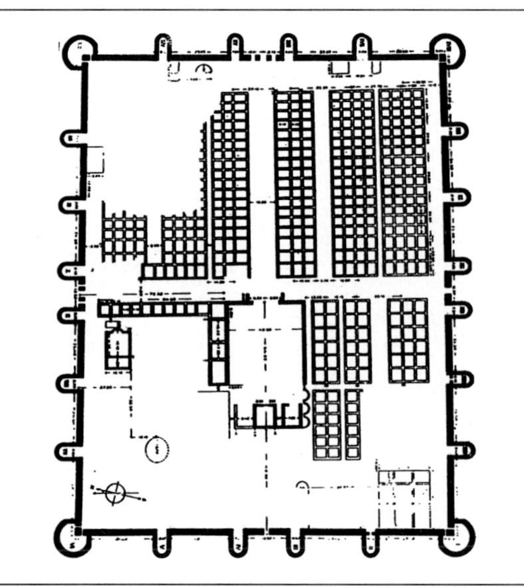

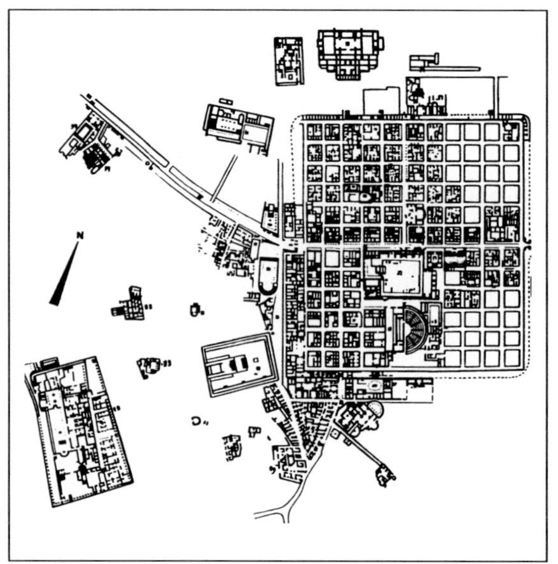

8.6 Left: Roman Settlement at El-Leggùn, Jordan.

8.7 Right: Plan of Timgad, Roman Town, c. A.D. 100.

the domain of the spectator and that of the stage. Rather than theaters-in-the-round, staging was organized frontally. As we shall see, axiality and frontality are two spatial organizers which differentiate Roman design and planning from that of the Greeks.

Frontality and axiality derive from myths surrounding landscape and settlement. According to legend, Rome was founded by Romulus, one of the twins suckled by the Roman she-wolf. To claim the land, his first act was to mark the principal north-south and east-west roads traversing the site, the ***Cardo*** and ***Decumanus***. He then plowed a furrow to define the perimeter. At the intersection of the axes and the boundary, Romulus 'picked up' (Latin, *portare*) his plow. In this way, the four 'portals', or gates to the city were defined. The spatial diagram of the four-square grid emerged, along with a ritual for settling the land. When the peripatetic Romans set up camp or founded new frontier towns, they imported Roman order and stability by re-enacting the mythical founding of Rome. The crossing of the *cardo* and *decumanus* established four precincts within the town, and at the center, an important public space was located: the **forum**. The four-square town plan, identical to the spatial paradigm of the paradise garden, consecrated the land for Rome and linked it ritually back to the seat of the empire. The definition of boundary marked an enclosed precinct within the wilderness that could be settled and controlled.

All roads lead to Rome. In other words, the dispersal of mystical events and sacred sites throughout the landscape, typical of the Greek world view, was replaced by an insistence on the supremacy of one place: Rome. Even though the term *genius loci*, 'spirit of the place,' is of Latin origin, spatial reiteration of Roman authority took precedence in site planning over strategies which emphasized the specific nature of the place. The Roman empire was centrally organized, and reference to that central authority conferred meaning. The similarity between the Latin word for city, *"urbs"*, and world, *"orbis"*, testifies to the conflation of the meanings of the two in ancient Rome.

It is surprising to observe how many towns owe their lay-out to this Roman diagram. Not only Italian towns, like Florence, Lucca, and Turin, but towns throughout Europe and Africa. London was founded on a four-square grid as a Roman town, as were all English towns with 'Chester' in their names ('Chester' is an anglicized rendering of *castra*, or 'Roman Camp'). When frontier towns were settled in the Americas, it is of little surprise that the ordering diagram of the four-square Roman camp was frequently followed.

The use of axes in Roman design remind us of axial schemes in ancient Egypt, but there is an important difference. In Egypt, a single, dominant axis defined a voided processional path. In Rome, axes intersected and marked significant points at their crossing or termination. Complex spatial organizations in ancient Rome were knit together by means of **cross axes** and local symmetries so that axial schemes with different orientations could coexist in tight proximity. Within a complex of buildings, round or hemicyclical spaces acted as 'hinges' or 'ball-and-socket joints' to make possible axial shifts and realignments. In his imaginary reconstruction of the Roman **Campus Martius**, **Giambattista Piranesi** (1720-1778) explored the

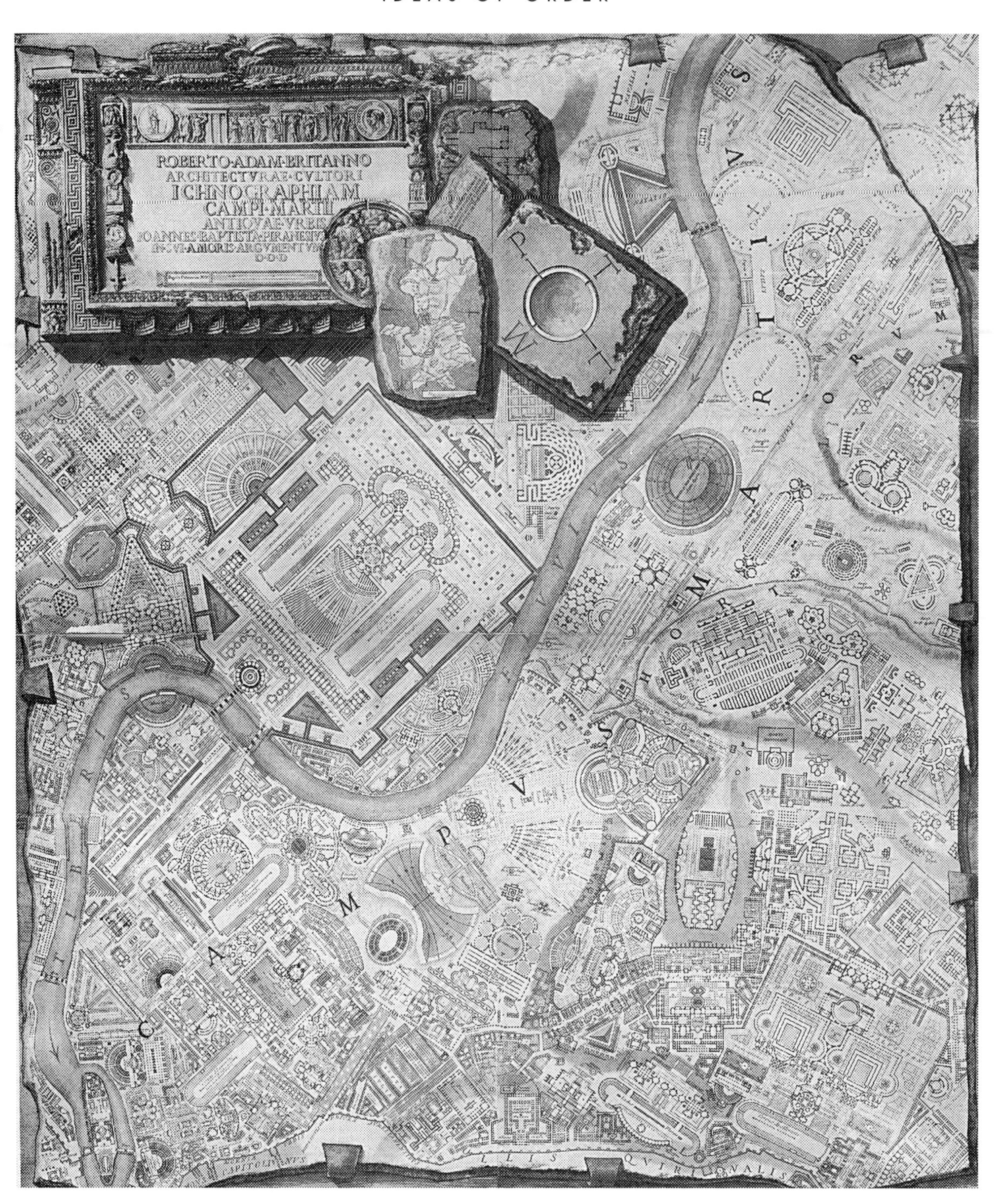

8.8
G.B. Piranesi, Reconstruction of the Campus Martius, Rome, c.1761.

full range of spatial complexity through the combination of orthogonal and rotational elements.

Sited on the Adriatic coast, the **Palace of Diocletian** in Split, Yugoslavia was laid out in accordance to the diagram of a typical Roman camp. Measuring 709 x 591 feet it is difficult to determine if it is a small city or a large palace. Four equal quadrants are described by the crossing of the two major axes, an east-west street extending from the 'Brass Gate' to the 'Iron Gate,' and a north-south street, running from the 'Golden Gate' to the Atrium overlooking the sea.

A palace for an emperor is perforce hierarchical; it must appropriately house the emperor, his entourage, his courtiers, his servants, his army, his animals, and store his goods. Furthermore, sacred spaces for the living and the dead must be sited with decorum. How can such diversity of program and hierarchy be accommodated in a scheme which really only contains four more or less equal places, the quadrants? Firstly, each of the four quadrants is assigned a different function. Ceremonial free-standing buildings, a Mausoleum and a Temple, are placed in the southern half of the complex, in the east and west courtyards respectively. Their location is not casual. The temple, with associations of rebirth and renewal, enjoys a view of the rising sun; the mausoleum, final resting place for the dead, enjoys a view of the setting sun. The two northerly quadrants are given over to service functions. Servants and stables are to the east and soldiers to the west. Ritual spaces are housed within free-standing object-buildings, while the quotidian support spaces define edges to streets and private courtyards.

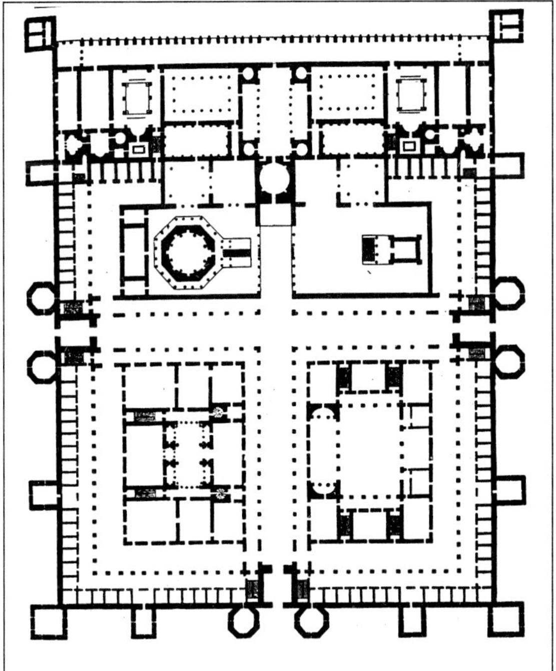

8.9 Diocletian's Palace, Split, Yugoslavia, A.D. 305, plan and elevation.

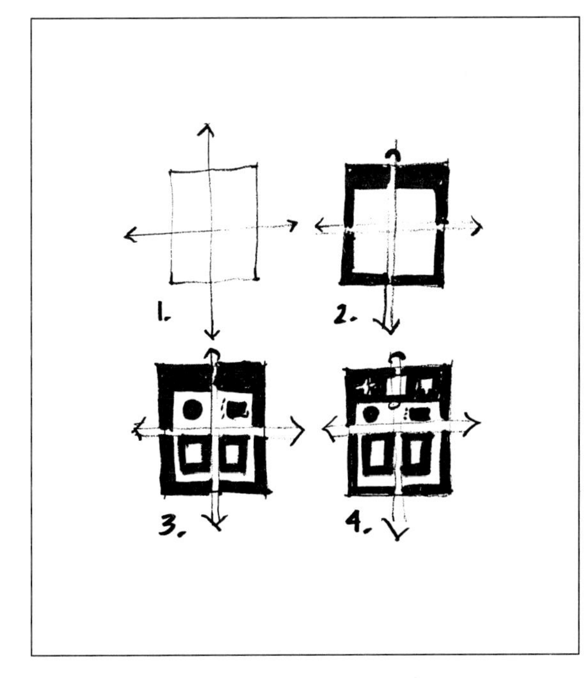

8.10 Diocletian's Palace, diagrams.

Where is Diocletian in this scheme? We have already filled all the quadrants and nothing has been designated as the emperor's abode. In an earlier discussion, we defined poché as the space between the two surfaces of a wall. When the space is sufficiently thick, it can take on an organization of its own. Hence, in Diocletian's Palace, the walls on the east, north, and west of the palace are thickened to encompass cellular storage rooms. Adjacency to the sea affords the southern bar special prominence. It is here that Diocletian's apartments are located, within the thickness of the wall, which measured approximately 80 meters. The swelling of the bar made possible a complex internal configuration of rooms. The terminus of the Golden Gate Street established a center of symmetry for the bar of apartments, but also divided the front bar into halves, each of which was organized around its own figural center. Asymmetries continue to unfold as one moves towards the perimeter wall. Finally, the west side is given over to women, the same side as the servants, and the east side is given over to the emperor, the same side as the soldiers.

At first glance, the scheme seems to be based on an overly simplistic diagram: a four-square grid. Yet complexity and richness are achieved by using the diagram to clarify and particularize differences. When there is flexibility and room to maneuver within the four-square grid, subtle refinements can have enormous liberating power. When the grid dictates an untransformable, unrelenting, monotonous rigidity, it then constrains the designer.

Of the plethora of Roman towns, Rome alone did not conform to ideal Roman town planning principles. Built on seven hills, irregular topography fostered building alignments which were advantageous to the particularities of the site but which frequently were askew with respect to other elements in the environment. Furthermore, unlike frontier Roman camps where the historical occupation of the site had no importance to the soldiers, the city of Rome was home to the pre-existing civilization of the Etruscans. Many sites had already developed associations with cults, and these sacred sites were adapted by the Romans. A view of the **Model of Rome** reveals the dense tangle of buildings, courtyards, and spaces, knitted together at preposterous angles. Indeed, it is difficult to find any buildings at all, since the built mass of the city is so continuous as to appear solid, relieved only by the interspersion of enormous shaped exterior spaces.

We have here identified the most essential difference between the architecture of the Greeks and the Romans. The former relied on figural object-buildings which organized their landscapes; the latter relied on figural spaces, around which buildings were grouped with varying degrees of freedom and rigidity. Although the Greeks and Romans made use of the same lexicon of building types and architectural elements, the fundamental difference in how the two societies understood space led to widely varied results. In the previous chapter, we observed the transformation of the Athenian agora from the Archaic Period, in which it was comprised of sparsely scattered buildings, to the Hellenistic and Roman periods, when it grew denser, and the central space became more strongly defined and introverted, losing its connection with the landscape. A figure/

8.11
Model of Rome, from the Museo della Civiltà Romana, E.U.R., Rome.

ground reversal had occurred. The general character of the space shifted from one of open terrain bespeckled with figural objects, to one of a solid built mass, bespeckled with carved figural spaces.

The **Pompeii Forum** is a crisply defined rectangular void located off-center at the crossing of the dominant north-south and east-west axes of the town. The most important temple, the Capitolium, slips forward into the forum and marks its central axis. Unlike counterparts on Greek sacred sites, the temple is frontally organized. Columns disappear at the sides and back; an open porch almost the size of the temple itself pulls forward to address the colonnaded space before it; a flight of steps extends forward along the axis. At the opposite end of the forum three small buildings are arrayed.

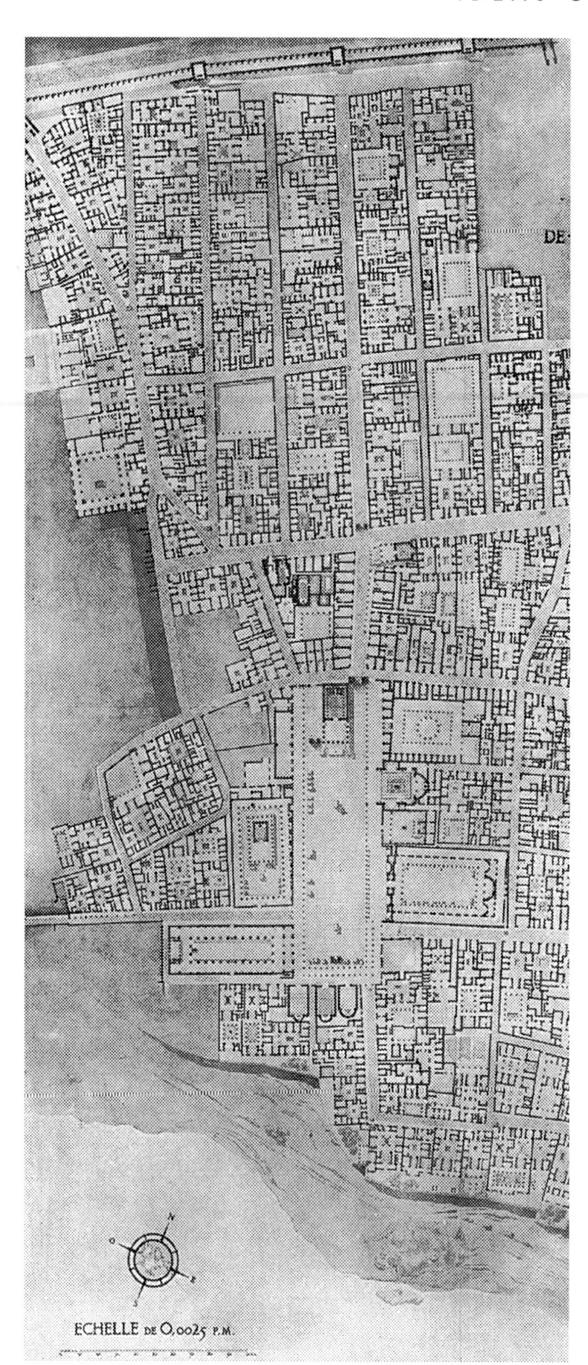

8.12 Left: Pompeii.

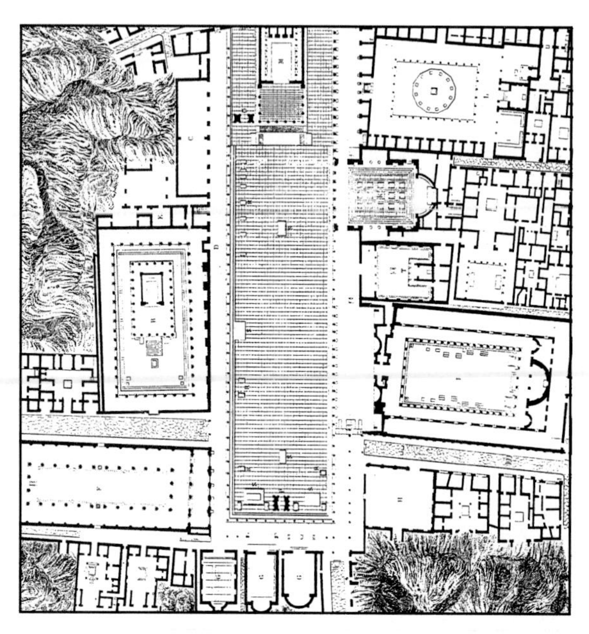

8.13 Right: The Forum, Pompeii.

The centralizing shaft of space from the temple portico meets the three small buildings at the opposite end of the forum. The easterly building slips to engage the center of the colonnade, allowing the remaining two buildings to flank the axis projected from the other side.

Simplicity of the void permits subtle differences to be developed around the edges. Fronts of buildings are loosely clipped on to a regular colonnade, but the backs disappear into the density of the urban fabric. On the east side of the forum, the circular market and the other public buildings form a ragged, irregular edge. Thresholds open up and close down as appropriate to the scale and stature of the building being addressed. This local irregularity is mitigated by the strong edge of the colonnade and the symmetry of the whole is not disturbed. Buildings have lost their status as free-standing objects, instead they function as edges to define

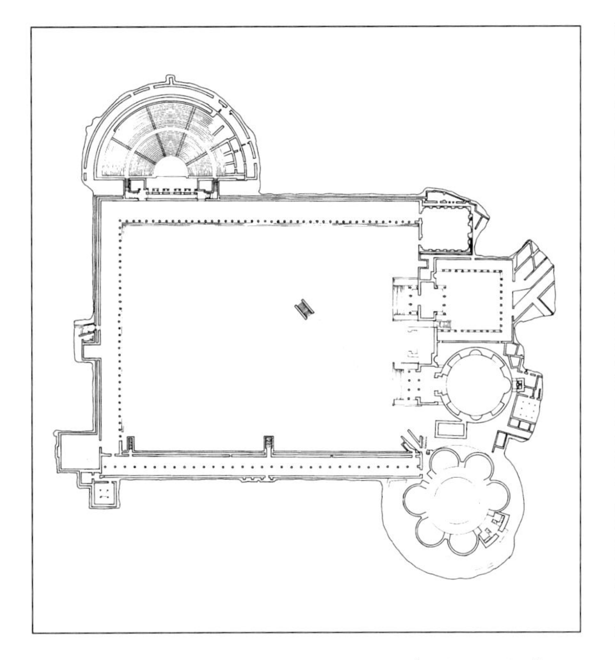

8.14 Left: The Sanctuary of Aesculapius, Pergamon, c. A.D. 140-175, plan.

8.15 Right: The Sanctuary of Aesculapius, Pergamon, according to Douglas Graf, showing the transformation from perimeter organization to free-standing, radial object.

public space. Even buildings with figural characteristics are installed in special courtyards and prohibited from interacting freely with their broader context.

The **Sanctuary of Aesculapius** in Pergamon uses a clearly defined rectangular court to organize even more widely disparate elements than those in Pompeii. Colonnaded porticoes frame three sides of a courtyard which encloses a sacred spring. On the remaining side, a strange assortment of temples are assembled to define the edge. Douglas Graf has analyzed the sanctuary as follows: *"...a sequence of four buildings along the eastern interior facade can be interpreted as a progression from perimetrical organization to central, from orthogonal to radial, and from dependent to independent. On the series the final temple can be seen as response to the diagonal of the sanctuary's rectangular perimeter, and thus as a termination of a sequence, or as the generator of the dialogue, and thus the origin of the sequence..."* (Douglas Graf, "Diagrams," *Perspecta* 22).

The **Roman Forum** is less perfect in its geometry than the Pompeii Forum. Edges of buildings inflect with respect to the hilly topography. The skewed orientations of the Basilica Aemilia on the north and the Basilica Julia on the south form a trapezoid, concentrating and funneling the space towards the Temple of Divus Julius at the east, while breaking the space apart at the west. The spatial disjunction makes possible multiple readings of the boundary through slippages, overlaps and shifted alignments. The space is 'leaky' rather than uniformly bounded, permitting elements from outside the space of the forum to be engaged.

The **Imperial Fora** are not a single work but the agglomeration of many idealized fora in tight proximity to one another, built by many different emperors who sought to assure their

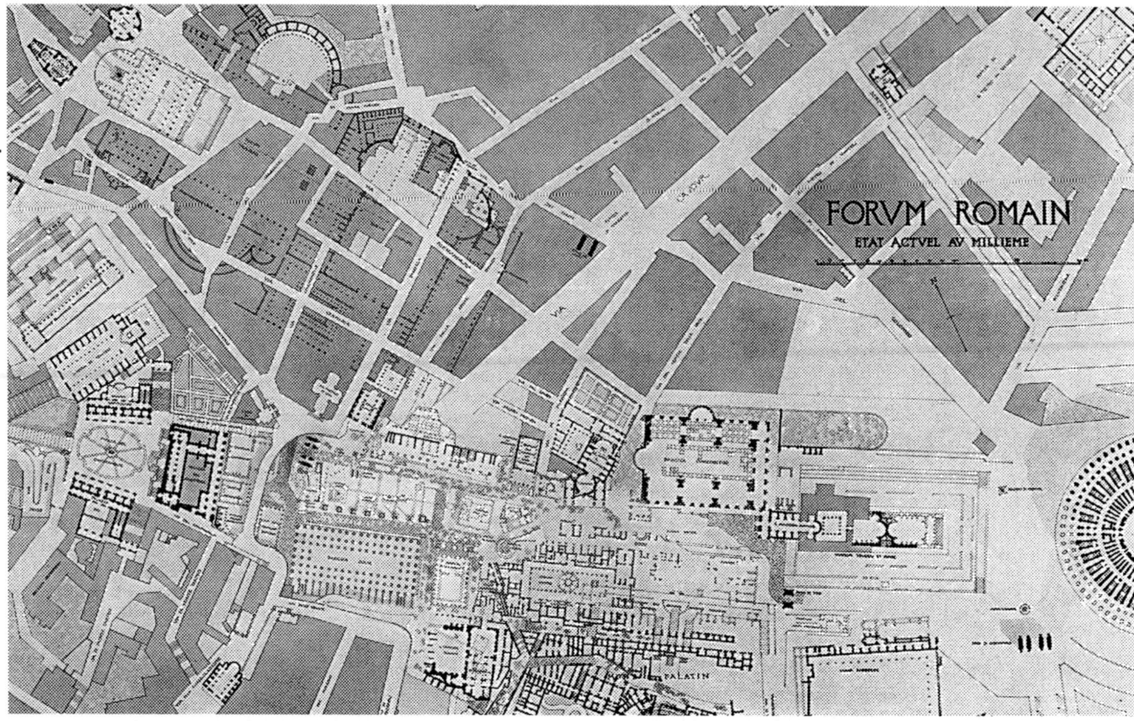

8.16
Roman Forum, nineteenth century condition.

good repute by constructing a forum and naming it after themselves. Located to the north of the Roman Fora, the later Imperial Fora are more systematic, rigid and formalized. Unlike the Roman Fora, they don't make use of gentle building realignments to negotiate the topography. Vast orthogonal spaces, interconnected by multiple axes, cross axes, and systems of local symmetry, are inserted into the terrain, related to their surroundings by the use of round or hemicyclical forms. Such forms do not give privilege to one axis and can be used as hinges between systems of alignment.

Trajan's Forum, the largest of the Imperial Fora carves a curved figure into the hill. The curve sponsors a new orientation for the **Markets of Trajan**, which overlook the forum. Hierarchy is likewise established. Ordinary functions of the city, such as market stalls, shops, or housing, become a kind of urban poché into which great public spaces are carved. The expression of the private domain and the individual structure is suppressed. All emphasis is given to the articulation of figural public spaces.

In an earlier chapter, we discussed the use of Greek precedent in Roman temple architecture. The placement of temples at the edge of shaped courtyards rather than as figures on open landscape enforce a frontal organization. While Greek temples are free standing objects in the round, Roman temples are particularized events

8.17
Imperial Fora, Model of Rome, from the Museo della Civiltà Romana, E.U.R., Rome, Italy.

8.18 *Left: Trajan's Market, and Trajan's Forum.*

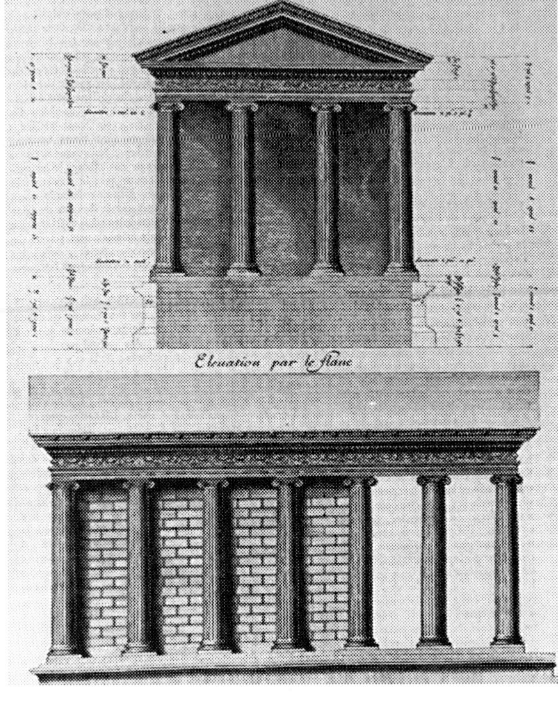

8.19 *Right: The Temple of Fortuna Virilis, Rome, Italy, 2nd Century B.C., front and side elevation.*

8.20 *The Temple of Fortuna Virilis, view.*

within a continuous fabric. Roman temples have a single entry porch, approached by an extended flight of steps. Their backs are frequently embedded in the surrounding cityscape. The interior of the temple is also transformed. In Greek architecture, the cella was modestly proportioned; in Roman architecture, the cella grew larger. As the cella increased in size, flanking colonnades were absorbed into the cella walls and trussed roof structures were replaced by vaulted ones.

The Roman interest in figural space led to an increased involvement with interior space. Stemming from functional and ritual determinations, the requirement for interior space was made possible by innovations in engineering and technology. Greek **trusses** were typically

8.21
A typical Roman Templee, according to E.E. Viollet-le-Duc.

built of huge, continuous timbers. The Romans developed a technique of truss building in which smaller pieces of wood could be joined. Longer spans could be achieved at the sacrifice of fewer virgin trees. However, the real structural innovation in Roman architecture was the masonry **vault**. Already present in Hellenistic buildings such as granaries, the Greek vault was capable of only modest spans. The Romans refined the idea of the vault until its culmination in the 43 meter wide dome of the **Pantheon.**

Broadly defined, vaults are roof structures which use curved surfaces to take advantage of the compressive strength of masonry. If there is sufficient mass, a vault can resist **lateral thrust,** i.e. the tendency of the load to kick out sideways, and span an opening by gradually transferring the load along the curvature of the vault. Thus, masonry is always in compression and the structure is very stable. Trabeated masonry structures have limited spans because of the brittleness of stone in tension. An arch is the simplest of vaulted structures. If an arch is dragged longitudinally, a **barrel vault** results. If two barrel vaults are intersected at right angles, a **cross vault** or **groin vault** results. If an arch is rotated around its axis of symmetry, a **dome** is created. Domes, like the dome of the Pantheon, work through stacked compression rings. It is therefore possible to remove the center of the dome to form an oculus without compromising the structural stability of the building. On the other hand, if the **keystone** or

8.22 Pantheon, Rome, A.D. 118-128; exterior dome detail.

top-most stone in an arch were removed, the structure would fail because the continuity of the transferred forces would be broken.

The enclosure of the **Baths of Caracalla** makes use of many Roman vaulting techniques: the dome, the barrel vault and the cross vault. Dashed lines in plan indicate the presence of a vaulted structure above. The crossing of major north-south and east-west axes is the major organizational armature of the Baths of Caracalla, but further relationships among parts are established through proportion, centering, repetition of like forms at varying scales, and the nesting

8.23 Left: Pantheon, Rome, Italy.

8.24 Right: The Baths of Caracalla, cut-away perspective.

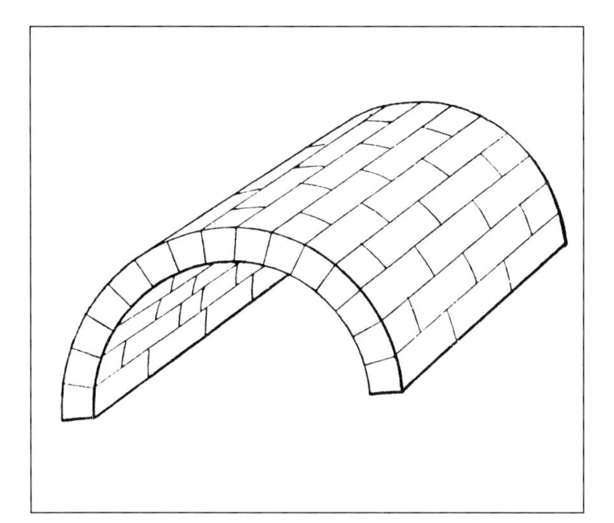

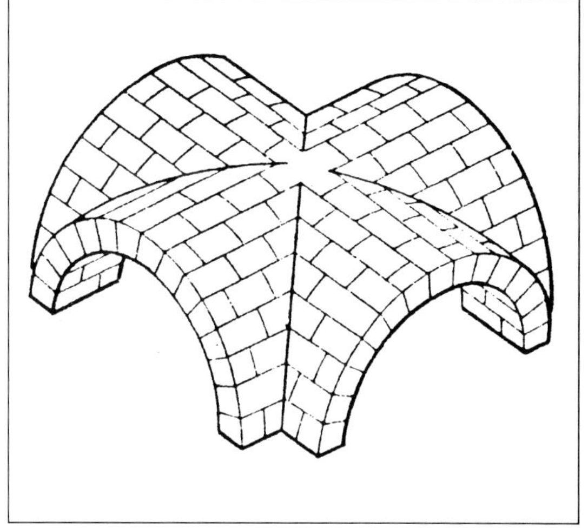

8.25 Left: Barrel vault diagram.

8.26 Right: groin vault diagram.

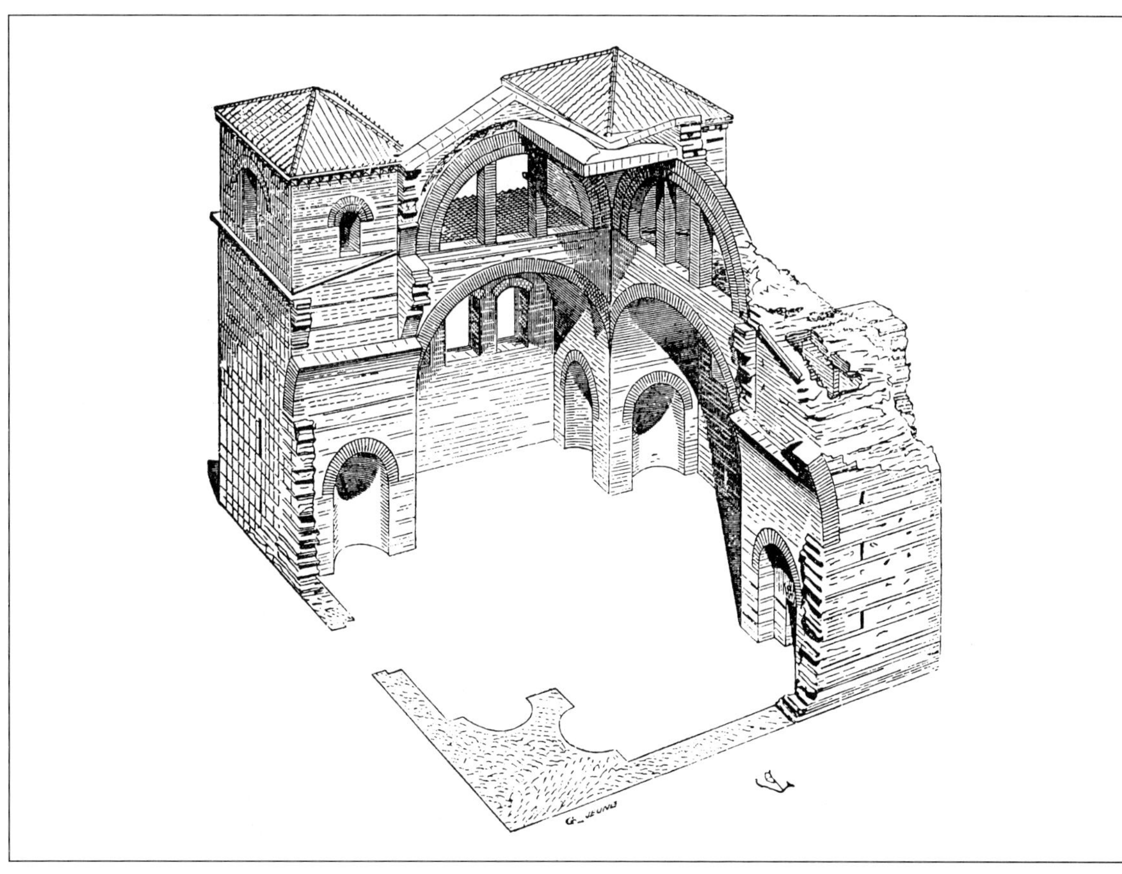

8.27 Roman arch construction, according to E. E. Viollet-le-Duc.

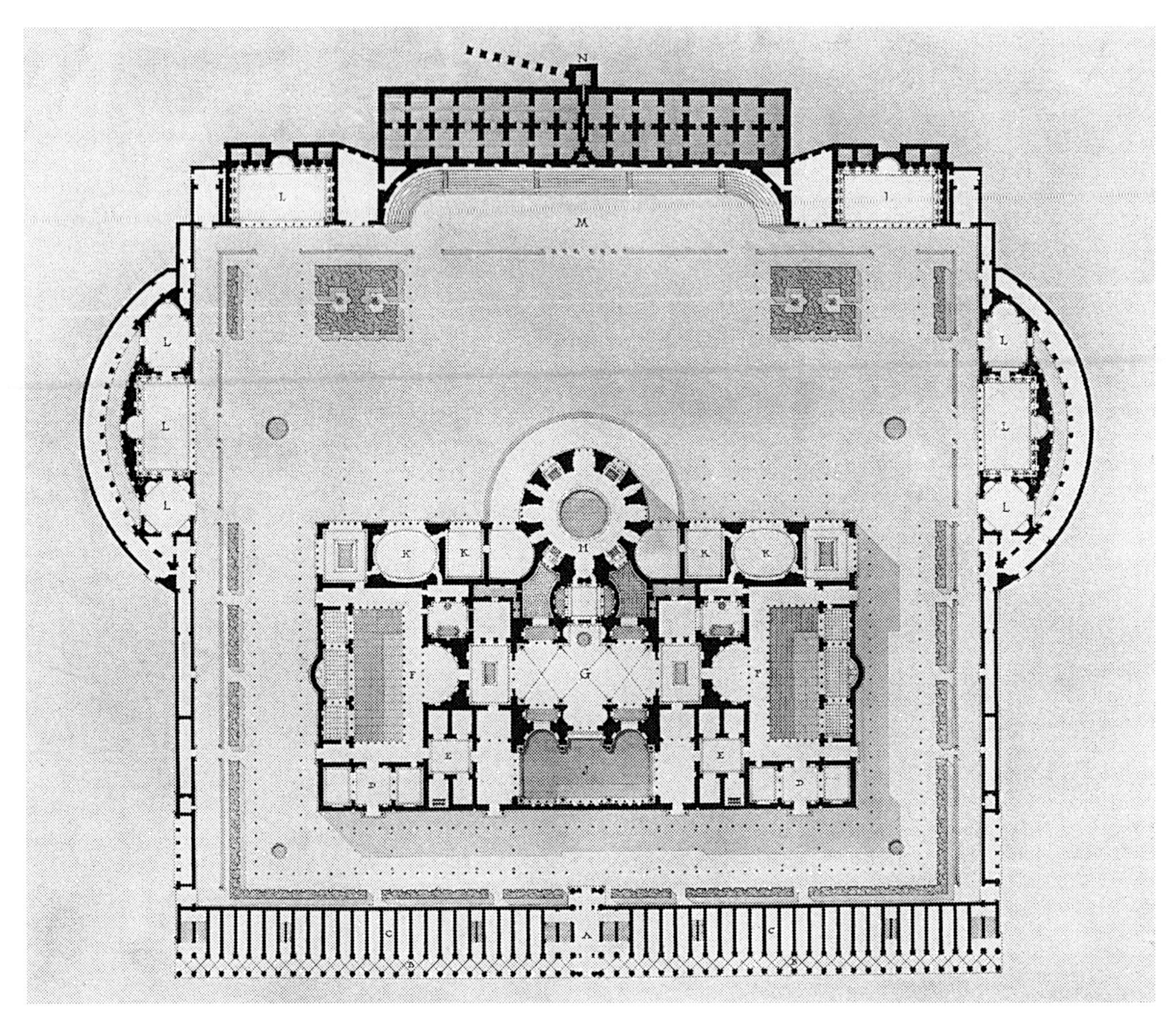

8.28
The Baths of Caracalla, Rome, Italy, A.D. 212-216, plan.

of forms within forms. The central axis contains a progression of bathing areas. Hot, warm, cold, and open-air swimming pool are respectively housed in the round, square, cruciform and lobed rectangular spaces. Open-air exercise courts are linked to the vaulted cold bath chamber along the major cross axis. Measuring 702 x 361 feet, the bath complex is almost a perfect two-square rectangle. The proportional relationships among the elements are tightly related, determining not only the measure of elements in the scheme, but their location as well, as shown in the diagram.

Multiple centers of the scheme rival one another for dominance. A center is described by the cross axes through the Baths. Another is implied by the paired hemicycles of the outer precinct wall. Yet another center relates to the

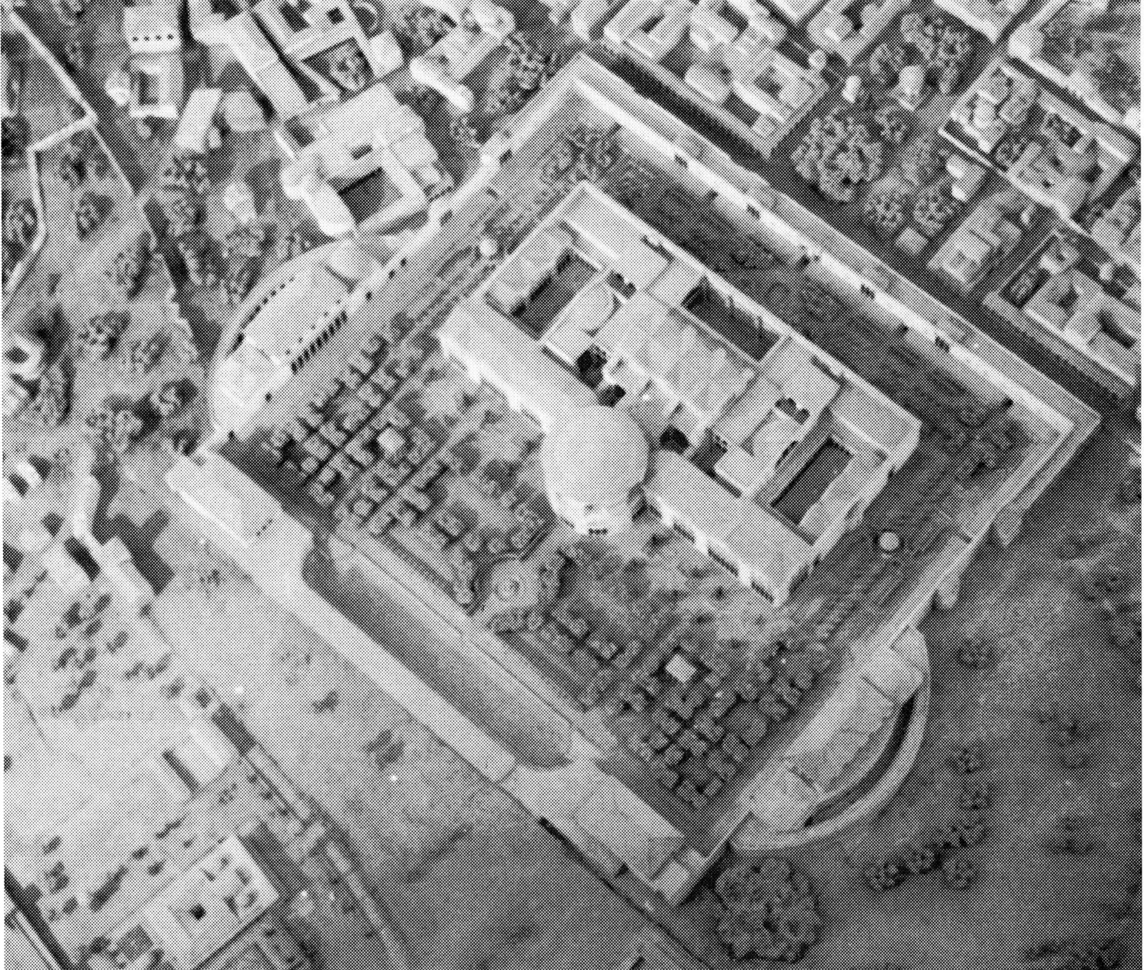

8.29 Baths of Caracalla, photo of the model.

absolute center of the square precinct. Hierarchy is established in relationship to these centers. The crossing of the two axes within the Baths locates the cold baths, but even greater importance is assigned to the hot baths by their position. The cylindrical drum breaks out from the closed perimeter of the Bath building, making it the only figural object in a site dominated by edges; its special shape sets it apart from orthogonal, cellular space; it is displaced with respect to the center of the Bath building, but it locks onto the center of the overall complex, thus uniting the two geometries.

The architectural production of the Roman civilization was enormous. With their empire spreading over three continents and their reign lasting over five hundred years, it is impossible to select a few representative works which accu-

*8.30
The Baths of Caracalla, engraved by G.B. Piranesi.*

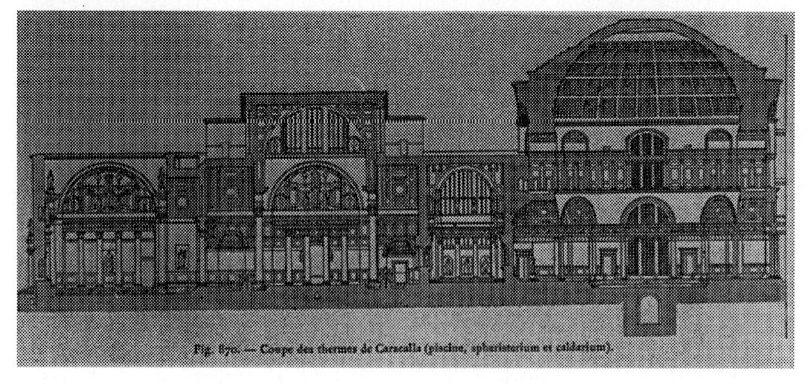

*8.31 Left:
The Baths of Caracalla, section*

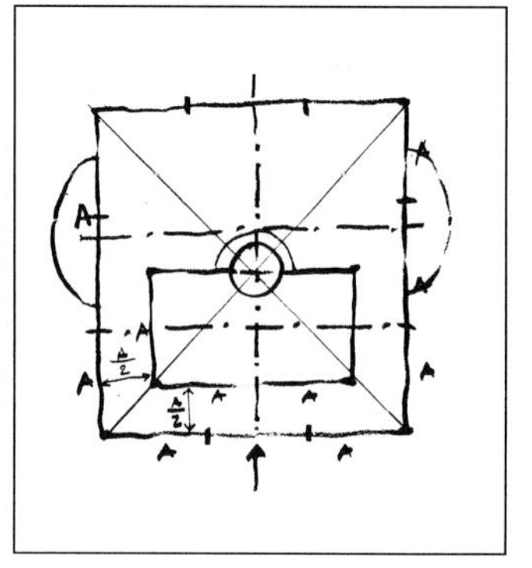

*8.32 Right:
The Baths of Caracalla, diagram of proportions.*

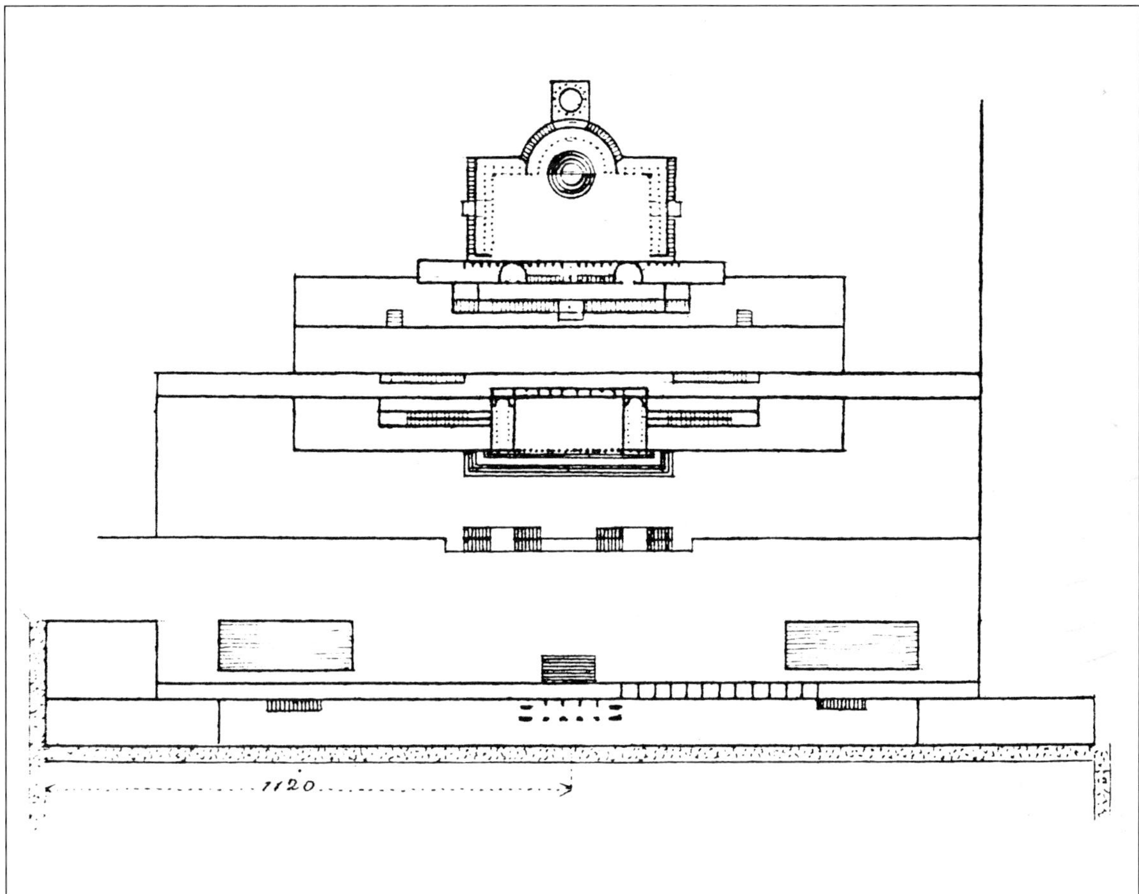

8.33 Temple of Fortuna Primagenia, Palestrina, 80 B.C., plan.

rately sum up the culture. All the examples we have examined have been urban, a choice which necessarily effects the kind of spatial features to be found. Villas, shrines and gardens of exquisite refinement also characterized Roman architecture, but it is beyond the scope of this text to discuss them at length. Two projects will be mentioned briefly. The first is an early Roman shrine, the **Temple of Fortuna Primagenia**, from c. 80 B.C. The second is a later work, **Hadrian's Villa,** Tivoli, from A.D. 118-134.

The Temple of Fortuna Primagenia occupies a sacred site, and the procession through the site is formal and hieratic. A dominant axis organizes the entire scheme, but the ramped path moves away from the center, only to reconstitute it in a different form. As the procession ascends, the terraces grow smaller and more figural in their definition. Niches are carved into the wall at a lower terraces, marrying together figure and edge. On the next terrace, the edge bends to frame a rectilinear terrace. The space

8.34 Left: Temple of Fortuna Primagenia, Palestrina, Italy, 80 B.C.

8.35 Right: Hadrian's Villa, Tivoli, A.D. 118-134, view.

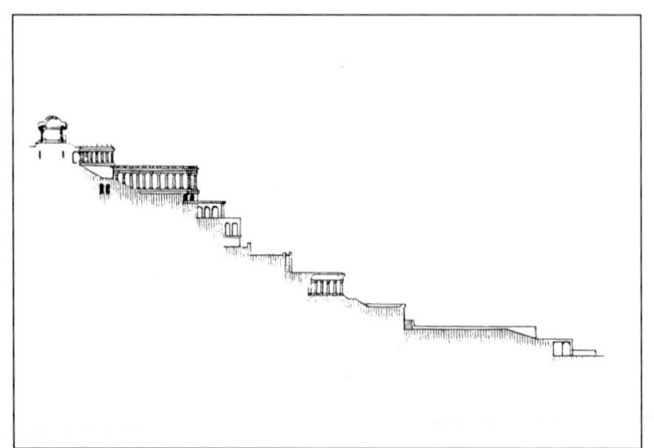

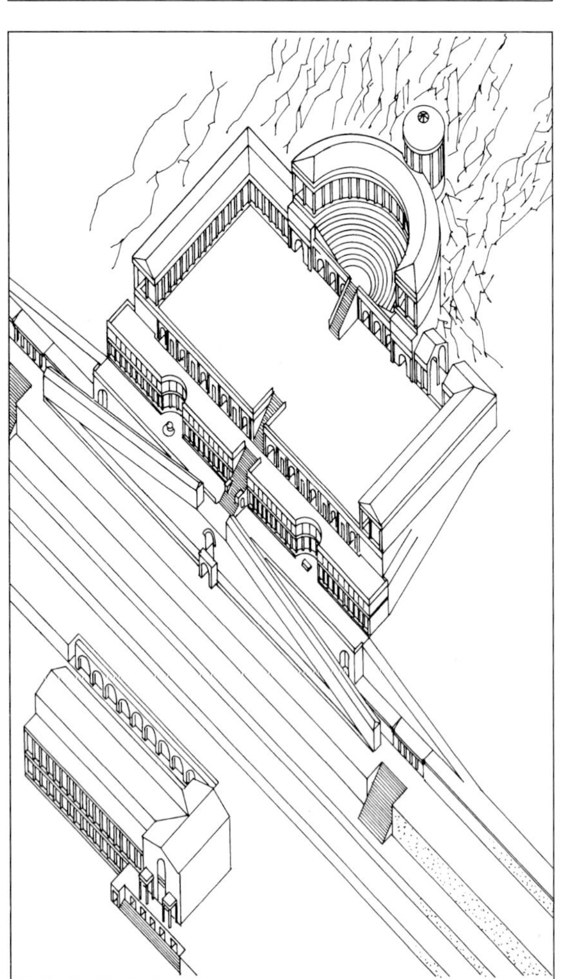

compresses still further to yield a theater which has almost liberated itself from the perimeter. Finally, the round Fortuna Temple appears, a free- standing object just beyond the precinct.

Hadrian's Villa is the largest villa ever built: to this day it is only partially excavated. The villa is comprised of an odd assortment of architectural curiosities, a kind of architectural 'post card collection,' full of structures reminiscent of outlying colonies. In urban schemes and at Palestrina, relationships were forged through adjacencies and strong axial links. At Hadrian's villa, elements interrelate across tremendous distance, locked together by vistas, or hinged into position by figural set-pieces, like the **Maritime Theater**.

Long after the fall of the Roman Empire, the bones of Rome still haunt us in the form of ruins and infrastructure, the still-functioning sewers, roads, and aqueducts. The plans of many towns still are ordered by the simple cross axes placed there by Roman soldiers millennia ago. The elongated horseshoe of space once used by Domitian to race horses is conserved in the voided space of the Piazza Navona in Rome. Succeeding generations have inhabited these

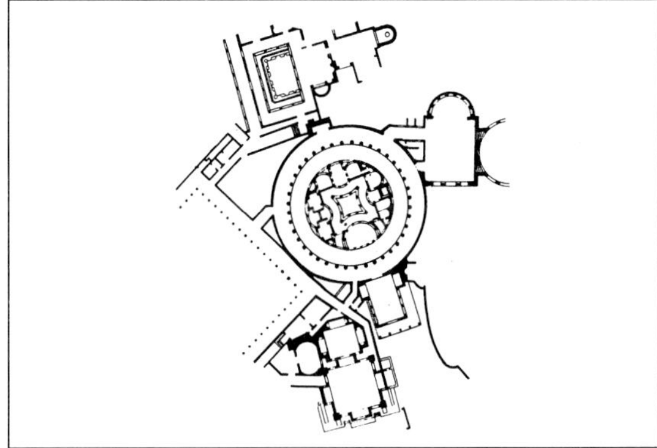

8.37 *Left: Hadrian's Villa, view.*

8.38 *Right: Hadrian's Villa, Maritime theater, plan detail.*

ancient relics in a host-parasite way, as barnacles clinging to the under-belly of a sunken ship. Over time, the Roman arena in Lucca has been entirely absorbed into the fabric of the town, inhabited by shops and dwellings. Heroically scaled monuments remain, but their function is mutable, because of their dependence on culture.

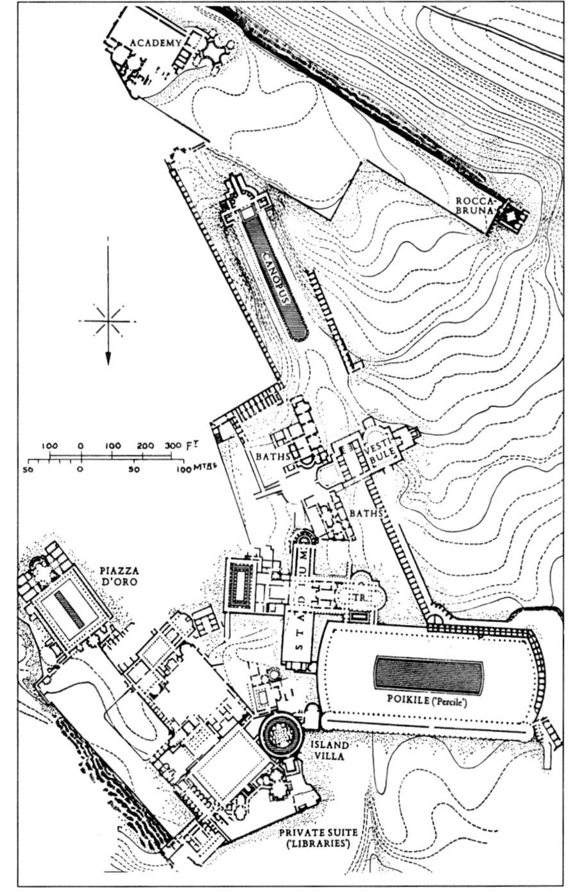

8.39 *Hadrian's Villa, plan.*

Part III.

The Architecture of Christianity

9.0
Villard de Honnecourt, Sketches from his Lodgebook, c.1235.

Chapter 9

The Middle Ages: Spiritualized Mass & Space

In the period of three centuries, from 1050-1350, several million tons of stone were quarried in France to build 80 cathedrals, 500 large churches, and tens of thousands of parish churches. More stone was quarried in France during these three centuries than in ancient Egypt during its whole history— and the Great Pyramid alone has a volume of 40,500,000 cubic feet.
-Jean Gimpel

This text does not purport to be a history of western architecture, and even if it did, no history is all-embracing in its scope. The process of selecting examples and excluding others perforce biases and falsifies any account. Our discussion of antiquity almost completely ignored commonplace buildings like houses, shops, barns etc. in favor of works for royal or religious patronage. Therefore in this chapter we shall leap ahead almost a thousand years and devote our discussion to the architectural and urbanistic developments of the Gothic period, hoping that our earlier discussion of some Early Christian and Byzantine monuments (St. Paul's outside the Walls, Rome, and Hagia Sophia, Istanbul) is sufficient to characterize the major accomplishments of those ages.

The Gothic style was the first true international style. It arose in the area around Paris using structural techniques probably learned from the Moors during the Crusades. For four hundred years the Gothic style dominated western Europe, spreading from France to England, Germany, Italy, Spain, and even as far afield as Eastern Europe and Scandinavia. Great social and political developments took place in the late eleventh and twelfth centuries. Industry and trade revived, and there was renewed communication among neighboring towns and regions. The feudal social structure was transformed by the emergence of a prosperous class of merchants and tradesmen. For the church, this constituted a new class of patrons whose resources could be tapped to finance great construction projects. In the Gothic period, nations such as France and Spain were formed out of disparate city states. Rivalries among towns and regions inspired a thirst for symbols of civic pride. The cathedral was an excellent vehicle to carry both secular and spiritual aspirations.

Before we discuss Gothic architecture in detail, we shall examine some paintings produced in Siena in the twelfth century. We will not go as far as Heinrich Wölfflin in suggesting that people who like pointed arches also like pointed-toed shoes, while people who like round-headed arches like round-toed shoes; but we maintain that important discoveries about the architecture of a culture can be gained by examining the formal order, subject matter, and pictorial style of other works of art. (Heinrich Wölfflin, *Renaissance and Baroque.)*

We shall begin with **Ambrogio Lorenzetti's *"Ideal Town".*** A strong sense of hierarchy is communicated in the painting, not through the formal organization of the pieces, but through their relative size. The church and the castle loom above the other buildings, which are tightly packed into the confines of the fortified city wall at irregular angles. Slender towers punctuate the skyline. Erected by noble families or wealthy merchants, the towers were more for ostentation than for any practical purpose. The only open space included in the painting is the market square which occurs along side the church. The painting is nonperspectival and space is flattened out, producing a catalog of parts rather than a realistic depiction of urban space.

The power of the church in the Gothic period was enormous. Lorenzetti depicts a massive church thrust into the fabric of a town. The physical presence of the church does not respond to a pre-existing urban order, but reorganizes the space around it. Idiosyncratic spaces grew up in the shards of space around the church, each of which took on a different function. **Camillo Sitte**, a nineteenth-century urbanist, appreciated the irregular, picturesque qualities of medieval urban space, and the opportunity for functional differentiation that non-axial arrangements of building provided. In the German towns **Schwerin** and **Würzburg,** Sitte illustrates how three different kinds of spaces are created by the skewed alignment of the cathedral.

Financing the building projects was carried out with great ingenuity. Sacred relics (bones, garments, limbs or mummified corpses of saints) belonging to the cathedral were put on travelling display to raise money. As the popularity of the crusades subsided, the sale of religious pardons, or 'indulgences,' increased. It was more convenient to buy one's way to heaven by donating to the cathedral building fund than to earn one's place in the kingdom of God on crusade. Most charming is the apocryphal use of volunteer labor to construct cathedrals. The 'Cult of the Carts' was said to be a religious movement that centered on the transport of stone to construction sites. Knights and noble ladies, side by side with peasants and average citizens, would strap themselves like oxen to carts loaded with quarried stone, knowing that temporal suffering would bring eternal redemption.

The other painting we shall examine is the ***"Maestà"*** by **Duccio di Buoninsegna.** The organization of figures in Duccio's painting is

9.1 Duccio di Buoninsegna, "Maestà", detail, 1308-11, Museo del opera del Duomo, Siena.

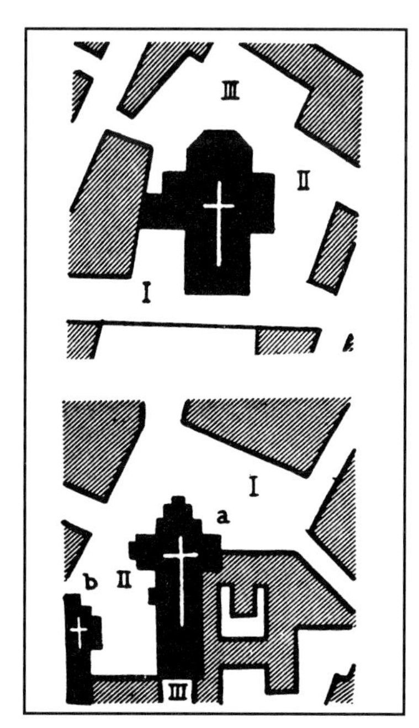

9.2 Left: Schwerin (above), and Würzburg (below), showing I. Parade Square; II. Minster Square; III. Cathedral Square., according to Camillo Sitte.

9.3 Right: Ambrogio Lorenzetti, "Ideal Town", c. 1335, Pinoteca Nazionale, Siena.

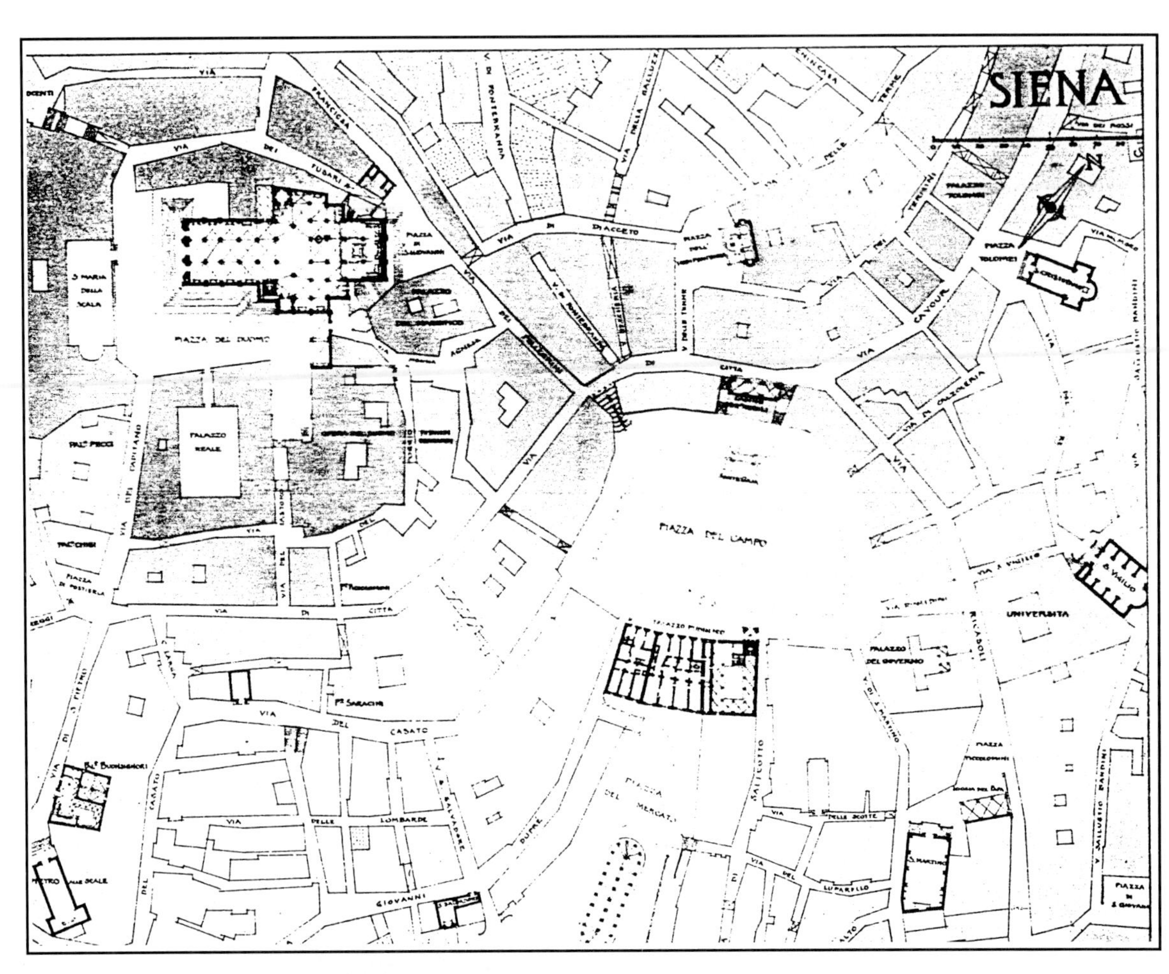

9.4
Siena, Italy, plan.

9.5 *Left:*
Siena, Italy,
Piazza del Campo.

9.6 *Right:*
Siena, Italy,
Piazza del Campo.

akin to the hierarchical spatial organization in medieval towns. The largest figure, the Virgin, towers over all others, imposing an overall order on the composition. Depending on their relative importance, the other figures are neatly arrayed on tiers. Apostles, disengaged from the ground plane, are closest to heaven. The Donors and Bishops are positioned very close to the Madonna, to inspire the patronage. The throne of the Madonna is designed as if it were a church. The arms of the throne resemble the twin towers on a cathedral facade. Architectural motifs like pointed-arched windows and horizontal string courses adorn the throne, underscoring its connection to architecture. Moreover, exaggerated attenuation of the figures and the two-dimensional flatness of their forms signifies that there was a greater interest in spirituality than in the sensual materialism of this world.

Aside from the literal content of the painting, its formal composition reveals a great deal about the sensibilities of the time. Erwin Panofsky has argued that Gothic architecture can be seen as analogous to Scholasticism, a branch of philosophy propounded by Saint Thomas Aquinas and others during the Middle Ages. (*Gothic Architecture in the Age of Scholasticism*). Scholastic thought was highly structured, based on the extreme categorization, division and subdivision of arguments into clearly articulated and arranged parts. According to Panofsky: *"the whole was divided into partes which could be divided into smaller partes; the partes into membra, quaestiones or distinctiones, and these into articuli..."* It is possible to understand the formal order of the "*Maestà*" as another manifestation of Scholastic order. The tiers of figures, their different sizes, their relationship to the center, their relationship to the frame all are components which make the "*Maestà*" an elaborate argumentative matrix. When we look closely at the articulation of walls, tracery and facades in Gothic cathedrals, we shall see the same insistence on the division of the whole into parts, hyper-articulation, stratification, and adumbration. In other words, the analogy between Scholastic thought and the structure of the *Maestà* can be extended to explain the composition and language of Gothic architecture.

Siena is an unplanned medieval hill town which took its characteristic form in the 1300's. Built around three hills, its grandest public space, the fan-shaped **Piazza del Campo**, is in fact a natural drainage basin at the joint between the hills. The great figural space of the Piazza del Campo provides relief from the congestion of dark, narrow, winding streets and ramps which comprise the town. The Campo is the physical, symbolic and ritual center of the town. Usually the center of active public life, twice a year the square is the site of a horse race, the *Palio*. The radial paving pattern emphasizes the importance of the Town Hall, the **Palazzo Publico**, 1298, which dominates the straight edge of the square.

Private dwellings play a passive role in shaping the space of the town. They provide continuous edges which frame streets, alleys or square but have no recognizable presence as individual entities. Even public buildings like the Town Hall act only as edge-buildings: its prominence is indicated by facade articulation, location, and the verticality of the tower. Only the churches are fully plastic objects. Here, as in Lorenzetti's painting, the imposition of the

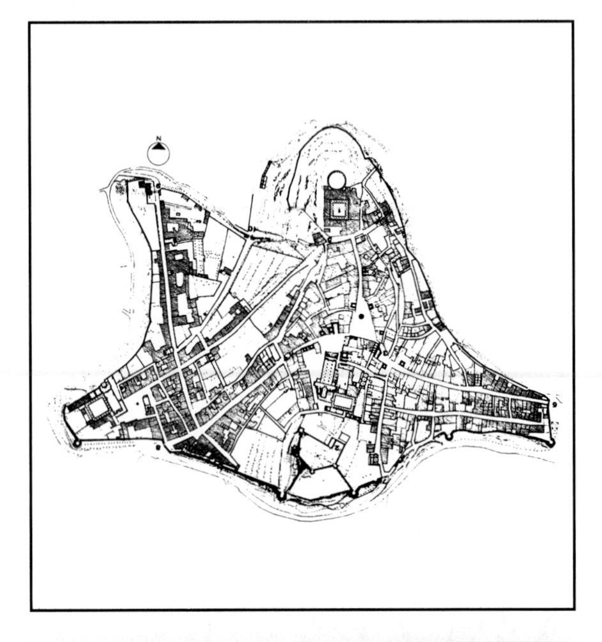

9.7
San Gimignano, Italy, plan.

9.8
San Gimignano, Italy, view.

9.9
San Gimignano, Italy, view.

church in the urban fabric sponsors a group of open spaces around it.

San Gimignano is another medieval Tuscan hill town, not far from Siena. Siena has lost most of its characteristic towers, but San Gimignano still retains 16 of the many dozen that once graced its skyline. An unplanned town, Siena grew up taking advantage of natural topographic features. San Gimignano, on the other hand, was originally founded as a Roman camp. The *cardo* and *decumanus* of the plan strive for orthogonality as the natural declivities of the site are traversed. The crossing of the two Roman roads sponsors two squares in diagonal relation to one another. Piazza della Cisterna ('Square of the Cistern') slips north towards the city gate. To the west is the Piazza del Duomo ('Cathedral Square'), fronting the cathedral and reserved for ceremonial activities. Diagonally related to the cathedral square, yet another square is associated with the market. A continuation of the oblique progression leads to the castle.

San Gimignano is a good example of how a formal order, the Roman plan, has been inflected by a natural topographical order, and the emergence of a new social order. Experientially, a remarkable transformation takes place as the rigid Roman diagram is over taken by a more irregular plan. In the Roman plan, straight axial views reveal the order of the entire town at a single glance. In the medieval plan, oblique views and changing spatial boundaries occur without warning. The progression through San Gimignano is not only an intellectual or visual experience. All the senses are engaged. A constant juxtaposition of extremes articulates the path. Brilliant light in the squares contrasts with dark, shadowy alleys; large, open, relatively flat areas contrast with compressed, narrow, inclined passageways; cool, damp surroundings in dark recesses never touched by sunlight contrast with the parched stone paving of the open spaces; constrained narrow ranges of vision contrast with broad, expansive vistas across the landscape from the castle or towers.

Monasteries acted as important centers of thought and commerce during the medieval period. Housing a wide variety of functions and many residents, monastic complexes frequently functioned as small towns, albeit towns of a highly idealized organization. **The Monastery of Mont St. Michel** is situated on a island off the coast of Brittany. The site embodies the monastic spirit of solitude and withdrawal from the worldly activities: it is in contact with the mainland only when tides are low and isolated during other times. The imposing presence of the cathedral reconfigures the hill into an enormous Christian shrine. Landscape and building are wholly synthesized.

The **Carthusian Monastery** in Pavia, Italy is a late example of a monastic complex, but its spatial and functional organization are particularly clear. Hierarchy, from most to least important, and division between public and private are articulated with the clarity and precision of a Scholastic argument.

Two great courtyards organize the scheme. A rectangular space along the axis of the cathedral stretches out to meet the monastery gate. The Latin Cross of the cathedral plan is reflected here and its cross axis aligns with the western colonnade of the Great **Cloister**, the other major space in the scheme. Laity may en-

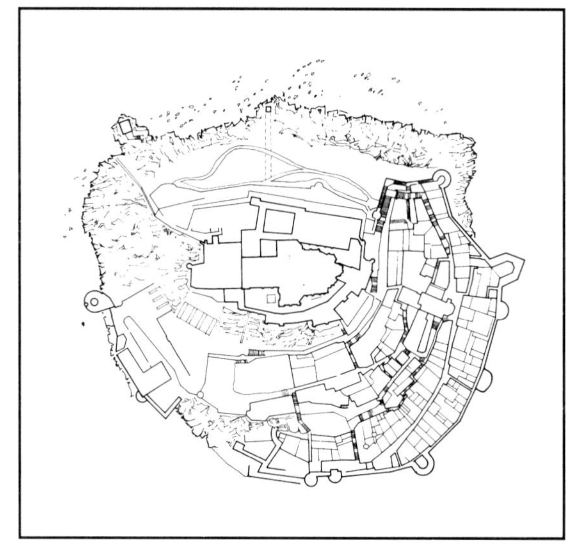

9.10
Mont St. Michel, France, plan.

9.11
Mont St. Michel, France, section.

9.12
Mont St. Michel, France, view at low tide.

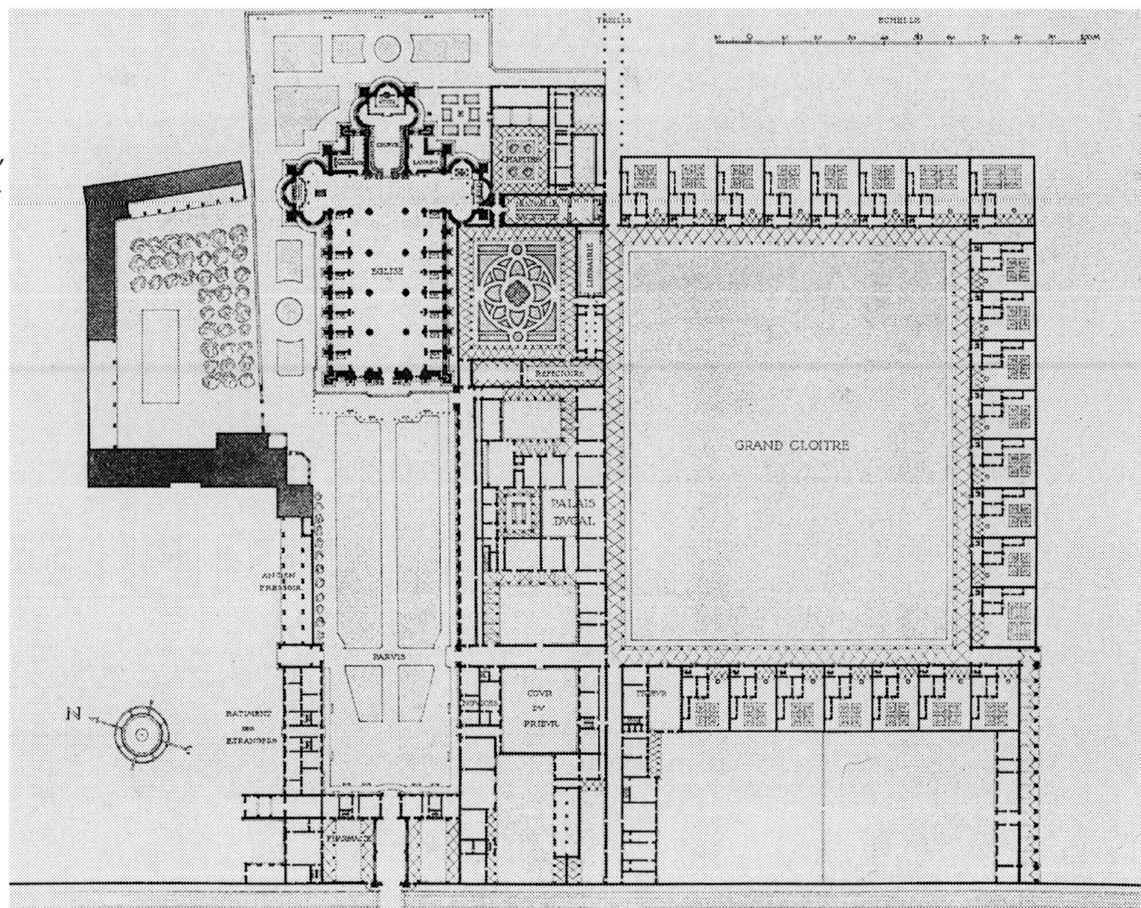

9.13 Carthusian Monastery (Certosa di Pavia), Pavia, Italy, 1396, plan.

ter the rectangular court, or *parvis,* which is bounded by rooms with a semi-public nature. The Great Cloister is reserved for monks alone. Carthusian monks took vows of silence and solitude. The controlled manipulation of thresholds, transition spaces and hierarchy expresses and preserves their way of life. Monastic cells border the cloister. The arrangement of the monk's dwellings recapitulates the order of the whole at a reduced scale. An ell of rooms wraps around each monk's private, idealized four-square garden which can be entered after passing through no fewer than three transition spaces within the monk's cell.

Functions are grouped from most secular to most private in bands of rooms which define the long edges of the courtyards. Affinities emerge as program elements are grouped around courtyards of varying scales but related proportions. The side of the great cloister is three times that of the cathedral cloister, which is twice that of the chapter and ducal cloisters, which is twice the size of the monks' private gardens, and so forth. The entire scheme is

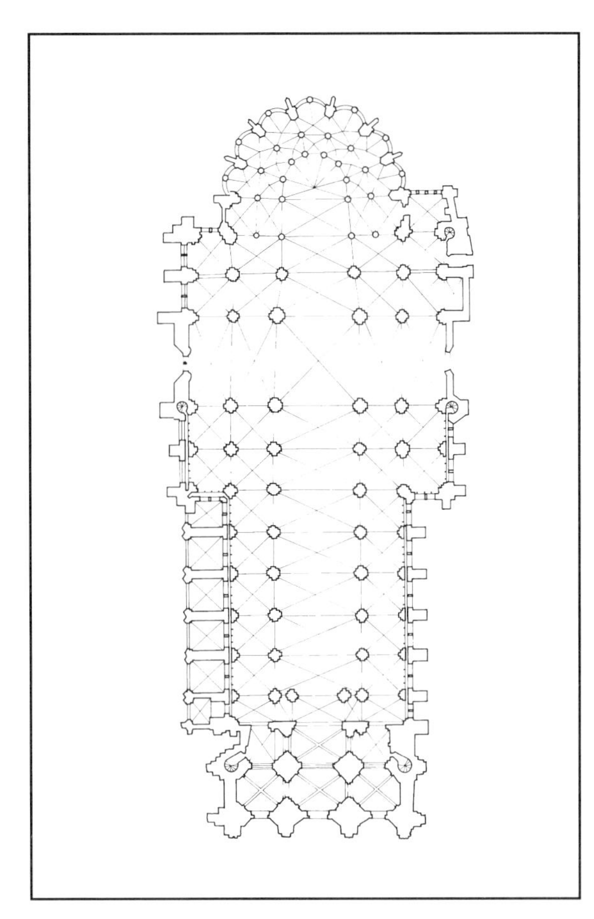

9.14 Left: St. Denis, near Paris, France, c.1140, plan.

9.15 Right: St. Denis, exterior view.

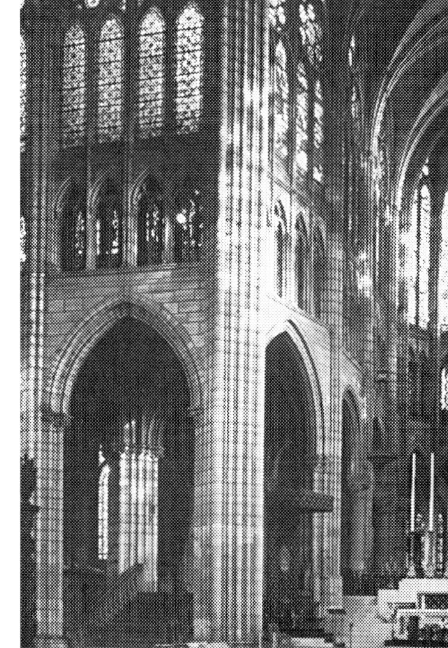

9.16 St. Denis, interior view.

comprised of a network of intersecting axes, realignments of center and scaled recursions of proportionally interrelated rectangles. The church is the most important and most figural building in the scheme. Therefore, it might be understood to follow its own logic, but this not the case. Although the cathedral is the meeting place of laity and clergy, a division between the realms divides the church into distinct, spatially discrete zones, linked through axes. The eastern **choir** of the church is reserved for the worship by monks while the laity make use of

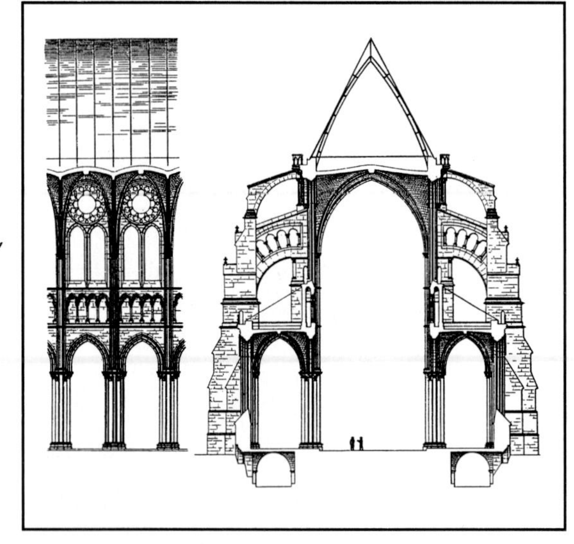

9.17 Chartres Cathedral, Chartres, France, begun 1194, section.

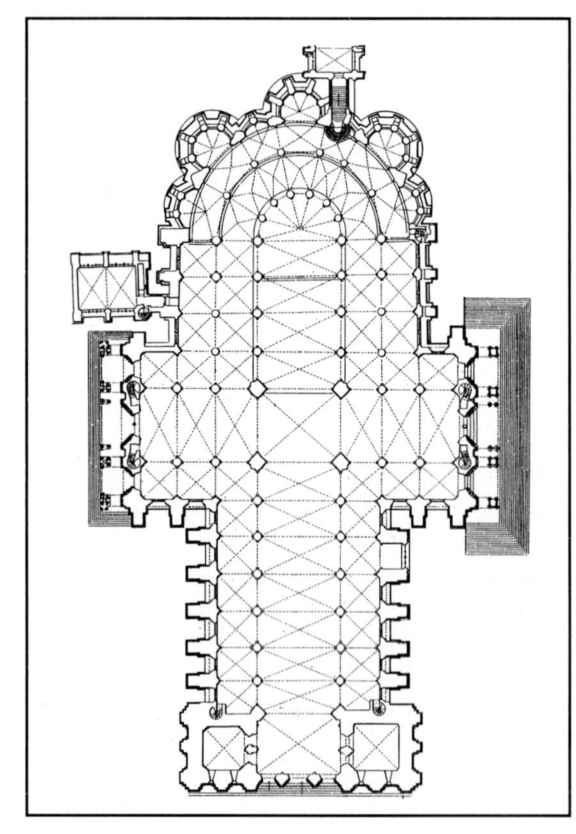

9.18 Chartres Cathedral, plan.

the main body of the church. The shape of the monks' choir repeats the Latin cross plan of the whole at a smaller scale.

The glory of medieval architecture is the Gothic cathedral. In the period from the fall of Rome to the rise of the Gothic, attitudes towards space and technology remained more or less what they were at the time of the Romans. Bearing walls, domes, barrel vaults, and timber trusses constituted the principal structural elements of the churches. A taste for asceticism persuaded some early Christians to eschew ornament in favor of severe, spare interiors; other early Christians believed that all beautiful things were reflections of God's divine grace. The former attitude is expressed by St. Bernard: *"We who have turned aside from society, relinquishing for Christ's sake all the precious and beautiful things in the world, its wondrous light and color, its sweet sounds and odours, the pleasures of taste and touch, for us all bodily delights are nothing but dung."*

The basilican plan type, inherited from a secular Roman precedent, was widely adapted for churches. Increased emphasis on the development of the transepts changed the type firmly from a simple longitudinal nave flanked by aisles to a true Latin Cross. In some Gothic churches, such as Amiens and **Chartres,** the transept of the Latin cross slips towards the entry to more precisely mark the true center of the church. Another innovation in this period was the introduction of towers on the facade, previously used only on city walls. Symbolically, the facade of a church so ornamented represented the City of God, the *Civitas Dei.*

The development of Gothic ecclesiastical architecture was built on the tradition of the basilica but pushed the envelop of the basilican type further in the conquest of verticality, light, and dematerialized mass. The first cathedral that bears all the true marks of the Gothic style is **St. Denis** in France. A twin-towered facade, a **rose window,** pointed arches, rib vaults, and chapels radiating around the **apse** are all present here. Slender columns and diaphanous walls permit a fluidity of space, inundated by dazzling light from stained glass windows. The cleric in charge of the works at St. Denis was Abbot Suger (1081-1151). He had a vision that God was "superessential light," and that light makes visible the presence of God on earth. Suger stated: *"The church shines with its middle part brightened. For bright is that which is brightly coupled with the bright, And bright is the noble edifice which is pervaded by new light..."* Unlike St. Bernard, who turned away from physical delights, Suger embraced ornament and rich, glittery materials as reflections of God's beauty, apprehensible in divine light.

In earlier Roman and Romanesque architecture, the continuity of forces through bearing walls and surface vaults rendered fenestration difficult and the spaces dark and closed. Architectural expression of light symbolism led Gothic architects to conceive of skeletal structures, rather than ones comprised of continuous planar surfaces. Narrow masonry ribs carried structural loads across the roof in **rib vaults,** directly related to lines of force in the ceiling. Point loads from the vaults were transferred downwards on columns or **piers**. Already greatly reduced in mass, the visual effect of the piers was rendered even less substantial through their articulation as bundles of thin shafts.

9.19 *Chartres Cathedral, facade.*

9.20 *Chartres Cathedral, view.*

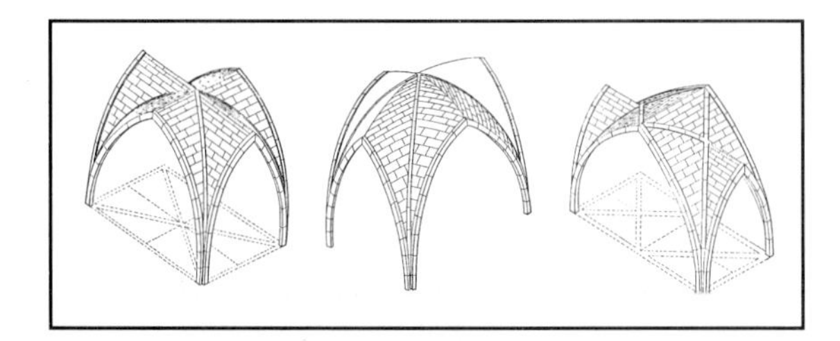

9.21
Ribbed vaults.

The articulation of the interior walls of the cathedrals likewise grew more diaphanous with the development of the Gothic style. In early churches, the walls were conceived of as independent, superimposed zones of **arcade**, **gallery, triforium** and clerestory. In later churches, the clerestory so increases in size that it is united with the triforium. The layering of tracery further transforms and reduces mass. Wall tracery has been seen as irrational and antistructural, but curiously enough, it translates into German as *Maßwerk,* or 'proportional work,' suggesting a dimensional connection be-

9.22 *Left: Tombstone of the architect Hugues Limbergier (died 1263), Reims Cathedral.*

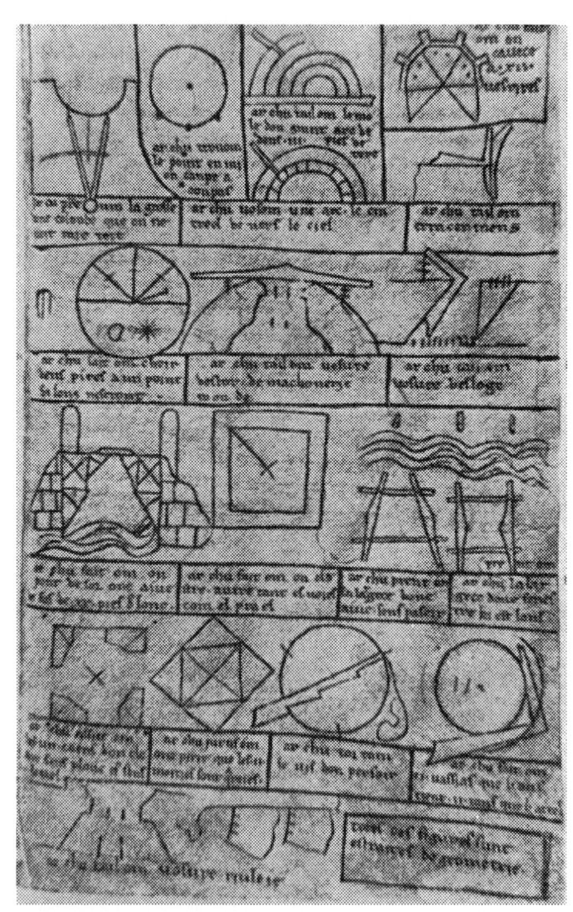

9.23 *Right: Villard de Honnecourt, Lodgebook, showing the key figure of rotated squares.*

tween aspects in Gothic architecture from the most substantial, the overall proportions governing the cathedral, to most apparently superficial, the overlay of decorative tracery.

The **Tomb of the Architect Hugues Limbergier** (died 1263), is placed in Reims cathedral. The funerary slab is marked with a full-figure portrait of the architect bearing the church and a measuring rod. Behind him are other tools of the trade: a square and a compass. These tools and Masonic lodge books surviving from the Middle Ages give us clues to how the cathedrals might have been constructed in an era when there were no plans, no scaled drawings, no standardized measures, such as the foot or the meter, and international teams of masons could not always speak the same language. The amount of integration, from overall layout of the scheme, to fine-grained detail, is so extraordinary that a mystique now surround the secret method used by the masons in the medieval period. Erwin Panofsky and Paul Frankl have tried to unravel this secret. In the **Lodgebook of Villard de Honnecourt**, Frankl identifies a drawing by 'Master II.' ("The Secret of the Medieval Masons," Art *Bulletin*, XXVII,

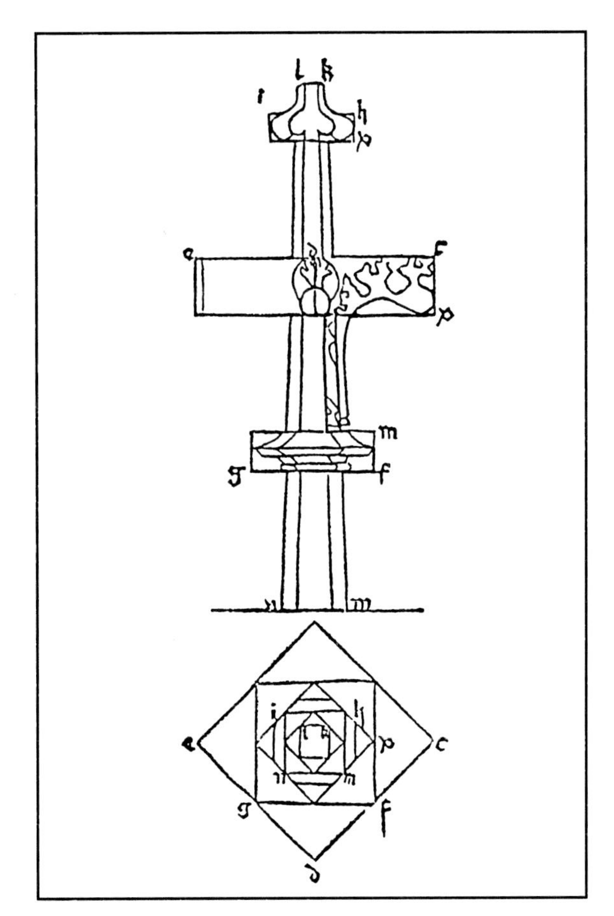

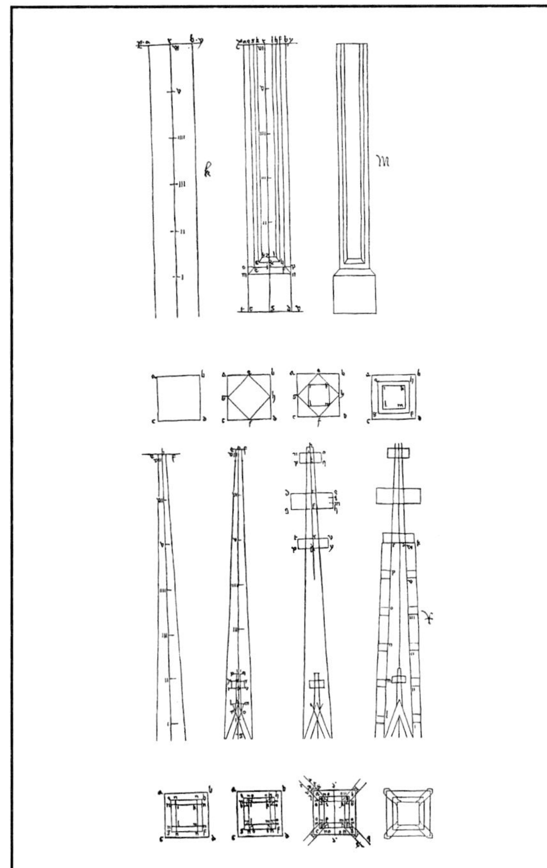

9.24 Left: The development of a finial based on the key figure of the rotated square, according to Mattias Roriczer.

9.25 Right: Plan and elevation of a finial, according to Mattias Roriczer.

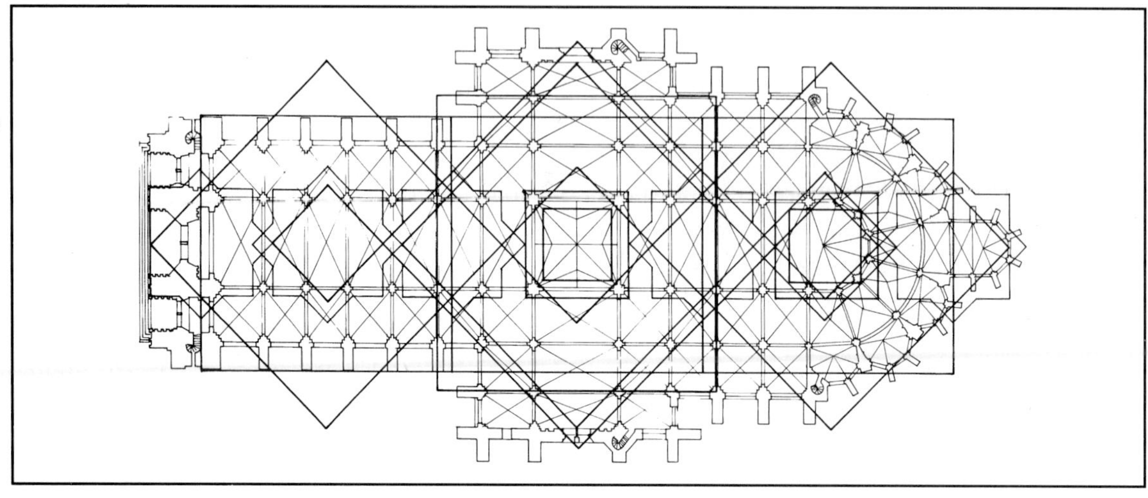

9.26 Diagram of Amiens Cathedral, begun 1220, Amiens, France, with inscribed rotated squares.

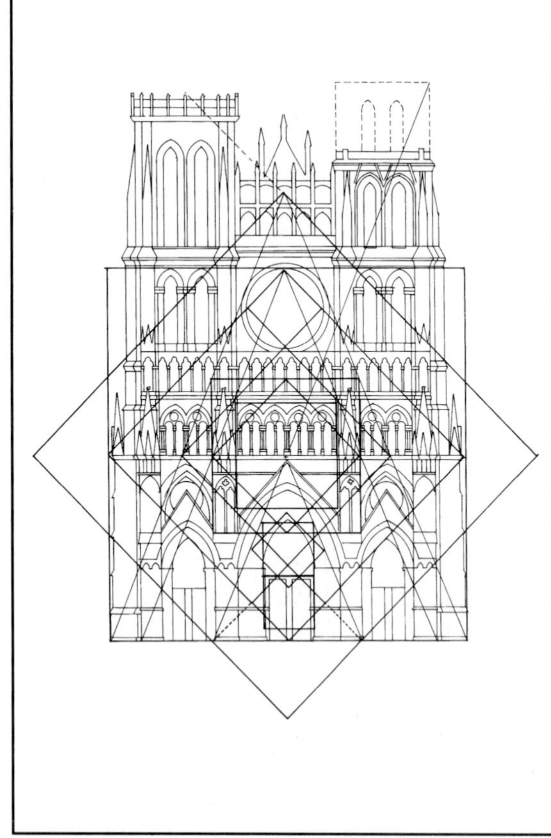

9.27 Diagram of Amiens Cathedral, elevation with inscribed rotated squares.

1945). Frankl suggests it is a 'key figure' which reveals the geometric relationship between two squares, the smaller of which has half the area as the larger. He substantiates this claim with reference to a late **Medieval lodgebook** by **Mattias Roriczer** c. 1489. Roriczer's drawing shows how the lineaments of a Gothic finial were determined through the rotation of a square within a square, the very diagram from Villard's sketchbook. Hence, the secret of the masons was to organize great construction projects by use of geometric schemata which could be expanded outward, to yield larger related dimensions, or involuted to yield smaller ones. Geometric diagrams also played a role in the decorative arts, but there the schemata were used as convenient formal armatures to make drawing easier; in the lay-out of cathedrals, geometry generated the placement and measure of all parts.

It is not difficult to analyze the layout of Gothic buildings according to geometrical methods of *quadrature* or *triangulation,* or by us-

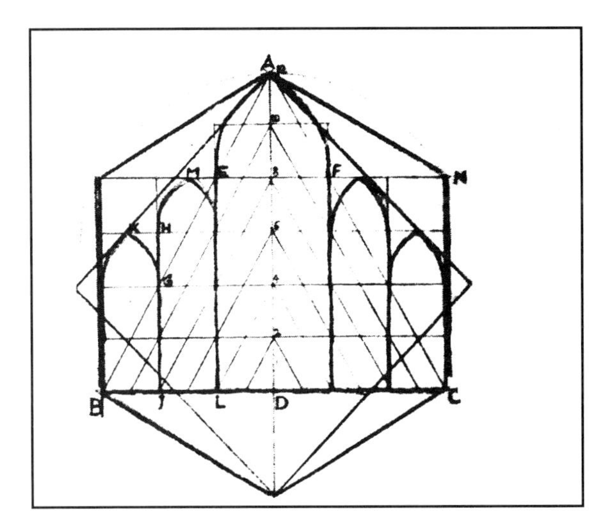

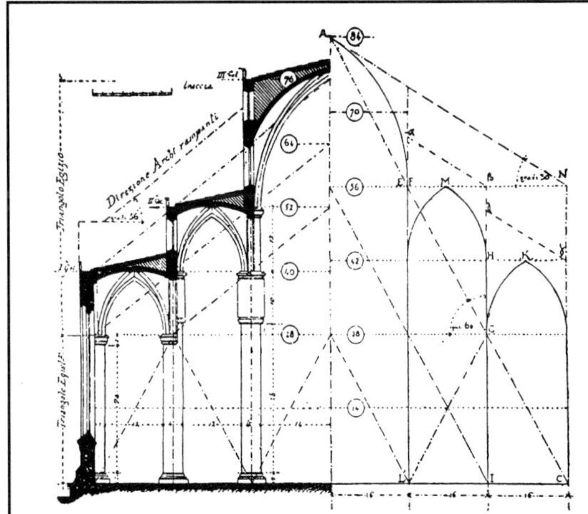

9.28 Left: Stornoloco's diagram for the section of the Milan Cathedral, 1393, after Wittkower.

9.29 Right: Stornoloco's diagram compared with a diagram of the adjusted nave of the Milan Cathedral.

ing any other applied geometrical structure. The plan, section and elevation of **Amiens Cathedral** (begun in 1220) can be solved by the method of quadrature. The validity of the method is even more credible when we see it confirmed in the contemporary record, as in the case of the Milan cathedral.

Pointed arches in the Gothic style made higher naves possible. At the same time their increased verticality made them more efficient. To counter lateral thrust, round-headed arches require surrounding mass. Pointed arches allow the wall structure to be less massive because loads are more directly translated downwards, resulting in reduced lateral thrust. The **flying buttress** helps to further dematerialize the wall. Light structural bridges leap across space to towers remote from the enclosure; flying buttresses envelop the entire structure in a gossamer web. In effect, the outward extension of the flying buttresses takes the wall mass required to counteract lateral thrust and turns it perpendicular to the wall. With the

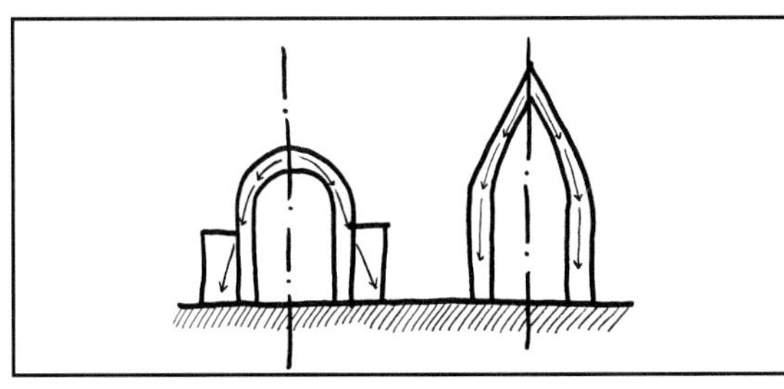

9.30 Diagram, showing the transfer of loads through pointed and round-headed arches.

9.31 Flying buttresses at Notre-Dame, Paris, France.

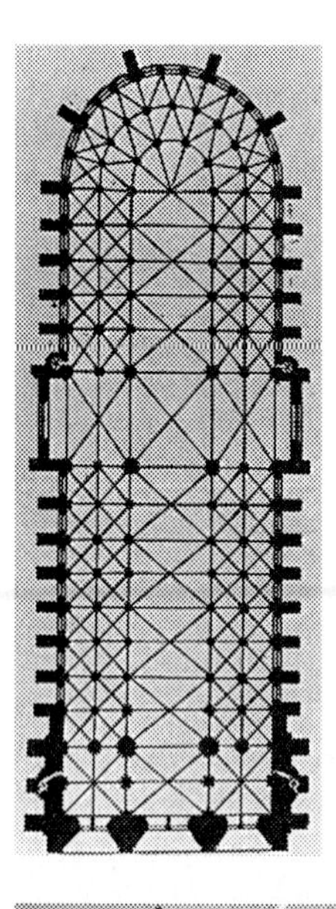

9.32 Notre-Dame-de-Paris, Paris, France, begun 1163, plan and section of a flying buttress.

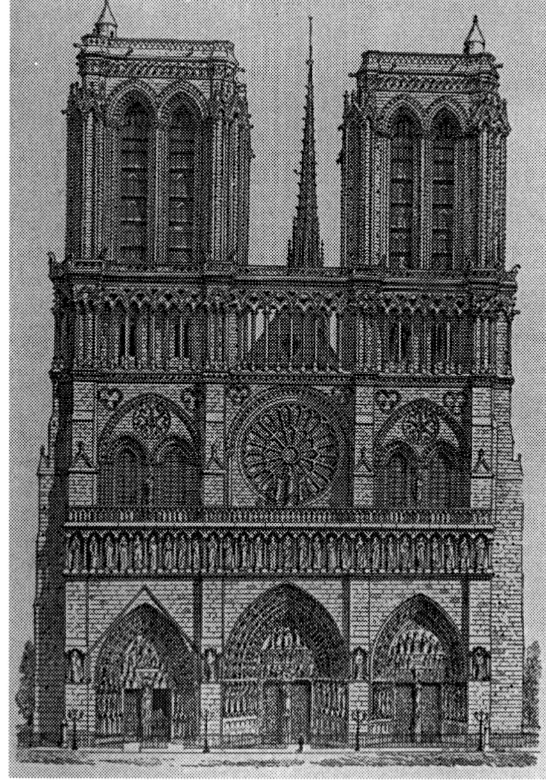

9.33 Notre-Dame, elevation.

skeletal structure supported beyond the enclosure of the cathedral, the walls no longer needed to support weight. Therefore, they could be thin screens of **tracery** or stained glass. The impression is that stone is floating. Spaces of astonishing verticality seem to be supported by almost no matter at all. Dappled light from stained glass windows sparkles over the already skeletal structure, rendering it even more dematerialized in appearance. The intention was to dazzle the beholder and to constantly remind one of the power of God through the mystical fusion of spirit and matter.

The facade was a symbolic vehicle, spatially independent from the church, like a giant billboard representing of the gated city of God. St. Augustine believed that all works should hold multiple levels of meaning. The illiterate peasants gained religious instruction from the church, whose sculptural and ornamental program acted as an illustrated Bible. The learned understood the composition, number, adumbration, and disposition of parts as an exercise in Scholastic rhetoric. Everyone was astonished by the soaring vertical spaces, suffused with light, a visceral testament to the presence and power of God. Monstrous **gargoyles** leaping from the roof lines spat out torrents of water on rainy days and enhanced the sense of awe and terror inspired by the great cathedrals. In fact they were **scuppers**, and their function was to keep rain water off the walls of the cathedral.

Because Gothic architecture was so diffuse almost every European nation can boast of fine examples in the style. To focus our argument, we shall examine a few French cathedrals. Notre-Dame de Paris was begun in 1163; Reims, in 1211; Beauvais in 1224 and Ste. Chapelle in

1243-48. In other words, eighty years separates their inceptions, a mere twinkling of an eye if one considers the longevity of the Egyptian dynasties and their constant style. Yet a tremendous difference in composition, technique, and spatial feeling exists among them, even though they are all examples of Gothic architecture from roughly the same region in France.

Begun in 1163, **Notre-Dame-de-Paris** was conceived as the tallest church in Christendom with a nave height of 35 meters. The structural innovation of flying buttresses assured against collapse. The plan of Notre-Dame is a closed, unitary volume. The crossing of the transept is expressed sectionally but does not disturb the perimeter of the church. The closure and compression in plan has correspondence in the elevation. Neither porch nor towers pull out from the plane of the wall. The former is carved into the wall, the latter, vertical extensions of it. An extreme clarity and hyper-articulation of parts characterizes the facade. Horizontal bands of sculpture demarcate the zone of the portals from the zone of the rose window, and so forth. It is almost as though the facade of the church were overlaid with a compartmentalized grid, each cell holding a discrete architectural feature.

Reims Cathedral has been called the "Queen of Gothic cathedrals" and owes some of its refinement and richness to the fact that it was the seat of coronations for the Capetian monarchs of France. The height of the nave is 38 meters (about 125 feet) and the wall is further dematerialized. The unified relationship of clerestory and triforium at Reims cathedral must have impressed contemporary architects, for a sketch of

9.34 Notre-Dame, gargoyles.

9.35 Notre-Dame, nave.

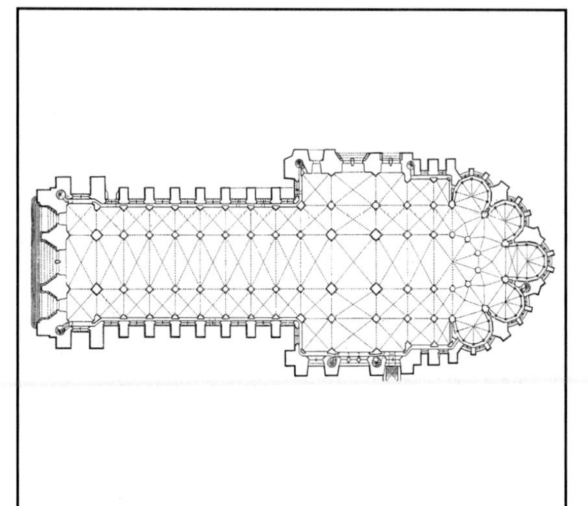

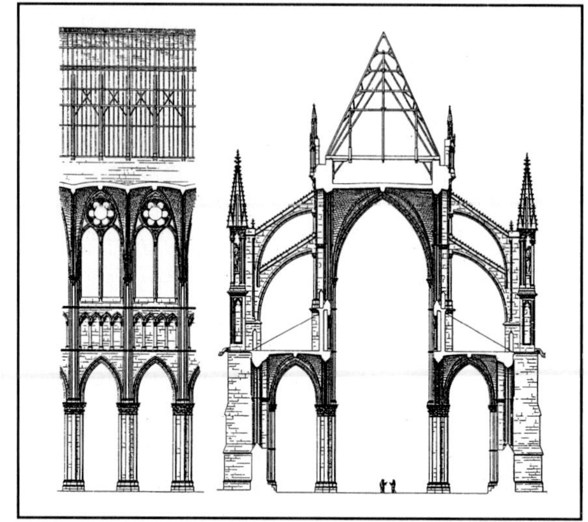

9.36 Left: Reims Cathedral, Reims, France, begun 1211, plan.

9.37 Right: Reims Cathedral, section and interior elevation.

9.38 Left: Reims Cathedral, elevation.

9.39 Right: Reims Cathedral, nave.

it is included in the lodgebook of Villard de Honnecourt. The facade of Reims cathedral is less planar and more sculptural than at Notre Dame. The horizontal banding characteristic of Notre Dame is diminished through an overlay of vertical elements which integrate the zones. Turrets pulled out from the plane of the wall exaggerate the verticality of the facade. The porch is a freestanding screen which overlaps and connects to the rose window, inscribed within a pointed arch. There is a uniform exterior articulation and synthesis of discrete parts into a new, grander expression of the whole.

9.40 Beauvais Cathedral, Beauvais, France, begun 1225, view of the choir vaults.

The building of great Gothic churches reached its apogee and culmination with **Beauvais Cathedral**, begun in 1225. It was designed to reach almost 48 meters in height. John Ruskin was moved to write the following lines: *"there are few rocks, even among the Alps that have a clear vertical fall as high as the choir of Beauvais."* At the height of the Gothic period, funds could be raised easily and work proceeded swiftly: Chartres Cathedral was completely finished in the brief span of 27 years; Bourges cathedral was erected during two building campaigns, from 1195-1214 and from 1225-1255. The construction of Beauvais cathedral was undertaken without sufficient funds in place to assure its completion. Work dragged on slowly. A desire to render the structure as light and airy as possible led the architects to space the piers too far apart and provide too little buttressing. In 1284, the partially completely cathedral choir collapsed; it is unclear if the vaults fell because of excessive height, poor foundations, or because the static forces of the cathedral, like a house of cards, could only be stable with all the pieces in place.

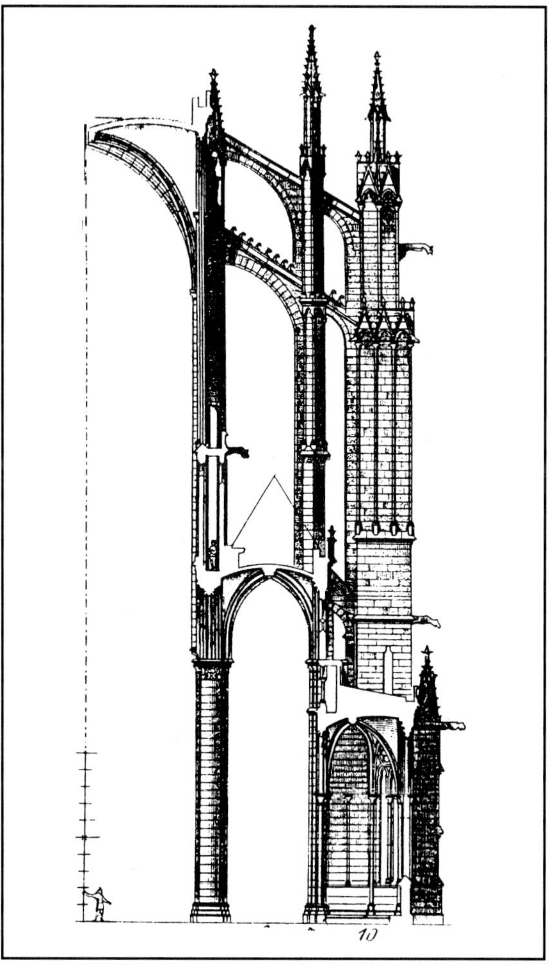

9.41 Beauvais Cathedral, section.

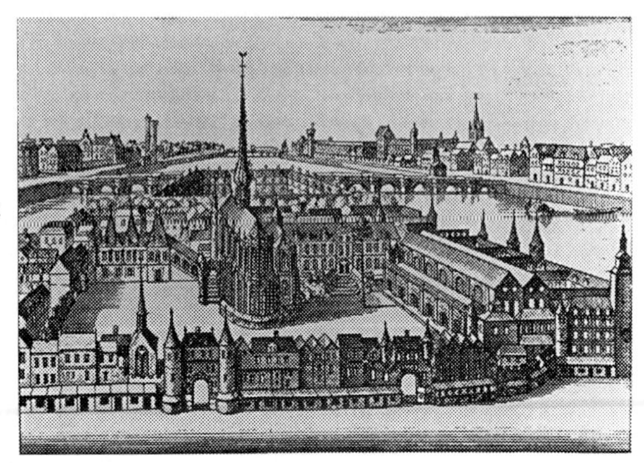

9.42 Sainte Chapelle, Paris, France, 1243-48, exterior view with the Palais de Justice.

9.43 Sainte Chapelle, section.

Sainte Chapelle is the last example we shall examine. Unlike the other vast cathedrals, Sainte Chapelle is but a tiny appendage to the Royal Palace in Paris. It was built for St. Louis as an architecturally scaled reliquary to house treasures brought back from the orient, the 'True Cross' and 'The Crown of Thorns.' The dematerialization of wall and suffusion of interior space with dappled mystical light reaches its height in this church. Wall disappears entirely and one has the sensation of being inside a Tiffany lamp.

The ambitious construction projects of the Gothic period depended on a flourishing economy, which was possible only in peaceful times when trade among regions could proceed without obstacles. After the collapse of the choir at Beauvais, no sufficient funds were ever raised to complete the church, in spite of over four hundred years of active fund raising. War and pestilence struck Europe; the beginning of the One Hundred Year War in 1337 coincided with the onslaught of the Black death. Munitions workshops took the place of cathedral construction projects and skilled sculptors from Reims and Chartres were put to work carving canon balls.

Among the most valuable lessons manifested in Gothic architecture is the integral connection between form and content. Purely architectural play of space and structure can connect to a symbolic program as complex as a Scholastic argument or a Biblical narrative. The medieval requirement that works of art have many levels of meaning provides a useful lesson for contemporary architects. As Quintilian observed: "The *learned understand the nature of art, the unlearned its voluptuousness.*"

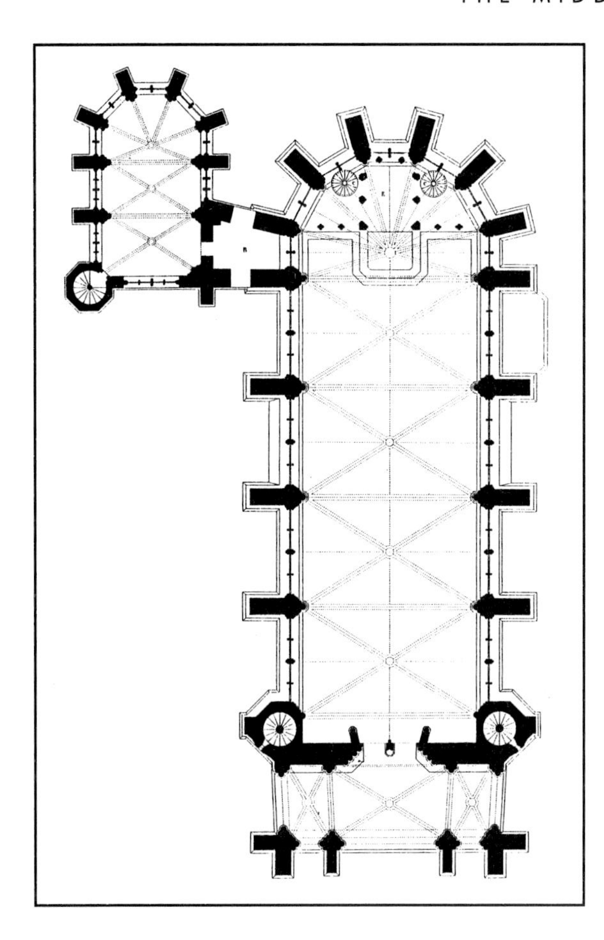

9.44 Left: Sainte Chapelle, plan.

9.45 Right: Sainte Chapelle, nave.

The strong relationship between form and content is no less compelling than the interdependence of structure and ornament in Gothic architecture. In the nineteenth century, the apparent structural rationalism of the Gothic style provided a source of inspiration and renewal in an architectural milieu characterized by uncritical historicism. Augustus Pugin, a great proponent of the Gothic Revival in nineteenth century England urged architects to 'construct ornament', not to 'ornament construction'.

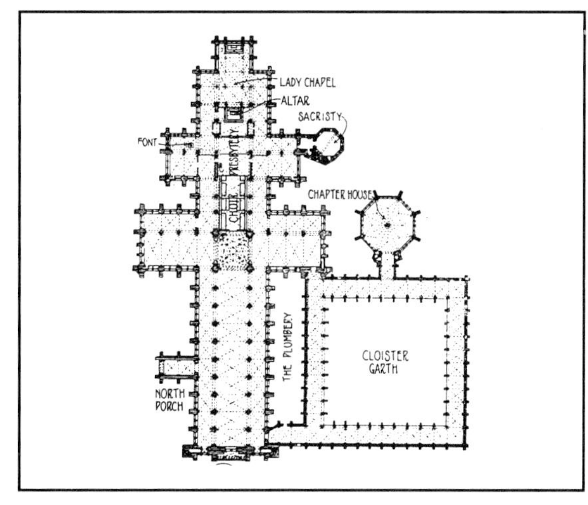

9.46 Salisbury Cathedral, England, 1220-65.

10.0
Andrea Palladio, Villa Rotonda (Villa Capra), Vicenza, Italy, 1566-70.

Chapter 10

The Renaissance: Proportion and Ideality

. . . Beauty is a certain regular harmony of all the parts of a thing of such a kind that nothing could be added or taken away, except for the worse . . .

-LEONBATTISTA ALBERTI

The Renaissance took place in Italy in the 1400's, at a time when Gothic architecture was still flourishing in northern countries and would continue to do so for more than a hundred years. What was the Renaissance, and why did it emerge in Italy at that particular time and place? One factor was prosperity. Great banking families like the Medici, the Pitti and others, rose in political stature as their wealth increased. Bankers, merchants and guilds provided sponsorship for many artistic and architectural endeavors, creating a need for artists and craftsmen. Talented artists came forward to fill the vacuum. Legend has it that the great painter **Giotto** (1267-1337) was discovered as he tended his flocks in the hills: his native artistic ability revealed itself through the perfection of circles he sketched on rocks. In the Renaissance, talent was nurtured in academies and workshops set up to promulgate a revived interest in the arts and letters of antiquity.

Cosimo de Medici (1389-1464), great patriarch of the Florentine banking family, did much to sponsor the renewal of the arts. He assembled an impressive library, founded the Platonic Academy and brought together a team of scholars from all over Europe and the Middle East. The assemblage of so many great minds stimulated discussion and fostered a climate in which the ideas of the ancient philosophers could be applied directly to the contemporary situation. Humanism and Neo-Platonism replaced spiritualism and Scholasticism as the dominant ways of thought. The effect on artistic production was immediate. The spirituality of the medieval times produced little interest in nature, the human form or the depiction of naturalistic, three-dimensional spaces. In the Renaissance these became central concerns, for it was believed that beautiful things of the earth were windows to divine beauty. Belief in the apprehensibility of divine good through reason was a double edged proposition. It greatly increased the stature of the individual, and creative geniuses thrived in the arts and sciences. At the same time, rational Humanism made it possible for individuals to do without the formal religious structure of the church. This jeopardized both the patronage base and the societal consensus of meaning necessary to bring about great, unitary, synthetic movements in the arts.

Another factor was geographic. The classical civilization of ancient Rome was the natural birthright of the Italians and in the Renaissance, they sought to reclaim it. They were in a good position to do so, because the landscape was still scattered with ruins of Roman buildings. Moreover, the Gothic style had never firmly taken root. The resumption of classical culture was a manifestation of patriotism and ethnic pride. The Gothic style arose in the land of barbarians, it was thought. The classical style was the perfect embodiment of the civilized values of a civilized land.

The architectural space of the Middle Ages was spiritualized and characterized by extreme verticality, diminution of mass, mystical light, and a deliberate lack of relationship to human scale. In the Renaissance, architecture derived from the measure of human beings and was their external projection. A revived interest in the architecture and Orders of classical antiq-

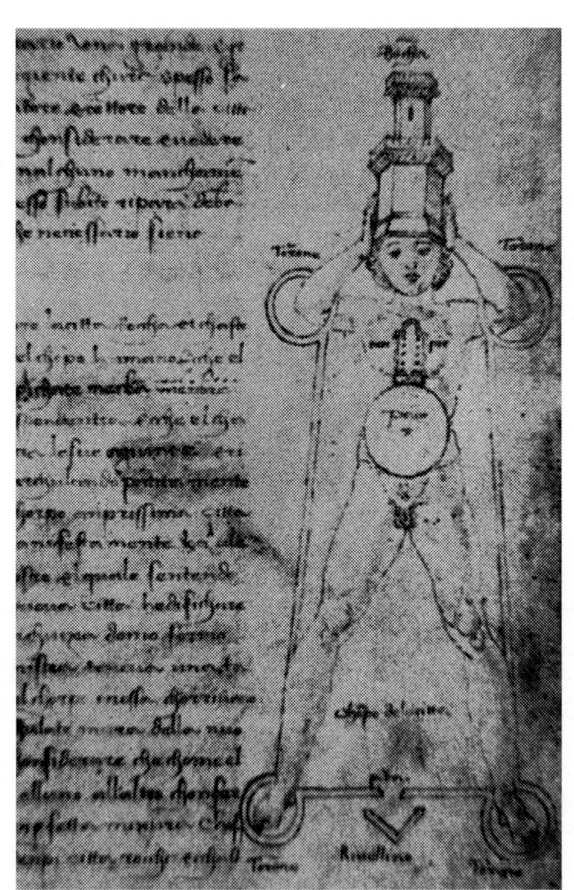

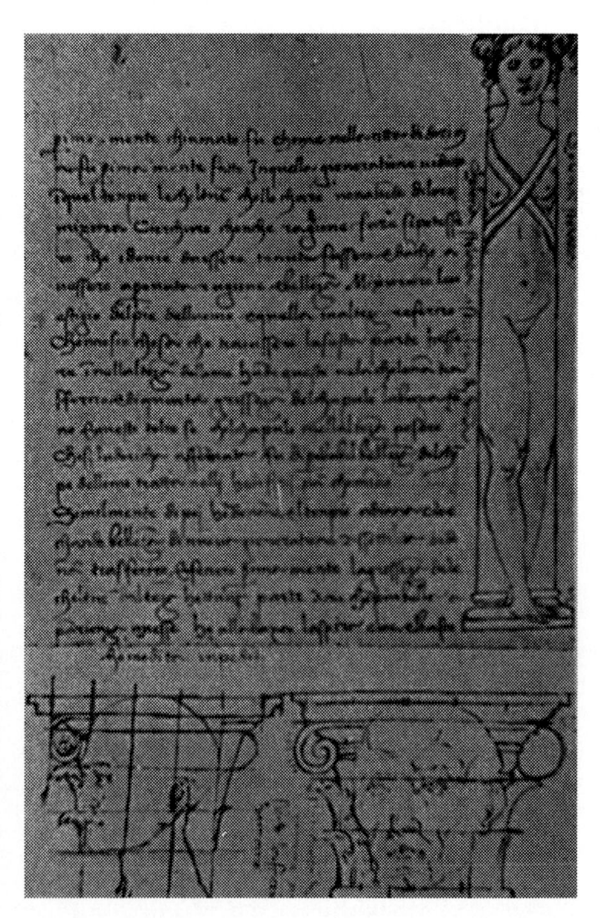

10.1 Left: Francesco di Giorgio Martini, Anthropomorphic Town Plan, c. 1480.

10.2 Right: Francesco di Giorgio Martini, The Relationship between a Column and a Body, c. 1480.

uity provided a language already laden with anthropomorphic associations. Leonardo's Vitruvian Man established a connection between the lineaments of the human figure and abstract geometry; others, such as **Francesco di Giorgio Martini** (1439-1501), conceived of relationships between the body and all aspects of architectural form, from columns and cornices to town plans. **Albrecht Dürer** (1471-1528) took the study of human proportions to new scientific heights. He took sections through the body at regular intervals to study human dimensions in plan as well as in elevation.

Strangely enough, the Renaissance may also have been caused, in part, by the devastation of the Black Death. Florence and Siena were particularly hard hit by the plague, Siena losing two thirds of its inhabitants. During the medieval period, an apprentice system assured the transmission of skills and styles directly from master to pupil. Transformations occurred within the style, but they came about slowly and significant changes were not manifest for generations. The apprentice system also assured the collectivity of works of art. Groups of workmen, having received the same training,

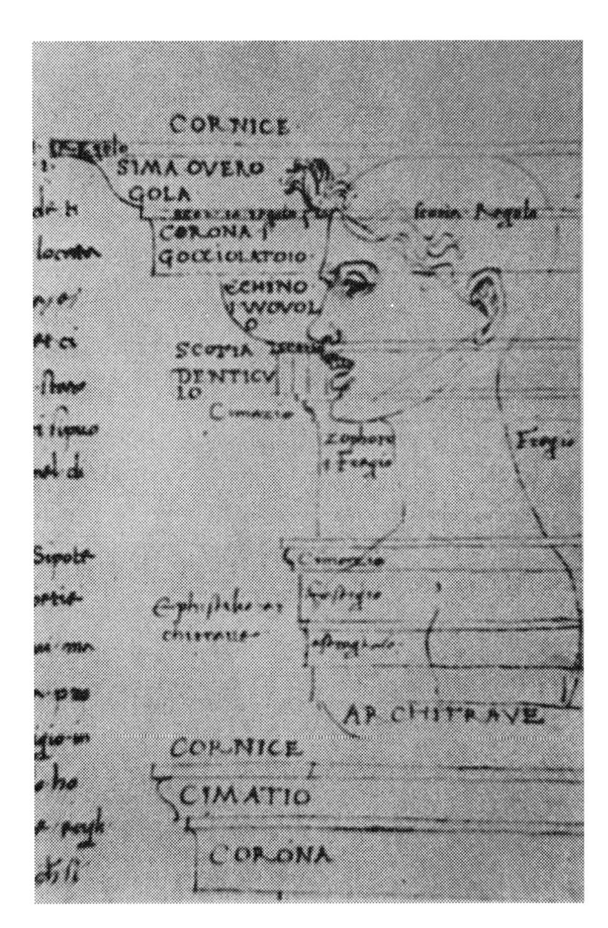

10.3 Left: Francesco di Giorgio Martini, The Relationship between a Cornice and the Human Head, c. 1480.

10.4 Right: Albrecht Dürer, Study of Human Proportion, c. 1500.

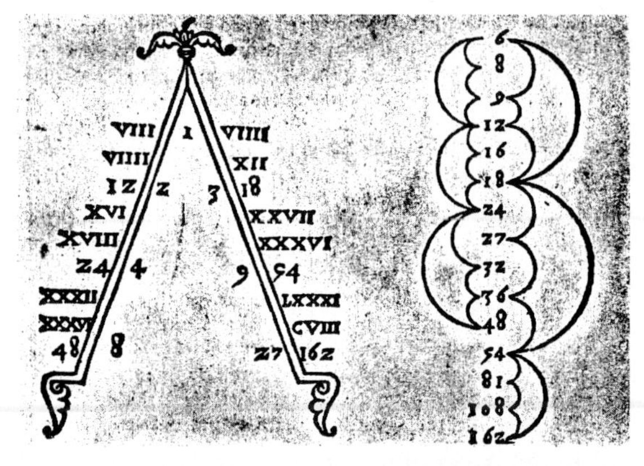

10.5
Diagram from Francesco di Giorgio Martini, 1525. Plato's Lambda is used to determine proportions.

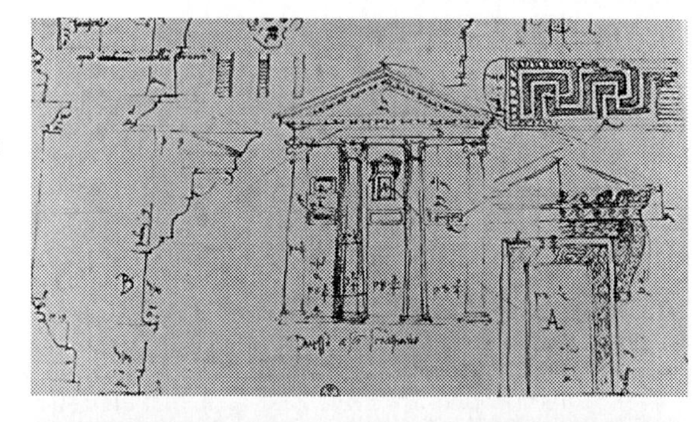

10.6
Baldassare Peruzzi, sketches of antiquities, Uffizi.

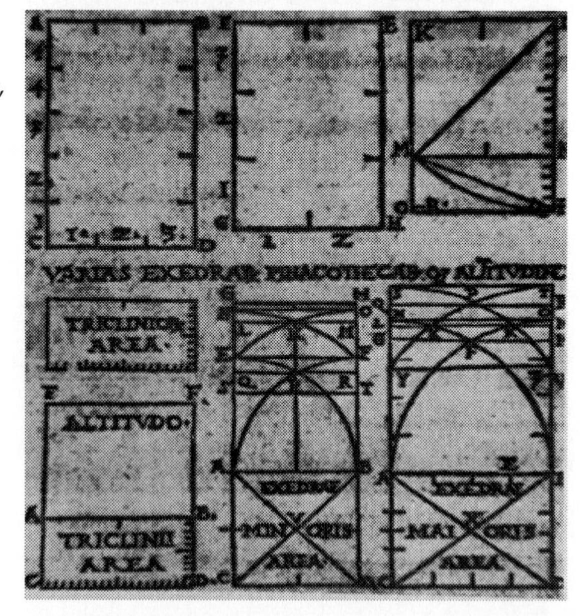

10.7
Cesare Cesariano, Proportions for Rectangles, c.1520.

could be relied on to work together in the production of a single unified product. There was little room for the eccentricities or discoveries of genius. When the Black Death killed a great number of master builders, painters, and craftsmen, the natural evolution of styles was broken. Lacking skilled masters, the new generation was obliged to reinvent the arts from ground zero. Instead of a continuity in a tradition, there was a 're-birth,' which is the meaning of 'Renaissance.' The point of reference for this rebuilding was not the art of the previous generation, but the great authorities of precedent, nature, and geometry.

In architecture, the greatest authority was Vitruvius. During the Renaissance, there was a flurry of activity around his *Ten Books on Architecture.* Translations, critiques, and illustrated versions appeared and were scrutinized by a generation starved for knowledge of the architecture that made possible the grandeur of ancient Rome. Precedent could be archaeological. The great artists and architects of the Renaissance set themselves the task of measuring, recording and studying fragments of Roman buildings in hopes of extracting universal principals that they could apply in their own work. Measured drawings and **sketchbooks of Roman ruins** abounded by Renaissance masters such as Raphael, Sangallo, **Peruzzi**, Serlio, and many others.

Geometrical figures and mathematically derived ratios were believed to hold universal truth about the order of the cosmos. Proportional systems drawn from the ancients were rationalized, systematized and put into effect. Musical theory and architectural theory were bound together, governed by the same harmonic ratios. (See Rudolf Wittkower, *Architectural Principals in the Age of Humanism* for a detailed discussion of proportional systems in the Renaissance and their specific application by Alberti and Palladio).

The importance of the mathematical properties of form led to the development of scientific perspective, a mathematically verifiable way to construct space in a painting. Perspective does two things. First, it provides a two-dimensional representation of three-dimensional space within which plastic figures can be situated. Second, it privileges the point of view of the viewer, engaging the space between the viewer and the picture plane in the composition. The use of architectural forms proved the most effective way to represent three dimensions in a painting. Floor paving, colonnades and roof trusses were all rhythmic structures which receded in an even, legible way, and thereby gave measure to the perspectival space. Architectural design became a concern for painters as well as architects, to the mutual benefit of both.

The ***"Trinità"*** by **Masaccio** (1401-28) is one of the first paintings that can be ascribed to a purely Renaissance sensibility. The figures are conceived as three-dimensional, muscular bodies situated in space. Accurate delineation of anatomy is accompanied by an attempt to depict the stresses and muscle tension appropriate to the various poses. Scientific perspective, invented at roughly the same time by the architect Filippo Brunelleschi, (1377-1446), is used in the construction of the architectural surrounds. Overlapping planes define the recession of space, as does the perspectival rendering of the Roman barrel vault. In the Gothic period, **pictorial space**, as the two-dimensional

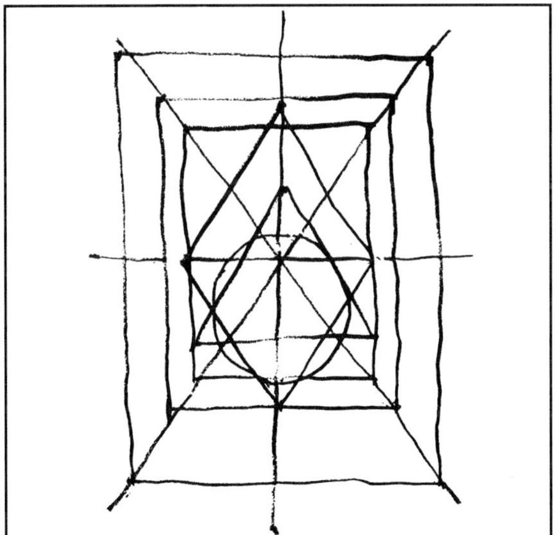

10.8 "Trinità" diagram.

10.9 Masaccio, "Trinità," 1425, fresco, Santa Maria Novella, Florence, Italy.

10.10 Raphael, "School of Athens," 1510-11, fresco, Stanza della Segnatura, Vatican.

representation of three-dimensional space, was not of interest. Paintings were not meant to depict scenes of this world as they would appear to the eye; paintings were lexicons of symbols and attributes. The *"Trinità"* includes both symbolic and narrative content about the Trinity. The two-dimensional schemata which underlie the organization of the painting are replete with three-fold iterations of triangles. A symbol of Trinity, in the middle of the composition, unites the 'Father,' 'Son,' and 'Holy Ghost' figures together. Meanwhile, the three-dimensional image presents the theme of the Trinity in narrative form. Tension between the two-dimensional and three-dimensional organization of the painting yields a powerful dialogue between the symbolic and emotional content of the painting. Masaccio's use of geometry is radically different than Villard de Honnecourt's, discussed in Chapter 9. The latter used geometry to aid in the delineation of discrete figures; the former used geometry to bind together the formal organization of space with symbolic meanings.

If Masaccio's *"Trinità"* laid out the essential themes of the Early Renaissance, then **Raphael Sanzio's** (1483-1520) fresco ***"The School of Athens"*** did so for the High Renaissance. It is a celebration of the classical roots of contemporary Rome, painted in the very heart of the Vatican. Many of the spatial techniques explored by Masaccio are in operation, but here they are applied with greater self assurance and control. Overlapping planes of space define zones of action and separate related groups of figures. Indeed, the lofty hall depicted in the painting seems to be a representation of St. Peter's, with the vaults removed to afford a more direct view of the great vault of heaven.

The central figures, Plato and Aristotle, argue learnedly while a pensive Heraclitus broods in the foreground. Commingling with the great thinkers of the classical age are modern thinkers, such as Dante, Boccaccio, Petrarch and others. Identities of other moderns are conflated with the ancients. Plato seems to be modeled after Leonardo; Heraclitus, after Michelangelo. Raphael even includes himself in the company, looking squarely at the viewer. At his feet is a tablet inscribed with the Greek harmonic scale; the secret of ancient beauty and proportion, now reclaimed by Renaissance men like Raphael.

In the earlier chapters we discussed a number of important buildings and building types from the Renaissance. These included Bramante's Tempietto, Palladio's villas, Sangallo and Michelangelo's Palazzo Farnese, Peruzzi's Palazzo Massimo and Vasari's Uffizi. The whole question of centralized churches, treated at length in Chapter 5, is essentially a Renaissance theme, spawned by the desire to revive antique forms within a Christian context. In this chapter, we shall look at other examples and concentrate on questions particular to the Renaissance: space, proportion, articulation and the relationship between techniques of drawing, such as perspective and orthographic projection, and the conceptualization of architectural form.

Filippo Brunelleschi is usually credited with the invention of mathematical perspective, although he began as a sculptor and is best known as an architect. The division between trades and branches of the arts, so characteristic of the twentieth century, was virtually unknown in the Renaissance. Many of the greatest Renaissance figures excelled in architecture, sculpture, painting, and sometimes even literature, science, medicine, and mathematics. Michelangelo wrote sonnets of exquisite beauty. Christopher Wren, architect of St. Paul's in London, was professor of astronomy at Cambridge University. The athletic prowess of Leonbattista Alberti was such that he could jump over a horse from a standing position.

Brunelleschi's training as a sculptor inculcated him with a keen sensitivity to the nature of materials and their constructional possibilities. These talents helped him solve a problem that had been vexing Florentines for a long while: the construction of the dome over the 42 meter wide (approximately 140 feet) octagonal crossing of the **Cathedral of Florence, Santa Maria dei Fiori**. The span was roughly equal to that of the Pantheon and far larger than that of the Hagia Sophia. Moreover, it was determined that the dome would have no external buttressing, in the Gothic manner, but be wholly self-contained.

When competing for the commission to construct the dome, Brunelleschi promised to build it "without money and dirt." Legend has it that

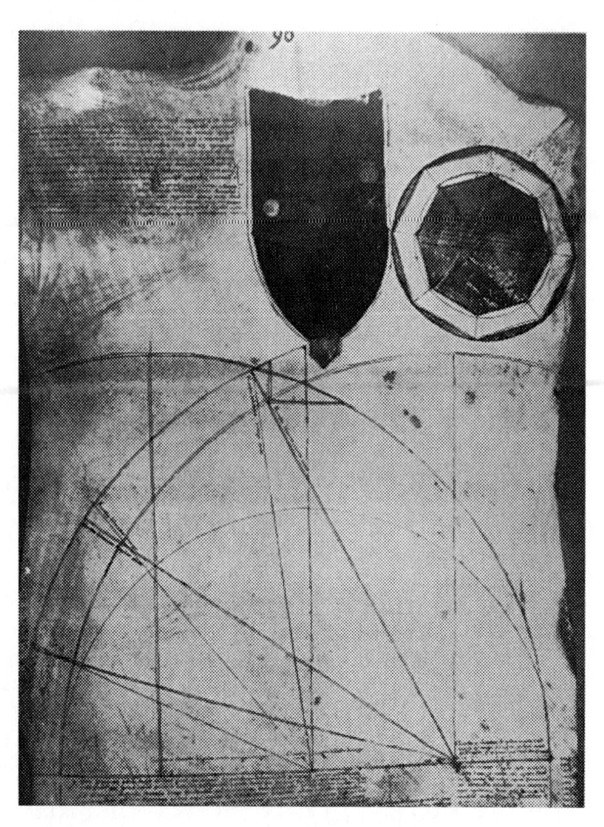

10.11 Left: Filippo Brunelleschi, dome of Santa Maria dei Fiori, (Florence Cathedral), with Giotto's Campanille (Bell Tower) in the foreground, Florence, Italy, view, c. 1420-36.

10.12 Right: Giovanni di Prato, drawing to calculate the curvature of the dome of Santa Maria dei Fiori (Florence, Archivio di Stato).

the floor of the Pantheon was filled with a mixture of dirt and coins to support the building of the dome. After this artificial mountain had served its constructional purpose, the mound was emptied out by inviting the citizens of Rome to keep any coins they found in the dirt they removed from the church floor.

Brunelleschi spent sixteen years on this project, from 1420-1436, and invented techniques to study the problem. Extreme precision was important in such a difficult engineering problem, so Brunelleschi drew a full-scale plan of the dome on a flat expanse of dirt along the banks of the Arno. A drawing from his workshop shows how the curvature of the dome was calculated. He is even said to have tested the three-dimensional aspects of the dome by carving a large turnip.

Finally, Brunelleschi devised a method of erecting the dome without constructing an enormous scaffold as **centering.** Instead he used a double shell system of construction so that the static forces of each ring would be resolved internally. Instead of using external buttressing to resist lateral thrust, chains and cables were wrapped around the base of the dome. He also used structural ribs to isolate forces and reduce the overall weight of the dome. At the same time, these ribs helped map the location of progressive layers in the construction process.

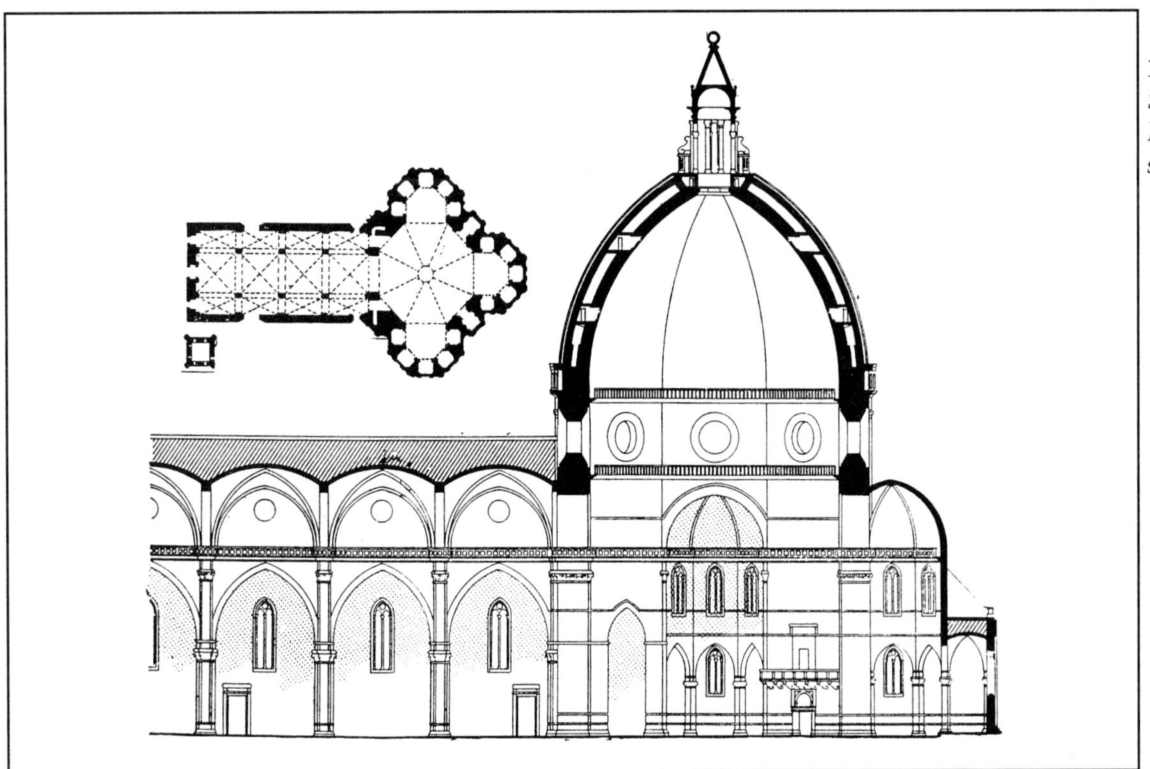

10.13 Santa Maria dei Fiori, plan and section.

In his solution for the dome of the Florence Cathedral, Brunelleschi did away with precedent and solved the problem based on analysis, observation, and a thorough understanding of materials. In the design of **Santo Spirito Brunelleschi** investigated proportion, classical language and the use of clear Platonic forms. Called by Bernini "the most beautiful church in the world" Santo Spirito is a basilican church based on an additive system of square **modules**. The module system which organizes the plan also organizes the section. The modules are arranged according to the arithmetic mean, in which the relationship of transept to nave is B-A = C-B. The diagram isolates the base module 'A' and identifies the aforementioned relationship as (8A:4A) = (12A:8A).

Brunelleschi makes a great effort to articulate the church so that the mathematical relationships among parts is visible. A dark stone called *pietra serena* is used for columns and horizontal courses to delineate the elements and clarify the rhythm among them. The gridded paving pattern on the floor maps the modular relationships at play. Brunelleschi uses the language of classicism, but he transforms elements and combines them in new ways. An enormous order of Corinthian columns supports an arcade rather than a straight entablature, as would have been the case in antiquity. This results in a greater spatial interpenetration of nave and aisle. Moments of awkwardness result. At the end of the colonnade, the terminal arch butts into the wall without a graceful transition.

Brunelleschi continues many of the same themes in a small centralized **Chapel for the Pazzi** family. Square modules link together to orchestrate space according to the arithmetic progression and the entire building can be inscribed into a square in plan and elevation. Bands of *pietra serena* delineate the zones so that the clear proportionate division among parts is legible. The dome is not a Roman hemispherical vault, but a lighter, more laterally stable dome invented by Brunelleschi. The load of the vault is carried by ribs, and the **webbing**, or enclosing membrane, is free from structural duties.

The problem of the corner, which we already noted in ancient Greece and ancient Rome, re-

10.14 Fillippo Brunelleschi, Santo Spirito, Florence, Italy, begun 1434, nave.

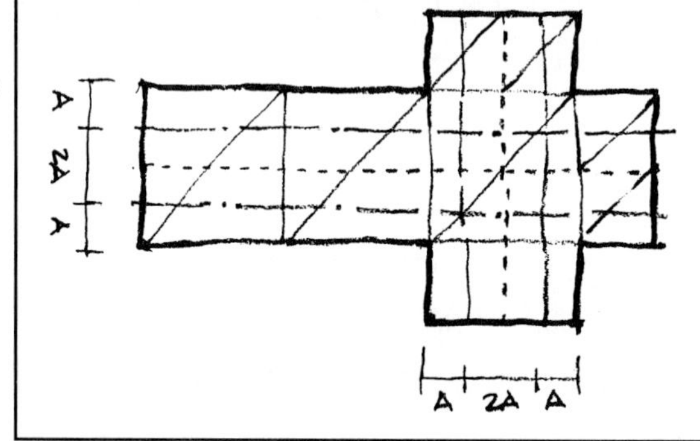

10.15 Diagram of Santo Spirito.

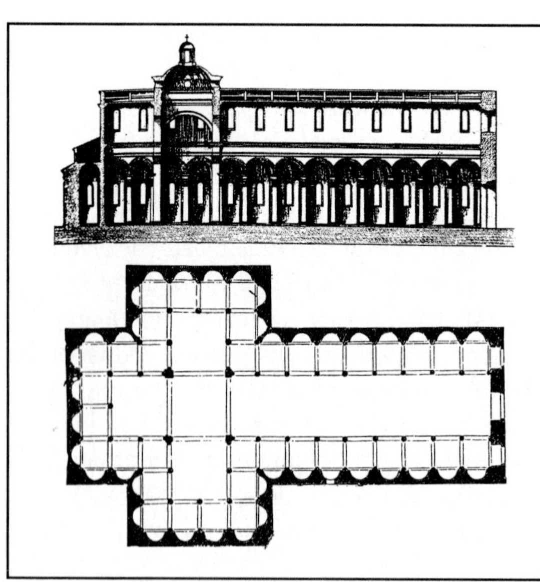

10.16 Left: Santo Spirito, plan and section.

10.17 Right: Filippo Brunelleschi, Pazzi Chapel, Florence, Italy, 1429, section.

mains a concern in the Renaissance. Brunelleschi finds it difficult to reconcile the visual weight of pilasters wrapping corners with the logical desire that columns mark a steady rhythm along the wall. At the altar, his solution is to absorb most of the pilaster within the wall, leaving only a tiny sliver. In the lateral extensions of the space beneath the barrel vaults, he bends the pilaster around the corner.

Brunelleschi and **Leonbattista Alberti** are the two great founders of Renaissance architecture, but their engagement with the profession was quite different. Brunelleschi came to architecture through sculpture, and had a natural understanding of construction, material, and problems that were purely tectonic. Alberti, on the other hand, was a gentleman and a scholar. For him, architecture was an intellectual pursuit, not a manual one. While Brunelleschi was the first to solve the problem of scientific perspective, Alberti was the first to codify and

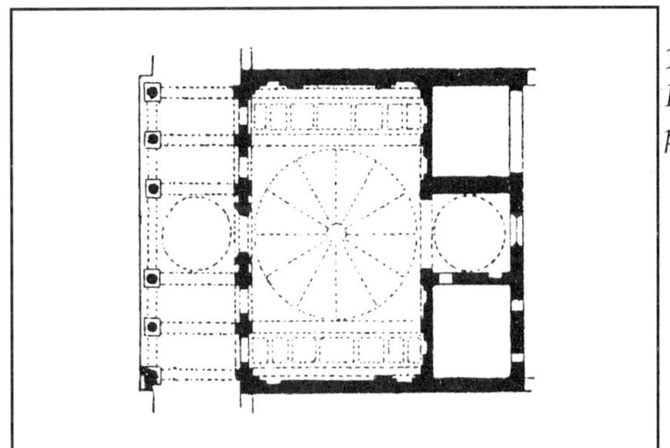

10.18 Pazzi Chapel, plan.

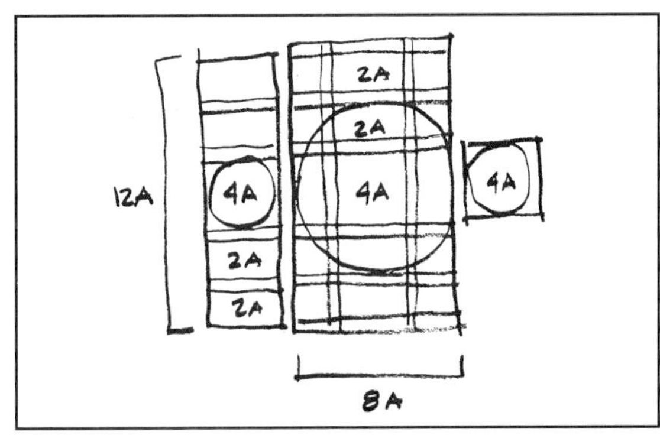

10.19 Pazzi Chapel, plan diagram.

10.20 Left: Pazzi Chapel, facade.

10.21 Right: Pazzi Chapel, interior view.

10.22 Left: Leonbattista Alberti, Santa Maria Novella, Florence, Italy, 1456-70, facade.

10.23 Right: Santa Maria Novella, elevation diagram.

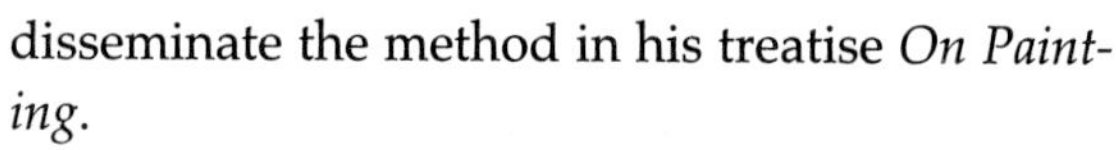

10.24 Leonbattista Alberti, San Andrea, Mantua, Italy, c.1470, nave.

disseminate the method in his treatise *On Painting*.

Alberti was the quintessential Renaissance Man. His architectural treatise *Ten Books on Architecture,* c. 1472 sought to replace Vitruvius with a more systematic and scientific book. He began by belittling Vitruvius, who was a Roman, for his poor command of Latin and then went on to write his own treatise in Latin, displaying mastery of style and nuance. To Vitruvius' three requirements of architecture, *utilitas, firmitas, venustas* (commodity, firmness and delight), he added that the beauty of a building depends on *numeros* (numbers), *finitio* (proportion, or the harmonic relationship of parts to the whole), *collocatio* (the arrangement of parts) and *concinnitas* (the concordance of all parts with respect to the whole). For Alberti, any individual part of the building had to be subordinated to the order of the whole for the result to be beautiful.

At **Santa Maria Novella** in Florence, **Alberti's** task was to complete the facade of a pre-existing Gothic building. The facade had

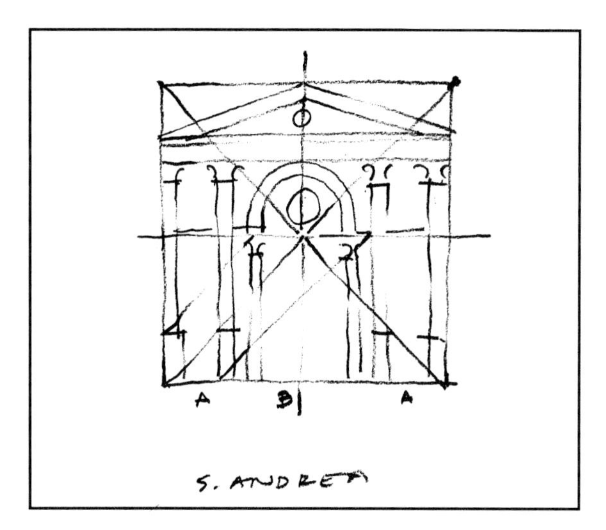

10.25 Left: San Andrea, facade, diagram.

10.26 Right: San Andrea, facade view.

already been constructed up to the first entablature. Therefore, the task was not the simple composition of a facade. Instead it was an exercise in reconciling opposites. Alberti's self-avowed interest in *concinnitas*, concordance among parts, made it repugnant for him to disrupt the harmonious agreement of the whole by combining a Gothic interior with a Renaissance exterior, and a Gothic lower facade with a Renaissance upper facade. He had to work within the Gothic manner in such a way as to render the proportional relationships among the parts agreeable to a Renaissance sensibility.

Alberti's method was to inscribe the church facade into a gridded square. The overall geometry is governed by the square and each of the component parts and their measurements derive from modules which comprise the grid. A large Corinthian Order defines square bays and sets up a thin screen which frames, veils and neutralizes the architectural value of pointed arches and slender colonnettes of the Gothic work. Concordance with the Gothic

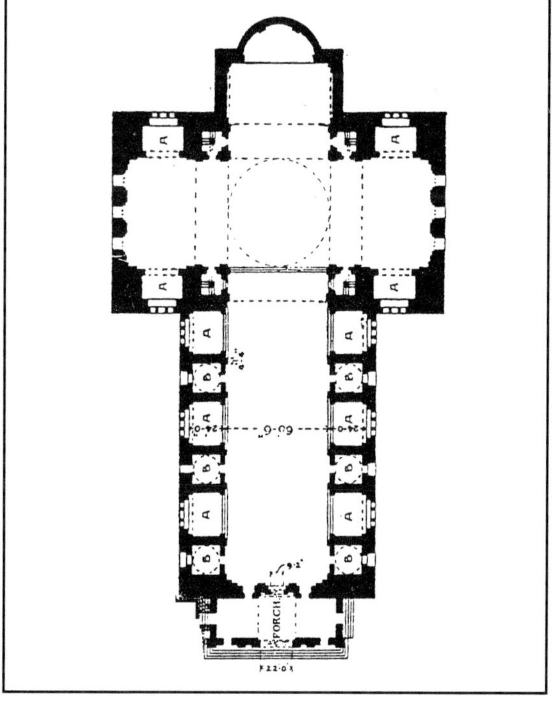

10.27 San Andrea, plan.

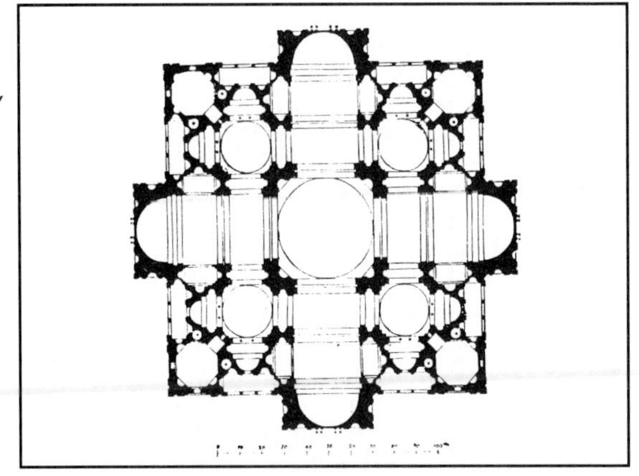

10.28 Donato Bramante, plan for St. Peter's, Rome, Italy, 1506.

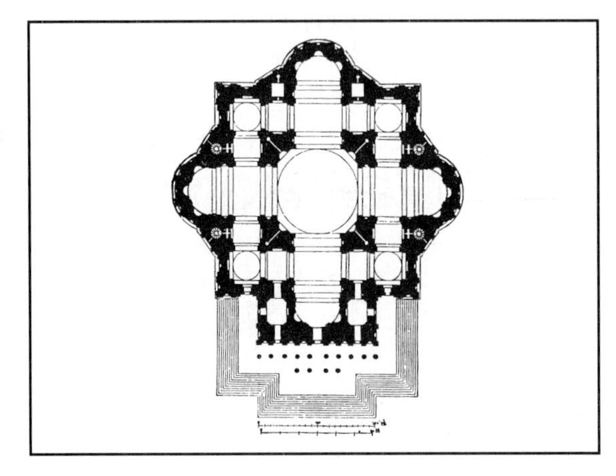

10.29 Michelangelo Buonarotti, plan for St. Peter's, c. 1546.

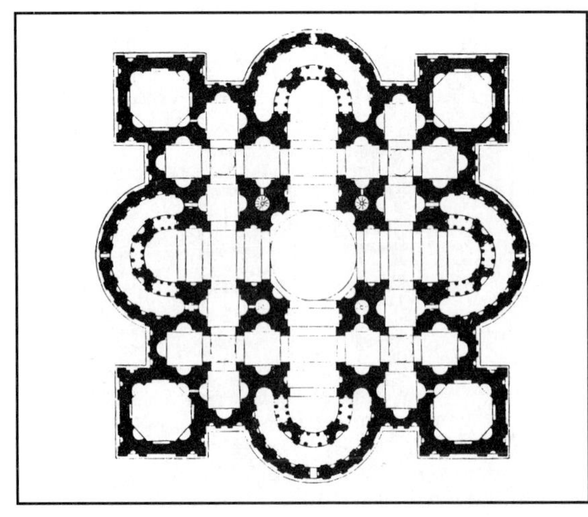

10.30 Baldassare Peruzzi, plan for St. Peter's, c. 1520.

original is thus achieved; at the same time the Gothic elements of the building are harmonized with the whole and made modern. A classical temple, contained within a square, rises above the horizontal banding. The ideality of the temple encapsulates and reifies the operations Alberti had applied to the church as a whole. Unity is achieved among opposites. Even the decorative scrolls at the side of the temple serve to knit the two bodies of the elevation together and to mask the disproportionate height of nave and aisle in the church itself.

San Andrea in Mantua was planned by **Alberti** in 1470, although it was not completed until after his death. The four-square organization of the facade at Santa Maria Novella is again present, but here Alberti is not constrained to manipulate geometry alone. A new kind of facade for a Christian church is designed by superimposing a triumphal arch and a classical temple front. The church is neither wholly pagan nor wholly Christian, it is Humanist. Likewise, Alberti takes the coffered barrel vault of the triumphal arch and uses it thematically in the development of interior space. A complete agreement between interior and exterior expression is thus achieved. The architectural language seems to be directly inspired by Masaccio's arches in the "Trinità". The borrowing among the arts had come full circle. The architect Brunelleschi invented mathematical perspective which made it possible for the painter Masaccio to define a structure which inspired the architect Alberti.

We have already discussed Donato Bramante's masterful little shrine, the Tempietto of San Pietro in Montorio, a building often considered to be the apotheosis of Renaissance centrally planned churches. Part of the reason the Tempietto was able to attain its ideal form and proportion is that it was designed to sit in its own special courtyard. It did not need to respond to pressures from the surrounding context. Part of the reason is that it simply needed to mark a spot: that of St. Peter's crucifixion. No complex rituals had to be housed within its diminutive walls.

At **St. Peter's** in Rome, **Bramante** takes his interest in ideal geometry and central planning to a colossal scale. The dome measures more than 136 feet across and the barrel vaulted aisles reach 150 feet from the ground. The church plan is at once complex and simple: it is simultaneously a nine-square grid, a Greek cross, and a vast centralized dome surrounded by an elaborate ambulatory. Great variety is accommodated within the unifying envelope of the church. The location and dimension of parts within the whole are set up by a geometric relationship among rotated squares, the very method used by Gothic masons in the erection of cathedrals. Furthermore, scaled recursions of the Greek cross plan are sponsored along diagonals, which are also organized by the geometry of the rotating squares.

Many of the greatest architects in the Renaissance prepared plans for **St. Peter's**, including Michelangelo, Peruzzi, Raphael, and Sangallo. Ultimately, **Michelangelo's** plan won out. The perimeter elaboration of smaller Greek crosses and sacristies in Bramante's plan was simplified in Michelangelo's scheme to provide a more continuous ambulatory around the centralized dome. Moreover, the structure of the piers at the crossing was strengthened. The delicacy of

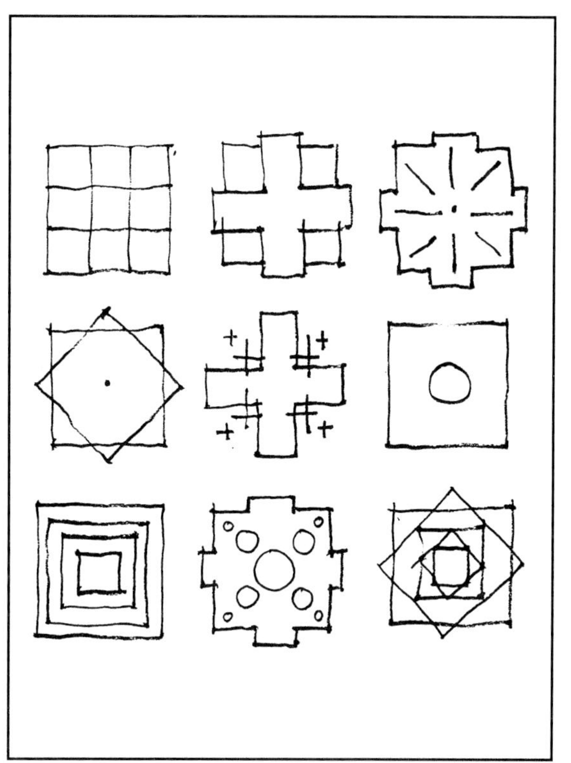

10.31 Diagrams of St. Peter's.

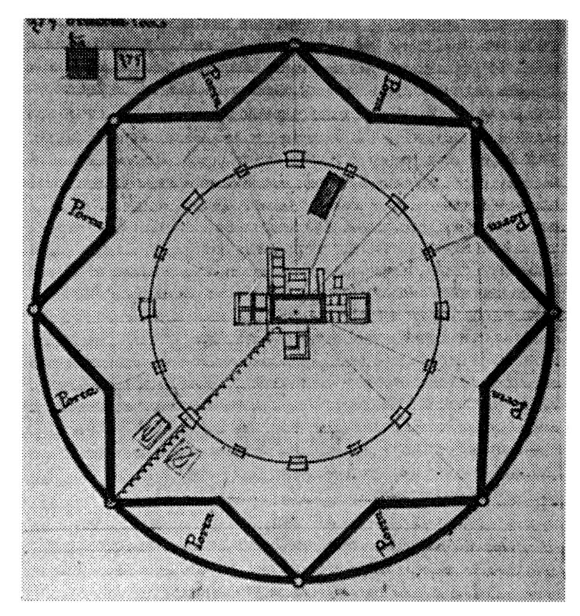

10.32 Antonio Averlino Filarete, Sforzinda, 1464, plan.

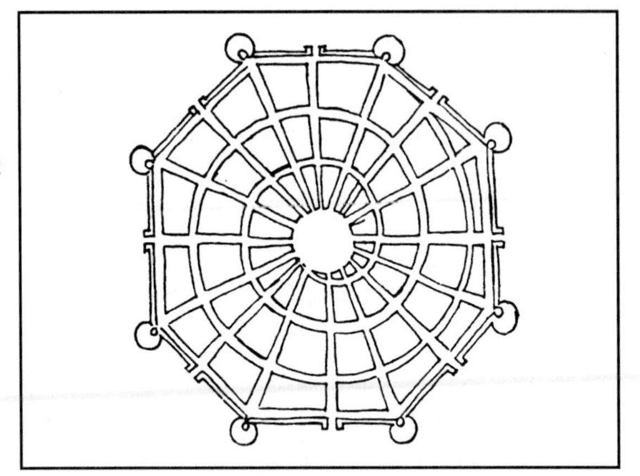

10.33 Left: Francesco di Giorgio Martini, "Plan of a City on a Hill", (from Codice Magliabecchiano, 1451-1464).

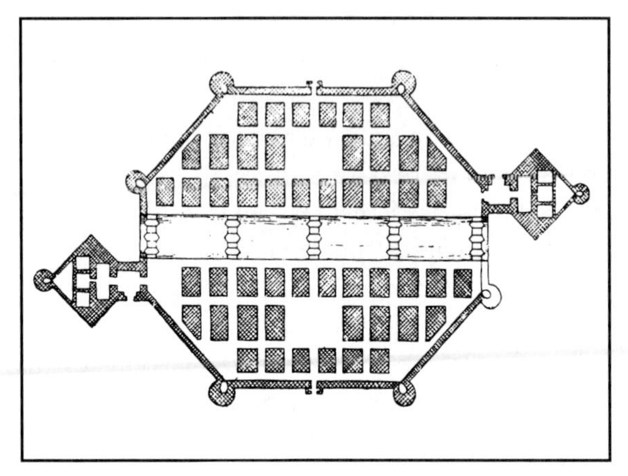

10.34 Right: Francesco di Giorgio Martini, "Plan of a City Crossed by a River", (from Codice Magliabecchiano, 1451-1464).

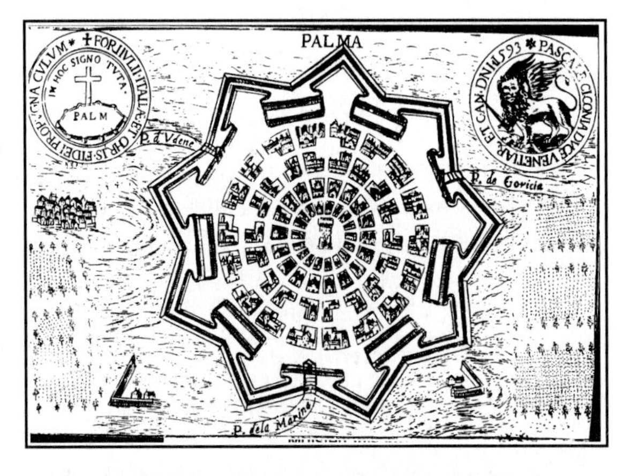

10.35 Vincenzo Scamozzi, Palmanova, plan, 1599.

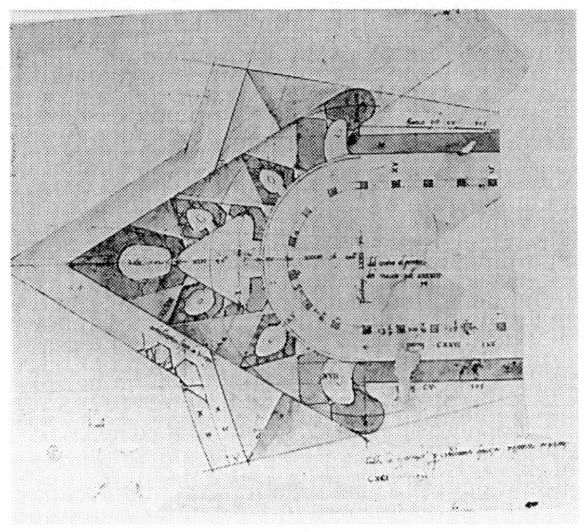

10.36 Baldassare Peruzzi, "Fortifications", Uffizi.

Bramante's piers did not provide sufficient structure to support the enormous dome.

Enthusiasm for the centralized planning carried over into Renaissance ideas about towns. Radial fortified plans such as **Antonio Averlino Filarete's** (1400-69) imaginary town of **Sforzinda** (1464), or **Francesco di Giorgio's ideal town plans** for different terrains abounded in Renaissance theory. Sforzinda was the site for an elaborate fairy tale, encompassing, among other things, a ten story tower hierarchically organized to house an observatory at the top and a brothel at the bottom. Most often, theory about ideal towns was a legitimate extension of fortification design, an important task for Renaissance architects. For example, most of **Peruzzi's** productive years were spent on **fortification design** for his embattled home town of Siena.

It was not until 1593 that **Vincenzo Scamozzi** (1552-1616) actually succeeded in building a radial town, **Palmanova**. Norberg-Schulz has observed that *"the ideal city of the Renaissance no longer expresses a communal form of life, such as the late medieval town, but forms the*

10.37 Anonymous, "Ideal Town", c. 1475-1500, Galleria Nazionale delle Marche, Urbino.

center of a small autocratic state. At the center of the ideal city we therefore find the palace of the signore connected to a large piazza."

Palmanova was a frontier town, a fortified military outpost. As such, it could be planned on a *tabula rasa*. With existing cities, only small urban interventions could be attempted. A late fifteenth-century painting in Urbino illustrates a prevalent view of an **"Ideal Town"**. The piazza is scenographically organized by one-point perspective, and a centralized building, like the protagonist in a play, occupies center stage. The singularity of the round building is emphasized by the subdued, repetitive nature of the buildings which line the square.

Just as painting and architecture influenced one another, so too did stage design influence ideas about urban space. Serlio explored scenographic space in the **"Tragic Scene"** from his *Five Books of Architecture* (1537-57). The convergence of parallel lines makes legible the three-dimensional recession of space and describes a tapering trapezoid in two dimensions. Distant objects, like the pyramid, obelisk and triumphal arch are brought to focus by the sur-

Of Perſpectiue

HOuses for Tragedies, must bee made for great personages, for that actions of loue, strange aduentures, and cruell murthers, (as you reade in ancient and moderne Tragedies) happen alwayes in the houses of great Lords, Dukes, Princes, and Kings. Therefore in such cases you must make none but stately houses, as you see it here in this Figure; wherein (for that it is so small) I could make no Princely Pallaces: but it is sufficient for the workeman to see the manner thereof, whereby he may helpe himselfe as time and place serueth: and (as I sayde in the Comicall) hee must alwayes study to please the eyes of the beholders, and forget not himselfe so much as to set a small building in stead of a great, for the reasons aforesayd. And for that I haue made all my Scenes of laths, couered with linnen, yet sometime it is necessary to make some things rising or bosing out; which are to bee made of wood, like the houses on the left side, whereof the Pillars, although they shorten, stand all vpon one Base, with some stayres, all couered ouer with cloth, the Cornices bearing out, which you must obserue to the middle part: But to giue place to the Galleries, you must set the other shortening Cloth somewhat backwards, and make a cornice aboue it, as you see: and that which I speake of these Buildings, you must vnderstand of all the rest, but in the Buildings which stand far backward the Painting worke, must supplie the place by shadowes without any bearing out: touching the artificiall lights, I haue spoken thereof in the Comicall worke. All that you make aboue the Roofe sticking out, as Chimneyes, Towers, Piramides, Oblisces, and other such like things or Images; you must make them all of thin bords, cut out round, and well coloured: But if you make any flat Buildings, they must stand somewhat farre inward, that you may not see them on the sides. In these Scenes, although some haue painted personages therein like supporters, as in a Gallery, or doore, as a Dog, Cat, or any other beasts: I am not of that opinion, for that standeth to long without stirring or mouing; but if you make such a thing to lie sleeping, that I hold withall. You may also make Images, Histories, or Fables of Marble, or other matter against a wall; but to represent the life, they ought to stirre. In the latter end of this Booke I will shew you how to make them.

10.38 Sebastiano Serlio, "Tragic Scene", 1557.

10.39 Leonardo da Vinci, "Mona Lisa," 1503-06, the Louvre, Paris.

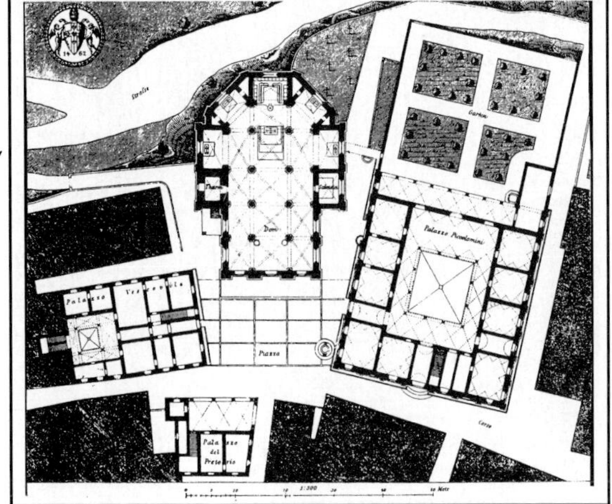

10.40 Bernardo Rossellino, Town Plan, Pienza, Italy, 1460.

rounding street walls, much as in the Urbino painting earlier examined.

Bernardo Rossellino (1409-64) was given the task of designing a town center for **Pienza**, seat of Pope Pius II. Planned as a whole, the buildings which comprise the town are proportionally related to each other, although their styles vary from classical to Gothic, almost as if Rossellino wished to set up a confrontation between the styles. In determining the form of the main space, Piazza Pio II, Rossellino did not look to idealized geometric forms but to scenographic distortions. The cathedral is perched at the edge of a steep cliff, its apse extending beyond the town wall to form an apparently centralized octagonal volume when seen from the valley. On top of the hill, a trapezoid of space is framed by four buildings of Rossellino's design, the Cathedral, the Palazzo Piccolomini, the Town Hall and the Bishop's Palace. The plasticity of the Gothic church facade is emphasized, while the planarity and tautness of surface is exaggerated in the flanking, classical buildings. Coding of the architectural language of the buildings is reversed by making the Gothic muscular and the classical seem immaterial.

The skewing of the Piccolomini Palace and Bishop's Palace forces the perspective towards the town hall, increasing the perceived length of the square and emphasizing the axial connection to the market beyond. At the same time, the splay allows the cathedral to slip forward into the square and the breadth of its facade to be emphasized. Instead of an unequivocal boundary, slots of space rush alongside the church and connect with distant views of the landscape. A collapse of space is provided by the skewing and the erasure of middle ground, identical to the technique used in contemporary portraits, such as ***Leonardo's "Mona Lisa"***.

Instead of the introversion typical of the medieval period, the substance of the town plan involves its engagement with the outlying landscape. The site and disposition of the palace is determined by the views it commands. Landscape is framed in three different ways, progressing from most mundane to most divine. One, the surrounding agricultural fields are brought into the spatial domain of Piazza Pio II through the displaced boundaries of the square. Two, a view of the natural landscape is provided from the idealized four-square garden of the Piccolomini Palace. Three, a clear view of a blue celestial rectangle is framed by the cornice of the Palace courtyard.

Michelangelo confronted a similar site in his design of the **Campidoglio**, or Capitoline Hill, in Rome, except that the hill top in Rome was not occupied by an entire town, as at Pienza, but by a collection of civic buildings. Incorporating two existing medieval buildings at irregular angles to one another, Michelangelo conceived of the space as an enormous trapezoid. The pressure between the two converging palaces, the Palazzo dei Senatori and the Palazzo dei Conservatori, frames a forced perspective towards the city in one direction and provides oblique glimpses into the Roman Fora in the other. An enormous outdoor room is constructed. The space between buildings, rather than any individual building, commands attention. In Pienza, the articulation of the four buildings in Piazza Pio II varied, but here there is a overarching unity. A colossal order of columns unifies the two levels of the

10.41
Rossellino, Pienza, view.

10.42
Rossellino, Pienza, Palazzo Piccolomini, courtyard view.

10.43 Left: Michelangelo, Campidoglio (Capitoline Hill), Rome, Italy, 1539, view.

10.44 Right: Campidoglio, view.

10.45 Campidoglio, view.

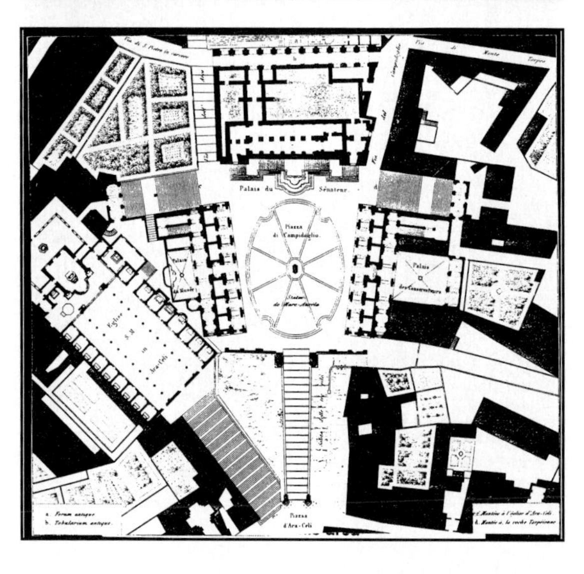

10.46 Campidoglio, plan.

Palazzo dei Conservatori and the Palazzo dei Senatori. Even the treatment of the ground plane contributes to the orchestrated definition of enclosure. The bulging central oval seems to erupt through the space and sponsor the distortions of the edges.

Michelangelo's Campidoglio was designed in 1539, at a time when the absolute power of the Roman church was shaken by the rise of Protestantism in the north and the Sack of Rome in 1527. Optimistic confidence in the ideal harmonies of the Early and High Renaissance gave way to **Mannerism,** a strain of Classicism which made thematic the tensions and incongruities suppressed or sublimated within the classical tradition.

The relationship between landscape and man-made artifact was explored in numerous designs for formal gardens, the medium in which Mannerism found its most articulate expression. The **Villa Lante,** in Bagnaia, was built for Cardinal Gambero in 1566 by **Giacomo Barozzi da Vignola** (1507-73). The garden uses an axial path, a procession up (or down) a hill, and the recurrence of fountains to develop an allegory about culture versus nature. Procession along the strong central axis provides a

10.47 *Left:* G.B.Vignola, Villa Lante, 1566, Bagnaia, Italy, view of garden casini and path up the hill.

10.48 *Right:* Villa Lante, view of garden towards the portal.

10.49 Villa Lante, view of the gambero fountain.

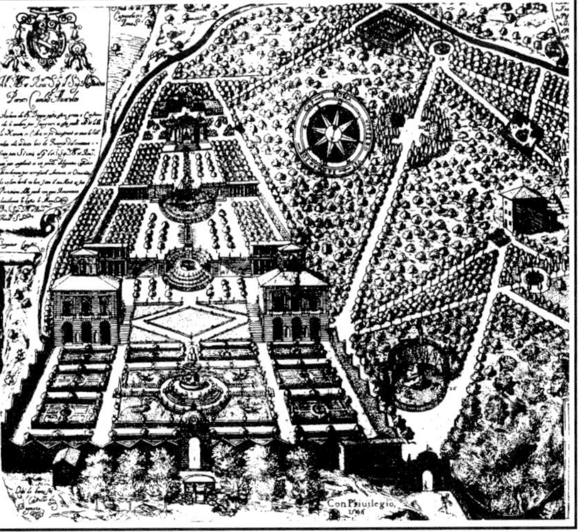

10.50 Villa Lante, plan perspective.

very different narrative depending on your direction of travel.

The sunny lower terrace, on the same level as the town, contains an ideal four-square garden centered around an ideal four-square fountain. Facing Bagnaia, a heroically scaled, handsome stone portal is inserted in the surrounding hedge, making evident the association of this garden with the urbane realm of the town. Indeed, the garden axis continues with a slight deflection into the town to link up with a tower in the main square. The clear symmetrical organization of the ***parterre*** garden at ground level sets up a motif of natural disorder held in check by rational order. At the lowest terrace, reason and geometry dominate. The axis through the garden is marked by a series of water features which grow more or less orderly depending on their position on the path and the condition of the surrounding landscape.

The garden is not organized around a villa, although here the structure is not even a villa, but just a garden house or *casino*. Instead, the axis of the garden splits the building in half, doubling it. A zigzag path continues up the hill, through the gateway formed by the paired villas. The axis is strongly stated throughout

10.51
G.B. Vignola, Villa Giulia, Rome, Italy, c. 1550-51, section.

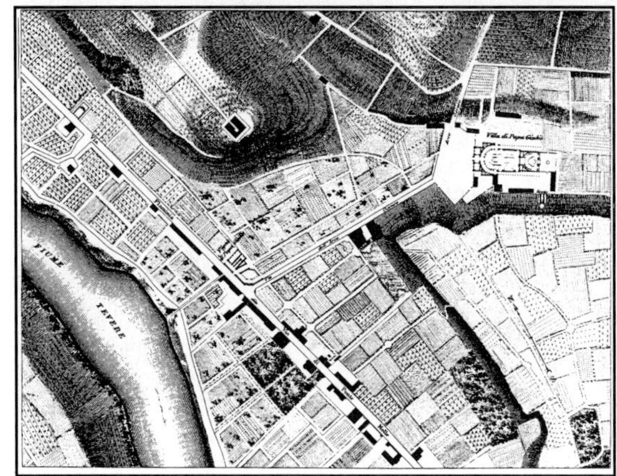

10.52
Villa Giulia, site plan.

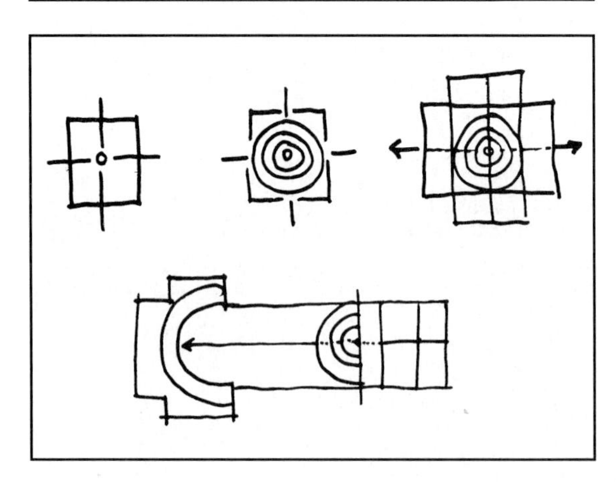

10.53
Villa Giulia, diagram

the scheme, but the path is organized around the axis, not on it. A circular fountain pins together the next two terraces. On the lowest level, the fountain occupies the center of an ideal condition. Here the location of the fountain is more ambiguous: it occupies a seam between two different domains.

The procession upwards reveals increasingly more natural surroundings. Fountains metamorphosize from pristine, geometric vessels into dining tables with water troughs for chilling wine and fruit; to swirling, organic linear, forms, resembling vertebrae or a crawfish (in Italian, the cardinal's name, *Gambero,* means 'crawfish'). Finally, one arrives at the dark grotto source which seems to be cut into the rock. The fecund disorder of nature overwhelms the attempt of humankind to impose order. Rows of columns cease to have tectonic function and become architectural cousins to the surrounding stand of trees. Even the surfaces of buildings are encrusted with scales and merge with the rocks.

Starting at the top and proceeding downwards, an affirmation of order is developed along the procession. On the path upwards,

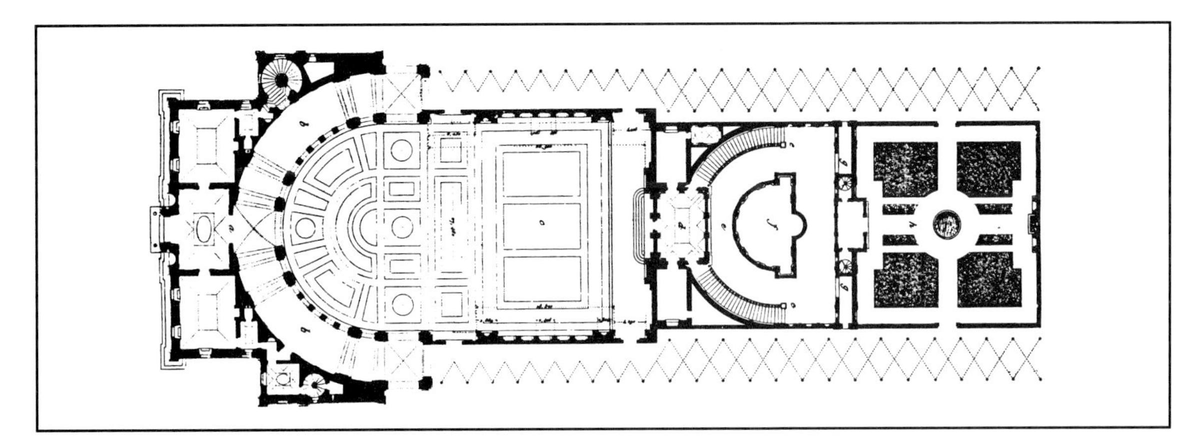

10.54
Villa Giulia, plan.

one's view is obscured by the darkness of the forest and the rising hill; on the path down, the entire axial progression is clearly in view. Order is reasserted and natural disorder is relegated to the margins. Yet even at the top of the garden, next to the grotto source and equal in size, Vignola designed a secret garden. Its ideal, four-square arrangement suggests that there is kinship between the extremes of nature and geometry.

10.55
Villa Giulia, grotto.

Vignola's design for the **Villa Giulia** in Rome engages similar themes of natural versus geometrical order, but here the narrative unfolds as one proceeds down into the sunken grotto, the carved center of the garden. Situated in the countryside, the entire villa was designed within a tight rectangular box. Nature of the ordinary variety was not welcome here, instead, Vignola constructed an argument which could be internalized within the clearly defined boundaries.

10.56
Villa Giulia, hemicycle.

The transformation of garden and water motifs from geometric ideality to an organic or rustic condition occurs along a line at the Villa Lante. At the Villa Giulia, the garden emerges

10.57 Giulio Romano, Palazzo del Tè, Mantua, Italy, 1525-43, courtyard.

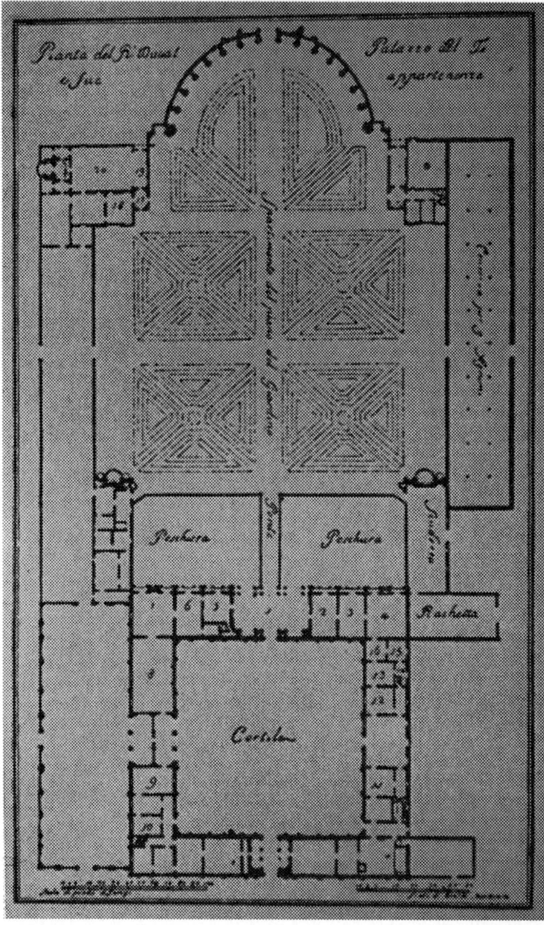

10.58 Palazzo del Tè, plan.

through the dismantling and pulling apart of an ideal paradigm. The large curved colonnade attached to the main building gestures across the evacuated sward at its displaced center. There, an exedral grotto carves into the ground, each excavated layer growing cooler, damper, and more like the primal condition of the earth itself. Enchanted creatures are imagined to dwell in this **nympheum**. Their stone images replace conventional architectural elements. On the opposite side of the nympheum, once again on ground level, a final portal opens onto a reconstituted ideal paradise garden.

Giulio Romano's (c. 1499-1546) design for the **Palazzo del Tè** ('Tea Palace') in Mantua, 1525-43, investigates another theme that greatly preoccupied the Mannerists, a theme internal to the discourse of architecture itself: the conventions of architectural language. Classical ornament, tectonics, and even the meaning of architectural terms are challenged. Giulio highlights the difficulty of architecture to do anything or mean anything. Although playful in its fanciful manipulation of linguistic tropes, the architecture of the Palazzo del Tè expresses the tensions and anxieties of an age whose stability and belief in itself was crumbling.

At first glance, the building appears to be a conventional Italian palazzo. A rectangular courtyard is enclosed within a 'square doughnut' of rooms, arranged ***enfilade***. Beyond the courtyard is a garden, flanked by outbuildings and terminated by a hemicyclical colonnade. However, the Palazzo del Tè is anything but conventional. No two facades are alike, and there is a constant shift in texture, articulation, and rhythm of elements. Made of brick, the walls are stuccoed to look like large blocks of stone. The blocks closest to the earth are more aggressively rusticated than the smooth blocks on the upper story. Giulio makes use of an architectural convention which equates the work of nature with **rustication**, the uneven rough treatment of the stone surfaces, like those found in the landscape. A cage of smooth pilasters establishes the outermost layer of the wall, almost as if the rusticated masonry were held back in a structural cage. Indeed, the **voussoirs** over the windows seem to be escaping: the keystones break free from the string course above and meet the plane of the pilasters.

In the interior courtyard the use of rustication is even more forceful and the tension among tectonic elements and the layers of the wall surface is exacerbated. On the exterior, the pilasters are unnaturally flat; here they are fully plastic engaged columns, resting on bases in front of the rusticated wall. The cornice they support seems to be in the process of crumbling; triglyphs slip down from their proper position and seem to exchange places with keystones over openings. The absence and mutability of elements is coupled with redundancy. Flat arches of massive voussoirs frame the openings, but that is not all. A pediment also defines the opening, its vestigial character made evident by the split between halves, as if the upward thrust of the keystone had rent it asunder. The building is not conceived of as inert matter. It is a living organism whose tectonic stresses cause it to quiver, bend or recoil. The blind windows above the central niches are examples of this. Where the rusticated blocks are removed, an undulating smooth surface appears, as though the skin of the building were alive.

10.59 Palazzo del Tè, garden facade.

10.60 Palazzo del Tè, detail of garden facade.

10.61 Palazzo del Tè, Hall of Giants.

10.62 Anonymous, Villa Orsini, or 'Sacred Grove,' Bomarzo, Italy, c. 1552, leaning tower.

10.63 Villa Orsini, garden giant.

Strange asymmetries emerge within the symmetrical organization of the building. This is partly because Giulio Romano built the Palazzo del Tè around a pre-existing farmhouse; yet he used the existing condition to his own ends. The garden facade is the best illustration of Giulio's playful manipulation of symmetry. A transformation in the solidity and articulation of the wall occurs from center to outer extreme. The central opening is an A-B-A arrangement of arched and horizontally spanned openings, supported by free-standing columns. Moving outwards, the A-B-A rhythm continues, but the 'A' term is slightly modified to set up a new pairing. Gradually, column becomes pier, arch becomes enframed niche, and a wall that was primarily columnar becomes primarily solid.

A masterful dialogue takes place between the architectural expression of the building and the narrative content of **Giulio's** interior wall and ceiling paintings. The **Hall of Giants** pictorially represents the collapse of the room itself; subsequent articulation of the building seems to respond to the calamity wrought by the painted giants. Metonymic troping also takes place, in which one thing stands in for another or a part stands for the whole. A painted figure of a little horse, in Italian *'cavalletto'*, is placed above a door instead of the expected door molding, also called *'cavalletto'* in Italian. In Vignola's gardens, nature and culture hold each other in check. Here, nature is beginning to get the upper hand. Language, the chief repository for cultural meanings, is shown to be inadequate to the task of communication.

The last Mannerist garden we shall look at is the **Villa Orsini**, or 'Sacred Grove' in Bomarzo. At Bomarzo there is no longer even a vestige of the order and calm asserted by the latent geometry in Vignola's gardens. The entire landscape has metamorphosized into a nest of monsters. Caves become enormous heads; rocks become the grooved backs of tortoises or the tails of dragons. The balanced world in scale with the Vitruvian man is topsy-turvy. Even structures which resemble conventional architecture distort one's sense of scale and orientation. A tower leans, a triumphal arch sinks, and temples are present as fragments. A stone plaque explains Orsini's motive in the design of the garden: *"Sol per sfogar' il cor,"* "solely to overwhelm the heart." Instead of striving to reflect universal, objective truths, as in the High Renaissance, at the Villa Orsini the subjectivity of experience is celebrated. A self-consciousness typical of the modern sensibility is at play.

The Renaissance is characterized by experimentation with ideal forms, ideal geometries and ideal proportions. Curiously enough, very few examples of such ideality can be found. Implicit within any high style is already its dissolution into Mannerism, Expressionism or the moribund rigidity of Neoclassicism. As architects master a language and a repertoire of forms, they set new challenges for themselves, some of them accessible to the public, some of them internal to architectural discourse. Already in 1460, in Rossellino's plan for Pienza, there is a distortion of ideal geometry in favor of an exaggerated scenographic effect. By 1484, in Bramante's Santa Maria presso San Satiro in Milan, (Chapter 5) a centralized church is conjured up in a T-shaped space by using perspectival tricks.

In the medieval period, very few architectural drawings were done and even fewer

10.64 Federico Zuccari, Detail of a House on Via Gregoriano, Rome, c.1550.

10.65 Wendel Dietterlin, "The Victory of Death", 1598.

drawing conventions were stabilized. In the Renaissance, in addition to the codification of scientific perspective there was also a methodical application of orthographic projection, a way of drawing which favored orthogonal views of buildings. It is not surprising that such design techniques inspired the production of buildings that could be fully studied by plan, section and elevation. The complicated curvature of Gothic vaults, derived from direct **stereometric** work with stone, was supplanted by an architectural space that could be fully understood as planar surfaces.

Renaissance architecture was not rule-bound and inflexible. A tremendous range for invention and interpretation was provided by the classical language and the archaeological models that were followed. Moreover, although the adoption of Platonic forms limits the choices available to architects, the intricacies of proportional systems expand the range of combinatory possibilities.

Use of simple volumes, modules, repetition and proportion is not the exclusive province of a classical architecture. **Louis Kahn** applies the same tools and rigor to his work in a spare, twentieth-century language. **Le Corbusier** attempted to solve many of the same proportional questions as the Renaissance theoreticians in his *Modulor* of 1948.

10.66 Louis Kahn, Mellon Center for British Art, New Haven, Connecticut, c.1974, view of center space.

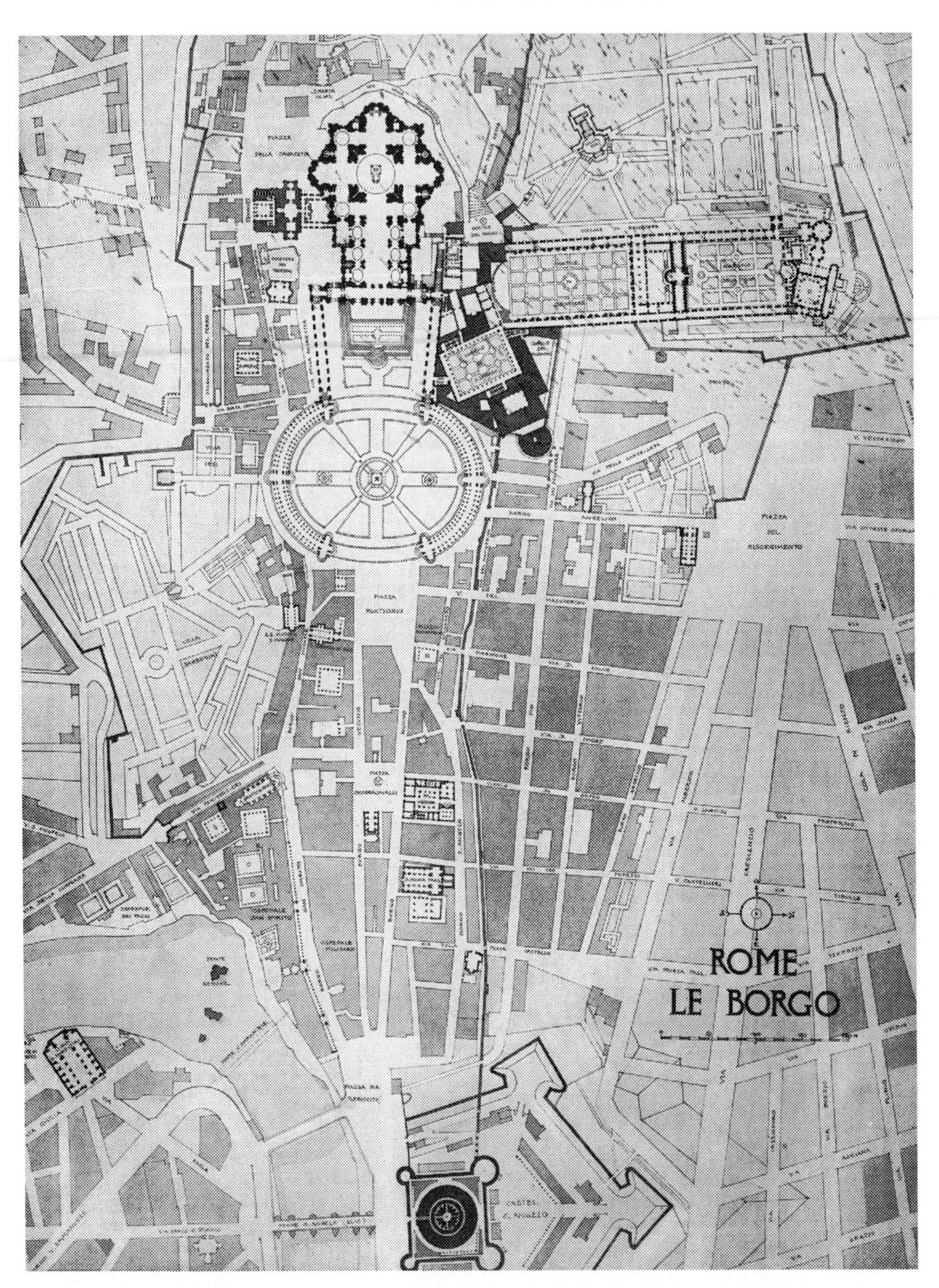

11.0
G.L. Bernini, St. Peter's Cortile (Courtyard), Rome.

Chapter 11

The Baroque Period: Theater & Rhetoric

"Del vero più bella è la menzogna..." (Lies are more beautiful than reality)

- ALGAROTTI

The sack of Rome in 1527 ended the creative activity of the Italian Renaissance. In its wake came a period of upheaval, uncertainty, and finally, reconsolidation. Renaissance Humanism vaunted reason as a means by which one might know God; the Baroque period fostered a reprisal of mysticism and rapture, typical of religious practice during the Middle Ages when the power of the church was at its height. New religious orders rose up around new Baroque saints. St. Philip Neri, St. Ignatius Loyola, St. John of the Cross and St. Teresa were all canonized in 1622. The rites practiced by these orders verged on theater. The Oratorians of St. Philip Neri made music the centerpiece of their worship; the Society of Jesus of St. Ignatius invited worshippers to re-enact the suffering of Christ through 'Spiritual Exercises.' The Counter Reformation reaffirmed confidence in traditional doctrines and traditional architectural forms, such as the longitudinal church. After the austerity of the early part of the Counter Reformation ended, a vigorous campaign of building and art patronage began.

Theater, rhetoric and persuasion are terms often associated with the Baroque. The clear geometry of Renaissance forms and rational precision of Renaissance space was supplanted by an architecture suffused with inexplicable inundations of light, dynamic play among masses, contrapuntal tension among wall, column and sculpture, and an engagement with the urban context which makes it difficult to say where a building ends and the surrounding town begins. Once scientific perspective made it possible to study the space between things, buildings were no longer conceived as isolated objects, but rather as part of an urban continuum.

One-point perspective, typical of Renaissance perspective drawing, gave way in the Baroque period to more dynamic two and three-point perspective accompanied by exaggerated figural **foreshortening.** The shift of the vantage point from the center increased the plasticity of the depicted object and set up a dynamic tension between the diagonal recession of representational space and the orthogonality of the picture plane. The static calm of the Renaissance painting of an *Ideal Town* (Chapter 10) is in sharp contrast to the sense of movement and acceleration created in a two point perspective,

11.1 Giuseppe Bibiena, Engraving from <u>Architetture e prospettive,</u> 1740.

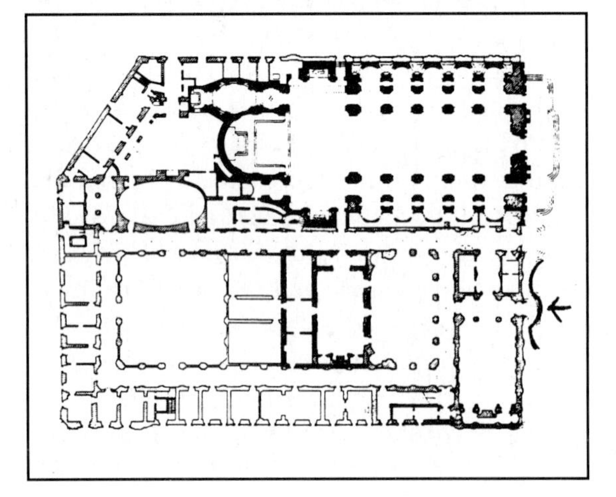

11.2 F. Borromini, Oratorio of S. Filippo Neri, Rome, 1637, site plan.

such as **Giuseppe Bibiena's** engraving from 1740. Not surprisingly, Bibiena's drawing is for a stage set. In the Baroque period, the entirety of urban space was understood theatrically. As Giulio Carlo Argan remarked, *"buildings did not occupy space, they created it."*

In the Renaissance, the practice of perspective drawing influenced architectural form in urban schemes by Michelangelo for the Campidoglio and Rossellino for Pienza. In both cases the distortion of an ideal condition made possible powerful relationships among buildings and landscape. The architects recognized that built form does not have to tell the truth. In other words, the geometrical shape and arrangement of parts in buildings do not have to embody absolute cosmic truths in their own perfection; they can respond to the subjective condition of the viewer. The illusionistic methods of the Baroque period can be seen as a radical extension of earlier experiments, and indeed as developments in the tradition of the optical corrections and refinements used by the ancient Greeks. But in the Baroque period, the rhetoric of the architecture became the subject matter, rather than a means towards an expressive end.

Baroque architecture can be seen as a synthesis of the grandeur and muscularity of Classicism and the mysticism and wonder of the Gothic. As in Gothic Architecture, dramatic, irrational use of light is used to conjure up a divine presence. However, the Gothic uses light to render form immaterial while the Baroque uses light to make manifest its plasticity. In both architectures, the delineation of form is ambiguous and surface is not a singular membrane, but comprised of many layers. In Gothic, the layering is structural while in the Baroque, the counterpoint between wall, column and space is rhythmic. Both generate complex plans from the superimposition of clear, simple geometric figures. In the Gothic, each point is marked tectonically, as in the pier system of Amiens Cathedral. In the Baroque, the multiple geometries can be synthesized into a single, undulating line whose origin may seem inexplicable, as in the plan of San Carlo alle Quattro Fontane (Chapter 5). In both there is a clear schism between the interior definition of space and the form, scale and elaboration of the facade. The Gothic facade, like an enormous billboard, looms in front of the cathedral, its only connection to the interior one of adjacency. In the Baroque, the facade is also understood as an independent entity, a rhetorical screen that promotes the messages of the church to the city at large. The independence of the elements makes it possible for the architect to decompose the constituent parts and reassemble them in a new way. In the **Oratory for San Filippo Neri** (1637) **Borromini** dislocates the facade from an axial relationship with the oratory and organizes its alignment with the monastery courtyard instead. The entire structure of the religious organism must be reassembled in the mind of the viewer. The architectural experience of the fragments is rather like the temporal unfolding of the plot in a theater production.

Gianlorenzo Bernini (1598-1680) has been called the Michelangelo of the Baroque period. He was certainly the most remarkable sculptor of his age and a brilliant architect as well. His representation of **Santa Teresa in Ecstasy** for the Cornaro Chapel, Rome, goes beyond con-

11.3 Oratorio of S. Filippo Neri, view of elevation.

11.4 Gianlorenzo Bernini, "Santa Teresa in Ecstasy", Cornaro Chapel, Santa Maria della Vittoria, Rome, 1657, Anonymous Eighteenth Century Painting, Staatliches Museum, Schwerin.

11.5 Santa Teresa in Ecstasy, detail.

ventional understanding of statuary and brings the entire chapel into a web of relationships that commingles 'real' and 'illusionistic' space. At the center of the composition is the recumbent figure of Santa Teresa at the moment of her mystical vision. The Saint is not pictured in isolation; she is dramatically engaged with a beautiful angel who is about to pierce a golden arrow into her heart. Action is arrested the moment before Santa Teresa receives her divine wound. Inert marble has been charged with grace and vitality. Santa Teresa's drapery billows in a supernatural wind, her soft skin dimples and dew seems to form on her lips. But that is not all.

Reality and illusion fuse together in Bernini's work. Chromatically rich marbles and shining metals are used to adorn the chapel walls. As if architecture too were enlivened by the mystical force emanating from the statue, the **aedicula** which houses the statue erupts from the wall and the pediment splits to reveal the figures. A hidden source from behind the pediment rakes golden light down on the enraptured figures, its luminescence carried directly towards the image of the saint by shining metal rays. The perspectival ceiling painting above helps sustain the illusion. Aggressively foreshortened cherubs pull apart the clouds to reveal a luminous sky, the apparent source for the light shining on the saint. Housed in the flanking walls of the chapel are likenesses of the Cornaro family, witnessing the miracle as if they were at the theater. Enveloped in the illusionistic space of Bernini's composition, the viewer too is caught up in the voyeurism and becomes at once subject and object, caught by the gaze of the Cornaros and the divinities above.

Architectural manipulation of perspectival space is not the sole province of projects as dramatic as Bernini's composition. There is an implication of perspectival depth in the development of facades, such as that of **Santa Susanna** by **Carlo Maderno** (1556-1629). The facade is comprised of overlapping layers with the densest zone at the center. An increasing plasticity of elements ranges from the flat pilasters at the extreme outer edges, to the engaged columns in the middle, to the free-standing columns at the center. **SS. Anastasio and Vincenzo**, by **Martino Longhi the Younger,**

(1602-1660) takes the method of articulation in Santa Susanna and goes even further. No fewer than four pedimented structures are layered one atop the other to create a sense of depth and density in the facade, as though a deep space had collapsed to form the more or less planar elevation.

The intense effects created by Baroque manipulation of space, light, color and form led many eighteenth and nineteenth century observers to view it as a degeneration of the Renaissance. The same classical language was used, but the refinement and balanced equipoise typical of the earlier age had yielded to something wild and histrionic. Heinrich Wölfflin ascribed this transformation to a *"blunted sensibility"* in the Baroque period, which occasioned architects to strive to outdo the 'special effects' of earlier buildings, even at the expense of the Albertian dictate that nothing could be added nor subtracted, except for the worse. To Wölfflin, Baroque architects had abandoned architecture in its proper sense and had adopted the criteria more appropriate to painting: *"It is generally agreed among historians of art that the essential characteristic of Baroque architecture is its* ***painterly*** *quality. Instead of following its own nature, architecture strove after effects which really belong to a different art form: it became "painterly... Freedom of line and interplay of light and shade are satisfying to the painterly taste in direct proportion to the degree to which they transgress the rules of architecture."* (*Renaissance and Baroque*, 1888).

In fact, the spiritual climate had changed and the vigorous, persuasive effects of Baroque architecture were effective vehicles to carry new messages. The Humanism of the Renaissance,

11.6 Carlo Maderno, S.Susanna, Rome, 1597-1603, view of the facade.

11.7 Martino Longhi the Younger, SS. Vincenzo and Anastasio, Rome, 1646-50, view of the facade.

embodied in ideal, self-sufficient geometries, gave way to an age characterized by powerful, sweeping systems of reform and the consolidation of power in the hands of a few, i.e. a powerful papacy in Rome, and the reign of Louis XIV (1638-1715) in France. The persuasive power of Baroque architecture helped to stabilize and reinforce those authorities. The invention of calculus introduced the concept of infinity into the repertoire of mathematical terms. Galileo Galilei (1564-1642) saw astral bodies through his telescope that violated a centuries-old belief in a fixed number of stars in the heavenly firmament. After such staggering discoveries, Euclidean elements and Platonic form were never again sufficient in the description of the universe. The perfect circle of Renaissance cosmology had been broken by dynamism and the possibility of infinite space.

The early part of the Baroque period (characterized by Wittkower as the time before the canonization of the great Baroque saints) did not produce any master architects. Its defining architectural agenda was issued by **Pope Sixtus V** (1521-1590), who governed from 1585-1590. During that time, massive reforms were enacted, including the restructuring of the College of Cardinals, the draining of the pontine marshes, the building of a water system (the Acqua Felice), the establishment of workers' housing and the completion of Michelangelo's dome at St. Peter's. Little progress had been

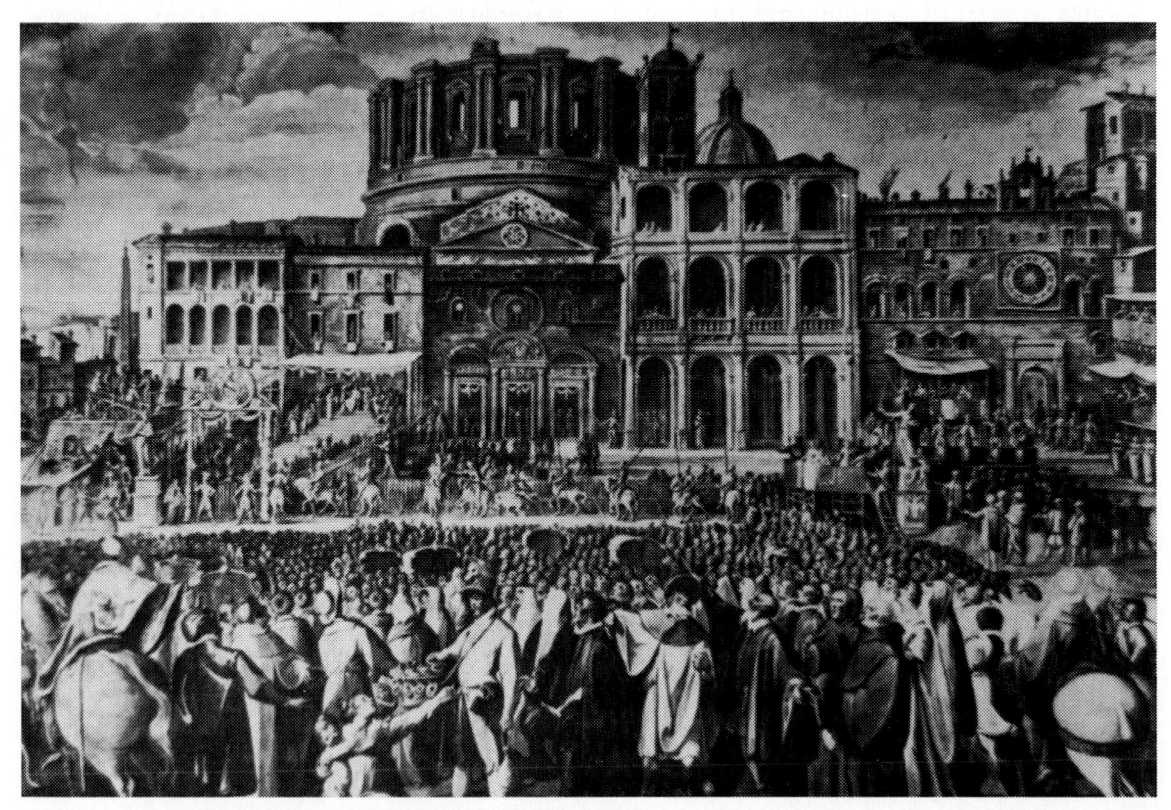

11.8 St.Peter's at the beginning of Sixtus V's pontificate. The dome is missing from the church and the obelisk is in the process of being erected.

made on the dome since the architect's death some twenty-five years before. Sixtus V employed 800 workers days, nights and weekends to complete the job. In the end, the dome was finished in twenty-two months. Sixtus' most important reform was the **restructuring of Rome** itself. His aim was to change Rome from a small medieval town into the appropriate seat for the Vatican and the most sacred site in Christendom. It was especially important that all reforms be completed by the year 1600, a Holy Year in which many pilgrims from afar could be expected to visit the city.

Recognizing that the entire city of Rome was too vast and too complicated to be rebuilt, even by a Pope, Sixtus and his architect **Domenico Fontana** (1543-1607) concentrated on making a few precise interventions to organize important views and relationships among monuments. Giant **obelisks**, which the Romans had brought from Egypt as a mark of their conquest, were surmounted by crosses, symbols of the Christian dominion over the old Rome. These obelisks were then erected in front of the most important churches along the pilgrimage route: St. Peter's, Santa Maria Maggiore, and St. John in Laterano. A fourth obelisk was erected at the Porta del Popolo, the northern and most heavily trafficked town gate. In place of the narrow, irregular, congested alleys in the old medieval city, Sixtus cut broad, straight roads to organize the pilgrimage route. Fontana boasted that five

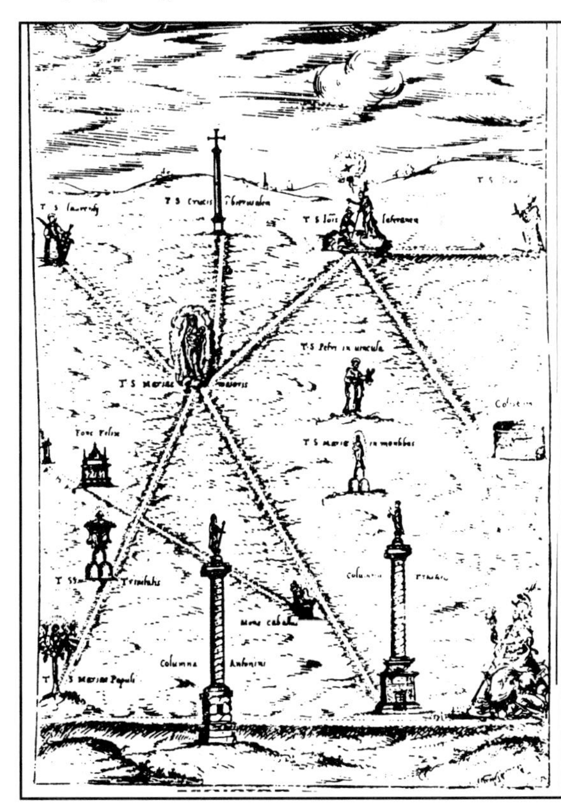

11.9 Left: Sixtus V's plan of Rome.

11.10 Right: G.F. Bordino, Engraving of the Streets of Sixtus V, 1588.

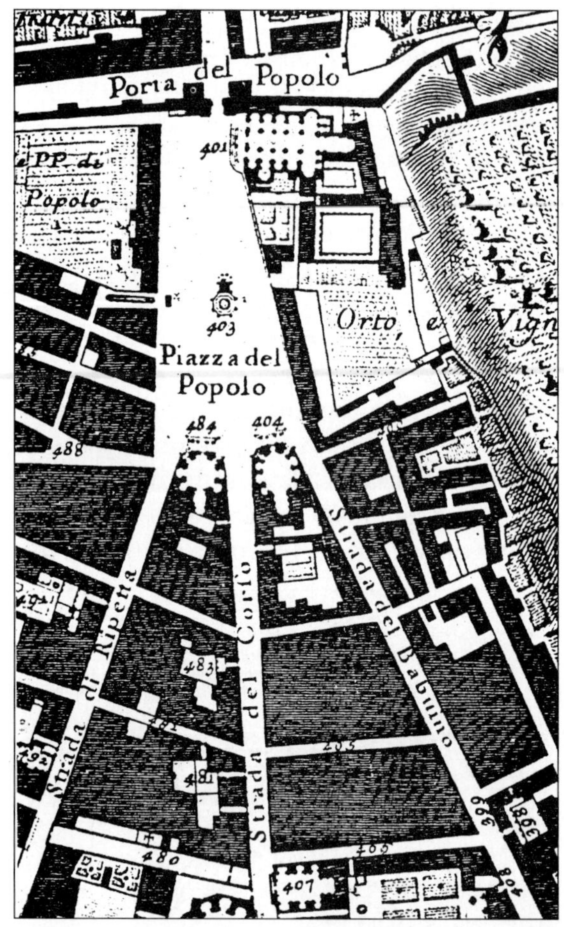

11.11
Piazza del Popolo, detail from the Nolli Plan, 1748.

11.12
Piazza del Popolo, G.B. Piranesi, engraving showing the Rainaldi churches.

carriages could ride abreast through the streets. Axial views from one monument down the straight roads would terminate in an obelisk in front of the next monument, and the pilgrim could proceed with confidence. False facades were erected along the new roads that traversed unpopulated areas of Rome to promote settlement and to create the impression of a vast, thriving city. At one point in the scheme, two of Sixtus V's new roads cross, the Strada Felice, intended to link the Porta del Popolo with Santa Maria Maggiore, and the Strada Pia, which links the Porta Pia (the easterly gate of town) to an obelisk in front of the papal Quirinale Palace. This special moment in the urban plan was marked by chamfering the corners of all four buildings. In this way, an octagonal space was created at the intersection. In each corner a fountain was placed. The most famous of the four corners is occupied by the **Borromini** church, **San Carlo alle Quattro Fontane**, which means "Saint Charles at the Four Fountains".

Edmund Bacon, in the *Design of Cities*, provides an illuminating discussion of Sixtus V's plan for Rome. He puts forward the "Theory of the Second Man", which maintains that one architect (or Pope) need not put an entire urban plan into action at a single historical moment. If the diagram and idea are strong enough, people in subsequent generations will take it upon themselves to complete the work. This is what happened to Sistine Rome. The network of monuments and obelisks included in Sixtus' V's original scheme expanded to include and give order to more monuments in the city including secular ones, like the Colosseum, the river port (Porta della Ripetta), and the later Spanish

Steps, which forge a sectional link between the axis from the Porta del Popolo to its continuation in the Strada Felice.

Points within the network were further developed over time. The radial disposition of roads from the Porta del Popolo prompted the location of twin churches by **Carlo Rainaldi** (1611-91) in 1660 to mark the threshold into the city. Eventually, in 1813 Valdier implemented a plan to ovalize the square. The expansion regularized the loosely defined fan of space into a clear geometric figure, and at the same time made connections east and west, to the Pincio Gardens and the Tiber River respectively.

We have already discussed the plan of San Carlo alle Quattro Fontane (1635-36), but the development of the facade, c.1665, is a direct response to the site at the Quattro Fontane. The facade is not conceived of as the exterior elaboration of the built volume, nor as a planar surface attached to it. Instead, it is an independent screen which undulates and inflects towards the intersection as it peels away from the wall, as though it had a life of its own. At Santa Susanna and SS. Vincenzo and Anastasio there is an implication of planar distortion created by surface layers and column rhythms. Here the surface literally warps, allowing the facade to command the octagonal square of the crossing, rather than just the area of the Strada Pia directly across from it.

Borromini's urban intervention at San Carlo alle Quattro Fontane demonstrates one solution to a typically Baroque problem: the location of an important, figural building within a continuous, scenographically conceived urban fabric. Farther down the Strada Pia, opposite the long arm of Domenico Fontana's Quirinale Palace,

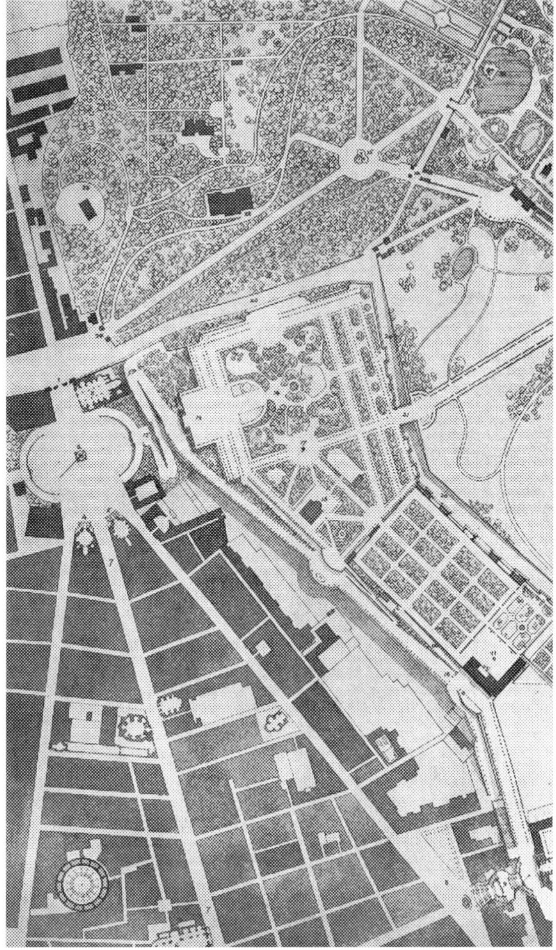

11.13
Piazza del Popolo, ovalized space of the Piazza , showing the connection to the Pincio and Villa Borghese.

11.14
G. de Rossi, engraving of San Carlo alle Quattro Fontane, with the Strada Felice terminating at the obelisk of Santa Maria Maggiore.

11.15
Detail of the Nolli Plan, showing the Quattro Fontane, the Quirinale, the Porta Pia, the Spanish Steps, and S. Maria Maggiore.

another strategy is used by **Bernini** in the siting of **San Andrea al Quirinale,** c.1658-70. Bernini's task is rendered especially delicate because he had to focus proper attention on his church, but at the same time, be careful not to compete with the greater importance of the papal palace across the street. While Borromini peels away surface to create figure, Bernini carves a shallow space into the continuous street edge and frames it with low walls. Here he places his ovalized church which rises above the low walls like a fully plastic object-in-the-round. The pedimented temple front overlaps the low wall, so the concave space of the street is invaded by the convexity of the object. The fully sculptural projection of the hemicyclical aedicula into the street niche reinforces the dynamic tension between object and edge.

The relationship of a figural object with respect to a figural void is thematic in Bernini's work. Even when Pope Alexander VII commissioned him to do a study of the Pantheon, the archetypal object building, Bernini proceeded to add towers to the facade, as though a central-

11.16 Left: Francesco Borromini, San Carlo alle Quattro Fontane, Rome, 1635-36, facade.

11.17 Right: Gianlorenzo Bernini, San Andrea al Quirinale, Rome, 1658-70, facade.

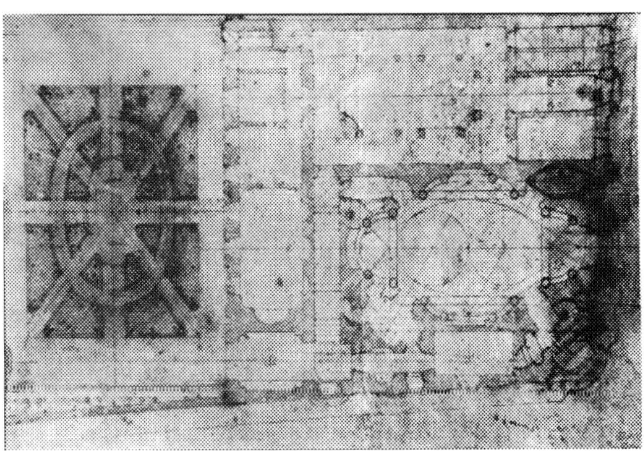

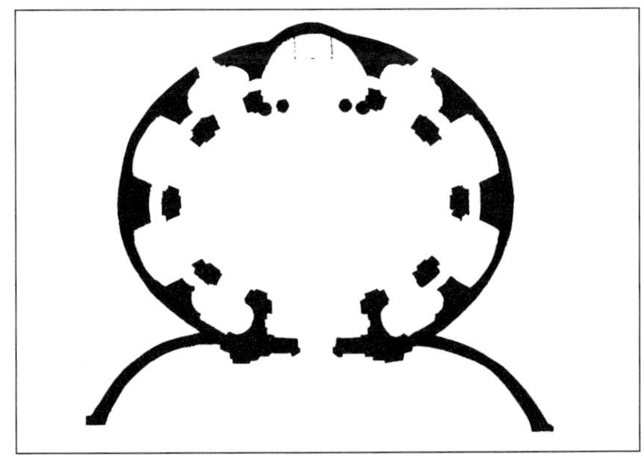

11.18 Left: F. Borromini, San Carlo alle Quattro Fontane, plan, Albertina, Vienna.

11.19 Right: Gianlorenzo Bernini, San Andrea al Quirinale, plan.

ized building could only be understood with respect to a *scenae frons*, as in San Andrea al Quirinale. Ultimately, Bernini's projects for the Pantheon were never realized. Pope Alexander feared he *"did not have sufficient talent."*

At **Santa Maria della Assunzione**, in the hill town of Arricia, **Bernini** had an opportunity to reprise his thoughts about object buildings begun with the San Andrea and the Pantheon. But while the former two projects placed great contextual constraints on the architect, in Arricia he was free to place his building anywhere. It was the sort of site dreamed of by Renaissance architects who required isolated, open sites for the realization of perfect centralized volumes, such as Santa Maria della Consolazione in Todi. Bernini constructs a great horse-shoe building as an architectural frame for his church and screens off the disordered medieval part of town from the new Baroque square. Into the center of horseshoe, a round Pantheonic temple is placed, its axis aligned with that of the Chigi Palace on the opposite side of the square. A trapezoidal space is formed, partly in response to existing street patterns and the lay of the land, and partly to stress the relationship between the two buildings and their landscape.

The slippage between the ovalized, curvilinear recess at San Andrea al Quirinale and ovalized church is here made coincident. Bernini constructs a grand figural void and immediately occupies it with a grand figural object, permitting him to achieve both the Renaissance ambition of centralized free-standing building and the Baroque ambition of continuous scenographically orchestrated urban fabric. The slot of space between the church and the surrounding building contains ramped stairs which descend to the older part of the town.

11.20
G.B. Falda, engraving of the Pantheon showing towers sometimes atributed to Gianlorenzo Bernini, c.1665.

One of Sixtus V's first acts as Pope was the erection of the obelisk in front of St. Peter's. The task of moving and hoisting the stone shaft into position tested the limits of sixteenth-century engineering. Sixtus was unable to see the completion of the Basilica in his life time. It was not until 1612 that Maderno's work on the nave extension and facade were completed. In 1656 Bernini was called upon to design a piazza in front of the great church. The space had to be large enough to accommodate crowds of pilgrims. Formally it had to respond to Sixtus V's obelisk and the church itself.

The great colonnaded **courtyard in front of St. Peter's** marks **Bernini's** final exploration of the relationship between figural space and figural object. At San Andrea they overlap; at Santa Maria dell'Assunzione they are concentric; at the Vatican, they are displaced from one another and linked by the infolding trapezoidal

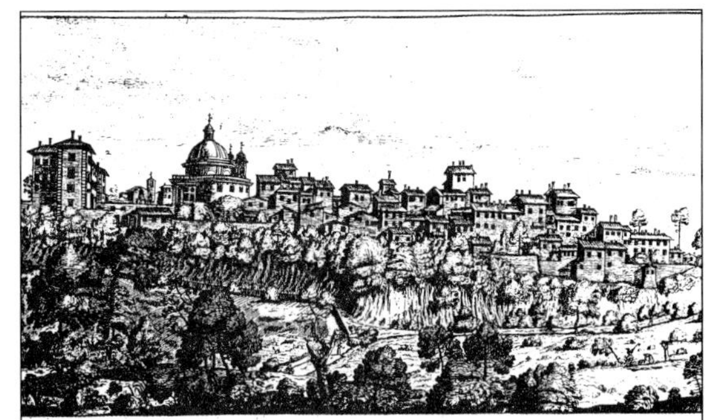

11.21 G.B. Falda, engraving of Arricia showing the Ducal Palace and Santa Maria della Assunzione, c.1665.

11.22 G.L. Bernini, Santa Maria della Assunzione, Arricia, 1662-3, exterior view.

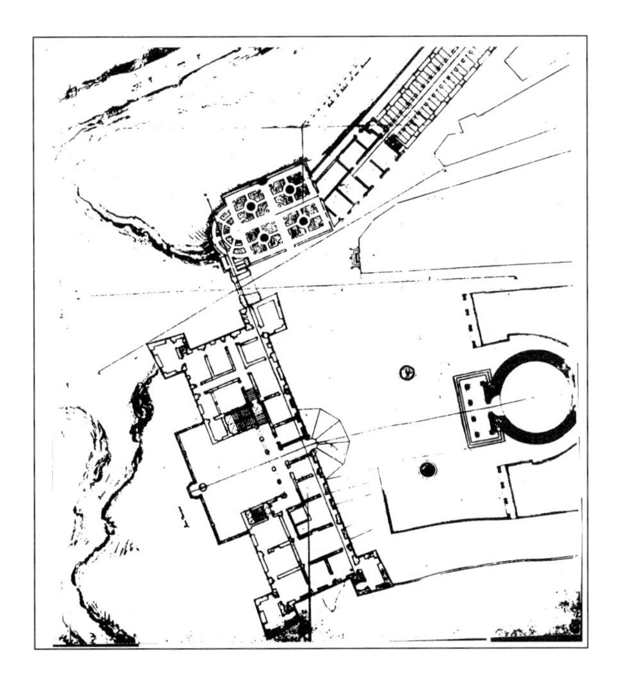

11.23 Left: Santa Maria della Assunzione, site plan, Biblioteca Apostolica Vatican, Rome, Codice Chigi.

11.24 Right: Santa Maria della Assunzione, view of space between the church and the flanking buildings.

11.25 G.L. Bernini, St. Peter's Courtyard, Rome, 1624-33.

11.26 G. de Rossi, engraving of St. Peter's Courtyard.

arms of the great corridors. The oval courtyard appears to be an autonomous figure, but it can be seen as a vessel out of which the basilica has slipped. Indeed, the basilica can be perfectly inscribed within the space of the courtyard: the centers of the colonnades correspond to the centers of curvature of the lateral apses, and the vertical assent of the obelisk corresponds to the vertical rise of the dome. Bernini rhetorically recreates the sacred space of St. Peter's Basilica *"to receive in a maternal gesture in order to confirm their belief, heretics in order to reunite them with the church and infidels in order to reveal the true faith."* The courtyard also does more. The inward canting of the corridor arms illusionistically adjusts the disproportionate breath of Maderno's facade and affords the viewer sufficient distance from the church so that Michelangelo's dome may be seen, in spite of the imposition of Maderno's longitudinal nave.

Borromini's university church, **S. Ivo alla Sapienza** (1644), is a centralized church at the end of a pre-existing rectangular courtyard. As in San Carlo alle Quattro Fontane, the plan results from the synthesis of multiple forms: inverted equilateral triangles, a hexagon, and

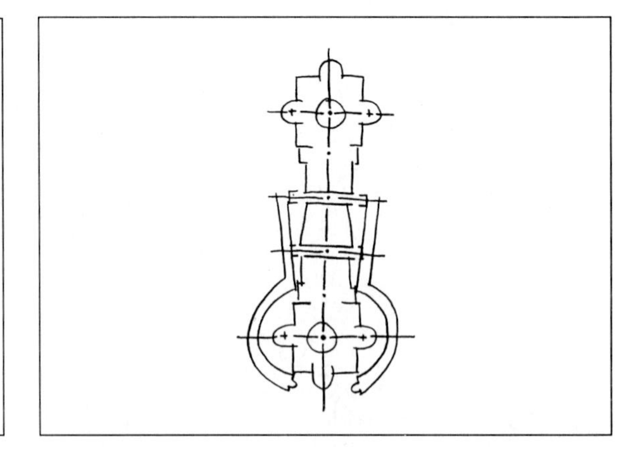

11.27 Left: Diagram, Object/ Void relationships in Bernini projects.

11.28 Right: Diagram, Relationship of church and cortile at St. Peter's.

circular lobes. The symbolism legible in the quirky little church is enormous, ranging from the Barberini bee, the heraldic symbol of Pope Urban VII, to the spiraling Tower of Babel. Yet even without access to arcane references, the form itself provides a good deal of insight into Borromini's intentions.

Urbanisticly, the building is inward. Its eccentricities are completely masked from the surrounding city by the more or less neutral surrounding walls of university buildings. Inside the courtyard the church presents itself as simultaneously concave and convex. A curve is carved at the ground level to embrace the viewer; tangent to the concave space a bulging, lobed drum emerges. The drum is surmounted by a tower comprised of stacked oddities: crowns, torches, jewels, etc. The pulsating interchange between concave and convex space on the exterior also characterizes the interior space, where alternating apses are treated each way. As one ascends in section, the irregular, animated, syncopated plan of the church grows more and more serene, until finally, all complexities are resolved in a round, light filled opening at the top. Except for this moment, the

11.29 F. Borromini, S. Ivo alla Sapienza, Rome, 1644, interior.

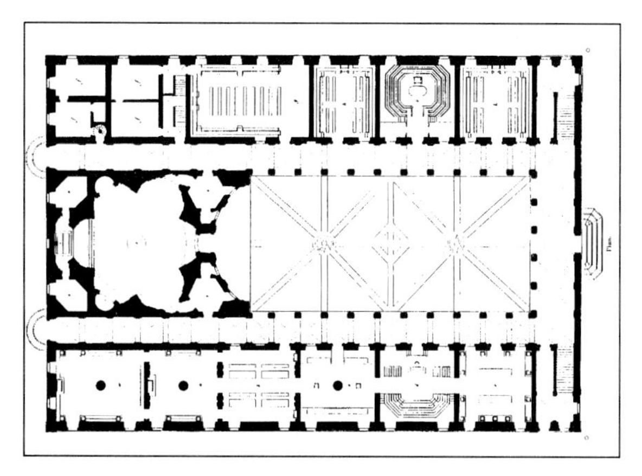

11.30 Left: S. Ivo alla Sapienza, plan.

11.31 Right: S. Ivo alla Sapienza, courtyard view.

11.32 S. Ivo alla Sapienza, dome.

church does not seem to be at rest, but is rather caught in a dramatic act of transformation, like the captured action of a Bernini statue.

The sense of pulsation, or expansion and contraction, present in Borromini's church is developed at an even higher pitch in the work of **Guarino Guarini** (1624-83). His plan for **San Filippo Neri** at Casale Monferrato (1671) describes an isolated moment within an expanding grid of circles. The dome-like vaults of his **Nameless Church** in Turin seem to undergo mitosis, and the syncopated, alternating articulation of concave and convex chapels on the lateral aisles gives the impression that the church is inhaling and exhaling, like a quivering, living organism.

The theatricality of the Roman Baroque and Rococco reaches its height in the following works, which we shall discuss only briefly: the **Piazza della Pace**, by **Pietro da Cortona** (1596-1669), and the **Piazza San Ignazio**, by **Filippo Raguzzini** (1680-1771). Pietro da Cortona is sometimes considered to be the third great master of the Roman Baroque. At **Santa Maria della Pace** (1656-9) his task was to design a new facade for an existing church. Because it was

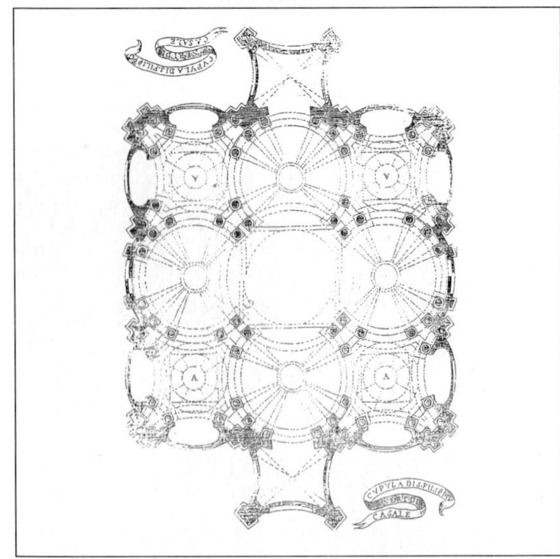

11.33 Left: Guarino Guarini, S.Filippo Neri in Casale Monferrato, c.1671.

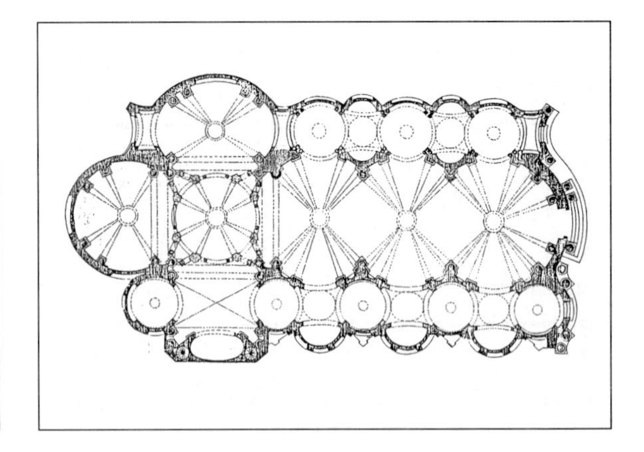

11.34 Right: Guarino Guarini, "Nameless Church", Turin, c.1671.

impossible for a Baroque architect to conceive of a facade without also giving attention to its setting, da Cortona slices through the existing fabric of the town to create a tiny trapezoidal piazza. The building is at once proscenium and actor in the urban theater. The wall of the church wraps around the square, framing doorways which either lead to the church or permit the space to continue beyond it. At the same time, a round porch punches forward, almost completely filling the space, and creating the impression that its penetration has caused the alignment of the two sides of the square to skew.

Piazza S. Ignazio by **Filippo Raguzzini** (1689-1771) organizes the space in front of an older Jesuit church. The central triangular building is one of the smallest building blocks in all of Rome and has the scale of a free-standing building. However, it cannot be viewed, except in relationship to the two flanking buildings with concave facades. The three buildings share a common language and articulation. They collaborate to create a permeable edge to the city with oblique entry and exits in the theatrical manner. In addition to organizing the

11.35 Pietro da Cortona, Santa Maria della Pace, Rome, 1596-1669.

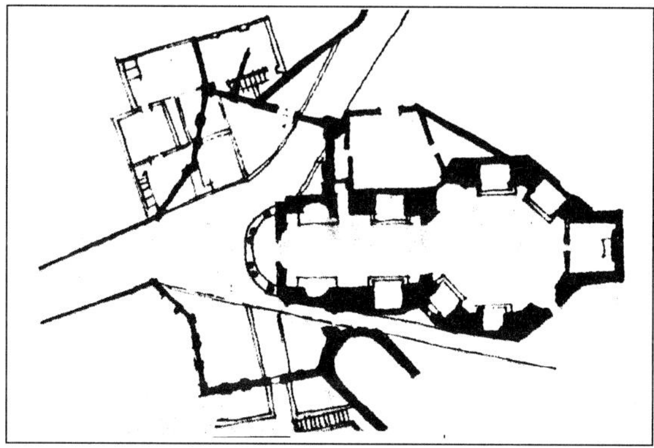

11.36 Maria della Pace, site plan.

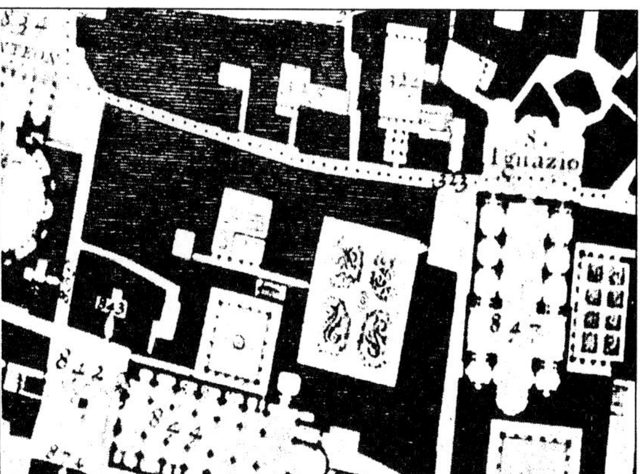

11.37 Left: Piazza S.Ignazio, view.

11.38 Right: Filippo Raguzzini, Piazza S.Ignazio, Rome, 1727-8, detail of the Nolli plan.

11.39 Place Royale (Place des Vosges), Paris, c. 1605-12.

exterior space as an ideal set piece, Raguzzini also projects information about the interior of the church. The A-B-A articulation of nave and circular aisle chapels is recreated in the A-B-A organization of the Piazza.

The Baroque was a truly international period. Bernini travelled to France, Guarini built in Portugal, and architects from other countries came to Italy to learn new techniques and import architectural ideas to their native lands. In the northern countries, Guarini's investigation of interdependent, interpenetrating spatial cells is carried on in projects like the Vierzehnheiligen church by Balthasar Neumann (Chapter 5).

In France, the presence of a powerful central government and developments in mathematics and philosophy gave rise to a local variant of the Baroque. Great Baroque squares, like **Place Royale** (Place des Vosges) and **Place Dauphine** were manifestations of Henry IV's power. Projects of an even more extraordinary scale were carried out under his successor, Louis XIV, a patron with almost unlimited wealth and power.

Vaux-le-Vicomte was designed for Louis XIV's superintendent of Finances, Nicolas

11.40 Left: M. Fouqier, engravings of Vaux-le-Vicomte.

11.41 Right: Vaux-le-Vicomte, view of the Chateau.

Fouquet, by **Louis Le Vau** (1612-1670) and the landscape architect **André Le Notre** (1613-1700). A perfect marriage of site and architecture is accomplished. The extension of the garden axis punches through the forecourt of service buildings. One edge is displaced and reconstituted as the bar of the Palace. Within the Palace itself, the force of the axis causes the ovalized salon to break free from the box. The force of the axis continues and shifts the center from the Palace into the garden. A circular pond marks the displaced center of the scheme and acts as a point of reflection which relates the radial paths on both halves of the scheme.

The **Palace at Versailles** (1661) for Louis XIV began as a reconstruction of a hunting lodge, but its scale and magnificence far exceeded anything that had come before it. The ambitious project integrated palace, town and garden into a single conception. Indeed, the palace acts as a seam or filter between the landscape and urban conditions, mitigating between the two by means of a simple bend in the bar. Towards the town, the inward bend creates a figural space which funnels down the vast space of the Place d'Armes into courtyards of greater and greater compression. Hence, when addressing the

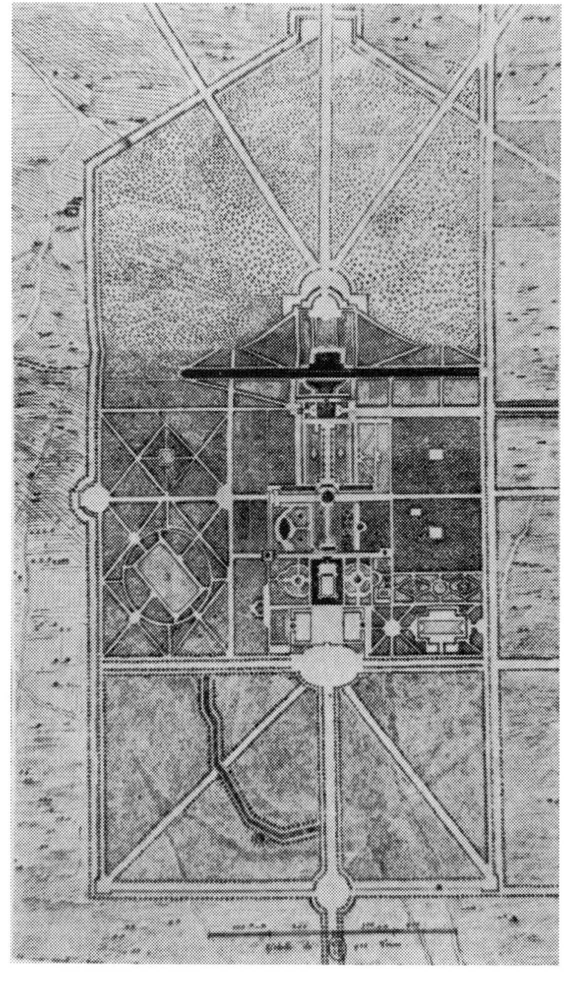

11.42 Louis Le Vau and André Le Notre, Vaux-le-Vicomte, France, 1656-61, site plan.

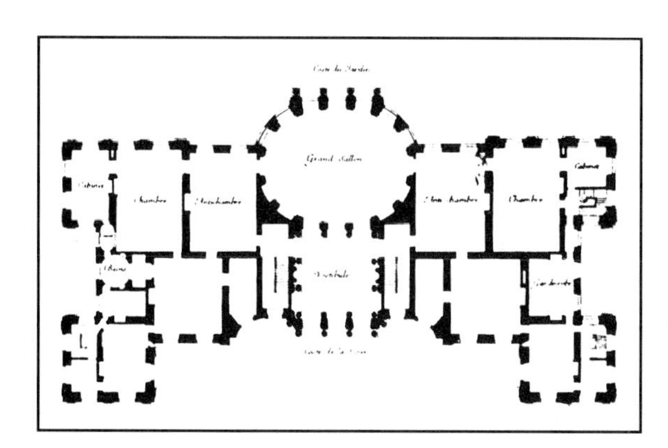

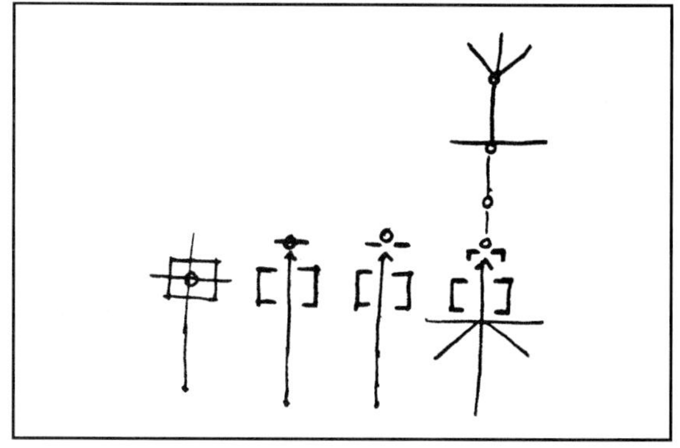

11.43 Left: Vaux-le-Vicomte, plan.

11.44 Right: Vaux-le-Vicomte, diagram.

11.45 Vaux-le-Vicomte, view of the Chateau.

11.46 Le Vau and Le Notre, Versailles, c. 1669, view toward of the Palace from the garden.

town, the building contracts to create a figural space which partakes in a network of such spaces and which sets up the radial lines through the town towards Paris. Fronting the garden, the infolding of the bar transforms the linear building into an isolated, pavilion-like structure on the central axis. Hence, the palace functions as a free-standing building in a garden environment characterized by free-standing buildings. The Palace at Versailles is chameleon-like in its ability to change its character in accordance with the context it addresses.

In many ways, the form and function of Versailles recreates that of the Porta del Popolo in Rome, although it does so in a more unified architectural language and at a grander scale. At the Porta del Popolo, the Aurelian Wall demarcates a boundary between the unsettled countryside of the Roman campagna and the urbanity of Rome. Entry into the radial streets of Sixtus V's plan are framed by the twin churches which flank the central axis. At Versailles, the town bears striking similarity to the Piazza del Popolo in 1669, except that the scale of the space is inflated and the oval churches are replaced by oval courtyards, the *Grand* and *Petit Ecuries*. The garden at Versailles looks nothing like the scattered settlement in the Roman countryside. Rather, it has been reformulated based on ideas about Cartesian space and the possibility of infinite extension. In appropriating the form of the Porta del Popolo, Le Vau is making explicit connections between the power and glory of the French kingdom and that of both the Romans and the Papacy.

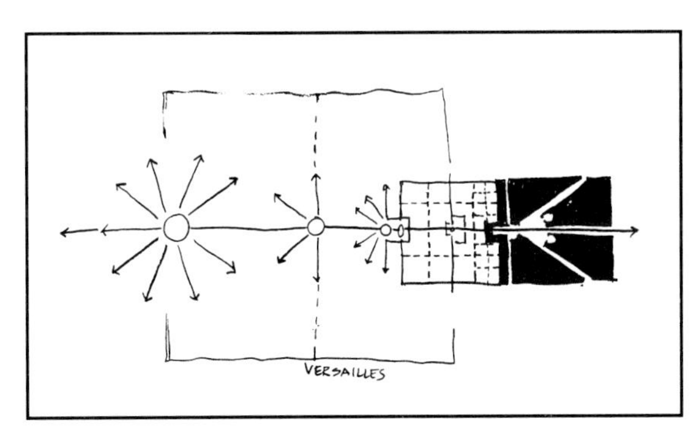

11.47 Versailles, Left top Diagrams of the relationship between town and garden.

11.48 Left bottoms: Versailles, entry court.

11.49 Right: Versailles, view down the garden axis.

In discussing **Cartesian Space,** the coordinate system invented by **René Descartes** (1596-1650) where rationally structured space is referenced to a measurable but infinitely extensible grid built around the X, Y and Z axes, it is useful to identify the point of origin, i.e., the point at which the axes intersect. One obvious possibility at Versailles is that the bar of the palace forms one axis and the long, central axis forms the other. But this explanation does not account for very much of the plan. The role of the central axis at Versailles is reminiscent of Vaux-le-Vicomte. There is a slippage of center along the axis so that not only one center is marked, but traces of displaced centers are mapped along a line. At Versailles, radial fans mirror each other on opposite sides of a four-square *parterre* garden. The shared gesture and tension suggests that they are in some way reciprocal halves to the same figure: a sun burst, heraldically connected with Louis XIV, the Sun King. Indeed, on the far side of the cruciform water course a perfect sun burst appears. The centers of the four-square garden, the cruciform water course and the perfect sun burst are all equidistant, further emphasizing the centrality of the middle term, and the equivalence between the highly manicured *parterre* gardens and the townscape on the other side of the palace bar.

Scale transforms as one moves away from the palace into the landscape. The delicacy of the *parterres* gives way to the long radial paths. Conversely, four-square gardens increasingly diminish as they approach the palace. The scale change responds to systems of circulation. The modestly scaled *parterre* gardens are meant for pedestrians; the remote gardens are intended for carriages and equestrians. The scale change is also symbolic. Just as the urban space contracts as it meets the Palace bar, the scale of the gardens expands as it moves away. There is an accelerating increase in scale as one moves out towards infinity. Unlike the Italian Baroque, which delights in terminating axial views with objects, the long axis of Versailles has no terminus. Two trees move inwards from the bosque to frame the slot of space that continues, even beyond the boundaries of the garden.

The Baroque age was born during a period of a great cultural consensus. The church, state and commerce worked according to the same teleological assumptions. Because the underlying content of society was universally acknowledged, the meanings of buildings in the Baroque period were readily decipherable. A synthesis of those shared beliefs and strong patronage from church and state made possible urban and landscape projects whose scale would be almost unthinkable today. Baroque architecture was not only a reflection of the powerful bodies which governed society. It also mirrored and interpreted ideas in disciplines as varied as mathematics and philosophy. The unending extension of the axis at Versailles suggests an optimistic attitude towards the infinite unknown, a concept that would have filled the previous generation with terror.

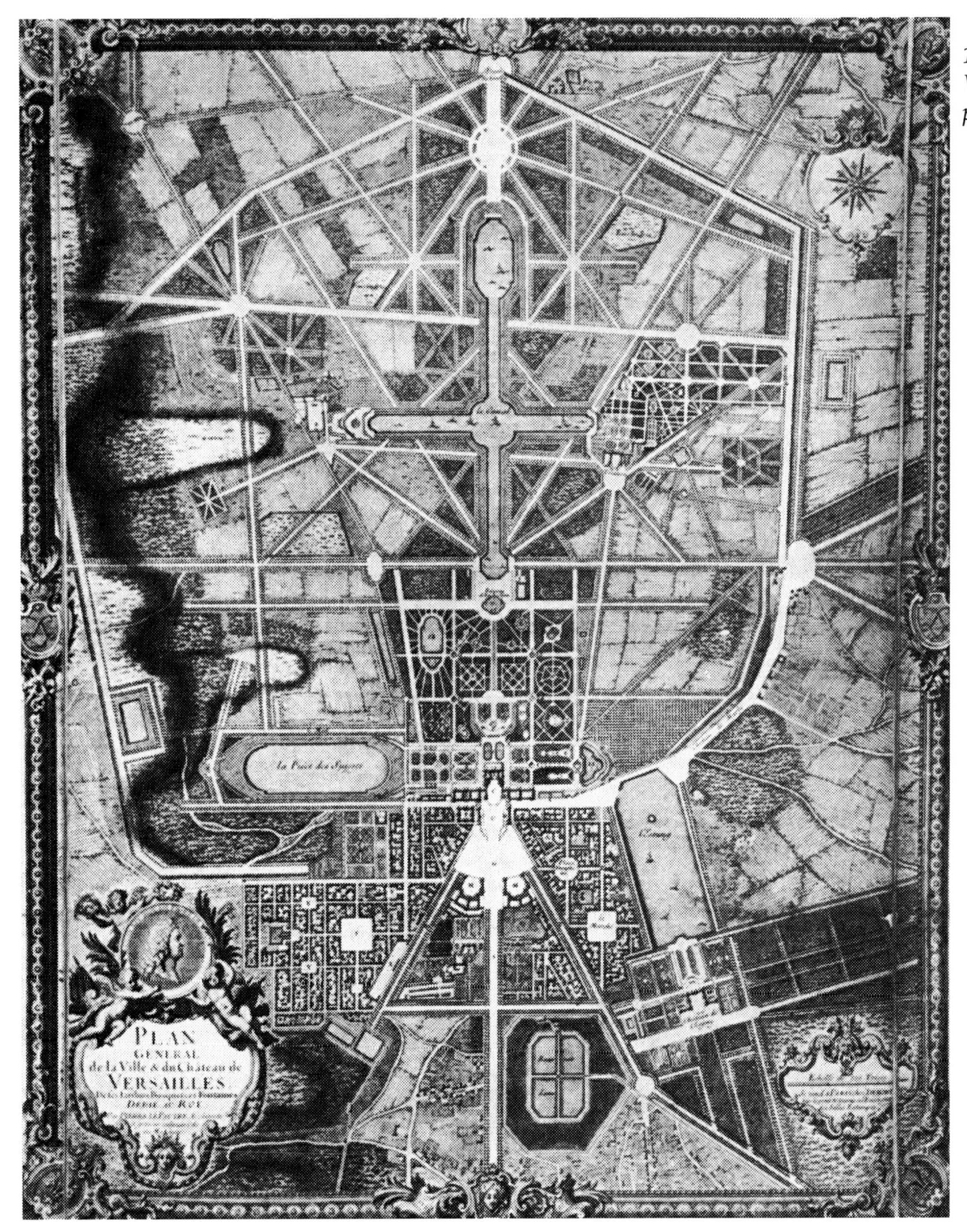

11.50 Versailles, site plan.

Part IV.

The Architecture of Modernity

12.0
Albert Bierstadt, Indian Encampment in the Rockies, detail, Amon Carter Museum, Fort Worth.

Chapter 12

Enlightenment Town Planning in America

All nature here is new to art, no Tivolis, Ternis, Mont Blancs, Plinlimmons, hackneyed and worn by the daily pencils of hundreds; but primeval forests, virgin lakes and waterfalls.

--THOMAS COLE

The grid, in its most reduced form, is a four-square paradise garden. According to Sir Thomas More, such was the configuration of the first city in history, Babylon: *"For the form of Babylon, the first city, was square, and so shall be the last, according to the description of the Holy City of the Apocalypse."* Throughout history, in diverse times and places, from Pre-Columbian America to the great cities of Asia, whenever land had to be settled and people governed, the grid was selected as the most convenient and most equitable urban organization. The grid is a memorable diagram. It is easily exported to claim new territories and establish a familiar order. The crossing of the two major axes in a bounded grid establishes center; yet the grid can be infinitely extended and confer equal meaning to all points within the system. The grid is based on the uniform, orderly repetition of a module; yet it is capable of delicate inflection in response to the particularities of site or program. The rhythm and structure of the grid provide equal measure; yet no scale is fixed. It defines its own subdivisibility and recapitulates its order many times within itself; yet it implies the potential for infinite expansion through the vectorial trajectories of its constituent lines.

In our examination of buildings and landscapes we observed that a simple paradigm can be manipulated and massaged to yield surprising variety. The same is true with the grid-iron town plan. The grid can be centric, as when two roads cross and establish the center of a **Roman Town**. It can be non-hierarchical and neutral, as in the expansive, repetitive block structure of **Salt Lake City**. It can allow surprising flexibility and the possibility of unexpected secondary order as seen in the grid-

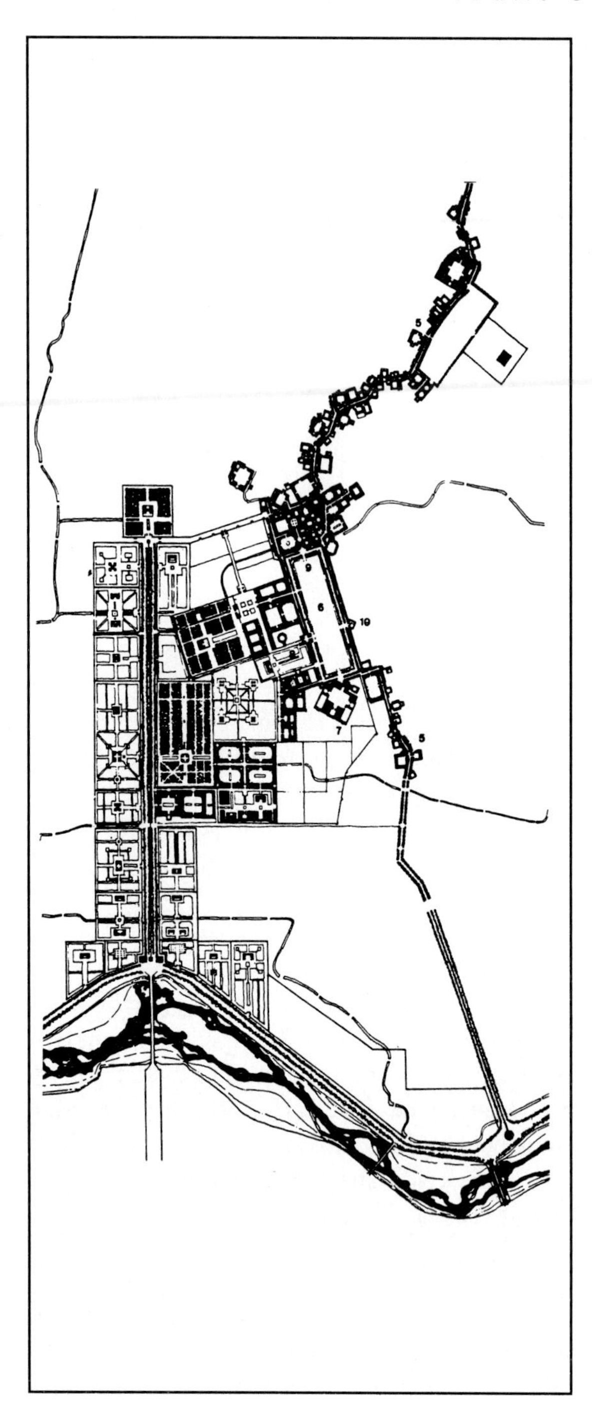

12.1
Isfahan, Iran,
Town Plan.

ded plan of the **Khmer Shrine** at Ankor Wat. The grid of **Isfahan** develops along two opposite yet complementary axes, one installing a pure geometric order along a straight line, and the other permitting the cells of various dimensions to fragment and peel away from a rambling, organic spine. The two paths are in dialogue with one another. The fragmented cells reassemble and gradually anneal to the crystalline order of the garden. **Beijing** is structured on concentric grids of increasingly larger modules, each the legacy of a different building campaign. These are but a few examples of the richness and variety available within a gridded order.

The logical, predictable structure of the grid in no way assures that a predictable, neutral, space will emerge. On the contrary, the systematic clarity of the grid can act as a datum and allow diversity to be embraced within the ordered whole. Even in Salt Lake City, seemingly the least developed of the aforementioned plans, a secondary order exists within the primary grid of square, ten-acre blocks. The lot structure from block to block varies in orientation so that no two houses face each other across the street.

The historical founder of town planning in Western civilization was **Hippodamus of Miletus**, although earlier examples of gridded Greek sites abound. The 7th century B.C. settlement of Smyrna is gridded, as are the 6th century B.C. settlements of Agrigentum (Akragas) and Metapuntum. Hippodamus is said to have invented the concept of the city block to lay out his home town, **Miletus**, on a regular grid. The central urban space in Miletus was reserved for public buildings and an agora.

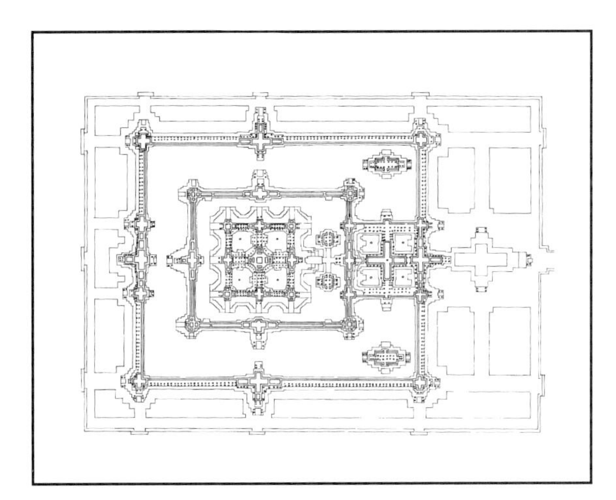

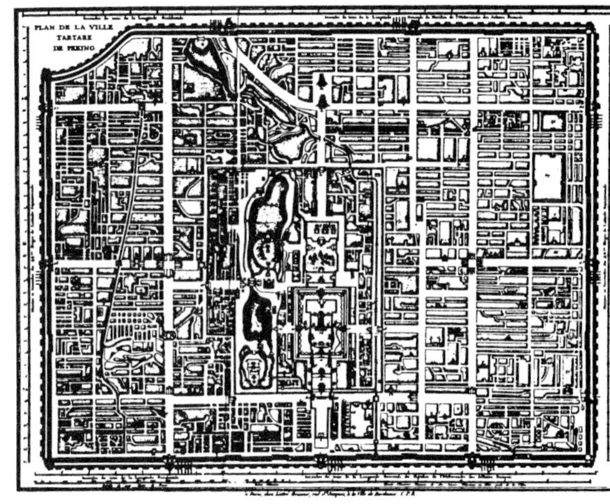

12.2 Left: Ankhor Wat, Cambodia, site plan.

12.3 Right: Beijing, China, town plan.

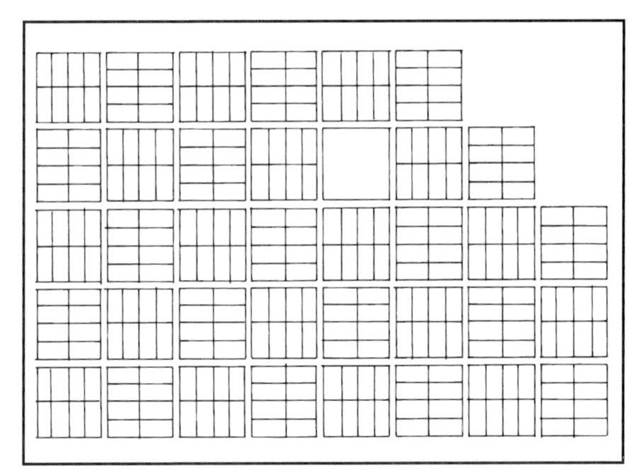

12.4 Left: Salt Lake City, town plan.

12.5 Right: Salt Lake City, detail showing the alternating block structure from north-south to east-west.

12.6 Hippodamus of Miletus, Miletus town center, model, c. 322 B.C.

The contrast between the delicate site-specificity of building arrangements on sacred Greek sites, and Hippodamus' methodical system for urban organization is striking. The programmed order of the grid-iron was used in commercial centers, but not in the historical centers of the aristocracy.

In ancient Rome, as in ancient Greece, the available, rational program for site settlement was not adopted at home. The formulaic layout of the Roman camp had no impact whatsoever on the internal organization of the capital city. There, the disposition of buildings relied on pre-existing functions, meanings associated with the site and the exigencies of topography. The idealized order of the Roman camp could be imprinted only on land that had not otherwise been claimed and imbued with significance.

Our earlier characterization of Medieval space stressed the *ad hoc* accretion over time of buildings, monuments, streets and squares. However, even in the medieval period, when new towns were established the memorable geometry of the grid was evinced as the formal organizer. Medieval **bastide** towns, such as **Monpazier**, are organized on the four-square grid, enclosed within a fortified perimeter wall. Like the Hippodaman towns of Greece and the Roman camps, bastides were established as frontier trading settlements or military outposts. Sited on virgin territory, they were free to assume a clarity of form impossible in cities which grew up naturally over time.

Vitruvius' discussion of town planning, like all of Vitruvius' writing, is not particularly clear. Renaissance theoreticians interpreted him differently and derived from his writings different models for the ideal town. **Pietro Cataneo's diagram** from *L'Architettura* is rectangular, an elaboration of the Roman camp. The crossing of the two principal streets locates a central

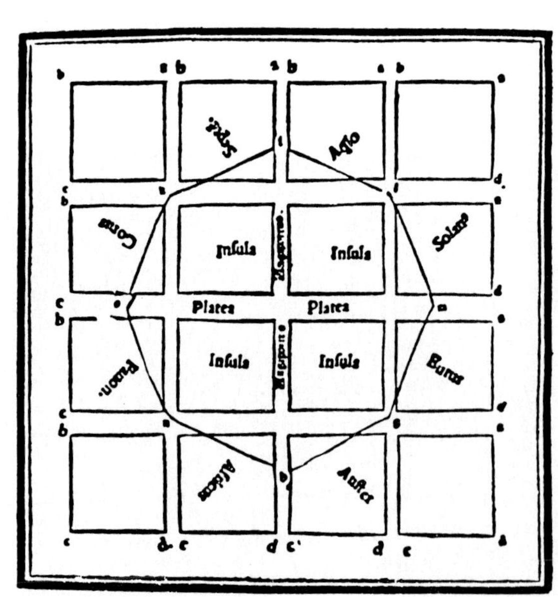

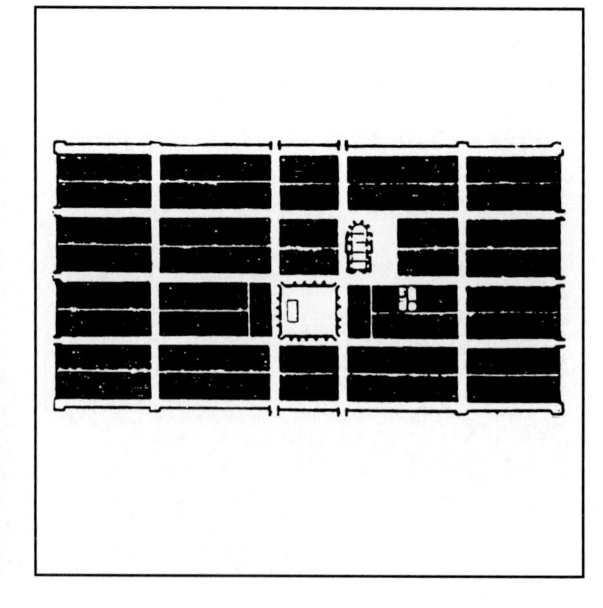

12.7 *Left: Renaissance reconstruction of a Roman town plan, after Vitruvius, c.1536.*

12.8 *Right: Monpazier, French Bastide Town, c. 1248, plan.*

square, but Cataneo goes farther in building hierarchy into his scheme. Each of the four quadrants rehearses the order of the whole, engendering four secondary centers. The oblong city blocks provide a natural 'grain' to the structure of the city, differentiating the character of the east-west from the north-south streets, and providing a variety of spatial conditions within the simple plan.

In European history, ideal towns could only take form when new towns were built, and that was not frequent. The ancient land of Europe was too haunted by history and too deeply saturated with successive layers of settlement to permit the broad imposition of a new, abstract order upon the land. A virgin land was required for such interventions. Thomas More posited such a place in his *Utopia,* but by the time he wrote his famous book in 1516, settlement had already begun in the Americas. Unlike More's *Utopia,* a bounded island of identical houses and identical gardens, the new land seemed to extend without limit and was home to a population of great diversity.

It is surprising to confront the settlement of the United States with contemporaneous historical events in Europe. In 1492, when Columbus set sail, the Italian Renaissance was coming into full flower. With the quest for ideal proportions and classical architecture came a philosophical belief in Humanism and Neoplatonism. The perfect union of reason and faith sponsored great monuments in art, architecture, literature, music, philosophy, and political science. The Renaissance political ideal was Machiavelli's Prince. Power resided in the hands of the few and the stratification of society was reflective of the stratification in the cosmic order: humankind was situated somewhere between angels and worms. Social institutions and the architecture that housed them had as

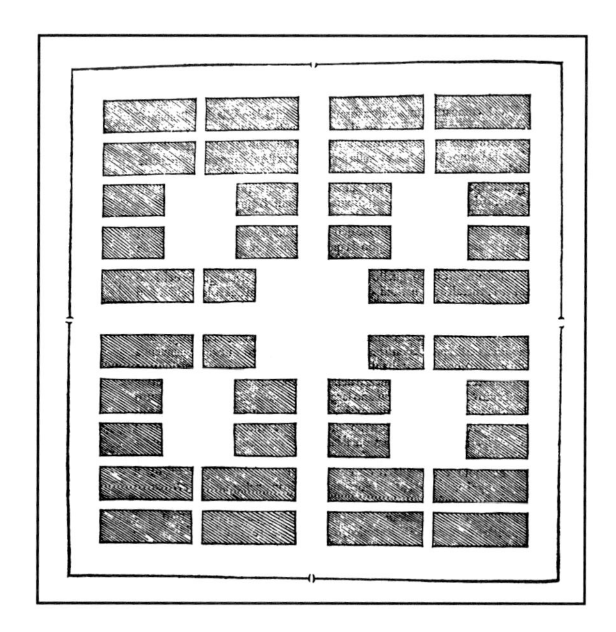

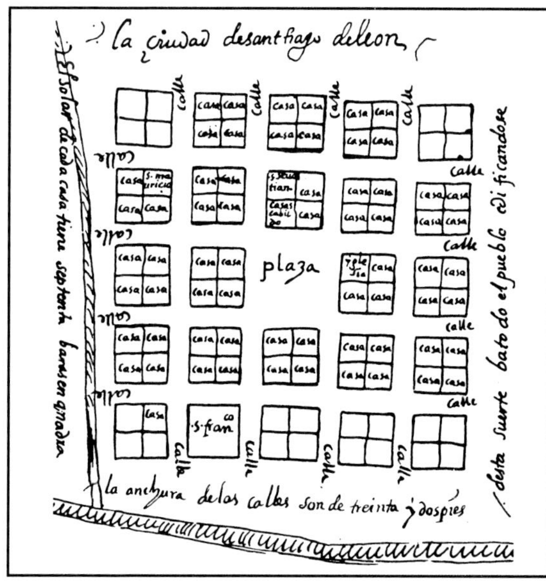

12.9 Left: Pietro di Giacomo Cataneo, Plan of a Vitruvian Town, from L'Architettura.

12.10 Right: Original Plan of Santiago de Leon (now Caracas, Venezuela).

their objective the reinforcement of these hierarchies.

A fascination with Vitruvius, ancient Roman planning principals, and the concept of the Ideal Town continued to flourish long after the Renaissance. However, it was not until the settlement of the American colonies that a large scale opportunity was provided to put town planning principles into effect. The older towns of Central and South America were founded during the European Renaissance. **Caracas** was laid out on a 25 square checker board plan with the central square set aside as a plaza. A Renaissance sensibility is reflected in the strongly defined center, fortified perimeter walls, and the ideal, closed geometrical lay-out. In Europe, the greatest architects of the time were thwarted in their dreams to build an ideal town, while in the Americas, immigrants of no special talent were charged with the design of entire cities.

After the discovery of America, almost two hundred years passed before the Northern American colonies were settled in a serious way. By that time, the Renaissance had passed and Enlightenment ideology dominated. Philosophers like Locke, Rousseau, Montesquieu and Voltaire proposed a new egalitarian ideal which enshrined democracy, equality of all people, the innate rights of humankind, and the nobility of the wilderness. The very institutions that empowered the old aristocracy were viewed with critical contempt. In architecture, the repercussions were obvious. The glorification of a strong central authority, implicit in grandiose Baroque town plans, was replaced by a mistrust of cities and an increased respect for the countryside. Great public spaces were eschewed in favor of the expression of the individual. Free-standing buildings became the characteristic built form of the new nation.

Michael Dennis has observed that American towns owe many individual buildings to Greek and Roman inspiration, but that there is nothing equivalent to the bounded public spaces of antiquity: the forum and the agora. He remarks: *"America was born on the cusp of history, a philosophical and architectural turning point between the spatial tradition of the Renaissance and the iconic stirrings of the Enlightenment..."* (*Court and Garden*). The vast expanse of the continent offered freedom to spread out, and the autonomous, free-standing buildings became the vehicle best able to embody the aspirations of a nation of individuals. An atomization of urban fabric resulted in American cities.

We shall examine a few examples of American town plans. Some of the towns grew up naturally, without reliance on a plan; others made use of very rudimentary planning ideas; still others can be ranked among the finest examples of built form from their epoches. Unlike the perfunctory, formulaic American town lay-outs of the sixteenth century, Enlightenment town plans of the United States are elegant yet functional, expressive of the complex aspirations of the age.

Boston was settled c. 1640 and did not grow up around a structured plan. Instead, its organization reflects informal patterns of communal growth. Harbor, hills and marshes all influenced the street lay-out and settlement patterns, although the apparent randomness of Boston's plan has led some to claim that it was laid out along cow paths. An irregularly shaped meadow, the 'Common', is situated in the middle of town and provides relief from the congestion of the streets. The casual arrangement of buildings, squares and streets lends the town a charming, picturesque quality, but it is anything but a manifestation of Enlightenment order. Indeed, it is not even readily navigable.

New Haven, Connecticut, c.1641, as opposed to Boston, was laid out on a very orderly nine-square grid. At immediate glance, the gridded scheme is reminiscent of Caracas, the Roman camp and the French bastide. However, there is an important difference. In the earlier examples the center was occupied by a great urban square, bounded by continuous edge-buildings: the central square was the most urban episode in the town. In New Haven, the central square is loosely fringed by free-standing buildings situated in the center of their lots. Moreover, the central space is not really a square, but a 'green', a public grazing meadow, bringing the countryside into the very center of the town. A square meeting house originally stood at the center of the green; it was a symbol of the enfranchisement of the populace, not of the authority of central government. Later, it was replaced with not one but three churches, expressing the diversity of belief and dispersion of authority prized by the American colonies.

In the bellicose world of pre-Enlightenment Europe, a fortified, walled town was needed to protect the civilized precinct from the menacing

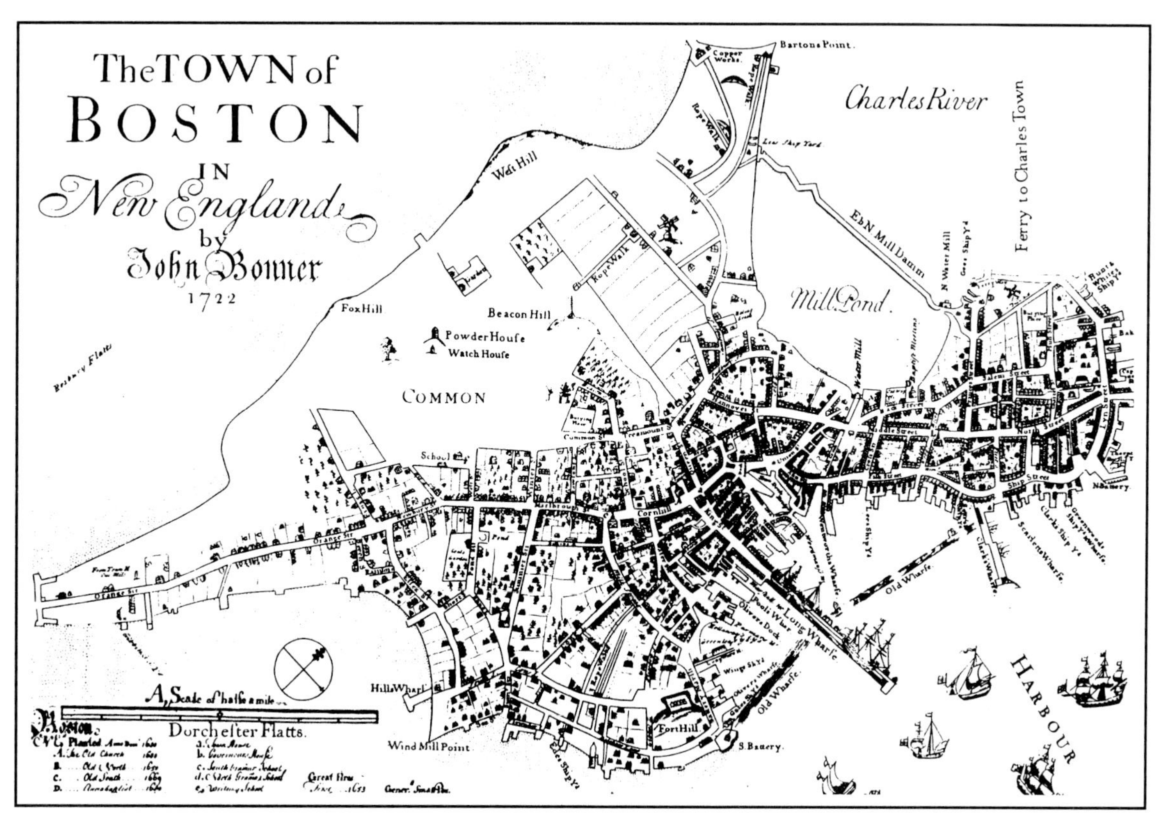

12.11
Plan of Boston, Massachusetts, 1722.

wilderness. At New Haven, the town is unbounded; the gridded streets extend into the countryside. The merging of town and landscape suggests a changing set of values. First, because the grid is extensible, the center is not absolute, but may shift as urban growth transforms the surrounding fabric. Second, contact with the landscape was deemed to be salubrious and purifying, not the opposite, as presumed in earlier days.

American cultural ideals were always closely tied to Europe, and particularly to Britain. In 1666, there was a great fire in London, which followed a devastating plague in 1665. Suspicion of European urban centers, which partly motivated the settlement of the New World, was confirmed. Before the fire London was without sewers, adequate housing, a good water supply, and paved roads. The conditions of overcrowding easily bred disease and pestilence. Ramshackle wooden structures were tightly packed together, separated only by timber and wattle party walls. A small dwelling might house *"eleven married couples and fifteen single persons."* When the fire broke out on September 1, 1666, it spread quickly and blazed for almost a month, engulfing most of the central city. The conflagration wrought great tragedy, but also provided an opportunity for the architects of the English Baroque to apply their

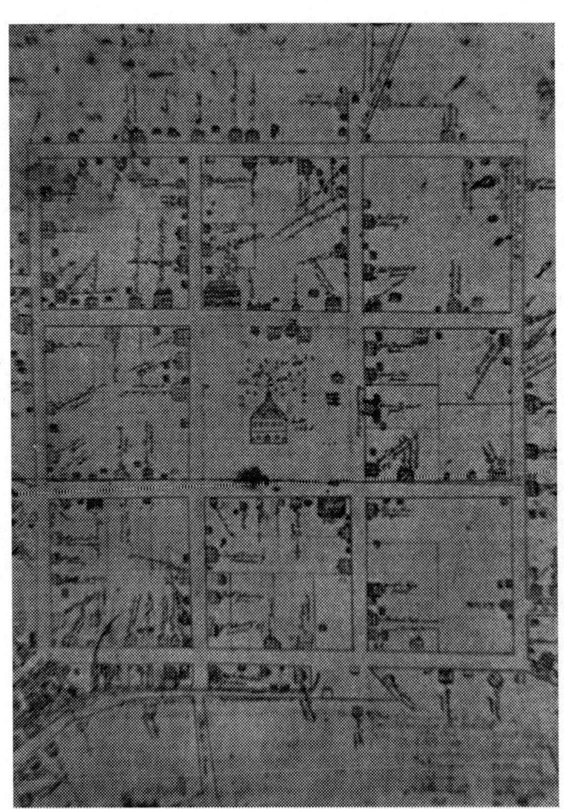

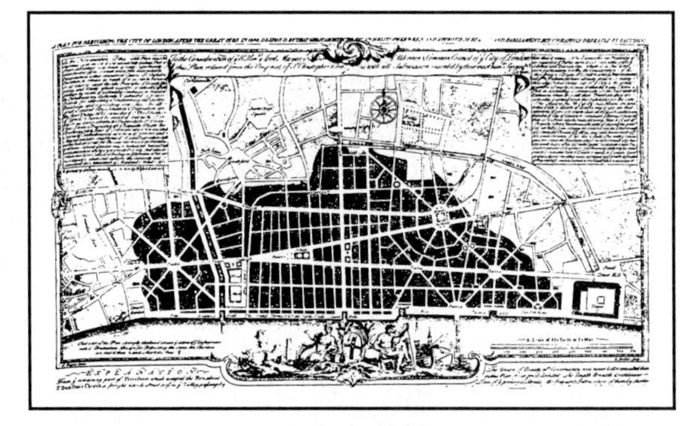

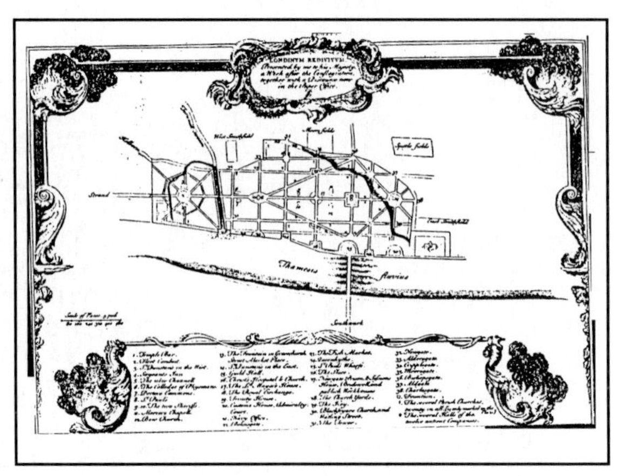

12.12 Left: New Haven, Connecticut, Original plan of 1641, according to the Wadsworth Map of 1748.

12.13 Right top: Christopher Wren, plan for the rebuilding of London, 1666.

12.14 Right bottom: John Eveyln, first plan for the rebuilding of London, 1666.

visions of the 'Ideal Town' directly to a real situation.

On September 7, with the fire still raging, **Christopher Wren** (1632-1723) presented his **Plan for Rebuilding London** to the King; **John Evelyn** (1620-1706) followed with the first of his three plans on September 10; and **Robert Hooke** on September 21. Like vultures circling a dying beast, they seized the opportunity to install order, clarity and hierarchy to the tangle of streets which comprised London. Wren, who had just returned from France, proposed a comprehensive network of diagonal streets, uniting Renaissance radial planning and Baroque axial planning. The center of Wren's scheme was Saint Paul's Cathedral, which he was to design nine years later in 1675. Evelyn's first scheme considered London as a *tabula rasa,* a blank slate upon which an ideal symmetry could be traced, but his successive projects addressed pre-existing conditions. Although contemporaneous with broad-reaching European urban projects like Bernini's Courtyard at St. Peter's, and Le Notre's extensive radial systems at Versailles, the English dismissed the ambitious Baroque projects and reconstructed London according to existing property lines.

Robert Hooke's project for London was most radical of all. While schemes by Wren and Evelyn emphasized the monuments of the city

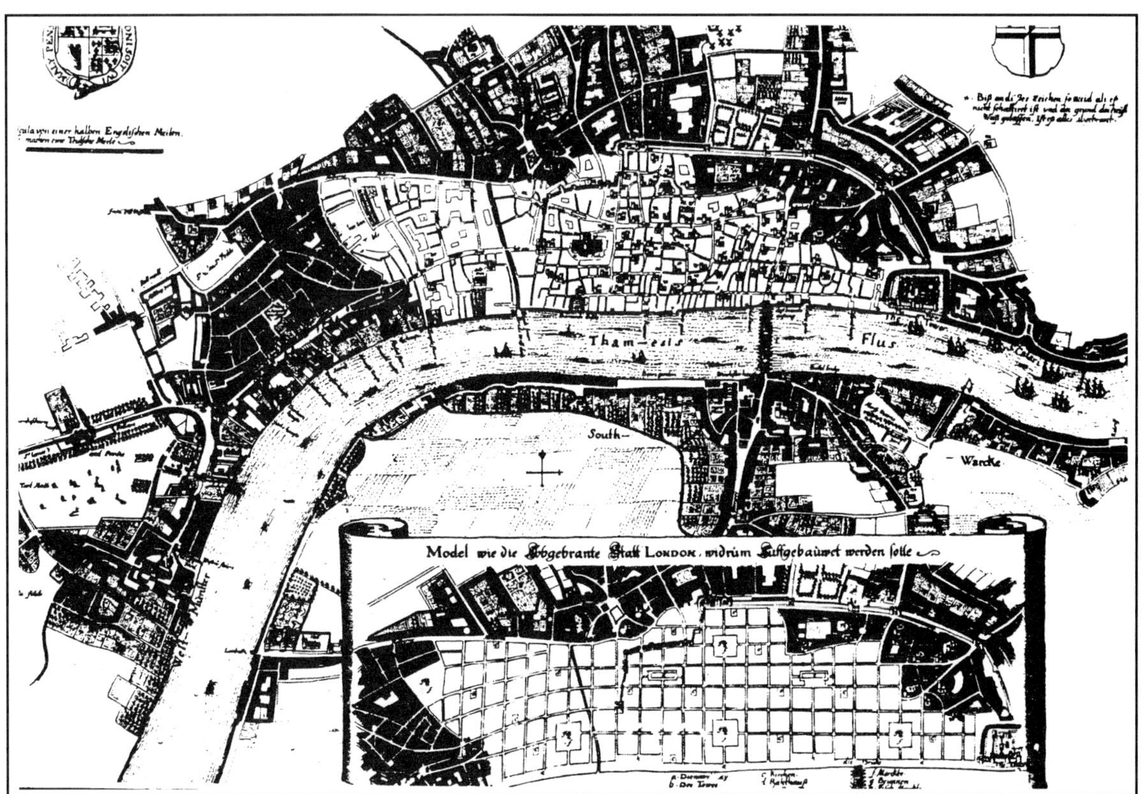

12.15 Robert Hooke, plan for the rebuilding of London, inset beneath a plan of London before the fire of 1666.

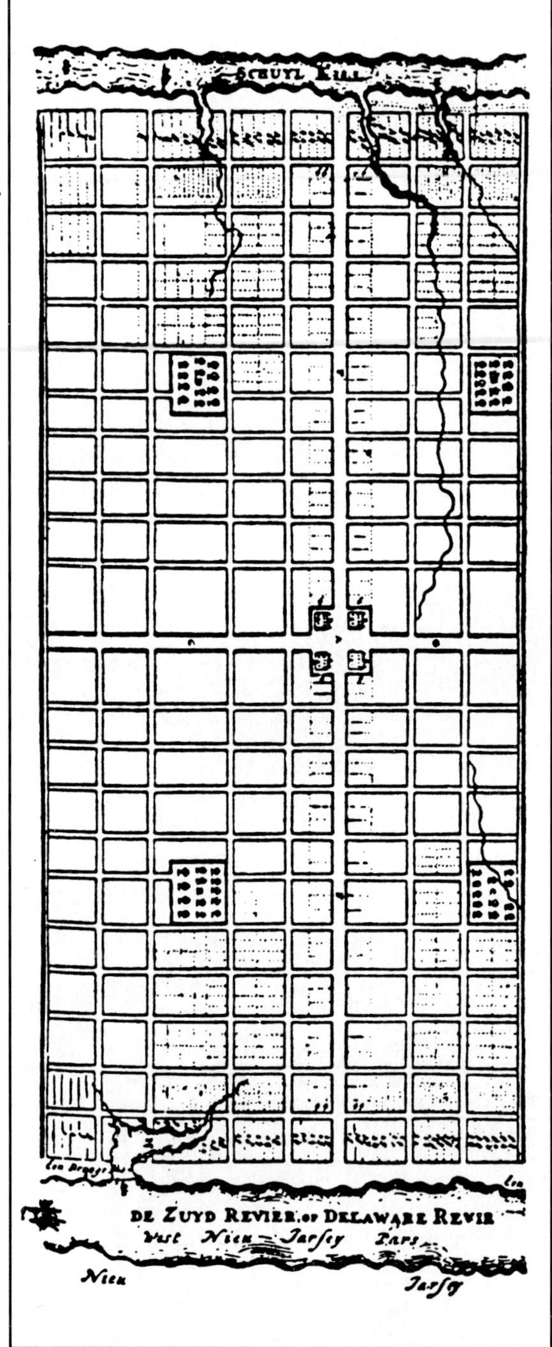

12.16 William Penn and Thomas Holme, Plan of Philadelphia, 1682.

with Baroque axes and broad radial avenues, Hooke imposed a neutral, even grid over the entire blighted area. No single center was identified; instead, within the grid a repetitive rhythm of squares and greens created a fabric which could sponsor growth evenly and democratically. Hooke was a mathematician by training, and his insistence on order and disregard for the absolutist expressions of hierarchy or the accretion of historical associations is typical of seventeenth-century science's aggressive relationship to the past.

Philadelphia was laid out in 1682. The memory of the London fire and the progressive projects for its rebuilding were still fresh in the minds of the planners, **William Penn** (1644-1718) and **Thomas Holme**. Penn, who viewed the settlement of the New World as a money-making enterprise, laid out a city on a rectangular, Roman grid, almost one by two miles, stretching out between the Delaware and Schuylkill Rivers. It was an undertaking of extraordinary ambition: the size was comparable to that of Paris and London, and larger than any other European city. The grid satisfied practical as well as idealistic objectives: the entire area could be subdivided into marketable lots. Hence, not only could the river property be sold, but the inland sites as well. Penn's strategy worked imperfectly. The eastern part of the town, along the banks of the navigable Delaware River, was settled first. It was not until one hundred and fifty years later that the entire grid filled in.

In contrast to congested, unhealthy, and fire-prone conditions of cities like London, Penn decreed that Philadelphia was to be a *"green country town."* Plots were to be at least half an acre, and houses were to be free-standing *". . . so that there may be ground on each side for gardens or orchards, or fields that it may be a green country town, which will never be burnt, and always be wholesome."* (From Penn's *Instructions to the Commissioners.*)

The plan of Philadelphia unites the clear hierarchy of a Roman town, particularly Cataneo's version of the Vitruvian town, with the neutral order of Hooke's plan for the rebuilding of London. The crossing of the major east-west street (Market Street) and the major north-south street (Broad Street) located the central square. One hundred feet wide, these streets were exactly the size prescribed by Evelyn for major roads in his scheme for London. The central square was the locus for public buildings and markets. Each of the four quadrants was organized around a subsidiary center. As in New Haven, these centers were not designated for urban activities, but the contrary: Penn decreed that the squares were to be green meadows, *"to be for the likes and uses as the Moor-fields in London."*

The rational, democratic grid of the city governed expansion and internal development of Philadelphia until 1919 when a modification was introduced by a Frenchman, **Jacques Gréber**. Like Wren in London, he drew diagonal boulevards to interconnect squares and major monuments. Only one of Gréber's diagonals was constructed, the Benjamin Franklin Parkway, which links the City Hall (which now fills the entire central square) with Logan Square (rendered circular by the Frenchman's Beaux Arts vision) and the Art Museum on the banks of the Schuylkill River. While the diagonal axially links important

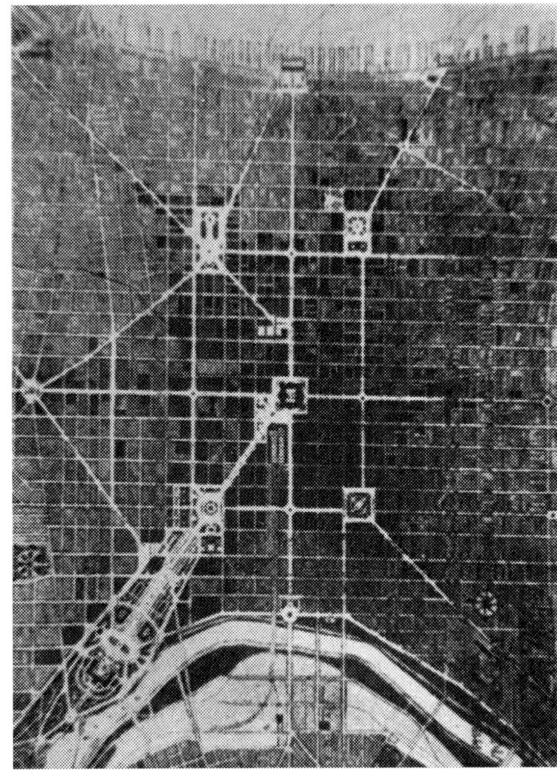

12.17
Jacques Gréber, Philadelphia Plan of 1919, with diagonal avenues interconnecting points in the grid.

12.18
The Benjamin Franklin Parkway, Philadelphia, showing the Art Museum and Fairmount Park in the distance.

monuments in the city in true Baroque fashion, the gesture has a particularly American aspect. The Art Museum sits at the head of Fairmount Park, which stretches out along the banks of the Schuylkill River. The diagonal parkway gathers up the expanse of the park and reintroduces it to the center of the city. The city center is reintegrated with the landscape through this bold gesture.

Savannah, Georgia was founded as a debtors colony by **James Oglethorpe** (1696-1785) in 1733. Like New Haven and Philadelphia, it is laid out on a grid. Unlike the two earlier town plans, Oglethorpe's original layout had no singular center. The crossing of the *Cardo* and *Decumanus* was uncelebrated. Instead, each of the four quadrants was organized around a central square. Oglethorpe presented an urban texture and a formula for growth, unimpeded by deference to a central point. By 1735, the original four quadrants had expanded to six through the simple repetition of the basic order of the grid. Growth continued to follow the model for more than one hundred years. In 1815, a cemetery originally sited on the outskirts of town was absorbed within the gridded fabric and provided a counterpoint to the rhythm of street and square.

The blocks of Savannah are not square but rectilinear which provides a hierarchical distinction between long and short blocks. Further hierarchy is built into the plan by the width of

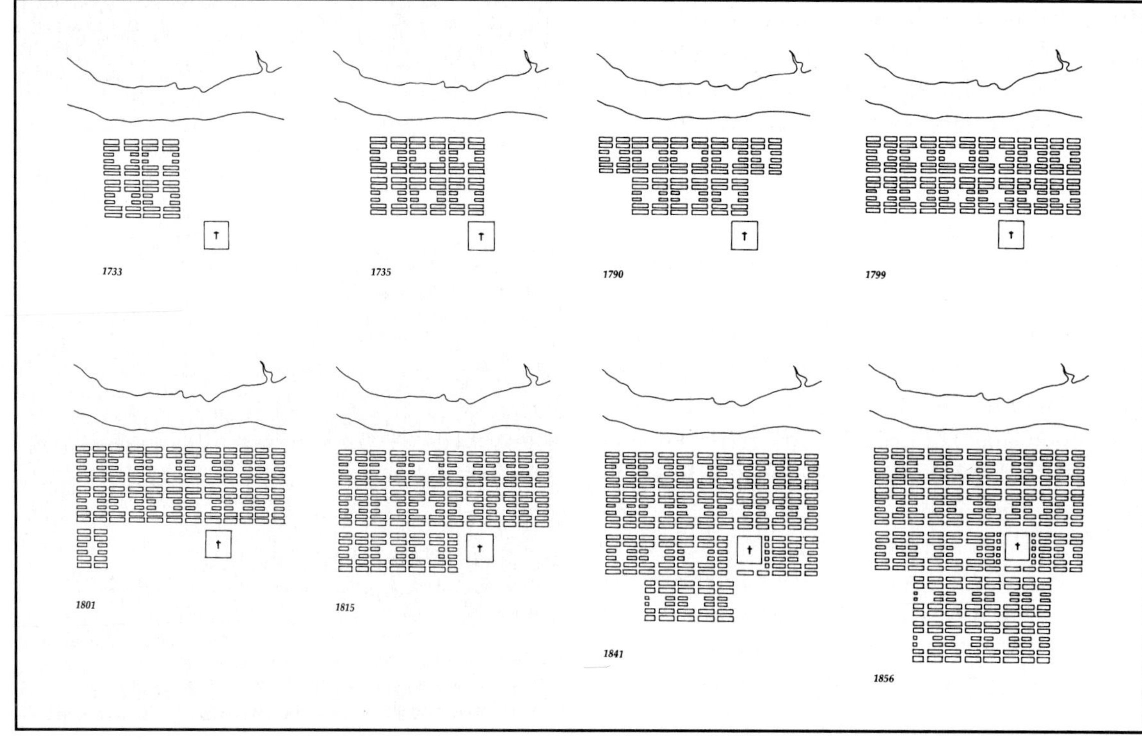

12.19 Savannah, Diagram of Town Plan and its Growth, from John Reps, The Making of Urban America.

streets. The widest streets run through the squares towards the river, or parallel to the river between the squares. The syncopation of street and square, boulevard and alley, provides a variety of experience through the grid. One may circumvent the squares altogether; one may progress through broad avenues and green squares; one may move on narrow streets along side the squares, etc. The different episodes within the grid provide logical locations for different elements in the city. The most prominent sites are the short blocks facing the squares. Here important public buildings or fine mansions were located.

Washington D.C. was laid out in 1792 by **Pierre l'Enfant** (1754-1825), a sophisticated French architect who brought to the New World a knowledge of the great Baroque towns of Europe and a facility with their planning. Great diagonal boulevards, 160 feet in width, link major monuments and intersect to form radial sun-burst patterns, worthy of Versailles. It is a bit surprising that planning strategies characteristic of Louis XIV's France became the physical structure for the capital of a new democratic nation. However, Washington is not only organized on the grandiose diagonal system. Like Wren's scheme for London, underlying the Baroque boulevards is the plain, rational order of a reticulated grid. The democratizing grid, an ordering device upon which Jefferson was said to have insisted, eases movement through the city and assigns equal value to all points.

The plan of Washington has been called one of the most brilliant town plans ever conceived. This has much to do with L'Enfant's exploitation of the natural features of the site and his integration of the town with the distant land-

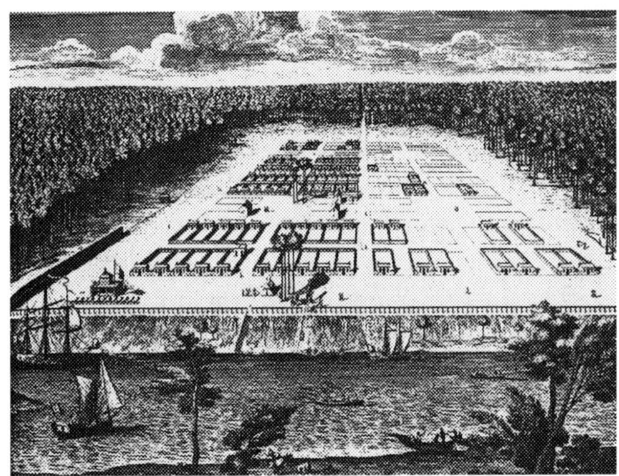

12.20 Engraving of Savannah, Georgia, c. 1734.

12.21 Savannah, Georgia, view down an avenue.

12.22 Savannah, Georgia, view of a square.

scape. The President's House and Capitol, the two most important monuments in the plan, terminate broad lawns arrayed on the orthogonal grid of the town. The buildings themselves become foci for radial networks of avenues. The intersection of the greenswards in front of the President's House and the Capitol does not lead to another monument, but to the banks of the Potomac River, and views across it into the landscape. L'Enfant stated, "a *sense of the real grand and truly beautiful [are] only to be met where nature contributes with art and diversifies objects.*" The strength of The United States was not its cities, however grand in design, but the westward extension of the landscape, and the agrarian virtue that comes with close contact to the land.

Simplicity, utility and honest accommodation have always been valued by the American people over grandeur and pomp. Nowhere is this clearer than in the history of **Circleville, Ohio**, recounted by John Reps in *The Making of Urban America*. Built in 1820 upon an annular Indian mound, the town of Circleville assumed

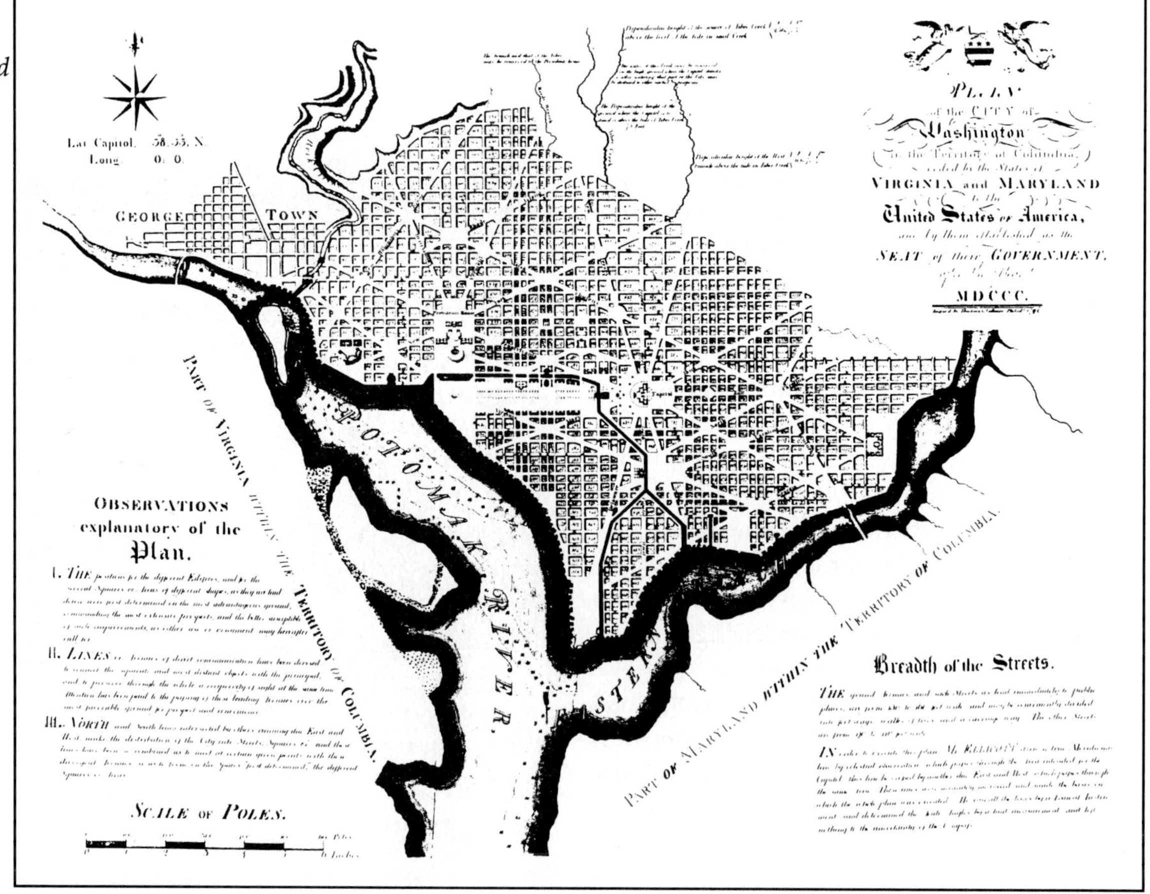

12.23
Pierre l'Enfant and Andrew Ellicott, Washington D.C., 1792, plan.

an original form very close to that of an ideal Renaissance radial town. The inner circle was contained within on outer square, the latter laid out on an orthogonal grid. By 1837 the orthogonal order of the perimeter had invaded one quadrant of the radial center. Land speculators realized that profits could be gained by transforming the 'wasted space' at the center of the organization into salable lots. Dismissing the circle as *"a piece of childish sentimentalism,"* in 1838, the 'Circleville Squaring Company' was founded. By the end of the year, two quadrants were entirely overtaken by the grid; only one retained its original structure. By 1856, no trace was left of the original plan. Circleville, like most Midwestern towns, is now configured exactly as the surrounding plowed fields, on a grid.

In 1785 **Thomas Jefferson** (1743-1826) arranged for the United States to be surveyed and marked off on a 6 mile square grid, which was subdividable into 1, 4, 8, 16, 32 or 64 smaller areas. The grid was an expression of Enlightenment dominion over the landscape but it also made the landscape accessible. Naming and parcelling the land would facilitate settlement and the sale of land in all regions. Beyond the pragmatics of the **Jeffersonian grid**, there were symbolic meanings as well.

René Descartes' coordinate system translated the geometrical mathematics of Euclid and Pythagoras (rooted in magic and reliant on solid, bounded, knowable things) into an algebraic model based on extrapolation, systematization, and a concept of infinity. Extending across the continent, the Jeffersonian Grid works the way intended by Descartes. No center is stipulated

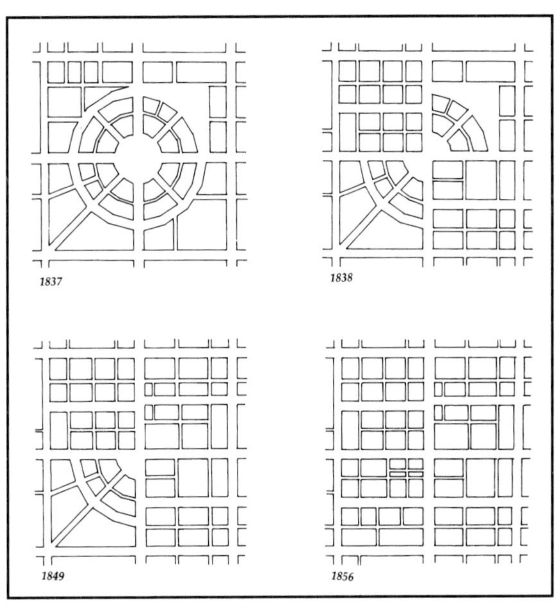

12.24
The Squaring of Circleville, Ohio, according to John Reps.

12.25
Circleville, Ohio, 1836 engraving.

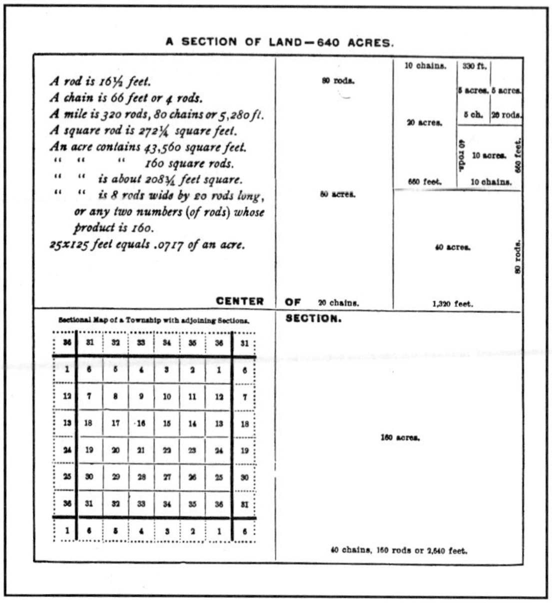

A SECTION OF LAND—640 ACRES.

A rod is 16½ feet.
A chain is 66 feet or 4 rods.
A mile is 320 rods, 80 chains or 5,280 ft.
A square rod is 272¼ square feet.
An acre contains 43,560 square feet.
" " " 160 square rods.
" " is about 208¾ feet square.
" " is 8 rods wide by 20 rods long, or any two numbers (of rods) whose product is 160.
25x125 feet equals .0717 of an acre.

80 rods. 80 acres. 10 chains. 330 ft. 5 acres. 5 acres. 5 ch. 20 rods. 20 acres. 40 rods. 10 acres. 660 feet. 660 feet. 10 chains. 40 acres. 80 rods. 20 chains. 1,320 feet. 160 acres. 40 chains, 160 rods or 2,640 feet.

CENTER OF SECTION.

Sectional Map of a Township with adjoining Sections.

36	31	32	33	34	35	36	31
1	6	5	4	3	2	1	6
12	7	8	9	10	11	12	7
13	18	17	16	15	14	13	18
24	19	20	21	22	23	24	19
25	30	29	28	27	26	25	30
36	31	32	33	34	35	36	31
1	6	5	4	3	2	1	6

12.26 The basic structure of the Jeffersonian Grid.

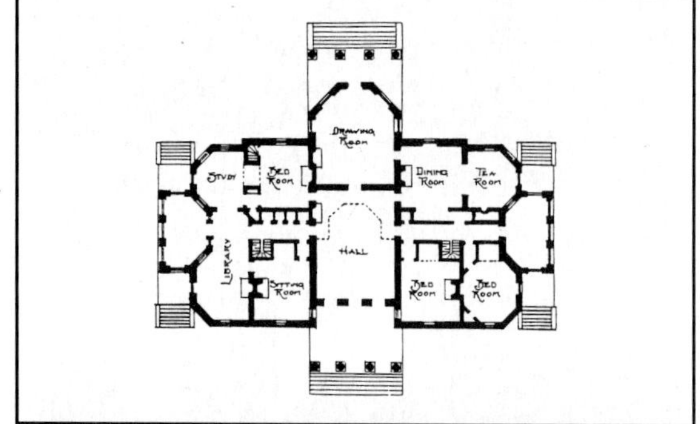

12.27 Thomas Jefferson, Monticello, Charlottesville, Virginia, 1771-72.

12.28 Monticello, view.

as in Roman gridded towns. The unbounded Cartesian grid of the American landscape is neutral and infinitely extensible. Space is mathematized and the hierarchy of an absolute center is broken.

Thomas Jefferson was deeply suspicious of cities and called them *"a pestilence to the morals, health, and liberties of man."* He was particularly suspicious of the fineries and foppishness of Europe, although he lived there in grand style for over four years. Jefferson firmly believed in the 'agrarian ideal,' i.e., in the virtue of self-sufficient, independent farmers who lived in small family groups throughout the countryside. For Jefferson, urban life brought with it not only pestilence and fire, but also a decline in moral character. The gridding of the continent was a practical tool to make possible Jefferson's dream of a nation of farmers. As a work of engineering, the Jeffersonian grid is without equal in scale and relentlessness. It covers America without concern for variations in topography: lakes and mountains are traversed, yet it persists, invariable, on its rational description of the geometry of a continent.

Jefferson was not only the architect of the Declaration of Independence, but he was also one of the most noteworthy American architects of his period. He designed his own home, **Monticello**, and the **Virginia Statehouse** in Richmond, 1775, as well. Based closely on the Masion Carrée, the Statehouse was the first public building since antiquity to be configured as a temple, although the model soon became a standard for American public buildings.

Jefferson was best able to express his views about social structure, history, education, and the landscape in his plan for the **University of**

Virginia, 1817-26; a U-shaped plan organization which included a library, professors' houses, classrooms, and student rooms. Like L'Enfant in Washington, Jefferson situated the most important building on the highest ground. For Jefferson, this was not the home of the President of the University, nor even the chapel, but the library. Modelled on the Pantheon, the Library Rotunda commanded an axial view across a manicured green lawn to the wilderness of the valley and the hills beyond. Flanking the Pantheonic central pavilion were two ranges of five discrete, Neo-Classical pavilions engaged on a colonnaded cellular bar of dormitory rooms. The lay-out of the University, reminiscent of Louis XIV's Chateau Marly in France, is apparently simple but incorporates many levels of hierarchical stratification.

The Pantheonic configuration of the library, as well as its central location, reveal a shift in values. The Pantheon was a sanctuary for all the gods; the library was the repository of all knowledge. Reason, scientific inquiry, and scholarship had replaced faith as the center of meaning for the Enlightenment community of the University of Virginia. Each professor's house is an isolated pavilion, although it takes part in the overall assemblage of forms. No two pavilions are alike. Jefferson did not try to invent a particularly 'American' style of architecture. Instead, he self-consciously provided exempla of great historical buildings. In that way, students could develop proper sensibilities about architecture without travelling abroad, a practice Jefferson wished to discourage.

The systematic structure of the plan hierarchically links all built forms in the complex,

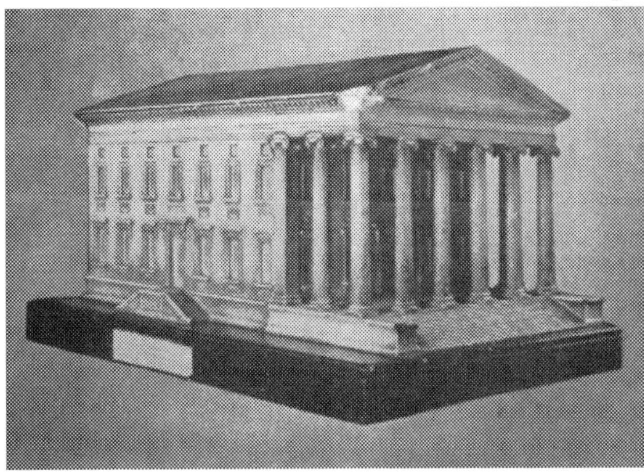

12.29 Virginia Statehouse, Richmond, Virginia, model by Jefferson and C.L. Clérisseau, 1785.

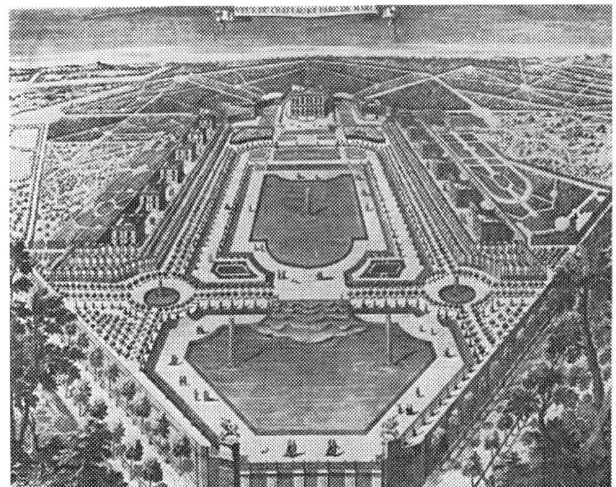

12.30 J.H. Mansart, Chateau Marly, France, began 1679.

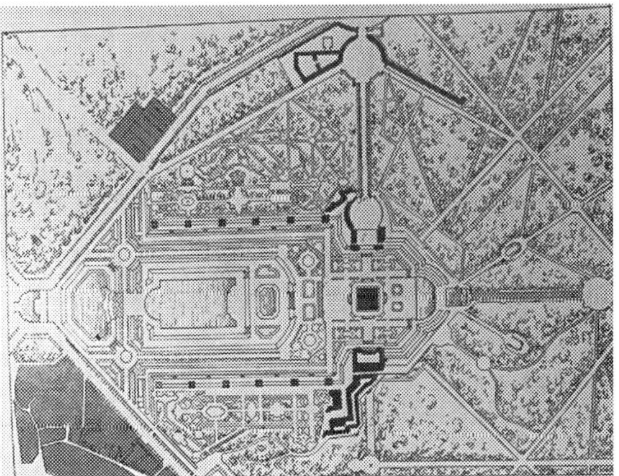

12.31 Chateau Marly, plan.

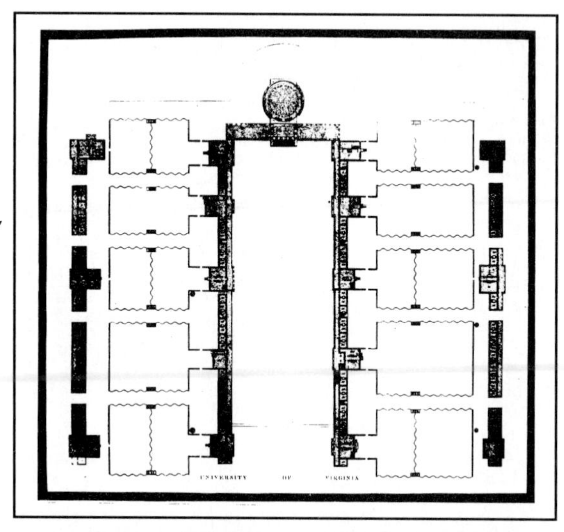

12.32
Thomas Jefferson, University of Virginia, Charlottesville, Virginia, 1817-26, plan.

12.33
University of Virginia, view.

12.34
University of Virginia, view.

from the Rotunda, to the professors' houses, to the students' houses. In a like fashion, a structured relationship is put into play among different conditions of landscape. The central lawn is a well-groomed rectangle: nature subjected to and transformed by culture. Behind the ranges of buildings, symmetrically disposed around the central axis, are small pleasure gardens and kitchen gardens: nature subjected to cultivation. Terminating the central axis, on par in stature with the Rotunda itself, is the distant wilderness: nature in its pure, unaltered state. The form of the University complex is created by the reciprocal tension between nature and culture. The power of the wilderness is emphasized by the uneven rhythm of the pavilions. Nearest the Rotunda, they are closest together, but as they move farther away from it, the space between them increases, as if they are accelerating outwards, pulled into the valley by the force of the infinite, open landscape.

The particularity of the University of Virginia as an American work can be seen by comparing it to the **Salt Works at Chaux** by **Claude Nicolas Ledoux** (1736-1806). Like Jefferson at the University of Virginia, Ledoux created a new settlement in a forested landscape. While Jefferson saw the wilderness as a source of moral renewal, Ledoux saw the forest as a source of fuel to power the Salt Works. The concept of consuming the wilderness was only to catch fancy in America some years later. Both Chaux and the University of Virginia have strongly defined centers, but the center at Chaux organizes a closed, self-contained, radial system; there is a clear distinction between the protected inner precinct and the landscape. At the University of Virginia, the axial placement of the Rotunda sponsors an open ended system in dialogue with landscape.

Both Jefferson and Ledoux self-consciously borrowed architectural language and forms from the classical era. Jefferson did so to equate the values of the new nation with those of Republican Rome and Democratic Greece. His purpose was didactic, to instruct young Americans about the great architectural patrimony of the western world. Hence, he made minor, playful variations on his Palladian and antique models, but was accurate in his classical detailing.

Ledoux, on the other hand, attempted to transform the classical language to more precisely represent the unclassical function of his Salt Works. To do so, he made use of heavy rustication, the rough, primitive treatment of stone surfaces, claimed by sixteenth-century theoreticians to represent the work of nature. The classical language he used is stripped down to the bare essentials, and the forms are stark and elemental in their geometric simplicity. Upon entering the main gate to the complex, there is a sudden transformation in surface treatment from the smoothly faced stone of the exterior to a cavernous space with rough natural stone walls, mimetic of the entry into the earth at a salt mine. Even columns are trapped by horizontal bands of rustication. Windows cease to have ventilation and illumination as their chief function. Instead, they are given the task of representing saline fluid pouring into a tank.

Politically, both the Salt Works at Chaux and the University of Virginia make statements about the nature of the community in architectural form. Jefferson constructs an 'Academic Village' where all citizens take their place at the

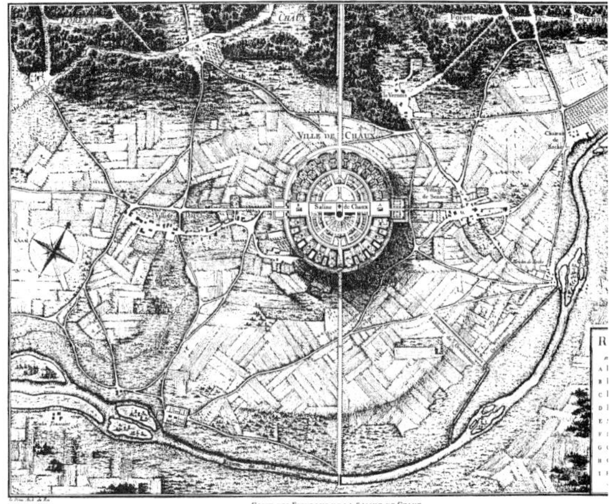

12.35 Claude-Nicolas Ledoux, Salt Works of Chaux, Arc-et-Senans, France, 1775-79, site plan.

12.36 Salt Works of Chaux, view.

12.37 Salt Works of Chaux, view.

12.38 Salt Works of Chaux, plan perspective.

perimeter in deference to the central position of the library. The organization of Chaux is radial, like a Renaissance town plan, but here the factory director, not the prince, occupies the authoritarian position of center. The plan enforces class stratification.

Jefferson's legacy of the agrarian ideal and suspicion of the town has continued to color American visions of the city and contribute to the lack of formal definition in many American towns. **Frank Lloyd Wright's** plan for **Broadacre City** is perhaps the most extreme contemporary expression of the Jeffersonian ideal. Wright shared Jefferson's anti-urban stance and was even more out-spoken: *"To look at the plan of any great city is to look at the cross-section of some fibrous tumor."* Broadacre City was not meant to be a city in any conventional sense of the word. Believing that *"when every man, woman and child may be born to put his own feet on his own acres, then democracy will have been realized,"* Wright favored radical decentralization, made possible by the speed and ease of automobile travel. He even designed his own cars, futuristic space pods, and helicopters for more convenient travel. An extensive grid of motor ways structured the settlement, similar in form to the plan of a conventional gridded city, but operating at a scale and speed far in excess of the norm. Broadacre City might sprawl over 100 square miles with no clearly defined center. Instead, the crossing of roads would spawn dispersed centers of commerce, 'Farmers Markets.'

Wright's utopian vision for America was prophetic of many of the conditions usually considered to be the *problem* with American urbanism: the lack of strong town centers, the dispersal of commerce to the perimeter, the erosion of a sense of collectivity, and the conspicuous consumption of natural resources.

The dream of arcadia and the 'green country town,' have also left a softer impression on American urban form. Penn's stipulation for the lay-out of Philadelphia *". . . So that there may be ground on each side for gardens or orchards, or fields that it may be a green country town, which will never be burnt, and always be wholesome,"* is not dissimilar to the condition in American suburbia today. Born in the era of Neo-Classicism and the Picturesque Romantic Garden, America has always favored independent, free-standing structures in dialogue with the landscape in favor of an order that is too insular, or too urban, and too authoritarian.

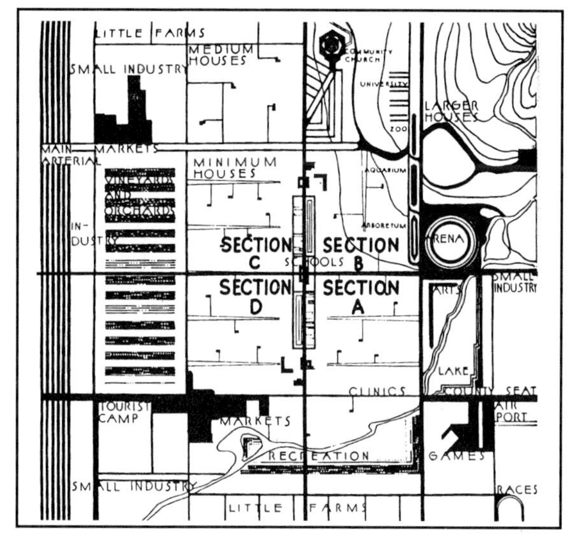

12.39 Frank Lloyd Wright, plan of Broadacre City, 1958.

12.40 Frank Lloyd Wright, drawing of Broadacre City, 1945.

12.41 Frank Lloyd Wright, drawing of Broadacre City, c. 1950 with helicopters and cars of Wright's own design.

13.0
"The Palace of Architecture", nineteenth-century project.

Chapter 13

The 18th & 19th Centuries: The Crisis of Style

The peculiar characteristic of the present day, as compared with all former periods, is this - that we are acquainted with the history of art ... It is reserved to us above all the generations of the human race, to know perfectly our own standing-point, and to look back upon the entire history of what had gone before us . . . This is amazingly interesting to us as a matter of amusement and erudition, but I fear it is a hindrance rather than help to us as artists.

-Sir George Gilbert Scott

In early history, untamed nature was thought to be terrifying, unknowable and diabolical. Paradise was a walled enclosure, a bounded precinct removed from the expansive wilderness. Order and control could be established within the walls: outside, a wasteland without limit threatened to reduce humankind to the condition of brute beasts. The punishment for Adam and Eve was expulsion from the walled oasis of Eden. Religion, philosophy, and art began as ways to mediate between the human condition and forces beyond control. Because natural forces were terrifying, social conventions and cities were established so that people could band together for refuge and renewal. Civilization was understood to be a protective sanctuary from the unpredictable hostility of nature.

By the eighteenth century, a paradigm shift had taken place and the status of nature altered with respect to culture. **Enlightenment** science and discoveries by men like Leibniz, Newton, and Descartes provided a new understanding of the forces of the unknown. Direct observation and rational deduction took the place of mysticism and analogical reflection. Science replaced religion as the vehicle by which cosmologies were modelled; and nature, instead of representing the impure, corrupt, and unholy side of man, was embraced as pure and essential. In nature, civilized people might recover the godly innocence of a simpler time.

13.1
Claude Lorrain, The Father of Psyche sacrificing to Apollo," 1660-70, The Fairhaven Collection, Anglesey Abbey (The National Trust), Cambridgeshire.

13.2
Nicolas Poussin, "Landscape with the Burial of Phocion," 1648, the Louvre.

13.3
Henry Hoare and Henry Flitcroft, Stourhead, c.1740-60, Stourton, England, view of pavilions around the lake.

Europeans and Americans alike were fascinated by the nobility of the wilderness and its savage denizens. Men like Rousseau, Schelling, Thoreau, and Emerson wrote lengthy philosophical works about nature. Related hobbies gained fashion: hiking, picnicking, and landscape painting. Until that time, the subject matter of paintings addressed serious religious and historical themes; landscape painting merely captured the charm of a fleeting moment. In the eighteenth century, art exchanged its iconic status for an aesthetic one. Preference was guided by taste rather than transcendental criteria. It is not surprising that at this time the first museums were established.

The paintings of two seventeenth-century Frenchmen, **Claude Lorrain** (1600-1682) and **Nicolas Poussin** (1594-1665), emphasized the landscape over the allegorical subject matter. In response to the beauty of such paintings, a strange reversal took place. Garden designers began to transform nature in imitation of paintings by Lorrain and Poussin, rather than the reverse. People carried 'Claude glasses,' framed panels of yellow glass, so that their view of the landscape would better resemble the format and golden light of Claude Lorrain's paintings. The **Picturesque** was born.

Romantic or Picturesque gardens found their greatest following in England. The structured formality of earlier garden design gave way to the irregular forms and curving lines of the picturesque. Landscape was no longer groomed with geometric precision; instead, the natural, unbounded sweep of the terrain was made more 'natural' through great effort. Hillocks were built on flat land, asymmetrical lakes and rivulets were cut through the fields, clusters of trees were planted at advantageous spots. Herds of deer were even imported to the site so that they might enhance the picturesque effect of the landscape. The role of architecture in the garden changed as well. In sixteenth-century gardens, such as the Villa Lante or the Villa Giulia, landscape was framed by architecture. In picturesque gardens, small pavilions or **follies** were objects to be discovered in the landscape. A scattering of charming little temples brought to mind Arcadia, that glorious time in the remote past when shepherds and shepherdesses frolicked, at one with nature. The sight of Gothic ruins brought to mind the mysticism and intrigue of a bygone age. Moreover, decaying architecture highlighted the Romantic contrast between human mortality and the everlasting renewal of nature.

The very fact that artificial ruins were deliberately constructed indicates a self-conscious attitude towards history. Unlike previous periods in which architecture and architectural style were authentic, direct expressions of the culture, in the eighteenth century the natural chain had been broken. Style was not inevitable, but a product of choice.

At **Stourhead** (1740-60), by **Henry Hoare** and **Henry Flitcroft** (1697-1769), the composed casualness of landscape painting is achieved through great artifice. The garden has been described as an *"eighteenth-century theme park ... With Virgil and Poussin (not Mickey and Donald) as its animating spirits"* (Moore, Mitchell and Turnbull, *The Poetics of Gardens*). An eclectic assortment of pavilions and follies are organized around a small lake, loosely strung together on a meandering path. The sequence of events unfolds counter-clockwise along the path, describing an allegorical narrative loosely based

13.4 Stourhead, view of the Apollo Temple.

13.5 Stourhead, view of the Grotto.

13.6
Caspar David Friedrich, "The Wanderer above the Mist," c. 1817-18, Kunsthalle, Hamburg.

13.7
J.M.W. Turner, "Steamer in a Snowstorm," 1842, London, Tate Gallery.

on Virgil's *Aeneid*. The procession traces the mythical journey of Aeneus from the devastation of Troy, to the Sybil's grotto, to the underworld, and finally, on to Rome. Scenes of the *Aeneid* are not literally depicted, but are evoked by the architecture and siting of follies along the path. From a landscape populated by classical temples on high ground, one proceeds to a netherworld of grottos, secret pools, and statues of nymphs and river gods. Upon emerging from the underworld, one encounters a miniature Pantheon, symbol of Rome. The victory of the Olympian Gods (lovers of the heights, light and reason) over the Chthonic earth deities (lovers of the depths, darkness, and frenzy) is affirmed architecturally. High on a sun-lit bluff overlooking the lake is the final temple, the Temple to Apollo, the god of reason.

It is impossible to name the style of the architecture at Stourhead. Historical styles are appropriated and used because of the associations they conjure up, not because of any historical or functional connection. The main house, by Colin Campbell, (1676-1729), is Neo-Palladian. The garden hosts an **eclectic** assortment from as many historical periods as there are pavilions. Some pavilions are Gothic; others are classical; some are inventions of the architect, like the temple front embedded in a rough cavern wall; and others, like the Pantheon and the Apollo Temple, present miniaturized versions of famous buildings from antiquity.

An appreciation of nature meant an appreciation of the effects of nature, even raging storms, torrential waterfalls, lurid sunsets, and the craggy asymmetry of mountains. The classical ideal of 'beauty' as the harmonious arrangements of parts, so that nothing could be added or taken away, except for the worse, was inadequate in dealing with the violence and scale of natural splendors. A new concept was introduced by Edmund Burke (1729-97) in his book *Origin of Our Ideas of the Sublime and the Beautiful,* 1756. According to Burke, beauty had to do with refined proportions, harmony, simplicity, geometry, and order, the very qualities called for by Renaissance theoreticians. The **Sublime**, on the contrary, suggested the opposite. Instead of complementing and reflecting human scale, the Sublime had the power to dwarf; in place of smoothness and clear definition of form, the Sublime offered the rough and the irregular; instead of using light to illuminate, it was used to blind or obscure. The sensation evoked by the Sublime was not well-being, but 'delight,' i.e. the feeling roused when one is at the brink of death and is miraculously spared. Beauty could be found in the most perfect works of humankind, but the sublime could only be produced by nature.

The landscape paintings of **Casper David Friedrich** (1774-1840) and **J.M.W. Turner** (1775-1851) depict the sublime, not the beautiful in nature. In Friedrich's painting, ***The Wanderer above the Mist,*** human presence is dwarfed by the vastness of the wilderness, where even gnarled oak trees cannot thrive. The sky is turbulent and strange light pervades the composition and the figures are relegated to the shadows. Turner too selects subject matter because of its violence and dynamism, not because of any conventional attitude towards beauty or appropriate subject matter. Blizzards, fires and storms at sea are all part of his repertoire. The foment of natural elements becomes

13.8 E.L. Boullée, Cenotaph to Newton, 1784, section, night view.

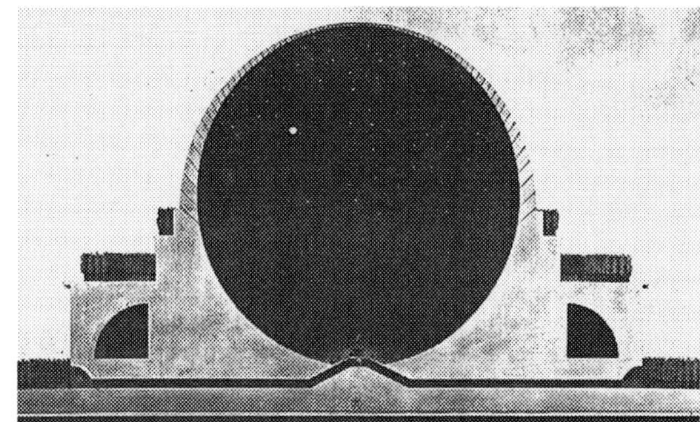

13.9 Cenotaph to Newton, section, day view.

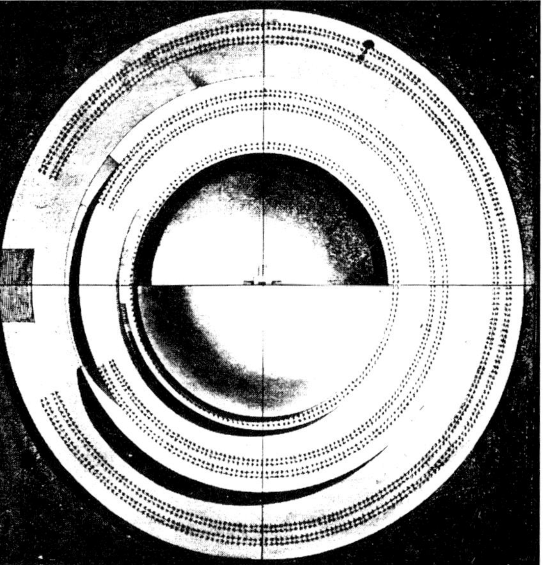

13.10 Cenotaph to Newton, plan.

13.11
C.N. Ledoux, Cooper's Workshop, c. 1773-79.

13.12
C.N. Ledoux, Inspector's House at the Source of the Loue, c. 1773-79.

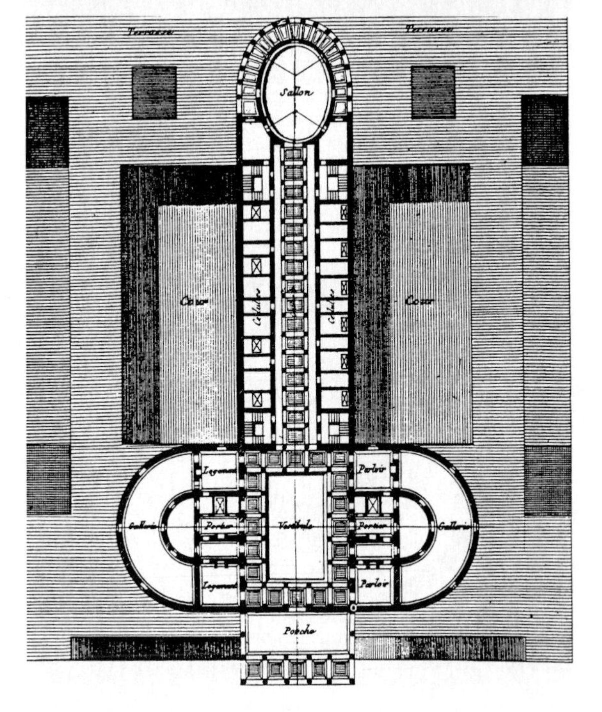

13.13
C.N. Ledoux, Oikema, or 'House of Pleasure,' c. 1773-79.

the subject. All scale and figurality are absent in paintings such as ***Steamer in a Snowstorm***, 1842.

The French civil servant, **Etienne-Louis Boullée** (1728-99), expressed his fascination with the sublime through enormity of scale rather than the irregular, picturesque effects of nature. His project for a **Cenotaph to Newton** is comprised of a vast sphere, overwhelming because of its sheer magnitude. Trees planted on exterior terraces seem like tiny **crenulations** in contrast with the sphere itself. Inside, the globe not only houses the **sarcophagus** to Newton, but also creates the illusion of the cosmos. By day, tiny slits in the vault emit light, creating an illusionistic star-filled sky; by night, a lamp suspended within an armillary sphere glows like the sun at the center of its solar system. Day and night are reversed and the vastness of the universe is explicitly contrasted to the finitude of man. An epigram by Alexander Pope (1688-1744) expressed the awe evoked by Newtonian physics and the degree to which science had usurped the traditional place of religion in the eighteenth century. *"Nature and Nature's laws lay hid in night, God said "Let Newton Be," and all was light".*

For the Romans, the spherical space of the Pantheon *was* a microcosmic recreation of the heavenly firmament. Boullée's monument to Newton, instead, *looks like* a physical model of the heavens. While the former is an embodiment of a metaphysical idea or a presentation of the structure of the universe, the latter is a representation of the universe; its aspirations are associational. Boullée is using **character** and **associations** to create an ***architecture parlante*** or speaking architecture, that is, an architecture whose form is a direct expression of its content.

Claude Nicholas Ledoux (1735-1806) investigated the limits of *architecture parlante* in his **House for a Cooper's Workshop** and **Inspector's House at the Source of the Loue**. The Barrel Maker's house is literally a barrel form; the River Inspector's house is literally a conduit for the river. Ledoux did numerous other such houses, all of them designed to express the particular character of the client. Ledoux's project for the **Oikema**, or 'House of Pleasure,' is likewise organized around a form expressive of its function. Perhaps the most explicit and fanciful use of *architecture parlante* is **Jean-Jacques Lequeu's** (1757-1825) unbuilt project for a **Cow Stable**. The upper hay loft gains light and ventilation from the cow's eyes.

The dilemma facing architects in the nineteenth century was enormous. Buildings could look like anything, even an ornately robed cow. A painting by **Thomas Cole** (1801-48) entitled ***The Architect's Dream*** depicts a dapper architect lounging upon a colossal column capital, loosely holding an architectural drawing. To his left, in the gloom and shadows, is the irregular profile of a Gothic townscape. To his right, stretching out along the sun-lit shores, is a classical town; beyond that, an Egyptian pyramid looms. For Cole, the task of the architect was to choose which historical style to use, or to combine bits and pieces from each, not to invent something specific to his own age.

The link between contemporary culture and its automatic expression in artistic production had been broken. A new self-consciousness characterized the age. Historical revivals flourished. It was commonly believed that since one

13.14 J.J. Lequeu, Project for a Cow Stable, c. 1800.

13.15 Thomas Cole, "The Architect's Dream," c. 1825, Toledo Museum of Art.

13.16 Leo von Klenze, Walhalla, 1830-42, Regensburg, Germany.

13.17 Left: K.F. Schinkel, Gardener's House, Potsdam, Germany, 1829-36.

13.18 Right: K.F. Schinkel, Schloß Glienicke, Berlin, Germany 1824-26.

13.19 K.F. Schinkel, Gardener's House.

13.20 K.F. Schinkel, Schloß Babelsberg, Potsdam, Germany, 1833.

could no longer build with authenticity, then the best compromise was to copy the works of those who could. Johannes Winckelmann (1717-1768) expressed this sentiment clearly: *"To take the ancients as our models is the only way to become great, yes, unsurpassable if we can."* With the Greek Revival came a passion for archeology, the beauty of stark white marble, and severe Doric buildings. Sometimes buildings were unabashed copies of ancient sources, as in **Leo von Klenze's** (1784-1874) **Walhalla**, a hall of German worthies, based faithfully on the Parthenon. While Classical Revivals evoked a sense of the beautiful, the Gothic revival evoked feelings of the sublime. Pointed turrets, dra-

13.21 K.F. Schinkel, Schloß Charlottenhof, Potsdam, Germany, 1826.

matic sites, irregular plans, and massive walls carried associations with the supernatural and the bizarre intrigues of Gothic novels. Other historical revivals had more limited impact. The Egyptian Revival was ideal for cemeteries: no one celebrated the dead more gloriously than they.

Architects at the beginning of the nineteenth century found little difficulty in using whichever style suited them for the project at hand. In Potsdam, **Karl Friederich Schinkel** (1781-1841) designed several buildings, all in very different styles. The **Schloß Charlottenhof**, 1826, is in the Classical style; the **Gardener's House**, 1829-36, in Tuscan vernacular; the **Schloß Babelsberg**, 1833, in Gothic, and across the river, the **Schloß Glienicke** is in a fanciful strain of Graeco-Roman revival.

Schinkel and von Klenze contented themselves with using one style at a time, but eclectic recombination of elements from many sources was another serious option. The **Palace of Architecture**, frontispiece to this chapter, is a serious design for a gate in the Graeco-Roman-Indo-Arabian-Egypto-Gothic-Renaissance Style. The architect's task was reduced to that of a stylist, and when so many styles are available, there is no style.

Not everyone was content to move promiscuously among styles. **Augustus Welby**

13.22 Left: E.E. Viollet-le-Duc, Cast-iron structure.

13.23 Right: E.E. Viollet-le-Duc, Market.

Northmore Pugin (1812-52), made a moral argument. Gothic architecture was the only 'true' architecture because it was the product of Christian faith and northern sensibilities, while Classicism grew up around the pagan Mediterranean. Others, like **Eugène-Emmanuel Viollet-le-Duc** (1814-1879) argued that the superiority of Gothic over Classic lie in its structural rationalism. In Gothic architecture, ornament was not applied, as in Classical architecture, but was the product of constructive and structural necessity. For Viollet, the honesty of the Gothic skeletal systems should be studied and expanded upon with new materials such as iron. **John Ruskin** (1819-1900) was yet another proponent of Gothic Revival architecture. His argument differed from those of Pugin and Violet-le-Duc. Ruskin believed that the value of architecture resided in the moral well being of its maker. Pleasure in work, associated by Ruskin with medieval guilds, naturally produced a superior architecture to one produced under less amiable circumstances.

Viollet's interest in constructional honesty and structural rationalism shared its agenda with those who looked to the primitive hut as a source of renewal and replenishment for the exhausted architectural practice. The myth of the primitive hut goes back to Vitruvius, but it gained currency in the eighteenth and nineteenth centuries. If one needed to recuperate lost meanings for architecture by appropriating forms from an earlier age, then the most honest and most natural expression could be found in the earliest example; the mythical first building. Among the most popular theories were **Marc-Antoine Laugier's** (1713-69), based on the intertwining of limbs to form a skeleton, and **Gottfried Semper's** (1803-79), which posited that the first structures were woven. All primi-

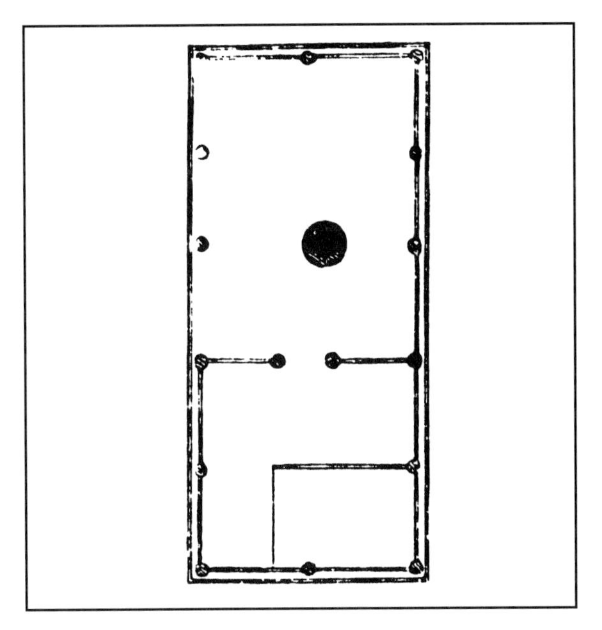

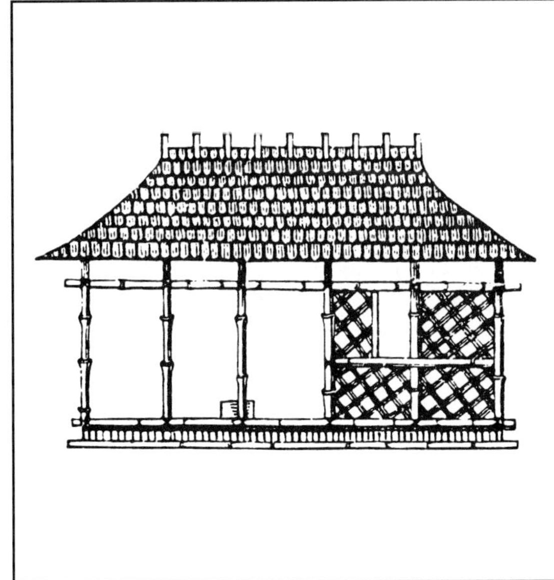

13.24 Left: Gottfried Semper, Primitive Hut, the "Caribbean Hut," from Der Stil, 1859, plan.

13.25 Right: Gottfried Semper, Primitive Hut, the "Caribbean Hut," from Der Stil, 1859, elevation.

tive hut theories shared a belief in the honest use of materials, in ornament formed from structural and connective details, and an abhorrence for applied decoration.

When Viollet-le-Duc identified the liberating possibilities of new materials in architecture, he hit upon a very potent theme. However, for some time, engineers had been using iron, reinforced concrete and plate glass in their designs for structures such as train sheds, covered market halls, exposition halls, and the like. Because these were new building types, there were no precedents to be imitated. Moreover, because such structures required clear spans longer than those of preceding epoches, design solutions arose in direct response to the problem and without reliance on stylistic choice. Through structural rationalism, honesty in use of materials, and the jettisoning of nostalgic allegiance to the architecture of the past, many felt that the spirit of the age, the ***Zeitgeist***, could at last find expression in architectural form.

The first truly modern building expressive of the contemporary *Zeitgeist* was the **Crystal Palace**, 1851, by **Joseph Paxton** , a landscape designer who specialized in greenhouses. Designed as a temporary exhibition hall in London, the plan and massing of the Crystal Palace were symmetrical and conventional. Extraordinary was the material and the method of construction. The Crystal Palace was built entirely out of glass and pre-fabricated cast iron panels, almost identical in design to those used on an earlier Paxton greenhouse. The interior space was light and airy, attaining a dematerialization aspired to in the Gothic period, but unattainable due to the limits of stone. The panels were built on an eight foot module and could be dismantled and reassembled, which is

13.26
Joseph Paxton, Crystal Palace, London, 1851, exterior view.

13.27
Crystal Palace, interior view.

what occurred. The modular panel system made it possible for the large hall to be built in only four months. The advances in design and construction of the Crystal Palace indicated a way out of the dilemma of styles, but visitors to the Crystal Palace were not yet cognizant of this. Instead, their attention was drawn to the exhibits of historical decoration found within. Engineering and architecture were seen as two separate endeavors, and the Crystal Palace belonged squarely to the former.

Gustave Eiffel (1832-1923) is the nineteenth-century engineer whose works did most to forge a link between the disciplines of architec-

13.28 Crystal Palace, construction process.

13.29 Left: Gustave Eiffel, Eiffel Tower,1889.

13.30 Right: Eiffel Tower.

ture and engineering. Using riveted iron, he contrived structures of exquisite elegance and daring, such as the **viaducts at St. Andrew de Cubzak** and **Garabit.** Best known is his design of the **Eiffel Tower** for the Paris Exposition of 1889. At the time of its construction the unclad nudity of the 300 meter tall iron frame shocked and insulted the urbane Parisians, but there is really nothing brutal about the Eiffel Tower. The fine correspondence between the size of elements and the structural task they perform lends the tower a delicate laciness. Scale is knit together with nuanced refinement so that the smallest detail is responsive to the language and syntax of the whole. The Eiffel Tower is now one of the most memorable monuments in Paris and the most lasting symbol of the euphoria of the first machine age.

At the Paris Exposition of 1900 another monstrous and beautiful machine was constructed, the **Great Wheel**. Unlike the Eiffel Tower, it was torn down shortly afterwards. In *The City of Tomorrow,* Le Corbusier marks its passing: *"Here is the age of steel, an age of confusion, of the introduction of a new scale confounding accepted standards and causing great excitement . . . But by 1920 the great wheel no longer existed; the verdict had been passed and an idol overthrown."* Ancient cultures, such as that of Egypt, produced a style that lasted millennia; at the turn of the nineteenth century, the consumption and generation of styles took place at a break-neck pace. Most buildings were out of fashion by the time they were constructed. Not even engineering and structural rationalism could remedy the situation.

13.31 Left: Gustave Eiffel, St. Andrew de Cubzak train bridge.

13.32 Right: The GreatWheel at the Paris Exposition.

13.33 Gustave Eiffel, GarabitViaduct.

14.0
El Lissitzky, "Tatlin working on the Monument to the Third International," 1922, Collage and Drawing. Collection Eric Estorick, London.

Chapter 14

The Twentieth Century: High Modernism

Elements have entered into our life of whose very possibility the ancients did not even dream... We have lost the sense of the monumental, of the heavy, of the static; we have enriched our sensibility by a taste for the light, the practical, the ephemeral and swift. We feel that we are no longer men of the cathedrals, the palaces, the assembly halls; but of big hotels, railway stations, immense roads, colossal ports, covered markets, brilliantly lit galleries, freeways, demolition and rebuilding schemes...

-Antonio Sant'Elia

A dizzying euphoria struck at the turn of the century as people realized that they were living in a historical period vastly different from anything that had come before. All traditions of formal and social order seemed diminished when confronted with the speed, scale, and power of the new technology. The nineteenth-century search for a style expressive of the *Zeitgeist* seemed to reach its consummation in the disciplined, rational art of engineering. Le Corbusier said: "*The Engineer's Aesthetic and Architecture are two things that march together and follow one from the other: the one being now at its full height, the other in an unhappy state of retrogression.*" While historicist styles were kept alive in the academies, **avant-garde** architectural movements proliferated. Every country in Europe produced its own particular brand of architecture, each with a claim to embody the spirit of the times. French Art Nouveau, German Expressionism, Italian Futurism, Russian Constructivism, the Viennese Secession, Dutch De Stijl, more styles than there were countries in Europe. Some, like Art Nouveau, lasted no more than a few years; others, like Functionalism, were long lived and so widely diffused that it came to be known as the 'International Style.'

Developments in contemporary science had an impact on the conceptualization of form and space. Just as the concepts of infinity and Cartesian space stimulated aesthetic production in the Baroque age, relativistic ideas about the space-time continuum had great impact on artists and architects in the early part of the

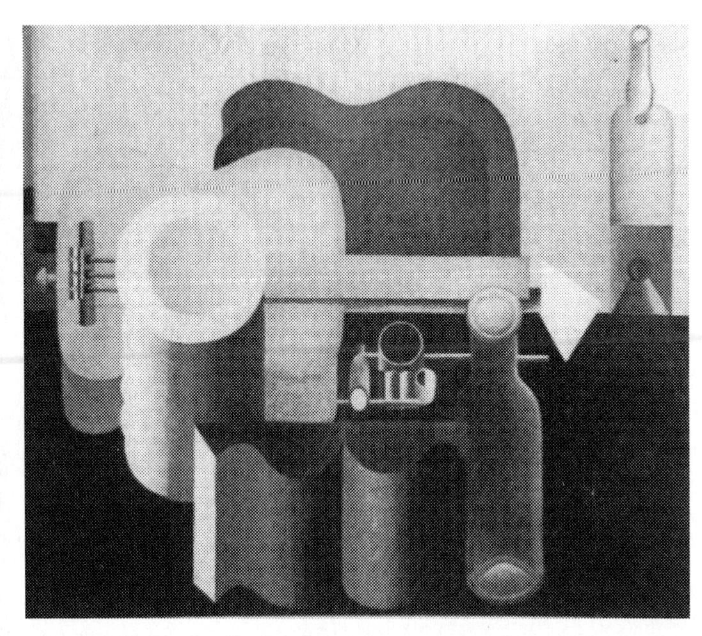

14.1 Left: Pablo Picasso, "Violin and Grapes," 1912 , New York , The Museum of Modern Art.

14.2 Right: Charles-Eduoard Jeanneret (Le Corbusier), "Still Life," 1920, New York, The Museum of Modern Art.

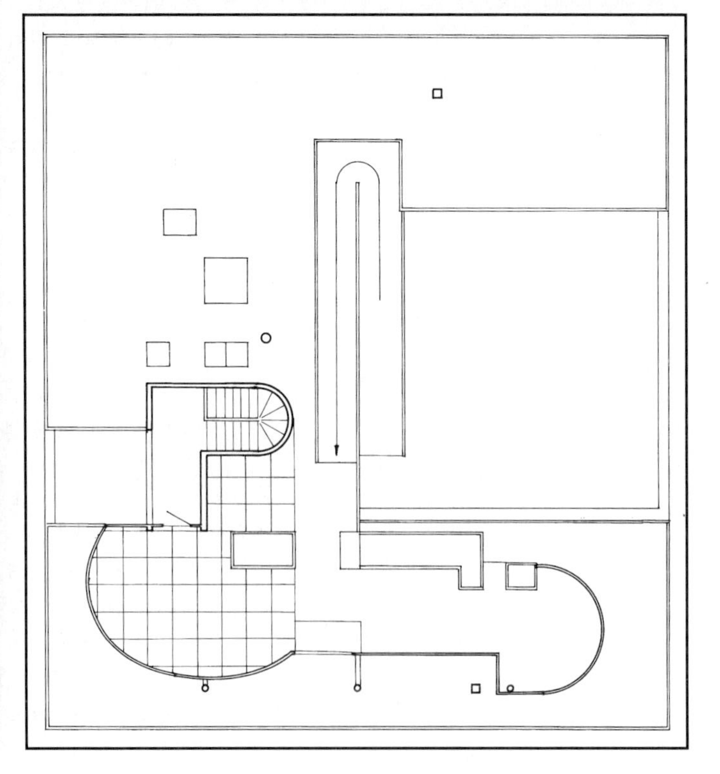

14.3 Left: Marcel Duchamp, "Nude Descending a Staircase, No.2," 1912, Philadelphia Museum of Art, Louise and Walter Arensberg Collection.

14.4 Right: Le Corbusier, Villa Savoye, Poissy, 1928-31, roof plan.

twentieth century. In painting, Analytic Cubists like **Georges Braque** (1881-1963) and **Pablo Picasso** attempted to combine a primitive vision of form and a Post-Newtonian view of space. **Picasso's *"Violin and Grapes"*** simultaneously depicts multiple views of the violin in an attempt to violate the two-dimensionality of the picture plane, not by the illusionistic representation of three-dimensional space, but by implying the fourth dimension of time. Transparent layers of paint impart depth in the two-dimensional image while asserting the flatness of the fragmented three-dimensional subject. Superimposition and interpenetration of vignettes creates an ambiguous field of fragments in place of a whole image. Over time, these fragments are reassembled in the mind, like the discrete frames of a film strip or the collided images of collage.

Other artists, such as **Marcel Duchamp** (1887-1968), were explicitly engaged with the question of four-dimensional space. His ***"Nude Descending a Staircase"*** represents movement and duration through the multiple, overlapping figures. In his ***"Bride Stripped Bare by her Bachelors, Even"*** the impossibility of union between the 'Bride' and 'Her Bachelors' is signified in part by Duchamp's depiction of the latter in perspectival space, and the former in fragmented 'four-dimensional' space.

Cubism and related movements provided inspiration for architects. **Le Corbusier's 'Purist' paintings** explore the same tension between a clear orthogonal frame and interpenetrating fragments of organic form as do his architectural works: in the **Villa Savoye,** (Chapter 4) the crisp geometric definition of the exterior shell serves as a datum against which the playful arrangement of partition walls can be deciphered.

14.5 Marcel Duchamp, "The Bride Stripped Bare by her Bachelors, Even," ("The Large Glass"), front view. Philadelphia Museum of Art, Bequest of Catherine S. Dreier.

Colin Rowe and Robert Slutzky have compared the pictorial space in Cubist painting with the architectural space of Le Corbusier's work in their essay, "Transparency: Literal and Phenomenal". In Le Corbusier's architecture, negative space, implied slots of space and fragmentary, interdependent figures create a spatially ambiguous three-dimensional nexus akin to the effect of overlapping planes and interpenetrating, fragmented figures in the Cubist works. *"By definition the transparent ceases to be that which is perfectly clear and becomes instead that which is clearly ambiguous."* Hence, the pellucid order which reflects and embodies the world view of an earlier age is replaced by the fragmentary and ambiguous. Unified, totalizing structures are replaced by dispersed fields where incomplete images constellate and disperse, and elements from unrelated contexts commingle through collage to spark associations.

Of the emergent avant-garde styles, Functionalism proved to be the most long-lived and broadly accepted. For one thing, it *looked* more rational and scientific than the other architectural styles. It also provided a systematic, inexpensive way of building and a political and social agenda attractive to the progressive governments which came to power between the two world wars. Cities were in desperate need of restructuring and Functionalists embraced the task. The industrial revolution in the eighteenth and nineteenth centuries introduced new means of transportation and production which expanded the economic capacities of nations. At the same time, cities were transformed from regional market places to international manufacturing centers. Great numbers of people came in from the countryside to work in mills, and the cities could not graciously absorb them. Towns that had grown up to accommodate small-scale commerce and the scale and speed of carriage traffic were ill equipped to deal with a surge in population and the necessary expansions of roadways, sewage lines, workers' housing, etc. The conditions in the tenements of major cities worsened as tuberculosis reached epidemic proportions and over-crowding was pushed to its limits. It was not untypical in industrial cities like Berlin and London for several generations of a family to live together in a single room. In the face of such pressing social concerns, the debate about styles seemed overly precious.

Action was needed, and Functionalism presented itself as the architectural movement most capable of assuming an aggressive role in the social and political scene. When Le Corbusier declared *"Architecture or revolution!"* He recognized that something had to be done about prevailing social injustices. Architects and planners could dedicate themselves to questions of inexpensive public housing and the provision of a cleaner, more hygienic environment, or the workers could take violent action. Le Corbusier believed that industrialization, the very source of the problem in the contemporary city, could be used to solve it. He continued: *"In building and construction, mass-production had already begun; in face of new economic needs, mass-production units have been created in mass and detail. . . "* Optimistically, Le Corbusier believed that architecture could redress the wrongs of society.

The German *Werkbund,* a group of artists, craftsmen and architects, tried to collaborate with industry. They reasoned that since industrial production could replicate objects quickly and inexpensively, then the prototypes for these objects should be designed with exquisite care. The 'typical' or 'prototypical' was sought in favor of the eccentric or original. Instead of squandering their talents on the design of grand palaces or cathedrals, architects should determine the requirements for the 'minimal existence dwelling.' Many spartan minimal existence dwellings could be provided for the cost of a single palace and the resources of society could serve the good of many, rather than of only a few. Architects like **Walter Gropius** (1883-1969) did exhaustive studies on **prefabricated building systems** and on how close together, or how tall, or how wide housing blocks could be.

The Werkbund organized international expositions dedicated to the theme of housing. In 1926 at the **Weißenhof Siedlung,** in Stuttgart, Germany, prominent architects from all over the world were invited to design and build dwellings which dealt with social and constructional questions. New technology and new building types were systematically explored and pushed to their limits. New structural capabilities and a scientific re-invention of the house created a new scale for the city and a new kind of community.

In 1914 **Le Corbusier** presented his ideas about housing reform in a diagram. The **Domino House** was a simple structural system comprised of parallel **reinforced concrete** slabs supported by a regularly spaced grid of columns with a **cantilevered** stair at one end. All the structural work of the house was carried out by this standardized, repeatable, efficient scaffold. Enclosure could then be particularized based on the individual client, resulting in less expensive, more rational housing. Le Corbusier sought to do away with old-fashioned, nostalgic associations of the house and to deal with the problem as an engineer might, rationally and systematically. For Le Corbusier, a house was a *"machine for living,"* and like any machine, the qualities that mattered were functional efficiency, ease of production and cost effectiveness.

The destruction wrought by World War I made the housing situation even more pressing.

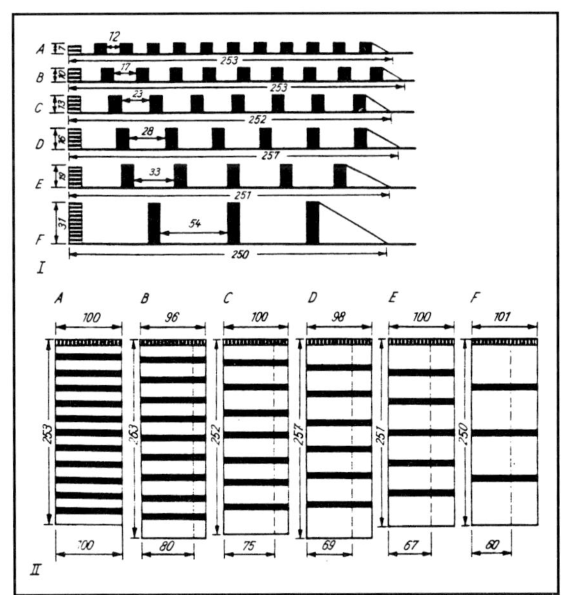

14.6
Walter Gropius, A plan and sectional comparison of six housing block configurations, showing the relationship between building height and the distance between buildings.
Walter Gropius Archive, Harvard University Museums.

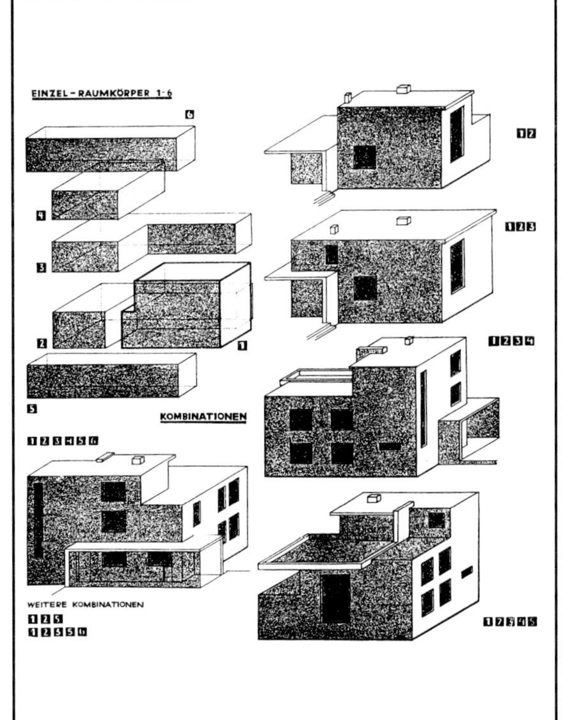

14.7
Walter Gropius, "Big Box of Bricks" project for a kit of parts, prefabricated dwelling, 1923.
Walter Gropius Archive, Harvard University Museums.

14.8 View of the Weißenhof Siedlung, Stuttgart, 1926, Mies van der Rohe Archive, Museum of Modern Art, New York.

14.9 Left: Hans Scharoun, Weißenhof Siedlung, House.

14.10 Right: J.J.P. Oud, Weißenhof Siedlung, Row Housing.

14.11 Left: Le Corbusier, Weißenhof Siedlung, House.

14.12 Right: L. Mies van der Rohe, Weißenhof Siedlung, Apartment Block.

In 1926, Le Corbusier generalized the basic principles of the Dom-ino House into a manifesto, the *"Five Points of Architecture."* The Five Points follow logically from the distinction between structure and enclosure already drawn in the Dom-ino House:

1. Free Plan: If structure is organized into horizontal, stacked slabs supported by a field of columns, then partition walls can be placed freely; they are moreover under no obligation to align from story to story.

2. Free Facade: The systematization of structure frees the perimeter enclosure from any load-bearing responsibility. Hence, the facade can be perforated at will without compromising the solidity of the whole. Walls can be hung like curtains from the structure. Windows can wrap around the entire building like ribbons. Conventional window proportions, fixed by the limits of masonry or timber construction, had no role in the articulation of the new architecture.

3. Ribbon Windows: Instead of punching a window through a solid, load-bearing wall, horizontal windows could extend from column to column, resulting in greater efficiency and greater light, view and ventilation.

4. Roof Garden: While conventional bearing-wall architecture uses up exterior space, buildings constructed according to the Five Points of Architecture provide a usable exterior area on top of the final slab. Moreover, the plantings of the roof garden help protect the slab against changing temperatures.

5. *Piloti:* Literally, *piloti* are the vertical supports or columns in a free plan system. A structural system based on *piloti* does away with the need for a continuous foundation wall.

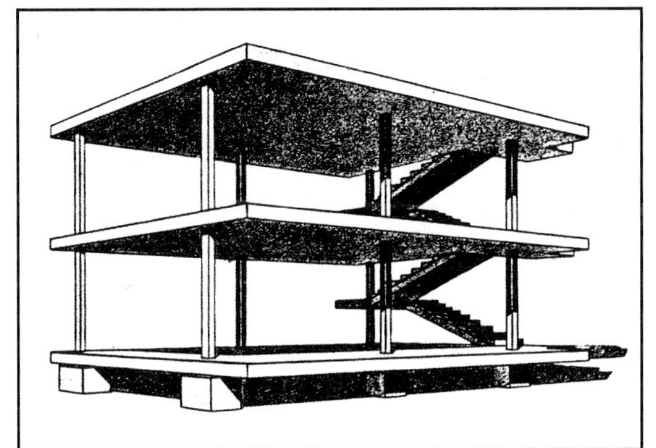

14.13 Le Corbusier, Dom-ino House, 1914.

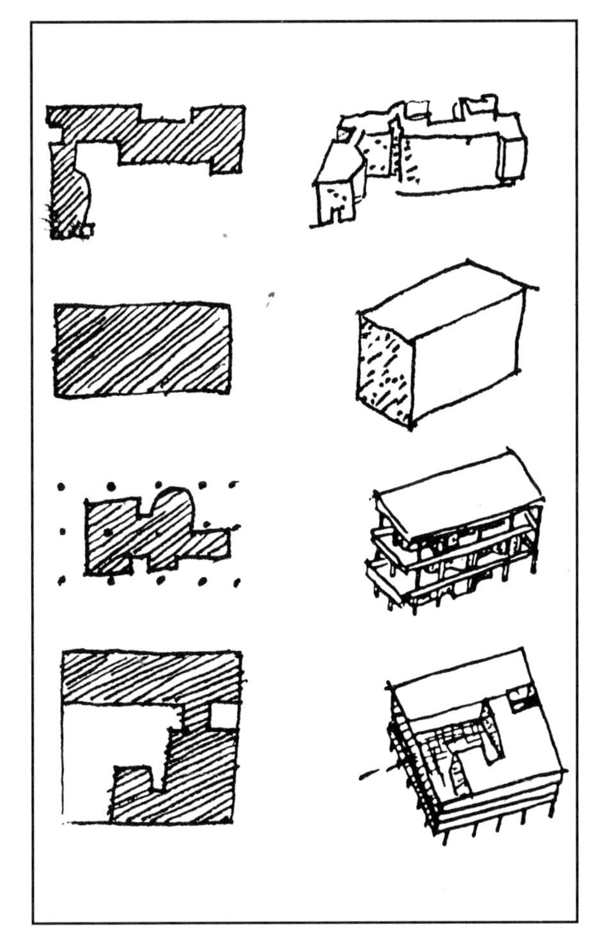

14.14 Diagram of the Five Points of Architecture, after Le Corbusier.

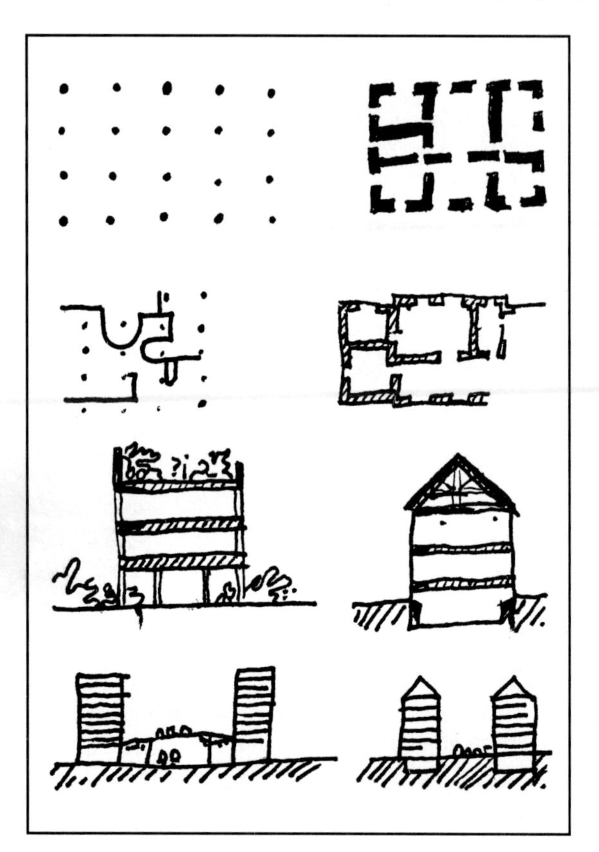

14.15 Left: Free Plan vs. Bearing Wall, after Le Corbusier.

14.16 Right: Le Corbusier, Villa Savoye, view of terrace.

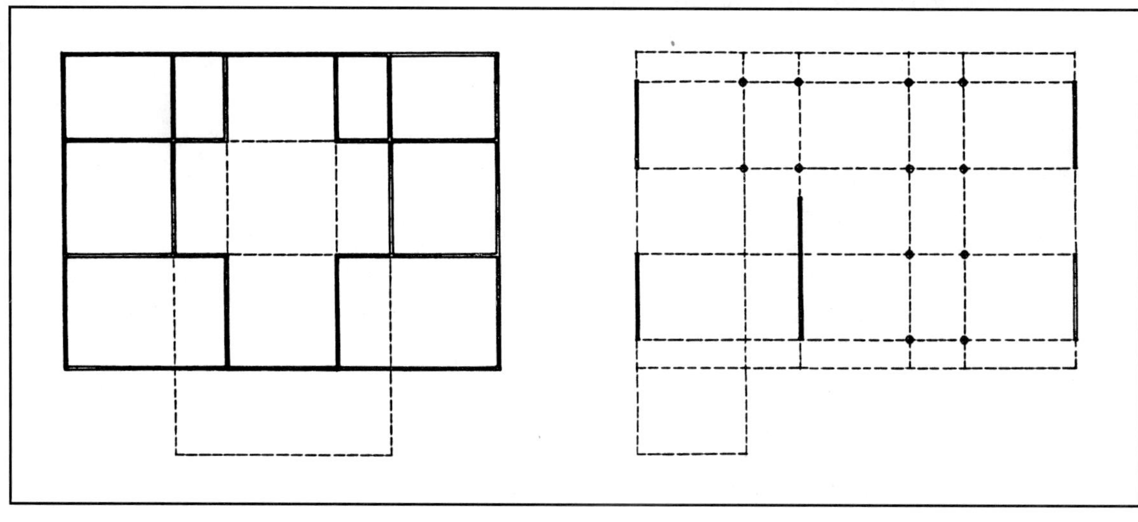

14.17 Analytical plan diagrams of the Villa Malcontenta and the Villa Stein at Garches, according to Colin Rowe.

Hence, the inhabited rooms can be raised up off the ground to avoid dampness and take advantage of better views and ventilation. The area beneath the house is recovered for garden use.

In his essay *The Mathematics of the Ideal Villa,* Colin Rowe compares **Le Corbusier's free-plan Villa Stein at Garches**, 1927 and **Andrea Palladio's bearing-wall Villa Foscari** (Villa Malcontenta), 1559-60. The former is abstract, asymmetrical, and subtractive while the latter is classical, symmetrical, and additive, yet they share a similar underlying organization. To quote Rowe: *"...both Garches and Malcontenta are conceived as single blocks; and, allowing for variations in roof treatment, it might be noticed that both are blocks of corresponding volume... Then further to this, there is a comparable bay structure... Each house exhibits (and conceals) an alternating rhythm of double and single spatial intervals; and each house, read from front to back, displays a comparable tripartite distribution of lines of support."*

Some of the differences between the two villas result from different construction systems. The use of free-plan permits Le Corbusier to vary the organization of each level, while Palladio is obliged to align upper walls over lower ones. On the other hand, free-plan restricts the manipulation of section. The structural system of parallel slabs allows no room for subtle differentiation in section or the shaping of roof vaults. One can cut away the slab to create a double height space, or one can work within the confines of the parallel slabs. The *'plan paralyse'* (paralyzed plan) of the Villa Malcontenta affords freedom in section which is not possible with *'plan libre.'*

The difference in spatial development within a common framework of a 'tartan' grid (A-B-A-B-A) more sharply reveals the difference between a Modern and a Renaissance sensibility. Palladio makes use of all-encompassing geometries and proportional systems which unequivocally assert the singularity of form and clarify the dominance of the center. Within the tartan grid, Palladio configures a cruciform central space, bracketed at the side by stairs and services. At Garches, the central space is dynamically dismantled, as if the stair to the left of the main hall had collapsed and torsional dynamism distorted the rest of the plan: a piano shape is cut-away in the floor; the curved wall of the dining room bows out in the direction of the distorting force, and an unstable 'z-shaped' shape results.

At Malcontenta, the centralizing function of the entry pediment is incontestable. At Garches, the upper balcony establishes the center to the entire elevation, but the canopy above the door throws that center into question and establishes a local center. Rowe states:*"... There ensues in the elevation something very like that simultaneous affirmation and denial of centrality which is displayed in the plan. Thus a central focus is stipulated; its development inhibited; and there occurs a displacement and breaking up of exactly what Palladio would have assumed to be a normative emphasis."*

Both architects are obsessed with proportion, and both go so far as to call out the essential organizing features in their drawings. Palladio does this by inscribing the dimensions of rooms in his plans so that their the correspondence to the harmonic mean is immediately legible. Le Corbusier, on the other hand, is deliberately enigmatic in his plans, but on the elevations, he traces regulating lines which reveal the essential proportional order of the scheme. With Palladio, each interior volume is controlled by the proportional system, whereas with Le Corbusier, the parts do not necessarily re-assume the order of the whole.

A similar comparison can be drawn between a late **Le Corbusier** building, the **Palace of Assembly** at Chandigarh, 1953, and **K.F. Schinkel's Altesmuseum** in Berlin, 1823. Both buildings share many formal properties. The footprints of both buildings are contained within horizontally disposed rectangular boxes and the roof of each is pierced by taller volumes emerging from within. Three bars separated by service spaces wrap the perimeter while the fourth side is a permeable edge, a porch, which extends the entire length of the building. Both the Altesmuseum and the Palace of Assembly are organized by a round central space. In the Altesmuseum, the rotunda is embedded within thick poché and can only be experienced as an interior volume. In Le Corbusier's scheme, the plasticity of the central space can be experienced from within and without. In fact, circulation is organized *through* the rotunda of the Altesmuseum and *around* the Assembly Chamber of the Palace of Assembly.

14.18 Left: Andrea Palladio, Villa Malcontenta, Malcontenta di Mira, Italy, c.1550-60 garden elevation.

14.19 Right: Le Corbusier, Villa Stein, Garches, 1927, entry.

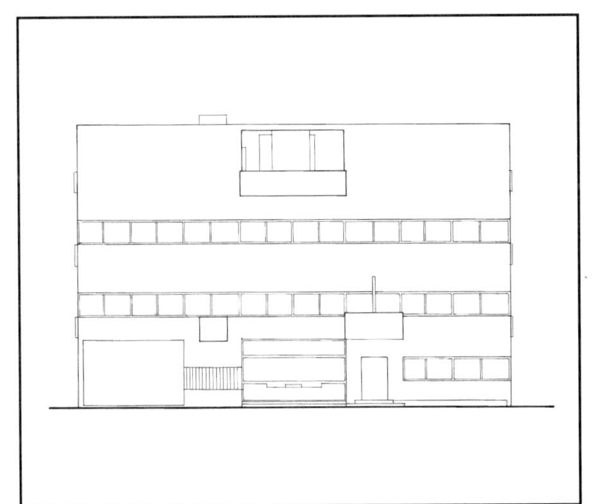

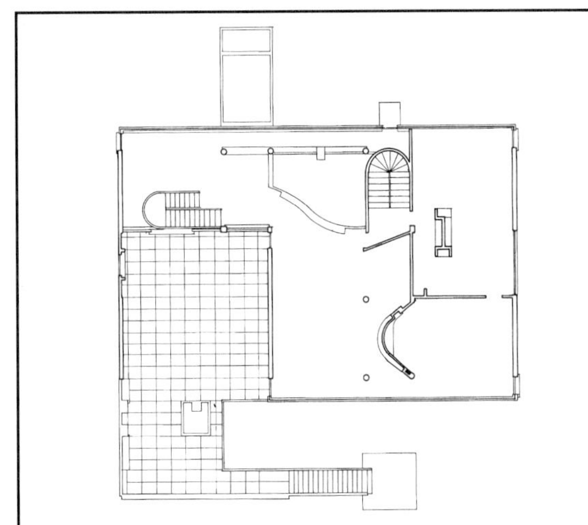

14.20 Left: Villa Stein, elevation.

14.21 Right: Villa Stein, plan.

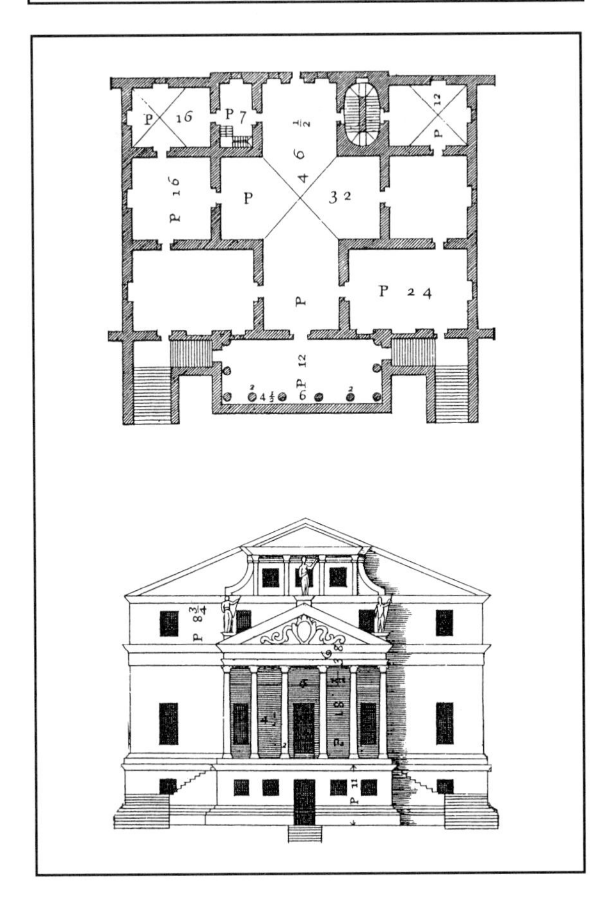

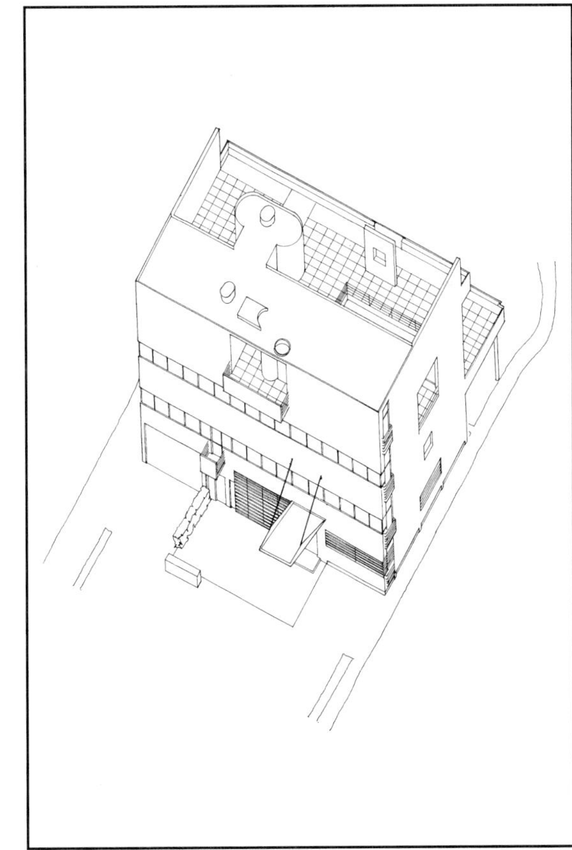

14.22 Left: Villa Malcontenta, plan and river elevation.

14.23 Right: Villa Stein, axonometric.

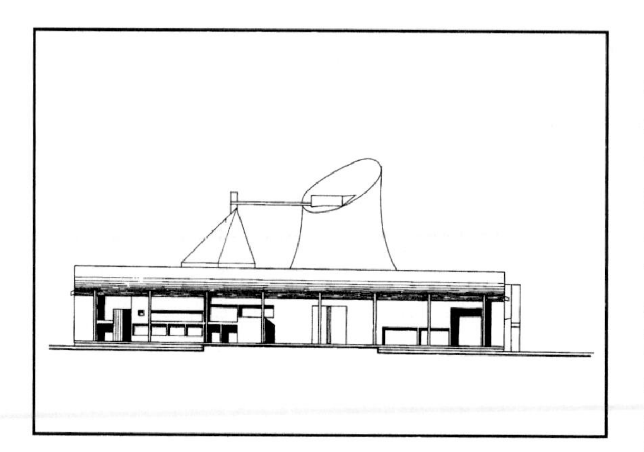

14.24 Le Corbusier, Palace of Assembly, Chandigarh, India, 1953, elevation.

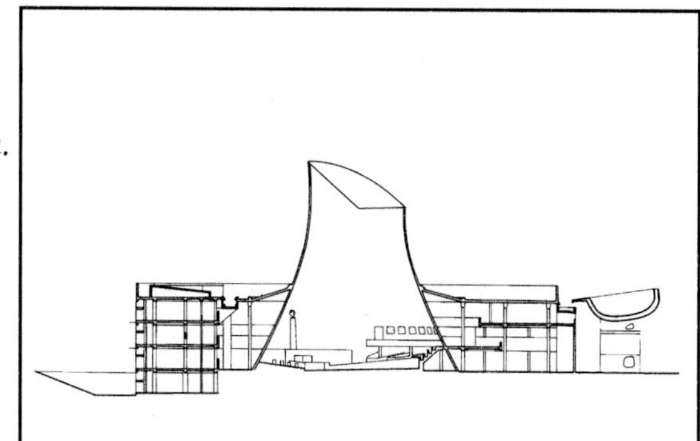

14.25 Palace of Assembly, section.

In Chandigarh, Le Corbusier found another strategy for sectional development within the free-plan. In addition to providing sectional complexity through the use of multi-story spaces, independently structured objects (the canted cylinder and the inclined pyramid) are thrust through the rectilinear volume of the Palace, bringing about a radical juxtaposition between the spatial properties of the enveloping slab structure and the open, figurality of the special volumes. In contrast, the structure of Schinkel's dome is consistent with the tectonic system of the entire building.

At Chandigarh, center is articulated, only to be denied; the idea of a totalizing center is annulled through fragmentation, replication and the iteration of multiple centers. The center of the canted cylinder of the Assembly Chamber is not the same as the center of the rectangular box; instead, it pairs with a pyramidal volume to frame the axis of the path. The path is re-

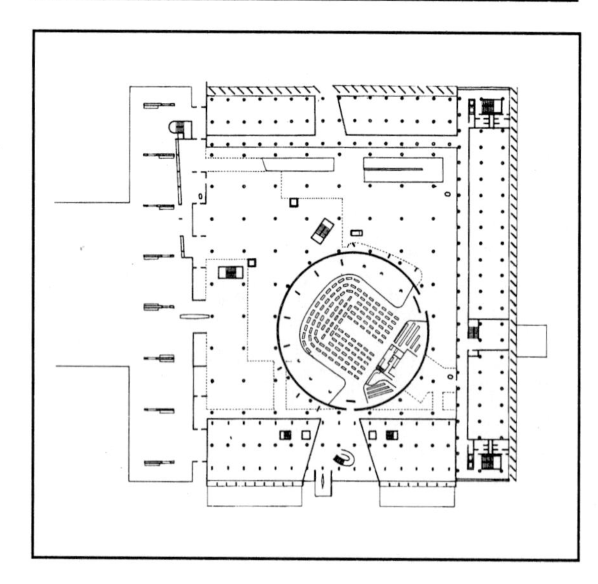

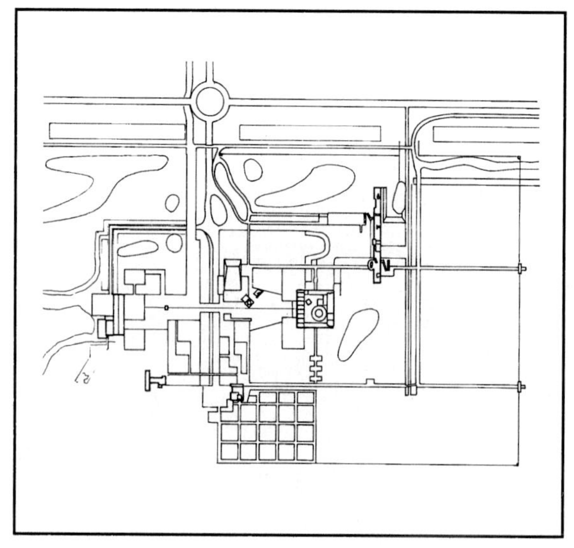

14.26 Left: Palace of Assembly, plan.

14.27 Right: Palace of Assembly, site plan.

ceived by the neutral edge of the porch and deflected through a gradual stepping of the wall. There, at entry, center is once again established with reference to the cylinder. In Berlin, the symmetry of the building is absolute and even extends to the site plan. Both the Altesmuseum and the Palace of Assembly make use of layered space to establish entry. Schinkel sets up a densely striated zone at the entry with portico, carved recess, and switch-back stairs. Le Corbusier striates space through voided slots, established by the stepping back of the porch wall.

The spare, reduced, mechanistic language of Le Corbusier's early works is expanded in later works like the Palace of Assembly. In response to the particularities of site and program, Le Corbusier invents a language: objects emerging above the roof refer to distant mountains; the portico roof and light baffles evoke the horns of the sacred Brahman bull. Schinkel, on the other

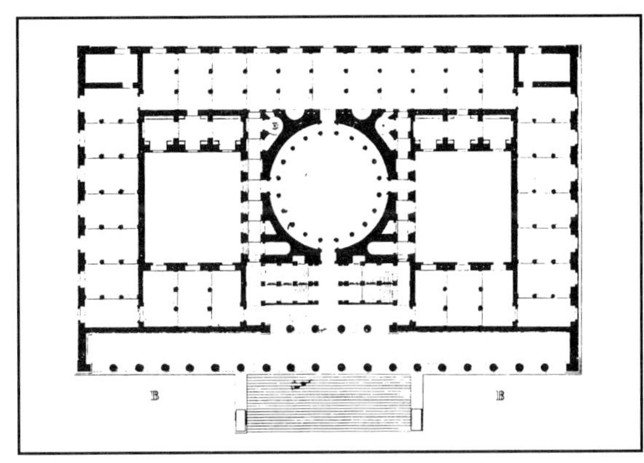

14.28 K.F.Schinkel, Altesmuseum, Berlin, 1823, plan.

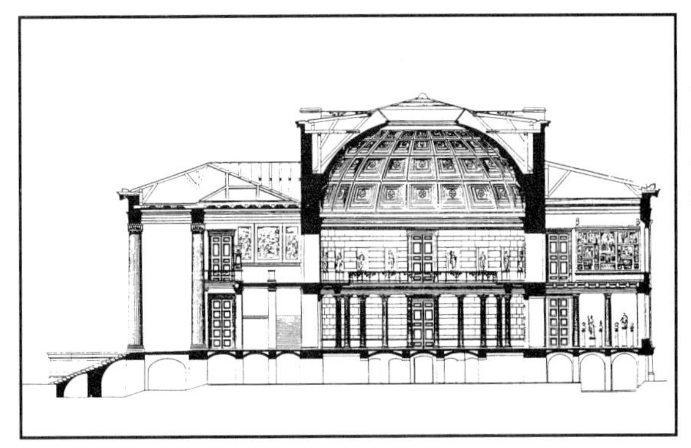

14.29 K.F.Schinkel, Altesmuseum, section.

14.30 K.F.Schinkel, Altesmuseum, perspective.

14.31 Frank Lloyd Wright, Robie House, Chicago, Illinois, 1909.

hand, is working at the height of the Greek Revival and is very happy to adapt the classical tradition to his own purposes.

European Modernism was fueled by a social and political agenda. For European avant-garde movements, architecture was a collective enterprise, tied to industrial production, engaged in the representation of current pseudo-scientific phenomena, and responsible for achieving a new attitude towards form and space which could accommodate the speed, scale, and power of the industrial world. In America, architecture followed a very different course. In place of the collective, the individual was celebrated; in place of the typical or standardized, the particular was sought; in place of mass-production, hand-craftsmanship was valued; instead of focusing on social problems, like housing, American architects designed great monuments of capitalism: skyscrapers.

Throughout the first two centuries of America's existence, Europe was looked to as the source for cultural inspiration. But at the dawn of the twentieth century, the tide turned. Borrowing of ideas, which had previously only moved west across the Atlantic, had reversed

14.32
Frank Lloyd Wright, Ward Willitts House, Highland Park, Illinois, 1900-02, view.

direction. The European avant-garde's infatuation with the machine led Le Corbusier and Walter Gropius to extol American grain elevators and factories as the quintessential formal expression of the *Zeitgeist*. Efficiency studies and American assembly-line production were widely studied by the Europeans and given enthusiastic reception as *"Fordismus"* and *"Amerikanismus."* America did not produce an avant-garde or architectural movement that inspired the Europeans. Instead, it produced one man, Frank Lloyd Wright. An individualistic genius, Wright single-handedly transformed the face of both American and European architecture.

In Chapter 4 we discussed Wright's Robie House, perhaps the best known of his 'Prairie Houses'. We observed that the horizontal extension of the flat prairies inspired the dominant horizontal lines of the roof and terrace, and that a dynamic shearing takes place between the two bars of the house. Similar operations are at play in **Wright's** design for the **Ward Willitts House** and the **Martin House**, both from the very beginning of the twentieth century. The Ward Willitts House, like the

14.33 *Left: Robie House, interior view.*

14.34 *Right: Robie House, plan. (Courtesy of the Taliesin Fellowship)*

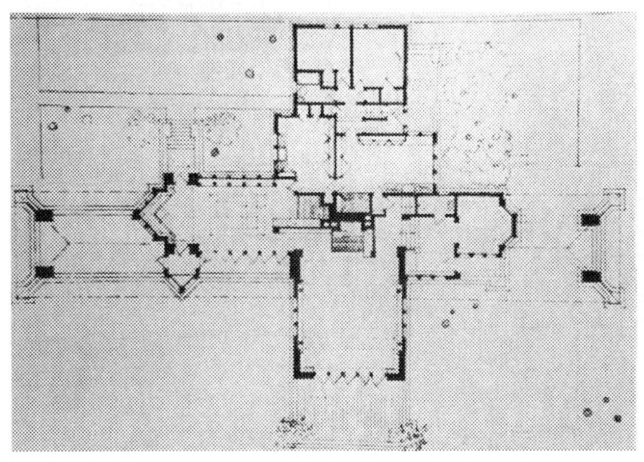

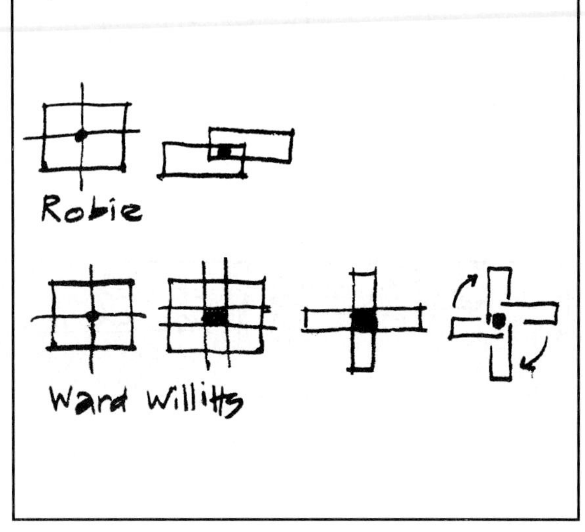

14.35 *Left: Ward Willitts House, plan. (Courtesy of the Taliesin Fellowship)*

14.36 *Right: Diagram of plan partis in Wright's Robie House and the Ward Willitts House.*

Robie House, is organized by a solid vertical shaft at the center, the hearth. At the Robie house, the chimney mass pins the two sliding bars of the house together; at the Ward Willitts House, the central mass acts as a center for a pinwheel arrangement of wings. In both cases, Wright conceives of the house as an exploded box. Walls, roofs and floor slabs are all pulled apart to capture exterior space and to provide flowing interior space, rather than discrete rooms. The treatment of the walls is spare and abstracted: the stucco facing emphasizes their planarity and makes them vertical equivalents of the simple overhanging roof lines and terrace extensions. A continuous band of attic windows anticipates the ribbon windows that Le Corbusier was to call for almost twenty-five years later.

Wright's Martin House in Buffalo, New York takes the strategy of the Illinois houses and applies it at a larger scale. The conventional idea of a building box is decomposed into constituent bars which are pulled apart, knit together and reassembled to create a new whole. Shafts of space intertwine with built form to create the effect of a tectonic weaving, with the hearth the densest episode in the textile. Interior and exterior space move fluidly together as courtyards

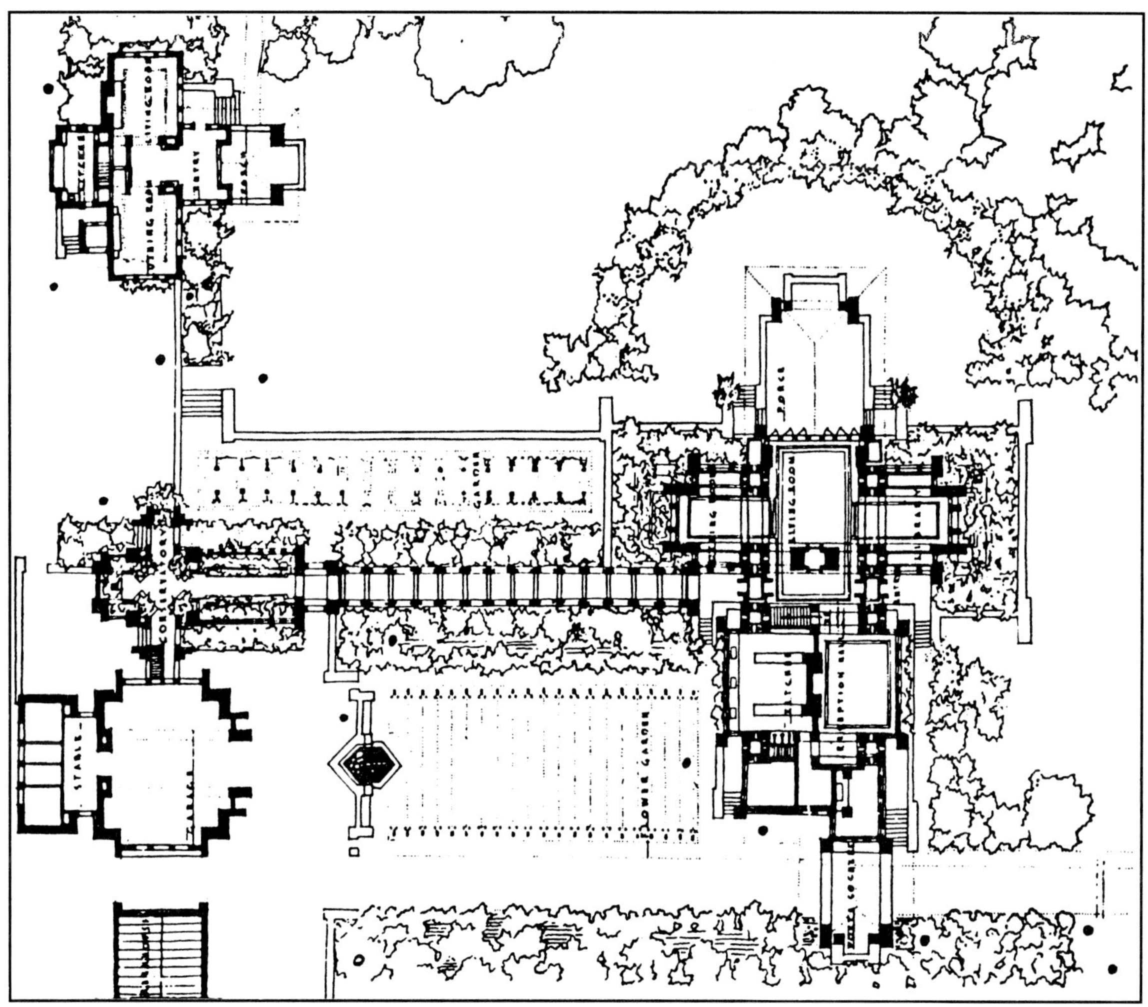

14.37 Frank Lloyd Wright, Martin House, Buffalo, New York, 1904.

and terraces are captured by the extension of walls and roofs across space. Indeed, there are no walls in the plan, just columnar bands permeable to the flow of space. In the Martin House, it is no longer a question of figural space or figural object: built object and space have become one.

Wright's Prairie Houses respond to the horizontal sweep of the Midwestern landscape. Given a different landscape, his architectural response changed accordingly. In the **Kaufmann House**, or 'Falling Water,' in Bear Run, Pennsylvania, Wright confronted his most challenging landscape: a waterfall on a river in a large wooded site. Wright chose to locate the house precisely over the waterfall. Reinforced concrete slabs cantilever over the stream so that water can flow beneath the house.

14.38 Left: Frank Lloyd Wright, Kaufmann House (Falling Water), Bear Run, Pennsylvania, 1936-37, exterior view.

14.39 Right: Falling Water, exterior view.

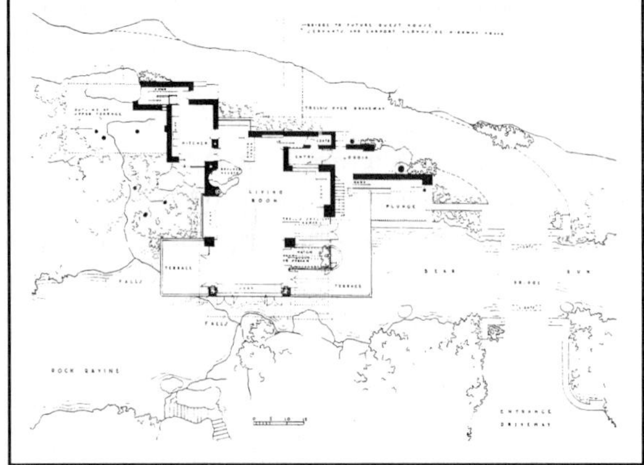

14.40 Left: Falling Water, interior view.

14.41 Right: Falling Water, plan. (Courtesy Taliesin Fellowship)

In the Prairie Houses, the architectural language is stripped down, but still connects to tradition. At Falling Water, the language of the house responds only to that of the natural site: shifted slabs of concrete mimic the outcropping of the bedrock. A massive chimney rises up, anchoring all the slabs together; the vertical of the chimney accompanied by vertical, glazed corners. While the slabs respond to the rock, these roughly faced vertical elements pick up the rhythm of the surrounding tree-trunks. The abstraction of architectural language into horizontal and vertical planes is not done for geometry's sake, but as a reification and restatement of the natural landscape.

The erosion and dematerialization of the built enclosure, suggested in Wright's earlier houses, is here carried to an extreme. Solid walls define the uphill side of the house, while the downhill side, perched over the waterfall, is enclosed only by glass and piers. The poché of tree trunks in plan corresponds in dimension to the reduced columnar elements of the structure, as if the house occurred at the moment of greatest condensation between organic and geometric form. Natural and man-made features exchange places throughout. The hearth of the fireplace is not constructed, it *is* the living bedrock. The stream bed beneath the house assumes the orthogonal geometry of architecture until it tumbles over the cascade in wild abandon.

Wright thoroughly re-thought what a house should be. Affluent clients like the Kaufmanns (of Pittsburgh department store fame) might be accustomed to generous rooms with lavish appointments. At Falling Water, the entry vestibule, living room, dining room, kitchen, and terrace all flow together in a spatial continuum. While not unusual today, this was a radical proposition in 1936. Furniture is built-in or of Wright's design. Zones are differentiated not with walled enclosures, but through subtle sectional changes and the modulation of light. Evening activities constellate in the darker part of the room, around the solid vertical upward shaft, the chimney. Daytime activities constellate around the light vertical downward shaft, the stairwell, which houses a thin metal stair to the river. Earth, air, fire, and water are elegantly opposed and brought together. Bedrooms are almost oppressively small. Wright believed that collective spaces were the heart of the home, and bedrooms should be used as quiet, private spaces of retreat. Even so, the sleeping spaces recapitulate the basic intentions of the house: every room has a private terrace to unify interior and exterior. Young Edgar Kaufmann's sleeping space was at the end of a magnificent corridor, commanding views in all directions.

Richard Neutra's (1892-1970) **Lovell Health House** in Los Angeles, California provides an instructive comparison between American (Wrightian) and European Modernism. An Austrian by birth, Neutra was admittedly under Wright's influence when he designed the house in 1929-30, a few years before Wright designed Falling Water. Although both projects occupy a sloping site and both are articulated with broad horizontal bands and glazed infill, there are substantial differences. Wright's building is made of reinforced concrete while Neutra's building has a steel frame. Section in Falling Water is compressed between the slabs and shares the horizontality of the external massing.

14.42 Richard Neutra, Lovell Health House, Los Angeles, California, 1929-30, view.

At the Lovell Health house, double height spaces open up behind large glazed windows. Wright celebrates organic materials and develops the building as a natural extension of the site. Neutra constructs a mechanistic object, meant to contrast with its landscape rather than clarify its structure. Wright's building relies on hand craftsmanship; Neutra's on the mass-production of modular parts. Neutra's systematic reduction of materiality, site specificity, and organic engagement with the landscape is typical of European handling of Wrightian themes. Europeans preferred the immaterial, the mechanistic, and the typical. Wright was wont to comment that Neutra's house was *"cheap and thin."* In their 1932 book, *The International Style*, Philip Johnson and Henry Russell Hitchcock remarked: *"we are forced to interpret your opposition to this man who has frequently expressed his indebtedness to you as due to a jealousy at once meaningless and undignified."*

The European publication of Wright's work in 1910 spurred tremendous excitement. To many, his work had already resolved the critical questions facing contemporary architects: he had vanquished the inertia of the box-like building and permitted a new dynamism to enter; he had destroyed the elementary

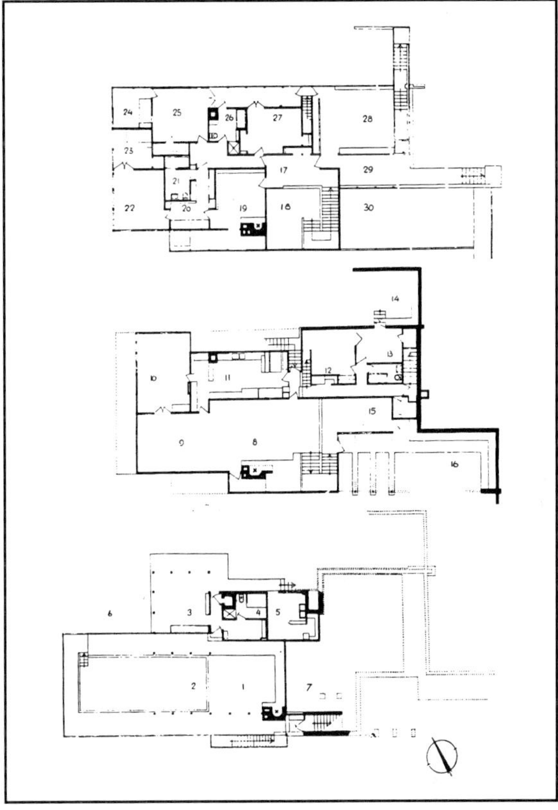

14.43 Left top: Lovell Health House, view from the top of the cliff.

14.44 Right: Lovell Health House, plans.

14.45 Left bottom: Lovell Health House, view of entry.

stereotomy of building mass and conceived of his structures as independent planes; by pulling apart the constituent planes of the box, he permitted an interpenetration of interior and exterior space to their mutual benefit.

The Dutch De Stijl architect **Robert van't Hoff** traveled to the United States to view Wright's work first-hand. The result was his **House at Heide**. Wrightian in conception, the volumes are reduced to abstract, denatured planes. Nevertheless, the disposition of forms lack the tension and dynamism characteristic of Wright's work; in spite of overhanging roof eaves and the central masonry mass, the plan is rigidly symmetrical and the rooms are not fluidly interconnected.

The De Stijl movement in Holland adopted Wright's aggressive attack on the stereotomy of the box and went further towards reducing three-dimensional mass into discrete planes. The Wrightian legacy left its mark in painting as well as architecture. The paintings of **Piet Mondrian** (1872-1944), leading painter of the group, address the essential themes of painting: color, line, proportion, rhythm, and the orthogonal boundary of the frame. For mystical as much as compositional reasons, Mondrian completely reduced and condensed his subject

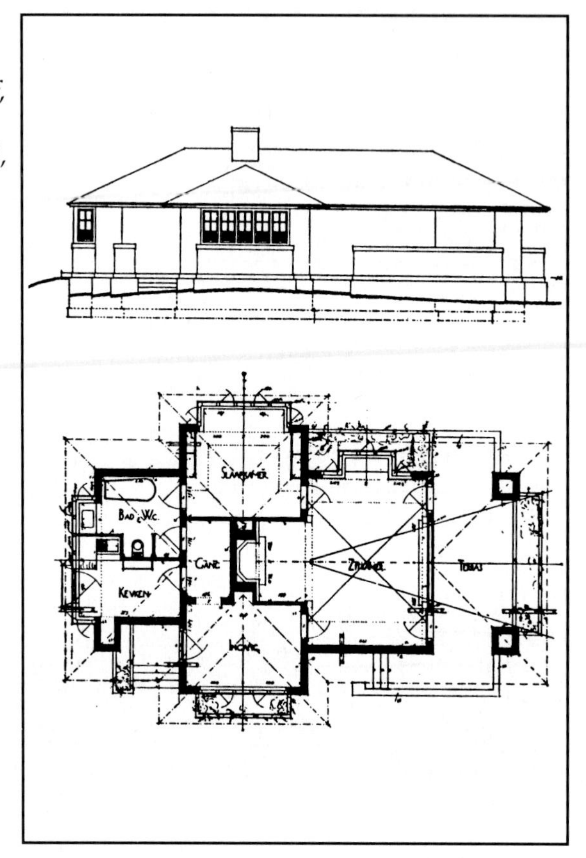

14.46 Robert van't Hoff, House, Heide, Holland, 1914-16, plan and elevation.

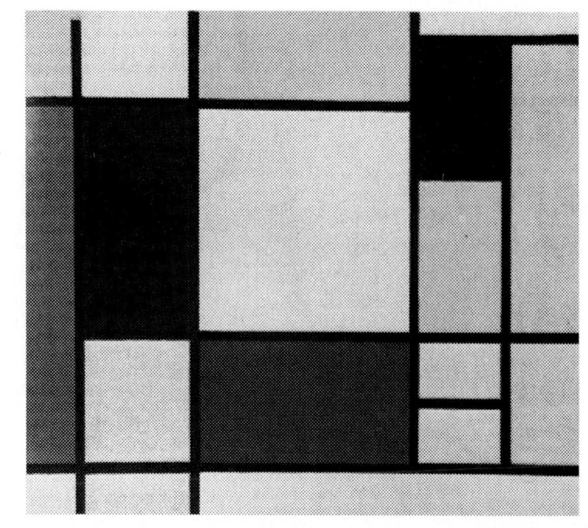

14.47 Piet Mondrian, "Composition with Red, Yellow and Blue", 1927, Cleveland Museum of Art.

matter until he was left with fields of primary color contained within an irregular grid of thick black lines. In Mondrian's painting, perspectival space, narrative, and figural representation are dismissed as inessential.

De Stijl architects engaged in a similar process of reduction. Buildings were not conceived of as volumes, but as freely arranged planes. Hence, architectural space was not bounded, but consisted in the dynamic interweaving of planar elements and slots of space. **Gerrit Rietveld** (1886-1964) explored these principals in the **Schroeder House** in Utrecht, Holland.

Although Rietveld's debt to Wright is obvious, their handling of materials, space and the ground plane differs sharply. In Wright's work, the **materiality** of the building is a carefully considered aspect of the design; wood, stone, and warm colored stucco compose a palette of earth tones, varied textures and natural materials. Rietveld, on the other hand, uses materials which are as abstract and denatured as possible. Walls of smooth white stucco are used as a background for the interlocking composition of red, yellow and blue bands. The building becomes a three-dimensional canvas for a De Stijl exercise in color and space. In Wright's Prairie Houses, the perimeter of the building is transformed by the spatial extension of the volumes. In Rietveld's house, spatial extension is implied through the dematerialization of a glazed corner, but the mass of the building is almost cubic. Wright's interior spaces flow together or break down internally into smaller interdependent zones. Rietveld presents a unified space on the upper story. Movable partitions are used to delimit separate areas for sleeping and bathing. Wright's houses are firmly anchored to the ground by the *axis mundi* of the chimney. In Rietveld's house, the vertical element uniting all floors is the voided shaft of a stairwell. Furthermore, the abstract reduction of surface in the Schroeder House continues on the interior. Floors, walls and even furniture are painted with interlocking planes of color. The effect is of weightlessness: up, down, left, and right are equalized in a wholly three-dimensional spatial matrix. Mrs. Schroeder's only complaint about the house was that she had to train the children to jump over the white patches of the floor which otherwise needed cleaning too frequently.

While Rietveld was the best known of the De Stijl architects, **Theo Van Doesburg** (1883-1931) was the movement's most vociferous publicist. He carried the ideas of De Stijl to many countries, including Germany, where he taught unofficially at the Bauhaus, a progressive academy of design. Van Doesburg's painting ***"Rhythm of a Russian Dance"*** uses the same

14.48 Gerrit Rietveld, Schroeder House, Utrecht, Holland, 1923-24, exterior view.

14.49 Schroeder House, interior view.

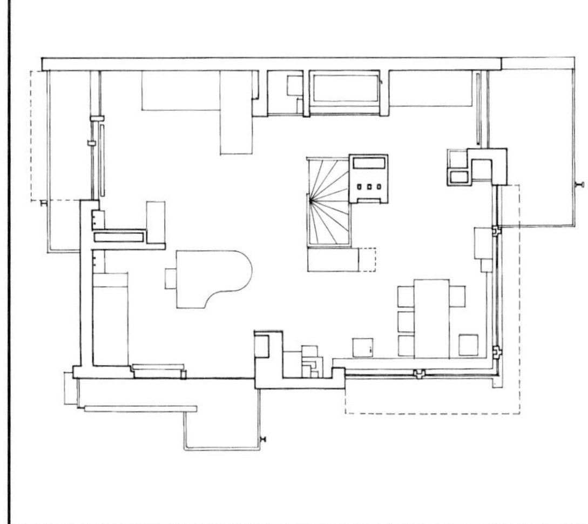

14.50 Left: Schroeder House, exterior detail.

14.51 Right: Schroeder House, plan.

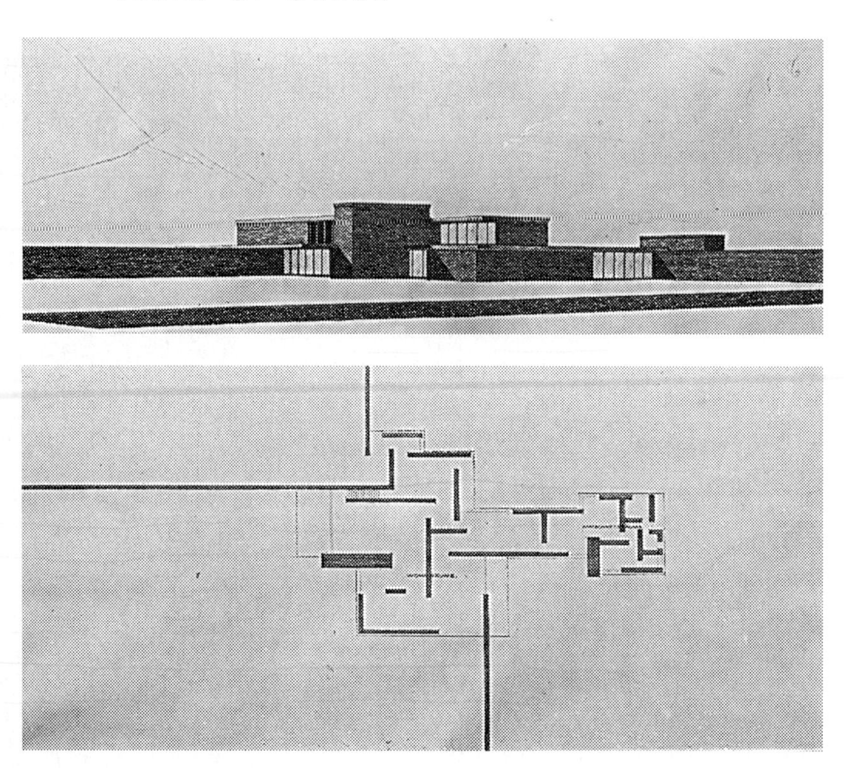

14.52 Left: Theo van Doesburg, "Rhythm of a Russian Dance," 1918. Lillie P. Bliss Bequest, Museum of Modern Art, New York.

14.53, 14.54 Right: Ludwig Mies van der Rohe, Brick Country House, project, 1923-24, plan and elevation. Mies van der Rohe Archive, Museum of Modern Art, New York.

palette of primary forms and colors that typifies the work of the De Stijl movement, but instead of gridding the entire surface, as did Mondrian, he pulled apart an implicit grid. Bars of color, orthogonally arranged, gesture to one another across the open space of the canvas and create spatial tension between them.

Ludwig Mies van der Rohe (1886-1969) was responsive to the architectural implications of van Doesburg's painting. In plan, his unbuilt project for a **Brick Country House** of 1923-24 looks like a De Stijl painting. At the same time, Mies further investigates the decompositional strategies of Wright's prairie houses. Spaces are not defined by enclosing walls, but suggested by orthogonal relationships among free-standing planes. Interior and exterior space merge fluidly together.

Mies van der Rohe was asked to design the **German Pavilion** for the International Exposition of 1929 in Barcelona. Once again, he used a shifting nexus of free-standing planes to develop his composition. Unlike Rietveld, who tried to attain the immaterial condition of painting in architecture, Mies exhilarated in lavish materials. Mies achieves dematerialization through reflection, refraction, and the multiplication of images on shiny surfaces. The planes in the Barcelona Pavilion are made of polished onyx, marble, glass, and pools of water held in

14.55
L. Mies van der Rohe, German Pavilion, (Barcelona Pavilion), Barcelona, 1929, view.

14.56
Barcelona Pavilion, view.

dark basins. Even the columns are of exquisite delicacy: cruciform in plan, they are cased in chromium. The arms of the cruciform columns mirror back upon themselves and shatter the smooth surfaces of the Pavilion in the playful glitter of their reflections.

The plan of the Barcelona Pavilion does not only draw its inspiration from contemporary Dutch painting. Allusion to architectural precedent is at the heart of the apparently abstract composition of lines and planes. Overlapping similar rectangles govern the asymmetrical disposition of planes, pools, and platforms in space, but eight cruciform columns, regularly arrayed on a grid, structure the main pavilion. The platform and colonnade suggest the vestigial presence of a Greek temple, or more probably, a temple filtered through the German Romantic Classical tradition of Schinkel. The cella of Mies' temple has been dismantled to provide a new dynamism fraught with political implications: the strong hierarchy insisted on by the forbidden cella of the Greek temple has been demolished so that the whole is accessible to the people. The cult statue likewise has been pulled out of its protected space and thrust into a more direct confrontation with the elements. Mies uses a voided, luminous light shaft framed by the double walls at the heart of the composition to pin the planes together instead of anchoring the composition to a solid mass, as in Wright's work. Stasis and symmetry have been abandoned, but in their place, a new symmetry has entered. The architectural critic Robin Evans has observed that the floor and ceiling are almost equidistant from eye level, causing a perfect mirroring between the two across a horizontal axis of symmetry.

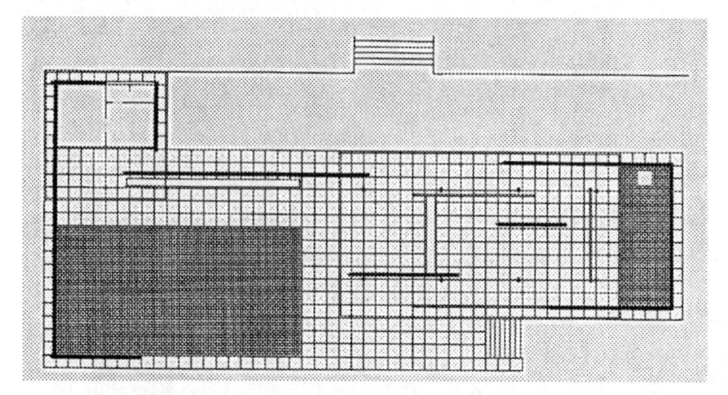

14.57 Left: Barcelona Pavilion, plan.

14.58 Right: Barcelona Pavilion, view.

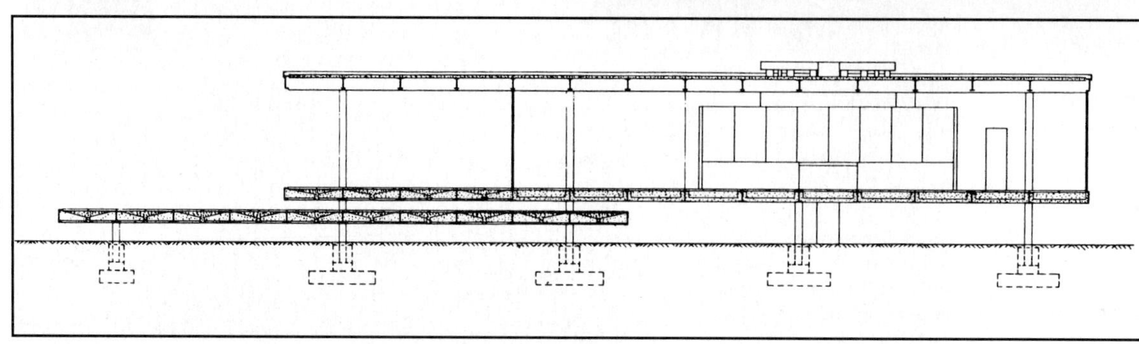

14.59 L. Mies van der Rohe, Farnsworth House, Plano, Illinois, 1950, section.

In dismantling a known paradigm, Mies is able to enrich the meaning of his composition. In politically charged times, his building represented the free Weimar Republic in monarchical Spain. Shattering the old order and replacing it with a new democratic order was a potent gesture, made more powerful by the placement of the building on the site. Mies chose to locate his Pavilion at the terminus of the cross axis in a rigid, axial *Beaux Arts* plan. The Barcelona Pavilion receives the site axis and deliberately scrambles it, undermining the implied authoritarianism of the lay-out.

Founded in Weimar, Germany, the **Bauhaus** was a leading center for the discussion and dissemination of ideas about architecture. Functionalists joined forces with Expressionists and mystics to create one of the most extraordinary faculties ever assembled: Wassily Kandinsky, Paul Klee, Johannes Itten, Walter Gropius, Mies van der Rohe, Hannes Meyer, Lazlo Moholy-Nagy, Oscar Schlemmer, and Joseph Albers, to name a few. It is worth observing that very few students of note were trained at the school. (Only Marcel Breuer, who was only good at chair design.)

In 1926 the Bauhaus moved from Weimar to Dessau, Germany and Walter Gropius, director of the school, was called upon to design an appropriate edifice for this progressive institution. Gropius eschewed earlier models of academic buildings as too stolid, too hierarchical, too static, too rooted in the past, and not properly appreciative of the new, scientific spirit of the contemporary artist. Instead, he looked to factories for inspiration. In factories, such as **J.A. Brinckmann** (1902-49) and **L.C. van der Vlught's** (1894-1936) **Van Nelle Chocolate and**

14.60
J.A. Brickmann and L.C. van der Vlught, Van Nelle Chocolate and Tobacco Factory, Rotterdam, Holland, 1928-29.

Tobacco Factory, different functions are housed in structures which correspond directly to their purpose. At the Bauhaus, a desire for functional differentiation motivated the articulation of each part: the workshop wing is clad with a three-story high glazed curtain wall; the classroom wing is wrapped with ribbon windows; and the dormitory/atelier wing is given the most individualistic treatment with projecting balconies for each room.

Compositionally, the bars of the Bauhaus are not grouped in any tight, formal order. They are loosely arranged as a pin-wheel, each of the arms bending around an absent center. The plan is deliberately non-hierarchical and equalizing. Even entry does not establish absolute center: twin entries mirror one another on opposite sides of the bridge. While a traditional institutional building could only occupy and displace space, the dynamic, outstretching arms of the Bauhaus embrace space and define three exterior areas: a sports field, an entry court, and a service court.

The concrete structural frame is pulled away from the **curtain wall** skin in the Bauhaus, providing a thin plenum of space between them. Glazed corners wrap the prismic volume to further enhance the sense of immaterial weightlessness. The twin entry stairs on opposite sides of the bridge ascend behind glazed

14.61 Walter Gropius, Bauhaus, Dessau, 1926, view, Gropius Archive, Harvard University Museums.

walls, affording multiple framed views of the building through the building. However, the transparency achieved here is not the 'phenomenal transparency' which Rowe and Slutzky attributed to Le Corbusier's space. Phenomenal transparency, like the space in cubist paintings, is ambiguous, polyvalent, and implied. Gropius' spatial effects are far too straightforward and unequivocal. Instead, the transparency of the Bauhaus is what the authors would call 'literal transparency.' They describe the Bauhaus as follows: *"In plan, the Bauhaus reveals a succession of spaces but scarcely a 'contradiction of spatial dimensions.' Relying on the diagonal viewpoint, Gropius has exteriorized the op-*

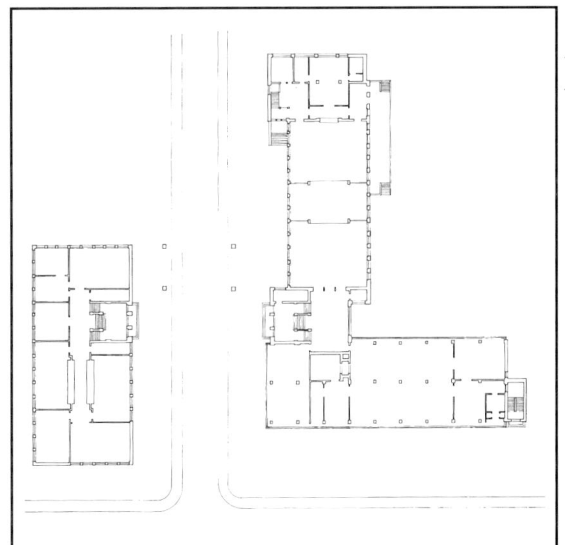

14.62 Bauhaus, plan.

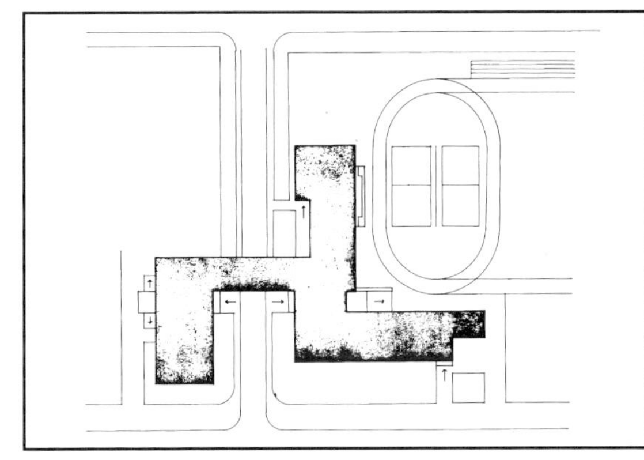

14.63 Left: Bauhaus, view.

14.64 Right: Bauhaus, site plan.

14.65 Left: Bauhaus, view.

14.66 Right: Bauhaus, view.

posed movements of his space, he has allowed them to flow away into infinity; and, by being unwilling to attribute to either one any significant difference of quality, he has prohibited any potential of ambiguity."

The language of the building and the different treatments of building skin clarify the functional distinctions of the parts, but there is also a mechanistic fetish at play. Round port-hole windows on the atelier block mimic the functionally determined windows of an ocean liner, where they must resist water pressure. In land-locked Dessau, port-holes hardly serve any purpose, except to remind one of the kinship between machines and Functionalist buildings.

The frenzy of productivity and invention that characterized the early, 'heroic' period of the modern movement had a tendency to rigidify and become formulaic after the Second World War. The systematization of building production, characteristic of Functionalism, was easily co-opted by pressures from the building industry. Functionalist architecture, which began as the harbinger of a new society, became in time the symbol of the very class it sought to challenge. Mies declared that *"less is more"* in a belief that reduction and abstraction led to a poetic clarity with all pieces in delicate equipoise with the others. Mies' dictum was not dissimilar to Alberti's some centuries before, when he declared that beauty had to do with a relationship among essential elements so that nothing could be added or subtracted except for the worse.

Sometimes, however, less is less. In the hands of second and third generation modern-

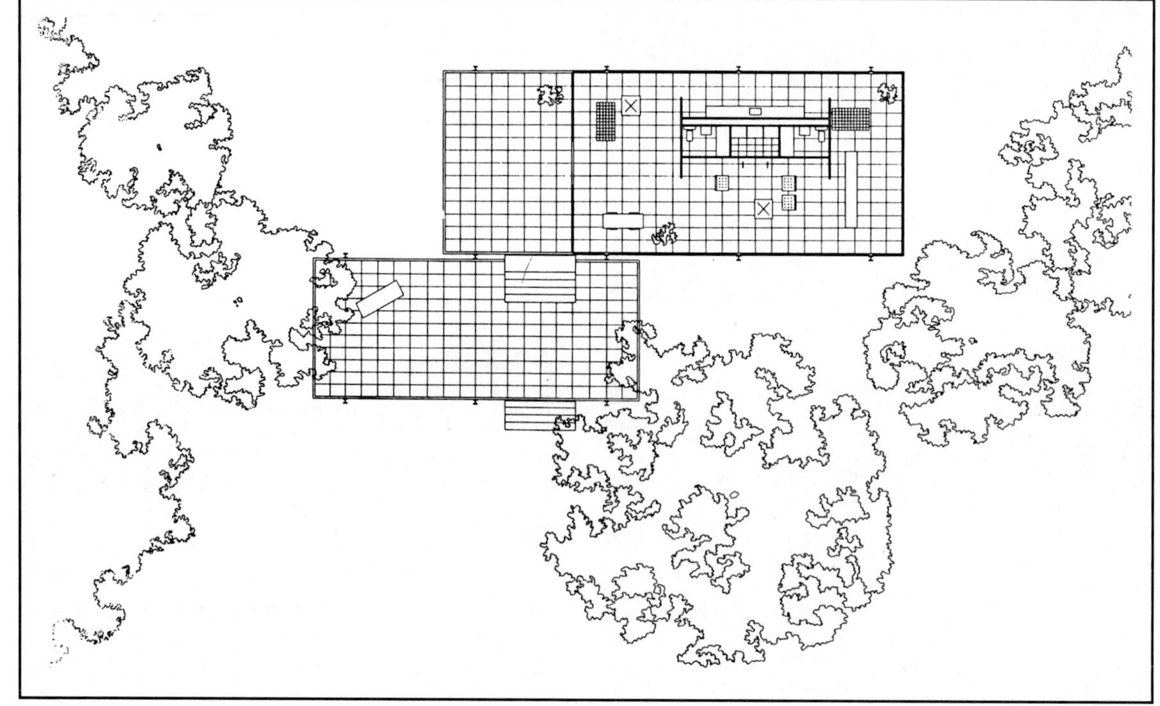

14.67 L. Mies van der Rohe, Farnsworth House, Plano, Illinois, 1950, plan.

ists, many of the subtle relationships of space, material, massing, and site succumbed to formula and rapid, careless design. Even the late work of Mies van der Rohe is guilty of reducing the architectural argument so drastically that there is little argument left. The dynamic interchange between interior and exterior space, and the play of reflections against exquisite polished surfaces, present in the Barcelona Pavilion of 1926, is much reduced in **Mies' Farnsworth House** of 1950. The Farnsworth house has a pristine elegance: the glazed structure is so pure that even columns fall on the exterior and only a simple object, housing bathroom and kitchen, impedes the universal flow of space. Still, it is static and symmetrical in organization, as though Mies reconstituted the dismantled *cella* of the Barcelona Pavilion and replaced the cult figure with plumbing, icon of our spiritless age.

In his **Berlin New National Gallery**, 1962-67, **Mies** again presents an elegant glazed box, but its square plan and virtually equal treatment of all four facades erases all site distinctions in favor of a centered, ideal form that would have pleased Renaissance theoreticians. The open space of the main floor is so pure that not even an object housing a service core is permitted. All functional program spaces and offices are relegated to the basement. The modernist dream of interpenetrating interior and exterior spaces had been undermined, and replaced instead with a too simple, too clean, ultimately diminished architecture.

14.68
L. Mies van der Rohe, National Gallery, Berlin, 1962-67, view.

15.0
R. Hausmann, "Tatlin at Home," 1920, Moderna Museet, Stockholm.

Chapter 15

The Late 20th Century: Architecture in the Post-Industrial Age

We declare that the splendor of the earth has been enriched by a new beauty: the beauty of speed!
-F.T. Marinetti

In the medieval period, before the invention of the printing press and the rapid dissemination of information through type, the cathedral served as a three-dimensional bible and memory theater. Sculpture and stained glass windows narrated Biblical tales; effects of light and space evoked religious feeling; geometry and number encoded secret hermeneutical truths. In *Notre-Dame of Paris,* set in 1482, Victor Hugo compares the cathedral with the newly invented means of recording and spreading information, the printing press. The cathedral was a massive singular artifact, place-bound, costly and laborious to produce. On the contrary, printed texts were light, inexpensive, quickly produced, transportable and replicable. Hugo's conclusion was, *"This will kill that, the book will kill the building."* In other words, in the nineteenth century, when Hugo was writing, there was a perception that the traditional role of architecture had changed. Architecture had been superseded as the repository of a culture's beliefs and the expression of its spirit. The new technology of the printing press had surpassed the old, and the ponderousness of stone and brick had been replaced by a neutral, placeless, timeless medium. Hugo concluded, *"...as human ideas changed form they would change their mode of expression, that the crucial idea of each generation would no longer be written in the same material or in the same way..."*

If we are to believe Hugo, that architecture has ceased to carry meanings in familiar, traditional ways and that new technology brings with it new paradigms of order and meaning, then what is the condition of architecture in the late twentieth century? Turbine engines, locomotives, grain elevators and diesel trains gave spark to the architecture of the High Modernists in the early part of the century, but the heavy mechanical imagery of that era, romantic in its heroic brutality, has been replaced by a technology which grows increasingly less material. The celebration of the machine in works by Eiffel, Gropius, Sant'Elia and their ilk was bold and courageous; the celebration of the same nineteenth-century technology today is an exercise in nostalgia.

What are the architectural and urbanistic ramifications of cordless telephones, microchips, fiber optics, and fax machines? The speed of transmission, the ease of replication,

15.1 San Miniato al Monte, Florence, 1018-62.

and the freedom from material proximity provided by such technology is surely as unsettling in our day as the printing press was in the Middle Ages. The idea of people working together for the collective good, the fundamental premise of urban life, is made redundant by a technology which permits collective activity from remote locations. Frank Lloyd Wright's vision of decentralization is timid when compared to the societal atomization made possible by the technology of our age. Has a new spatial paradigm emerged? In previous ages, the pure centricity of the Platonic solid or the intimations of infinity of the Cartesian grid embodied both a cosmology and an ideal beauty for their time. Does our age require a new system of mathematics to define the world? Or have systems been replaced by the spatial and temporal discontinuity of cybernetics and the byte map?

What is the role of architecture? Can architecture embody the spirit of our times? Can architecture model or comment on prevailing cosmologies? Can architecture carry transcendental meanings? Can architecture mean anything at all? These questions may seem particular to our *Angst*-ridden age, but they are questions which have been dogging architects for at least two hundred years. The eighteenth-century quest for 'Character,' the nineteenth-century quest for a 'Style' expressive of the *Zeitgeist*, and the early twentieth century infatuation with the machine are all attempts to solve the same question: what is the role of architecture in a society which no longer provides the consensual background required for great synthetic expressions of the age to take place?

Since these questions have not been resolved in the last two hundred years, we do not propose to do so now. Instead, we shall outline a few strategies that have been pursued in this century by thoughtful architects in an effort to make meaningful decisions about how to design. A myriad of styles and strategies have arisen and it is impossible to include them all. We shall limit ourselves to methods which can be categorized by four dominant strains: 1. Architecture as a vehicle for cultural continuity; 2. Architecture as a closed, hermetic, self-referential system; 3. Architecture as a reflector of the *Zeitgeist*; 4. Architecture as a critical act. The categories are not intended to be proscriptive, but merely to form a loose structure for the discussion of a wide variety of design approaches. The categories are not exclusive, but overlapping. Many of the following buildings could be included equally well in several sections. The text neither endorses nor prohibits any of the methods. Instead, it is hoped that the questions raised will prove more useful than the specifics of the examples in this study.

Let us begin with the first category, architecture as a vehicle for cultural continuity. While not the most critically incisive approach, the desire to continue and extend the traditions of western architecture is a natural one, and readily understandable. Known commodities are familiar and reassuring; standards for judgements are available; precedent provides models that can be adopted. Obviously failed strategies have already been tried and found out, hence, the likelihood of catastrophe is more remote. Moreover, even when histories of architecture tell us otherwise, there has always been continuity. The validity of the great stylistic and paradigmatic shifts from Classical to Gothic back to Classical depends on the examples you choose to examine. The neat divisions between historical periods is illusory. Roman templar architecture continued in buildings like **San Miniato al Monte**, Florence, at the height of the Middle Ages; Gothic architecture persisted in the northern countries while the Renaissance flowered in the south; the casualness with which Schinkel and von Klenze move among styles had a precursor in **Nicholas Hawksmoor** (1661-1736) a hundred years earlier, at the height of the English Baroque; Canonical Modernism coexisted with the ***Ecole des Beaux-Arts,*** an institution which took a far less adversarial stance towards tradition than the Bauhaus.

Two 'movements' have championed the preservation and continuation of pre-existing styles: Historicism and Post-Modernism. The former attempted faithfully to work within a pre-existing style; the latter attempted critically to re-present linguistic aspects of a style so that meanings may be conserved, although the

15.2 Nicholas Hawksmoor, St. Alfege, Greenwich, c. 1720.

15.3 Nicholas Hawksmoor, All Soul's College, Oxford, England, 1716.

forms may change. In its most impoverished form, twentieth-century Historicism continues the pessimistic resignation of nineteenth-century Historicism. Believing that their age was no longer capable of a creative utterance, many nineteenth-century architects imitated the presumed authenticity of the architecture from earlier eras. An over reliance on stylistic attributes sometimes led to an uncritical borrowing and piecing together of historical motifs, rather than exploration of the compositional and theoretical agendas of the original. Such is the architecture of 'Georgian' gas stations, 'Tudor' duplexes and 'Spanish Colonial' Taco Bells.

In its richest form, Historicism provides a language and a patrimony of types which can be adapted, adjusted, and made specific to the design task at hand. **Edwin Lutyens** (1869-1944), one of the most gifted architects of the twentieth century, worked continuously within the established traditions of Classicism and the English Vernacular. In discussing Classical architecture, he stated: "*That time-worn doric order- a lovely thing- I have the cheek to adopt. You can't copy it. To be right, you have to take it and design it ...You cannot copy: you find if you do you are caught, a mess remains. It means hard labour, hard thinking, over every line in all three dimensions and in every joint; and no stone can be allowed to slide.*

15.4
First Prize Project, Prix de Rome, M. Prévot, student of MM. Guadet and Paulin at the Ecole des Beaux-Arts, 1901.

If you tackle it this way, the Order belongs to you. " (Quoted by John Summerson in *The Classical Language of Architecture*).

Lutyens' plan for **Deanery Garden,** 1901 is comprised of the interweaving of solid and void bars of space which assert and deny center time and again as the radial garden organization is brought into contrapuntal relationship with the concentric organization of the courtyard house. At **Heathcote,** Lutyens' site plan is less fanciful than at Deanery Garden, but the same device of shifted centers provides an asymmetrical experience of the apparently symmetrical H-shaped plan. At both Deanery Garden and Heathcote, the architectural language is masterfully

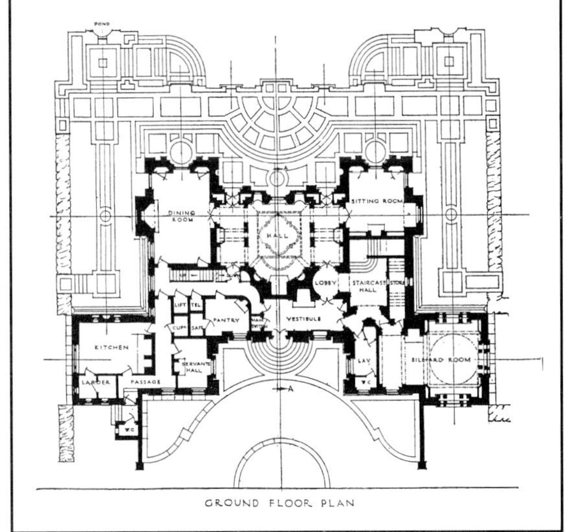

15.5
Edwin Lutyens, Heathcote, Ilkley, England, 1906, plan.

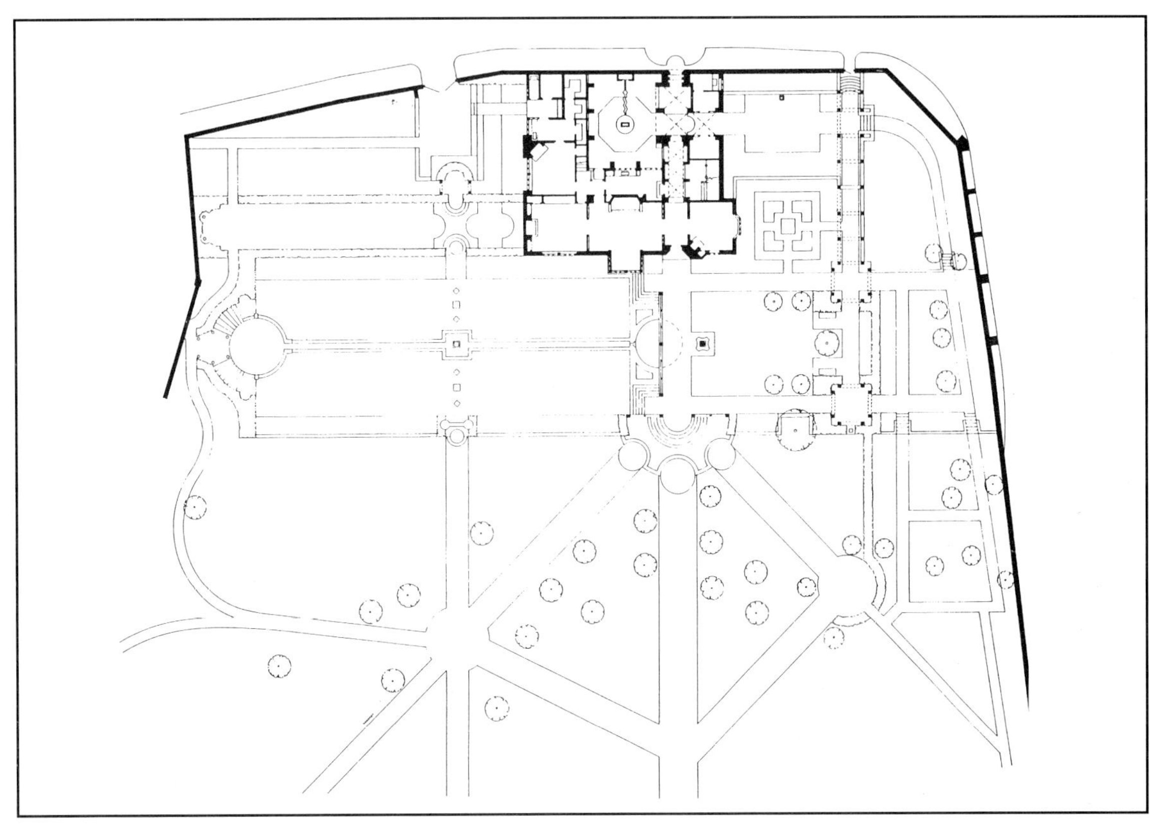

15.6
Edwin Lutyens, Deanery Garden, Sonning, England, 1901, plan.

handled, not because of its style, but because of the keen attention to detail, proportion, and the witty re-presentation of convention. Moreover, the development of space, mass, light, path, and material is satisfying regardless of the style of the building.

Robert Venturi investigates architectural themes similar to those of Lutyens, but he does so from a critical vantage point. In 1966 he published *Complexity and Contradiction in Architecture,* a seminal attack on canonical modernism. To Mies' declaration that *"less is more,"* Venturi responded that *"less is a bore."* He called instead for an architecture that is richly ambiguous, double-functioning, and semantically loaded. Instead of an exclusive architecture of *"either/or,"* Venturi proclaimed an inclusive architecture of *"both/and,"* capable of embracing familiar images, associations, and meaningful signs. Venturi did not criticize the masters of Modernism, but the thoughtless, formulaic borrowing of their motifs and methods. He argued that spare, reductive, minimalism addressed an architectural elite and distanced itself from the people. Architecture, however, was a social enterprise and needed to embrace the known forms, ciphers, and themes of popular culture. *Complexity and Contradiction* can be considered the foundation manifesto for Post-Modern architecture, although the import of the movement has been greatly diminished by the many dreadful buildings done in its name in the 1980's.

Venturi would argue that the appropriate content of architecture is everyday life. *"Main Street is almost all right,"* he declared. Venturi's 'Main Street' did not present a unitary vision, but a jumble of styles, signs, and scales. On Main Street the high-style architecture of banks and post offices is placed along side low-style elements like billboards, neon, street lights, and parking lots. Both make use of symbols, forms, signs and semiotic keys which are intelligible and can be used to construct meaning in architecture. Venturi's 1969 essay "Learning from Lutyens" and his 1972 book *Learning from Las Vegas,* are not as far apart as they would seem.

Venturi's House for his Mother, Vanna Venturi, combines traditional architectural types and language with modernist ideas of abstract, pure space and form. In plan, Venturi's Mother's House seems to be a streamlined, simplified re-presentation of Lutyens' Heathcote. Both houses promise a symmetry which is then subverted; the entry axis in both houses terminates on the mass of the fireplace; both plans share the A-B-A structure of an H-plan, although Venturi's building has been compactly tucked into the clean rectangle of a modernist box. In both houses a thin band of services establishes a layer of poché at the entry. Shaped spaces are carved out of the mass to organize the procession to the major rooms. At the same time, the layer separates public rooms at the back of the house from private rooms, which punch forward, beyond the entry circuit. Heathcote is comprised of large, independent rooms. Venturi's house is far more modest in scale, and the definition of space is looser. Shifting alignments create an asymmetrical interior organization which maximizes the size of the living room, while still retaining vestigial symmetry. Other memories of the traditional house are conserved in the Vanna Venturi house as well. A 'ghost stair' wraps behind the fire place, leading nowhere.

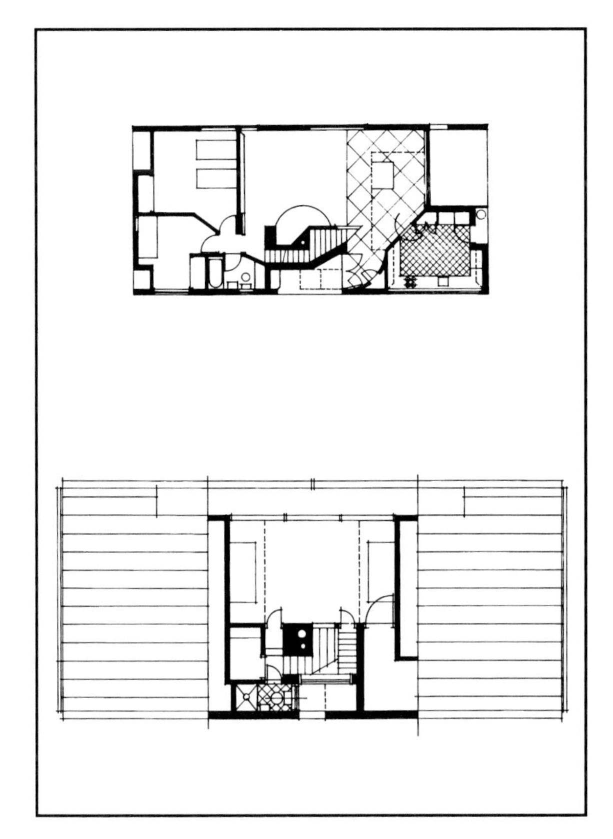

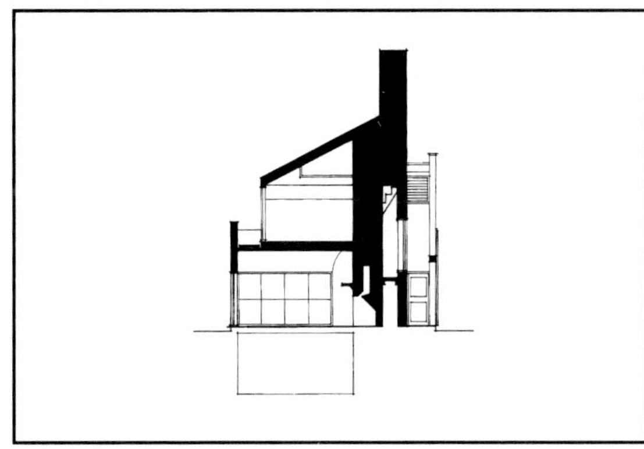

15.7 Left: Venturi and Short, Vanna Venturi House, Chestnut Hill, Pennsylvania, 1961, plans.

15.8 Right: Vanna Venturi House, section.

15.9 Vanna Venturi House, view.

Venturi's strategy of inclusion allows him to design *both* a modern *and* a traditional building at the same time. Like Le Corbusier at Garches and Poissy, the particularities of the house derive from carving a box, not from the addition of discrete forms. Unlike Le Corbusier, the box that Venturi carves is semantically meaningful. The emphatic gable roof and massive chimney evoke oneiric images of house, while the lurid Crayola green paint, insistent planarity and severe, abstracted language of square windows and applied string courses, suggest precedents in bill-boards and cartoons. Center is established through the gable but it is then broken by the split pediment; center is re-established by the fire-place but displaced by the canting of the wall within the recessed vestibule; center is reasserted by the arch, which is broken by the voided slot; and so forth. The superabundance of contradictory entry motifs reminds one of the Mannerist games of **Michelangelo** at **Porta Pia** and the severe tension between halves in **Luigi Moretti's** (1907-1974) binary **Girasole Apartment Building** in Rome. Venturi is *both* critically reinterpreting form, like a Modernist, *and* expanding the range of meaning in his building by laying bare the internal contradictions of the classical linguistic code.

15.10 Left: Michelangelo, Porta Pia, Rome., 1561-4.

15.11 Right: Luigi Moretti, Girasole Apartment Building, Rome. 1950.

Legible signage even informs the arrangement of windows. The apparent symmetry between the two sides is disrupted by unequal fenestration. However, symmetry is represented by the common presence of five windows on each side. Moreover, Venturi uses the window patterns to code the spaces functionally, like Gropius at the Bauhaus. Spaces for dreaming and ablution are given the sign of traditional architecture: the square window of one's childhood imaginings. The space for the production and preparation of food is given the modernist signature ribbon window: the kitchen is a 'machine for cooking.' The Vanna Venturi House holds these contradictions together in its compact space and gains strength from the simultaneous presence of two apparently incompatible design strategies.

Venturi's confrontation with popular culture is more aggressive in his **Fire Station No. 4**, in Columbus, Indiana, 1966. The smooth plane of the painted front facade crisply disengages from the posterior volume. Graphics become an important part of its expression, as if the fire station were a large sign. Venturi's unbuilt project for the **Football Hall of Fame** is even more extreme: architectural motifs are replaced with pure signage. The Football Hall of Fame

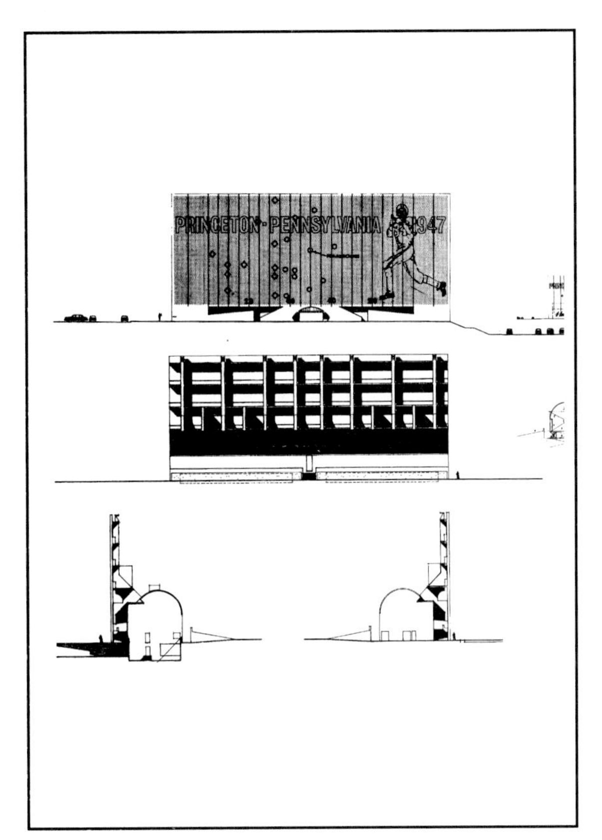

15.12 *Left: Venturi and Rauch, National Football Hall of Fame Competition, 1967.*

15.13 *Right: Venturi and Rauch, Fire Station No. 4, Columbus, Indiana, 1966.*

15.14 *Robert Venturi, 'The Duck' versus 'The Decorated Shed' from "Learning from Las Vegas."*

was not designed for a traditional urban context of genteelly scaled shop-fronts and a continuously defined street wall, but for the visual cacophony of the strip road. Such a site called for an architecture that could be perceived at 60 miles per hour from a swift-moving car; an architecture that made a primary, frontal response to the road, like the false store fronts in cowboy towns; an architecture that happily commanded its field of parking. In fact, an architecture already existed which responded well to those design criteria: the architecture of bill-boards, car washes and fast-food restaurants. Venturi steered away from grand precedents of traditional museums and civic buildings. Instead he adapted the motifs of vernacular strip architecture, achieving an expression as playful as the museum's subject matter.

In *Learning from Las Vegas,* Venturi identified two kinds of strip buildings: **'Ducks' and 'Decorated Sheds.'** For Venturi, 'Ducks' assume a distinctive, idiosyncratic form, such as hot-dog stands shaped like large hot-dogs, or monumental structures whose forms take on iconic value, such as the Pantheon. Among 'Ducks' Venturi includes High Modern buildings whose peculiarities of form seem designed solely to ex-

15.15
Farmer John's Bacon Factory, Los Angeles, California, A 'Decorated Shed,' adorned with bucolic images of pigs frolicking in happier days.

15.16
Tail of the Pup Hot Dog Stand, Los Angeles, California. A 'Duck,' configured to represent its product.

15.17
Robert Venturi, 'A Monument' as a 'Decorated Shed,' from ''Learning from Las Vegas.''

press their modernity and to announce their status as 'Architecture'. 'Decorated Sheds,' on the contrary, are modest, straightforward enclosures to which large signs have been attached. Meaning in the Decorated Shed is not encoded by the unusualness of the building envelope, but laid bare, reduced to pure graphics and signage. The Football Hall of Fame is a Decorated Shed. Its facade is literally a billboard, the scale of which is inflated to address the strip. The space of the museum is a neutral shed, tacked on to the back.

Aldo Rossi's approach to the making of architecture is radically opposed to that of Venturi, although they both make use of typology, abstraction, and the transformation of conventional meaning through reduction and exaggeration. But while Venturi looks for verification in popular culture, Rossi looks to the archetype and the reconstellation of images through memory and dreams. **Rossi's Cemetery for Modena**, 1976, relies on the Italian cemetery type of the ***Campo Santo,*** an enclosed field with urns and ossuaries placed into the wall. The plan and forms are severe and elemental. In Rossi's Modena cemetery, centrally within the two-square field, a second two-square precinct is defined by a U-shaped wall. The field is bisected by a series of parallel walls which taper along the path. The image is simultaneously suggestive of a tree and a skeleton, bringing together the opposites that constitute the vegetative cycle. Outside the inner precinct, austere Platonic forms terminate each end of the central axis. A cubic 'House of the Dead' is nearest the entry gate; most remote is a conical chapel, evocative of a great crematorium chimney. The quietness and severity with which Rossi works allows the forms to assume a relentless power.

15.18 Campo Santo, Pisa, Italy, 12th century.

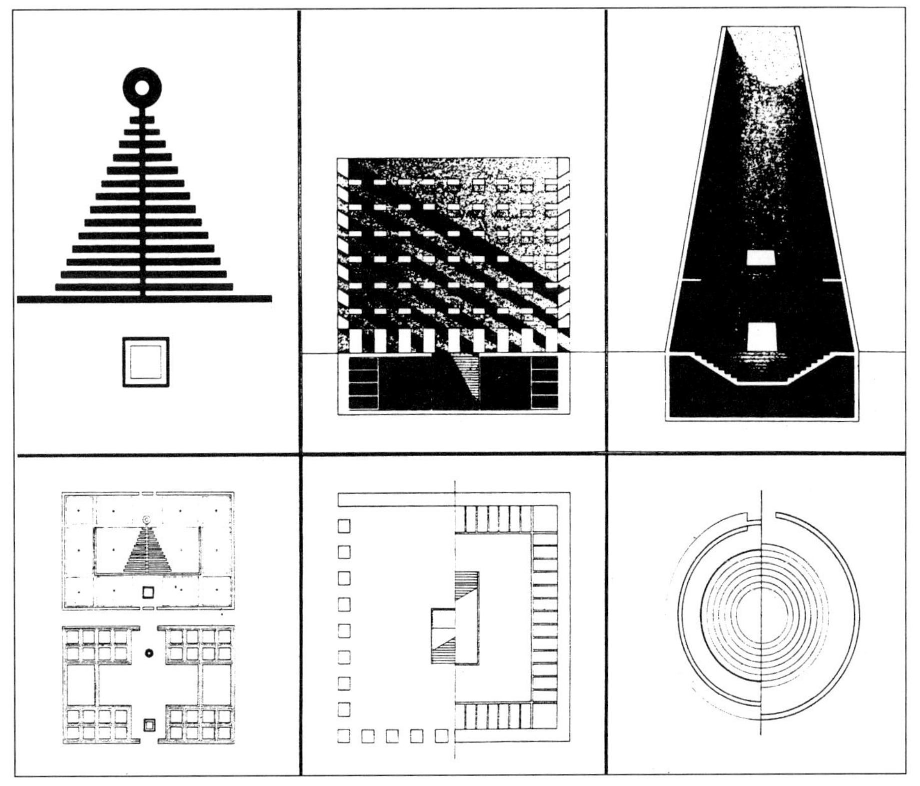

15.19 Aldo Rossi, Cemetery, Modena, Italy, 1976.

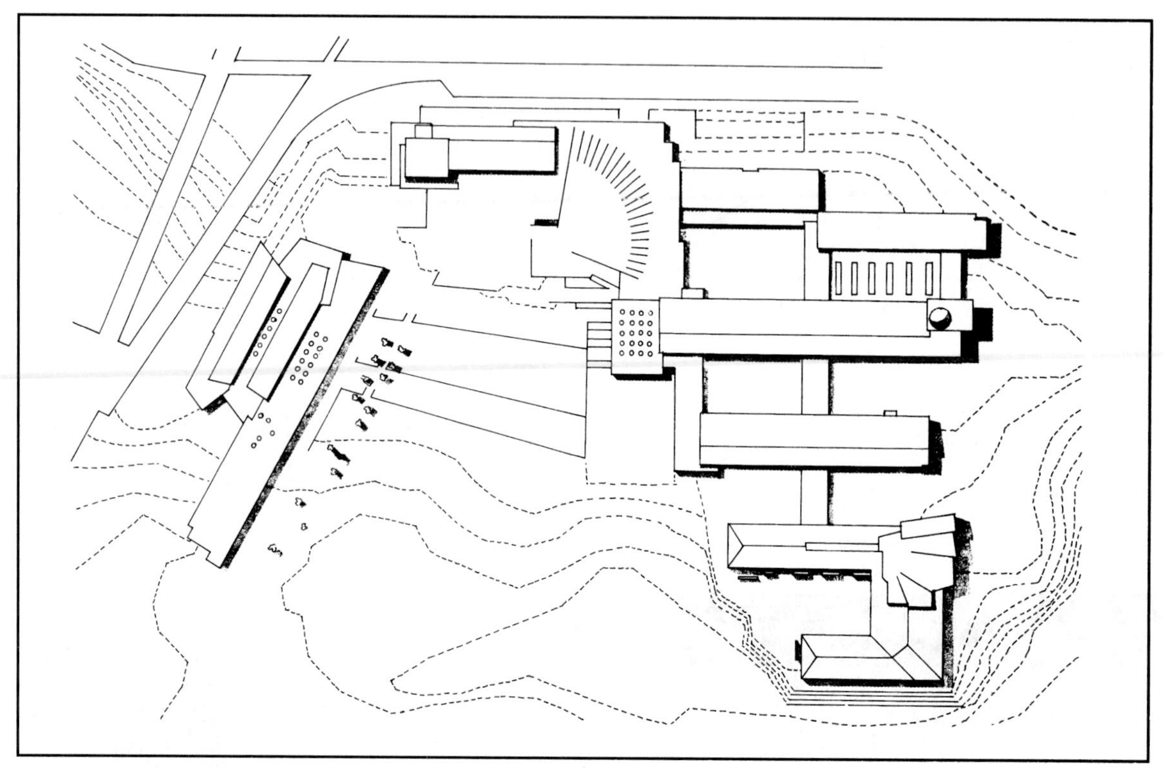

15.20 Alvar Aalto, Otaniemi University, Finland, 1949-1962, site plan.

Venturi and Rossi are quite open in their reliance on typology and tradition. **Alvar Aalto** makes use of the same material, but he more aggressively transforms the paradigms and uses a sparer, less polemical language. At **Otaniemi University** in Finland, Aalto reinterprets campus typology and the semantic coding of public buildings in a personal, abstract language. The campus plan is a fragmented grid, alluding to the quadrangles and courtyards that characterize the quintessential campus plans of Oxford and Cambridge. The exterior of the auditorium is configured to represent its interior. The stepped crescent roof permits clerestory lighting of the auditorium hall, but resembles an amphitheater. Indeed, it *is* an amphitheater. The deep steps of the clerestory windows grow shallower towards the ground and become a habitable part of the landscape. A smaller fan-shape lecture hall is coded to resemble the main auditorium, in contradistinction to the neutral bars which house repetitive, cellular elements, like classrooms, offices, and studios.

The main buildings of the Otaniemi campus define a ragged edge to a central trapezoid of space. The other side is cleanly defined by the smooth, skewed edge of the Library. Multiple centers and alignments are embraced within the whole, as contingent orientations, responsive to the gentle fall of the topography, rigidify into the

15.21 Left: Otaniemi University, detail of the auditorium.

15.22 Right: Otaniemi University, the Main Buildings.

15.23 Otaniemi University, courtyard of the Architecture Building.

orthogonality of the grid. The Functionalist rigor of ribbon windows, simple prismatic boxes and free-standing columns is overlaid with a curious use of material and form. Entry to the library takes place under a simple Functionalist canopy, yet directly to the left, an extension of the main reading room pulls forward, breaking from the dominant orthogonal lay-out, and appearing as an abstracted classical portico. Traditional hierarchies are subverted. The grand procession of entry is secondary to the space in which the real scholarship takes place.

The application of travertine marble to the brick campus buildings is nonfunctional, but expressive of the status of the buildings. The

15.24 Otaniemi University, entry to library.

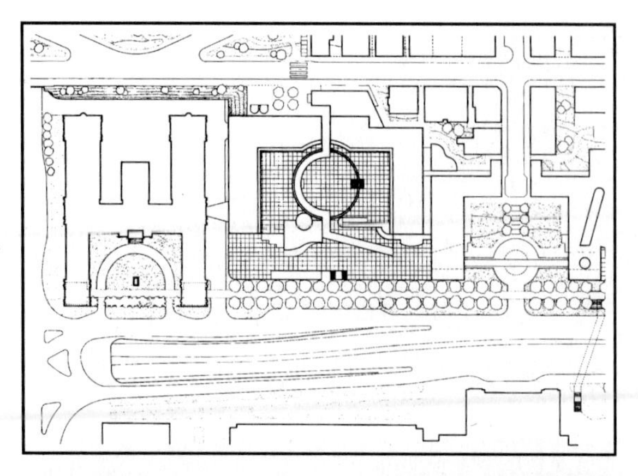

15.25 Left: James Stirling/ Michael Wilford, Neue Staatsgalerie and Chamber Theatre, Stuttgart, 1977-83, location plan.

15.26 Right: Staatsgalerie, entry terrace.

15.27 Left: Staatsgalerie, courtyard.

15.28 Right: Staatsgalerie, upper terrace.

library 'portico' is striated with plain bands of travertine, as if its material kinship with the architecture of classical antiquity were sufficient in communicating its cultural value. A full-blown use of classical types and ornament could not have communicated the message much more clearly. Travertine appears in one more place; on the interior courtyard of the Architecture School. While at the library, marble is applied to brick, here the facing is entirely travertine. Aalto, the architect, prized architecture above literature. Stark, abstracted slabs of marble are arrayed in the courtyard. Originally, these were intended to have been fragments of antiquities, but in the end, Aalto chose to replace the collection of classical columns, capitals, and friezes with signs embodying their meaning.

James Stirling's (1926-92) **National Gallery** (Staatsgalerie) in Stuttgart, Germany, 1977-84, works within the established architectural tradition and extends that tradition. Stirling bases his museum on the precedents of K.F. Schinkel's Neoclassical Altesmuseum (Chapter 14) and The Roman Temple of Fortuna Primagenia, Palestrina (Chapter 8). The precedents are re-

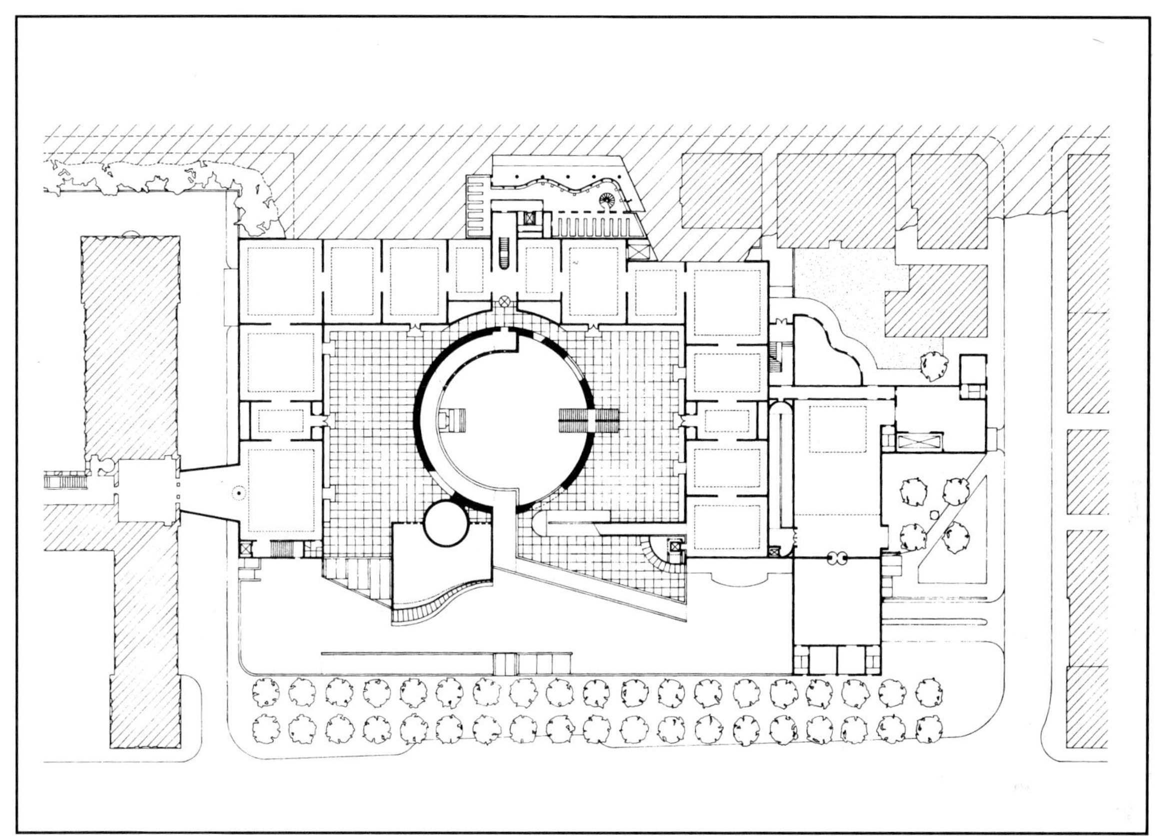

15.29 James Stirling/Michael Wilford, Neue Staatsgalerie and Chamber Theatre, plan at upper terrace level.

interpreted and radically transformed by the pressure each exerts upon the other. From Schinkel, Stirling derives a round central space and a U-shaped wrapper of rooms; from Palestrina, he extracts the procession upwards through a series of terraces which contract in scale along the route. Also from Palestrina comes the acropolean massing of the complex and the reconstitution of a new, idealized ground plane in stronger sympathy with the park across the street. At Palestrina, temples and other figural Roman structures mark the stages of the path. Stirling does likewise, but his 'temples' are mechanistic, brightly-painted, metal structures. The central round space alludes both to Schinkel's Rotunda and to the Theater atop the hill at Palestrina. The building as a whole takes on the aspect of a large classical ruin, out of context with the heavily trafficked road at its base.

Spatially, the building works in several ways. At the entry level, the plan is open, and path is made either by moving along an irregular perimeter or around the volumes of the circular courtyard and the theater. However, there is an axial relationship established among

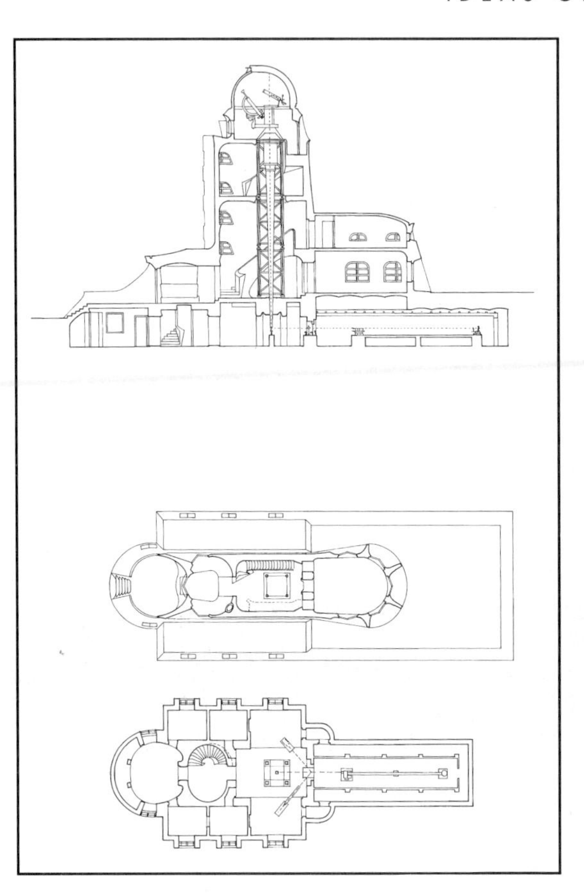

15.30 Left: Erich Mendelsohn, Einstein Tower, Potsdam, Germany, 1920-1924, plan and section.

15.31 Right top: Einstein Tower, detail.

15.32 Right bottom: Einstein Tower, detail.

the shaped spaces. The museum is a hybrid organization, commingling free-plan and axial procession. A cellular band of traditional gallery rooms wrap the courtyard at the upper level. Functionally, the diversity of museum space makes it possible to display a wide variety of works of art. Metaphorically, the museum recapitulates within itself the history of architecture, an appropriate task for a museum. The witty, totemic insertion of lurid machines into the polished stone wall on the exterior focuses attention on this dialectical relationship.

Not all twentieth century architects so willingly embraced historical precedent, traditions of type, and an established architectural language. Many believed that the central task of architecture was to find the mode of expression typical of the age, as suggested by Hugo. The search for a formal expression of the spirit of the times formed the central premise of *Zeitgeist* theory. Tradition and history played no role in this quest: they were but the residue of the past. The development of a proper response to the future was believed to be the task of architecture. At the Bauhaus history was seen with

15.33 Einstein Tower, view.

suspicion. Students were urged to reinvent architecture from ground zero, stripping away preconceptions about social interchange and its formal expression. Abstraction, simplification and essentialist reduction took the place of convention and compositional norms. With the abandonment of traditional modes of expression, architects had to find some way to make theirs projects intelligible.

Expressionism emerged contemporaneously with Functionalism and both methods were promulgated by the Bauhaus masters. While Functionalism sought the rational, the typical, and the minimal; Expressionism sought the supernatural, the extraordinary, and the excessive. If Functionalism was the 'super ego' of the modern condition, then Expressionism was the 'id'.

Erich Mendelsohn (1887-1953) was one of the most moderate Expressionists. Instead of rhapsodizing about the power of enchanted crystals and the magic of reflections, as was very much in vogue, Mendelsohn shared the Functionalist's intoxication with speed, technology, and the mechanized society. While a soldier on the Russian Front during the First World War, he did a series of **sketches** which

15.34 Left: Erich Mendelsohn, sketches, 1914 - 1917, railroad station (top) and theater (bottom).

15.35 Right: Wind-battered barn.

investigated the dynamic transformation of form through speed and motion. The industrial buildings he sketched seem like blurs or waves, as if their profiles had been streamlined or eroded through movement.

Mendelsohn's Einstein Tower, 1920-1924, is the only one of his visionary sketches that was ever realized. An astronomical research station, its function suits its futuristic form. However, Mendelsohn's handling of the space is more akin to the stolid symmetries of the *Ecole des Beaux-Arts* than the Cubist space/time constructions which also drew their inspiration from physics and astronomy. The great monolithic structure (*Ein Stein* means 'one stone,' or 'monolithic') is constructed of brick, although the plasticity of its volume suggests that it was conceived as a concrete structure. Mendelsohn's fetishist infatuation with technology led him to design the building as though it were a great ocean-going vessel or protean matter, whipped into a frenzy by the dynamism of the age. Mendelsohn was interested in finding an image illustrative of the spirit of the times, not in experimenting with the methodologies unique to his age. Deformation through applied force can be seen in the twisted frame of a wind-battered **Midwestern barn.** However, with the barn, both the force and the untransformed condition are clearly understood. With Mendelsohn's tower, it is impossible to guess what the tower was before it began moving so fast. A **process** is implied, but it is not mapped in the architecture. The original terms and the terms of interaction are not explicitly stated. In the end, we are left with a gesture, not a methodical approach to the making of form particular to a mechanized society.

Giuseppe Terragni (1904-42), like Mendelsohn, does away with traditional criteria for the making of architecture and substitutes a poetic alternative strategy in his project for the **Danteum**, 1938, an unbuilt monument to Dante Alighieri, author of *The Divine Comedy*. Designed under the patronage of Mussolini, the Danteum was to be sited among the Imperial Fora in view of the Colosseum, in Rome (Chapter 8). In such a charged site, Terragni's response was not to imitate or defer to the context, but to find a new expression, as appropriate to the 'Third Rome,' as the Classical Orders were to the first. Cautious not to *"lapse into rhetoric, symbolism or convention"* Terragni

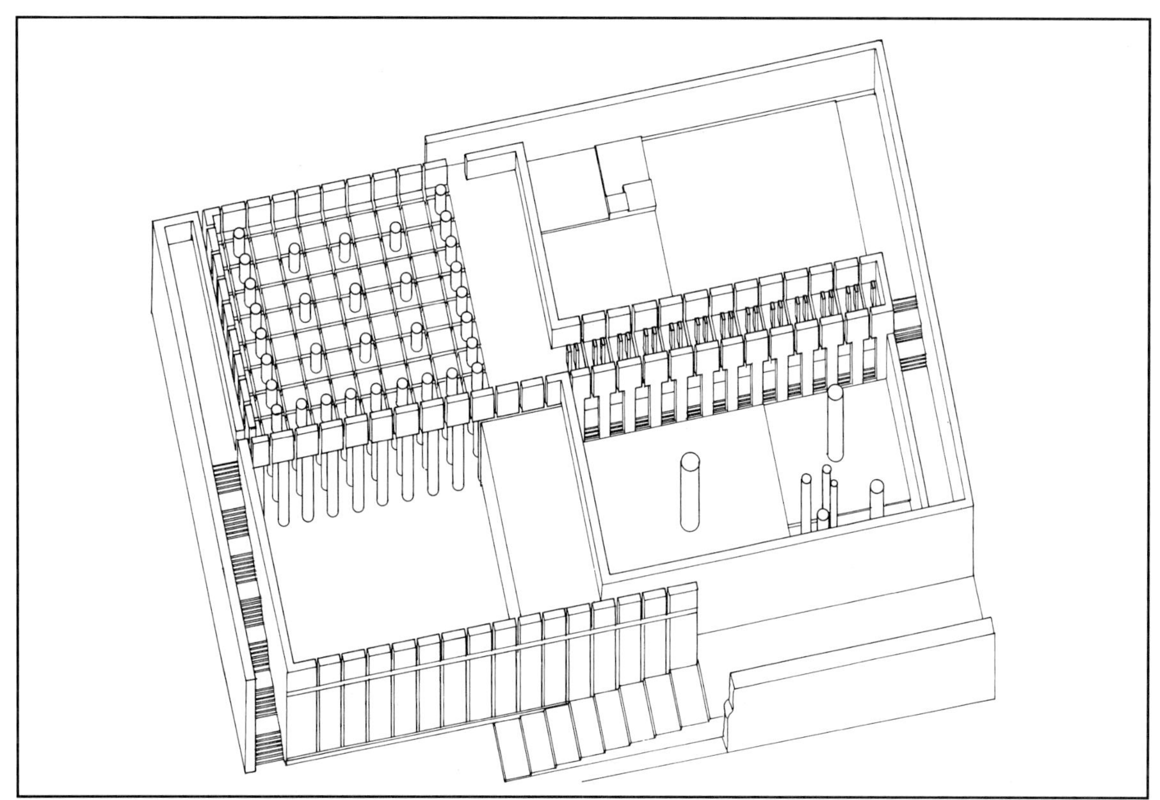

15.36 G. Terragni and P. Lingeri, Project for the Danteum, Rome, 1938, axonometric.

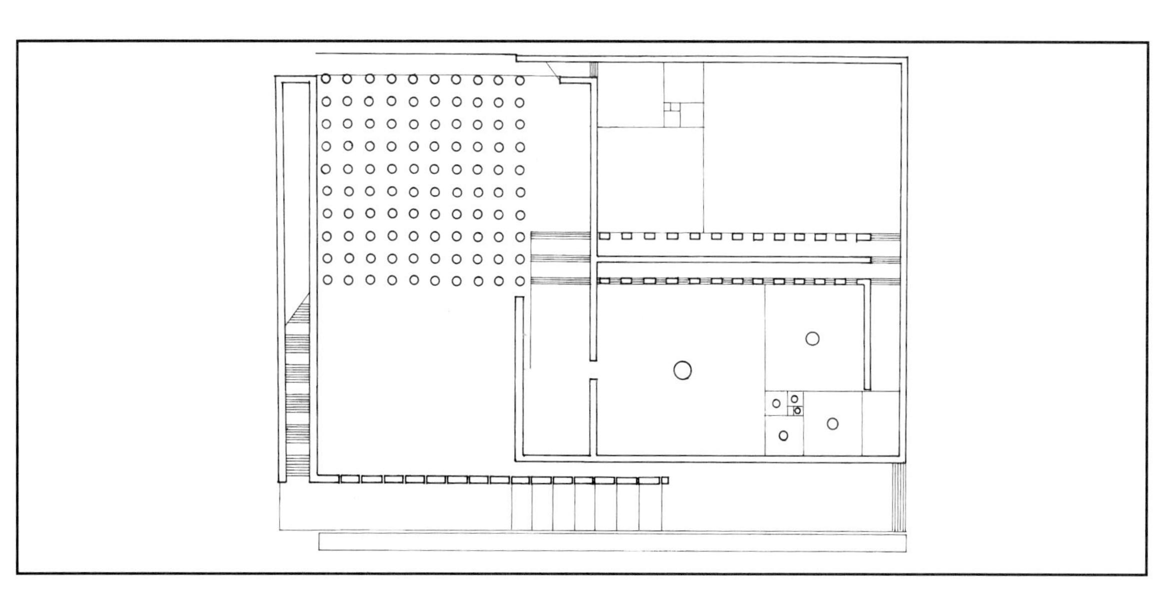

15.37 Danteum, plan.

stripped away linguistic references in his project and relied instead on geometry and number to embody the essence of the poet and his poem. Terragni's design strategy was to represent, in architecture, the narrative content and formal structure of the poem. The three parts to the poem, *Inferno, Purgatorio,* and *Paradiso,* give rise to three chambers. The ritual journey undertaken in the poem has correspondence in the ritualized, spiral processional path through the building.

The spatial scheme of Terragni's Danteum is wholly internalized, masked behind unarticulated walls, and held within an inexpressive, rectangular container. Slipped layers of blank travertine walls create narrow slots for passage among the zones. All sense of the exterior surroundings vanishes once the maze-like space is entered. The plan of the Danteum is based on a golden rectangle, and the path follows its spiral. The first space encountered is a 'forest' of columns. (Dante's poem begins: *"Midway along the journey of our life I found myself in a dark forest, for I had wandered off the straight path.)* From there, the spiraling path moves through three rectangular zones representative of the three books of Dante's poem. ***Inferno*** makes use of the recursive infolding of the golden rectangle progression to illustrate the infinitude of damnation. Each time the golden rectangle decomposes into a square and a smaller golden rectangle, the center of the square is marked by a column of decreasing diameter. ***Purgatorio*** is also structured by decomposing golden rectangles, but here, the constituent squares are marked by raised floor planes and cut-outs in the ceiling above. Order is revealed if you turn your gaze towards heaven, disorder if you cast your gaze downwards. Lastly, ***Paradiso*** replaces the instability of the golden rectangle spiral for a calm, static column grid. Unlike the forest of columns at entry, here the space is inundated with light. The roof is open and the columns themselves are transparent.

Terragni imports a narrative story line to orchestrate the progression through the Danteum and to define the character of the individual spaces. He does not illustrate the poem, but reveals its essential structure by using terms which are specific to architecture: walls, columns, floor planes, and geometry. The narrative line confers an order to the architecture that defies traditional compositional logic.

The **Russian Constructivists** also sought to develop an architecture appropriate to and expressive of the times. Their method was to apply the rigor of scientific method to their work. Like scientists engaged in controlled experimentation, they strictly limited the terms of their investigations: point, line, plane, volume; square, circle, rectangle, cube, sphere, bar. They likewise limited the ways in which the forms could interact. **Iakov Chernikhov** (1889-1951) wrote several instructional books which outlined his program. In *The Construction of Architectural Forms and Machines,* Chernikhov systematically laid out away of working. An excerpt is indicative of the general tone: *"Legitimacy in all constructive structures depends on our being simultaneously able to prove the TRUTH and CORRECTNESS of the chosen solution by ANALYTICAL MEANS..."* He provided specific guidelines for analysis: *"In the old aesthetics, rhythm was any periodic movement or regular repetition of elements. The new aesthetic uses rhythm*

15.38
Iakov Chernikhov, "Architectural Rhythms for the New Aesthetic", from The Construction of Architectural and Machine Forms, 1931.

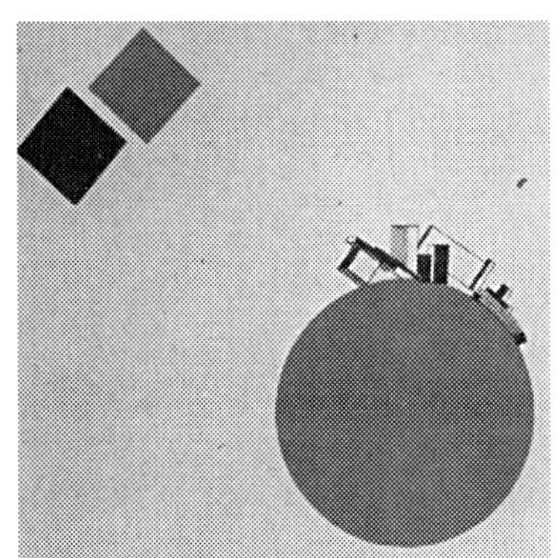

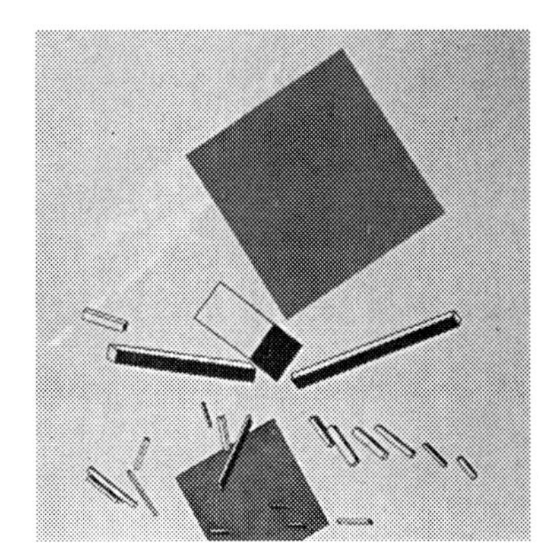

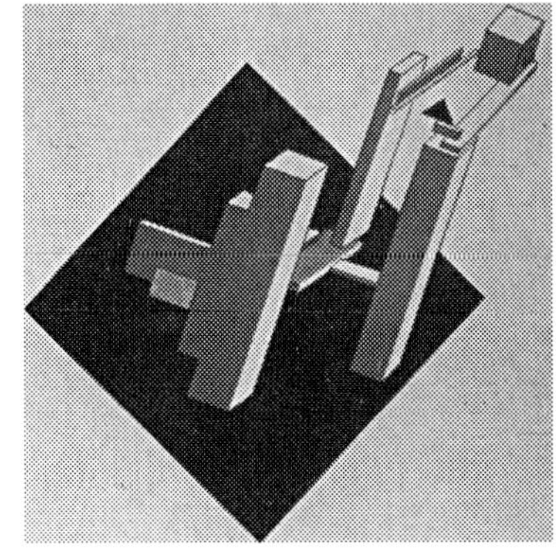

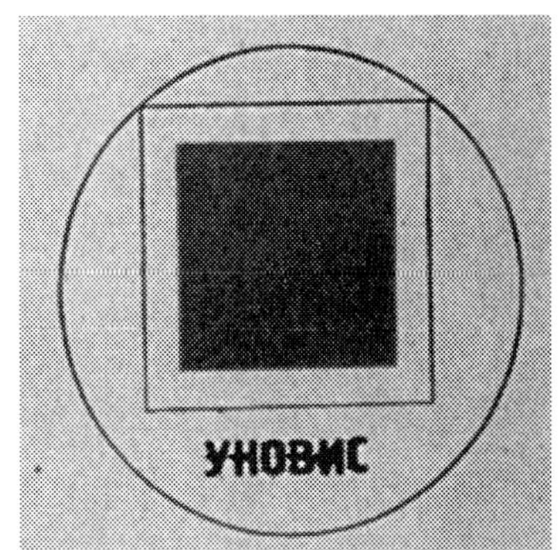

15.39–15.44
El Lissitzky, About Two Squares, 1920.
15.39 Left: "Here are Two Squares;"
15.40 Middle: "They Fall to Earth from Afar; and..."
15.41 Right: "And See a Black Disturbance"
15.42 Left: "A Crash Breaks All Assunder;"
15.43 Middle: "And on the Black, Red is Formed;"
15.44 Right: "Here is the End, Read On!"

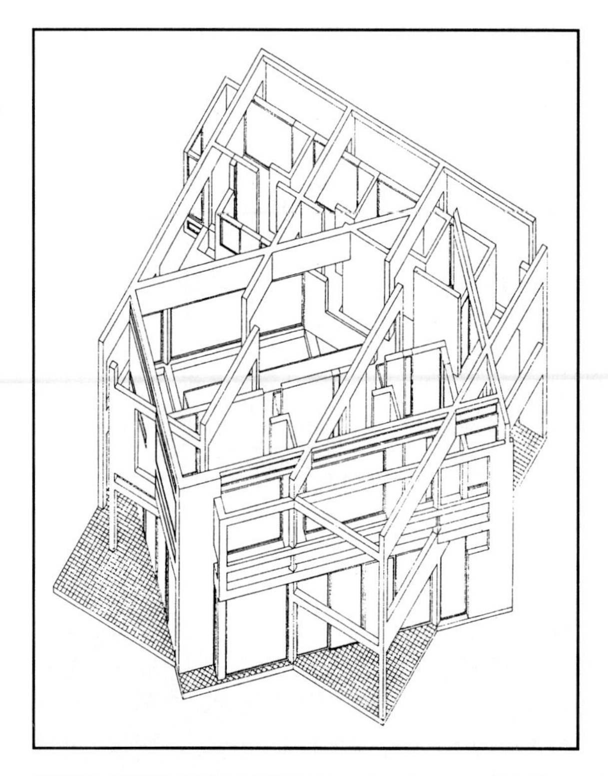

15.45
Peter Eisenman, House III, 1970, axonometric.

of a different kind, 'of a higher order,' rooted in subtler harmonies constructed from: 1. Relations of overall masses; 2. Mutual interlocking of weights of parts; 3. Appropriate 'percussiveness' of individual contiguous parts; 4. General coordination of elements of high coloredness... " and so forth. For Chernikhov, the progressive agenda of industry and technology was not merely the subject matter for architecture, it was the very stuff of architecture.

The work of **El Lissitzky** (1890-1941) is parallel to that of Chernikhov, although wittier and more daring graphically. Lissitzky is best known for his polemical architectural drawings, 'Prouns', but he also wrote a children's book in 1920 based on the inherent properties of geometric forms interacting in space. El Lissitzky investigated the *process* of interaction, not the final product. The six panels record different stages of transformation beginning with the ideal, original condition of a red and

15.46
Peter Eisenman, House IV, 1970, transformational diagrams.

black square floating in open space. Like Platonic forms touched by matter, when the squares make contact with the earth, a new dynamic order replaces the original stasis of the squares. In the final panels, something akin to architecture rises up from the fragments of the collision of earth and pure form. The meaning of El Lissitzky's panels is not universal, but self-contained, local to the system he constructs. Other nouns (the squares) and other verbs (falling to earth) would have yielded a different architectural product. Meaning is stabilized through the construction of a frame, even though the meaning cannot be extended beyond the frame. El Lissitzky emphasized the non-academic stance of Constructivism at the very beginning: *"Don't read! Take paper, blocks, wood pieces; build, paint, construct!"* He ends in an enigmatic way: *"Here is the end, Read on!"*

As the progressive social agendas of early Modernism dwindled, the content of architecture became more and more hermetic in the work of some architects and the subject matter of architecture was reduced to architecture itself. In recognition that architecture was no longer able to provide an absolute, all-embracing expression of the world at large, some architects began to make closed, self-referential systems, access to which was available only to the initiated few. El Lissitzky's "About Two Squares" already sketched a method in which narrative and process were to play a greater role in the generation of architectural form than traditional criteria, such as the Vitruvian triad, "Firmness, Commodity, and Delight". The subsequent generation of architects were to make such explorations thematic in their work.

Peter Eisenman's House Projects from the 1960's and 1970's pick up on Constructivist use of scientific metaphor and process-driven architectural design, but Eisenman uses these methods to explore the nature of architectural

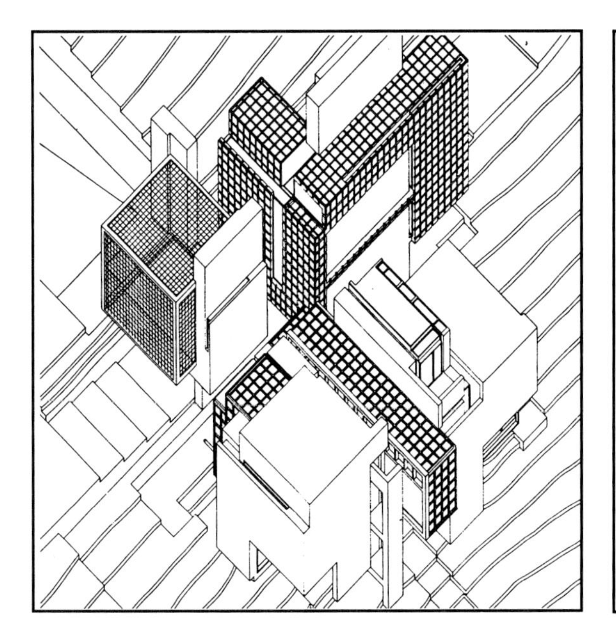

15.47 Left: Peter Eisenman, House X, 1976, axonometric.

15.48 Right: House X, transformational diagrams.

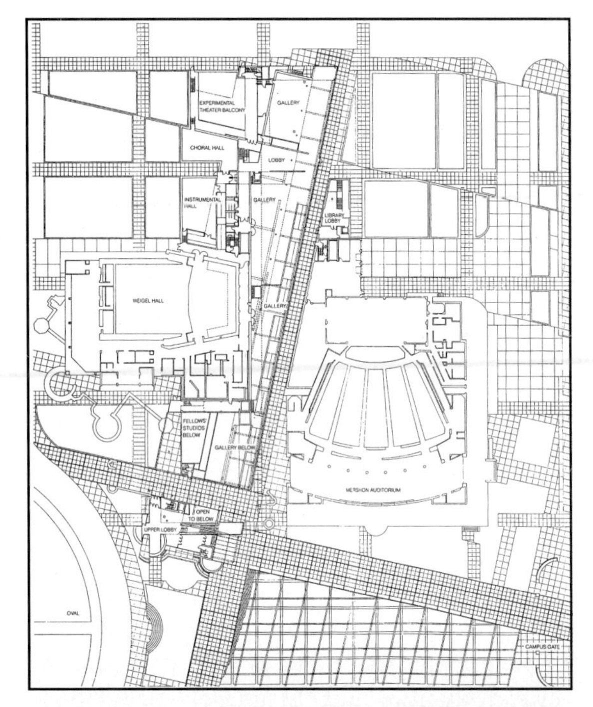

15.49
Peter Eisenman and Richard Trott, Wexner Center for the Visual Arts, Columbus, Ohio, 1989, plan.

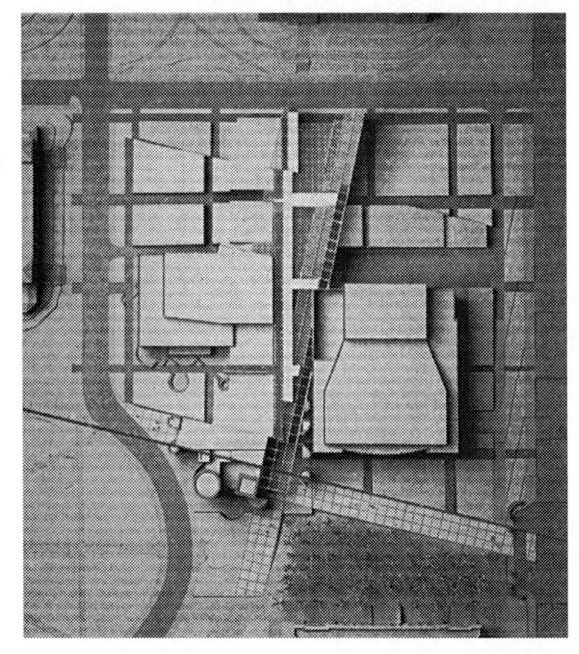

15.50
Wexner Center for the Visual Arts, competition model.

language. Eisenman's distance from tradition is affirmed by the fact that some of his houses were designed to work equally well right-side-up or upside-down. Relying on Noam Chomsky's theories of structural linguistics, Eisenman discarded architectural elements already coded semantically and began as objectively as possible: with a pure white cube, and its latent properties of surface, edge, volume, angle, layer, perimeter, and grid. Like Chomsky, Eisenman distinguished between *"deep structures"* and *"surface structures."* For Eisenman, the former are conceptual, the later perceptual. Eisenman's *"deep structure"* is the system of rules which governs the composition and de-composition of the cubic volume. By applying a rule-driven process, Eisenman was able to construct formal relationships outside the traditions of Modernism and Classicism. Eisenman was very methodical. As in El Lissitzky's *About Two Squares,* each stage of the process followed logically from the preceding stage and sponsored the subsequent one. *"The aim of the process is to find a law, a general rule that will combine each of the partial moves or stages into an uninterrupted sequence explanatory of the process from simple beginning to complex end."* (Mario Gandelsonas, *House X).*

Eisenman's earliest houses proposed closed systems, in which each move was objectively determined by the nature of the starting point and the terms of interaction. In **House III**, Eisenman dealt with rotation and the grid in three parallel explorations based on three different formal readings of the cube: the cube as a frame; the cube as a surface structure; the cube as a stereometric solid. The final product resulted from the overlay of the three. In

Eisenman's later houses, such as **House X**, the systems were deliberately contaminated by subjective intervention and contradictions emerged. In the earlier houses it is possible to reconstitute the original volume; in House X, the product is so fragmented and de-composed that the original point of departure is not wholly recoverable.

15.51 Wexner Center for the Visual Arts, view.

Eisenman's project for the **Wexner Center for the Visual Arts,** Columbus, Ohio, 1982-89, brought together two design strategies: the internal manipulations of an objective construct, the grid; and the evocation of subjective memory. Process and narrative design strategies are superimposed and the result is ambiguous and undecidable. The site of the Wexner Center is not neutral as in House III; instead, it is treated as a rich palimpsest whose strata already hold the essentials of the design. The task of the architect is to reveal the layers and the multiplicity of disjunctions and overlaps afforded by their simultaneous presence. Eisenman began with a grid; but his grid is not a purely abstract Cartesian device. Instead, it is specific to the meeting of the city grid and the campus grid in Columbus. The 12 1/4 degree displacement between the grids sponsors a disturbance of the ideal Cartesian condition. Moreover, Eisenman recognized that the city grid of a Midwestern town is simply a condensation of the surrounding Jeffersonian grid which structures the agricultural landscape. Hence, the intrinsic ability of a grid to reiterate its own system at larger and smaller scales is explored. The grid of the Wexner Center exists at twelve foot, twenty-four foot, forty eight foot, and ninety six foot modules. Not only do the cells of gridded space increase, but the width of

15.52 Wexner Center for the Visual Arts, site plan.

15.53 Left: Bernard Tschumi, Parc de la Villette, Paris, 1982, view.

15.54 Right: Richard Meier, Athenaeum, New Harmony, Indiana, c. 1980.

15.55 Parc de la Villette, view.

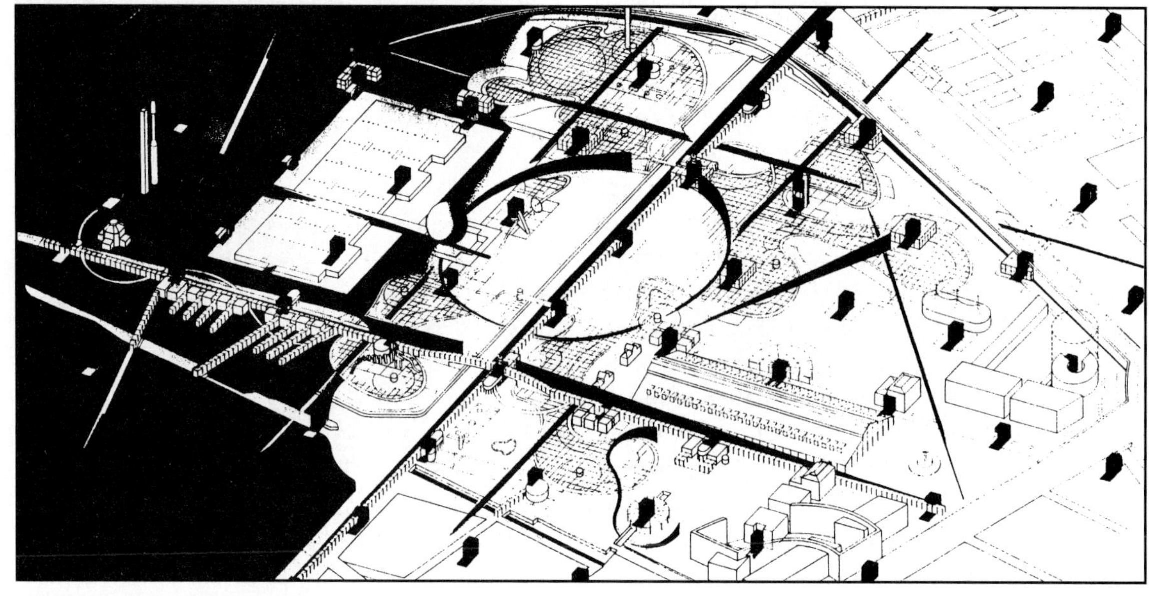

15.56 Parc de la Villette, perspective site plan.

the defining grid lines likewise expands. Even the surrounding ground plane registers the systems: plinths of disturbed earth heave upwards around the building and knit the order of the building firmly to the site. Prairie grass planted on the plinths suggests the landscape before settlement and gridding occurred.

The interwoven grids are semantically neutral, but Eisenman also introduces a semantically loaded text into the system by resurrecting a fragmented evocation of the demolished armory on the site. Rotund towers and battered brick walls are as insistent in their specificity as the overlaid, rotating grids are in their generality. The result of the simultaneous presence of two texts contaminates both, fragmenting the object and dispersing the system. Contradictions abound in the relations among architectural elements: columns pierce through stairs; beams shoot through panes of glass. At the same time, material changes and the differing scales of the multiple grid lines register each overlap and deformity. The method is at once coolly rational and sensually picturesque.

A paradigm shift has taken place since the time in which Kepler confidently modelled the *"Harmony of the Spheres"* with the concentric disposition of Platonic solids. Fragmentation, disjunction, heterotopia, and juxtaposition are the natural by products of the technology we use and the media which bombard us with disjointed images at such a rate that it is almost impossible to conceive of a synthetic whole. Novelists embrace the condition in the narrative structure of the new novel, which is non-linear, discontinuous, and reliant on multiple vantage points. Venturi's 'Main Street' and Eisenman's concatenated systems present related scenarios, in which the radical juxtaposition of signs, structures, and images appear at too fast a rate to be absorbed.

Such architecture aims at making an unsentimental response to the contemporary condition in which science no longer relies on unitary, absolute models, but on dispersed information fields. Temporally and spatially isolated forms are replaced by a complex, multidimensional nexus of interrelationships. The heroic brutality of nineteenth century technology has been replaced by a technology which relies less and less on physical mass. The dematerialization begun in the Gothic era reaches its apotheosis in the microchip.

Even language cannot hold a single transcendental meaning. According to Jacques Derrida, French literary critic and leading exponent of Deconstruction, every meaning is undecidable; no meaning can ever be present except in terms of its relations to other elements in other chains of meaning. Derrida calls such a net of relationships a 'text,' and for Derrida "there is nothing outside the text". Deconstruction does not look for standard signs to convey meaning, but for *difference* within a field of relationships to reveal that which has been suppressed in the text.

Today, just as in the past, technology, philosophy, mathematics and science stimulate artistic production and provide methods or images which are appropriated and reconfigured by the arts. **Bernard Tschumi's** 1982 design for the **Parc de la Villette** in Paris explicitly deals with the explosion of a unified entity and its recomposition into a neutral field of references. A strange disjunction exists between the atomized spatial dispersion in the scheme and the recomposition of the fragments into fetishist nineteenth-century machines, resembling three-dimensional illustrations from Chernikhov's text books. The conservatism of the forms contrasts sharply with the modernity of the method.

We have outlined only a few current ideas which are present in contemporary architectural design and discourse, ones that seem most directly to address the question of an architecture specific to our age. Stylistic revivals continue to flourish; not only Gothic and Classical revivals, as mentioned earlier, but also revivals of earlier avant-gardes. The work of **Richard Meier** can be seen as a Baroque strain of Neo-Corbusian architecture; the work of **Zaha Hadid** is a picturesque revival of Constructivism.

The Hegelian myth of Progress has dominated art historical discourse since the nineteenth-century. As a new technology supersedes the old, there has been a belief that new artistic expression made preceding work redundant. F.T. Marinetti, in his *Futurist Manifesto* of 1909, urged the destruction of the *Mona Lisa* and the *Nike of Samothrace* because they were no longer relevant to the contemporary age. Marinetti eagerly envisaged the demise of old (over 40) Futurists in view of the emergence of a new, younger artistic movement: *"they will throng around us, panting with anguish and spite, all of them exasperated by our proud, tireless courage ... and the more drunken their love and admiration for us, the greater will be the hatred in their hearts."*

The cult of novelty, spawned by the belief that 'new' and 'improved' necessarily march hand in hand, has given rise to the production and consumption of styles and images at alarming speed. No sooner does a style or movement acquire a name than it also expires in freshness and vitality. The task of engaging contemporary culture with architecture is made difficult

15.57 Zaha Hadid, Peak Project, Hong Kong, 1982-83.

by the condition of culture today. We live in a world of the cheap and consumable image. It is a world of the Hostess Twinkie and the disposable diaper. Little difference exists between art and advertising, except that advertising is more memorable and has a broader following.

Our moment in history is one of transition. It is doubtful that ever again stylistic hegemonies will arise and endure, such as those of ancient Egypt and Greece. The clarity and unity of vision required for such art no longer exists. T.S. Eliot expressed the dilemma of the modern world as follows: *"Our civilization comprehends great variety and complexity, playing upon a refined sensibility, must produce various and complex results. The poet must become more and more comprehensive, more allusive, more indirect in order to force, to dislocate if necessary, language into his meaning."*

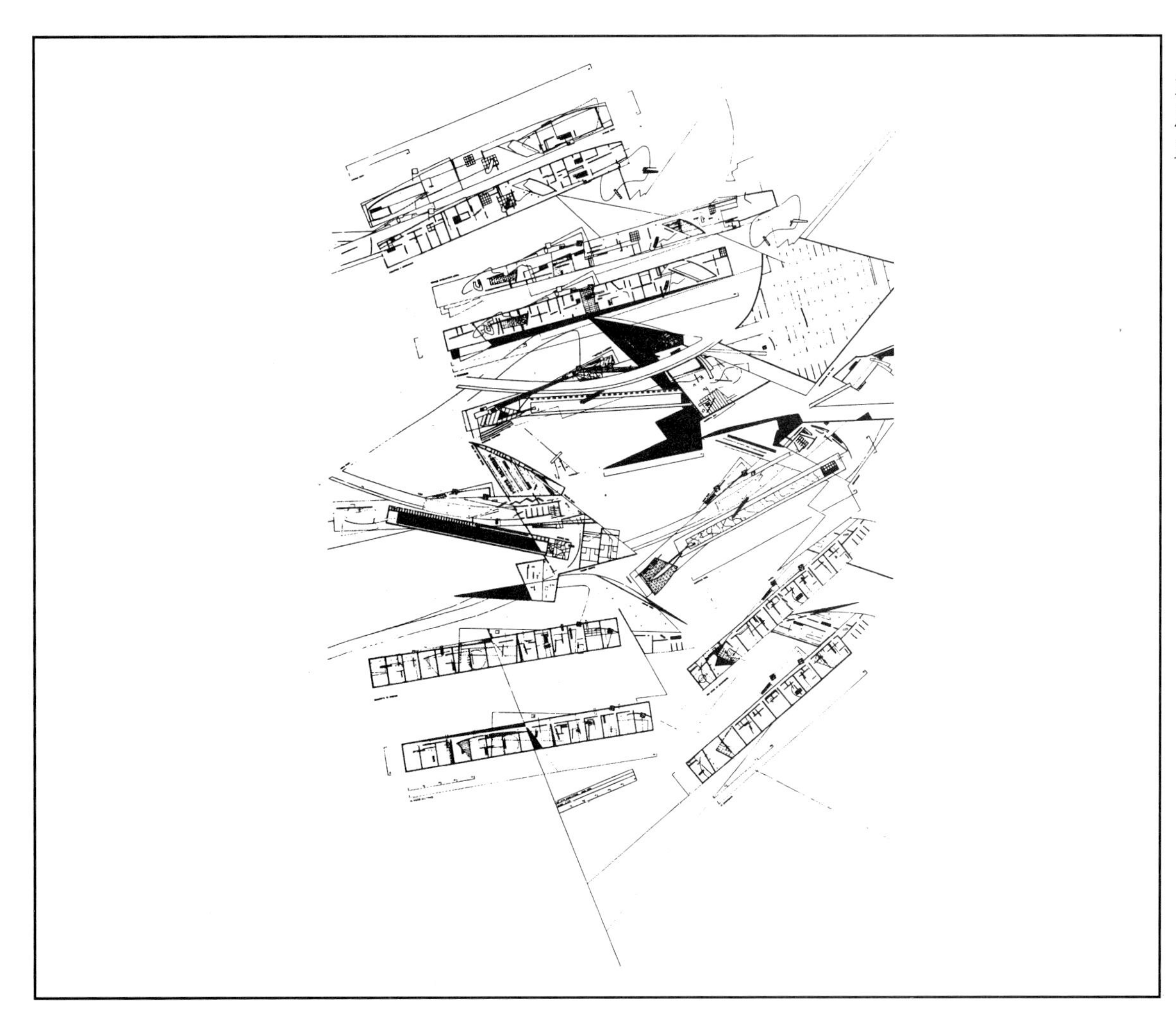

15.58
Zaha Hadid, Peak Project.

A.0 Ciampini, "Painting, Drafting, Chronicling, and Typography in their mutual function of documenting antique monuments".

Appendix
Ways of Seeing and Ways of Representing

Drawing Conventions

By the exactness of his shadows, lines and angles, the painter endeavors to make the parts seem to arise from the canvas, whereas the architect, without any regard to the shadows, gets his relief from the drawing of the plan, and indicates in other drawings the form of measurement of the facade and side by lines of invariable length and real angles, since he does not want his work to be judged by illusory appearance but precisely on the grounds of determinate quantities, founded upon reason."
-LEONBATTISTA ALBERTI

Architecture differs from other branches of the visual arts: it directly engages a specific site; fulfills a civic role; endures over generations and gives lasting character to our environment. Another important difference between architecture and other art forms has to do with methods of production. The painter works directly with paint and canvas. The sculptor works directly with clay, stone, metal, and other materials. Architects, on the contrary, rarely engage in the actual construction of the buildings they design. They may supervise construction, but their primary responsibility is the building design and the preparation of documents which communicate their architectural intentions to the workers on the site. Because workers cannot be expected to interpret accurately the idiosyncratic jottings of thousands of architects, standard drawing conventions have grown up over the ages.

Drawing conventions make possible the reduction of complex, three-dimensional information about a building into concise, two-dimensional form. Much information is lost in the process, but a legible, universal graphic language is gained. To better communicate important aspects of the design, architectural drawings are usually supplemented by additional information, be it in the form of written specifications, three-dimensional scale models,

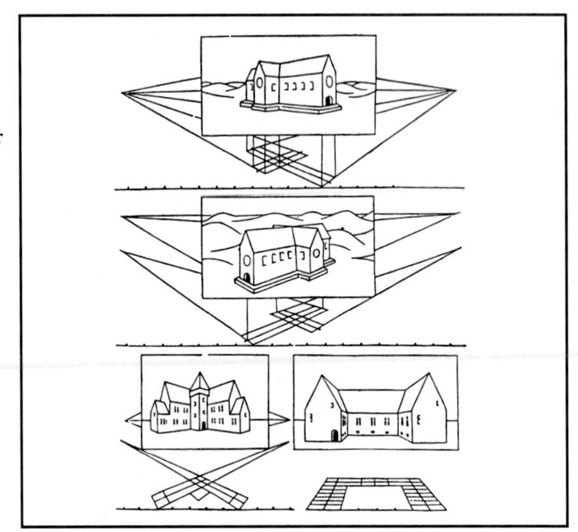

A.1
Jean Pèlerin, Different ways of setting up a three-point perspective. De artificiali p(er)spectiva, 1505.

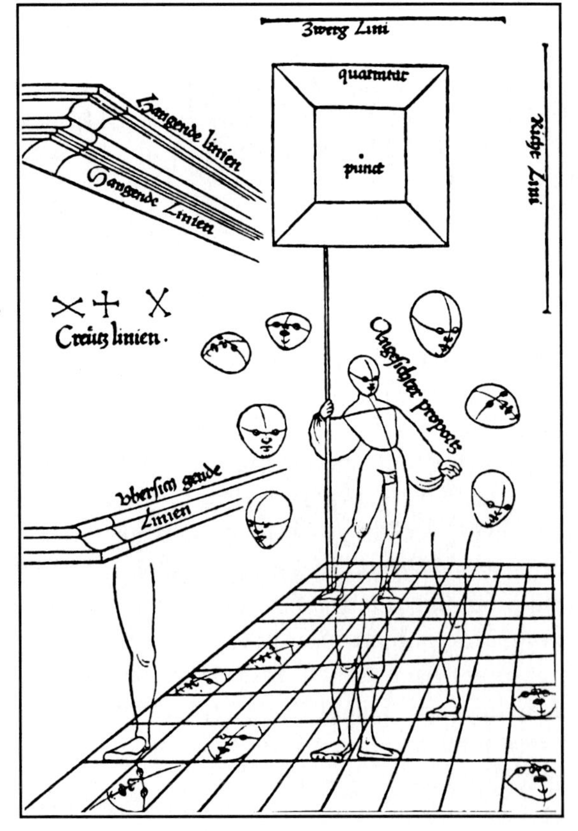

A.2
Jean Cousin, Studies for an interior perspective, and the human figure in perspective. Livre de Perspective, 1560.

sketches, conceptual diagrams, or whatever is pertinent to the particular project. Conventional methods of drawing have so fully entered into the discipline of architecture that the way in which architects conceptualize projects is often limited by the drawing conventions they use. Buildings which can be easily represented on flat sheets of paper with a straight edge and triangle (buildings which are rectilinear, volumetrically simple, repetitive in detail and dimension, etc.) are often favored above those which do not lend themselves as easily to such representation (buildings with complex curvature, irregularly shaped rooms, irregular floor levels, etc.) It is difficult to imagine any drawing that could adequately represent the soaring, intricately curved ceiling vaults which rise above cathedral floors. In fact, Gothic architects did not use drawings to realize their ideas, but worked directly with the stone. Now that computers have become standard tools in architectural offices, new means of representing space and form are available. Because the computer can store three-dimensional information about buildings, an exploration of complex geometries and intersections of forms is now possible, although such studies would have been too time-consuming and too difficult with old fashioned drafting tools and methods. In the past, whenever a new representational tool was developed, the resulting impact on architectural form was immediate. At present, most offices use computers simply to replicate the kinds of drawings done on drafting tables with traditional tools. When the power of the computer to organize spatial information in new ways is tapped, radically new developments in architecture may ensue.

A.3
Philibert de L'Orme, Le premier tome de l'architecture, Paris, 1567, "The Good Architect", with three eyes and four hands.

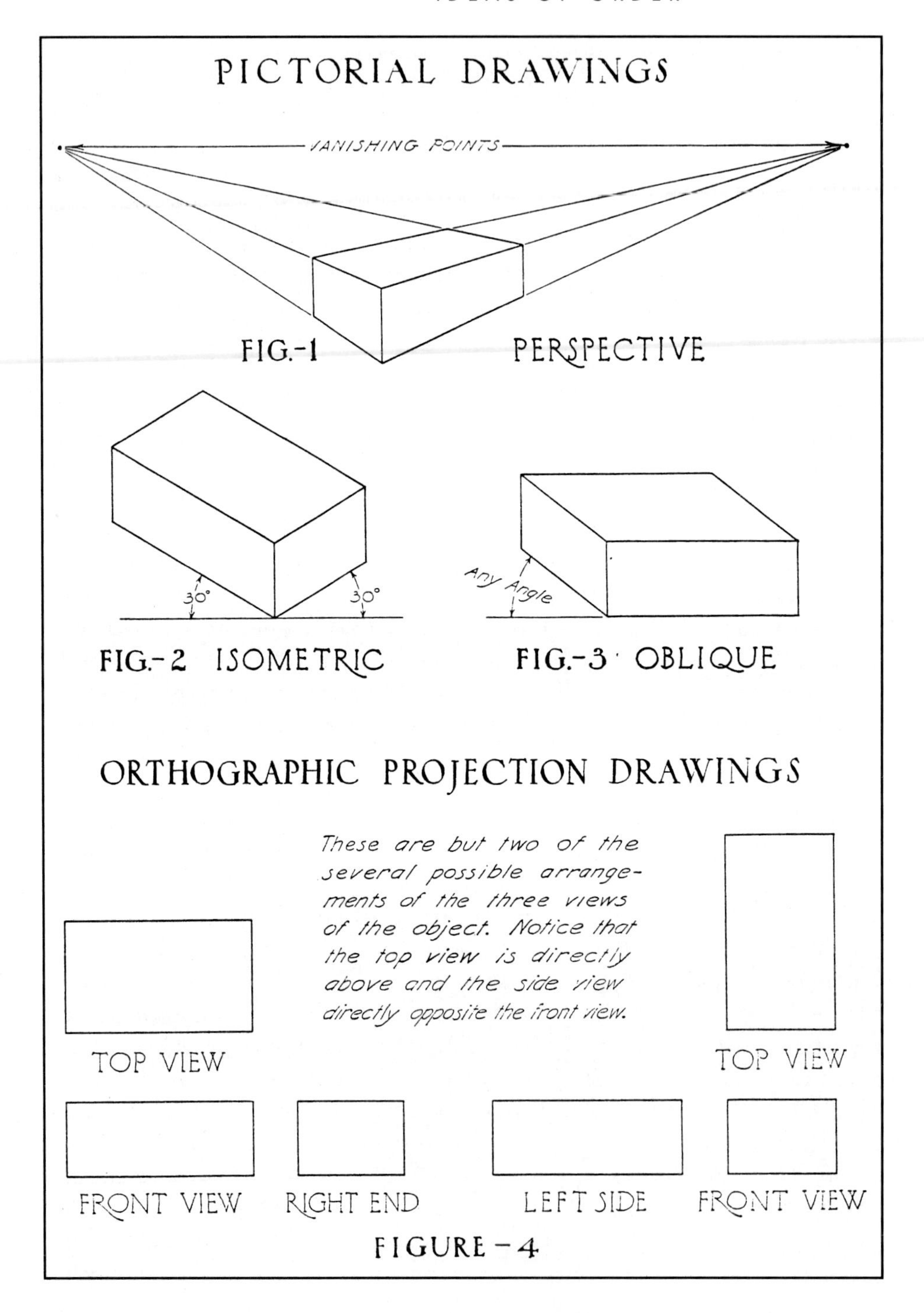

A.4 Pictorial Drawings and Orthographic Projection

For the moment, however, we shall concern ourselves with traditional architectural drawing, i.e., the techniques and conventions which assumed their customary form sometime around the Renaissance and which are still the standard representational tools.

A drafting text book from the turn of the century gives examples of many kinds of drawings still in use today, even though building technology and design issues have greatly changed since then. Let us begin with the **'perspective'.** (Figure A.4, 1) Perspective drawings strive to imitate the appearance of objects to the human eye. Because of this, many optical distortions which characterize sight are replicated in the drawings. Parallel lines converge or 'vanish' to **'vanishing points'.** Things farther away from the viewer appear smaller; elements closer to the viewer seem brighter and more crisply delineated. Perspective drawings imply a **'picture plane'**, or a frame beyond which nothing can be seen, and a privileged point of view, or **'station point'**. Elements which cannot be perceived from this vantage point are excluded from the picture. Because of the many distortions, adjustments and omissions in perspective drawings, they are not measurable and they do not provide accurate, quantitative information about the building. Instead, they suggest the over-all appearance and establish the location of the point of view, so that one can imagine oneself in relationship to the building and its surroundings. Although perspective drawings may appear realistic, they are in fact illusions. Buildings are not two-dimensional entities on paper, but three-dimensional ones in space. Moreover, perspectival depiction of pictorial space is by no means universal in all cultures, but particular to western civilization since the Renaissance.

The next kind of drawing we shall examine (Figure A.4, 2 and 3), the **'axonometric'**, or **'paraline'** drawing, also represents three-dimensional objects, but presents quantitative information more objectively than in perspective drawings. In axonometric drawings, vertical lines remain vertical, parallel lines remain parallel, and all lines parallel to the X, Y and Z axes are drawn to scale. **'Scale'** in this sense refers to the fixed relationship between the true dimensions of a structure and the dimensions represented on paper. In the United States common architectural scales are 1/16 inch = 1 foot, 1/8 inch = 1 foot, and 1/4 inch = 1 foot; engineering scales are more rational and divide the inch into tenths. In most other countries an even more rational measuring system is used, the metric scale. There are two kinds of axonometric drawings, the **'isometric'**, in which all three surfaces of a rectilinear prism show the same degree of distortion, and the **'plan oblique" or 'elevation oblique',** in which at least one surface remains undistorted. **Theo van Doesburg's 'Color Construction: Project for a Private House'** is an example of a plan oblique drawing, the most commonly used kind of axonometric in current architectural practice. Axonometric drawings give measurable information about the three-dimensional properties of buildings, but they do not provide good information about the space in between things, nor do they replicate objects as they appear to us. In axonometric drawings, parallel lines do not converge and one's vantage point does not approximate a natural angle from which the building would be viewed, but goes to ex-

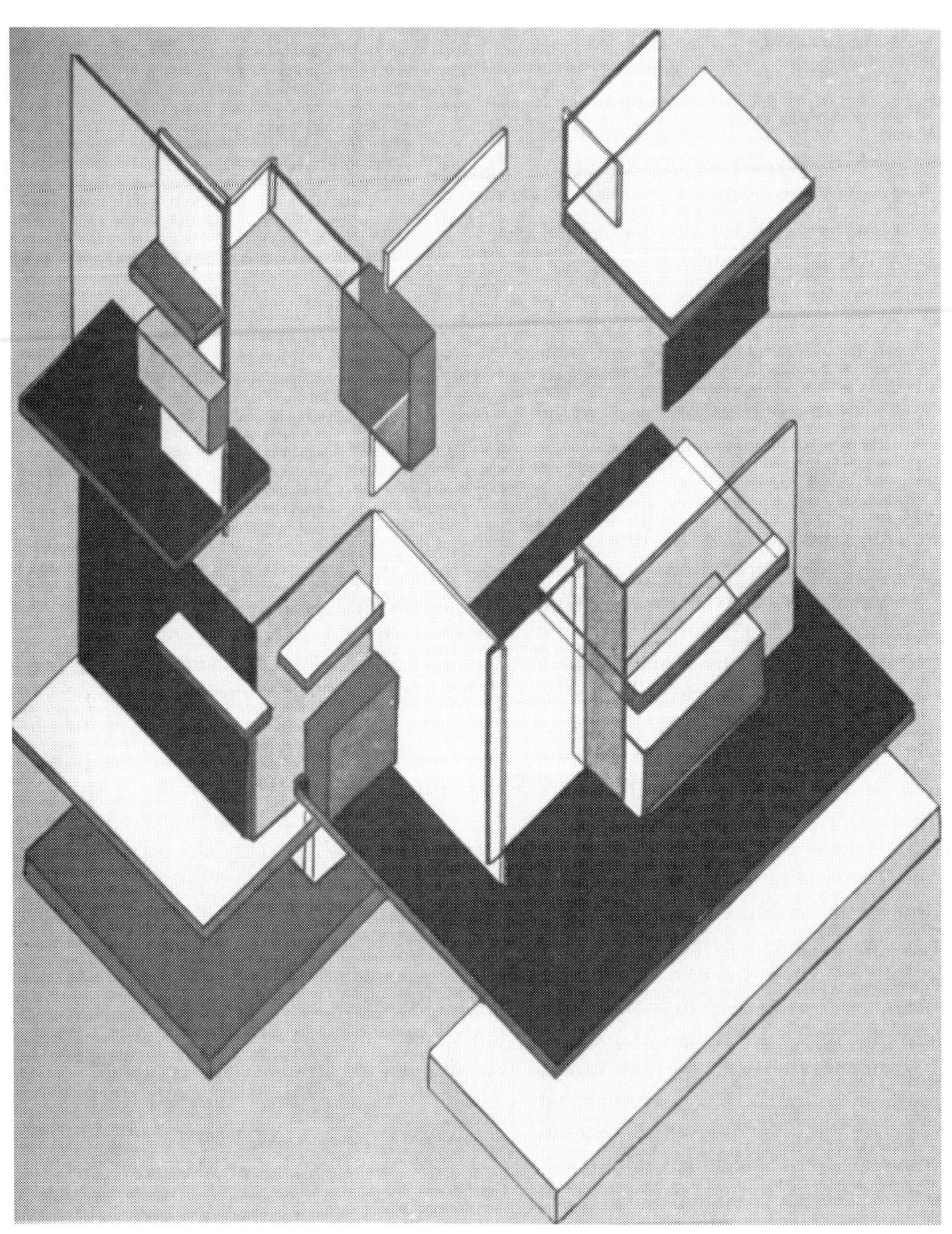

A.5 Theo van Doesburg, Axonometric, "Color Construction Project for a Private House", 1923, the Museum of Modern Art, New York.

tremes, furnishing either the **'bird's eye view'** (from above) or the **'worm's eye view'** (from below). Neither point of view allows the spectator to develop a sense of how the building would appear to an average individual whose eye is about five feet above the ground.

"**Orthographic projection**' is a way of drawing which presents views of buildings as if they were flattened out and projected onto a parallel surface. 'Orthographic projection' means that the drawings illustrate **'orthogonal'** views of the building, or views at right angles to the object which are perfectly parallel or perfectly perpendicular to the ground plane. Such drawings, '**plan**', '**section**' and '**elevation**', eliminate distortion and **foreshortening**. Because of their clarity and objectivity, these are the primary representational means used by architects to study and communicate their design intentions. All orthographic drawings are drawn to scale and comprise the set of documents used for the construction of buildings. Standard orthographic drawings show how a building would appear if one were directly in line with it and infinitely far away. Orthographic projections parallel to the ground plane include **plans, roof plans,** and **reflected ceiling plans**; orthographic projections perpendicular to the ground plane include **sections** and **elevations (facades)**. Line weights are modulated to provide different kinds of information. The thickest lines indicate that a material has been cut through in a plan or section; the next thickest lines define the boundary of a building; the next thickest describe a void cut into a building. Darker lines represent elements of the building that are closer to the picture plane; lighter lines represent more remote elements or edges, changes in

A.6 Josef Maria Olbrich, Großes Glückert House, Darmstadt, Germany, 1900, interior elevation.

A.7 Großes Glückert House, view of the interior.

A.8 Methods of Representation.

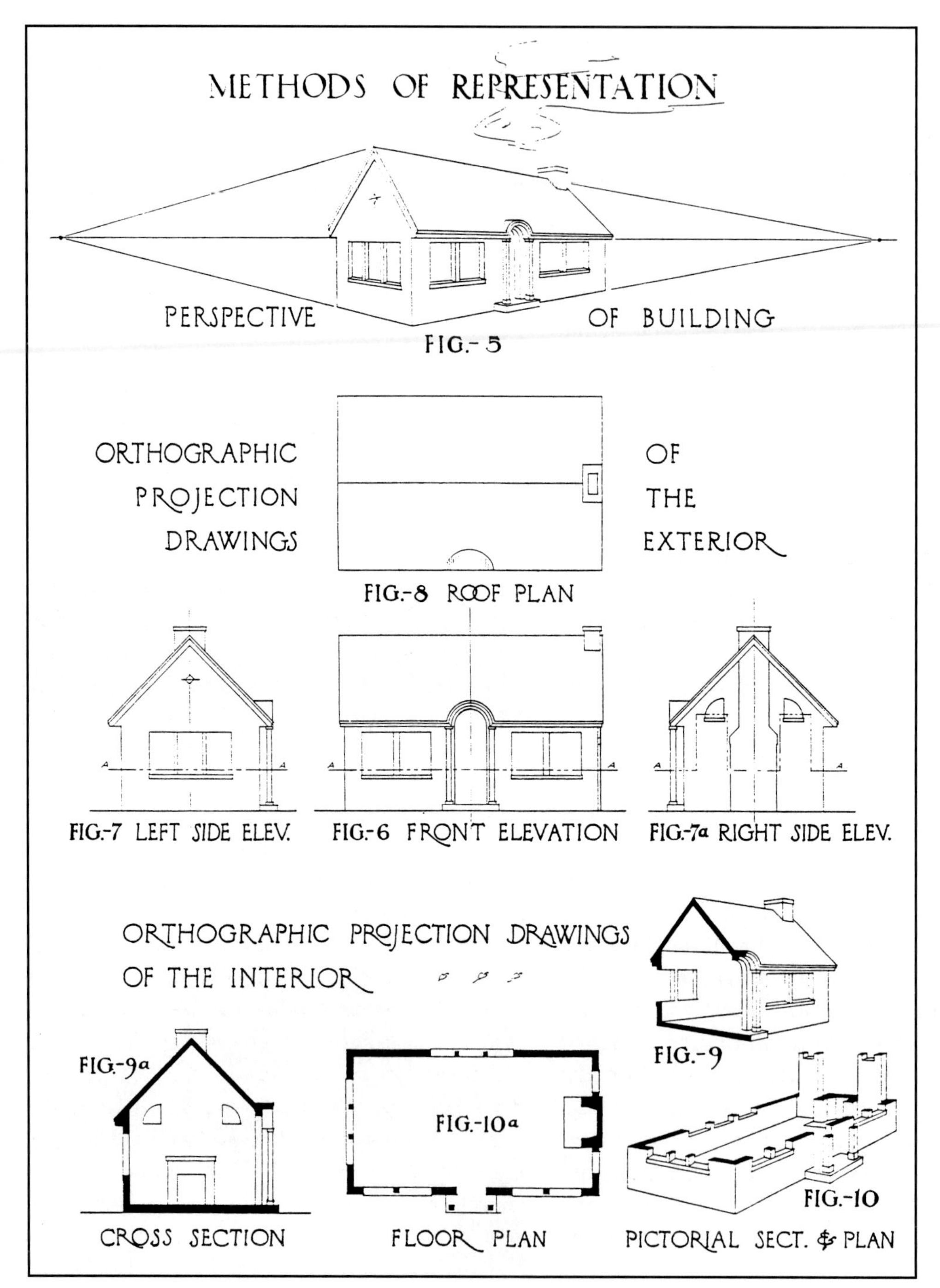

material, changes in planarity, or elements seen in elevation in the distance. Things that are overhead or below ground can be represented by a dashed line.

In illustration A.8, beneath the perspective drawing of the cottage is a roof plan, which shows the appearance of a roof if one were directly above it at an infinitely far distance. Elevations, or facades, are next shown. Generated in exactly the same manner as the roof plan, they present the appearance of any side of the building if one were directly in front of it and infinitely far away. Elevations are useful design tools because they permit careful control of the placement and proportion of elements upon a surface. In our illustration, the architect has noted one ordering device, the '**center line**'. It is impossible to perceive a building exactly as it appears in elevation because of the apparent convergence of parallel lines and the parallax caused by binocular (two-eyed) vision.

At the bottom of the illustration are plans and sections. They are generated in exactly the same way as the other orthographic projections (elevations and roof plans), but with one exception. Both the plans and the sections rely on an imagined *cut* through the building parallel (plan) or perpendicular (section) to the ground plane. The plan and section reveal the size of spaces, their proximity to one another, the lay-out of the interior, and the method of construction. The thickness of walls and floors relates to the method of construction. Stone walls are thicker than brick walls; brick walls are thicker than frame walls; frame walls are thicker than glass enclosing membranes; etc. Non-structural **partition walls** are thinner than structural **bearing walls.** In plan and section, the pocket of space between the inside and outside surfaces of a wall is rendered black. This graphic infill is called **'poché'**, which in French means 'pocket'. In construction documents, plans and sections may give more precise information about construction, materials and connections of elements in the building. The larger the scale of the drawing, the more detailed the information it conveys. Yet even such schematic drawings as those in the illustration tell us something about the construction of the building by the wall thickness and the way in which the walls meet the roof.

In illustration A.8, the drawing marked Figure 9-a is a section. The section is generated by a cut perpendicular to the ground plane. The perspectival view of the cottage (Figure 9) clarifies how the cut is made. If a section bisects a building along its shortest dimension, it is called a **'transverse section'** or **'cross section'.** If the section slices through the building along its length, it is called a **'longitudinal section'** or a **'long section'**. Lines in a section drawing can illustrate a variety of different conditions. Thick black 'pochéed' walls indicate places through which the building's walls, floor, and roof have been cut. The double lines at the buildings enclosure which have not been darkened represent the door and window **jambs** seen in elevation beyond the cut. The fire place and quarter-round windows constitute an **'interior elevation'** of the wall. Like an exterior elevation, it is an orthographic projection of elements arranged against the planar surface of the wall, with no

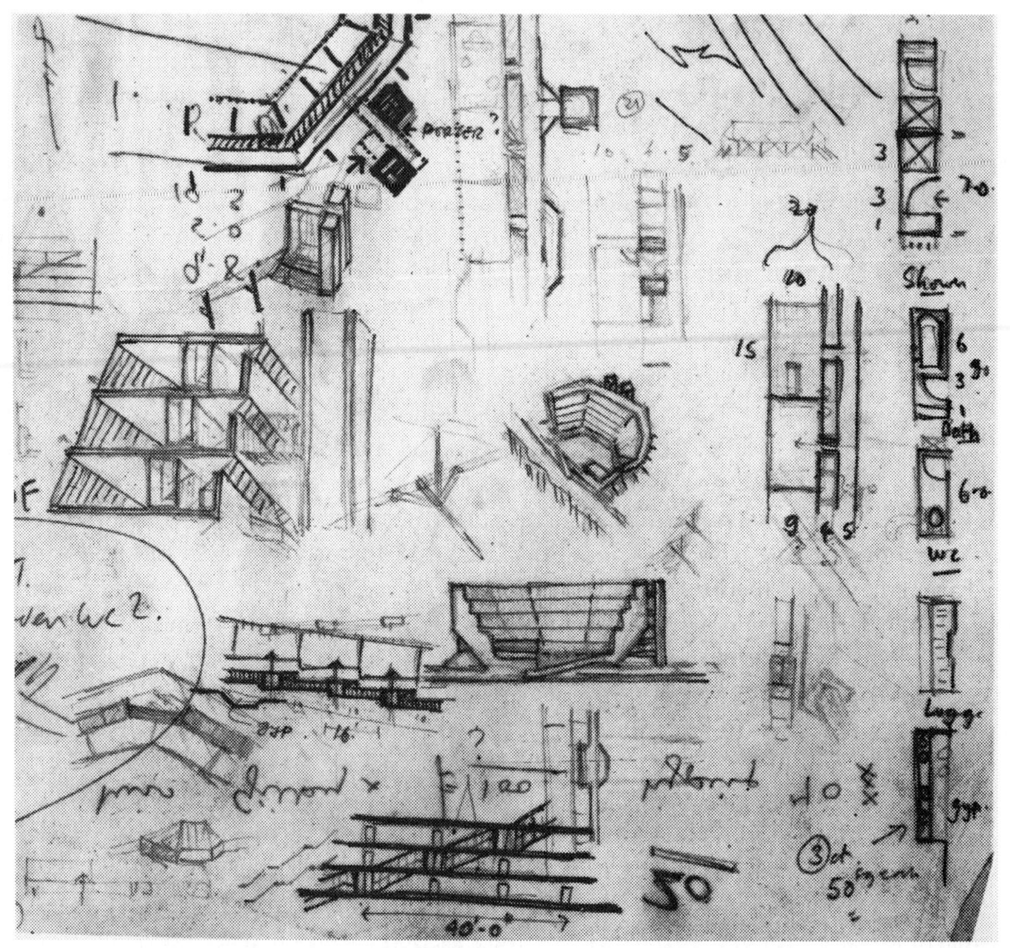

A.9
James Stirling, Concept Sketch, Queen's College, St. Clements: Student Halls of Residence, Oxford University, 1966–71.

A.10 Left: Queen's College, St. Clements: Student Halls of Residence.
A.11 Right: Queen's College, St. Clements: Student Halls of Residence.

distortion due to perspective or the relative distance of objects from the wall.

Figure 10-A in illustration A.8 is a plan, a drawing generated in exactly the same way as the section, except that the cut is parallel to the ground plane, taken at about waist height. The plan is a kind of section drawing. Like the section, it represents a slice through the building, revealing the thickness of the enclosing envelope and indicating which areas are delimited by walls and which areas are given over to open space. Figure 10 clearly demonstrates how the plan cut operates. Note that the dashed lines in Figures 6, 7, and 7A show in elevation where the plan has been cut. The cut has been jogged; the slice through the cottage is not even, but it cuts through various levels in the buildings to show salient features (the high windows flanking the fireplace) that would have been concealed if the convention of the waist-high cut were applied throughout. Because the height of the plan cut is fixed by convention, it is unusual to key plans to elevations. Sections, on the other hand, are usually taken wherever they give the best information about the building. Hence, section cuts are usually keyed to plans by arrows, although that is not the case here.

Precise measured drawings like plans, sections, and elevations represent the final stages of an architect's investigation of a design solution. The earliest phase yields a rough conceptual diagram or **'parti'**. No standard representational techniques are required and no special drafting tools are needed beyond a paper napkin and a pen. The British architect James Stirling used such a method in his design of the **Residence Hall at Queen's College, Oxford.** On a small piece of paper, Stirling explored not only the over-all shape of the building, but its interior organization, construction details, and its relationship to the site. Working at many scales simultaneously, Stirling assured that practical considerations required for the building's execution would not betray his initial design concept. In the design process it is valuable to spend a good amount of time working in a loose, diagrammatic fashion. Once the design of the building has been rigidified into hard-lined, dimensioned drawings, many issues which could have been taken into account and resolved in an earlier phase become impossible obstacles.

We have devoted a good amount of time to the rather pedestrian topic of architectural drawings because much of what is contained in this text relies on the student's ability to interpret graphic material correctly. Some of the illustrations are photographs, which pose no difficulty, but many of the drawings can be properly read only if one understands the conventions upon which they are based. When looking at an architectural drawing, it is a good exercise to try to imagine the three-dimensional entity to which it refers and to realize how much information about the full-scale, material object has been deleted. It is likewise good training for architects to constantly interpret the spaces they occupy in terms of plan, section, and elevation. Sensitivity to the configuration and dimension of familiar built spaces allows designers to enlist memory of these spaces in their architectural projects, and to imbue their designs with the same desirable qualities.

A.12 Henry Bacon, Lincoln Memorial, Washington, D.C., 1911-22, column detail.

A.13 Louis Sullivan, Merchants' National Bank, Grinnell, Iowa, c.1908.

Scale and Proportion

In our discussion of drawing conventions, we mentioned 'scale drawings', i.e. drawings whose dimensions relate in a precise, measurable way to the size of things at 'full scale.' There is another meaning of scale, one that is not coolly mathematical but which refers to the relative position of structures within a subjective field of reference. In this sense scale does not refer to the size of things *per se* but to the relative size in terms of a greater whole. Scale relationships involve the overall massing of a building with respect to the number and size of its constituent parts; the size of a building relative to other elements in its immediate proximity; the size of a building with respect to other buildings which share a common type and function; and the articulation and proportion of a building with respect to the human body. If a building is bigger or smaller than other nearby elements, it can be said to be out of scale with its context, or scaleless. But that is not necessarily the case. The relationship of parts to the whole may create an apparent scale to a building which is much larger than its actual size, as in **Louis Sullivan's** (1856-1926) **Bank** in **Grinnell, Iowa.** The modest, one-story high structure gains enormous presence through the tension between the simplicity of the building block and the over-sized doors, windows and ornamental work. The **Lincoln Memorial**, in Washington D.C., is a small structure in terms of other buildings in the Capitol, but it gains monumental stature through the stark simplicity of its volume and the heroic proportions of its constituent members. Although classical architecture is intended to reflect human scale in its proportions and detail, the size of the columns at the Lincoln Memorial have been so inflated that this is no longer true. The column does not affirm the dimensions of the human body; instead it evokes the presence of giants, dwarfing human stature. Scale relationships can be drawn among buildings which share the same function or building type. Both the **Civic Building** in Cedar Rapids, Iowa and the **Post Office** in Seaside, Florida share a common purpose and a common architectural language: they are volumetrically simple white buildings embellished with classical columns, Greek pediments, and flights of stairs. Yet the miniature scale of the Seaside post office removes it from the grave, heroic, seriousness of purpose usually associated with public buildings and suggests instead adjectives like "cute" or "precious".

The universal scale referent is the human body. Elements such as doors and windows are usually proportioned to accept graciously the passage or the gaze of the human being. In the house designed for his sister, Ludwig Wittgenstein made the insistent use of over-scaled doors thematic and polemical. While exploring **Wonderland, Alice** discovered how disconcerting it was to inhabit a realm where relations between the physical world and the size and proportion of the human body were highly unstable and never familiar. Indeed, poor Alice even found the proportion of parts within her own body to be disappointingly changeable. The proportions of the over-all size of the human body are commensurate with the size and arrangement of the parts. The great Greek sculptor, Polyclitus derived a formula for beautiful proportion, his *Kanon*, by studying the

A.14 Civic Building, Cedar Rapids, Iowa.

A.15 Post Office, Seaside, Florida.

A.16
Lewis Carroll, Illustration from Alice in Wonderland.

A.17
Lewis Carroll, Illustration from Alice in Wonderland.

internal relationships of size and number within the human form (see Chapter 7). The apparent simplicity of the human figure provides unity and order for a multiplicity of different parts.

Scale in architecture also has to do with the **articulation** of buildings into commensurable parts. Articulation is the task of dividing the overall mass of a structure into intelligible, interrelated parts, so that the whole is related to the details, and multiple scales of elaboration are tightly knit together. Articulation may be accomplished by the break down of the building into interrelated masses, as in **Frank Lloyd Wright's Unity Temple, 1906**; it may be accomplished through the rhythmic disposition of windows, columns, piers, or whatever, as in Aldo Rossi's (b. 1931**) Gallaratese Apartment Building**; a building may be articulated through the application of surface ornament, such as the superposition of columnar orders on the Colosseum in Rome (Chapter 4), or through an even more reduced, surface ornamental program, such as the tile decoration on the facade of **Otto Wagner's** (1841-1918) **Majolica Hous**e in Vienna, or the pattern of facing stone and bolts on **Wagner's Postal Savings Bank** in Vienna. The articulation of buildings may correspond to the disposition of parts in the human figure. The tri-partite division of **Alberti's Palazzo Rucellai**, Florence, or the articulation of classical columns into capitals, shafts and bases, has long been equated with the human body's membrature of head, body and feet (see Chapters 7 and 10). Likewise, many have held symmetry to be desirable in architecture by noting the symmetry of the human body, as illustrated in the **Renaissance church plan** by **Juan Battista Vallapando.**

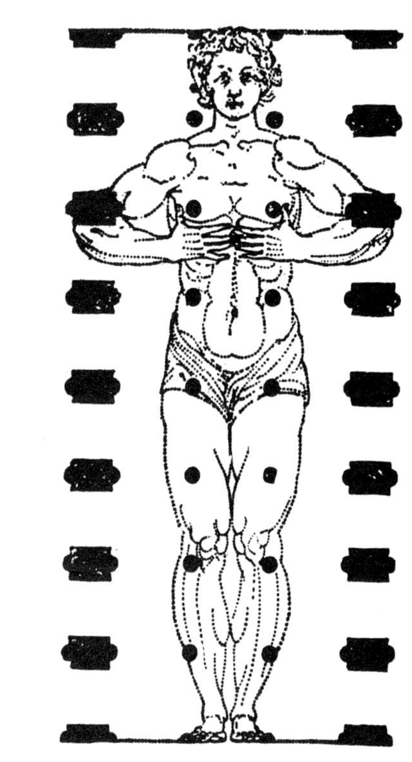

A.18 Left: Leonbattista Alberti, Palazzo Rucellai, Florence, Italy.

A.19 Right: Juan Bautista Villalpando, In Ezechielem Explanationes, Rome, 1596.

A. 20 Left: Frank Lloyd Wright, Unity Temple, Oak Park, Illinois, 1906.

A.21 Right: Aldo Rossi, Gallaratese Apartment Building, Milan, Italy, 1968-73.

Buildings which operate at only one scale are sometimes said to be scaleless. Without a gradation of elements to link the overall composition back to the measure of the human figure, it is impossible to know how big or how small a building is, and it is impossible to feel comfortable in its presence. The **Palazzo della Civiltà e Lavoro** in Rome is an example of a 'scaleless' building. Built under Fascist patronage, it is a cubic colosseum-like structure atop a steep, treacherous mountain of stairs. Unlike its precedent, the Colosseum, the Palazzo della Civiltà e Lavoro does not reveal greater articulation as one approaches it. It remains a severe, elemental block of bleached travertine, material joints and punched arcades providing the only relief to the relentless expanse of wall.

The desire to assure scale and order in architecture has long been a central concern of architectural theory. Systems of proportion have arisen to provide architects with a way of working which confers an interrelationship

A.22 Left: Otto Wagner, Majolica House Apartment Building, Vienna, Austria, 1898.

A.23 Right: Otto Wagner, Postal Savings Bank, Vienna, Austria, 1904-06.

among parts, and thereby, a fine development of scale. Throughout the Renaissance, the dominant proportional systems were the **Arithmetic Mean** (B-A = C-B as in 2:1 = 3:2), the **Geometric Mean** (A:B = B:C as in 4:6:9) and the **Harmonic Mean** ({B-A}/A = {C-B}/C) as in 6:8:12}. The term **'mean'** refers to a middle term which relates the extremes at either end. In architecture, the application of the mean was used to relate the height, width, and length of rooms; to relate the dimensions of spaces in a sequence, and to relate the dimensions of the constituent parts of that of the over-all building.

The **Golden Rectangle** is a geometric figure which contains within it a scale of relationships. Celebrated by the ancient Greeks, the **Golden Mean** was probably not used widely in Renaissance architecture, but gained popularity in the twentieth century by Modernist and Beaux-Arts architects alike. The Golden Rectangle can be subdivided into a square and another smaller golden rectangle. The relationship between the

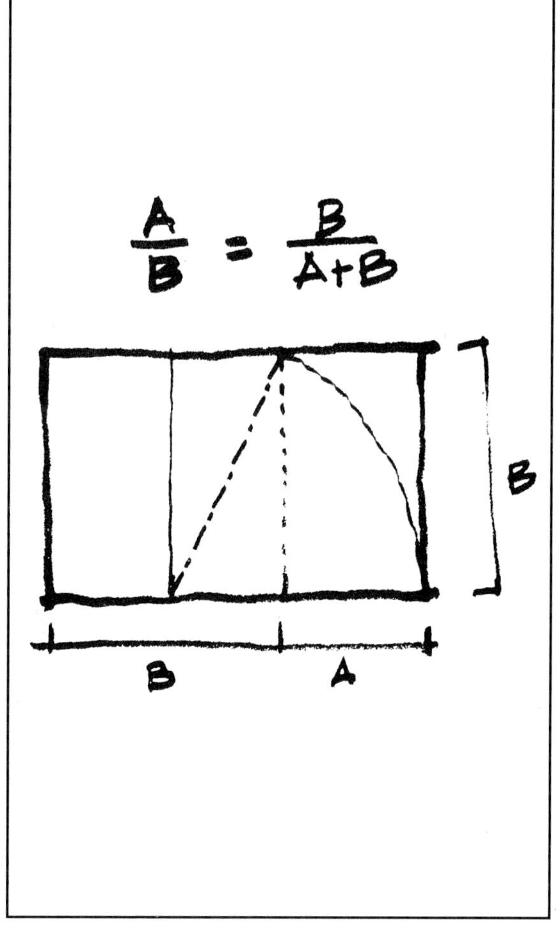

A.24 Left: La Padula and Guerini, Palazzo della Civiltà e Lavoro, Rome, E.U.R. c.1940.

A.25 Right: Golden Rectangle.

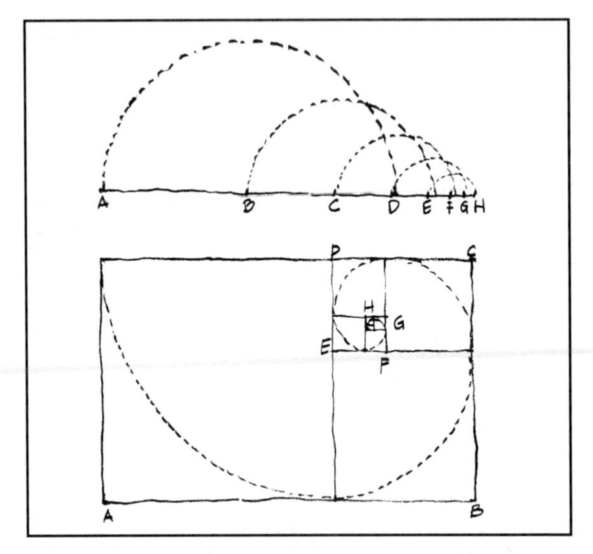

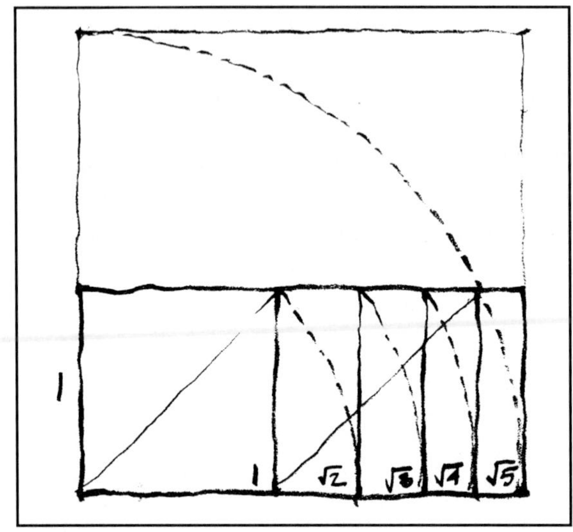

A.26 Left: The Golden Rectangle Spiral, or the Golden Rectangle Progression.

A.27 Right: Root rectangles.

A.28 Giuseppe Terragni, Casa del Fascio, Como, Italy, 1932-36, view.

A.29 Case del Fascio, window detail.

length and width of the rectangle is governed by the golden mean. In other words, the long side of the rectangle is divisible into two parts A and B so that the ratio of (A/B) = B/(A+B). The relationship of length to width in the golden rectangle is widely known. Natural scientists have found evidence of a geometric relationships reflective of the golden mean in the curvature of conch shells, the development of pine-cones, and the distribution of branches in fir trees. Pop psychologists claim that the form is naturally pleasing to people, and that most individuals will draw a golden rectangle if asked to draw any rectangle. However, all rectangles imply a proportional system by the ratio of length to width. Such proportional systems are not solved numerically but graphically. **Regulating lines** are a graphic device used to govern the proportions of buildings. **Le Corbusier** used them to study the elevations of his buildings (see Chapter 14), as did **Giuseppe Terragni**, in his **Casa del Fascio**, 1932-36. In the **Morgan Library, McKim, Mead and White** (Charles Follen McKim (1847-1909), William Rutherford Mead (1846-1928) and Stanford White (1853-1906)) used a proportioning system based on nested golden rectangles to compose a serene, classical facade, in sharp contrast to the stark modern expression attained by Le Corbusier or Terragni through similar strategies of geometrical relationships.

Buildings may be proportioned through the addition of like units, or **modules**, so that the whole is comprised of the sum of commensurate parts. Such was the method most widely used in ancient Egypt and the Renaissance. Buildings may also be proportioned through the subdivision of an originary figure into related parts. Such was the method most widely used by the ancient Greeks and in the Gothic period. The former system is easy to solve numerically, but the latter system may include irrational numbers, like $\sqrt{2}$ or $\sqrt{5}$. On the other hand, graphic diagrams, such as regulating lines or key figures clearly and quickly reveal the relationship among parts.

Throughout the history of architecture many different systems of order, proportion, and articulation have been used to provide scale and legibility to buildings. The static, resolute stillness of Egyptian artifacts was created from the addition of modules in a highly prescriptive system. The organic muscularity of Greek architecture and sculpture derived from a geometric decomposition of interrelated elements from within a whole. Geometry is not just a tool used in the design of buildings but it is integrally related to the expression of a building: to its scale, to its articulation, and to its ultimate richness.

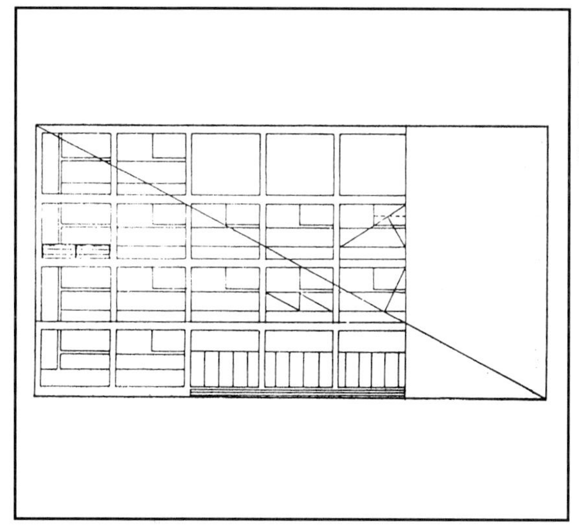

A.30
Casa del Fascio, elevation, with regulating lines.

A.31
McKim, Mead and White, Morgan Library, New York, New York, c. 1906.

A.32
Le Corbusier, Unité d'Habitation, Berlin, 'Modulor Man' imprinted in the concrete, to remind us of the relationship between the human form and architectural scale.

Glossary

Abstraction: 1. A summary of an idea. 2. A distillation of a basic idea or parti into its most significant or telling parts.

Acropolis: The citadel of an ancient Greek city, usually containing a sacred site.

Additive form: Characterized by a basic process which involves adding simple solids together to make a more complex whole. Objects can be seen as being attached to other objects.

Aedicula, aedicule: Literally, Latin for 'little house', commonly used to signify a small temple-like structure in which columns or pilasters support a pedimented roof.

Agora: An open-air area, used as a market and place of assembly in ancient Greece.

Agrarian Ideal: Promulgated by Thomas Jefferson and other founding fathers, the Agrarian Ideal celebrated the virtue, industry and simplicity of agricultural life. The health and piety of self-sufficient farmers in decentralized agricultural settlements was opposed to the dependency, vice and impurity fostered by crowded, unhygienic urban conditions, such as those that typified European metropolises in the eighteenth century.

Aisle: A passageway or corridor parallel to the nave of a church or basilica, and separated from it by a colonnade or arcade.

Allegory: A figurative or verbal depiction or discussion of one subject under the guise of another. A fable or any other symbolic narrative.

Ambiguity: Equivocal or uncertain in meaning. William Empson's *Seven Types of Ambiguity* outlines how ambiguity may create richness and poetic meaning.

Ambulatory: The aisle around the chancel or choir of a Latin cross church.

Amphitheater: an oval or circular shaped outdoor performance area surrounded by sloping tiers of seats, usually semi-circular in form and sited to take advantage of natural basins in the topography.

Analytic Cubism: A form of Cubism typified by the work of Georges Braque and Pablo Picasso from 1909-1911. Characterized by a restricted palette of neutral colors, multiple points of view, fragmentation and transparency, figural subject matter is disintegrated and re-presented in flattened , ambiguous pictorial space. See Cubism.

Angst: German for 'fear' or 'anxiety', used by psychologists to refer to the lingering dread characteristic of the modern condition

Annular: Ring-shaped.

Anthropomorphic: The ascription of human characteristics or human form to things or beings that are not human.

Apse: A semi-circular or polygonal niche, usually found in a Roman basilica at both ends of the nave, and in a Christian church at the end of the nave behind the choir, and/or at both ends of the transept, and at the ends of chapels.

Aqueduct: A masonry structure which supports an artificial channel for the transport of water.

Arcade: A linear arrangement of arches supported by columns or piers, free-standing or engaged in a larger architectural composition.

Arcadia: A mythical place which exemplifies the simplicity and rustic innocence of the pastoral life, from a mountainous district in ancient Greece famed for its easeful, peaceful way of life.

Arch: An architectural construction built to span an opening. Often semi-circular, it can be built of wedge-shaped blocks (voussoirs), bricks, or other stone. The weight of the structure requires both vertical support in the form of walls, columns, or piers, and lateral support for the thrust, called buttressing.

Archaic: Old-fashioned or primitive; in Greek art and architecture, a period from 600 to 500 B.C.

Archetype: A model or primal form of which all things of the same species are copies. The archetype contains essential characteristics which are primitive, general, and universal rather than particular or specialized.

Architectonic: Having qualities specific to architecture.

Architecture parlante: Literally, French for 'speaking architecture'; an architectural theory popular in Revolutionary France which linked the formal development and ornamentation of a building to the expression and representation of its function.

Architrave: 1. Horizontal component of the architectural Orders which spans from column to column; the lowest part of the entablature. 2. Molding around a door or window.

Arcuation: A constructional system reliant on arches and vaults.

Arena: The stage or space in the center of a Greek or Roman amphitheater.

Arithmetic mean: A proportioning system which relates three terms so that the relationship of the middle term to the extremes is:

B-A= C-B, as in 2:1 = 3:2.

Articulation: The surface expression of underlying structure or joints, or the way in which the parts are shown to relate to the whole, etc. The clarification of various relationships within a wall or built structure.

Asceticism: The practice of rigorous self-denial, abstinence, austerity, and the mortification of the flesh.

Association, Associationism: An architectural theory which governed the adoption of historicist styles so that the function and decorum of the building could be most legibly expressed.

Asymmetry: Not symmetrical; one half of the image is not a mirror image of the other along a central dividing line or axis.

Atelier: French for 'studio' or 'workshop'.

Atrium: The courtyard of an ancient Roman or Etruscan house; enclosed open public space in a multi-story building.

Avant-garde: Literally, 'the vanguard'; often used in reference to progressive architectural movements which arose in the 1910's, 1920's and 1930's and which took an adversarial stance towards architectural history and tradition.

Axiality: Relationship or organization along an axis, i.e. a conceptual connecting or dividing line.

Axis: 1. The line or segment about which a rotated body or form is turned. 2. A line which bisects a body or form along which symmetry or asymmetry is determined. 3. A structure or datum along which objects are arranged. 4. A line connecting two points.

Axis mundi: A vertical axis which connects the earth with the sky.

Axonometric: A paraline drawing; a geometric, architectural drawing which represents the three-dimensional appearance of objects in such a way that vertical lines remain vertical, parallel lines remain parallel, and all lines parallel to the X, Y and Z axes are drawn to scale.

Balustrade: A railing comprised of a series of balusters, or short posts.

Baptistery: A building or part of a church used for baptisms; often a free-standing octagonal building adjacent to a church.

Bar/object organization: An architectural *parti* which makes use of a linear datum to organize more figural elements in the composition.

Baroque: A style developed in sixteenth century Italy, characterized by exaggerated ornamental, pictorial and scenographic effects, the bold use of light, the dynamic interplay of forms and masses, and complex columnar rhythms.

Barrel vault: The horizontal extension of an arch becomes a barrel vault which requires both continuous support along its length and (usually) buttressing.

Base: From the Greek "basis", literally meaning "something upon which one stands", the lower portion of any building or architectural element, such as a column base.

Basilica: Originally a Roman public meeting place and hall of Justice, the basilica is a rectangular building with a nave, side aisles and one or more apse.. The basilican form was adopted as the basic church plan in Early Christian architecture, with nave, central apse, and side aisles. In both Roman and Christian basilicas, the massing of the elevation usually reflects the disposition of the plan in that both embody A-B-A proportional systems, with A<B.

Bastide: A French medieval new town, for trade or military activities, usually laid out on a four-square grid, following the model of the Roman camp.

Bay: The space on a wall between two vertical elements; the space between structural columns in a column grid.

Beam: A horizontal structural support or member.

Bearing wall: A wall which acts as a structural support.

Beaux-Arts: French for 'Fine Arts', used in reference to style promulgated by the *Ecole des Beaux-Arts,* the French academy of architecture which favored the use of the classical orders, elaborate symmetries, axial organizations, heavy poché and great pomp.

Biomorphic: Form derived from that of a living organism. See zoömorphic, vegemorphic.

Bird's eye view: An elevated view point, similar to an aerial view.

Bosque: A naturalistic wooded area in a garden design.

Bracket: A structural support projecting out from a wall, often shaped like a scroll.

Brise soliel: A wall, sometimes louvered, designed to act as a sun screen.

Buttress: A support; a masonry mass which resists lateral thrust.

Byzantine: Pertaining to the Byzantine Empire, i.e. the Eastern Roman Empire, after the fall of Rome in A.D. 476 ; the style produced during the Byzantine Empire, characterized by centralized plans, round arches, extensive vaulting, and abundant use of painted or mosaic ornamentation.

Campanile: Italian for 'bell tower'.

Canopy: An overhanging cover or roof-like shelter which may be attached to a building or free-standing.

Cantilever: 1. A structural system of support at only one end. 2. A projecting beam or slab supported only at one end. 2. A projecting bracket that supports a cornice, balcony, or other small overhanging element.

Capital: From the Latin *"caput"*, literally "head". The top of a column or pilaster, usually elaborated according to one of the architectural Orders.

Cardo: The main north-south street in the lay-out of a Roman settlement.

Cartesian space: Based on the X, Y, Z coordinate system of René Descartes, an infinitely expandable, infinitely homogeneous space defined by a squared grid.

Caryatid: The figure of a woman used as a columnar support.

Casino: A small garden house.

Castra: A Roman camp, usually organized as a four-square grid by the crossing of a major north-south road *(Cardo)* and a major east-west road *(Decumanus).*

Cella: In Greek or Roman architecture, an interior walled structure built within the temple, surrounded by colonnades, to house a cult image.

Cellular: Made up of discrete repetitive units, or cells, (small, regular, usually square or rectangular room units).

Cenotaph: A funerary monument.

Center: 1. The core or middle point or area. 2. An important or principle point or space.

Centering: A temporary framework used during the construction of masonry arches, vaults and domes.

Center line: A graphic or conceptual device that marks the center to a composition; the center line may be the axis of symmetry.

Centralized: 1. Dominated or controlled by a central point or space. 2. Radiating from a central point or space.

Centralized plan: A building plan which is organized around a central point.

Chancel: The eastern extension of a church beyond the crossing which contains the altar and which is reserved for the clergy; the part of a church which consists of the choir and the ambulatory.

Chapter House: A building attached to a cathedral or monastery which houses the meetings of the chapter (an assembly of monks, canons or representatives)

Character: An eighteenth and nineteenth century architectural theory which held that the outward appearance and style of a building should be a decorous expression of its function.

Charette: French for 'little cart', the term comes from the Ecole des Beaux-Arts where the *charette* was used to collect drawings after the end of a fixed deadline. In architectural schools and in practice, *charette* has come to mean the flurry of sleepless activity that precedes a deadline.

Choir: In a Latin cross church the part of the church reserved for the clergy, which extends eastwards from the crossing towards the altar, ringed by the ambulatory.

Chthonic: Earth-dwelling; relating to the deities or spirits or the underworld.

Circulation: The means of passage from one place to another; the system of movement through a space or a series of spaces.

Cladding: The exterior surface or skin of a building, applied to a structural frame.

Classicism: 1. The adherence to principles of classical literature and art, particularly Greek and Roman. 2. Architecture comprised of the Classical Orders and Graeco-Roman building types, usually symmetrical or incorporating local symmetries, and thought to embody timelessness, perfection of proportion and serene dignity.

Clerestory window: In Egyptian temples, Roman basilicas, and Christian basilican churches, the windows within the section of interior wall that rise above the adjacent roof line (i.e. the wall between the nave and the side aisles).

Cloisters: Colonnaded walkways which surround a courtyard in a monastery.

Clustered: A number of similar objects grouped together.

Coffer: An ornamental sunken panel in a ceiling or vault.

Collage: A composition made by the free assembly of diverse elements and forms.

Colonnade: A series of columns spanned by lintels.

Colossal order: An architectural order that organizes two or more stories of a building.

Column: A cylindrical support, usually consisting of base, shaft, and capital.

Columniation: The rhythmic system of arranging columns.

Composite Order: One of the five Roman Orders; a late Roman mix of elements from Ionic and Corinthian Orders, it is the tallest and most slender of the Orders.

Compression: A static force which tends towards the reduction of volume and the increase in pressure. Examples of architectural elements in compression are masonry units laid up in a wall, paving, columns, etc.

Constructivism: A Russian avant-garde movement which flourished between the two world wars.

Core: The center or most important part. In office buildings or skyscrapers, the area that remains constant throughout, usually forming an important structural unit and usually containing lobbies, elevators, stairs and mechanical systems.

Corinthian Order: The tallest and the slenderest of the three Greek Orders, invented in Athens around 500 B.C. and marked by acanthus leaf capitals. A later Roman development served as the prototype for the Renaissance interpretation.

Cornice: The upper part of the entablature in Classical architecture.

Corridor: A linear passageway which provides access to rooms in a building. A single-loaded corridor has rooms only on one side; a double-loaded corridor has rooms on both sides.

Cortile: Italian for courtyard, usually surrounded by a colonnaded walkway.

Counterpoint: In musical theory, the art of combining melodic lines; used more generally to describe the rhythmic and textured interplay of two or more themes.

Counter-Reformation: A movement within the Roman Catholic church aimed at opposing the Protestant Reformation in the 16th century.

Courtyard: A walled exterior space next to or within a palace, castle or large house.

Crenellation: Saw-tooth openings in the parapet, usually seen in medieval castellated architecture and other fortifications.

Cross axis: A secondary axis orthogonal to the principal axis of a building.

Crossing: The intersection of the nave, transepts, and chancel in a cruciform church.

Cross section: Transverse section; a section cut through the short dimension of a building.

Cross vault: Groin vault; an arched ceiling or roof formed by the perpendicular intersection of two barrel vaults of identical size and shape, usually constructed of brick, stone, or concrete.

Cruciform: Cross-shaped

Crypt: The space beneath a building, especially in churches.

Cubism: A name mockingly invented in 1908 by Henri Matisse to describe the self-consciously modern school of art led by Pablo Picasso and Georges Braque. Shunning imitative, figural and perspectival representation, the Cubists reduced and abstracted forms to simple, essential geometric forms and patterns. According to G. Apollonaire, a French poet, member of the Cubist circle, and one of the first to write about Cubism, the multiple points of view, overlapping, transparent, flat layers, and fragmented, interpenetrating figures evoked the fourth dimension, the dimension of space/time. Hence the task of Cubism was not the representation of outward appearances, but of inner essential structure. See "Analytic Cubism"

Cupola: Italian for dome.

Curtain wall: A non-structural enclosing membrane hung off a structural frame; the outer wall of a medieval castle.

Cybernetics: The study of methods of control and communication, especially artificial intelligence.

Datum: A neutral object or system (line, plane, or volume) which acts as a means of organization of forms and spaces due to its regularity and continuity.

Decentralization: To divide and distribute that which had been concentrated; to disperse mass and power.

Deconstruction: A branch of late twentieth-century French philosophy which makes use of mis-reading and undecidability to extract meanings from a text. Often misused in architecture, Deconstruction sometimes refers to an architectural style generated by the process of Deconstruction; more typically the term is used to describe a style which illustrates structures in decomposition by means of fragmentation, distortion and dynamic tension.

Decumanus: The principal east-west road in a Roman settlement.

Dematerialization: Reduction of mass in the wall; the tendency of the wall to become skeletal rather than solid.

De Stijl: A Dutch avant-garde movement popular in the 1920's and 1930's. See, "Neo-Plasticism".

Dialectic: A method of logical argumentation which opposes *thesis* with *antithesis* to yield *synthesis.*

Dome: A hemi-spherical vault or cupola supported by a circular wall or drum, or by corner supports.

Doric Order: The oldest, stoutest and most severe of the three Greek Orders, characterized by the use of metopes and triglyphs in the frieze (thought to be reminiscent of original wood structural system) and mutules under the corona. The

Greek Doric has no base and a fluted shaft. The Roman Doric has a base, and a fluted or unfluted shaft.

Drum: The cylindrical volume which supports a dome.

Duomo: Italian for 'cathedral'.

Eaves: The overhang at the end of a roof.

Eclectic: Comprised of elements from diverse sources; not following one system, but picking and choosing from many.

Ecole des Beaux Arts: The French school of architecture which sponsored the design of grand, axial, classical projects in the nineteenth and early twentieth century.

Elevation: 1. An orthographic projection drawing of one side of a building, drawn to scale with no perspectival distortion. 2. Any side of a building.

Elevation oblique: A kind of axonometric drawing in which the elevation of the building remains undistorted.

Enfilade: A circulation system through a building whereby passage is provided by a regular alignment of doors through rooms, rather than by means of separate corridors.

Enlightenment: A school of philosophy in the eighteenth century which promulgated the questioning of political authority, the virtue of nature, scientific empiricism and rationalism; the period in which Enlightenment philosophy was current.

Entablature: The upper part of an architectural order, usually divided into architrave, frieze, and cornice.

Entasis: A bulging one-third up the shaft of a column which enhances the apparent muscularity of the column and counteracts the optical illusion of inward curvature present with straight columnar shafts.

Erosion: The process of wearing something away by exposure to a force such as wind, water, glaciers, etc.; used metaphorically to describe any irregular, distorted volume or surface which appears to have been created through erosion.

Esquisse: A term from the Ecole des Beaux-Arts, the *Esquisse* was a quick, preparatory sketch of a design idea or *parti*, usually prepared by the students in a few hours or a few days. Over the next few months, students at the Ecole des Beaux-Arts would have to elaborate the design scheme set forth in the *Esquisse.*

Exedra: A semi-circular or rectangular recess, usually with benches; an apse or niche in a church.

Expressionism: A school of art which arose most conspicuously in Germany at the beginning of the century, based loosely on the theories of Wilhelm Wörringer (*Abstaktion und Einfühlung,* 1908) and Wassily Kandinsky (*Uber das Gestige der Kunst,* 1912). Violently anti-realistic, Expressionist artists made use of bold, un-natural color, abstract forms, symbols, and gestures to evoke strong feelings, the irrational and the visionary.

Facade: Literally, 'face' , it is the outer surface of any side of a building, usually the primary, or front elevation.

Fenestration: The design and system of arranging windows (and other openings) in a building's exterior surfaces.

Figure/ground: A graphic device which uses contrasting tones of black and white to make evident the relationship between occupied and empty space.

Figural object: An object (or building, or complex of buildings) whose most imagable form arises from the configuration of its positive mass.

Figural space: An object (or building, or complex of buildings) whose most imagable form arises from the configuration of a negative void, such as a courtyard, an urban square, etc.

Finial: In Gothic architecture, an ornament which tops a spire, i.e. a pinnacle, gable, etc.

Fluting, flutes: Vertical grooves cut into the shaft of a column.

Flying buttress: In Gothic churches, the structural member which transmits the thrust of the nave vault across the side aisles to the solid pier buttresses at the outer perimeter of the church. It forms a structural exoskeleton to allow for the dematerialization of the walls.

Folly: A garden building, meant to be looked at as part of the landscape, rather than occupied.

Foreshortening: In two-dimensional representation, the distortion of relative sizes and the apparent diminution of distant elements due to perspectival distortion.

Fortification: The art and science of designing defensive architecture, i.e. castles walls, ramparts, barricades, etc.

Forum: An ancient Roman gathering place which served as a center of assembly for judicial and other public businesses.

Fragmentation: The shattering or the apparent shattering of an entity into segments, shards or parts, as it by violence.

Frame structure: A skeletal structural system (usually trabeated) based on the assemblage of discrete horizontal and vertical elements.

Free facade: One of Le Corbusier's five points of architecture which states that a facade can be independent from the structural system of a building.

Free plan: One of Le Corbusier's five points of architecture which states that a field of columns may act as a structural system of a building, leaving the partition walls free to organize space.

Fresco: A technique of wall and ceiling painting in which pigment is applied directly to wet plaster.

Frieze: The middle part of a classical entablature.

Frontal: Having a single facade which is defined as primary.

Functionalism: A doctrine associated with *Neue Sachlichkeit* (or 'New Objectivity') which promulgated an objective, scientific approach to design so that form would derive logically from use, structure and material, rather than from the nostalgic consideration of historical styles, convention, and ornament. Functionalist infatuation with the methodology of engineering led Le Corbusier to declare that "a house is a machine for living".

Futurism: An early twentieth-century Italian avant-garde movement in the arts. Futurism is characterized by a love of progress, new technology, and speed; and a disdain of tradition and weakness.

Gable: The triangular end wall of a building, formed beneath two equal sloping sides of a pitched roof.

Gallery: 1. A wide passageway, used for the display of art; 2. The upper level of seating in a church or theater.

Gambrel: A roof whose sides have two different slopes, the lower one being steeper than the higher, and whose ends are cut off in a vertical plane.

Gargoyle: In a Gothic cathedral, a grotesquely carved figure which acts as a water spout to throw water off the roof, away from the walls.

Geometric mean: A proportioning system which relates three terms so that the relationship of the middle term to the extremes is:

A:B = B:C as in 4:6:9.

Geometry: Literally, 'earth-measurement', Geometry is the mathematical discipline which deals with measurements, relationships and properties of points, lines, planes, angles, and figures in space.

Genius Loci: Latin for the guardian deity or spirit of a place, used to refer to the particular charms and characteristics of a place.

Glazing: The system of furnishing and fitting with glass; the glassy surface of a structure.

Golden Mean: See Golden section.

Golden Rectangle: A rectangle whose proportions embody the relationships of the golden section. A Golden Rectangle can be infinitely decomposed into a square and another smaller golden rectangle.

Golden Section: A proportion based on irrational numbers, probably known to the Greeks and thought to be of divine significance by Renaissance theorists, defined as a line cut so that the ratio of the smaller section to the larger is the same as the larger to the whole. The Golden Section governs the relationship of parts in the Golden Rectangle, the pentagram, and in patterns of natural growth, such as the spiral of shells, the disposition of pine cone fronds, the brachiation of certain trees, etc.

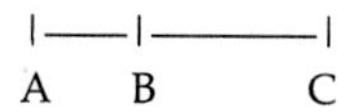

AB : BC = BC : AB+BC

Gothic: In architecture, a style of Western European architecture prevalent from the 12th to the 16th centuries, characterized by pointed aches, tall columns, and lofty vertical interior space (particularly used in reference to churches).

Gothic Revival: The reprisal of Gothic forms, ornament and massing, especially in the eighteenth and nineteenth centuries. In the eighteenth century the Gothic revival was often inspired by an interest associational connections with a thrilling and mysterious historical period, and hence the evocation of the sublime. In nineteenth-century England John Ruskin and the Pre-Raphaelites promoted the Gothic Revival as a way to recover the moral well-being of the worker; in France at the same time Eugène Viollet-le-Duc promoted the Gothic Revival because of the rational structural principles of the pointed arch, rib vault and buttress.

Grade: 1. The slope in a road or ground level. 2. Ground level. 3. To decrease or regularize the slope or surface of an area of ground.

Graphics: Two dimensional composition; drawing, especially incorporating alphabetic ciphers, words or graphs.

Greek cross: A cross with four equal arms, usually used in reference to a particular centralized church plan.

Greek Revival: The reprisal of classical Greek forms (especially temples), ornament and massing in the eighteenth and nineteenth centuries, often inspired by an interest in associational connections with the Arcadian state of carefree innocence in which the forms were thought to have arisen, or to confer the stature and dignity of ancient Greek civilization to the contemporary structures.

Grid: A framework of crossed lines; common architectural grids are 4-square and 9-square.

Groin vault: See cross vault.

Grotto: Italian for 'cave', a highly rusticated, cave-like space in a garden, often underground and often containing water.

Haptic: Solid, volumetric, characterized by the sense of touch.

Harmonic mean: A proportioning system which relates three terms so that the relationship of the middle term to the extremes is:

(B-A)/A = (C-B)/C as in 6:8:12.

Harmony of the Spheres: See "microcosm".

Hemicycle: A semi-circular form.

Hermeneutics: The science of interpretation and the deciphering of texts, symbols, codes, and signs.

Hermetic: Pertaining to a closed system; self-referential.

Heterogeneity: All of a different nature or type.

Heterotopia: A place whose nature is not uniform, orderly and consistent, but characterized by the disjunction of fabric, the juxtaposition of scales, contrary, colliding ordering systems, and a visual cacophony of elements in disunity.

Heuristic: Something which serves to aid discovery or stimulate investigation.

Hierarchy: A system of things, spaces, or areas ranked one above the other in series (of size, importance, use, etc.).

Hipped roof: A roof in which all surfaces slop to meet a ridge.

Historicism: Relying on the past or history for a basis or justification; in architectural design, the revival of styles or motifs drawn from history.

Homogeneity: Sameness, all of the same nature or type.

Horizon line: In perspective drawing, the line which divides earth from sky.

Humanism: A philosophy or system of thought in which the human position, values, and interests are believed to be of primary importance; Specifically refers to Renaissance developments of science and philosophy, and studies of ancient Greece and Rome.

Hybrid: Anything comprised of elements from two or more different, incongruous sources.

Hypostyle: A hall of columns.

I-beam: A structural steel member which can be used as a column or as a beam. The I-beam gains its rigidity through the displacement of parallel flanges by means of "webbing', resulting in its characteristic 'I' or 'H' section.

Iconography: The study of visual symbols.

Ideality: The condition of existing in the purist, most perfect, most essential state.

Illusionism: The creation of scenographic effects to represent something that is not there, as in the pictorial representation of perspectival space, or the creation of a optical trick, or 'trompe l'oeil' in architecture. See: scenography; trompe l'oeil.

Intercolumniation: The spacing between columns.

Interlock: To fit or connect together closely (parts or functions).

International Style: A strain of Functionalist architecture which gained its name from a book by Henry Russell Hitchcock and Philip Johnson, the International Style is characterized by the rational standardization of building systems. International Style architecture is comprised of simple, rectangular, box-like forms structured by skeletal frames and clad with glazed curtain walls. See: Functionalism.

Ionic Order: One of the three Greek Orders, originating around 600 B.C. in Asia Minor, characterized by a fluted shaft, the volutes of its capital, and dentils in the cornice.

Isometric: A kind of axonometric drawing in which all three visible surfaces of a box-like volume show an equal degree of distortion.

Jamb: The side of an door, window, niche, or arch.

Jeffersonian grid: A surveying project put into effect by Thomas Jefferson (1743-1826, president 1801-1809). A regular grid was laid over the un-colonized land of the United States to allow the surveying of unmapped territories, and the commodification of the land.

Juxtaposition: The close placement of elements which may have no relationship other than their adjacency.

Keystone: The wedge-shaped central stone of an arch, considered to be of prime importance in holding the other stones, or 'voussoirs' in place.

Kunstwolle: Literally, German for 'the will of Art', or the 'Will to Form', *Kunstwolle* is used in Zeitgeist theories of art to mean the inevitability that each age will find its own specific artistic expression which will emerge in all media.

Lantern: A small roof structure ringed by windows to emit light into a roof or dome.

Lateral thrust: A force directed to the side.

Latin cross: A cross with one crossing member shorter than the other; a longitudinal church plan in which the transepts and chancel are shorter than the nave.

Linguistics: The study of language; used in architectural discourse in reference to the specific elements (vocabulary) and compositional norms (grammar or syntax) which characterize various styles of architecture.

Lintel: A horizontal beam which spans the opening between two or more vertical posts.

Literal transparency: A term coined by Colin Rowe and Robert Slutzky in their essay "Transparency: Literal and Phenomenal", 'literal transparency' refers to the unambiguous and straightforward way in which some compositions permit light and views to pass through them because of voids, glazing, thinness, layers and other physical properties. The Bauhaus by Walter Gropius is used in the essay to exemplify literal transparency.

Local symmetry: Symmetries restricted to a small part or area.

Longitudinal plan: A plan organized around a central axis or spine; in ecclesiastical architecture, the longitudinal plan is usually based on the Latin Cross, i.e. a cross wherein the nave is longer than the transepts and chancel.

Longitudinal section, long section: Long section; a section cut through the long dimension of a building.

Macrocosm: 1. The universal or overriding concept, principle, or structure. 2. The universe as a whole.

Mannerism: The style of the late Renaissance, c.1530-1600, characterized by exaggerated scenographic effects, a critical stance towards linguistic and compositional norms, and elaborate symbolic or rhetorical programs.

Mansard roof: A roof the lower slope of which is very steep while the upper part is nearly flat.

Mass production: An industrialized method of production which uses machinery and technology to make numerous copies of a prototype or model.

Massing: The basic volumetric organization of a building.

Materiality: 1. The substance, or material characteristics of an object. 2. The perceived three-dimensionality, weight, or solidity of an object.

Megaron: In ancient Greece, a single-cell dwelling unit, usually with four columns supporting the roof; the main room in a Greek house.

Metamorphosis: A change in form, structure or substance; a transformation.

Metonymy: A rhetorical trope in which one term is used instead of another to which it has some logical connection.

Metaphor: A rhetorical trope in which a term or phrase which literally denotes one thing is used to suggest an analogy with another.

Metope: The spacing between triglyphs in a Doric frieze.

Microcosm: A small part of a system which can be seen to represent or mirror the whole.

Mimesis: Imitation.

Minimal Existence Dwelling: A design problem central in Functionalist architecture. Instead of concentrating of grandiose schemes for wealthy patrons, architects sought to address housing needs of the working class by determining the minimum spatial requirements and amenities required for a wholesome, dignified life.

Minimalism: A style of mid-twentieth century art which radically restricts compositional elements to simple geometries and simple colors.

Model: In the typological theories put forward by A.C. Quattremère de Quincy, a 'model' refers to something to be imitated or used as a pattern, as opposed to a 'type', which is the ideal embodiment of essential properties and organizational features whose structure may be adapted without strict imitation. See: "type."

Module: A standard, repeatable unit, used to regulate the proportions in a building.

Monastery: A complex of buildings to house of community of monks in seclusion from the world.

Montage: A composition made up of photographs and printed images which have been cut up and reassembled.

Monumentality: Having the properties of a monument, i.e. heroic scale, timelessness, universality, urban prominence.

Morphology: Literally a branch of biology which examines the forms and structures of plants and animals, used in architecture to discuss the study of form.

Mutability: The ability of something to change form or nature.

Mutule: The sloping, projecting blocks in Doric entablatures, said to derive from wooden beams,

Narrative: A story, sometimes used to guide the metaphoric development of a building.

Nave: The central aisle of a Roman basilica or Christian basilican church, used by the congregation. (From the Latin word for ship.)

Neo-Classicism: An eighteenth and nineteenth century revival of the architectural language (e.g. the Orders), compositional norms and types from classical antiquity. Unlike true classical architecture, which was highly inventive within the limits of the form, Neo-Classicism tended to be more rigid, more rule-bound and more timid.

Neo-Platonism: A school of thought which arose in the third century A.D. and gained popularity in the Renaissance and Romantic periods, Neo-Platonism strove to reconcile the writings of Plato and Aristotle with oriental mysticism. A belief that earthly beauty revealed glimpses of divine beauty elevated the status of the artist from that of workman to that of visionary seer. At the same time, the status of representational art was elevated. Works of art, disparaged in Plato's system as too removed from truth (the artist's work was a representation of a perceived object, which was but a representation of the divine archetype), were prized by Neo-Platonists as direct revelations of the divine archetype.

Normal language or imagery was believed to be inadequate in the expression of the supernatural; hence geometry, symbolism, proportion, and numerological references were used to embody truth and conceal knowledge from the profane, who might otherwise abuse it. Through Neo-Platonic allegory and symbolism, many myths, images and structures which arose in Pagan antiquity were embraced by Christianity as precursors of Christian wisdom. See, "Platonic forms"

Neo-Plasticism: Another name for the "De Stijl" movement, i.e. a Dutch avant-garde movement which flourished in the early part of the twentieth century. "Neo-Plasticism", literally meaning "new three-dimensionality," aimed at the destruction of the static, stolid, stereometric volumes and geometries of traditional architecture. Instead it proffered a new dynamism by pulling apart the constituent surfaces of a volume and replacing them with pure, abstract planes, rendered even more abstract and immaterial through the application of geometric painted patterns in primary colors. Because the edges of Neo-Plastic constructions did not join together, a dynamic tension and interlock was achieved with the surrounding space. See, "De Stijl".

Niche: A recess carved into the thickness of a wall, usually to house a statue, altar or other such element.

Non-hierarchical organization: An organization which deliberately strives to undermine any absolute, totalizing idea of center.

Nostalgia: A longing for the past.

Nympheum: Literally, an abode for nymphs; in classical architecture, a building or area in a garden with cool running water and abundant foliage.

Obelisk: A tall square-sectioned shaft which tapers upwards and ends with a pyramid.

Oculus: A circular opening at the top of a dome.

Oneiric: Related to dreams.

Opaque: Not able to be seen through.

Optic: Characterized by the sense of sight.

Optical corrections: Distortions in the ideal geometry of Greek architecture to compensate for perspectival distortion or to represent static forces through the building. See "entasis"

Oratory: 1. A building or chapel designed for orisons, or prayers or the performance of musical pieces with scriptural themes. 2. An order of monks whose worship centers on the performance of oratories.

Order (the Orders): An architectural system based on the column and its entablature. The Three Greek Orders are Doric, Ionic and Corinthian; the five Roman Orders are Tuscan, Doric, Ionic, Corinthian, and Composite (in relative order of development).

Orientation: Direction with relation to the cardinal points of the compass.

Orthographic Projection: A method of drawing which presents views of buildings as if they were flattened out and projected on to a parallel surface. Such drawings eliminate distortion and can be drawn to scale.

Orthogonal: At right angles; perpendicular or parallel.

Ossuary: A place for the repository of bones and remains in funerary architecture.

Painterly: Characterized by pictorial qualities such as polychromy, strong effects of light, diagonal spatial recession, softly defined outlines, strong gesture, exaggerated perspectival distortions, etc.

Palladian motif: A triadic window motif whereby a large arch is flanked by two smaller, linteled openings.

Palazzo: 1. Italian for large town house. 2. In architectural typology: a building form in which a bar of rooms wraps around a central courtyard.

Palimpsest: A parchment tablet which has been used many times and consists of multiple layers of text. Any surface comprised of the superimposition of multiple layers of information.

Paradigm: An ideal, a perfect example or model which defines a category of elements.

Paradox: A seemingly self-contradictory statement which expresses a possible truth.

Paraline: An axonometric drawing; a kind of architectural drawing which represents the three-dimensional appearance of objects in such a way that vertical lines remain vertical, parallel lines remain parallel, and all lines parallel to the X, Y and Z axes are drawn to scale.

Parallax: The apparent displacement of an object due to different positions of the observer or the space between the two eyes of the viewer.

Parapet: The portion of a wall which extends above the roof or balcony.

Parterre: A well-manicured formal garden design of ornamental patterns, meant to be seen from above.

Parti: From the French verb 'partir' meaning 'to leave,' or a point of departure, used in architecture to designate the basic organization of a design.

Partition wall: A non-structural wall which delimits rooms or zones in a building.

Parvis: A courtyard or enclosed space in front of a church or any other building.

Path: A route along which something can move.

Patronage: Financial support, encouragement of the arts through the commissioning of works or the provision of grants.

Pediment: A low-pitched, triangular area of a facade formed by the junction of two sloped roofs.

Pendentive: A concave curved triangular surface used to support a dome over a square or polygonal chamber.

Perimeter: The outer boundary of an object or spatial region (usually in plan).

Perspective: A 15th century geometric construction based on monocular, immobile vision, linear perspective is the mathematical representation of three-dimensional objects on a two-dimensional surface in such a way that the viewpoint and perceptions of the spectator are replicated, including the apparent convergence of parallel lines and the diminution of background objects. A lightening of tone, increasingly blue hue, and blurring of outlines represents depth in atmospheric perspective.

Phenomenal transparency: A term coined by Colin Rowe and Robert Slutzky in their essay "Transparency: Literal and Phenomenal", 'phenomenal transparency' refers to the ambiguous and polyvalent way in which some compositions suggest transparency through overlap, superimposition, fragmentation and simultaneity. The interlock of voided slots of space in Le Corbusier's Villa at Garches is used in the essay to exemplify phenomenal transparency.

Pictorial space: The two-dimensional representation of three-dimensional space.

Picture plane: In perspective drawing, the forwardmost surface represented; the flat, framed surface of a painting.

Picturesque: Resembling a painting, visually charming or interesting.

Pier: A vertical structural masonry mass, usually rectangular in section.

Pilaster: A flattened column, engaged in the wall, with capital and base, as appropriate to the Order in which it was designed.

Pillar: A vertical shaft-like support which may be round or rectangular in section.

Piloti: Vertical columnar supports, from the French term for structural pillars or stilts. One of Le Corbusier's five points of architecture states that a building should be supported off the ground by a system of piloti so that the flow of landscape may remain undisturbed.

Pinnacle: In Gothic architecture, the slender ornamental turret which terminates buttresses.

Plan: 1. An orthographic projection drawing, to scale, of a horizontal cut through a building, usually taken about 3′ above the floor. 2. The general arrangement of the parts of a building.

Plan oblique: A kind of axonometric drawing in which the plan of the building remains undistorted.

Plasticity: 1. Three-dimensionality. 2. Capable of being molded or carved.

Platonic solid: Based on the theories of the Greek philosopher Plato, active 427-437 B.C., Platonic or primary shapes are rotated or extended to generate primary volumes, which are the sphere, cylinder, cone, pyramid, and cube.

Plenum: A space filled with matter, as opposed to a vacuum; a zone of space, the properties of which are different from those of its surroundings.

Plinth: The lowest part of a column base; any platform or base for a building.

Poché: From the French word for "pocket," used to describe the substance between the two surfaces of a wall which can be carved to form figural spaces.

Pointed arch: Characteristic of Gothic architecture, formed by the intersection of two arcs, each with a radius equal to the span of the arch, and drawn from centers on the spring line.

Polemics, Polemical: The art of argument; pertaining to controversy, controversial, argumentative.

Polychromy: Literally, 'many colors', in architecture it refers to the decorative use of color.

Polymorphism: Having multiple forms.

Polyvalent: Multivalent, i.e. having many meanings, natures, or senses.

Portal: A door, gate, or entry, especially one of grand appearance and scale.

Portico: A colonnaded porch or entry vestibule.

Portico in antis: A porch carved into the body of a building.

Post: A vertical structural element in post and lintel (or post and beam) construction systems. Vertical posts support horizontal lintels (or beams) forming the basic structural unit.

Post-Modernism: In architecture, a revival of traditional architectural forms, ornament and language in an effort to more directly engage popular culture and in reaction to the abstraction and Minimalism of Modern Architecture. Theoretical issues addressed by Post-Modernism include the structure of the traditional city and urbanism, semiotics, typology and the linguistic value of architectural signs. In literary criticism, Post-Modernism refers to interpretation of works of art by means of non-totalizing structures, such as multiple readings, patterns and fragments.

Prairie House: A kind of single family house which arose in Chicago around the turn of the century in the circle of Frank Lloyd Wright. In response to the horizontal sweep of the mid-western prairies, Prairie House are dominated by broad horizontal lines of extended terraces, roof overhangs and horizontally disposed windows. Anchored around a massive central chimney, the walls and roofs of prairie houses are pulled apart to break the closure of a traditional house and to provide greater interpenetration of interior and exterior space.

Precedent: Something which came before which can serve as a justification or basis for subsequent things.

Precinct: A space enclosed by a boundary or limit.

Precolumbian: Cultures and artifacts from the Americas which date to the period before Christopher Columbus and European colonization.

Prefabrication: Made in standardized parts for easy and uniform assembly.

Primary Color: Colors from which all other colors can be derived. In painting, red, yellow and blue are considered to be the primary colors.

Primitive Hut: See Vitruvius; the first structure (fictitious) built by humans. Believed to be the origin of the Doric Order, the idea of a Primitive Hut has been used as a metaphor for an authentic, rational way in which to build, in which ornament is seen as an expression of structure and joinery.

Process: 1. A series of actions or changes leading to a particular end; 2. A rule-driven methodology for the generation of form which is an end in itself.

Program: A list of required spaces, desired adjacencies and functional requirements of a building; the subject (sometimes literary) of a work of art.

Proportion: 1. A ratio of small whole numbers. 2. The comparative relations between dimensions or sizes. 3. The relation of a part to the whole.

Proscenium: The framed opening or frontispiece to a stage in theater design.

Prototype: An original or model after which other things are formed.

Pteron: A colonnade surrounding a cella in Greek templar architecture.

Purism: A school of art which arose in France in the early twentieth century. Purism makes use of the same strategies of overlapping, simultaneity, and figural interpenetration as Cubism, but silhouettes of the forms are rendered more in tact.

Pylon: Greek word for "gateway". Used in Egyptian architecture, a monumental temple entry way of two truncated pyramidal towers flanking and attached to a central gateway. Can also mean either of the flanking towers.

Pythagorean progression: Derived from the number theories of the ancient Greek philosopher Pythagoras (c.582-c.500 B.C.) the dimensional sequence of point, line, plane and volume.

Quadrature: A Gothic method of design and proportion which relies on the interrelationship of square figures.

Radial: Disposed about a central point.

Recursion: The reoccurrence of a form or element at a different scale or configuration with reference to a shared origin.

Reflected ceiling plan: An architectural drawing which projects onto the floor plan information about the ceiling plan above.

Regulating lines: A network of parallel and perpendicular lines drawn over buildings to determine proportions. When the diagonals of two rectangles are parallel or perpendicular to one another, they are similarly proportioned.

Reinforced concrete: A construction system which uses steel mesh or rods inserted in concrete formwork prior to casting to take up structural tensile forces.

Renaissance: Rebirth, specifically the European 15th century and early 16th century, during which the use of the Classical orders were re-examined and re-instated.

Repetition: The fact of being repeated; the use of recurring patterns or shapes to organize space or form.

Rhetoric: The art of persuasive speech, which makes use of 'tropes' or poetic figures of speech.

Rhythm: Repetition or system with uniform pattern or beat recurrence.

Ribbed vault: A compound masonry vault in which the groins or intersections are marked by projecting masonry ribs.

Ribbon windows: One of Le Corbusier's five points of architecture which states that due to the non-load-bearing nature of the facade, the windows can be continuous around the surface of a building.

Ridge: The horizontal line at which the roof rafters meet.

Rococo: An architectural style from the eighteenth century characterized by lavish ornament and abundant scroll-like, naturalistic stucco decoration.

Roman town, Roman camp: See 'castra'.

Romanesque: An architectural style prevalent in western Europe from the 9th to the 12th centuries, characterized by a continuation of Roman masonry vaulting techniques, heavy walls, a preponderance of towers, etc.

Romantic Classicism: An eighteenth and nineteenth-century school of art and literature which conflated the idea of a Classical revival with Romantic notions of Arcadia. The Classical works of Schinkel and von Klenze partake in this tradition.

Romanticism: An eighteenth and nineteenth-century movement which emphasized imagination and emotion, encouraging freedom of form. The irregular effects of nature, and the sublime were celebrated over a more controlled, rational disposition of form.

Roof garden: A flat, habitable roof terrace; One of Le Corbusier's five points of architecture states that due to the use of a column and slab construction system, exterior space is not lost, but can be reclaimed on the roof.

Roof plan: A kind of orthographic projection drawing which represents the roof of a building as if it were flattened out and projected on to the ground plane.

Rose window: In Gothic architecture, a circular stained glass window built of radiating or concentric tracery patterns, usually found in the westworks; also called a "wheel window" due to the similarity of the converging mullions to the spokes of a wheel.

Rotation: The act of turning around a central point or axis.

Rustication: Masonry with indented joints and a rough surface finish, thought by Renaissance theoreticians to express the 'hand of nature'.

Sacristy: A vestry; a room in a church used by the clergy for the storage of vestments and sacred implements.

Sarcophagus: An elaborately carved coffin, usually of stone.

Scale. 1. A ratio between two measuring systems or sets of measurements. 2. A progression or relationship of things in order of size, importance, etc. 3. The perception of a relationship of the size of an object to that of the human figure. 4. Generic scale: the size of a building relative to its surrounding context. 5. Human scale: a building's relation to the size and proportions of the human body.

Scaling: An increase or decrease of size of a drawing or an object based on a ratio of measurements or proportions; a registration between multiple systems at proportionally related scales.

Scenae frons: A frontally organized stage set.

Scenography, Scenographic: Related to theater set design; designed to be seen in exaggerated, false perspective.

Schism: Division or separation.

Scholasticism: The dominant Christian philosophy of the Middle Ages which made use of logic, categories, numeration and adumbration in the structure of their arguments.

Scupper: A water spout.

Secession: A movement in Vienna in the early twentieth century in which progressive artists in the circle surrounding Otto Wagner withdrew, or 'seceded;' from the more traditional academy.

Section: An orthographic projection drawing of a vertical slice through a building, drawn to scale.

Semantics: 1. The branch of philosophy which investigates the relationship between signs (signifiers) and what they refer to (signifieds); 2. Related to the meaning of words or other elements.

Semiotics: The study of signs.

Sequence: A series or order of one thing following another.

Served Space: Public rooms whose clear spatial definition is made possible because secondary functions can be relegated to other rooms (servant space).

Servant Space: Subordinate spaces within a building that support the activities in the major public spaces of the building. These spaces might include closets, kitchens, mechanical space, etc.

Shaft: The middle, tubular part of a column which may or may not be fluted.

Shear: A structural force which characterizes the tendency of one stressed material to slide past another or two contiguous parts of the same material to slide past each other in a direction parallel to their plane of contact.

Shift: To displace; to move from one place to another.

Site: The location of a building. Refers to both the topographical location, and the surrounding built environment.

Skeletal system: A structural system in which structure and enclosure are understood as independent systems; a light trabeated framework of posts and beams satisfies structural requirements while enclosure is understood as an applied skin.

Skin: Cladding; the enclosing membrane of a building. With a skeletal structure, the skin is non-structural and sometimes hung, like a 'curtain wall'.

Slab: A thick plate or flat rectangular volume. Laid horizontally, a slab can act as a two-dimensional floor or ceiling structure. Laid vertically 'slab' describes a simple building mass wherein a multi-level building is comprised of stacked rectangular floors.

Soffit: The underside of an architectural element.

Space/time: A conception of a four-dimensional order comprised of three spatial coordinates (X, Y and Z) and one temporal coordinate (time). See 'Cubism'.

Spandrel: The triangular area between two arches in an arcade, or the area to the side of the round part of a single arch.

Spring line: The level at which an arch curves, or 'springs', inwards from its vertical supports.

Stasis: The state of being motionless.

Station point: In perspective drawing, the point of view from which the scene is represented.

Stereotomy: The study of three-dimensional solids; the art of cutting stone into sections of geometric solids.

Stoa: A long portico or covered colonnade used as a promenade or gathering place in Greek architecture.

String course: An ornamental horizontal band used to articulate a wall or facade.

Structural Rationalism: A belief that architectural form derives from the honest expression of structure, construction and materials in architecture, as opposed to the appliqué of ornament and the borrowing of forms derived rationally from one constructional system to another system in which they are contrary to the nature of the materials. (i.e.the use of arches in unit masonry construction is structurally rational; the use of arches in frame construction is not.)

Structure: 1. The means of construction, the elements which hold a building upright and together. 2. The organization or interrelationship of various elements. 3. A formal solution to a statical problem.

Stucco: Plaster, often used on the exterior of buildings, and for ornamental work.

Stylobate: In classical architecture, the platform on which a temple or colonnade is constructed.

Sublime: 1. Inspiring awe. 2. Lofty, immense, immeasurable, or unfathomable.

Subtractive form: Shape which is understood to have been created by a process of subtraction from a whole, i.e. by the removal of pieces or the carving out of a void from a solid.

Superimposition: The simultaneous presence of two or more forms, one atop the other.

Superposition: To place one layer above another, or to stack vertically elements one on top of the other. e.g. the exterior walls of the Roman Colosseum are articulated by means of superposed columnar orders.

Symmetry: A mirror-image about an axis; literally, Latin for 'of like measure or proportion'.

Synecdoche: A rhetorical trope in which a part of something stands for the whole.

Tabula rasa: Latin for "blank slate".

Tartan Grid: A column or wall system which is comprised of bays of unequal dimension, like the weaving of a tartan plaid.

Tectonic: In the nature of building or construction; the expression of construction features and joinery.

Temenos: The sacred precinct of a Greek holy site.

Temple: A building dedicated to the worship of gods or a god. In Classical antiquity, the temple was a free-standing building comprised of a platform or *'stylobate'*, an inner sanctum, or *'cella'*, a surrounding colonnade or *'pteron'*, and a pedimented roof. The 'portico' is the porch-like extension of the roof pediment, supported by columns. The cult image was housed within the cella or *'naos'*, accessible only to the clergy.

Tension: A static force which tends towards the extension and stretching of material. Examples of architectural elements in tension are cables, suspension bridges, the lower chords of trusses, etc.

Tholos: A round temple which had either a conical or domed roof.

Threshold: The stone or surface which lies under a door; the transition between one spatial domain and another.

Topography: 1. The physical features of an area of land: lakes, mountains, etc. 2. The surface configuration of the land: relative changes in heights and steepness, etc. Topography lines are graphically indicated by means of dashed lines which represent contours a given number of feet apart.

Trabeation: A post and beam constructional system, as opposed to arched construction, (arcuation).

Tracery: In Gothic cathedrals, the ornamental stone grills and patterns in stained glass or screens.

Transept: The cross-arm perpendicular to the nave in a basilican church.

Transition space: A space or zone which articulates, celebrates, or prepares for the movement from one place or state to another.

Translucent: Permitting some light to pass through, such that objects behind can be seen as dim, blurry figures.

Transparent: Permitting light to pass through such that objects behind can clearly be seen.

Transverse section: Cross section; a section cut through the short dimension of a building.

Travertine: A white porous form of limestone used for building.

Triangulation: 1. A Gothic method of design and proportion based on the interrelationship of triangles; 2. In the design of structural systems such as trusses or space frames, the joinery of diverse members into triangular cells so that the whole structure remains rigid.

Triforium: In Gothic cathedrals, the space between vaulting and the roof of an aisle.

Trigylph: In Doric architecture, blocks with three vertical bars which comprise the Doric frieze.

Triumphal arch: 1. Ancient Roman: free standing monumental gateway consisting of three arches (usually A-B-A pattern) erected to commemorate a military victory. 2. Christian church: the transverse wall with arched openings which separates the chancel and apse form the main body of the church.

Trompe l'oeil: Literally, French for 'trick of the eye', a pictorial or constructed optical illusion.

Trope: A rhetorical figure, a figure of speech; a non-literal use of words i.e. metaphoric or poetic speech.

Truss: A frame structural member comprised of a combination of beams and ties to increase the length and rigidity of the whole. Trusses are usually 'triangulated' i.e., comprised of smaller triangular units, to assure the stability of the structure.

Tuscan Order: One of the five Roman Orders, this simplest and most massive of the orders may have been derived from Etruscan-type temples.

Type: In architecture, a class or group of buildings distinguished by shared formal characteristics and derived from the same historical sources.

Typology: The study of building types and formal organizations.

Urban: Relating to the nature or qualities of a city or town.

Urban fabric: The structure of a city, including street patterns; relationship of public vs. private space; density of built vs. unbuilt space; the character and materiality of the architecture; the pattern of street set-backs, side lot set backs, cornice heights, etc.

Urbanism: The study of cities and urban design.

Utopia: Literally, "no place", the imaginary island in Sir Thomas More's book by the same name (1516) where a perfect government and way of life prevailed. "Utopian" has come to mean any place or state of ideal perfection.

Valley Temple: Part of an Old Kingdom Egyptian complex of funerary temples; the corpse of the Pharaoh is received at the Valley Temple from funerary barges and makes its way up the causeway to the pyramid tombs.

Vanishing point: In perspective drawing, the points to which parallel lines converge.

Vault: See vaulting.

Vaulting: Arched or otherwise curved covering or roof, usually made of masonry or concrete. Typical vaults are barrel, groin and ribbed.

Vegemorphic: Sharing the formal characteristics of plants.

Vernacular: Relating to local customs and usages; native; making use of local forms and materials.

Vertical circulation: A means of movement vertically in a building, usually stairs, ramps, and elevators.

Vestige, Vestigial: A mark or trace of evidence of something which no longer exists.

Vestry: See "sacristy".

Villa: Italian for 'country house' , a house of some size and distinction; in architectural typology, a free-standing building, usually organized on the basis of a nine-square grid.

Vitruvius: Minor Roman architect and theorist, born circa 83-73 B.C., active 46-30 B.C., noted for his 10 book treatise: De architectura, the only complete architectural treatise to survive from antiquity, which became important during the Renaissance.

Volute: An ornamental scroll, found on Ionic, Corinthian and Composite capitals

Voussoir: A wedge shaped block which structures the opening of an arch.. See keystone.

Webbing: In architectural structures, struts or membranes which hold apart the primary chords of a truss or the flanges of an I-beam.

Weltanschauung: German for 'world view'.

Westworks: Found at the west end of a Carolingian or Romanesque church, and usually reserved for and built by the nobleman of the area, a multi-story gallery capped with turrets or towers.

Worm's eye view: A point of view from low on the ground looking upwards.

Zeitgeist: The spirit of the times.

Zoomorphic: Sharing the formal characteristics of animals.

Select Bibliography

Chapter 1: Basic Terms

A. Aalto, *Gesamtwerk, Oeuvres Complètes, Complete Work,* Zürich 1970.

K.G. Bitterberg, ed., *Bauhaus,* Cambridge 1968.

P. Blundell Jones, *Hans Scharoun,* Stuttgart 1979.

Le Corbusier, *The City of Tomorrow,* (1929) Cambridge 1982.

J. Gailhabaud, *Monuments anciens et modernes,* Paris 1850.

Graf, Douglas, "Strange Siblings" *Datutop,* Tampere, Finland 1991.

K. Frampton, *Modern Architecture 1851-1945,* New York 1983.

J. Hejduk, *Mask of Medusa,* New York 1985.

W. Kandinsky, *Point and Line to Plane,* (1926) New York 1979.

P. Klee, *Pedagogical Sketchbook,* New York 1953.

G. Schildt, *Alvar Aalto: The Mature Years,* New York 1991.

G. Schildt, *Alvar Aalto, The Decisive Years,* New York 1988.

S. Serlio, *Tutte l'opere d'architettura, 1537-51,* Ridgewood, New Jersey 1964.

Chapter 2: Mass and Space

R. Arnheim, *The Dynamics of Architectural Form* (1975), Berkeley, Los Angeles, London 1977.

R. Arnheim, *Art and Visual Perception,* (1954), Berkeley, Los Angeles, London 1971.

R. Arnheim, *Visual Thinking,* Berkeley, Los Angeles, London 1969.

E. Bacon, *The Design of Cities,* (1967) Harmondsworth 1978.

L. Benevolo, *The History of the City,* (1975) Cambridge 1985.

W. Boesiger, *Le Corbusier,* New York 1971.

A. Christ-Janer, *Eliel Saarinen: Finnish American Architect and Educator* (1979), Chicago 1984.

M. Dennis. *Court and Garden, From the French Hotel to the City of Modern Architecture,* Cambridge 1986.

M.C. Escher, *The Graphic Work of M.C. Escher,* New York 1960.

D. Graf, "Diagrams", *Perspecta 22,* New York 1986.

P. Letarouilly, *Edifices de Rome Moderne,* Paris 1860. Reprint Princeton 1984.

R. Meier, *R. Meier, Architect,* New York 1984.

A. Riegl, *Stilfragen,* Berlin 1893.

C. Rowe and F. Koetter, *Collage City,* Cambridge 1978.

Chapter 3: Basic Organizations

A. Aalto, *Gesamtwerk,* Zürich 1970.

H. Aronson, *The History of Modern Art,* Englewood Cliffs 1968.

P. Arnell and T. Bickford, *Frank Gehry, Buildings and Projects,* New York 1985.

P. Blundell Jones, *Hans Scharoun,* Stuttgart 1979.

C. Cesariano, *Vitruvius,* Como 1521.

F. Ching, *Architecture: Form, Space and Order,* New York 1979.

Le Corbusier, *Oeuvre Complète, 1910-1965,* 7 vols, Zürich 1937-57.

Le Corbusier, *The Modulor,* Cambridge 1954.

R. Giurgola and M. Jarmini, *Louis I Kahn,* Boulder 1975.

J. Guadet, *Eléments et theories,* vol. 2, Paris c. 1894.

G.Kepes, *Education of Vision,* New York 1965.

G. Kepes, *Module, Proportion, Symmetry, Rhythmn,* New York 1966.

R. Krautheimer, *Early Christian and Byzantine Architecture,* Harmondsworth 1975.

R. Meier, *Richard Meier, Architect, New York 1984.*

C. Norberg Schultz, *Meaning in Western Architecture,* New York 1980.

A. Palladio, *The Four Books of Architecture,* (1570), New York 1965.

S. Serlio, *Five Books on Architecture,* (1611) New York 1982.

I. Sola-Morales, *Gaudi,* New York 1984.

M. Vitruvius Pollio, *Ten Books on Architecture,* New York 1960.

R. Wittkower, *Architectural Principles in The Age of Humanism,* London 1973.

CHAPTER 4: TYPOLOGY V. MORPHOLOGY

W. Boesiger, *Le Corbusier,* New York 1971.
J.N.L. Durand, *Précis des leçons,* Paris 1802.
H.W. Kruft, *Storia delle theorie architectoniche dal ottocento a oggi,* Bari 1987.
Le Corbusier, *Oeuvre Complète, 1910-1965,* 7 vols, Zürich 1937-57.
J. Gailhabaud, *Monuments anciens et modernes,* Paris 1850.
R. Moneo, "On Typology", *Oppositions 13,* New York 1978.
A.C. Quattremère de Quincy, *Dictionaire d'architecture encyclopédie méthodique,* Paris 1788-1825.
K.F. Schinkel, *Collection of Architectural Designs,* Chicago 1984.
S. Villari, *J.N.L Durand (1760-18340, Art and Science of Architecture,* New York 1990.
A. Windsor, *Peter Behrens, Architect and Designer 1868-1940,* London 1981.
F.L.Wright, *Frank Lloyd Wright,* Wendigen Edition, Amsterdam 1923.

CHAPTER 5: PRECEDENTS & TRANSFORMATIONS

E. Bacon, *The Design of Cities,* Harmondsworth 1978.
A. Blunt, *Borromini,* Cambridge 1979.
A. Bruschi, *Bramante,* (1973) London 1977.
T. Buddenseig, *Industriekultur. Peter Behrens and the AEG 1907-14* (1979) Cambridge 1984.
H. d'Espouy, *Fragments d'architecture antique, d'après les relevés et restaurations des anciens pensionnaires de l'Acadèmie de France,* Paris 1905.
J. Gailhabaud, *Monuments anciens et modernes,* Paris 1850.
G. Guarini, *Architettura civile,* 2 vols. Turin 1739, reprint 1964.
K. Junghanns, *Bruno Taut 1880-1938,* Milan 1978.
M.A. Laugier, *Essai sur l'architecture,* Paris 1755.
Le Corbusier, *Oeuvre complète, 1910-1965,* 7 vols, Zürich 1937-57.
C.F. Otto, *Space into Light, The Churches of Balthasar Neumann,* Cambridge 1979.
G. Perrot, *Histoire de l'art dans l'antiquité,* Paris 1882.
D. Porphyrios, *Sources of Modern Eclecticism,* London 1980.
P. Portoghesi, *Francesco Borromini,* (1967) Milan 1990.
S. Serlio, *Tutte l'opere d'architettura, 1537-51,* Ridgewood, New Jersey 1964.

CHAPTER 6: ANCIENT EGYPT

A. Badawy, *A History of Egyptian Architecture,* 3 vols., Berkeley, Los Angeles and London, 1965.
L. Benevolo, *The History of the City,* Cambridge 1980.
A. Desgodetz, *Les edifices antiques de Rome,* Paris 1695.
I.E.S. Edwards, *The Pyramids of Egypt,* Harmondsworth 1979.
S. Giedion, *The Beginnings of Architecture,* (1963) Princeton 1964.
S. Lloyd, H.W. Müller, R. Martin, *Ancient Architecture: Mesopotamia, Egypt, Crete, Greece,* New York 1972.
H. Schäfer, *Primiples of Egyptian Art,* (1918) Oxford, 1974.
E.B. Smith, *Egyptian Architecture as Cultural Expression,* New York and London 1938.
W.S. Smith, *The Art and Architecture of Ancient Egypt,* Harmondsworth 1958.

CHAPTER 7: ANCIENT GREECE

E. Bacon, *The Design of Cities,* Harmondsworth 1978.
A. Blunt, *Borromini,* Cambridge 1979.
J.J. Coulton, *Ancient Greek Architects at Work,* (1977) Ithaca 1988.
W.A. Dinsmoor, *The Architecture of Ancient Greece,* (1902), New York and London 1975.
K.A. Doxiadis, *Architectural Space in Ancient Greece,* (1936), Cambridge 1972.
G. Hersey, *The Lost Meaning of Classical Architecture,* Cambridge 1988.
H.W. Kruft, *Storia delle teorie architettoniche,* Bari 1987.
A.W. Lawrence, *Greek Architecture,* Harmondsworth 1957.
J. Onians, *Art and Thought in the Hellenistic Age,* London 1979.
J.J. Pollitt, *The Art of Ancient Greece 1400-31 B.C.: Sources and Documents,* Englewood Cliffs, New Jersey, 1965.
J.J. Pollitt, *The Ancient View of Greek Art: Criticism, History and Terminology,* New Haven and London, 1964.
D.S. Robertson, *A Handbook of Greek and Roman Architecture,* (1929) Cambridge 1969.
M. Robertson, *A History of Greek Art,* 2 vols. Cambridge, 1975.
V. Scully, *The Earth, the Temple and the Gods, Greek Sacred Architecture,* (1962) New York, Washington, London, 1969.
J.B. Ward-Perkins, *Cities of Ancient Greece and Italy, Planning in Classical Antiquity,* New York, 1974.
J. Stuart and N. Revett, *The Antiquities of Athens,* London 1762-1830.
R.E. Wycherley, *How the Greeks Built Cities,* New York and London 1962.

Chapter 8: Ancient Rome

E. Bacon, *The Design of Cities*, Harmondsworth 1978.

L. Benevolo, *The History of the City*, Cambridge 1980.

A. Boëthius and J.B. Ward-Perkins, *Etruscan and Roman Architecture*, Harmondsworth 1970.

F.E. Brown, *Roman Architecture*, New York, 1961.

A. Desgodetz, *Les edifices antiques de Rome- dessinés et mesurés très exactement*, Paris 1695.

H. d'Espouy, *Fragments d'architecture antique, d'après les relevés et restaurations des anciens pensionnaires de l'Acadèmie de France*, Paris 1905.

G. Perrot, *Histoire de l'art dans l'antiquité*, Paris 1882.

J. Gailhabaud, *Monuments anciens et modernes*, Paris 1850.

G. Gromort, *Grandes compositiones exécutées*, Paris 1915.

H.W. Kruft, *Storia delle teorie architettoniche*, Bari 1987.

W.L. MacDonald, *The Architecture of the Roman Empire: An Introductory Study* (1965), New Haven, 1982.

W.L. MacDonald, *The Architecture of the Roman Empire: An Urban Appraisal*, New Haven 1986.

W.L. MacDonald, *The Pantheon*, London 1976.

G.B. Piranesi, *Antichità romane*, Rome c. 1755.

J.J. Pollitt, *The Art of Rome c.753 B.C. - A.D. 337: Sources and Documents*, Englewood Cliffs, New Jersey.

A. Rossi, *The Architecture of the City*, Cambridge 1982.

M. Vitruvius Pollio, *Ten Books of Architecture*, New York 1960.

J.B. Ward Perkins, *Roman Imperial Architecture*, (1970) Harmondsworth 1981.

J.B. Ward-Perkins, *Roman Architecture*, New York 1977.

Chapter 9: Gothic

E. Bacon, *The Design of Cities*, Harmondsworth 1978.

L. Benevolo, *The History of the City*, Cambridge 1980.

P. Frankl, *Gothic Architecture*, Harmondsworth 1962.

P. Frankl, *The Gothic, Literary Sources and Interpretations during Eight Centuries*, Princeton 1960.

P. Frankl & E. Panofsky, "The Secret of the Medieval Masons", *Art Bulletin*, XXVII, 1945.

J. Gimpel, *The Cathedral Builders*, (1961), New York 1984.

L. Grodecki, *Gothic Architecture*, New York 1977.

J.H. Harvey, *The Medieval Architect*, London 1972.

J.H. Harvey, *The Gothic World 1100-1600*, London 1950.

G. Henderson, *Gothic*, Harmondsworth 1967.

H.W. Kruft, *Storia delle teorie architettoniche*, Bari 1987.

G. Lesser, *Gothic Cathedrals and Sacred Geometry*, 2 vols. London 1957.

L. Mumford, *The City in History*, London 1961.

E. Panofsky, *Abbot Suger on the Abbey Church of St. Denis*, (1946) Princeton 1979.

E. Panofsky, *Gothic Architecture and Scholasticism*, New York 1958.

O. von Simson, *The Gothic Cathedral: Origins of Gothic Architecture and the Medieval Concept of Order*, New York 1956.

C. Sitte, *The Birth of Modern City Planning (1889)*, New York, 1989.

R. Wittkower, *Classic vs. Gothic*, New York 1974.

Chapter 10: Renaissance:

J. Ackerman, *The Architecture of Michelangelo*, (1961) Harmondsworth 1960.

J. Ackerman, *The Villa Form and Ideology of Country Houses*, Princeton, 1985.

J. Ackerman, *Palladio*, Harmondsworth 1960.

L.B. Alberti, *Ten Books on Architecture* (1485), London 1955.

G.C. Argan, *The Renaissance City*, New York 1969.

E. Bacon, *The Design of Cities*, Harmondsworth 1978.

E. Battisti, *Filippo Brunelleschi, the Complete Work*, New York 1981.

L. Benevolo, *The Architecture of the Renaissance*, 2. vols, (1968) London 1978.

L. Benevolo, *The History of the City*, Cambridge 1980.

A. Blunt, *Artistic Theory in Italy 1450-1600*, (1940) London, Oxford, New York 1968.

F. Borsi, *Leon Battista Alberti*, (1973) New York 1986.

A. Bruschi, *Bramante*, (1973) London 1977.

J.C. Burckhardt, *The Civilization of the Renaissance in Italy*, 2 vols. (1860) New York and Evanston 1958.

J. Burckhardt, *The Architecture of the Italian Renaissance*, (1865), Chicago and London 1985.

C. Cesariano, *Vitruvius, de architectura*, Como 1521.

A. Chastel, *The Age of Humanism*, London 1963.

D.R. Coffin, *The Villa in the Life of Renaissance Rome*, Princeton 1979.

M. Fagiolo and M.L. Madonna, ed. *Baldassare Peruzzi, pittura, scena e architettura nel Cinquecento*, Rome 1987.

A.A. Filarete, *Treatise on Architecture*, (1460) New Haven and London 1965.

J. Gadol, *Leon Battista Alberti, Universal Man of the Early Renaissance*, Chicago 1969.

E.H. Gombrich, *Norm and Form: Studies in the Art of the Renaissance,* London 1966.
G. Gromort, *Jardins d'Italie,* Paris 1931.
F. Hartt, *Giulio Romano,* 2 vols., New York 1958.
L.H. Heydenreich and W. Lotz, *Architecture in Italy 1400-1600,* Harmondsworth 1974.
R. Klein and H. Zerner, *Italian Art 1500-1600: Sources and Documents,* Englewood Cliffs, New Jersey, 1966.
H.W. Kruft, *Storia delle teorie architettoniche,* Bari 1987.
P. Letarouilly, *Edifices de Rome moderne, Paris 1860.*
M. Levey, *Early Renaissance,* Harmondsworth 1967.
M. Levey, *High Renaissance,* Harmondsworth 1975.
W. Lotz, *Studies in Renaissance Architecture,* Cambridge 1977.
G. Masson, *Italian Villas and Palaces,* London 1959.
M. Meiss, *Painting in Florence and Siena after the Black Death (1951),* New York 1964.
P. Murray, *The Architecture of the Italian Renaissance (1963),* New York 1965.
P. Murray, *Renaissance Architecture,* New York 1971.
A. Palladio, *The Four Books of Architecture* (1570), New York 1965.
P. Portoghesi, *Rome of the Renaissance* (1970), London 1972.
L. Puppi, *Andrea Palladio,* Venice 1973.
S. Serlio, *Tutte l'opere d'architettura, 1537-51,* Ridgewood, New Jersey 1964.
J. Shearman, *Mannerism,* Harmondsworth 1967.
J.C. Shepherd and G.A. Jellicoe, *Italian Gardens of the Renaissance,* London 1925.
M. Tafuri, *L'architettura del Manierismo nel Cinquecento europeo,* Rome 1966.
C. Thoenes, *Sebastiano Serlio,* Milan 1989.
G.B. da Vignola, *The Regular Architect: or the General Rule of the Five Orders of Architecture* (1562), London 1669.
D. Wiebenson, *Architectural Theory and Practice from Alberti to Ledoux,* Chicago 1982.
R. Wittkower, *Architectural Principles in the Age of Humanism,* (1949) New York 1971.

CHAPTER 11: BAROQUE

E. Bacon, *Design of Cities,* Harmondsworth 1978.
L. Benevolo, *The History of the City,* Cambridge 1985.
A. Blunt, *Art and Architecture in France 1500-1700,* (1953), Harmondsworth 1973.
A. Blunt, *Baroque and Rococo Architecture and Decoration (1978), New York 1982.*
A. Blunt, *Borromini,* Cambridge 1979.
F. Borsi, *Bernini,* (1980) New York 1984.
J. Connors, *Borromini and the Roman Oratory,* Cambridge 1980.
M. Dennis, *Court and Garden, From the French Hotel to the City of Modern Architecture,* Cambridge, 1986
R. Krautheimer, *The Rome of Alexander VII 1655-1667,* Princeton 1985.
H.W. Kruft, *Storia delle teorie architettoniche,* Bari 1987.
P. Letarouilly, *Edifices de Rome moderne,* Paris 1860.
C. Norberg Schulz, *Baroque Architecture,* New York 1971.
C. Norberg Schulz, *Late Baroque and Rococo Architecture,* New York 1971.
P. Portoghesi, *Roma Barocca,* (1966) Rome and Bari 1988.
P. Portoghesi, *Borromini,* (1967) Milan 1990.
J.M. Schwarting, *The Harvard Architecture Review, "Urban Architecture:,* Cambridge 1981.
J. Summerson, *The Classical Language of Architecture,* (1963) London 1980.
R. Wittkower, *Art and Architecture in Italy 1600-1750,* (1958), Harmondsworth 1973.
R. Wittkower, *Studies in the Italian Baroque,* London 1975.
Heinrich Wölfflin, *Principles of Art History,* (1915), New York 1950.
Heinrich Wölfflin, *Renaissance and Baroque,* (1888) Ithaca 1984.

CHAPTER 12: ENLIGHTENMENT TOWN PLANNING

E. Bacon, *Design of Cities,* Harmondsworth 1978.
L. Benevolo, *The History of the City,* Cambridge 1985.
M. Dennis, *Court and Garden, From the French Hotel to the City of Modern Architecture,* Cambridge, 1986.
R. Fishman, *Urban Utopias in the Twentieth Century,* New York 1977.
M. Girouard, *Cities and People, A Social and Architectural History,* New Haven 1985.
J.B. Jackson, *The Necessity for Ruins,* Amherst 1980.
J.B. Jackson, *Discovering the Vernacular Landscape,* New Haven and London 1985.
G. and S. Jellicoe, *The Landscape of Man,* London 1989.
E. Kaufmann, *Architecture in the Age of Reason,* (1955) New York 1968.
L. Marx, *The Machine in the Garden,* (1964), London, Oxford, New York 1969.
L. Mumford, *The City in History: Its Origins, Its Transformations, and Its Prospects.* New York 1961.
R. Nash, *Wilderness and the American Mind,* (1967) New Haven 1973.

W.B. O'Neal, *Pictorial History of the University of Virginia,* Charlottesville 1968.

W.H. Pierson, *American Buildings and their Architects: The Colonial and Neo-Colonial Styles,* New York 1970.

S.E. Rasmussen, *London: The Unique City,* (1934) New York 1974.

J.W. Reps, *Town Planning in Frontier America,* Princeton 1965.

L. Roth, *A Concise History of American Architecture,* New York 1979.

V. Scully, *American Architecture and Urbanism,* London 1969.

C. Tunnard, *The City of Man,* New York and London 1953.

W. Whiffen and F. Koeper, *American Architecture, 1607-1976,* London and Henley 1981.

Chapter 13: 18th & 19th Centuries

J. M. Crook, *The Greek Revival,* London 1972.

J.M. Crook, *The Dilemma of Style,* Chicago 1987.

L. Eitner, *Neoclassicism and Romanticism 1750-1850: Sources and Documents,* Englewood Cliffs, N. J., 1970.

K. Frampton, *Modern Architecture 1851-1945,* New York 1983.

W. Hermann, *Laugier and Eighteenth Century French Theory,* London 1972.

W. Hermann, *Gottfried Semper, In Search of Architecture,* (1978) Cambridge 1984.

H. Honour, *NeoClassicism,* Harmondsworth 1969.

G. and S. Jellicoe, *The Landscape of Man,* (1975) London 1989.

Le Corbusier, *Towards a New Architecture,* (1927), New York 1982.

H.W. Kruft, *Storia delle teorie architettoniche,* Bari 1987.

J.C. Lemagny, *Visionary Architecture,* Houston 1968.

R. Middleton and D. Watkin, *Neo-classical and Nineteenth-Century Architecture,* (1977), New York 1980.

C. Moore, W. Mitchell, W. Turnbull, *The Poetics of Gardens,* Cambridge, 1989.

A. Perez-Gomez, *Architecture and the Crisis of Modern Science,* Cambridge 1983.

W.H. Pierson, *American Buildings and their Architects, Technology and the Picturesque, The Corporate and Early Gothic Styles,* New York 1978.

H. Rosenau, *Boulée- Visionary Architect,* New York and London 1974.

J. Ruskin, *The Seven Lamps of Architecture,* London 1940.

J. Rykwert, *The First Moderns, The Architects of the Eighteenth Century,* Cambridge 1980.

J. Rykwert, *On Adam's House in Paradise,* New York 1972.

E.E. Viollet-le-Duc, *Lectures on Architecture* (1877) New York.

Chapter 14: High Modernism

R. Banham, *Theory and Design in the First Machine Age,* London 1960.

L. Benevolo, *History of Modern Architecture,* 2 vols. (1960), Cambridge 1982.

W. Boesiger, *Le Corbusier, New York 1972.*

H.B. Chipp, *Theories of Modern Art,* Berkeley 1968.

F. Choay, *The Modern City, Planning in the Nineteenth Century,* New York, 1969.

P. Collins, *Changing Ideals in Modern Architecture,* (1965) Kingston and Montreal 1984.

U. Conrads, *Programme und Manifeste zur Architektur des 20. Jahrhunderts,* Frankfurt 1964.

A. Drexler and T. Hines, *The Architecture of Richard Neutra,* New York 1982.

K. Frampton, *Modern Architecture 1851-1945,* New York 1983.

K. Frampton, *Modern Architecture, a Critical History,* (1980), London 1985.

S. Giedion, *Mechanization Takes Command,* (1948), New York 1975.

H.R. Hitchcock, *Architecture, 19th and 20th Centuries,* (1958) Harmondsworth 1968.

H.R. Hitchcock and P. Johnson, *The International Style: Architecture since 1922,* New York 1932.

C. Jencks, *Modern Movements in Architecture,* New York 1973.

W.H. Jordy, *American Buildings and their Architects. The Impact of Early Modernism in the Mid-Twentieth Century,* New York 1972.

S. Kern, *The Culture of Time and Space,* Cambridge 1983.

Le Corbusier, *Oeuvre Complète, 1910-1965,* 7 vols, Zürich 1937-57.

Le Corbusier, *Towards a New Architecture,* (1927), New York 1982.

H.W. Kruft, *Storia delle teorie architettoniche,* Bari 1987.

S. von Moos, *Le Corbusier, Elements of a Synthesis (1968)* Cambridge 1982.

N. Pevsner, *The Sources of Modern Architecture and Design,* New York and Washington, 1968.

N. Pevsner, *Pioneers of Modern Design,* (1936) Harmondsworth 1982.

B. Pfieffer, *Frank Lloyd Wright Mongraph,* Tokyo.

K.F. Schinkel, *Collection of Architectural Drawings,* Chicago 1984.

R. Poggioli, *The Theory of the Avant-Garde,* (1968) Cambridge and London 1981.

H. Probst, and C. Schädlich, *Walter Gropius,* Berlin 1985.

C. Rowe, *The Mathematics of the Ideal Villa and other Essays,* Cambridge 1977.
V. Scully, *Frank Lloyd Wright,* New York 1968.
G. Semper, trans. W. Hermann & H. Mulgrave, *The Four Elements of Architecture & Other Writings,* Cambridge 1989.
D. Spaeth, *Mies van der Rohe,* New York 1985.
W. Tegethoff, *Mies van der Rohe: The Villas and Country Houses,* Cambridge 1985.
H. Wingler, *The Bauhaus: Weimar, Dessau, Berlin and Chicago,* Cambridge, 1969.
B. Zevi, *La Poetica dell'architettura neoplastica,* Turin 1974.

CHAPTER 15: POST INDUSTRIAL AGE

A. Aalto, *Alvar Aalto, Gesamtwerk, Oeuvre Complète, Complete Work,* Zürich 1963.
K. Downs, *Nicholas Hawksmoor,* London 1980.
A. Drexler, *The Architecture of the Ecole des Beaux-Arts,* London 1977.
P. Eisenman, *House X,* New York 1982
P. Inskip, *Edwin Lutyens,* London 1979.
C. Jencks, *The Language of Post-Modern Architecture* (1977), London 1984.
H. Klotz, *The History of Post Modern Architecture,* Cambridge 1988.
E. Lissitzky, *Maler, Architect, Typograf, Fotograf,* Dresden 1967.
S. von Moos, *Venturi, Rauch & Scott Brown, Buildings and Projects,* New York 1987.
F. Moschini, ed. *Aldo Rossi, Projects and Drawings 1962-1979,* London and Florence 1979.
P. Noever, *Architecture in Transition: Between Deconstruction and New Modernism,* Munich and New York 1991.
C. Norris, *What is Deconstruction,* London and New York 1988.
D. Porphyrios, *Sources of Modern Eclecticism: Studies on Alvar Aalto,* London 1982.
M. Tafuri, *Architecture and Utopia: Design and Capitalist Development,* London 1976.
M. Tafuri, *The Sphere and the Labyrinth,* (1978) Cambridge 1990.
R. Venturi, *Complexity and Contradiction in Architecture,* New York 1966.
R. Venturi, D. Scott-Brown and S. Izenour, *Learning from Las Vegas,* Cambridge 1972.
M. Wigley, *Deconstructivism,* New York 1989.
B. Zevi, *Erich Mendelsohn,* New York 1982.
B. Zevi, *Giuseppe Terragni,* Bologna, 1984.

GENERAL SOURCES:

M. Barasch, *Theories of Art From Plato to Winckelmann,* New York and London 1985.
J. Burchard and A. Bush-Brown, *The Architecture of America,* (1961), Boston and Toronto 1966.
W.B. Field, *Architectural Drawing,* New York 1912.
B. Fletcher, *A History of Architecture,* New York 1975.
P. Frankl, *Principles of Architectural History: The Four Phases of Architectural Style, 1420-1900;* (1914) Cambridge 1977.
S. Giedion, *Space, Time and Architecture,* (1941) Cambridge 1967.
A. Hofstader, *Philosophies of Art and Beauty,* New York 1964.
K. Jormakka, *Inadvertent Ontologies: Reading Architectural Theory,* Helsinki 1991 (unpublished).
G.E. Kidder Smith, *The New Architecture of Europe,* Cleveland 1961.
S. Kostoff, *A History of Architecture,* New York 1985.
H.W. Kruft, *Storia delle teorie architettoniche,* 2 vols. Bari 1988. (*Geschichte der Architekturtheorie von der Antike zur Gegenwart,* Munich 1985).
C. Norberg Schulz, *Meaning in Western Architecture,* (1975), New York 1980.
E. Panofsky, *Meaning tn the Visual Arts,* Garden City, New York 1957.
N. Pevsner, *Outline of European Architecture,* (1943) Harmondsworth, 1963.
N. Pevsner, *A History of Building Types,* Princeton 1976.
S.E. Rasmussen, *Experiencing Architecture,* Cambridge 1964.
M.L. Reynaud, *Traité d'architecture premier partie, Art de Batir,* Paris 1885.
R. Scruton, *The Aesthetics of Architecture,* London 1979.
M. Tafuri, *History and Theories of Architecture,* Cambridge 1982.
D. Watkin, *A History of Western Architecture,* London 1986.
D. Wiebenson, *Architectural Theory and Practice from Alberti to Ledoux,* Chicago 1982.
W. Whiffen and F. Koeper, *American Architecture, 1607-1976,* London and Henley 1981.

Sources of Illustrations

All photos and drawings not otherwise credited are by the author.

Cover

Monzu Desiderio, "Explosion in a Church", 16th c. Naples, detail. Reproduction by permission of the Syndics of the Fitzwilliam Museum, Cambridge, England.

Chapter 1

1.0 Reproduced with permission by Kunstmuseum, Paul Klee-Stiftung, Bern, Switzerland.

1.1 S. Serlio, *Tutte l'opere d'architettura*, 1537-51, fac. Ridgewood, N.J. 1964.

1.2 Le Corbusier, *The City of Tomorrow*, 1929, reprint, Cambridge 1982.

1.3 J. Kepler, *Mysterium Cosmographicum*, 1621.

1.4 Barbari, Jacob de, *Portrait of Luca Pacioli*, c. 1500. Naples, National Museum. Alinari / Art Resource.

1.6 J. Gailhabaud, *Monuments anciens et modernes*, Paris 1850.

1.7 R. Sturgis, *Illustrated Dictionary of Architecture and Building*, New York 1902-1902, reprint New York 1989.

1.8 G.B. Cipriani, *Itinerario figurato degli edifici più rimarchevole di Roma*, Rome 1835-37, translation, *Architecture of Rome*, New York 1986.

1.9, 1.12 Photo, Robert S. Livesey.

1.10, 1.20 W.A. Dinsmoor, *The Architecture of Ancient Greece*, New York 1902.

1.11 K. Frampton, *Modern Architecture 1851-1945*, New York 1983.

1.14 Frederick Gutheim, *Alvar Aalto*, New York 1960.

1.15-1.18 Reproduced with permission by John Hejduk.

1.19 Berlin, Pergamon Museum.

Chapter 2

2.0, 2.12-2.15 P. Letaurouilly, *Edifices de Rome moderne*, Paris 1840, reprint Princeton 1982.

2.3 © 1938 M.C. Escher Foundation - Baarn - Holland. All rights reserved.

2.4 Eliel Saavinen. Aerial Perspective of Cranbrook School for Boys. Reproduced with permission by The Cranbrook Academy of Art Museum..

2.9 *The Ohio State University* Archives, Columbus, Ohio.

2.10 Reproduced with permission by Kunstmuseum, Paul Klee-Stiftung, Bern, Switzerland.

2.11 J.F. Blondel, *Architecture françoise*, vol. III, Paris 1752, 1754, 1756, fac. Paris 1904.

2.17, 2.18, 2.33 W. Boesiger, ed. *Le Corbusier*, New York 1971.

2.19, 2.24, 2.34 Photo, Robert S. Livesey.

2.20 Reproduced with permission by Kunstmuseum, Paul Kleestiftung, Bern, Switzerland.

2.21, 2.23 O. Bertotti Scamozzi, *Le fabbriche e disegni di Andrea Palladio*, Vicenza 1776 and 1786, reprint London 1968.

2.25 A. Blunt, *Baroque & Rococo Architecture*, New York 1982.

2.27, 2.28 P. Bertelli, *Theatrum Urbium Italicarium*, Rome 1599.

2.29, 2.30 G.B. Nolli, *Plan of Rome*, Rome 1748.

2.31 G. Gromort, *Grandes compositiones exécutées*, Paris 1925.

2.36-2.38 Turgot Plan of Paris, 1734-39, from M. Dennis, *Court and Garden*, Cambridge 1986.

Chapter 3

3.0 A. Palladio, c. 1560. Reproduced with permission by British Architectural Library, RIBA, London.

3.2 Leonardo da Vinci, Galleria dell'Accademia, Venice, from P. Murray, *Renaissance Architecture*, New York 1965.

3.3 C. Cesariano, "Vitruvian Man", *Vitruvius*, Como 1521, fac. 1968.

3.4, 3.5, 3.9 S. Serlio, *Tutte l'opere d'architettura*, 1537-51, fac. Ridgewood, N.J. 1964.

3.6 J. Gailhabaud, *Monuments anciens et modernes*, vol 2, Paris 1850.

3.7 B. Fletcher, *A History of Architecture*, 5th edition, New York and London 1905.

3.8 G.B. Piranesi, *Vedute di Roma*, Rome c. 1756.

3.10 K. Frampton, *Modern Architecture 1851-1945*, New York 1985.

3.11 J. Burckhardt, *The Architecture of the Italian Renaissance*, 1867, reprint Chicago 1985.

3.12 O. Bertotti Scamozzi, *Le fabbriche e disegni di Andrea Palladio*, Vicenza 1776 and 1786, reprint London 1968.

3.13 Drawing after R. Wittkower by Jon Stephens.

3.14 © 1977. Louis I. Kahn Collection, University of Pennsylvania and Pennsylvania Historical and Museum Commission.

3.17-3.19 Reproduced with permission by Richard Meier & Partners Architects, New York.

3.20-3.21, 3.35 W. Boesiger, *Le Corbusier*, New York 1972.

3.22, 3.34 Photo, Robert S. Livesey.

3.24 P. Cataneo, *L'architettura*, 1567.

3.27 Alvar Aalto, *Gesamtwerk*, Zürich 1970.

3.31 I. Sola-Morales, *Gaudi*, New York 1984.

3.33 Picasso, Pablo. *Green in Still Life*. Avignon, summer 1914. Oil on canvas, 23 1/2 x 31 1/4. The Museum of Modern Art, New York. Lillie P. Bliss Collection.

3.36, 3.37 Reproduced with permission by John Hejduk.

3.38, 3.39 Reproduced with permission by Frank Gehry, Architect.

3.43, 3.45 J. Guadet, *Eléments et Theories*, vol. 2, Paris c.1894.

3.47 Drawing after M. Scharoun by Jon Stephens.

Chapter 4

4.0 J.N.L. Durand, *Précis des leçons*, vol. II, Paris 1819.

4.1 J. Gailhabaud, *Monuments anciens et modernes*, Paris 1850.

4.2 M.L. Reynaud, *Traité d'architecture premier partie*, Paris 1875.

4.10 Drawing, Andrew Gargus.

4.11-4.12 Frank Lloyd Wright Drawings are copyright © 1945, 1957, 1958, 1960, 1962 The Frank Lloyd Wright Foundation. All rights reserved.

4.13-4.15 Drawings after Le Corbusier by Jon Stephens.

4.16, 4.17 Photo, Robert S. Livesey.

4.18-4.20 19th century engraving, from J. Mordaunt Crook, *The Dilemma of Style*, Chicago 1987.

Chapter 5

5.0 S. Serlio, *Tutte l'opere d'architettura*, 1537-51, fac. Ridgewood, N.J. 1964.

5.1-5.3 J. Gailhabaud, *Monuments anciens et modernes*, vol 1, Paris 1850.

5.4, 5.10 W.A. Dinsmoor, *The Architecture of Ancient Greece*, New York 1902, reprint New York and London 1975.

5.5 B. Taut, *Die Auflösung der Städte*, Berlin 1917.

5.6 M.A. Laugier, *Essai sur l'architecture*, frontispiece, second ed., Paris 1755.

5.7 F.M. Simpson, *A History of Architectural Development*, London, New York, Bombay, Calcutta and Madras, 1921.

5.8 J. Guadet, *Eléments et Theories*, vol. 2, Paris c.1894.

5.11-5.13, 5.18, 5.19 H. D'Espouy, *Fragments d'architecture antique*, Paris 1905.

5.15 From *Design of Cities*, Edmund Bacon. Copyright © 1967, 1974 by Edmund Bacon. Used by permission of Viking Penguin, a division of Penguin Books USA, Inc.

5.20, 5.21 P. Letaurouilly, *Edifices de Rome moderne*, Paris 1840.

5.22, 5.24 B. Fletcher, *A History of Architecture*, 5th edition, London and New York 1905.

5.23 J. Guadet, *Eléments et theories*, vol. 2, Paris c.1894.

5.25, 5.32, 5.38, 5.39 Photo, Robert S. Livesey.

5.26 G.B. Piranesi, *Vedute di Roma*, Rome c. 1756.

5.27, 5.28 Photo, Robert S. Livesey.

5.29 S. Botticelli, "Birth of Venus", Uffizi Museum, Florence, from H.W. Janson, *History of Art*, Englewood Cliffs, 1970.

5.30 J. Burckhardt, *The Architecture of the Italian Renaissance*, 1867, reprint Chicago 1985.

5.31 R. Sturgis, *Illustrated Dictionary of Architecture and Building, New* York 1902-1902, reprint New York 1989.

5.35 Drawn by Jon Stephens.

5.37 Borromini, Francesco, Alb. 173. Reproduced with permission by Albertina Museum, Vienna, Austria.

5.40 G. Guarini, *Architettura Civile*, Turin 1739, reprint London 1964.

5.41, 5.42 Neumann, Balthazar, S.E. 86. Reproduced with permission by Mainfränkisches Museum, Würzburg, Germany.

5.45 Redrawn after Le Corbusier by Jon Stephens.

Chapter 6

6.0, 6.8, 6.9, 6.16 J. Gailhabaud, *Monuments anciens et modernes,* vol 1, Paris 1850.

6.1 Egyptian sculpture of Senmut with a daughter of Queen Hatshepsut, ca. 1480 B.C. Foto Marburg/Art Resource.

6.2 Egyptian sculpture, Pharoah Chefren, 4th dynasty. 2720-2550 B.C. Foto Marburg/Art Resource.

6.4 R. Sturgis, *Illustrated Dictionary of Architecture and Building,* New York 1902-1902, reprint New York 1989.

6.5 Hammerton, *Wonders of the Past,* New York, 1937.

6.7, 6.21 G. Perrot, *Histoire de l'art dans l'antiquité,* Paris 1882.

6.10, 6.20 E.B. Smith, *Egyptian Architecture as Cultural Expression,* New York and London 1938.

6.14 Benevolo, Leonardo, *The History of the City.* Reproduced with permission by the publisher, MIT Press, Cambridge, MA.

6.22 E.E. Viollet-le-Duc, *Lectures on Architecture,* Vol. 1, 1877, reprint New York 1986.

Chapter 7

7.0 G. Gromort, *Grandes compositiones executées,* Paris 1925.

7.1 Greek bronze sculpture, Zeus. ca. 460 B.C. Athens, National Museum. Foto Marburg/Art Resource.

7.2 J. Gwilt, *Encyclopedia of Architecture,* London 1842, 1867, reprint New York 1982.

7.3, 7.17, 7.18, 7.25, 7.30, 7.31 Photo, Robert S. Livesey.

7.4, 7.20 W.A. Dinsmoor, *The Architecture of Ancient Greece,* 1902, reprint New York and London 1975.

7.5 J. Stuart & N. Revett, *The Antiquities of Athens,* London 1787.

7.6 B. Fletcher, *A History of Architecture,* New York and London 1905.

7.8 R. Sturgis, *Illustrated Dictionary of Architecture and Building, New* York 1902-1902, reprint New York 1989.

7.9 J. Gibbs, *A Book of Architecture Containing Designs and Building Ornaments,* London 1728.

7.10-7.12 A. Desgodetz, *Les edifices antiques de Rome, dessinés et mesurés très exactement,* Paris 1695.

7.14 Spini, G., c. 37. Reproduced with permission by Biblioteca Nazionale Marciana, Venezia.

7.15 J. Shute, *The First and Chief Groundes of Architecture,* London 1563, fac. 1912.

7.16 Reprinted from J.J. Coulton, *Ancient Greek Architects at Work: Problems of Structure and Design.* Copyright © 1977 by J.J. Coulton. Used by permission of the publisher, Cornell University Press.

7.21 H. Berve, *Greek Temples, Theatres, & Shrines,* New York.

7.22 Doxiadis, K. A., *Architectural Space in Ancient Greece.* Reproduced with permission by the publisher, MIT Press, Cambridge, MA.

7.23 Redrawn after J. Pollitt by Jon Stephens.

7.24, 7.27, 7.28, 7.32, 7.33 H. D'Espouy, *Fragments d'architecture antique,* Paris 1905.

7.34, 7.36-7.39 From *Designs of Cities,* by Edmund Bacon. Copyright © 1967, 1974 by Edmund Bacon. Used by permission of Viking Penguin, a division of Penguin Books USA, Inc.

7.40 Le Corbusier, *Journey to the East, (Le voyage d'orient* (Paris, 1911) translation, Cambridge 1987.

Chapter 8

8.0, 8.12, 8.16, 8.28 G. Gromort, *Grandes compositiones executées,* Paris 1925.

8.1 S. Serlio, *Tutte l'opere d'architettura,* 1537-51, fac. Ridgewood, N.J. 1964.

8.2, 8.13 J. Gailhabaud, *Monuments anciens et modernes,* Paris 1850.

8.3 Colossal head of Constantine. Capitoline Museums, Rome. Scala/Art Resource.

8.4 Roman copy of Doryphoros by Polykleitos, ca. 450-440 B.C. Naples, National Museum. Alinari/Art Resource.

8.5 G.B. Piranesi, *Antichità romane, IV,* Rome c. 1755, from Scott, *Piranesi,* London and New York, 1975.

8.6 Rossi, Aldo, *The Architecture of the City.* Reproduced with permission by the publisher, MIT Press, Cambridge, MA.

8.7 Benevolo, Leonardo, *The History of the City.* Reproduced with permission by the publisher, MIT Press, Cambridge, MA.

8.8 G.B. Piranesi, Rome 1761, *Campius Martius,* from G. Gromort, *Grandes compositiones executées,* Paris 1915.

8.9 J. Gwilt, *Encyclopedia of Architecture,* London 1842, 1867, reprint New York 1982.

8.11 Museo della Civiltà Romana, Rome, Photo, Robert S. Livesey.

8.14, 8.15 Reproduced with permission by Douglas Graf.

8.17, 8.29 Museo della Civiltà Romana, Rome.

8.18 L. Benevolo, *The History of the City,* Cambridge 1985.

8.19 A. Desgodetz, *Fragments d'architecture antique,* Paris 1905.

8.21., 8.27 E.E. Viollet-le-Duc, *Lectures on Architecture,* Vol. 1, 1877, reprint New York 1986.

8.22, 8.23 Photo, Robert S. Livesey.

8.24-8.26 R. Sturgis, *Illustrated Dictionary of Architecture and Building,* London 1902-1902, reprint, New York 1989.

8.30 G.B. Piranesi, *Vedute di Roma,* Rome c. 1756.

8.31 Guadet, *Eléments et Théories,* Paris 1894.

8.33, 8.34 G.B. Cipriani, *Itinerario figurato degli edifici più remarchevole di Roma,* Rome 1835-37, translation, *Architecture of Rome,* New York 1986.

8.36 C. Norberg-Schulz, *Meaning in Western Architecture,* New York 1980.

8.38, 8.39 Fletcher, Banister, *A History of Architecture.* Reproduced with permission by Butterworths, Stoneham, MA.

Chapter 9

9.0, 9.23 Villard de Honnecourt, *Lodgebook,* XIII c. Paris, Bibliotéque Nationale, ms. fr. 19093.

9.1 Duccio, "Maestà", 7x13 ft., Museo dell'opera del Duomo, Siena, Italy.

9.2 C. Sitte, *City Planning According to Artistic Principles,* 1889, reprint, G. Collins and C. Collins, *The Birth of Modern City Planning,* New York 1989.

9.3 A. Lorenzetti, "View of a Town", c. 1338–1340, Tempera on Wood, 9"x13 1/8", Pinoteca Nazionale, Siena, Italy.

9.4, 9.13 G. Gromort, *Grandes compositiones executées,* Paris 1925.

9.5, 9.6, 9.8, 9.12 , 9.20, 9.38, 9.39, 9.45 Photo, Robert S. Livesey.

9.7 Benevolo, Leonardo, *The History of the City.* Reproduced with permission by the publisher, MIT Press, Cambridge, MA.

9.10, 9.11 Drawn by Jon Stephens.

9.14 Drawn by Jon Stephens.

9.17-9.19, 9.36, 9.37 Thomas King, *The Study Book of Medieval Architecture and Art,* London 1858.

9.21 R. Sturgis, *Illustrated Dictionary of Architecture and Building, New* York 1902-1902, reprint New York 1989.

9.22 Tombstone of the Architect H. Limbergier, Reims Cathedral from J. Gimpel, *The Cathedral Builders,* (1961) New York 1984.

9.24, 9.25 M. Roriczer, *Büchlein von der Fialen Gerechtigkeit,* Regensburg 1486, fac. Wiesbaden 1965, from Frankl & Panofsky, "The Secret of the Medieval Masons", *Art Bulletin* XXVII, 1946.

9.26, 9.27 Drawn by Jon Stephens.

9.28 Stornoloco, 1391, from R. Wittkower, *Gothic vs. Classic,* New York 1974.

9.29 L. Beltrami, *Per la storia della costruzione del Duomo,* Milan 1887-88, from R. Wittkower, *Gothic vs. Classic,* New York 1974.

9.32, 9.33 J. Guadet, *Eléments et Theories,* vol. 2, Paris c.1894.

9.41 Brockhaus, *Iconological Encyclopedia of Architecture,* vol. IV., Leipzig and Philadelphia 1885.

9.42 A. Maquet, *Sous Louis XIV - Monuments et vies,* Paris 1883.

9.43, 9.44 Decloux et Doury, *Histoire Archéologique et graphique de Sainte Chapelle,* Paris 1857.

9.46 B. Fletcher, *A History of Architecture,* 5th edition, New York and London 1905.

Chapter 10

10.1 F. di Giorgio Martini, Turin, Cod. Saluzziano 148, fol. 3, from Kruft, *Storia delle teorie architettoniche,* Bari 1988.

10.2 F. di Giorgio, Turin, Cod. Saluzziano, from Wittkower, *Architectural Principles in the Age of Humanism,* (1949), New York 1971.

10.3 F. di Giorgio, Florence, Biblioteca Nazionale, Cod. Magliabecchiano II, I, fol. 47, from Kruft, *Storia delle teorie architettoniche,* Bari 1988.

10.4 Dürer, Formerly Dresden Sächische Landesbibliotek, c. 1523, from Panofsky, *Meaning in the Visual Arts,* Garden City, N.Y., 1955.

10.5 F. di Giorgio, *De Harmonia Mundi,* 1525, from R. Wittkower, *Architectural Principles in the Age of Humanism,* (1949), New York 1971.

10.6 B. Peruzzi, Sketch, Florence, Uffizi #481 Ar, from Würm, *Baldassare Peruzzi: Architekturzeichnungen ,* Tübigen 1984.

10.7 C. Cesariano, *Vitruvius,* Como 1521, fac. 1968.

10.9 Masaccio, "Trinità", Florence, Santa Maria Novella, from H.W. Janson, *History of Art*, Englewood Cliffs, N.J., 1970. Photo by author.

10.10 Raphael, "School of Athens", Stanza della Segnatura, Vatican, from H.W. Janson, *History of Art*, Englewood Cliffs, N.J., 1970. Photo by author.

10.12 Giovanni da Prato, drawing, Florence, Archivio di Stato, from Battisti, *Brunelleschi: The Complete Work*, New York 1981.

10.13 B. Fletcher, *A History of Architecture*, 5th edition, New York and London 1905.

10.14, 10.20, 10.21, 10.24, 10.49, 10.57-10.61 Photo, Robert S. Livesey.

10.16-10.18, 10.28-10.30, 10.40 J. Burckhardt, *The Architecture of the Italian Renaissance*, 1867, reprint Chicago 1985.

10.27 F.M. Simpson, *A History of Architectural Development*, London, New York, Bombay, Calcutta and Madras, 1921.

10.32 Filarete, *Trattato di Architettura*, Florence, Biblioteca Nazionale, Cod. Magliabecchiano II, I, 140. fol 41r, Sforzinda, from Argan, *The Renaissance City*, New York 1969.

10.33, 10.34 F. di Giorgio, Florence, Biblioteca Nazionale, Cod. Magliabecchiano, from Argan, *The Renaissance City*, New York 1969.

10.35 Bertelli, 1599, Palmanova, from Argan, *The Renaissance City*, New York 1969.

10.36 Uffizi #613 Ar, from H. Würm, *Baldassare Peruzzi: Architekturzeichnungen* , Tübigen 1984.

10.37 Galleria Nazionale delle Marche, Urbino, from Argan, *The Renaissance City*, New York 1969.

10.38 S. Serlio, *Tutte l'opere d'architettura*, 1537-51, fac. Ridgewood, N.J. 1964.

10.39 "Mona Lisa", c. 1503–1506. Oil on wood. 30 1/4"x12". The Louvre, Paris.

10.45, 10.46, 10.51, 10.52, 10.54 P. Letaurouilly, *Edifices de Rome moderne*, Paris 1840, reprint Princeton 1982.

10.50 J. Ackerman, *The Villa*, Princeton 1985.

10.65 W. Dieterlin, *Architettura*, 1598.

Chapter 11

11.0, 11.13, 11.50 G. Gromort, *Grandes compositiones exécutées*, Paris 1925.

11.1 G. Bibiena, *Architettura e Prospettive*, Augsburg, 1740.

11.2 F. Borromini, *Opus Architectonicum*, Rome 1720.

11.3, 11.16, 11.17, 11.22, 11.24, 11.29, 11.41, 11.45 Photo, Robert S. Livesey.

11.4 Anon, 18th c. Reproduced with permission by Staatliches Museum, Schwerin.

11.5 Bernini, Gian Lorenzo, *Ecstasty of St. Theresa.* Rome, S. Maria della Vittoria. Alinari / Art Resource.

11.8 From *Design of Cities*, by Edmund Bacon. Copyright © 1967, 1974 by Edmund Bacon. Used by permission of Viking Penguin, a division of Penguin Books USA, Inc.

11.9 Reproduced with permission by Jon Michael Schwarting.

11.10 G.F. Bordoni, "Veduta Schematica del Piano stradale ideato da Sisto V", 1588, From E. Bacon, *The Design of Cities*, Harmondsworth 1978.

11.11 G.B. Nolli, *Plan of Rome*, Rome 1748.

11.12 G.B. Piranesi, *Vedute di Roma*, Rome 1756,

11.14 M.G. Rossi, "Veduta della Chiesa e Convento di S. Carlino alle Quattro Fontane", from E. Bacon, *The Design of Cities*, Harmondsworth 1978.

11.15, 11.30 P. Letaurouilly, *Edifices de Rome moderne*, Paris 1840, reprint Princeton 1982.

11.18 Borromini, F. Reproduced with permission by Albertina Museum, Vienna, Austria.

11.19 Florence, Uffizi Gabinetto Disegni e Stampe, from F. Borsi, *Bernini*, New York 1984.

11.20, 11.21 G.B. Falda, *Vedute di Roma*, 18th c.

11.23 The Vatican, Biblioteca Apostolica, Cod. Chigi PVII 12, from Borsi, *Bernini*, New York 1984.

11.26 M.G.. de Rossi, *Nuova Pianta di Roma Presente*, (1668) 1773, from C. Sitte, *City Planning According to Artistic Principles*, 1889, reprint, G. Collins and C. Collins, *The Birth of Modern City Planning*, New York 1989.

11.31-11.34 G. Guarini, *Architettura Civile*, Turin 1739, reprint London 1964.

11.36 Reproduced with permission by Jon Michael Schwarting.

11.37 G.B. Nolli, *Plan of Rome*, Rome 1748.

11.40 M. Fouquier, *De l'art des jardins*, Paris 1911.

11.42 Silvestre, 18th c. engraving, from Jellicoe, *The Landscape of Man*, New York 1978.

11.43 J. Marot, *Grand Marot*, Paris 1670, fac. Paris 1970, from M. Dennis, *Court and Garden*, Cambridge 1986.

Chapter 12

12.0 Bierstadt, Albert, *Indian Emcampment in the Rockies*, engraving, 1866. Reproduced with permission by Amon Carter Museum, Fort Worth, Texas.

12.1 Leonardo, *The History of the City.* Reproduced with permission by the publisher, MIT Press, Cambridge, MA.

12.2 Drawn by Jon Stephens.

12.7, 12.10, 12.15 L. Benevolo, *The History of the City,* Cambridge 1980.

12.32 Nineteenth-century engraving, from S. & G. Jellicoe, *The Landscape of Man,* New York 1978.

12.3, 12.4, 12.11-12.13, 12.16, 12.17, 12.27, 12.29 V. Scully, *American Architecture and Urbanism,* New York and London 1969.

12.26 Nineteenth-century document, from C. Tunnard, *The City of Man,* New York and London 1953.

12.6 Model, Pergamon Museum, Berlin, author's photo.

12.8 Montpazier, from Le Corbusier, *The City of Tomorrow* (1929), Cambridge 1982.

12.9 Cataneo, *L'architettura.* 16th c.

12.14 J. Evelyn, London Plan 1666, from S.E. Rasmussen, *London: Unique City,* (1934) New York 1974.

12.19, 12.24 Drawn by Jon Stephens after J. Reps.

12.23, 12.25 Nineteenth-century engravings from J. Reps, *Town Planning in Frontier America,* Princeton 1965.

12.20 P. Gordon engraving, 1734.

12.28, 12.33, 12.34, 12.36, 12.37 Photo, Robert S. Livesey.

12.30 M. Fouquier, *De l'art des jardins,* Paris 1911.

12.31 J. Guadet, *Eléments et Theories,* vol. 2, Paris c.1894.

12.35, 12.38 C.N. Ledoux, *L'architecture considerée sous le rapport de l'art, des moeurs et de la législation,,* Edition Ramée, Paris 1847, reprint Princeton 1985.

12.39-12.41 Frank Lloyd Wright Drawings are copyright © 1945, 1957, 1958, 1960, 1962 The Frank Lloyd Wright Foundation. All rights reserved.

Chapter 13

13.0 19th c. engravings, from J.M. Crook, *The Dilemma of Style,* Chicago 1987.

13.1 Lorrain, Claude. Reproduced with permission by The Fairhaven Collection, Anglesey Abbey (The National Trust), Cambridgeshire.

13.2 Nicholas Poussin, The Louvre, Paris.

13.3-13.5, 13.29-13.31, 13.33 Photo, Robert S. Livesey.

13.6 Friedrich, Caspar David, *The Wanderer Above the Mist.* Hamburg, Kunsthalle. Foto Marburg / Art Resource.

13.7 Turner, J.M.W., *Snow Storm: Steam-Boat Off a Harbour's Mouth.* Exhibited 1842. London, Tate Gallery. Clore Collection, Tate Gallery, London / Art Resource.

13.8-.10, 13.14 Boulée, E.L. Reproduced with permission by Bibliothèque Nationale, Paris, France.

13.11-13.13 C.N. Ledoux, *L'architecture considerée sous le rapport de l'art, des moeurs et de la législation,,* Edition Ramée, Paris 1847, reprint Princeton 1985.

13.15 Cole, Thomas, *The Architect's Dream.* Reproduced with permission by The Toledo Museum of Art.

13.22, 13.23 Viollet-le-Duc, *Entretiens (Lectures on Architecture),* 1881, 1887, reprint New York.

13.24 M.A. Laugier, *Essai sur l'architecture,* frontispiece, second ed., Paris 1755.

13.25 Semper, *Der Stil in den technischen und tektonischen Künsten oder praktische Aesthetik,* Frankfurt 1860, reprint Mittenwelt 1979.

13.26-13.28 19th century engraving, from Frampton, *Modern Architecture 1851-1945,* New York 1983.

13.31 Turn of the century engraving from Le Corbusier, *The City of Tomorrow,* (1929) Cambridge 1982.

Chapter 14

14.0 El Lissitzky, from *Harvard Architecture Review VI,* 1987.

14.1 Picasso, Pablo. *Violin and Grapes.* Ceret and Sorgues (spring-summer, 1912). Oil on canvas, 20x24". The Museum of Modern Art, New York. Mrs. David M. Levy Bequet.

14.2 Le Corbusier (Charles-Edouard Jeanneret). *Still Life,* 1920. Oil on canvas, 31 7/8"x39 1/4". The Museum of Modern Art, New York. Van Gogh Purchase Fund.

14.3 Duchamp, M., Philadelphia Museum of Art: Bequest of Katherine S. Dreier. Reproduced by permission.

14.4, 14.13, 14.14, 14.15, 14.22, 14.21, 14.25-14.27 Redrawn by Jon Stephens.

14.5 Duchamp, M., Philadelphia Museum of Art: Louise and Walter Arensberg Collection. Reproduced by permission.

14.6, 14.7, 14.61 Gropius, W. Reproduced with permission by Harvard University Art Museums, Cambridge, MA.

14.8 Weissenhofsiedlung. 1925-27. Photo courtesy, Mies van der Rohe Archive, The Museum of Modern Art, New York.

14.10, 14.48, .50 Photo, Robert S. Livesey.

14.16 Le Corbusier, from J. Ackerman, *The Villa,* Princeton 1985.

14.17 Redrawn after C. Rowe by Jon Stephens.

14.20 A. Palladio, *Four Books on Architecture,* (1570) New York 1965.

14.24 Le Corbusier, from C. Rowe, *The Mathematics of the Ideal Villa,* Cambridge 1977.

14.28-14.30 K.F. Schinkel, *Sammlung Architektonischer Entwürfe,* 1866, reprint and translation, *Collection of Architectural Designs,* Chicago 1984.

14.34, 14.36, 14.37, 14.41 Frank Lloyd Wright Drawings are copyright © 1945, 1957, 1958, 1960, 1962 The Frank Lloyd Wright Foundation. All rights reserved.

14.42, 14.45 Reproduced with permission by Dion Neutra.

14.46 Robert vant'Hoff, from Zevi, *La poetica dell'-architettura neoplastica,* Turin 1974.

14.47 Mondrian, Piet, *Composition with Red, Yellow, and Blue.* Oil on canvas, 1927, 51.1x51.1 cm. Dutch 1872-1944. © Contemporary Collection of the Cleveland Museum of Art, 67.215.

14.51 T. Brown, *The Work Of Gerrit Rietveld,* Cambridge.

14.52 van Doesburg, Theo (C.E.M. Kupper). *Rhythm of a Russian Dance,* 1918. Oil on canvas, 53 1/2x 24 1/4. The Museum of Modern Art, New York. Acquired through the Lillie P. Bliss Bequest.

14.53-14.54 Brick Country House, 1924. Elevation and Plan (drawings no longer extant). Photo courtesy Mies van der Rohe Archive, The Museum of Modern Art, New York.

14.57, 14.59 German Pavilion, Barcelona. 1928-1929. Floor plan. Final scheme. Made for publication in 1929. Ink, pencil on paper, 22 1/2"x38 1/2". Mies van der Rohe Archive, The Museum of Modern Art, New York. Gift of the architect.

14.62 Redrawn after W. Gropius by Jon Stephens.

14.63 Photo, Christine Carlyle.

14.64 W. Gropius, from J.M. Fitch, *Walter Gropius,* New York 1960.

14.67 Farnsworth House, Fox River Plano, Illinois. 1946-51. Plan. Ink on illustration board, 30x40". Mies van der Rohe Archive, The Museum of Modern Art, New York, Gift of the architect.

Chapter 15

15.0 Hausemann, R., *Tatlin at Home.* Reproduced with permission by Statens Konstmuseer, The Swedish National Art Museums.

15.2, 15.10, 15.11, 15.18 Photo, Robert S. Livesey.

15.4 G. Gromort, *Grandes compositiones exécutées,* Paris 1925.

15.5 C. Hussey and A.S.G. Butler, *Lutyens Memorial Volumes,* 3 vols. London 1951.

15.6 P. Inskip, *Edward Lutyens,* London 1979.

15.7-15.9 Reproduced with permission by Rollin R. LaFrance, Venturi & Scott Brown Architects (VSBA).

15.12, 15.14, 15.17 Reproduced with permission by Robert Venturi, Venturi & Scott Brown Architects.

15.19 Aldo Rossi, *Progetti e disegni 1962-1979/Aldo Rossi. Projects and Drawings 1962-1979,* edited by Francesco Moschini, Centro Di, Florence, 1979.

15.20 A. Aalto, *Alvar Aalto, Gesamtwerk,* Band 1, Zürich 1963.

15.25 Stuttgart: Neue Staatsgalerie and Chamber Theatre. By permission of James Stirling / Michael Wilford.

15.29 Stuttgart: Neue Staatsgalerie and Chamber Theatre. By permission of James Stirling / Michael Wilford.

15.30 Redrawn after Mendelsohn by Jon Stephens.

15.36-37 Redrawn after Terragni by Jon Stephens.

15.38 *Architectural Design,* London 5 / 6 1983.

15.39-44 El Lissitzky, *Πpo 2 ◻, (About 2 Squares),* 1920, reprinted in S. Lissitzky-Küppers, *El Lissitzky: Maler, Architekt, Typograf, Fotograf,* Dresden 1967.

15.45-47, 15.49, 15.50 Reproduced with permission by Peter Eisenman.

15.56 Reproduced with permission by Bernard Tschumi, Columbia University, New York.

15.57, 15.58 H. Klotz, *The History of Post Modern Architecture,* Cambridge and London 1988.

Appendix

A.0 Ciampini, engraving, from *Via 8.*

A.1 Pèlerin, *De artificiali p(er)spectiva,* 1505, from D. Wiebenson, *Architectural Theory and Practice from Alberti to Ledoux,* New York 1982.

A.2 Cousin, *Livre de Perspective* , 1560, from D. Wiebenson, *Architectural Theory and Practice from Alberti to Ledoux,* New York 1982.

A.3 de l'Orme, *Le premier tome de l'architecture,* 1567, from Wiebenson, *Architectural Theory and Practice from Alberti to Ledoux,* New York 1982.

A.5 van Doesburg, Theo and Cornelis van Eesteren, *Color Construction.* Project for a private house, 1923. Gouache, 22 1/2x22 1/2. The Museum of Modern Art, New York. Edgar J. Kaufmann, Jr. Fund.

A.4, A.6 W.B. Field, *Architectural Drawing,* New York 1912.

A.7 I. Latham, *Joseph Maria Olbrich,* London and New York 1980.

A.9 Oxford: Queen's College, St. Clements: Student Halls of Residence. Concept sketch by James Stirling, by permission of James Stirling/Michael Wilford.

A.10, A.11, A.22, A.23 Photo, Robert S. Livesey.

A.13 Photo, Jay Gargus.

A.16- A.18 L. Carroll, *Alice in Wonderland,* Illus. John Tenniel. New York 1865, reprint New York 1960.

A.19 *The Work of Frank Lloyd Wright,* Wendingen Edition, Amsterdam 1923, reprint New York 1965.

A.24 Juan Bautista Villalpando, *In Ezechielem Explanationes,* 1596, from D. Wiebenson, *Architectural Theory and Practice from Alberti to Ledoux,* New York 1982.

A.25 *Architectural Design,* 1/2 1981.

A.31 Redrawn after Terragni by Jon Stephens.

A.33 C.F. McKim, W.R. Mead & S. White, *A Monograph of the Works of McKim, Mead and White,* 1915, Reprint L. Roth and B. Blom, ed., New York 1977.

Index

Aalto, Alvar
  Baker House Dormitory, Cambridge *15*
  Otaniemi University, Otaniemi, Finland *304, 305*
  Säynätsalo Town Center, Säynätsalo, Finland *50*, 51
Abbot Suger 155
About Two Squares (El Lissitzky) 312, *313*
Abstraction 88, 298, 302, 308, *347*
Abu Simbel, Egypt
  Rock Temple of Ramesses II 93, *94*
Asceticism 154
Acropolis, Athens *100, 111*, 110,*112*, 347
Additive Form 95, 175, 347
Aedicula, aedicule 200, 206, 349, 347
AEG Turbine Factory, Berlin 64, *65*
Aeniad (Virgil) 248
Aesculapius, Sanctuary of *129*
Agon 101f.
Agora 15, 115f., 126, 347
Agrarian ideal 242, 347
Agrigentum (Agrigento, Italy) 224
  Temple of Concord *110*
  Temple of Olympian Zeus 104
Aisle 347
Alberti, Leonbattista 77, 167, 171, 173, 177f., 201, 290, 325
  Palazzo Rucellai, Florence 338, *339*
  San Andrea, Mantua *178, 179*, 180
  Santa Maria Novella, Florence *178*, 179
Albers, Joseph 287
Alexander VII (Pope) 141, 206
Alice in Wonderland (L. Carroll) 337, *338*
Alighieri, Dante, see Dante Alighieri
Algarotti 197
Allegory 77, 186, 247, 347
All Souls College, Oxford *295*
Altesmuseum, Berlin 270f., *273*, 306, 307
Ambiguity 264f, 295, 296, 347
Ambulatory 181, 347
Amenhotep III, Mortuary Temple 91, *92*
Amerikanismus 275
Amiens, France *158*
Amphitheater 102,*103*, 347
Analytic Cubism 263f., 347
Anecdote of the Jar (W. Stevens) 3
Angst 347
Ankor Wat, Cambodia 224, *225*
Annular 347
Anthemius of Thralles
  Hagia Sophia, Istanbul 74, *75*
Anthropomorphism 49, 96, 169, 105, 347
Apollo 101, 248
Apprenticeship 169
Apse 347
Aqua Felice 202
Aqueduct 122, 347
Aquinas, Thomas 145
Arc-et-Senans, France
  Salt Works *(Salines)* at Chaux 241f.
Arcade 156, 347
Arcadia 243, 247, 347
Arch 347
Archaic 347
Archaic period 126
Archetype 102 f., 302, 347
Architectonic 347
Architectural Principles in the Age of Humanism (R. Wittkower) 45, 171
Architectural Space in Ancient Greece (K.A. Doxiadis) 109
Architect's Dream, The (T. Cole) *251*
Architecture Parlante 250f. 251, 347
Architettura, L' (P. Cattaneo) 226, *227*
Architrave 104, 108, 348
Arcuation 156, 348
Arena 141, 348
Argan, Giulio Carlo 198
Aristotle 101
Arithmetic Mean 341, 348

Arno River 34
Arricia, Italy
  Palazzo Chigi 208
  S. Maria della Assunzione 208, *209*
Art Nouveau 261
Articulation 173. 175, 190, 192, 288, 339f., 348
Asceticism 348
Association, Associationism 251, 348
Asymmetry 83, 126f., 297, 298, 348
Atelier 348
Athena 110f.
Athena Nike, Temple 111, *113*
Athena Polias, Temple 113
Atheneum, New Harmony, Ind. *318*, 320
Athenian Agora 15,*115, 116*, 126
Athens
  Acropolis *100, 111*, 110, *112*
  Agora *115, 116*
  Erechteion 113, *114*
  Hephasteion Temple *115*
  Parthenon 69, *71*, 104, *107*, 110, *112*
  Stoa of Attalos *14*
  Propylaea *111*
  Temple to Athena Nike 111, *113*
Atlanta, Georgia 46, *47*
Atrium 350, 348
Auflösung der Stadt 68
Aurelian Walls 217
Avant-garde 261, 264, 274, 275, 320, 348
Axiality 102f., 123f., 133, 186, 199, 204f., 348
Axis 12, 13, 62, 73, 102f., 123f., 133, 186f., 218, 223f., 298, 302, 348
Axis Mundi 13, 62, 73, 283, 348
Axonometric Drawing, *327*, 328f., 348
Babylon 223
Bacon, Edmund 21
  Development of Athens Agora 115, *116*
  Sixtus V's Plan of Rome 204
Bacon, Henry
  Lincoln Memorial, Washington D.C. *336*
Bagnaia, Italy *187*, 247
Baker House Dormitory, Cambridge, MA. 15
Ballustrade 348
Baptistry 76, 348
Bar/Object organization 52, 348
Barbarians 168
Barberini 221
Barcelona, Spain
  Barcelona (German) Pavilion 284f., *285, 286*, 291
  Santa Coloma de Cervello *50*, 51
Barcelona Pavilion (German Pavilion), Barcelona 284f., *285, 286*, 291
Baroque 80, 81, 197f., 348
Barrel vault 133, 134, *135*, 171, 180, 181, 348
Base 96, 104, 348
Basilica 73f, 129, 154f., 175, 348
Basilica Aemilia 129
Basilica Julia 129
Bastide 226, 229, 348
Baths of Caracalla, Rome *134, 136, 137, 138*
Bauhaus, Dessau 283, 287f., *288, 289, 290, 291*, 295, 302, 309
Bay 348
Beam 348
Bearing wall 269, 333, 348
Bear Run, Pennsylvania
  Kaufmann House (Falling Water) 277f., *278*
Beauvais, France 160,*163*, 164
Beauvais, Hôtel de, see Hôtel de Beauvais
Beaux-Arts 348, see Ecole des Beaux-Arts
Behrens, Peter
  AEG Turbine Factory, Berlin 64, *65*
Beijing, China 224, *225*
Benjamin Franklin Parkway, Philadelphia 233
Berlin
  AEG Turbine Factory 64, *65*
  Altesmuseum 270f., *273*, 307
  Neuwache *59*
  New National Gallery *291*
  Philharmonic Hall 53, *54*
  Schloß Glienicke *252*, 253
  Tenements 261
  Unité d'Habitation *343*
Berlin Philharmonic Hall, Berlin 53, *54*
Bernini, Gianlorenzo 175, 214
  Pantheon project 206, *208*
  S. Andrea al Quirinale, Rome 206f, *207*
  S. Maria della Assunzione, Arricia 208, *209*
  S. Teresa in Ecstasy, (Bernini), Cornaro Chapel, Rome *199, 200*
  S. Peter's Cortile, Rome *196*, 209, *210*, 231
Bertelli, Pietro *31*
Bibiena, Giuseppe *198*
Bierstadt, Albert
  Indian Encampment in the Rockies 222
Big Box of Bricks Project (Gropius) *265*
Billboard 302
Biomorphic 348
Bird's eye view 331, 348

Birth of Venus (S. Botticelli) *77*
Black death 164, 169, 170
Bloomfield Hills, Michigan *23*
Boccaccio, Giovanni 173
Bomarzo, Italy*192*, 193
Bordino, G.F.
Streets of Sixtus V *203*
Borromini, Francesco
Oratorio of S. Filippo Neri, Rome *198*, *199*
S. Carlo alle Quattro Fontane, Rome *80*, *81*, 199, 210, 204, *205*, *206*, *207*
S. Ivo alle Sapienza, Rome 210, *211*, *212*
Bosque 218, 348
Boston, Massachusetts 227, *228*
Botticelli, Sandro
Birth of Venus 77
Boullée, Etienne-Louis
Cenotaph to Newton *249*, 250
Bourges, France 163
Bracket 348
Bramante, Donato
S. Maria presso S. Satiro, Milan 78, *79*, 80, 193
S. Peter's, Rome *180*, 181
Tempietto of S. Pietro in Montorio, Rome *44*, *78*, 181
Braque, Georges 263
Breuer, Marcel 287
Brick Country House Project *284*
Bride Stripped Bare by Her Bachelors, Even (M. Duchamp) *263*
Brinckmann, J.A.
Van Nelle Chocolate and Tobacco Factory, Rotterdam *287*
Brise soliel 348
Broadacre City 242, *243*
Brunelleschi, Filippo 171, 174f., 177, 180
Pazzi Chapel, Florence *176*, *177*
S. Maria dei Fiori, Florence 173, *174*, *175*
S. Spirito, Florence *176*
Buffalo, New York 275, *277*
Buonarotti, Michelangelo, see Michelangelo
Buoninsegna, Duccio di, see Duccio di Buoninsegna
Burke, Edmund 249
Buttress 163, 173, 349
Byzantine 145, 349
California
Los Angeles 31, 279, *280*, 281, *302*
Callicrates *71*, 107,*112*, 113
Cambridge, Massachusetts *15*
Cambridge, England 173
Campanile 349
Campidoglio, Rome 185, *186*, 198
Campo Santo, Pisa, Italy 302, *303*
Campus Martius, Rome (Piranesi) *124*, 125
Canopy 349
Cantilever 265, 277, 349
Capetian monarchs *161*
Capital 96, 104, 349
Capitalism 274
Capitoline, see Campidoglio
Capitolium 127
Caracalla, Baths of *134*, *136*, *137*, *138*
Caracas (Santiago de Leon), Venezuela *227*, 228, 229
Cardo 123, 234, 349
Carroll, Lewis 337, *338*
Cartesian Space 217f, 237, 238, 261, 294, 317f., 349
Carthusian Monastery, Pavia, Italy 151f., *152*
Caryatid 113, *114*, 349
Casa del Fascio, Como, Italy *342*, *343*
Casale Monferreto, Italy *212*
Casino 187, 349
Castel S. Angelo (Piranesi) 122
Castra 349, see Roman camp
Cataneo, Pietro
Anthropomorphic Church Plan *49*
Plan of Vitruvian Town 226, *227*, 233
Cavaletto 192
Cedar Rapids, Iowa *337*
Cella 69, 71, 103,132, 286, 291, 349
Cellular 26, 137, 349
Cemetery, Modena 302, *303*
Cenotaph to Newton *249*, 250, 349
Center 11f., 76, 81, 136, 223f., 297, 298, 304, 349
Centering 174
Center line 333, 349
Centralized plan 74f., 79, 173, 181, 206, 349
Ceres 108, *109*
Certosa di Pavia, see Carthusian Monastery, Pavia
Cesariano, Cesare
Proportions for Rectangles *170*
Vitruvian Man *41*, 42
Chancel 349
Chandigarh, India
Palace of Assembly 270f., *272*
Chapter House 76, 349
Character 251, 294, 349
Charette 349
Charlottesville, Virginia

Monticello *238*
University of Virginia *58, 240*
Chartres, France *154, 155*
Chatsworth, England *15*
Chaux, France
Salt Works 240, *241, 242*
Chefren, Pharoah 88, 102
Cheops 89
Chephren 89
Chernikhov, Iakov 312f., 320
Architectural Rhythms for the New Aesthetic 312, *313*
Chester 123
Chestnut Hill, Pennsylvania
Vanna Venturi House 298, *299*
Chicago, Illinois
Robie House *61, 274, 275*
Chigi Palace, Arricia, see Palazzo Chigi
Choir 153f., 163f., 349
Chomsky, Noam 316
Chthonic 349
Circleville, Ohio 236, *237*
Circleville Squaring Company 237
Circular plan 67
Cirogna, Italy
Villa Thiene *45*
Circulation 16, 218, 349
City of Tomorrow, The (Le Corbusier) 208, 258, *259*
Civic Building, Cedar Rapids, Iowa *337*
Civitas Dei 154
Cladding 349
Classical Language of Architecture, The (J. Summerson) 296, 297
Classicism 175f., 184f., 198f., 248, 296, 349
Claude, see Lorrain, Claude
Clerestory 73, 156, 161, 304, 349
Cloisters 151, 152
Clustered organization 349
Coffers 80, 180, 349, 349
Cole, Thomas 223
The Architect's Dream 251
Collage 52, 263, 264, 349
Collage City (C. Rowe & F. Koetter) 34-35
College of Cardinals 202
Collocatio 178
Cologne, France
Pavilion for the Glass Industry *44*
Colonnade 349
Colossal order 185, 349
Colosseum, Rome *58, 120,* 204, 310
Columbus, Christopher 227
Columbus, Indiana
Fire Station No. 4 *301*
Columbus, Ohio
The Ohio State University Oval *24,* 25
Wexner Center for the Visual Arts *316, 317*
Column 96, 108, 169, 191, 349
Columniation 65, 349
Como, Italy *343*
Complexity and Contradiction in Architecture (R. Venturi) 298f.
Composite Order 120, 350
Composition with Red, Black, Blue, Yellow and Grey (Mondrian) 281, *282*
Compression 95. 96, 133, 350
Concrete shell 51
Connecticut
New Haven 194, *195,* 229, *230,* 233, 234
Constantine 120
Constantinian Head (statue fragment), Rome *121*
Constantinople, see Istanbul
Construction of Architectural Forms and Machines, The (I Chernikhov) 312, *313*
Constructivism 261, 320, 350
Cooper's Workshop (C.N. Ledoux) *250,* 251
Core 350
Corinthian order 104, *105, 107,* 179, 350
Corn crib *12*
Cornaro Chapel *199, 200*
Cornice 104, 169, 350
Corridor 350
Cortile 350
Cortona, Pietro da
S. Maria della Pace, Rome 212, *213*
Coulton, J.J.
Doric Temple with Refinements 107, *109*
Council Chamber, Miletus 104
Council of Trent 79
Counterpoint 199, 350
Counter-Reformation 197, 350
Court and Garden, Michael Dennis 228
Courtyard 350
Cousin, Jean,
Livre de Perspective 326
Cow Stable (Lequeu) *251*
Cranbrook School, Bloomfield Hills, Mich. *23*
Crenelation 250, 350
Cross axis 123, 130, 287, 350
Crossing 76, 161, 350

Cross section 333
Cross vault 133, 350
Cruciform plan 75, 350
Crusades 145, 146
Crystal Palace, London 255, *256*, *257*
Crypt 350
Cubism 263f., 310, 350
Cubitt, Lewis
King's Cross Station *64*
Cult of Carts 145
Cupola 350
Curtain wall 288, 350
Cybernetics 294, 350
Dante Alighieri 173, 310
Danteum Project, Rome 310, *311*, 312
Darmstadt, Germany,
Großes Glückert House *331*
Datum 10, 39, 40, 52, 350
Dayton, Ohio 60
Deanery Gardens, Sonning *297*
Decentralization 242, *243*, 294, 350
Deconstruction 319f., 350
Decumanus 123, 234, 350
Deir-el-Bahari, Egypt
Mortuary Temple of Queen Hatshepsut 94, *95*
Delaware River 232
Delphi, Greece
Sanctuary of Apollo *110*
Tholos at Delphi *69*, *70*
Dematerialization 75f., 82, 155, 161, 164, 198, 255, 279, 282, 284, 319, 350
Demeter 101
Democracy 101, 228, 241
Dennis, Michael 228
Derrida, Jacques 319f.
Descartes, René 218, 237, 245
Design of Cities, Edmund Bacon 21, 115, *116*, 204
Dessau, Germany
Bauhaus 287f., *288*, *289*, *290*, *291*
De Stijl 261, 281, 283, 284, 350
Dialectic 350
Dictionaire d'architecture encyclopédie méthodique 57
Dietterlin, Wendel *193*
Diocletian *125*, *126*
Diocletian's Palace, Split *125*, 126
Dionysius 101
Divine Comedy, The, (Dante Alighieri) 310, 311
Doesburg, Theo van 284
Rhythm of a Russian Dance 283, *284*
Color Construction, Project for a Private House, 330
Dome 134, 350
Dom-ino House 265, *267*
Domitian 140
Donald Duck 247
Doric Order 104, *105*, *106*, *107*, 252, 296, 350
Doryphoros (Polyclitus) 120, *121*
Doxiadis, K.A. 109f.
Athenian Acropolis *111*
Drum 351
Duccio di Buoninsegna,
Maestà 147, 149
Duchamp, Marcel
Bride Stripped Bare by Her Bachelors, Even (Large Glass) 263
Nude Descending a Staircase 262, 263
"Ducks and Decorated Sheds" (R. Venturi) *301*, *302*
Duomo 351
Durand, Jean-Nicolas-Louis
Precise des Leçons 56
Dürer, Albrecht
Study of Human Proportion *169*
Dynamic symmetry 117
Early Christian 145
Earth deities 101, 248
Earth, the Temple and the Gods, The (V. Scully) 103f
Eaves 351
Eclectic 248, 351
Ecole des Beaux-Arts 39, 287, 295, 310, 351
Egypt
Column detail *98*
Great Pyramids, Giza *89*
Mortuary Temple of Amenhotep III, Luxor 91, *92*
Mortuary Temple of Hatshepsut, Deir-el-Bahari 94, *95*
Mortuary Temple of Ramesses III, Medinet Habu 91, *93*
Pyramid of Cheops, Giza *12*, *89*
Rock Temple of Ramesses II, Abu Simbel 93, *94*
Temple of Khons, Karnak *90*, *91*
Egyptian Revival 253
Eiffel, Gustave 293
Eiffel Tower, Paris *257*
Train bridge at St. Andrew de Cubzak 258, *259*
Viaduct at Garabit 258, *259*
Einstein Tower, Potsdam *308*, *309*
Eisenman, Peter 314f., 319
House III *314*, 315
House IV *314*
House X *315*

Transformational Diagrams *315*
Wexner Center for the Visual Arts, Columbus, Ohio *316, 317*
Elevation, 331, 351
Elevation oblique, 329, 351
Eliot, T.S. 321
El-Leggun, Jordan *122*
Ellicott, Andrew
Washington D.C. *236*
Ellicott City, Maryland *60*
El Lissitzky
About Two Squares 312, *313*
Tatlin at Work 260
Emerson, Ralph Waldo 256
Enfilade 191, 351
Engineering 255f., 261f.
Enlightenment 228f., 239, 245, 351
Entablature 104, 179, 351
Entasis 105, 351
Epidaurus, Greece
Theater *103*
Erechteion, Athens 113, *114*
Erosion 351
Escher, M.C.
Sky and Water 1 (M.C. Escher) *22*
Essai sur l'architecture (M.A. Laugier) *69*
Esquisse 39, 351
Euclid 202, 237
Evans, Robin 286
Evelyn, John
Plan for Rebuilding London *230, 231*, 233
Exedra 351
Exeter, New Hampshire
Exeter Library *46*
Expressionism 193, 261, 287, 309, 351
Facade 154, 160, 178, 179, 199f., 204, 206. 209, 213, 331, 351
Fairmount Park, Philadelphia 233f.
Falda, G.B.
Engraving of Arricia *209*
Engraving of Pantheon *208*
Falling Water (Kaufmann House), Bear Run, PA 277f., *278*
Fanzolo, Italy
Villa Emo *29, 30*
Farmer John's Bacon Factory, Los Angeles, CA *302*
Farnese Palace, see Palazzo Farnese
Farnsworth House, Plano, Illinois 290, *291*
Fenestration 46, 155, 351
Feudal society 145
Figure/Ground 24, 115, 126, 351
Figural object 126, 351
Figural space 126, 132, 351
Filarete, Antonio Averlino
Sforzinda 180, *181*
Film 263
Finial 351
Finitio 178
Fire Station No. 4, Columbus, Indiana *301*
Firmitas 178
Five Points of Architecture 267, *268*
Flitcroft, Henry
Stourhead, Stourton *246, 247*
Florence, Italy 123, 169, 173
Palazzo Rucellai 338, *339*
Pazzi Chapel *176, 177*
S. Maria dei Fiori 173, *174, 175*
S. Maria Novella *178*, 180
S. Miniato al Monte *294*, 295
S. Spirito *176*
Florey Building, Queen's College, Oxford *334*, 335
Florida
Seaside *337*
Fluting, flute 102, 351
Flying buttress *159*, 351
Folly 247, 351
Fontana, Domenico
Sixtus V's Plan of Rome 203
Football Hall of Fame Competition *301*
Fordismus 275
Foreshortening, 331, 351
Fortifications 182, 351
Fortuna Primagenia, Temple of *139, 140*
Fortuna Virilis, Temple of *132*
Forum 118, 123, 127, *128, 130*, 185, 351
Fouquet, Nicolas 215
Fourth dimension 263f.
Fragmentation 54, 199, 263f., 272, 315, 317, 319, 351
Frame structure 279, 288, 351
Francesco di Giorgio Martini 169
Anthropomorphic Town Plan *168*
Harmonia Mundi 170
Plan of a City Crossed by a River *182*
Plan of a City on a Hill *182*
Relationship of a Column and a Body *168*
Relationship of a Cornice and a Head *169*
Frankl, Paul 157f.
Free facade 267, 351
Free plan 267f., *268*, 269f., 272, 351

Free Plan vs. Bearing Wall (Le Corbusier) *267*, *268*, 351
Fresco 352
Friedrich, Casper David
The Wanderer Above the Mist 248
Frieze 104, 352
Frontality 69, 102, 123f., 352
Functionalism 261, 264, 287, 290, 305, 309, 352
Functional differentiation 288, 290
Funerary temples 91f. 102
Futurism 261, 320, 352
Gable 352
Galileo Galilei 202
Gallaratese Apartment Building, Milan 338, *339*
Gallery 156, 352
Gambero, Cardinal 186
Gambrel 352
Gandelsonas, Mario 316
Garches, France
Villa Stein *268*, *269*, *270*, *271*, 298
Gargoyle 160, 352
Garnier, Charles
Paris Opera House, Paris 53, *54*
Gas station 59, *60*
Gaudi, Antoni
Santa Coloma de Cervello, Barcelona *50*, 51
Gehry, Frank
Winton Guest House, Wayzeta, Minn. *52*, 53
Geometric Mean 341, 352
Geometry 169f., 179, 193, 293, 312 , 352
Genius 102, 123
Genius loci 123
Georgia
Atlanta 46, *47*
Savannah *234*, *235*
German Pavilion, Barcelona, see Barcelona Pavilion
German Werkbund, see Werkbund
Gibb, James *105*
Gilbert Scott, George 245
St. Pancras Station, London *64*
Gimpel, Jean 145
Giotto 167
Girasole Apartment Building, Rome 299, *300*
Giulio Romano, see Romano, Giulio
Giza, Egypt
Great Pyramids *89*
Pyramid of Cheops *12*, *89*
Glazing 352
Golden Mean 341, 352
Golden Rectangle 49, 312, *341*, *342*, 352
Golden Section 352
Gombrich, Ernst 87
Gothic 76, 81, 145f., 167, 168, 184, 198, 352
Gothic Revival 165, 252, 254, 320, 352
Grade 352
Graf, Douglas
Transformation of Palazzo Farnese 28, *29*
Transformation of Sanctuary of Aesculapius *129*
Grain elevator 59, *60*
Graphics 352
Great Pyramids, Giza *89*
Great Wheel, Paris 258, *259*
Gréber Plan of Philadelphia *233*
Greek Cross 78, 79, 181, 352
Greek Revival 252, 352
Green Still Life (Picasso) *51*, 52
Greenwich, England
S. Alfege *295*
Grid 29f., 39, 40, 45f., 75, 81, 123, 179, 181, 223f., 269, 282, 312, 317f., 219, 352
Grinnell, Iowa
Merchants' National Bank *336*
Groin vault 133, 134, *135*, 352
Gropius, Walter 265, 275, 287f., 293
Bauhaus, Dessau 287f., *288*, *289*, *290*, *291*
Big Box of Bricks Project 265
Plan and Section Comparison of Housing Blocks *265*
Großes Glückert House *331*
Grotto 188, 189, 248, 352
Guarini, Guarino 214
Nameless Church, Turin *212*
S. Filippo Neri, Casale Monferrato *212*
S. Maria della Divina Providenza, Lisbon 80, *81*
Guerini *341*
Hadid, Zaha
Peak Project, Hong Kong *319*, *321*
Hadrian's Villa, Tivoli *140*, *141*
Maritime Theater *141*
Hagia Sophia, Istanbul 74, *75*, 178
Hall of Giants, Palazzo del Tè, Mantua 191, 192
Haptic 21, 30, 353
Harmonic Mean 171, 178, 269, 341, 353
Harmonic proportion 41, 353
Harmony of the Spheres *11*, 12, 77, 353
Hatshepsut, Temple of 95, *95*, 97
Hausmann, Raoul
Tatlin at Home 292

Hawksmoor, Nicholas
All Souls College, Oxford *295*
St. Alfege, Greenwich *295*
Head / tail scheme 51
Heathcote, Ilkley *297*, 298
Hegel, Georg Wilhelm Friedrich 320
Heide, Holland
House 281, *282*
Hejduk, John
Mask of Medusa 17
Wall House I *16*, *17*
Wall House II *17*
Wall House III *52*
Hemicycle 123. 130, 136, 189, 206, 353
Henry IV 214
Hephasteion Temple, Athens *115*
Heraclitus 173
Hermeneutics 293, 353
Heterotopia 319, 353
Heuristic 121, 353
Hierarchy 19, 53, 90, 130, 146, 149, 152, 182, 239f., 305, 353
Hieroglyph 87
Highland Park, Illinois
Ward Willitts House *275*, *276*
High Museum, Atlanta 46, *47*
Hinge 123, 130
Hipped Roof 353
Hippodamus of Miletus
Miletus *224*, *225*, 226
Historicism 68, 251f., 261, 285f., 353
Hitchcock, Henry Russell 280
Hoare, Henry
Stourhead, Stourton *246*, *247*
Hoff, Rob van't
House at Heide 281, *282*
Holme, Thomas
Plan of Philadelphia *232*
Homogeneity 353
Hong Kong
Peak Project *319*, *321*
Honnecourt, Villard de 157, 163, 172
Sketches from Lodgebook *144*, 158
Key figure *156*
Hooke, Robert
Plan for Rebuilding London *231*, 232, 233
Horace 119
Horizon line 353
Hostel, Wroclaw *14*, 16
Hôtel de Beauvais, Paris *25*, 27
House III (Eisenman) *314*
House IV (Eisenman) *314*
House X (Eisenman) *315*
House at Heide 281, *282*
House for a Cooper's Workshop *250*, 251
House in Mykonos, Greece *53*
Hugo, Victor 293
Humanism 77, 167, 197, 201, 227, 353
Hybrid 39, 113, 116, 353
Hypostyle hall 90, 353
I-beam 353
Iconography 353
Ictinos *103*, *107*
Ideality 353
Idea of Order at Key West, The (W. Stevens) 1f.
Ideal town 182f., 197, 228, 237
Ideal Town (Anonymous) *183*
Ideal Town (Lorenzetti) 146, *147*
Ilkley, England
Heathcote *297*
Illinois
Chicago *61*, *274*, *275*
Highland Park *275*, *276*
Oak Park 338, *339*
Plano *290*, 291
Illusionism 198, 200, 250, 353
Imperial Fora, Rome *118*, 129, 130, *131*
Indiana
Columbus 300, *301*
New Harmony, *318*, 320
Indulgence 145
Industrial Revolution 264f.
Innerspatial-Outerspatial (Klee) *25*
Inspector's House at the Source of the Loue *250*, 251
Intercolumniation 102, 353
Interior elevation 333
Interlock 353
International Style 261, 353
International Style, The (H.R. Hitchcock & P. Johnson) 280
Ionic Order 104, *105*, *106*, 120, 353
Iowa
Grinnell *336*
Cedar Rapids *336*, 337
Isfahan, Iran *224*
Isometric drawing 329, 353
Isidorus of Miletus
Hagia Sophia, Istanbul 74, *75*

Istanbul, Turkey
Hagia Sophia 74, *75*, 145, 173
Itten, Johannes 287
Izenour, Steve
Learning from Las Vegas 298
Jamb 353
Jeffersonian Grid 237, *238* , 317
Jefferson, Thomas 235, 241
Jeffersonian Grid 237, *238*, 317
Monticello, Charlottesville *238*
University of Virginia, Charlottesville *58, 240*
Virginia Statehouse, Richmond *239*
Johnson, Philip 280
Justinian 74
Juvarra, Filippo
Villa Stupinigi, near Turin 29, *30*
Juvenal 121
Juxtaposition 353
Ka 88
Kahn, Louis
Exeter Library, Exeter *46*
Mellon Center for British Arts, New Haven 194, *195*
Kandinsky, Wassily 287
Kanon, Polyclitus, 104-105, *121*, 337
Karnak, Egypt 97
Temple of Khons *90, 91*, 93
Kaufmann House, see Falling Water
Kepler, Johannes
Harmony of the Spheres 11
Keystone 133, 134, 191, 353
Khmer Shrine, Ankor Wat 224, *225*
Khons, Temple of 90, *91*, 92
Kings Cross Station, London *64*
Kingship 101
Klee, Paul
Point, Line Plane, Volume 8, 10
Innerspatial-Outerspatial 25
Klenze, Leo von
Glyptotek *59*
Propylaea *59*
Wallhalla 251, *253*
Koetter, Fred
Collage City 34–5
Kunstwolle 353
Landscape with the Burial of Phocion (Poussin) *246*
Landscape with the Father of Psyche Sacrificing to Apollo (Lorrain) *246*
Language 295f., 304, 308, 316
Lantern 353
La Padula 340, *341*
Lateral thrust 133, 159, 174, 353
Latin Cross 79, 81, 151, 154, 353
Laugier, Marc-Antoine
Primitive Hut *69, 255*
Learning from Las Vegas (R. Venturi et al.) 298, 301
Le Corbusier 9, *28*, 34, *35*, 47, *48*, *51*, 52, 61, *62*, *63*, 82, *83*, 106, *117*, *194*, *228*, 229, 258f., *266*, *267*, *268*, 270f., *272*, 275, *343*
City of Tomorrow, Frontispiece *9*
Dom-ino House 265, *267*
Five Points of Architecture 267, *268*
Free Plan vs. Bearing Wall *267*, *268*,
Mass production 264
Modulor *117*, *194*, *343*
Notre-Dame-du-Haut, Ronchamp 82, *83*
On the Ionic order 106
Ozenfant Studio, Paris 47, *48*
Palace of Assembly, Chandigarh 270f., *272*
Purism 263
Regulating lines 342
Salvation Army Building, Paris *51*, 52
Still Life 262, 263
Towards a New Architecture 228, 229
Unité d'Habitation, Berlin *343*
Unité d'Habitation, Marseilles 34, *35*
Villa Savoye, Poissy *28*, 61, *62*, *63*, *262*, 263, 298
Villa Stein, Garches *268*, 269, *270*, *271*, 298
Weißenhof Siedlung House *266*
Ledoux, Claude Nicholas
House for a Cooper's Workshop *250*, 251
Inspectors House at the Source of the Loue *250*, 251
Oikema (House of Pleasure) *250*, 251
Salt Works at Chaux 240, *241*, *242*
Leibnitz, Gottfried Wilhelm von 245
l'Enfant, Pierre
Washington D.C. *236*
Le Notre, André
Vaux-le-Vicomte *214*, *215*, *216*
Versailles 215f., *216*, *217*, *219*
Leonardo da Vinci 169, 173
Mona Lisa 184, 185
Vitruvian Man 40, 41, 77
Le Pautre, Antoine
Hôtel de Beauvais, Paris *25*, 27
Lequeu, Jean-Jacques
Cow Stable *251*

Le Vau, Louis
  Vaux-le-Vicomte *214, 215, 216*
  Versailles 215f., *216, 217, 219*
Lichtenfels, Germany
  Vierzehnheiligen 81, *82*
Light 75, 76, 82, 150, 155, 160, 164, 197, 198, 201, 293, 298
Limbergiers, Hugues *156*
Lincoln Memorial *336*
Linguistics 1, 316, 353
Lintel 353
Lisbon, Portugal
  Santa Maria della Divina Providenza 80, *81*
Literal transparency 353, see transparency
Local symmetry 28, 123, 130, 354
Locke, John 228
Logan Circle, Philadelphia 233
London 232, 233
  Crystal Palace 255, *256, 257*
  Evelyn's Plan for Rebuilding London *230*, 233
  Great Fire 230f.
  Hooke's Plan for Rebuilding London *231*, 232, 233
  Kings Cross Station *64*
  S. Pancras Station *64*
  S. Paul's 173, 231
  Tenements 216
  Wren's Plan for Rebuilding London *230*, 235
Longhi, Martino the Elder
  Palazzo Borghese *26*, 27
Longhi, Martino the Younger
  SS. Vincenzo and Anastasio, Rome *201*
Longitudinal plan 49, 58, 74f., 79, 154, 354
Longitudinal section, long section 333, 354
Lorenzetti, Ambrogio
  Ideal Town 146f., *147*, 149
L'Orme, Philibert de,
  Le premier tome de l'architecture, 327
Lorrain, Claude
  Landscape with the Father of Psyche sacrificing to Apollo 246
Los Angeles, California
  Farmer John's Bacon Factory *302*
  Lovell Health House 279, *280, 281*
  Marlboro Man *37*
  Tail o' the Pup *302*
Louis XIV 202, 239
Lovell Health House, Los Angeles 279, *280, 281*
Lucca, Italy 123, 141
Luther, Martin 79
Lutyens, Edwin
  Deanery Gardens, Sonning *297*
  Heathcote, Ilkley *297*, 298
Luxor, Egypt
  Mortuary Temple of Amenhotep 91, *92*, 93, 97
Macchiavelli, Niccolò di Bernardi 227
Macrocosm 354
Maderno, Carlo
  S. Peter's nave, facade 209, 210
  S. Susanna, Rome 200, *201*
Maestá (Duccio) *147*, 149
Magister II, see Master II
Maison Carré, Nîmes 69, *70*
Majolica House, Vienna 338, *340*
Making of Urban America, The (J. Reps) *234*
Malcontenta di Mira, Italy
  Villa Foscari (Malcontenta) *268*, 269, *270*
Mannerism 186f., 190, 193, 298, 354
Mansard roof 354
Mansart, J.H.
  Chateau Marly, France *239*
Mantua, Italy
  Palazzo del Tè *190, 191*, 192
  San Andrea *178, 179, 180*
Marinetti, F.T. 293, 320
Maritime Theater, Hadrian's Villa, Tivoli *141*
Marlboro Man, Los Angeles *37*
Marly, France
  Chateau Marly *239*
Marseilles, France
  Unité de Habitation 34, *35*
Martin House, Buffalo 275, *277*
Martini, Francesco di Giorgio, see Francesco di Giorgio Martini
Maryland
  Ellicott City *60*
Masaccio
  Trinità 171, 172, 173, 180
Mask of Medusa (J. Hejduk) 17
Massachusetts
  Boston *227, 228, 229*
  Cambridge *15*
Massimo, Pietro and Angelo, see Palazzo Massimo
Massing 65, 354
Mass production 255, 264, 274, 280, 354
Maßwerk 156
Master II (Magister II) 157
Materiality 282, 298, 354
McKim, Charles Follen *343*
McKim, Mead and White *343*

Medici, Cosimo de 167
Medici family 167
Medinet Habu, Egypt
  Mortuary Temple of Ramesses III 91, *93*, 97
Mead, William Rutherford *343*
Megaron 103, 354
Meier, Richard
  Atheneum, New Harmony *318*, 320
  High Museum, Atlanta 46, *47*
Mellon Center for British Arts, New Haven *195*
Mendelsohn, Erich
  Einstein Tower, Potsdam *308*, *309*
  Sketches *310*
Merchants' National Bank, Grinnell, Iowa *336*
Metamorphosis 354
Metaphor 39, 49, 92, 308, 315, 354
Metapuntum 224
Metonymy 192, 354
Meyer, Hannes 287
Mickey Mouse 247
Michelangelo Buonarotti 173, 181
  Campidoglio, Rome 185, *186*, *198*
  Palazzo dei Conservatori 185
  Palazzo dei Senatori 185
  Palazzo Farnese, Rome *26*
  Porta Pia, Rome 299, *300*
  S. Peter's Rome *180*, 181, 202f., 210
Michigan
  Bloomfield Hills 22, *23*
Microcosm 71, 74, 77, 79, 354
Middle Kingdom 92
Mies van der Rohe, Ludwig
  Barcelona Pavilion , Barcelona 284f., *285*, *286*, 291
  Brick Country House, Project for Czechoslovakia *284*
  Farnsworth House, Plano, Ill. 290, *291*
  German Pavilion, see Barcelona Pavilion
  New National Gallery, Berlin *291*
  Weißenhof Siedlung House, Stuttgart *266*
Milan, Italy
  Gallaratese Apartment Building 338, *339*
  Milan Cathedral Diagrams (Stornoloco) *159*
  S. Maria presso S. Satiro *78*, *79*, 80, 193
Miletus 104, 245, *225*
Mimesis 69, 120, 121, 354
Minimal Existence Dwelling 264
Minimalism 298, 309, 354
Minnesota
  Wayzata 52, *53*
Mitchell, William 247
Mnesicles *114*
Model 58, 102, 354
Model of Rome 126, *127*, *131*
Modena, Italy
  Cemetery 302, *303*
Module 175, 176, 179, 223f., 255f., 280, 343, 354
Modulor (Le Corbusier) *117*, *295*, *343*
Moholy-Nagy, Lazslo 287
Moore, Charles 247
Mona Lisa (Leonardo) *184*, 185
Monastery 151f., 199, 354
Mondrian, Piet 284
  Composition with Red, Black, Blue, Yellow and Grey 281, *282*
Monpazier, French Bastide Town *226*
Montage 354
Mont Blanc 223
Montepulciano, Italy
  S. Biagio 44, *45*, *78*
Montesquieu, Charles Louis de Secondat 228
Monticello, Charlottesville *238*
Mont S. Michel, France *151*
Monumentality 54, 354
More, Sir Thomas 223, 227
Moretti, Luigi
  Girasole Apartment Building, Rome 299, *300*
Morgan Library, New York City *343*
Morphology 57f., 103, 354
Mortuary Temple of Amenhotep III, Luxor 91, *92*
Mortuary Temple of Queen Hatshepsut, Deir-el-Bahari 94, *95*
Mortuary Temple of Ramesses III, Medinet Habu 91, *93*
Munich, Germany
  Glyptotek *59*
  Propylaea *59*
Mutability 354
Mutule 354
Mycerinus 89
Mykonos, Greece
  House *53*
Narrative 40, 172, 187, 192, 247, 282, 312, 315, 319, 354
Nave 354
Neoclassicism 193, 239, 243, 354
Neoplasticism 355
Neoplatonism 77, 167, 227, 354
Neumann, Balthazar
  Vierzehnheiligen, Lichtenfels 81, *82*, 214
Neutra, Richard
  Lovell Health House, Los Angeles 279, *280*, *281*

New Hampshire
Exeter 46
New Harmony, Indiana
Atheneum *318*, 320
New Haven, Connecticut
Mellon Center for British Arts *195*
Plan of New Haven 194. *195*, 229, *230*, 233, 234
New National Gallery, Berlin *291*
Newton, Sir Isaac 245f., 250
New York
Buffalo 275, *277*
New York City *49*, *343*
New York City
Morgan Library *343*
TWA Terminal *49*
Niche 355
Nile River 87, 92, 97, 101
Nîmes, France
Maison Carré *69*, *70*
Nolli Map of Rome *20*, 30, *32*, *33*, *204*, *206*
Non-hierarchical organization 54, 288, 355
Norberg Schulz, Christian 182
Nostalgia 293, 355
Notre-Dame de Paris (Victor Hugo) 293
Notre-Dame de Paris, France *160*, *161*, 163
Notre-Dame-du-Haut, Ronchamp 82, *83*
Nude Descending a Staircase (M. Duchamp) *262*, 263
Numeros 178
Nympheum 190, 248, 355
Oak Park, Illinois 338, *339*
Obelisk 101, 183, 203, 209
Oculus 13, 73
Oglethorpe, James
Savannah, Georgia *234*, *235*
Ohio
Circleville 236f.
Columbus *24*, 25, *316*, *317*
Dayton *60*
Oikema (House of Pleasure) *250*, 251
Olbrich, Josef Maria
Großes Glückert House *331*
Obelisk 355
Oculus 355
Olympia, Greece *110*
Olympian cults 101, 248
Omphalos 110
Oneiric 355
One Hundred Years War 164
Opaque 355
Optic 21, 355
Optical Corrections 107, *109*, 198, 355
Oratorians 197
Oratorio of S. Filippo Neri, Rome *198*, *199*
Oratory 199, 355
Orders, The 103, 104, *105*, *106*, *107*, *108*, 119, 120, 310, 355
Orientation 355
Origin of Our Ideas of the Sublime and the Beautiful (E. Burke) 249
Orsini , see Villa Orsini
Orthographic Projection 173, 194, 331f., 355
Orthogonality 88, 130, 137, 355
Ossuary 302, 355
Otaniemi, Finland
Otaniemi University 304, *305*
Oud, J.J.P.
Weißenhof Siedlung House *266*
Outhouse 59, *60*
Oval, The Ohio State University *24*, 25
Oxford, England 304
All Souls College *295*
Queen's College *334*. 335
Ozenfant, Amedée 39
Ozenfant Studio, Paris 47, *48*
Paccioli, Luca
Divina Geometria 11
Paestum, Greece
Temple of Ceres *108*, *109*
Painterly 201, 355
Palace of Architecture *244*, 253
Palace of Assembly, Chandigarh 270f., *272*
Palace of Diocletian, Split *125*, 126
Palazzo 25f., 58, 355
Palazzo Borghese, Rome *26*, 27
Palazzo della Civiltà e Lavoro, Rome *341*
Palazzo del Tè, Mantua *190*, *191*
Palazzo dei Conservatori, Rome 185
Palazzo dei Senatori, Rome 185
Palazzo Farnese, Rome *26*, 173
Palazzo Massimo, Rome *27*, 173
Palazzo Piccolomini, Pienza 184f.
Palazzo Publico, Siena *148*, 149
Palazzo Quirinale, Rome 204, 208
Palazzo Vecchio, Florence 34
Palestrina, Italy
Temple of Fortuna Primagenia *139*, *140*, 306, 307
Palio 149
Palladian motif 355

Palladio, Andrea 171, 173, 241
20 Plans for a Palace *38*
Diagram of Palladian Villas *45*
Villa Emo, Fanzolo 29, *30*
Villa Foscari (Malcontenta) *268*, 269, *270*, *271*
Villa Rotonda, (Villa Capra), Vicenza *29*, *166*
Villa Thiene, Cirogna *45*
Palimpsest 317, 355
Palmanova, Italy *182*, 183
Panathenaic Way *111*, *113*
Panofsky, Erwin 149, 157
Pantheon, Rome *13*, 70, *73*, 133, *134*, 173, 174, 206, *208*, 239, 248, 301
Paradigm 40, 80, 245, 250, 287, 294, 304, 319, 355
Paradox 355
Parallax 355
Paraline drawing, 329, 355
Parapet 355
Parc de la Villette, Paris *318*, 319
Paris 232
Eiffel Tower *257*
Exposition of 1900 *258*
Great Wheel 258, *259*
Hôtel de Beauvais *25*
Notre-Dame de Paris *160*, *161*
Opera House 53, *54*
Ozenfant Studio 47, *48*
Parc de la Villette *318*, 319
Place Dauphine *36*
Place des Vosges *36*, *214*
Place Royale *36*, *214*
Salvation Army Building *51*, 52
S. Chapelle *164*, *165*
Paris Opera House, Paris 53, *54*
Parterre 187, 218, 355
Parthenon, Athens 69, *71*, 104, *107*, 110, *112*, 252
Parti 39f., 53, 55, 335, 355
Partition wall 333, 355
Parvis *152*, 355
Path 92, 97, 101, 187,272, 298, 355
Patronage 145f., 168, 197, 356
Pavia, Italy
Carthusian Monastery 151f., *152*
Pavilion for the Glass Industry, Cologne *44*
Paxton, Joseph
Crystal Palace, London 255, *256*, *257*
Greenhouse at Chatsworth *15*
Pazzi Chapel, Florence *176*, *177*
Peak Project, Hong Kong *319*, *321*
Pediment 69, 356
Pèlerin, Jean,
De artificiali perspectiva, *326*
Pendentive 76, *77*, 356
Penn, William
Plan of Philadelphia *232*, 233, 243
Pennsylvania
Bear Run 277f.
Philadelphia *232*, *233*
Chestnut Hill 298, 299
Pergamon *18*, *19*, 103
Sanctuary of Aesculapius *129*
Perimeter 123, 127, 356
Perspective Drawing, 171, 173, 180, 193, 194, 197f., 282, *326*, *328*, 329f., 356
Peruzzi, Baldassare
Fortifications *182*
Palazzo Massimo, Rome *27*
Sketches of Antiquities *170*
S. Peter's, Rome *180*
Petrarch (Francesco Petrarca) 173
Pharaoh 89, 101
Phenomenal transparency 356, (see transparency)
Phidias *111*
Philadelphia, Pennsylvania
Art Museum 233
Benjamin Franklin Parkway *233*
City Hall 233
Fairmount Park 233f.
Gréber Plan of Philadelphia *233*
Logan Circle 233
Penn and Holme Plan of Philadelphia *232*
Piazza del Campo, Siena *148*, 149
Piazza del Popolo, Rome 204, *205*, 217
Piazza di Spagna, Rome 204, *205*
Piazza Navona, Rome *33*, 140
Piazza Pio II, Pienza *185*
Piazza S. Ignazio, Rome *213*
Picasso, Pablo
Green Still Life *51*, 52
Violin and Grapes *262*, 263
Pictorial space 171, 172, 356
Picture plane, 329, 358, 356
Picturesque 243, 246f., 319, 356
Pienza, Italy *184*, *185*, 193
Pier 81, 155, 163, 181, 182, 199, 356
Pietra Serena 175, 176

Pilaster 177, 191, 356
Pillar 356
Piloti 28, 267, 356
Pincio *205*
Pinnacle 356
Piranesi, Giambattista
Baths of Caracalla *138*
Campus Martius, Rome *124*, 125
Castel S. Angelo *122*
Nolli Map of Rome *20*, 30, *32*, *33*
Pantheon *76*
Piazza del Popolo, Rome *204*, *205*
S. Costanza *43*
Pitti family 167
Pisa, Italy
Campo Santo 302, *303*
Pius II (Pope) 184
Place d'Armes, Versailles 214
Place Dauphine, Paris *36*
Place des Vosges, Paris *36*
Place Royale, Paris (see Place des Vosges)
Plan 356
Plan libre, see Free plan
Plan paralysé, see Free plan
Plan oblique 329, 356
Plano, Illinois
Farnsworth House 290, *291*
Plasticity 22, 102, 184, 191, 198, 270, 310, 356
Plato 68, 71, 115, 173, 202
Platonic Academy 167
Platonic solid, Platonic form 11, 294, 302, 315, 319, 356
Plenum 356
Plinlimmon 223
Plinth 175, 356
Poché 14, 126, 279, 298, 333, 356
Poetics of Gardens, The , (Moore, Mitchell, Turnbull) 247
Point, Line, Plane, Volume (Klee) *8*
Pointed Arch 149, 155, 159, 179, 356
Poissy, France
Villa Savoye *28*, 61, *62*, *63*, *262*, 298
Polemics 356
Polyclitus, 104-105, *121*, 337
Polychromy 356
Polymorphism 81
Polyvalent 356
Pompeii
Forum 127, *128*
Pontine Marshes 202
Pope, see Alexander VII, Pius II, Sixtus V, Urban VIII
Pope, Alexander 250
Porta della Ripetta, Rome 204
Porta del Popolo, Rome 203, 204, 217
Portal 356
Porta Pia, Rome 204, 206, 299, *300*
Portico 356
Portico in antis 356
Poseidon 102, *103*
Post 356
Postal Savings Bank, Vienna 338, *340*
Post and Beam Construction 92
Post-Modernism 295f., 356
Potomac River 236
Potsdam, Germany
Einstein Tower *308*, *309*
Gardener's House *252*
Schloß Babelsberg *252*
Schloß Charlottenhof *253*
Poussin, Nicolas 247
Landscape with the Burial of Phocion *246*
Prairie House 357, see Frank Lloyd Wright
Prato, Giovanni di
Drawing to Calculate Curve of Dome *174*
Precedent 59, 69f., 154, 170, 286, 308, 357
Precinct 357
Précis des leçons, J.N.L. Durand *56*
Precolumbian America 223, 357
Prefabrication 255, 264, 265, 357
Primary color 357
Primitive Hut *69*, *108*, 254, *255*, 357
Prix de Rome First Prize Project *296*
Process 40, 310, 314f., 315, 357
Procession 92, 94, 97, 111, 186, 312
Program 16, 357
Proportion 116, 136, *138*, *169*, 170, 173f., 175, 176, 179, 193, 194, 269, 270, 281, 298, 336f., 357
Propylaea 102, 111, 112
Proscenium 121, 123, 213, 357
Prototype 264, 357
Proun 314
Pteron 103, 357
Pugin, Augustus Welby Northmore 165, 254
Purism 263, 357
Pylon 90, 92, 93, 97, 101, 357
Pyramid 89, 92f., 97, 145, 183
Pyramid of Cheops, Giza *12*, *89*
Pythagoras 41, 71, 237

Pythagorean progression 9, 312, 357
Quadrature 158, 159, 357
Quattremère de Quincy, A.C., 57, 58
Queens College, Oxford see Oxford
Quintilian 164
Quirinale, see Palazzo Quirinale
Radial organization 357
Raguzzini, Filippo
  Piazza S. Ignazio, Rome 213, *214*
Ramesses II, 93, *94*, 97
Ramesses III, *91*, *93*
Raphael 170f.
  S. Peter's 181
  School of Athens *172*, 173
Recentering 27
Recursion 40, 181, 312, 357
Reflected ceiling plan, 331, 357
Regensburg, Germany
  Walhalla *251*, 253
Regulating line 49, 342, 357
Reigl, Alois 21. 30
Reinforced concrete 60, 61, 357
Reims, France
  Reims Cathedral 161f., *162*
  Tombstone of the Architect *156*, 157
Reinforced concrete 265, 277, 279
Renaissance 76, 167f., 357
Repetition 357
Reps, John 234f.
Rhetoric 120, 197f., 210, 310, 357
Rhythm 190, 223, 281, 357
Rhythm of a Russian Dance (Doesburg) 283, *284*
Ribbed vault 155, *156*, 357
Ribbon Window 267, 288, 305, 357
Richmond, Virginia
  Virginia Statehouse *239*
Ridge 357
Rietveld, Gerrit 284
  Schroeder House, Utrecht 282, *283*
Robie House, Chicago *61*, *274*, *275*
Rock Temple of Ramesses II, Abu Simbel 93, *94*
Rococo 212, 357
Roman camp *122*, 123, 223,226, 233, 357
Roman castra 357, see Roman camp
Romanesque 76, 358
Roman Fora, Rome *118*, *130*
Romano, Giulio
  Palazzo del Tè, Mantua *190*, *191*
Roman Orders (Serlio) *118*
Romantic Classicism 286, 358
Romanticism 246, 358
Roman Towns 123, 223
  El-Leggun, Jordan *122*
  Timgad *122*
Rome, Italy
  16th Century Rome *31*
  Aurelian Walls 217
  Baths of Caracalla *134*, *136*, *137*, *138*
  Campidoglio 185, *186*
  Colosseum *58*, *120*
  Cornaro Chapel *199*, *200*
  Danteum project 310, *311*, 312
  Forum, see Imperial Fora and Roman Forum
  Girasole Apartment Building 299, *300*
  Imperial Fora *118*, *131*, 310
  Model of Rome 126, *127*
  Nolli Map *20*, 30, *32*, *33*, *204*, *206*
  Oratorio of S. Filippo Neri *198*, *199*
  Palazzo Borghese *26*
  Palazzo della Civiltà e Lavoro 340, *341*
  Palazzo dei Conservatori 185, *186*
  Palazzo dei Senatori 185, *196*
  Palazzo Farnese *26*
  Palazzo Massimo *27*
  Palazzo Quirinale 204, 208
  Pantheon *13* , 70, *73* , 133, *134*, 173, 174, 206, *208*, 248, 250, 301
  Piazza del Popolo *204*, *205*
  Piazza di Pace 212, *213*
  Piazza di Spagna 204
  Piazza Navona *33*
  Piazza S. Ignazio 212, *213*
  Plan of Ancient Rome *31*
  Pope Sixtus V's Plan of Rome 202, *203*
  Porta della Ripetta 204
  Porta del Popolo 205, 217
  Porta Pia 204, 206, 299, *300*
  Roman Forum *118*, *130*
  S. Andrea al Quirinale *207*
  S. Carlo alle Quattro Fontane *80*, *81*, 204, *205*, *206*, *207*
  S. Costanza *43*, 44
  S. Giovanni in Laterano 203
  S. Ivo alle Sapienza 210, *211*, *212*
  S. Maria della Pace 212, *213*
  S. Maria della Vittoria *199*
  S. Maria Maggiore 203, 204, 205
  S. Susanna 200, *201*

S. Teresa in Ecstasy (Bernini) *199, 200*
S. Paolo fuori della Mura, see S. Paul's outside the Walls
S. Paul's outside the Walls *74* , 145
S. Peters *180, 181, 202f.* 209, 231
S. Peter's Cortile *196*, 209, *210*
S. Pietro, see S. Peter's
S. Pietro in Montorio 44, 78, 180
S. Vincenzo and Anastasio *201*
Strada Felice 204, 205
Strada Pia 204
Tempietto of San Pietro in Montorio *44, 78,* 180, 181
Temple of Divus Julius 129
Temple of Fortuna Virilis *132*
Temple of Venus and Rome 70, *71, 72*
Trajan's Forum 130, *131*
Trajan's Market *132*
Villa Giulia *188, 189*, 190, 247
Romulus 123
Ronchamp, France 82, *83*
Roof garden 267, 358
Roof plan 331, 358
Root rectangle *342*
Roriczer, Mattias 158
Lodgebook Drawings *157*
Rose window 155, 358
Rossellino, Bernardo
Pienza, Italy *184, 185*, 193, 198
Rossi, Aldo
Cemetery, Modena 302, *303*
Rossi, G.B. *205*
Gallaratese Apartment Building, Milan 338, *339*
Rotation 358
Rotterdam, Holland *287*
Rousseau, Jean Jacques 228, 246
Rowe, Colin
Collage City 34-5
Mathematics of the Ideal Villa 268, 269f.
"Transparency: Literal and Phenomenal" 263f., 289f.
Ruskin, John 163, 254
Russian Constructivism 312
Rustication 191, 241, 358
S. Alfege, Greenwich *295*
S. Andrea, Mantua *178, 179*, 180
S. Andrea al Quirinale, Rome 206, *207*, 208, 209
S. Andrew de Cubzak Bridge 258, *259*
S. Augustine 140
S. Bernard 154, 155
S. Biagio, Montepulciano, Italy *44*, 45, *78*
S. Carlo alle Quattro Fontane, Rome *80, 81*, 199, 204, *205, 206, 207*, 210
S. Chapelle, Paris 160, *164, 165*
S. Coloma de Cervello, Barcelona *50*, 51
S. Costanza, Rome *43*, 44
S. Denis, near Paris *153*, 155
Abbot Suger 155
S. Filippo Neri, (S. Philip Neri) 197f.
Casale Monferreto *212*
Oratory of, Rome *198*, 199
S. Ignatius Loyola (S. Ignazio) 197
Piazza 212, *213*
Church 212, *213*
S. Ignazio, see S. Ignatius Loyola
S. Ivo alle Sapienza, Rome 210, *211, 212*
S. John of the Cross 197
S. Louis of France 164
S. Maria della Assunzione, Arricia 208, *209*
S. Maria della Consolazione, Todi *77*, 78, 208
S. Maria della Divina Providenza, Lisbon 80, *81*
S. Maria della Pace, Rome 212, *213*
S. Maria della Vittoria, Rome *199*
S. Maria dei Fiori, Florence 173, *174, 175*
Drawing to Calculate Curvature of Dome (Prato) *174*
S. Maria Maggiore, Rome 203, 204, 205
S. Maria Novella, Florence 171, *178*, 180
S. Maria presso San Satiro, Milan 78, *79*, 80, 193
S. Miniato al Monte, Florence *294*, 295
S. Pancras Station, London *64*
S. Paul's Outside the Walls, Rome *74*
S. Paul's, London 173
S. Peter 78, 181
S. Peter's, Rome 173, *180, 181, 202*, 203 209
S. Peter's Cortile, Rome *196*, 209, *210*
S. Pietro, see S. Peter and S. Peter's
S. Pietro in Montorio, Rome 44, *78*, 180, 181
S. Spirito, Florence *176*
S. Susanna, Rome 200, *201*
S. Teresa 197, 199f.
S. Teresa in Ecstasy (Bernini), Corona Chapel, Rome *199, 200*
S. Vincenzo and Anastasio, Rome *201*
Saarinen, Eero
TWA Terminal, New York *49*
Saarinen, Eliel
Cranbrook School, Bloomfield Hills 22f., *23*
Sacred Grove, Bomarzo 186, 197
Sack of Rome 74
Sacristy 358

Salt Lake City, Utah 223, *225*
Salt Works, Chaux 240f., *241*, *242*
Salvation Army Building, Paris *51*, 52
Sanctuary of Aesculapius, Pergamon *129*
Sanctuary of Apollo, Delphi *110*
Sangallo the Elder, Antonio
 Church of San Biagio, Montepulciano *44*, 45, *78*
Sangallo the Younger, Antonio da
 Palazzo Farnese, Rome *26*
San Gimignano, Italy *150*
Sant'Elia, Antonio 261, 293
Sanzio, Raphael, see Raphael Sanzio
Sarcophagus 250, 358
Savannah, Georgia *234*, *235*
Säynätsalo, Finland *50*, 51
Scale 101, 116, 117, 120, 152, 218, 223, 250, 258, 261, 298, 319, 329f., 336f., 358
Scaling 358
Scamozzi, Vincenzo
 Palmanova, Italy *182*, 183
Scenae frons 208, 358
Scenography 197f., 183, 213, 358
Scharoun, Hans
 Berlin Philharmonic Hall, Berlin 53, *54*
 Hostel, Wroclaw *14*, 16
 Weißenhof Siedlung House, Stuttgart *266*
Schelling, Friedrich Wilhelm Joseph 246
Schinkel, K.F. 286, 295
 Altesmuseum, Berlin 270f., *273*, 307
 Gardener's House, Potsdam *252*
 Neuwache, Berlin *59*
 Schloß Babelsberg, Potsdam *252*
 Schloß Charlottenhof, Potsdam *253*
 Schloß Glienicke, Potsdam *252*
Schism 358
Schlemmer, Oscar 287
Schloß Babelsberg, Potsdam *252*
Schloß Charlottenhof, Potsdam *253*
Schloß Glienicke, Potsdam *252*
Scholasticism 145f., 151, 164, 167, 358
School of Athens (Raphael) *172*, 173
Schroeder House, Utrecht 282, *283*
Schuylkill River 232, 233
Schwarting, J.M. *203*
Schwerin, Germany (C. Sitte) 146, *147*
Scientific Method 312
Scott, George Gilbert, see Gilbert Scott, George
Scott Brown, Denise *Learning from Las Vegas* 298
Scully, Vincent 103, 108
Scupper 358
Seaside, Florida *337*
Secession (Vienna) 261, 358
"Secret of the Medieval Masons, The" (P. Frankl and R. Wittkower) 156
Section 358
Semantics 299, 304, 316, 319, 358
Semper, Gottfried
 Primitive Caribbean Hut *255*
Senmut 88
Sequence 32f, 358
Serlio, Sebastiano
 Book 1, Plate 1 *9*
 Five Roman Orders *120*
 Round Temple Plan *42*
 S. Peter's 170
 Square Temple Plan *42*
 Temples *66*, 78
 "Tragic Scene" *183*
Servant space 358
Served space 358
Sforzinda, Italy 180, *181*
Shaft 96, 104, 358
Shear 96, 275, 358
Shell 51, 174
Shift 358
Shopping Mall 39
Shute, John
 Composite Order *108*
Siena 146, *148*, 149, 169, 182
 Palazzo Publico 149
 Piazza del Campo *148*, 149
Sign 298, 302
Sioux Village near Fort Laramie (Bierstadt) *222*
Site 358
Sitte, Camillo
 Diagram Schwerin, Germany 146, *147*
 Diagram Würzburg, Germany 146, *147*
Sixtus V 202f.
 Plan of Rome 202, *203*, 204, 208, 217
Skeletal system 155, 160, 254, 279, 358
Skin 358
Sky and Water 1 (Escher) *22*
Skyscraper 274
Slab 34, 52, 95, 358
Slutzky, Robert
 "Transparency: Literal and Phenomenal" 263f., 289f.

Smyrna 224
Society of Jesus 197
Soffit 359
Sonning, England
Deanery Gardens *297*
Space/time 310, 359
Spandrel 359
Spanish Steps, see Piazza di Spagna
Sphinx *89, 99*
Spini, Gherardo
Doric Primitive Hut *108*
Spiritual Exercises 197
Split, Yugoslavia *125, 126*
Spring line 359
Staatsgalerie, Stuttgart *306, 307*
Stasis 359
Station point 329, 359
Steamer in a Snowstorm (Turner) *248*, 249
Steel frame 279
Steinberg, Leo 80
Stereotomy 88, 89, 194, 280, 281, 317, 359
Stevens, Wallace 1f.
Still Life (Le Corbusier) *262*, 263
Stirling, James
Queens College, Oxford *334*, 335
Staatsgalerie, Stuttgart *306, 307*
Stoa *14*, 18, 103, 115, 359
Stoa of Attalos *14*
Stone Henge *67*
Stornoloco
Diagrams of Milan Cathedral *159*
Stourhead, Stourton *246, 247*
Strada Felice, Rome 204
Strada Pia, Rome 204
String course 191, 359
Structural Linguistics 316
Structural Rationalism 254f., 359
Structure 359
Stucco 359
Stuttgart, Germany
Staatsgalerie *306f., 307*
Weißenhof Seidlung *265, 266*
Style 87, 98, 161, 169, 184, 239, 245f., 294, 295, 298, 320
Stylobate 103, 359
Sublime 249, 359
Subtractive form 62, 89, 95, 359
Suger, Abbot 155
Sullivan, Louis
Merchants' National Bank, Grinnell Iowa *336*
Summerson, John 297
Superimposition 199, 263, 359
Superposition 120, 359
Symbol, Symbolism 172, 286, 297, 298
Symmetry 89f., 97, 126f., 192f., 359
Synecdoche 359
Syracuse, Italy *103*
Tabula rasa 359
Tail o' the Pup *302*
Tartan grid 269, 359
Tatlin at Home (Hausmann) *292*
Tatlin at Work (El Lissitzky) *260*
Taut, Bruno
Die Große Blum 68, *69*
Pavilion for the Glass Industry, Cologne *44*
Tectonic 17, 177, 190, 199, 359
Temenos 108, 116, 359
Tempietto of S. Pietro in Montorio, Rome *44, 78*, 180, 181
Temple 18f., 59, 65, 69, 82, 102, 103, 130f., 286, 359
Temple of Amenhotep III, Luxor 91, *92*, 97
Temple of Athena Nike, Athens 111, *113*
Temple of Ceres, Paestum 108, *109*
Temple of Concord, Agrigentum *110*
Temple of Divus Julius, Rome 129
Temple of Fortuna Primagenia, Palestrina *139, 140*, 307
Temple of Fortuna Virilis, Rome *132*
Temple of Hatshepsut, Deir el Bahari 94, *95*, 97
Temple of Hephaste, Athens, see Hephasteion
Temple of Khons, Karnak *90, 91*
Temple of Olympian Zeus Agrigento 104
Temple of Ramesses II, Abn Simbel 93, *94*, 97
Temple of Ramesses III, Medinet Habu *91, 93*
Temple of Solomon 74
Temple of Venus and Rome, Rome 70, *71, 72*
Ten Books on Architecture (Vitruvius) 40, 178
Tension 95. 96, 359
Terni, Italy 223
Terragni, Giuseppe
Casa del Fascio *342. 343*
Danteum Project 310, *311*, 312
Texas
Grain elevator *60*
Text 319f.
Theater 18, 102f., 121, 197f., 213
Theater at Epidaurus, Greece *103*
Theater at Syracuse, Greece *103*
Thebes, Egypt 95

Theory of the Second Man 204f.
Third Reich 53
Tholos 69, 78, 359
Tholos at Delphi 69, *70*
Thoreau, Henry David 246
Threshold 152, 359
Timgad (Roman Town) *122*
Tivoli, Italy 223
  Hadrian's Villa *140, 141*
  Maritime Theater *141*
Todi, Italy *77, 78,* 208
Tombstone of the Architect Hugues Limbergier *156,* 157
Topography 19, 359
Towards a New Architecture (Le Corbusier) 228, 229
Tower 76, 82, 146f., 150, 154, 206
Trabeation 95, 104, 133, 359
Tracery 156, 160, 359
Train Bridge at S. Andrew de Cubzak 258, *259*
Trajan's Forum, Rome 130, *131,* 132
Trajan's Market, Rome *132*
Transept 76, 359
Transition space 152, 154, 161, 359
Translucent 359
Transparency 263f., 289f., 359
Transverse section 333, 359
Travertine 360
Treasury 18, 67, 103
Treasury of Atreus *67*
Triangulation 154, 360
Triforium 156, 161, 360
Triglyph 91, 105, 360
Trinità (Masaccio) *171,* 180
  Diagram of *Trinità 171*
Trinity 76
Triumphal arch 180, 183, 360
Trompe l'oeil 80, 360
Trope 192, 360
Truss 132, 133, 360
Tschumi, Bernard
  Parc de la Villette, Paris *318,* 319
Turin, Italy
  Nameless Church, G. Guarini 212
  Villa Stupinigi, F. Juvarra 29, *30*
Turner, J.M.W.
  Steamer in a Snowstorm 248, 249
Tuscan Order 119, 360
TWA Terminal, New York *49*
Type 57f., 68f., 90, 97, 102, 104, 255, 264, 296, 298, 308, 309, 360
Typology 57f., 302, 304, 360
Uffizi, Florence *34,* 35, 173
Unité d'Habitation
  Berlin *343*
  Marseilles 34, *35*
University of Virginia, Charlottesville, VA *58, 240*
Unity Temple, Oak Park, Illinois 338, *339*
Urban 360
Urban VIII (Pope) 211
Urban fabric *32f.,* 360
Urbanism 360
Urban overcrowding 230, 264f.
Urbino, Italy 183
Utah
  Salt Lake City *223*
Utrecht, Holland 282, *283*
Utopia, Sir Thomas More 223, 227, 360
Valley Temple 89f., 360
Van der Rohe, Ludwig Mies, see Mies van der Rohe, Ludwig
Van der Vlught, L.C. , see Vlught, van der
Van Doesburg, Theo, see Doesburg, Theo van
Vanishing point 329, 360
Vanna Venturi House, Chestnut Hill, PA. 298, *299*
Van Nelle Chocolate and Tobacco Factory, Rotterdam *287*
Vant'Hoff, Rob, see Hoff, Rob Vant'
Vasari, Giorgio
  Uffizi, Florence *34,* 35
Vatican 209
  Stanza della Segnatura *172*
Vault, vaulting 133, 134, *135,* 155, 163, 194, 360
Vaux-le-Vicomte, France *214, 215, 216,* 218
Vegemorphism 39, 360
Venturi, Robert
  Complexity and Contradiction in Architecture 298f., 319
  "Ducks and Decorated Sheds" *301, 302*
  Fire Station No. 4, Columbus, Indiana 300, *301*
  Football Hall of Fame Competition 300, *301*
  Learning from Las Vegas 298
  "Learning from Lutyens" 298
  Vanna Venturi House, Chestnut Hill, PA. 298, *299*
Venustas 178
Vergil, see Virgil
Vernacular 53, 57, 296, 360
Versailles, France 215f., *216, 217,* 218, *219,* 231, 235
Vertical circulation 360
Vestige 360
Vestry 82, 360
Viaduct at Garabit 258, *259*

Vicenza, Italy *29, 166*
Villa Rotonda
Vienna
Majolica House 338, *340*
Postal Savings Bank 338, *340*
Vierzehnheiligen, Lichtenfels 81, *82*, 214
Vignola, Giacomo Barozzi 189
Constituent Elements of the Orders *105*
Villa Giulia, Rome *188f. 189*, 190, 247
Villa Lante, Bagnaia *187f.*, 247
Villa 25f., 58, 187, 360
Villa Borghese, Rome *205*
Villa Emo, Fanzolo 29, *30*
Villa Giulia, Rome *188, 189*, 190, 247
Villa Lante, Bagnaia *187*, 247
Villa Foscari, Malcontenta di Mira *268*, 269, *270*
Villalpando, Juan Bautista
In Ezechielem Explanationes 338, *339*
Villa Orsini, Bomarzo *192*, 193
Villard de Honnecourt, see Honnecourt, Villard de
Villa Rotonda, Vicenza *29, 166*
Villa Savoye, Poissy *28*, 61, *62, 63, 262*, 263, 298
Villa Stein, Garches *268*, 269, *270, 271*, 298
Villa Stupinigi, near Turin 29, *30*
Villa Thiene, Cirogna *45*
Viollet-le-Duc, Eugène-Emmanuel
Market *254*
Roman arch construction *135*
Roman Temple *133*
Stonework and cast iron *254*
Violin and Grapes (P. Picasso) *262*, 263
Virgil 247, 248
Virginia
Charlottesville *58*, 238, *240*
Richmond *239*
Virginia Statehouse, Richmond *239*
Vitruvian Man 40, *41*, 42, 77, 169, 193, 226, 228
Vitruvius 40f, 78, 105, 107, 170, 233, 254, 360
Proportions for Rectangles *170*
Ten Books on Architecture 40
Vlught, L.C. van der
Van Nelle Chocolate and Tobacco Factory, Rotterdam *287*
Voltaire, François Marie 228
Volutes 106, 360
Von Klenze, Leo, see Klenze, Leo von
Voussoirs 191, 360
Wagner, Otto
Majolica House, Vienna 338, *340*
Postal Savings Bank, Vienna 338, *340*
Walhalla, Regensburg *251*, 253
Wall House I *16, 17*
Wall House II *17*
Wall House III *52*
Wanderer Above the Mist (Friedrich) *248*
Ward Willitts House, Highland Park, Ill. *275, 276*
Washington D.C. *236, 336*
Wayzata, Minnesota
Winton Guest House *52*, 53
Webbing 176, 360
Weimar Republic 287
Weißenhof Siedlung 265, *266*
Apartment Block (Mies van der Rohe) *266*
House (Le Corbusier)
House (Scharoun) *266*
Row House (Oud) *266*
Weltanschauung 360
Werkbund, German, see German Werkbund
Westworks 83, 360
Wexner Center for the Visual Arts, Columbus, Ohio *316, 317*
White, Stanford *343*
Wilderness 228f, 239, 240
Winckelmann, Johannes 252
Winton Guest House, Wayzata Minn. *52*, 53
Wittkower, Rudolph 171, 202
Diagrams of Palladian Villas *45*
Wölfflinn, Heinrich 146, 201
World War I 309
World War II 290
Worm's eye view 331, 360
Wren, Christopher 173
Plan for Rebuilding London *230*, 231
Wright, Frank Lloyd 98, 275f., 294
Broadacre City 242, *243*
Kaufmann House (Falling Water), Bear Run, PA. 277f., *278*
Martin House, Buffalo, N.Y. 275, *277*
Prairie House 61f., 275f., 284
Robie House, Chicago *61, 274, 275*
Unity Temple, Oak Park, Ill. 338, *339*
Ward Willitts House, Highland Park, Ill. *275, 276*
Wroclaw, Poland
Hostel *14*, 16
Würzburg, Germany (Sitte) 146,*147*
Zeitgeist 255, 261, 275, 294, 308, 310, 360
Zoomorphism 39, 360
Zuccari, Federico *193*